Marriage and the Family

Marriage and the Family

Diane I. Levande
Michigan State University

Joanne B. Koch

Lewis Z. Koch

HOUGHTON MIFFLIN COMPANY Boston
Dallas   Geneva, Illinois   Hopewell, New Jersey   Palo Alto   London

When it comes to marriages and families, there are no successes and no failures—only people striving to keep love and intimacy alive. Whatever our family condition, that vision of caring and continuity allows us to begin this exploration together.

Library of Congress Catalog Card Number: 82-81562

ISBN: 0-395-33162-5

Cover art rendered by Steve Miller

Chapter-opening photographs: **Chapter 1:** Jerry Howard, Positive Images / **Chapter 2:** Frances M. Cox, Stock Boston / **Chapter 3:** Derrick TePaska / **Chapter 4:** Philip Jon Bailey, Picture Cube / **Chapter 5:** Laimute Druskis, Jeroboam / **Chapter 6:** Alan Oransky / **Chapter 7:** Rose Skytta, Jeroboam / **Chapter 8:** David Strickler, Picture Cube / **Chapter 9:** Suzanne Wu, Jeroboam / **Chapter 10:** Jerry Howard, Positive Images / **Chapter 11:** Florence Sharp / **Chapter 12:** Frank Siteman, Picture Cube / **Chapter 13:** Fred Bodin, Stock Boston / **Chapter 14:** Susan Lapides / **Chapter 15:** Jerry Howard, Positive Images

Other credits: **Page 71:** Sandra L. Hofferth, "Day Care in Next Decade," *Journal of Marriage and the Family*, August 1979, Vol. 41, No. 3, p. 655. Copyrighted 1979 by the National Council on Family Relations. Reprinted by permission. / **Pages 114–120:** Joann S. DeLora, Carol A. B. Warren, and Carol Ellison, *Understanding Sexual Behavior*, 2nd ed. Copyright © 1981 by Houghton Mifflin Company. Adapted by permission. / **Pages 123, 126, 127, 128, 129, 130:** William H. Masters and Virginia E. Johnson, *Human Sexual Response*. Boston: Little, Brown. Copyright © 1966 by William H. Masters and Virginia E. Johnson. Reprinted by permission. / **Page 145:** Kathleen Gough, "The Origin of the Family," *Journal of Marriage and the Family*, November 1971, Vol. 33, pp. 760–771. Copyrighted 1971 by the National Council on Family Relations. Reprinted by permission. / **Page 148:** Jessie Bernard, "Infidelity: Some Moral and Social Issues," in J. H. Masserman, ed., *Science and Psychoanalysis*, Vol. XVI, pp. 99–119. Used by permission of Grune & Stratton, Inc. / **Page 149:** Dale Wachowiak and Hanelore Bragg, "Open Marriage and Marital Adjustment," *Journal of Marriage and the Family*, February 1980, Vol. 42, No. 1, p. 58. Copyrighted 1980 by the National Council on Family Relations. Reprinted by permission. / **Page 158:** Material adapted from Alfred C. Kinsey, Wardell B. Pomeroy, and Clyde E. Martin. *Sexual Behavior in the Human Male*, W. B. Saunders, 1948, p. 638. Used by permission. / **Pages 161 and 162:** Excerpts from Alan P. Bell and Martin S. Weinberg, *Homosexualities*. Copyright © 1978 by Alan P. Bell and Martin S. Weinberg. Reprinted by permission of Simon & Schuster, a Division of Gulf & Western Corporation, and Mitchell Beazley Publishers Ltd. / (Credits continued on page C-1, following the Bibliography)

Contents

Preface

Our purpose in writing *Marriage and the Family* has been to present an introductory, yet comprehensive, account of how intimate human relationships come into being, develop, change, and sometimes terminate. To help us achieve this complex task, we have selected a developmental perspective as our unifying frame of reference. This view emphasizes both constancy and change in individuals and in families over the course of life. It provides a way to view the significant factors and processes in the development of relationships within the context of personal growth, family background, and the larger social environment.

Many assumptions underlie the selection and interpretation of text content. Some stem from the dictates of theory, others from professional experience; all are filtered through the personal and experiential backgrounds of the authors as individuals, family members, and participants in contemporary society. While we have striven for scientific accuracy and objectivity in our selection and discussion of content, several assumptions have guided us in the creation of our text. We believe

- that primary relationships represent a basic need to love and be loved.
- that marriage and family relationships are important and highly valued, though not exclusive, ways of meeting this need.
- that individual development, family background, and sociocultural factors all pose opportunities for growth of primary relationships, as well as obstacles to be overcome in those relationships.
- that changes in societal mores concerning such areas as sexuality, life style, and sex roles may both enhance and challenge our most intimate interactions.
- that good relationships are possible over the life span, but do not happen automatically; commitment, flexibility, and a great deal of work are necessary to maintain positive intimate relationships.

Approach and Content. We have written this text with a dual objective: to provide students with a sound theoretical background supported by research, and to apply the abstract concepts and statistical data to familiar situations, issues, and problems in primary relationships. To aid us in fulfilling this objective, we have drawn content and examples from a variety of fields, including sociology, psychology, social work, biology, anthropology, history, and literature. We have tried to balance theoretical explanation and practical application; historical development and current issues; idealized standards and realistic variations; and strengths of primary relationships and their stresses and problems.

We believe that students will find this text both intellectually stimulating and useful in a practical way, as they develop their own relationships.

Marriage and the Family is organized into an introductory chapter and three parts, in which we examine the development of love and intimacy from infancy through old age. In the first chapter, we offer a historical overview of marriage and the family and introduce the developmental framework that structures our book.

In Part One, "The Roots of Intimacy," we trace the growth of intimacy from its roots in the individual's capacity to love to its development within the family, and we examine the interaction of the family with society. A chapter on sexual behavior includes content on how to recognize and resolve difficulties in sexual functioning. Another chapter explores choices of intimate lifestyles other than traditional marriage.

In Part Two, "Intimacy in Marriage," we discuss the process of mate selection and explore the factors that influence the choice of a partner. In a chapter on role patterns, we analyze traditional sex roles and the ways that those roles are changing; we suggest methods to deal with conflicts caused by differing role expectations by intimate partners. In chapters on communication and conflict management, we discusss common problems in these areas and suggest methods to improve and enhance communication and resolve conflicts. Another chapter is devoted to choices about children—whether or not to have children, methods of birth control, dealing with infertility, and the experience of pregnancy for the expectant mother and her partner.

In Part Three, "Marital and Family Intimacy Over Time," we trace the family's development from the birth of the first child, to the departure of the last child, and finally to the middle and later years of adulthood. The life patterns of singles and of couples without children are also discussed. In a chapter on relationship termination, we discuss the causes of divorce and the effects on the couple and their children; we also examine the effects of an unhappy marriage on all concerned. A chapter on achieving economic life goals within a family is also included. Throughout this section, we emphasize the challenges and satisfactions offered by intimate relationships and family interactions during all phases of the life cycle.

The exploration of differences and similarities in relationship and family patterns by socioeconomic status, racial and ethnic identity, religious belief, sex, and age has been incorporated into discussions of major topics and concepts.

Features. *Marriage and the Family* is written in a clear and straightforward style. We discuss and apply complex theoretical material in a manner that is readable and interesting, yet challenging to the student.

We have incorporated a number of learning aids for students. Brief dialogues, or "playlets," introduce each chapter; these capsulize the major focus of the chapter and serve to stimulate interest. Boxed supplemental material within chapters, such as discussions of important new research, highlights issues discussed in the text. Each chapter begins with a topical outline and ends with a numbered summary, a list of key concepts, thought-provoking questions, and suggested readings. A glossary of important terms is found at the end of the text.

Acknowledgments. The emotional support and the intellectual input of many people go into the production of a textbook. We are grateful for the support we received from our families and friends during the difficult process of writing a textbook. Our parents and spouses—Dr. and Mrs. I. E. Schapiro, Blanche Koch, James Levande, and Dorothy Sax—helped us in countless ways. Sheldon and Noreen Schapiro, Michael Koch, Milton and Hana Eidelsheim, Donald and Sharlene Garfield, Martin and Andrea Freed, Karin and Harvey Kelber, and many others were there for us when we needed them. School of Social Work colleagues and others at Michigan State University shared the good times and the bad and gave continued support.

One of the authors had to spend a year based in Washington, D.C., where journalist Lawrence Mosher shared his home and his insights. Writer Daniel Greene and his wife, Mary, offered comfort, commentary on the emerging book, and loyal friendship.

We gained important insights from informal conversations with people in various fields. These special persons include Dr. F. Theodore Reid, Celia Rice, Joseph Giordano and the late Grace Giordano, Freya Barr, Dr. David Roth, Hunter Campbell, and Richard Koff. Faculty members of the J. L. Kellogg Graduate School of Management at Northwestern University applied their business acumen to our discussion of the economic problems of raising families.

We are thankful for the suggestions of the hundreds of students who have challenged, applied, and in large measure shaped the content and direction of this book.

Carolyn McKee organized the vast amount of research material and provided assistance throughout the writing of the book. Many detailed features of the text would have been far more difficult to complete without the superb skills of Lynda Palmer. Sue Kerman transformed sheafs of rough draft into clean manuscript.

The following academic reviewers offered comments and advice during the development of the text, and in some cases, added considerably to the structure of the book: Luella K. Alexander, University of South Florida; Charles J. Buehler, Virginia Commonwealth University; John H. Curtis, Valdosta State College; Jerry N. Harrison, New Mexico State University; Mark Hutter, Glassboro State College; Davor Jedlicka, The University of Georgia; Ronald A. Klocke, Mankato State University; Denise LeBlanc, University of Wisconsin, Stout; James R. Long, Golden West College; Theresita Polzin, Metropolitan State College; Roger H. Rubin, University of Maryland; and Janice Swenson, Southern Connecticut State College.

The assistance of our publisher guided the book to completion.

Diane I. Levande

Joanne B. Koch

Lewis Z. Koch

C H A P T E R 1

Intimacy, Marriage, and Family:
A Developmental View

SHE: Was I ever that young?

HE: Was I ever that slim?

SHE: It's like looking at someone else's wedding picture. I was such a different person then.

HE: I wasn't a person then. I was just a kid. I didn't know anything. If I had known then what I know now . . .

SHE: Yes?

HE: I wouldn't have waited six months to marry you.

SHE: I've been at least three different people since we've been married—a shy, kind of passive teenager, a bossy mom . . .

HE: A great lover.

SHE: Lord knows I wasn't that when we married. That's one thing you did know. You had to teach me.

HE: You were one helluva student.

SHE: There was that year after Mom died when I couldn't make love at all.

HE: And the seven months that I was out of work—and impotent.

SHE: During the day you pretended to go to the office, but at night your body refused to pretend.

HE: That firing was the best thing that ever happened to us. Our marriage was getting stale. I didn't even know the kids. I guess I was a work-aholic.

SHE: And I was depressed and lonely. Funny, you were afraid to tell me you were out of a job and the minute I knew you needed me to help, I came to life. Just when the kids didn't need me any more, you did. Getting my first job was really the beginning of a whole new marriage for us.

HE: It's a good thing you didn't know what a great accountant you were when we first met. You probably would have refused to marry me. You would have wanted a career.

SHE: If I were a young woman today, with job training, maybe, maybe I would want to remain single.

HE: And maybe I would say, "Let's live together," instead of "Will you marry me?"

SHE: But look at our daughter. Did you ever believe Janie would be engaged at 20? For years she's been telling me that her life would be totally different from mine. Yet with all her options and her degree coming up, she's choosing marriage.

HE: She's in love.

SHE: Do we know at 19 or 21 what love is?

INTRODUCTION

Marriage is an end and a beginning. It is the end of the uncertain period of courtship, an act of bonding that provides a degree of security and stability that had not existed before. It is also the starting point of a new relationship. When couples exchange vows, few are fully aware of how different marriage will be from their previous relationship. The new partnership will require an unprecedented sharing of emotion, responsibility, resources, and vulnerability. Such a partnership evolves gradually, with time and dedication.

The nature of this evolution will be a major focus of this book. We shall look at certain "predictable" periods of change in the partnership—those events in the life cycle of husband and wife that typically demand a new adaptation. We shall also consider some of the internal challenges of the marriage relationship: the need for verbal and nonverbal communication, conflict resolution, mutual sexual satisfaction, role assessment, work and career issues, and the handling of economic responsibilities within the family, as well as the economic vicissitudes beyond the family.

When a marriage begins, husband and wife may already feel a sense of closeness, sharing, and mutual regard. This affectionate intimacy can deepen, or diminish, over the course of the marriage. Throughout this text we shall be asking what contributes to the development of intimacy within marriage.

The development of intimacy between husband and wife depends on many factors; primary among them are the resources that two individuals bring to their marriage. We shall discover how the individual's development before marriage can influence the course of the relationship. We shall also explore families as complex units that tend to generate their own divisions of labor and power (obvious as well as hidden), their own rules of communication and standards of behavior. Beyond the individual and family unit is the larger social system. We shall examine ways in which the family is influenced by that social system and ways in which the family unit influences the system.

The developmental approach to marriage and family requires an appreciation of all these moving forces. The advantage of this approach is its appreciation of the dynamism, richness, and complexity of marriage. It recognizes marriage and family as forms of human relating that must adapt to individual and social change.

We shall start by looking at the status of marriages and families in the United States today. We shall examine some of the historical and social forces that have led to current trends in marriage and divorce. We shall then move to the realm of individual and family development, pointing out some of the basic skills that can enhance intimacy and suggesting some of the personal adaptations that serve to strengthen marriages and help individual families to endure.

THE CHANGING STATUS OF MARRIAGE AND FAMILY

Patterns of marrying and divorcing have definitely changed in recent decades. The family, which even in periods of great social unrest has been a bulwark of stability and even vitality, is now under attack for its *lack* of stability. Are families these days less flexible in responding to needs and resolving conflicts? Do couples expect marriage to satisfy all their social and psychological needs? When they are disappointed, do they reject marriage as impossible? Is marriage and the traditional family obsolete?

Statistics on Changing Patterns

With all the predictions about the impending demise of the institution of marriage, it is surprising that two of the leading authorities on family statistics, Paul C. Glick and Arthur J. Norton, find that "two of every three first marriages taking place today are expected to last 'until death do us part.'" Why are young couples still choosing to have an average of two children? And why, with at least one bad marriage behind them, do four out of every five divorced persons remarry?

These same demographers recognize that families today are more vulnerable to disruption and more diversified: "Forty percent of all marriages among young women now in their late twenties may end in divorce, if these women repeat the recent experience of their older sisters." More people—almost two million men and women—are living together without entering into a marriage. Many more adults—15 million—live alone. Many more children live in single-parent families or with one biological parent and one stepparent—only 67 percent of the children under 18 in the United States live with both of their own parents, who have not been previously married. About one in three first births are conceived before marriage, and one-tenth of remarried women's children are born between marriages. Only half of all pregnancies result in legitimate live births (Glick and Norton 1977, p. 3).

Changes in Family and Work Cycles

Historically, there have been important differences between men and women in the timing of family and work cycles. Given the demands of the American economy today, both men and women need more years to pre-pare for their professional careers than they used to. Earlier in the century, marriage for men meant that a man was ready to be the breadwinner. Men are no longer waiting until they have completed their professional and technical training before getting married, nor are they necessarily ex-pected to be the sole support of a family. Between the first decade of the century and the period of high marriage rates after World War II, the median age for men entering marriage declined by about three years. Women, on the other hand, seem to be postponing marriage. The median age of women at their first marriage was not quite 21 for most of the century, but the median age of women marrying for the first time in the 1970s was slightly higher—21.2 years (Glick 1977, p. 5).

Women are also having fewer children, and both men and women are living longer. In comparison with the women of 1910, women entering marriage during the 1970s were expected to have between one and two *fewer* children, to end childbearing three years earlier, and to have 22 more years of married life after the last child left home (Glick 1977, p. 5).

Career trends of men and women are changing in other ways that affect the family. Two-worker families are on the increase, especially in times of economic stress, while one-worker families are on the decrease (see Figure 1.1). Participation of women in the work force has changed dramatically, and a second revolution, greater "attachment" to the work force through involvement in full-time and permanent jobs, is just getting underway.

Women of the younger generation, born after 1940, are most significant in this work revolution. Their attachment to the labor force, as we shall discuss in our chapter on role patterns, is also revolutionizing family struc-ture (Masnick and Bane 1980, p. 63). The length of time spent in the labor force is also changing for men and women. Men tend to be older when they start work and younger when they retire. Women now tend to be younger

FIGURE 1.1 Employment Characteristics of Households, 1960, 1975, and 1990

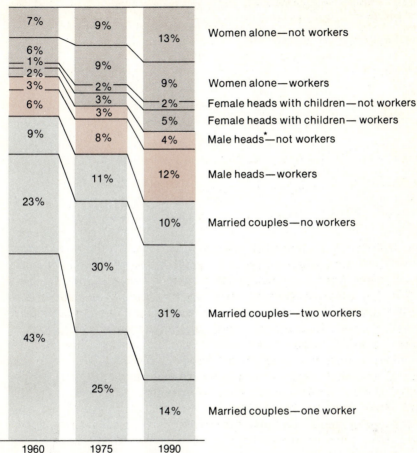

7%	9%	13%	Women alone—not workers
6%			
1%	9%		
2%			
3%	2%	9%	Women alone—workers
6%	3%	2%	Female heads with children—not workers
	3%	5%	Female heads with children— workers
9%	8%	4%	Male heads*—not workers
	11%	12%	Male heads—workers
23%		10%	Married couples—no workers
	30%	31%	Married couples—two workers
43%			
	25%	14%	Married couples—one worker

1960   1975   1990

* The term "male heads" includes unmarried males living alone or with their children.
Source: George Masnick and Mary Jo Bane, *The Nation's Families: 1960–1990* (Cambridge, Mass.: Joint Center of Urban Studies of M. I. T. and Harvard University, 1980), p. 5.

when they start to work. Although women, on the average, still spend less time in the labor force than men, a greater number of them are either continuing to work when children are born or returning to at least part-time employment when their children are very young and then working full time when their children reach school age (see Figure 1.2). These changes in work patterns influence many aspects of family life, including role division, parenting, and the handling of economic issues. In future chapters we will be commenting on the impact of these new work patterns.

The youth of new parents may affect their style of parenting. In the

FIGURE 1.2 Percentage of Married Women (Husband Present) Working Year-Round, Full-Time and Part-Time, by Age of Youngest Child, 1960–1978

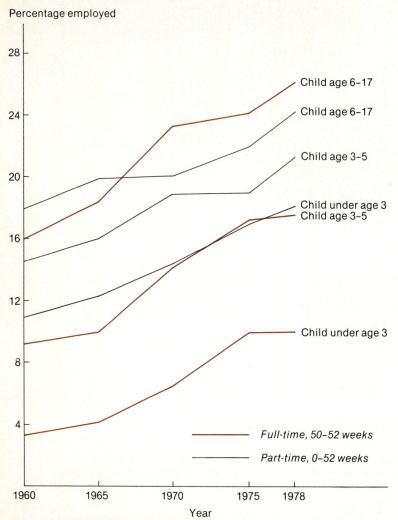

Source: George Masnick and Mary Jo Bane, *The Nation's Families: 1960–1990* (Cambridge, Mass.: Joint Center of Urban Studies of M. I. T. and Harvard University, 1980), p. 81.

1960s, half of all new fathers were under 23, and half of all new mothers were under 21. Younger fathers tend to be less authoritarian—less likely to demand absolute obedience from children. The youth of many new parents and their experience as two-worker families encourage more equal distribution of homemaking and child-rearing tasks. People who become grandparents younger may choose to participate more in the upbringing of their grandchildren (Neugarten and Datan 1973, p. 67). Or these youthful

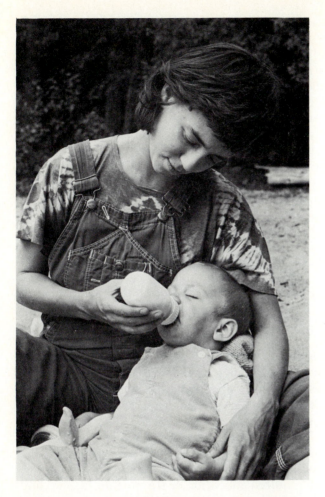

Changes in society initiate different patterns in family interaction. Parenting today is much less formal than in the past. (Susan Lapides)

grandparents may choose to make new plans of their own—returning to school, embarking on a new "retirement" career, moving to a warmer climate where they can share activities with their peers. This may leave the young, inexperienced parents on their own.

There is another, less common trend that shows signs of strengthening in the eighties—the tendency of young people to delay marriage and to begin childbearing at a later age (Glick 1977). Among those who delay marriage, both husband and wife have been accustomed to living autonomously. Their history of personal independence and work experience also tends to encourage an egalitarian approach to parenting and household responsibilities.

Our society has gradually moved from simply tolerating individual differences to encouraging self-discovery and personal change. Divorce, experimental forms of family life, children born to unmarried women, sexual activity unrelated to marriage—all are accepted as alternative lifestyles. Greater emphasis has been placed on self-fulfillment, which sometimes works against the maintenance of a viable family. Whether or not this trend will serve to rejuvenate the family and redistribute responsibilities more equitably remains to be seen. But whether the family continues in spite of, or because of, such social upheavals, it does continue. Couples keep on marrying and having children. And this general historical trend is not expected to reverse itself.

Examining these shifting social patterns of work participation, age of marriage and childbearing, and stress on self-fulfillment will help to explain some of the new strains and satisfactions of marriage in contemporary America. Another major contribution to our understanding of any given marriage is an awareness of forces that shape individual development. For it will be, after all, two unique individuals who constitute and continuously shape an intimate relationship.

STAGES AND TASKS IN DEVELOPMENT

Marital and family relationships continue to be central to the lives of most people, yet the rising divorce rates suggest that we are ill prepared for these relationships. Professions require a long period of educational preparation. Young people who want to become teachers, doctors, or accountants know that they must spend years preparing for their professions. Even driving a car in our society requires a test of knowledge and skills. Yet we require no test of couples about to be married (except for the Wasserman blood test, which detects syphillis). Perhaps more importantly, we do not offer any required education or training for marital and family relationships.

Possibilities, growth, process, becoming—these are words that connote the new attitudes toward male/female relationships. This new view favors attitudes that welcome change and reject limitations, that support equality and reject hierarchy, that allow men to be nurturing and women to be assertive. Yet the young man who strides into the singles' bar has a personal history; the young woman who initiates a conversation with a stranger at a friend's party also has a personal history. Their histories affect the way they interact in relationships, the kind of relationships they form, the men or women they are attracted to. Why does the young man in the singles' bar find certain traits attractive? Why does the young woman feel an immediate sympathy with the tall stranger, while another recent acquaintance bores or even disgusts her? Why is the young man seeking to satisfy certain needs and not others? The qualities men and women look for in a partner—consciously and unconsciously—relate in part to their psychological history.

The roots of intimacy in marriage extend far back into one's earliest experiences. Self-understanding is an important part of learning how to be intimate and of forming intimate relationships. Personal history begins at conception, with each person-to-be given a unique genetic endowment. This genetic endowment determines to some degree a person's physical characteristics and intellectual capability and may even affect creativity and temperament, in ways that we shall examine in Chapter 11. Environment also greatly influences the ways in which a child develops and grows, how he or she adapts individual genetic endowment to a particular situation in life. We shall look first at the stages of personal development and then discuss ways in which the culture influences individual development.

Stages of Individual Development

Individual development largely precedes and powerfully influences the development of intimacy, especially in the marital relationship. The experiences an individual encounters during development will also modify behavior. Even though early experiences may be particularly significant, the impact of other peoples' responses to a person continues to modify behavior throughout childhood and into adulthood.

What do we mean when we say that individuals develop? When a child learns to walk and talk, or when an adolescent stops running away when angry, we say the child or adolescent has *developed*. By this we mean not simply a random change, which could be reversed at any moment, but genuine growth, a forward progression, a step toward greater complexity or increased skills.

Each person develops in his or her own unique ways, but also in ways similar to other human beings. While research in this area is relatively recent, psychologists have gradually recognized a number of stages in individual development. The twentieth century began with a recognition of the importance of infancy and childhood. Then adolescents came into their own as a group worthy of consideration. Quite recently, studies have been conducted that suggest that development continues in more or less predictable stages throughout adulthood.

Age is a factor in human development, especially in infancy and early childhood. But people grow at different rates, especially in terms of psychological growth. Many psychologists and sociologists therefore find it more useful to look at life stages in terms of *developmental tasks*, or challenges that arise at different stages of the life cycle, for which people acquire new skills in dealing with their environment. We know more about a young adult if we say he or she has developed the capacity for intimacy than if we say that person has reached the age of 21. Developmental tasks play an important part in individual development and in the development of the family. If both husband and wife have met the challenges of identity and intimacy, they will be better equipped to handle the challenges of parenthood than a couple who are still grappling with issues of individual identity. A person's gender plays a strong role in the way parents and the culture treat that individual, but in this chapter we shall concentrate on developmental tasks without regard to gender.

Unlike our common usage of the word "task," which might refer to a chore as simple as taking out the garbage, a developmental task is a complex undertaking, one that is never completely finished. It is a challenge that individuals meet with varying degrees of success. An individual developmental task arises in a certain period of a person's life. When a person meets the challenge of that period with some success, there is a sense of accomplishment and progress. It will also be easier for that person to meet the next developmental task. A person who fails to accomplish the task appropriate to his or her stage of development may suffer the disapproval of others who are important. In childhood, the significant others are parents, siblings, and, later, peers and teachers. In adulthood, disapproval may come from family or society, or it may be internalized as a sense of dissatisfaction or, in extreme cases, despair. Failure to accomplish an earlier task usually presents difficulties with later tasks. As we shall see, the infant who does not develop a basic sense of trust will have trouble asserting independence during childhood and relating in intimate ways as an adult.

In his book *Childhood and Society* (1963), psychologist Erik Erikson divided individual development into eight stages (Figure 1.3), which serve as one basis for the developmental approach to human behavior. Each period has its challenges expressed as *polarities—basic trust* versus *mistrust*, or *autonomy* versus *shame* and *doubt*. Erikson used these polarities to allow for the wide range of possible outcomes at any given stage of life. Using Erikson's framework, and supplementing it with work by other psychologists (particularly Jane Loevinger's work on ego development), we now examine these eight stages of development. We shall refer to them as Infancy, Early Childhood, Play Age, School Age, Adolescence, Young Adulthood, Adulthood, and Maturity.

Infancy. At birth, an infant cannot differentiate itself from its surroundings and is totally dependent on parents for meeting physical and psychological needs, such as food, warmth, and loving care. The infant does not clearly perceive itself as having an identity separate from the parents, particularly the mother, or from the surrounding world (Loevinger 1976, pp. 15–16). This is the stage when the polarities of *trust* and *mistrust* vie for dominance in the child's psyche—when, according to Erikson, the infant acquires, to varying degrees, a basic sense of trust. The

FIGURE 1.3 Erikson's Stages of Development

	1	2	3	4	5	6	7	8
I Infancy	Trust vs. Mistrust							
II Early Childhood		Autonomy vs. Shame, Doubt						
III Play Age			Initiative vs. Guilt					
IV School Age				Industry vs. Inferiority				
V Adolescence					Identity vs. Role Confusion			
VI Young Adulthood						Intimacy vs. Isolation		
VII Adulthood							Generativity vs. Stagnation	
VIII Mature Age								Ego Integrity vs. Disgust, Despair

Source: Adapted from *Identity and the Life Cycle* by Erik H. Erikson, by permission of W. W. Norton and Co., Inc. Copyright © 1980 by W. W. Norton and Co., Inc. Copyright © 1959 by International Universities Press, Inc.

sense of trust comes from a feeling of inner security, which is conveyed to the infant by its biological parents or by the primary person who cares for it. Sometimes an infant fails to acquire a basic sense of trust, and this can profoundly affect the individual's ability to form close, intimate relationships later in life.

Early Childhood.   The mastery of control over one's muscles brings with it a series of new possibilities. The child is able to walk away or return, able to say yes or no, able to go to the bathroom or not. The young child thus enters a new phase of life when the primary challenges are *autonomy* versus *shame* and *doubt* (Erikson 1963). No longer as dependent upon the nurturing parent as the helpless infant was, the toddler begins to experiment with holding on and letting go. In the letting-go activities, independence becomes more attractive and the child begins to distinguish between self and surroundings (Loevinger 1976).

Play Age.   Having mastered toilet functions and increased muscular control, the child can move around and away with more confidence. Language has developed sufficiently to give the child (at about age three to age five) a new option—to express feelings or deny them. New intellectual powers combined with these language skills create activity within one's imagination as well as extensive physical activity. Imagination provides the child with absorbing fantasies. The combination of fantasy life, choices for self-expression, and greater exploration of the physical world, including body and genitals, provides the challenges of this period: *initiative* versus *guilt*. It is at this stage that the child begins to develop what we can call a conscience (Duvall 1962, pp. 30–31).

In the stages of both early childhood and play age, the child responds impulsively to rewards and punishments. He has a strong need for other people, but tends to see them only in terms of "nice to me" or "not nice to me," that is, in selfish terms. Almost all his awareness is of the present, not the past or the future. He is likely to locate his troubles in a place or a situation, rather than in himself. So if the child is in trouble and being punished, he is tempted to run away, thinking that will get rid of the problem. A child who remains too long at this stage may be said to be uncontrollable. Because young children do not yet perceive themselves as agents causing their own actions, parental rewards and punishments at this stage are not always effective in changing their behavior.

Eventually the child moves into a self-protective stage, when he does begin to see himself as an agent, a being who causes things to happen. He begins to have a sense of the past and the future and to anticipate rewards and punishments from parents and teachers. He learns to control his impulses to get what he wants.

The child also begins to understand that there are rules that link certain actions to rewards and punishments. He uses these rules for his own satisfaction and advantage, without as yet internalizing any notions of right or wrong, good or bad. An action is wrong only if he gets caught and is punished for it (Loevinger 1976, p. 16).

Some adults and young people seem to remain at this stage. Such people tend to be overly concerned with control and advantage in their relationships with others. A young woman finds it difficult to say "I love you" for fear of losing the upper hand. Similarly, a young man may refuse to call a woman friend out of pride or self-protectiveness, thinking that if he does call, it will show her that he cares about her, putting him at a disadvantage in their relationship. Yet he may really want to speak with her. He does not see that he need not regard life as a game in which someone gains only if someone else loses. He does not see that in giving his affection, in caring, he may get much in return—another's affection.

School Age.   Just as *trust* and *mistrust* are, in Erikson's scheme, the basis polarities of the infancy phase, so *industry* and *inferiority* are the polarities of the school-age phase. The child learns how to do and make things with others. She learns to accept instructions and to win recognition. She may develop a capacity to enjoy work or a sense of inadequacy and inferiority if her work is not recognized (Duvall 1962, pp. 30–31).

At school, the child learns to conform and to identify personal welfare with that of the group (family or peers). This can happen only as the child begins to trust others. Seeking the group's acceptance and approval, she is cooperative and helpful. She does not fear the consequences of her actions as much as she fears disapproval by others. Lacking independence in thinking as well as in actions, the child tends to see people in stereotypes, particularly sex-role stereotypes (Loevinger 1976, pp. 17–18).

Adolescence.   The polarities of this phase are *identity* and *role confusion.* "Who am I?" is the key question at this time. All children have fantasies and ideas about themselves: who they are and who they will become. Adolescents compare these childhood fantasies with more realistic perceptions of who they are—their biological drives, temperamental styles, genetic endowments, native abilities and limitations, and the opportunities offered by social economic circumstances.

Adolescents in all cultures have certain common goals. The child must grow up and become a separate individual. According to Erikson, this stage of development is a time for rehearsing the various roles a young person is considering, a period of time for consolidating previous psychological changes into what Erikson calls *identity.* Societies undergoing rapid changes put the adolescent under special pressures beyond those

↑ Cooperative efforts of school-age children (Alan Oransky)

←Meeting the challenge of autonomy in early childhood (David Krathwohl)

↓ Adolescence: consolidating peer relationships and testing new behaviors (Florence Sharp)

↑ Expressing generativity in adulthood by providing guidance for the next generation (Susan Lapides)

←Young adults expressing views through political activity (Barbara Alper)

↓ Maturity: coming to terms with one's life (Cynthia Benjamins)

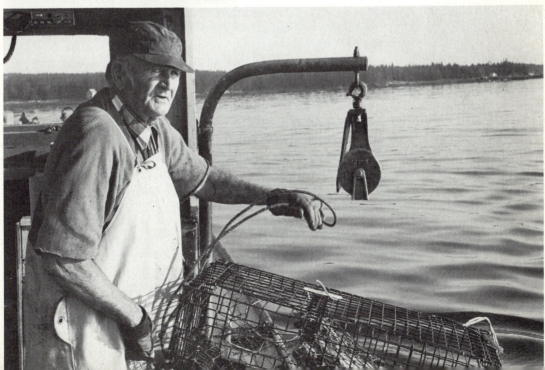

created by the biological changes of puberty. An American adolescent today, for example, must make a choice about sexual activity and birth control, a vocational choice, and a choice concerning drinking and drugs.

Thus, certain particular social strains of our culture are added to the normal psychological strains of adolescence. Adolescents in our society become intensely involved with one another, partially as a way of dealing with pressures they believe adults cannot understand. As youth connects with youth, a kind of subculture is produced. The "youth culture" as sociologist James Coleman has labeled it, may use drugs, music, and sexual intimacy to produce at least a temporary openness (Coleman 1974). Not all adolescent peer cultures are "anti-establishment." Some actually reflect many parental values; but the adolescent uses the peer group as a "filter through which parent norms must pass" (Siman 1977, p. 273). Parental relations during adolescence may be strained, but this is a period of redefinition and realignment, not a discontinuation of parent-child relations or an end of parental influence. The adolescent tends to feel like a child when at home, and so people of this age use the peer group as a testing ground for new behavior.

Friendships also change at this time, becoming more tolerant and less possessive. Among teenage girls, friendships tend to be intense. If a friend is loyal, the adolescent can accept differences in personality and taste. Friends provide solace and empathy. They become intimate confidantes (Selman 1980).

Adolescence is also a time when heterosexual relations begin, first as a tentative and often bantering interplay between a group of boys and a group of girls, later with actual dating often in the context of groups of couples (Dunphy 1963). Dating gives adolescents a chance to rehearse intimacy. Dating, especially in the later years of adolescence, may also involve sexual intimacy. By the age of 19, half of the unmarried women in America have had sexual intercourse, and the median age for first intercourse in that sexually active group is 16 or 17 (Kantner and Zelnik 1977). Increasingly, the sexual activity of adolescents is not tied to marriage, though it is usually seen as an expression of intense feeling or love (Sorensen 1973). Sexual activity before marriage among adolescents was common even in colonial times; as many as one-third to one-half of the brides in 1750 were "going to the altar pregnant" (Demos 1976, p. 17). But sexual activity that is clearly detached from the prospect of marriage is a new phenomenon in our culture.

Young Adulthood. As adolescents become adults, they face the polarities of *intimacy* and *isolation*. Young people may be torn between yearnings for intimacy and fears of involvement and commitment. As young adults begin to feel more secure in their sense of their own identity, they become more trusting of others and can create intimacy with themselves and with others.

In moving from adolescence to adulthood, young people begin to appreciate their own and others' individuality. They no longer need to conform strictly to the norms of their peers. The young man or woman can perceive a larger number of possibilities in any situation and so begins to see exceptions to rules. A young man may realize that he cannot always live up to the ideals he set for himself or that it may be many years before he can achieve them. A young woman may question what is expected of her by her peers and may turn to other sources—teachers, relatives, or friends—for guidance. She may see that she has potentially conflicting goals—the goal of establishing her independence and her career versus the goal of becoming involved in an intimate relationship that leads to marriage and a family. Which goal will she concentrate on first?

Young adults make choices and accept responsibility for those choices. Young men and women gain an awareness of their privileges and rights and develop a sense of fairness, of the responsibilities that others have toward them. They may come to the conviction that adults in their world lack this sense of fairness. Their concern for rights (their own and others') may find expression in their social and political behavior—participation in political activities or even in civil disobedience against laws they believe are unjust.

Adulthood.   Erickson's polarities for adulthood are *generativity* or creativity, on the one hand, and *stagnation*, on the other. In Chapter 14 we will use some more recent findings to map the adulthood period. We will see that generativity, which Erikson saw as primarily an interest in establishing and guiding the next generation, can be expressed in many ways. It is during this time that the individual makes a choice about whether to have children. But parenting is not the only means of meeting the challenge of generativity. Whether one is a parent or remains childless, generativity may be expressed in many ways. People may achieve generativity by forming mentoring relationships at work and guiding younger colleagues, or by nurturing other family members and friends. Adults are aided in finding creative and generative functions by individual changes—the recognition of individual differences, a greater tolerance for both themselves and other people. If they are able to accept their own limitations, they are likely to become less demanding of others, more affectionate and loving. The adult years may also be a time of new beginnings, returning to school, or training for a new or altered career.

Maturity.   In Erikson's final stage, maturity, the polarities are *ego integrity* and *disgust, despair*. As this period may actually extend some 20 to 30 years, some researchers now divide this stage of life into young-old and old-old (Neugarten 1974). The challenge of the aging period is to integrate or bring together various aspects of the self that have been discovered throughout life. The mature person must take complete responsibility for his or her life. If these integrations do not succeed, the individual will experience despair and disgust.

The Importance of Developmental Stages

Each period of development in the life of an individual has its tasks and its crises; each has a range of possible outcomes. Erikson has set up extreme polarities: *generativity* and *stagnation, trust* and *mistrust.* Few individuals, of course, wind up at either extreme. Most people emerge from infancy, for example, neither totally trusting nor continually suspicious. From the toddler stage they are likely to gain some sense of independence but perhaps a few lingering doubts, from the preschool years a sense of initiative but also a hidden reservoir of guilt that may be tapped during future experiences.

The way in which one stage is resolved will influence the individual's experience at future stages. A child who has learned to trust the world is more likely to assert autonomy than a child whose trust has been violated by unkindness or indifference. A child with a strong sense of inferiority may flee from the demands of dating. On the other hand, a child who arrives at adolescence having achieved basic trust, independence, initiative, and a sense of mastery is more likely to weave these accomplishments into a sense of identity and feelings of confidence in terms of future relationships.

It is at the stage termed "young adulthood" in Erikson's scheme that most people are expected to commit themselves to physical intimacy, occupational choice, energetic competition, and self-definition. Many young people will not be equipped for these demands. They may have sexual experiences, friendships, and affairs, but these relationships may be desperate attempts to find out who they are or perhaps to run away from the person they are afraid they have become. Fortunately, even at this stage of life, development has not ceased; change is still possible. But change at this stage may require coming to terms with some of the unresolved issues of previous stages.

TASKS AND CYCLES OF FAMILY LIFE

Tasks for Families

Married life presents tasks of its own, which differ from the psychological tasks of individual development that we have been discussing. Among the tasks that the family as a unit must perform are the satisfaction of survival needs, the ongoing contribution to the marital and family relationship— by husband and wife and later by children as well—and the establishment of boundaries that allow access to the outside world but also provide privacy (Aldous 1978; Duvall 1962):

1. Couples must meet their basic needs—food, clothing, shelter—and must be able to provide these for their children as well. They must be (and feel themselves to be) physically safe and secure. Providing these necessities is a basic developmental task of the family.
2. Couples must be motivated to contribute to the relationship, trying to make it successful and satisfying over a lifetime. If and when they have children, those children must reach a stage of maturity at which they feel motivated to cooperate in family activities and tasks, whether it be going on a camping trip or cleaning out the family garage. Cooperation and mutual support become important resources during later stages of family life when both partners may feel oppressed by the heightened demands of child rearing and careers and become temporarily disenchanted with family life.
3. As it copes with its own internal concerns, the family sometimes seems to exclude the world from its affairs. In effect, the family sets up and maintains boundaries between itself and the world. In the United States, where the family is said to be "nuclear," the family excludes not only people who have no family ties with the parents, but even aunts and uncles and more distant relatives who are still members of the "extended" family. The extent to which this is true depends partly on the cultural and ethnic background of the parents. In some other societies, the boundaries between the immediate family and the extended network of aunts, uncles, and cousins are much less clearly defined.

Setting up boundaries and monitoring outside interactions may be especially important early in the marriage. If the husband and wife are young and have never been married before, they may feel more at home in their old relationships with their own parents than in the new husband-wife relationship. But the task of setting boundaries is an ongoing and necessary process. Young married couples continue to have friends outside the marriage. Both partners also may have professional relationships with colleagues and coworkers of both sexes. All these outside interactions are monitored and controlled by the couple. The situation is even more complex with the arrival of children, who gradually form relationships with peers, teachers, and other adults, and eventually have their own families.

Each family member has a role in carrying out these family tasks; each role carries with it certain tasks or responsibilities that must be performed if the family is to continue as a unit. If the husband/father or wife/mother leaves or dies, the family may lose some of its ability to function. The parent who remains is overburdened. She or he must play both roles. The single parent often must not only earn money for the family's food, clothing, and shelter, but must also prepare the food, shop for clothes, and maintain and repair the house, in addition to raising the children. If the remaining parent is the father, he may find himself overburdened with responsibilities of child care for which he has not been prepared. If, as is usually the case, the single parent is the mother, she may have to seek further education or training to find an adequate full-time job. We shall explore role strain in Chapter 7 and other issues relating to single parenting in Chapter 12. Even two parents often need the support and encouragement of others, as we shall see in Chapter 11.

Stages of Family Development

Thinking about marriage and family in terms of developmental stages can aid us in several ways. First, it can better prepare us to cope with certain events when (and if) they do occur. Second, when it is clearly understood that all marriages and all families face normal, stressful periods, the sense of individual isolation that so many people feel—the feeling that "we're the only couple going through this"—is less severe. Although this knowledge may not decrease the initial pain people feel while going through a certain crisis period, it may shorten the length of time that those intense feelings of sadness and unhappiness last.

Within any given family, at least two people are undergoing their own psychological development while performing the tasks related to family life. If and when children arrive, their stages of development further complicate the pattern of growth and change. Thus we cannot divide family life into stages as easily or as clearly as we could divide the life of an individual.

Yet most couples who bear and rear children undergo certain significant changes in their lives. These changes can be used to mark off stages in the family life cycle. As we shall discuss in more detail in Chapter 14, these changes also influence the level of satisfaction within the marriage.

1. The couple marries.
2. Children arrive.
3. The eldest child (and others in their turn) starts school.
4. The eldest child reaches adolescence.
5. The last child leaves home.
6. One or both of the spouses retire.

These are, of course, only the broadest and most obvious periods of change in the life of the family. And in mapping the life of a family, we must also take into account the influence of events outside the family. Parents undergo career changes, job pressures, and tensions arising in their outside relationships. Their children, too, experience pressure to succeed in school or sports, and to be respected and liked by their schoolmates. Pressures of this sort can create strain and conflict. We shall look at ways in which conflict can be managed in Chapter 9.

The First Years of Marriage.   One of the most significant studies of marital satisfaction over the life cycle (Campbell, Converse, and Rogers 1976) points to married life without or before the advent of children—a period sometimes called the preparent years—as a time of unprecedented satisfaction in the life cycle. While each spouse may be devoting long hours to education or career, the couple also have long periods of uninterrupted time to spend together. These hours allow the couple to share their likes, wishes, hopes, dreams, and ideals for themselves, for each other, and for their marriage. The resources developed in these preparent years may stand the couple in good stead when they face the greater responsibilities of the parenting period.

Arrival of Children.   The arrival of the first baby brings changes in many aspects of the marriage relationship, from the partners' sexual relations to their housekeeping schedules and budgeting patterns.

Even in very diverse families the first child means adulthood, new responsibilities, a new status in the community and with relatives and friends, a readjustment of tasks, a transformation from "couple" to "family." A dependent, irrational, highly demanding, important person enters the scene and his future depends on his parents. (Hoffman and Manis 1977, p. 16)

The new, demanding person in the family often ushers in what has been called the "period of chronic emergency" (Gutmann 1975).

A fascinating picture of what happens to a couple's relationship when the first child is born emerges from a recent study by Hoffman and Manis (1977). They selected 1,569 wives and 456 husbands (constituting a representative sample of married couples in the country) to determine what effects a child had on marital satisfaction or dissatisfaction. Their study suggests that "the advent of children seems to move the couple in a traditionalistic direction" (p. 5). This shift in the role directions of the spouses occurred regardless of the couple's education or whether the woman was working or not. In Chapter 11 we shall discuss in greater detail the specific sources of strain and satisfaction that parenthood brings. Here it is important to recognize that the first child alters the marriage, complicating the relationship with conflicting demands, deepening it with the sharing of intense lows and highs. "The first child is seen as a strain on the marriage . . . with young parents describing more tensions and anxieties than those at any other stage in the family cycle" (Hoffman and Manis 1977, p. 5). Though couples report more disagreements and even thoughts of divorce, they also find that children bring them closer together, giving them a shared task. Though they have less time to spend together as a couple, they have new concerns and joys to share.

The Eldest Child Starts School.   When the first child goes to school, parents and siblings must adjust to a new routine. But the tug at the heartstrings produced by seeing the first child going off to school is offset in great part by the new freedoms this situation may produce. Studies of marital satisfaction (Hoffman and Manis 1977; Campbell, Converse, and Rogers 1976) indicate that marital satisfaction increases during this period. Many women see this as a good time to return to work. Maternal employment at full-time and part-time jobs has increased dramatically since the 1960s, especially for those women whose children are in school. Other women may view the child's departure for school as an opportunity to return to school themselves or as a chance to pursue other activities that have been delayed during the more dependent period of their children's early years.

Adolescence and Departure of Grown Children.   The adolescence of the first child is more stressful than the beginning of school. Parents worry about negative peer influences, drugs, alcohol, sex, and general "getting into trouble." Girls are generally seen as more of a worry than boys, but this is particularly true when the children are teenagers. Parents worry about a daughter's sexuality and, these days, they are concerned about her vulnerability to attack as well as the possibility of premarital pregnancy (Hoffman and Manis 1977). At this point, the child is less of an actual restriction on the marriage, yet this greater freedom is offset somewhat by worries about the child's safety and future. The Hoffman and Manis study gives some indication that mothers, but not fathers, become "more oriented toward their marital relationship when the youngest reaches adolescence than during the previous years of motherhood" (Hoffman and Manis 1977, p. 18). In Chapter 14 we shall discuss ways in which the adolescence of children can coincide with and aggravate certain midlife changes in their parents.

The Last Child Leaves Home.   When the last child leaves home, a new stage begins in the family cycle. The couple may begin interacting in new ways, partly to compensate for the absence of their children. Earlier in the twentieth century, the last child generally left home to marry and establish a separate household. Today, more young people leave home to work or go to college before they marry.

In the early part of the century, most couples rarely had an "empty nest." Trends now indicate that couples can expect to spend many years of their married life alone, without children. But, as we shall discover in Chapter 14, this is often a period of renewed happiness for the couple.

This extended "empty nest" period has happened partly because families have fewer children and have them earlier, so they are younger when the last child leaves home. The main reason, however, is that people are living longer. There has been a jump in the median age of couples at the death of one spouse, from a median age of 57 years in 1897 to a median age of just over 65 years in 1977 (Glick 1977, p. 9).

Retirement.   Another stage of family development begins when the parents reach the end of their formal work careers. This stage of development brings about sharp changes in the way couples live and interact with each other as well as with their adult children and grandchildren. Although they have retired from the work force, most older people do not lead aimless, empty lives. Many older people are relatively healthy, vigorous individuals. It is essential for people to plan for this period while they are

Men and women today are increasingly sharing child-rearing responsibilities. (Jean-Claude Lejeune)

still working. We shall discuss ways in which this can be done in Chapter 13. For those people who have been poor as adults, retirement may be forced and unplanned, bringing with it even more severe economic problems. Yet many retired people are relatively comfortable in economic terms and thus free to enjoy their leisure time and be active in the community or in the political arena. The years from 55 to 75 and even older may be a time when couples lend their wisdom and maturity to those with whom they come in contact (Neugarten 1974). We shall take a fresh look at this increasingly lengthy and potentially productive period of the family cycle in Chapter 15.

Individual Development versus Family Development

Since the family is composed of individuals, each engaged in personal needs and challenges, there are bound to be strains and conflicts. There appears to be a "life cycle squeeze" in the late twenties and early thirties, as we shall see in Chapter 14. At this time demands from the parents' work outside the home may be at their highest. Yet this is also the stage at which the responsibilities of child rearing are greatest. Husbands and fathers in our society have traditionally attended to outside work, while wives and mothers concentrated on the needs of the home and the young children. Increasingly, in our society, these roles are being shared. The strain of handling a career and the burden of child rearing may be particularly severe in single-parent families, in which the mother or father does not have the help of a spouse in rearing the children but must still maintain a job or career.

Later in the family cycle adolescent children may be striving for independence and freedom while their parents strive to restrain and guide them. Meanwhile these same parents are coming to terms with identity issues of their own. A husband may be feeling a sense of boredom and stagnation in midlife while his wife may be confronting the anxieties and excitement of beginning a new career. The matching or mismatching of individual development and family development may, at times, create stress and conflict within the husband-wife, parent-child relationships. These difficult periods, resulting in part from the unique combinations of sex and age differences that exist in the family, require the use of communication skills, conflict management, and role renegotiation (these skills will be discussed in Chapters 7, 8, and 9). Productive handling of difficult transitions in the lives of individuals and in the cycle of the family may increase growth and intimacy. Failure to respond to changing needs and tasks may bring continuing problems and even termination of marital relations. As we shall discuss further in the chapter on divorce (Chapter 12), the parent-child relationship is a lifelong commitment that can be honored even when husband and wife can no longer maintain their bond.

Limitations of the Developmental Framework

The developmental framework, however useful it may be in describing the life cycle of American families in general, must be adapted and modified when trying to apply it to an individual family. Take the example of couples who choose not to have children. They will have a pattern of development different from that of the majority of couples in this country. We shall be suggesting ways in which people who choose not to marry are likely to experience life-cycle changes. And we shall also consider, in Chapter 5, a variety of alternative lifestyles, but we shall not attempt to fit all the possible types of relationships into one framework. Divorced persons with children, widows and widowers, and those who remarry present special instances.

If, for example, a woman is divorced and has custody of her two children, and a man is divorced and has custody of his child, their marriage will result in three families—hers, his, and theirs. If these two decide to have a child as a result of this remarriage, the complexities of the families increase. They become new parents, but unlike most new parents, they are also dealing with the early adolescence of their older children.

Research into female development suggests that original notions about adult development may be more applicable to men. We shall adapt the developmental framework to women, when possible. Both men and women are affected by the general cultural environment, broad social and economic changes, new work patterns, and shifts in sexual and social mores.

CULTURAL INFLUENCES ON THE FAMILY

Individual psychological development does not take place in a vacuum. People develop their capacities within a family, and that family exists in a particular culture at a particular time in history. Time and place are not merely a backdrop. Profound social and economic changes have occurred in American society since the Industrial Revolution. These changes have altered the functions of the American family. The family remains the fundamental unit of our culture, but its functions have changed. In this section we shall see how the cultural shift from an agrarian to an industrial society has stripped the family of its economic function and changed the relationship of one generation to the next.

Changing Functions of the Family Unit

Prior to the Industrial Revolution, society was generally agrarian. The family was not only a social unit, but also the primary economic unit. The basic necessities of life (food, clothing, shelter) were supplied *by* family members *to* family members: "The household was . . . the primary unit of economic production and exchange. . . . These families possessed an occupational cohesion not even approximated in our own day" (Demos 1976, p. 11). Economic necessities of farm life exerted a "centripetal" force, drawing family members toward the core rather than pushing them away from home. The family was responsible for educating and vocationally training its own; the family was also responsible for providing social services such as care for the elderly, orphans, and indigents.

The Industrial Revolution changed both the economy and the society. Jobs were concentrated in urban areas. Opportunity drew young people away from home. Economic pressures began to exert a "centrifugal" force, pulling family members apart, dividing one generation from another.

This centrifugal pull has continued and even increased. Today, both husbands and wives travel to jobs that may be far from home. The possibility of careers pulling a husband to one state and a wife to another has created a new phenomenon—the commuter marriage. So the cultural upheaval that occurred over a century ago continues to reverberate today.

There have also been changes in the social functions of the family, some of them caused by the agrarian-industrial shift, others resulting from altered concepts of the roles of husband and wife. One can argue as John Demos has (Demos 1970, 1976) that the American family has always been a *nuclear family*—a unit composed primarily of husband, wife, and their children—rather than an *extended family*, which typically includes grandchildren, aunts, uncles, cousins, and other kin. But when the economic productivity of the family was placed outside the home, the roles of mother and father took on a different cast. Father left home to work; mother remained in the home to care for the children. In the twentieth century, the function of children in the family has changed. Rather than leaving home in childhood or adolescence to work or be apprenticed in a trade, children are encouraged to remain at home, where they go through a long period of education and training for life. From this new attitude grew the current state of adolescence and youth culture.

The nuclear family came to signify a particular type of unit that functioned in large part to develop children who could compete by virtue of education, training, and something called "drive," which parents would ideally instill. The period after the Great Depression and World War II was the heyday of the nuclear family in this modern sense, and the noted sociologist Talcott Parsons was its outstanding proponent. Writing in 1955, Parsons stated that every adult in America "is a member of a nuclear family and . . . every child must begin his process of socialization in a nuclear family" (Parsons 1955, p. 17). Parsons referred to the family as a factory—not for producing goods as before, but for turning out personalities suitable for an industrial and competitive society. "It is because the *human* personality is not 'born' but must be 'made' through the socialization process that in the first instance families are necessary. They are 'factories' which produce human personalities" (p. 16).

Parsons saw the "jobs" of male and female in the "family-factory" as unalterably separate and distinct:

It seems quite safe in general to say that the adult feminine role has not ceased to be anchored primarily in the internal affairs of the family, as wife, mother and manager of the household, while the role of the adult male is primarily anchored in the occupational world, in his job and through it by his status-giving and income-earning functions for the family. Even if, as seems possible, it should come about that the average married woman had some kind of job, it seems most unlikely that this relative balance would be upset; that either the roles would be reversed, or their qualitative differentiation in these respects completely erased. (Parsons 1955, pp. 14–15)

Parsons felt that these separate functions led to what he called the "isolation" of the nuclear family. The man, as breadwinner and "instrumental leader" of the family, was isolated from the woman, who remained at home managing the household and serving as socializing agent for the children. Each unit was, in addition to this internal isolation of its members, also isolated from other units. Father competed with father on the job market, mother with mother for domestic excellence and "well brought-up" children. For the generation of adults who had faced the depression and war, this retreat to the family unit may have provided a sense of security and welcome privacy. But the role divisions and other aspects of the atomized postwar society bred frustration for many Americans, particularly American women. Eventually, the frustration led to what Betty Friedan called "a new life plan" for women.

First, she must unequivocally say "no" to the housewife image. This does not mean, of course, that she must divorce her husband, abandon her children, give up her home. She does not have to choose between marriage and career; that was the mistaken choice of the feminine mystique. In actual fact, it is not as difficult as the feminine mystique implies, to combine marriage and motherhood and even the kind of lifelong personal purpose that once was called "career." It merely takes a new life plan—in terms of one's whole life as a woman. (Friedan 1963, p. 330)

Since Friedan was responding to a new attitude already in the air, we can't hold narrowly to the date of her *Feminine Mystique* as the beginning of the post-nuclear family. But the 1960s, a transitional period for many of America's institutions, was the period when the American family began to break out of its nuclear encasement. This nuclear explosion fragmented the American family monolith into a variety of family styles and patterns. Today, one can no longer speak of "the American family." One must now examine families in the plural, paying attention to the many different ways families may exist: single-worker traditional families; two-worker, more egalitarian families; and single-parent families; as well as communes, unmarried couples living together, and single people.

Some of the important trends for American families have been identified by Masnick and Bane in their predictive report *The Nation's Families: 1960–1990* (1980, pp. 2–7). They do not predict the demise of the family, but they do expect that in the next decade, households made up of married couples will increase only slightly, while other types of households will increase dramatically. The majority of young adults will continue to marry and head their own households, although marriage will come later and families will be smaller, with an increasing number of couples choosing to have no children. The generation between 40 and 60, which Masnick and Bane call "the middle-aged generation," will be largely involved in the empty-nest period, and many in that group will be divorced or widowed. The group of women who are over 60 will contain a significant number of widows.

The fact that only 47% [of the adult population] is married at one point in time does not imply that a majority of people do not marry. Most do, in fact, but at older ages, and with other types of living arrangements before, after and often in between. People will have more complicated histories and probably more complicated sets of relationships from one stage of life to another. (Masnick and Bane 1980, p. 7)

Divorce, as we shall see in Chapter 12, has been a major force in changing the nature of families, and even individual life-span development. Since 1955, the number of single-parent families has doubled. While divorce is on the increase, so is remarriage, with close to four out of five divorced persons marrying again. Two out of every three marriages taking place today are expected to endure. Women are marrying later, as many of them are postponing marriage for an upwardly mobile career. Those women who do marry also expect to work. In over half the marriages where the husband is present and there are children under 18, the wife works at least part-time outside the home (Masnick and Bane 1980, p. 73). Yet women are also expecting to have children, and the vast majority of married couples do have at least one child (Glick 1977).

The increase in divorce and the tendency for both parents to work outside the home have figured in changing the social function of the family. Families continue to be socializing forces, but children are not expected to adopt traditional male or female roles. In Chapter 7, we shall discuss the many ways in which roles may be divided within the family and some new attitudes about sex roles that are creating more egalitarian styles of dividing family labors. The socialization of children, while it still remains a primary family function, has also become increasingly a matter of government concern and involvement. Schools are charged with educating the young and, in recent years, sometimes with supervising them after school. Head Start and similar programs bring children under school supervision at an earlier age. Day care, while not at this point under government control, has nevertheless moved outside the home. Insofar as day-care centers must be licensed, they too come under government influence. Since an impersonal agency or bureaucracy has difficulty coping effectively with the personal and individualized needs of families, the tide of social change demands a public policy that is responsive to families yet does not deprive them of functions that they wish to control.

The post-nuclear family members will have a more complicated web of relationships both outside the home, due to work and interaction with educational, legal, and economic institutions, and within the home, due to their own personal histories of prior marriages or prior intimate relationships.

Ethnic Factors

Recognition of ethnic differences in American society was another outcome of the upheaval of the 1960s. The many racial and ethnic groups that have existed throughout our history were finally acknowledged as significant and valuable, rather than as alien groups in need of "melting." This relatively new attitude of honoring ethnic differences further emphasizes the diversity of family life in the United States.

Even research that had been undertaken in the past has been re-examined with this ethnic perspective in mind, just as many accepted theories have been re-examined with attention to possible sexism. For example, one of the major complaints about the conclusions of Parsons and other so-called nuclear-family theoreticians has been that the families they study are too similar—white, urban, middle-class, and Protestant. These critics of the nuclear approach looked at families and saw what they called an "extended kin network," families in which grandparents, aunts, uncles, brothers, and sisters responded with various forms of help and services during illness or financial troubles; these kin provided child care as well as personal and business advice and gifts. This kind of extended kin network can be observed in various forms in Italian, Irish, black, Hispanic, and Jewish families. Research has also shown that a family's socioeconomic status has a great deal to do with the way parents raise their children: "Middle-class parents are more likely to emphasize children's self-direction, working-class parents their conformity to external standards" (Kohn 1977, p. 19). Economic standing and membership in a subgroup exert a profound influence on dating and marriage patterns.

Sociologists now recognize many subcultures within American society. *Ethnicity* is the term that has been used to suggest membership in one of these subgroups: blacks, Irish, Italians, Jews, Poles, Germans, Puerto Ricans, Mexican-Americans, various Slavic groups, and others. These subcultures tend to govern issues basic to marriage, including dating, sexual behavior, time of marriage, spacing of children, and attitudes toward work (Novak 1972; Greeley 1971; Seifer 1973).

But there is some continuity within this change and variety. In subsequent chapters we shall discuss ways in which cultural change and various ethnic standards affect family life. But in closing this chapter it might be well to recognize the persistence of marriage and family through the many cultural upheavals and despite the differences between cultural groups.

More couples might live together before marrying and they might do it more openly than in the past. After marriage, more couples than in the past might sanction extramarital relations. Couples might more readily accept abortion. They might accept divorce more easily. More couples than before might decide not to have children at all. More marriages would include two partners pursuing independent careers. But when all these changed norms are recognized, the perduring fact emerges that whether people marry in blue jeans and bare feet or gowned and ascoted, this society continues to see the formation of many new groups consisting of an adult man and an adult woman, legally married, who procreate and live together with their children as a group, maybe for a shorter term than before, but nonetheless as a group inhabiting a common household over an extended period of time. So far as is now apparent, groups of this kind will continue to be the mode (both stylishly and statistically) in this and other western societies, for the combining of love, procreation, childrearing, and household formation. If this be so, then the study of families as groups will continue to have a compelling claim on our attention. (Hess and Handel 1974, p. vi)

The continuity of family life in this country, despite cultural and demographic shifts and a greater variety of other life choices, may be partially explained by the fact that the family is capable of satisfying needs for individual development and interpersonal intimacy. In the next chapter we shall focus on love, the emotional underpinning of intimacy.

SUMMARY

1. The major purposes of this chapter are to introduce the complex factors that influence the development and maintenance of intimacy in relationships such as marriage and family; to explain the stages and tasks of individual development in some detail from a life-span perspective; to present a developmental view of the family and explore the interaction between individual and family growth; and to indicate the important influences of historical events, cultural conditions, and societal expectations on families.

2. Some primary changes are occurring in work patterns and attitudes toward self-fulfillment and are having a profound effect on the institutions of marriage and family in American society. Attitudes and values about long-term commitments, children, sexuality, and roles for men and women have also changed markedly, particularly in the last two decades. A high value is still being placed on marriage and family relationships, but these relationships are now changing to accommodate new economic and social patterns, as well as the personal needs of husband and wife.

3. Each individual progresses through several developmental stages between infancy and adulthood. Each stage has its own special tasks to be completed, its unique potential for crisis, and its particular contribution to intimate development. Tasks not completed in one stage may make later developmental stages more difficult.

4. A family, comprised of parents and their children, also follows a cycle of development extending from the initial couple relationship through the childbearing and child-rearing years to the adolescence and departure of grown children and finally to the later years involving retirement and other events of aging. Each stage in the family developmental cycle also involves special tasks and unique contributions to intimacy.

5. Individual needs and family needs may come into conflict, especially when children are young and also when they reach adolescence. Husband and wife may also be at different stages of their own personal development. The skills necessary to cope with this dissonance will be discussed in forthcoming chapters.

6. Broad economic and social changes initiated by the Industrial Revolution have altered the functions of the family unit and the course of individual development. The shift from an agrarian to an industrial economy placed economic productivity outside the home. Role divisions became more rigid in the twentieth century. The mid-century advent of the nuclear family placed the family focus on socializing children. Women's working outside the home, divorce, remarriage, and government involvement in the family's socializing functions have since had the effect of making role divisions less rigid and creating a greater variety of family patterns and styles. These new post-nuclear families may be a sign of the adaptability of the family unit, but the many changes of recent decades also produce stress and render marriages somewhat less secure than in previous times. Ethnic influences add to the current variables of family life.

7. Developmental views of individuals and families are useful in understanding the expected or typical events and transitions within human lives and in acquiring a sense of continuity and change over generations. We need to be aware, however, that these same views can limit our understanding by concentrating primarily on "ideal" types and

ignoring the multitude of variations in individual and family lifestyle patterns.

KEY CONCEPTS

Intimacy

Individual developmental stages

Developmental tasks or polarities

Family developmental stages

The nuclear family

Ethnicity

QUESTIONS

1. Consider the concepts of *marriage* and *family*. What images come to mind when you hear these terms? How do you define or describe *marriage*? How do you define or describe *family*? What changes do you see in how you think about marriage and family today as compared with five years ago?
2. Briefly summarize Erikson's view of individual development. Which stage or stages do you think most influence an individual's capacity to establish intimate relationships based upon long-term commitments such as marriage?
3. Compare the stages of the individual life cycle with those of the family life cycle. At what points in the development of the two systems are serious difficulties or conflicts of interest between individual family members and the family as a whole likely to arise? Give some examples from your personal experiences or observations to illustrate your analysis.
4. Prepare a brief critique of the family developmental framework. In what ways does this approach to studying the family contribute to understanding and predicting family functioning and interaction? In what ways does this approach restrict our view of the family system?
5. Give some examples of how socioeconomic changes and ethnic values influence intimate relationship patterns such as marriage and family.
6. Do you think that the institutions of marriage and family are here to stay? Why or why not?

SUGGESTED READINGS

- Aldous, Joan. *Family Careers: Developmental Change in Families.* New York: Wiley, 1978. An excellent book for understanding the developmental view as applied to the family system and its various subsystems— spouse, parent, child, and sibling.
- Duvall, Evelyn Millis. *Marriage and Family Development* (5th ed.). Philadelphia: Lippincott, 1977. An introductory reference source on the family development perspective, which describes and discusses family

relationships in each developmental stage, from the beginning marriage stage through family dissolution.

- Erikson, Erik H. *Identity, Youth and Crisis.* New York: W. W. Norton, 1968. A classic work by Erikson that includes a discussion of his basic view of human development and reviews in some detail his eight stages of the life cycle.

- Evans, Richard I. *Dialogue with Erik Erikson.* New York: Harper & Row, 1967. A collection of interviews by Evans with Erikson that are interesting and easy to read. A significant portion of the book centers on Erikson's classification of the eight stages of the life cycle, how this view of development differs from the classical Freudian view, and how society and culture influence individual growth.

- Feldman, Harold, and Feldman, Margaret. "The Family Life Cycle: Some Suggestions for Recycling." *Journal of Marriage and the Family* 37, no. 2 (May 1975): 277–284. An interesting proposal for classifying and recycling the family life-cycle approach to include four subcareers: the sex experience career, the marital career, the parent-child career, and the adult-parent career.

- Ferguson, Lucy Rau. *Personality Development.* Belmont, Calif.: Brooks Cole Publishing, 1970. An excellent source of background information on development from birth through adolescence, which combines the theoretical views of Erikson and others on individual development with significant discussion of the role of family, peers, and other social systems on human growth.

- Mindel, Charles H., and Habenstein, Robert W. *Ethnic Families in America: Patterns and Variations* (2nd ed.). New York: Elsevier, 1981. A comprehensive guide for exploring ethnic-cultural characteristics and changes in American families. The authors discuss early and recent ethnic-minority families as well as historically subjugated and socio-religious-minority families.

- Rodgers, Roy. "Toward a Theory of Family Development." *Journal of Marriage and the Family* 26 (August 1964): 262–270. A basic article on the history of the family development approach, which details some of the strengths and limitations of this framework and discusses basic concepts of the developmental view.

Part One
The Roots of Intimacy

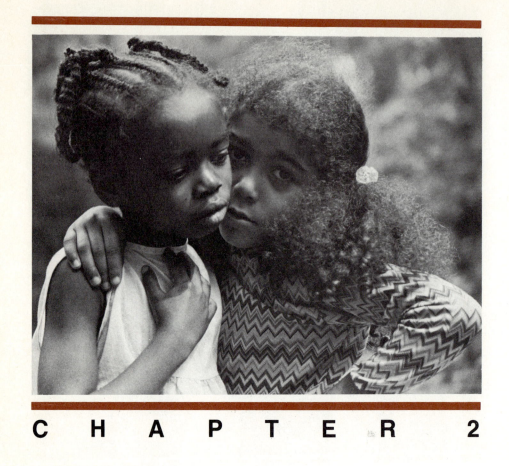

C H A P T E R 2

Love of Self and Others

HE: Do you love me?

SHE: I don't know. Sometimes I think I do.

HE: I know I love you. I've never been able to talk to anyone the way I can talk to you. With other people I feel I have to put on an act, but with you I can be myself.

SHE: Once last year, I thought maybe I was in love; but I feel a lot more certain this time. . . . Still . . .

HE: Still?

SHE: Aren't you wondering if it will last?

HE: It did with my Mom and Dad. Even now, they seem to really like each other, after all those years. I still think the old romance is there.

SHE: I'd like to believe we could keep—all right, keep loving each other the way we do now, with all the kindness and tenderness and excitement.

HE: I guess I've had some thoughts about that, too. When my sister got divorced, I thought, Wait a minute, if it can happen to her, it can happen to anybody. Things really got ugly with them toward the end.

SHE: Yeah, that's what I mean.

HE: At first, she and her husband were really nuts about each other, couldn't keep their hands off each other. But those last few months, visiting them was like watching a tennis match—played to kill.

SHE: I'd never want my kids to watch one of those.

HE: Our kids.

SHE: But how can we know that won't happen to us? A couple of times you have hurt my feelings, like the time your Mom didn't invite me for Thanksgiving and you took her side.

HE: Well, that's ancient history. Mom didn't even know we were going together then.

SHE: See, there you go again.

HE: I thought we had buried that turkey.

SHE: Just teasing. But that's the trouble with marriage—family dinners, budgets, mortgage payments.

HE: We can't make love all the time.

SHE: Have you ever noticed that in books all the great romances are outside of marriage, or else the lovers have to die right away before the two get bored or have to get bogged down in arguments about turkey dinners?

HE: *War and Peace* has a marriage with love.

SHE: *Who's Afraid of Virginia Woolf?* doesn't.

HE: I bet we're more like Natasha and Pierre. We'll keep loving each other.

SHE: I hope so.

HE: Do you love me?

WHAT IS LOVE?

The word "love" is used so loosely that it might refer to the most superficial and transitory distraction: "I love that new song"; "I'd just love to go to the movies tonight." Or love might be the deep, abiding feeling of commitment, admiration, sexual desire, and fulfillment that one feels blessed to attain in a marriage. Love can also be the intense attachment to one's mother or father, sister or brother, or to a long-time friend. It might be the feeling of respect and awe for a wise teacher or leader; it might be the love that cannot be directly reciprocated for a greater force or being, including the love for one's fellow human and the wonder one can experience at all the marvels of nature—this we usually call the love of God.

Since love incorporates so many human emotions, everyone can be an expert on love. One's definition of love will depend on one's perspective, as well as on one's personal history. A novelist might describe love as a grand emotion, continually sought after, though often pursued in vain. A biologist or ethnologist might tend to see love as part of our genetic, evolutionary inheritance, a biological imperative that results in a kind of "love at first genes," as one humorist put it. Psychologists and sociologists agree that love exists, but they don't agree on what love is or how it comes about.

Love often includes intense attachment to parents, siblings, and other family members. (Jerry Howard, Positive Images)

Some claim love is a selfish emotion; others describe it as selfless and disinterested—one of the rare emotions that places the well-being of the other above personal interests. Some see love as entirely circumstantial, requiring only that two people be in the right place at a time in their life when they are propelled toward mate selection.

In later chapters we shall examine some of the circumstantial aspects of love. Here we shall give a brief history of love and explain the roots of some prevalent Western beliefs about it. With this background, we shall examine more closely some current beliefs concerning love as the basis for marriage. Here and in subsequent chapters, we shall see that love is a capacity that develops gradually from the infant's basic need for human contact (which becomes associated with mother and father) to a growing desire in childhood for contact with one's age-mates or peers. As the child learns to read and write, the child also learns to read people's faces and gestures and to ascertain their emotions. A capacity for friendship develops, so that by adolescence one can allow a friend his or her differences in personality and taste as long as there is interpersonal sharing and loyalty. During adolescence the need for others becomes integrated with a new sexual need for another. As one grows older, and if one has incorporated such developmental capacities as trust, independence, initiative, industry, and personal identity, an individual's capacity for love also deepens and increases. One becomes capable of loving a spouse and at the same time loving one's children and continuing to love one's parents.

We shall see that the changing attitudes of our culture toward love and our own individual capacity for love combine to give the loves of our life their unique character.

THE ROOTS OF INTIMACY: A BRIEF HISTORY OF LOVE

There is no way in these few pages to review fully what poets, philosophers, theologians, dramatists, and novelists have said in the volumes they have written about love. But there is a certain pattern to Western attitudes concerning love, and it is this pattern we shall attempt to delineate here.

Ancient Attitudes

The source of Western attitudes toward love and especially "western hostility to sex" has been traced to Greek dualistic thought (Bullough and Bullough 1977). The ancient Greeks "divided the world into two opposing forces, the spiritual vs. the material, resulting in man having two natures, the higher and the lower, or alternatively, in having a soul and a body" (Bullough and Bullough 1977, p. 10).

Corresponding to these opposing natures were the two types of love people might experience. *Eros* refers to the carnal or sexual type of love, the joining of flesh with flesh. *Agape*, spiritual love, is associated with human beings' higher nature. *Agape* went beyond physical consummation to a more significant spiritual communion. *Eros* was not an ennobling and transforming goal of life, as it is often depicted in modern times. Sexual love might be, in its least harmful form, an amusing pastime and distraction; at its most intense it was an affliction, even a curse. Women were seen as part and parcel of this disturbing and even destructive force.

The male Greeks' disdain for women caused them to prize the "purer" love of man for man. That might be the loyal and complete friendship or even the combination of physical and spiritual love two men might experience. Homosexuality in ancient Greece was thus accepted as normal. Marriage, in such a culture, was bound to be considered a source of grief or, at best, a compromise of one's higher nature. Wives were depicted by Euripides and Aristophanes as adulterous, vicious, drunken, scheming, greedy, and vengeful. Later the Greek poet Pallades summed up the Greek view of marriage with this cruel epigram:

Marriage brings a man only two happy days; the day he takes his wife to bed, and the day he lays her in her grave. (Hunt 1959, p. 26)

Love and marriage didn't fare much better in Roman times. There were some minor concessions to the status of wives. A husband, for example, could no longer simply kill his wife with impunity if he suspected her of adultery, although he could accuse her in a court of law. Romans tended to be heterosexual but, like the Greeks, they separated sex from love and marriage. Writing about Julius Caesar, the historian Suetonius pointed out that the ruler of Rome did not much care whom he had sex with so long as the consort was politically or practically powerful. Romans called him *"omnium mulierum vit et omnium vicorium mulier"*—the husband of every woman and the wife of every man. Hunt believes it was this casual, indifferent attitude that eventually led to the fall of Rome: "It was when sex moved outside of marriage and called itself love, while marriage itself lost its values, that the long decline of the Roman population began" (Hunt 1959, pp. 88–89). According to his theory, there were not enough Roman citizens dedicated to the preservation of its civilization, and the barbarians eventually overwhelmed Rome.

Christian Influence

Under the influence of early Christianity, love remained separate from sex, but for different reasons. Sex in marriage was considered a necessary evil, but love, even married love, was separate from sex and, in fact, tainted by it. Therefore, love in its highest form could best be attained in a celibate state. Saint Paul set the tone for marriage in I Corinthians 7: 1-9: "It is good for a man not to touch a woman. Nevertheless, to avoid fornication, let every man have his own wife, and let every woman have her own husband." But Paul favored celibacy more: "I would that all men were even as I myself. . . . I say therefore to the unmarried and widows, it is good for them if they abide even as I. But if they cannot contain, let them marry: for it is better to marry than to burn." Many early Christians tried to imitate Paul's celebration of celibacy; many failed. In *The Natural History of Love*, Hunt argues that because many Christian men failed in their attempts to live up to Paul's rigorous standards, they needed a scapegoat. And they found it—woman.

Women were thought to be ruinous. Why else would men, pure of heart and mind, find themselves tormented by them? Serious theological debate arose over the question of whether women even had souls. When it was finally, grudgingly, decided that women did have souls, many men fled their wives for a life of monastic celibacy. A concerted attempt was undertaken to convince women to renounce their sexuality and thus do away with the *source* of temptation. Through all these developments, marriage continued to exist. But, the theological message was loud and clear: Marriage should certainly not be a pleasurable experience.

It was Saint Augustine, a formerly worldly man about matters of the flesh, who finally set the tone for Christian love for several centuries. Retreating to a monastic life, enduring an often agonizing asceticism, Saint Augustine saw all life as originating in corruption, the corruption of the sex act. To be sure, that act was necessary for the perpetuation of the species, but it nonetheless repeated the original sin of Adam and Eve, the intimate knowing of each other's bodies. According to Hunt, "Augustine set up a permanent barrier between personal affection and sexual expression" (Hunt 1959, p. 121). The ideal of "continent marriage" required men and women to police their behavior at all times. Sexuality and loving were divided, since asexual love was the only true love. The result was ambivalence toward marriage and one's spouse. The Christian view of love embraced *agape* as spiritual love belonging to God; *eros*, the flesh, sex, went to the Devil. Marriage—involving man, with his capability for spiritual love, and woman, with her nature limited to the base physical love— "naturally" became a master-servant, owner-and-property connection (Hunt 1959, p. 171).

Courtly Love

American attitudes toward love may owe less to Greco-Roman or Augustinian views of love than to an immensely important development that emerged in the eleventh century. The development of the ideal of *courtly love* radically altered the Western world's conception of love and distinguished it, perhaps forever, from the ancient Greek idea. Courtly love, an ideal celebrated by troubadours and poets in the Middle Ages, assumed that sexual love is a supreme value of life on earth. There are several ingredients to the ideal. It ennobles and uplifts both the lover and the beloved. It is an overwhelming passion, inspired, usually at first sight, by the beauty and character of the beloved. Lovers are fated for each other. Most important, perhaps, love involves not only passion, which was an element in the Greek conception of love, but also respect for the beloved. If these sound like the essential ingredients of a movie script for *Romeo and Juliet*, *Love Story*, or even *Annie Hall*, it is because the theme of romantic love has dominated Western life and literature for 800 years, ever since the troubadours and poets celebrated it in the eleventh century.

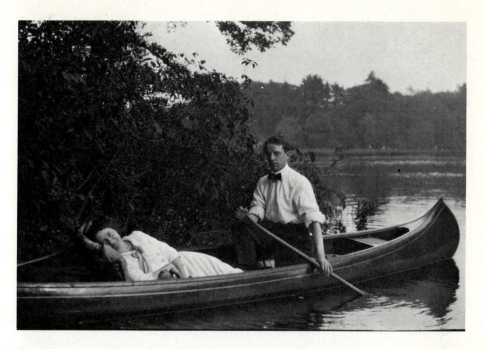

Courtly love stereotyped women as objects of romance. (Collection of Bobbi Carrey)

Courtly love, while not permitting women the full range of options opened to men, did allow women a duality: to be the object of a great romantic love or to be the source of a degrading passion. They were no longer limited, as in ancient times, to degradation. Their importance, it should be noted, was still determined by the effect they had on men. After the concept of courtly love developed, there remained a fear of women. The old duality of *eros* and *agape* became the new duality of the good woman and the bad woman. In the fifteenth century a woman could still be described as "either a lady or witch, Blessed Virgin or sinful Eve, object of adoration or vessel of abominable lust" (Hunt 1959, p. 175). This polarized view of women—objects of devotion or adoration on the one hand, witches and temptresses on the other—still survives. We see it in adolescent culture with its "good girl/bad girl" labels and in the American mythology purveyed by TV programs, detective stories, and romantic novels.

Courtly love at least admitted women, via their effect on men, to the higher realm of *agape* and began to bring *eros* and *agape* together. But this union was not conceivable in marriage until late in the nineteenth century; even then, love as defined by overwhelming passion would not be expected to continue at such intense levels throughout a marriage. The practice of arranging marriages, common in the Middle Ages and the Renaissance, as well as in many European cultures after that, also helped to keep courtly love outside marriage. The great courtly love romances—Tristan and Isolde, Lancelot and Guinevere—are tales of adultery (de Rougemont 1956).

The intensity of passion portrayed in the Tristan story, *Romeo and Juliet, Wuthering Heights,* or *For Whom the Bell Tolls* can hardly be maintained at such levels over the course of a 50-year marriage. Yet there is reason to believe that a marriage that lasts for a long period of time may have cycles of romance—periods of passion, or romantic fallings-in-love, followed by disillusionment and then a new resolution and a renewal of romance. Asking a marriage to fulfill all romantic desires at all times is asking more than any relationship can deliver. But settling for a marriage devoid of passion has come to be considered equally foolish. The modern ideal, despite disillusion and divorce, is love within marriage.

Love within Marriage

Historically, the link between love and marriage is a relatively recent development. They seem to have been joined first in England, surprisingly, by the Puritans. The Puritans condemned adultery and other sexual excesses, not necessarily because they were against sex, but simply on the grounds that sex should occur and be contained in marriage. According to Skolnick, the Puritans regarded marriage as a partnership based on companionship, trust, fidelity, and premarital chastity (1978, p. 206).

But premarital chastity was actually something of a myth in colonial America. While it is true that Puritan colonial culture epitomized sexual repressiveness, the trend was toward greater and greater "freedom." Historian John Demos demonstrates the actual permissive trend of Puritan culture in his book *A Little Commonwealth* (1970). Demos looked at marriage records in colonial America and then counted the number of months until the birth of the first child. His deductions were that premarital sex resulting in pregnant brides was common among the Puritans.

During the sixteenth, seventeenth, and eighteenth centuries, men slowly began to display a more liberal attitude toward women and sexuality. Most plays and books continued to be written by men, but Shakespeare's heroines, the clever women of Restoration comedies, the females of eighteenth-century novels, all reveal a somewhat more enlightened attitude toward women and sexuality.

Marriage and romantic love really merged, at least in terms of an ideal, in the eighteenth century, when the middle class rose to social and economic prominence. Ian Watt, in *The Rise of the Novel* (1957), writes that "new social and economic order gave rise (in the eighteenth and nineteenth centuries) to a new literary form, the novel, which placed the search for love and social mobility at the center of the plot, with marriage providing the happy ending." Jane Austen's heroines marry for love, with a comfortable income as a bonus; Tom Jones, after many wild adventures, settles down and marries his true love.

By the nineteenth century certain liberal thinkers were recognizing the oppressive nature of marriage and women's place in society. John Stuart Mill, in his classic essay *The Subjection of Women* (1869), passionately criticized the absolute legal subjection of a wife to her husband. The law had not changed substantially since biblical times, when a woman's father bestowed her, regardless of her desires, on her future husband. Women finally emerged as complex individuals in nineteenth-century novels. Nana, Emma Bovary, and Anna Karenina are neither evil nor angelic, but rich and tragic characters. Ibsen's heroines strive for understanding and often seem to be more insightful than their male counterparts. In *War and Peace*, Tolstoy suggested that love and marriage between two complete human beings might be possible.

In the United States, with its democratic traditions, the notion that love could lead to marriage was particularly congenial and attractive. Romantic marriage became an American ideal. Some have argued that romantic love functions like a religion in our culture. The symbol of love, like religious symbols in other societies, provides important models shaping the experience and the course of individual lives. The symbol of love and marriage is a dominant one in American culture. For many it is the emotional and even spiritual hub of existence.

THE ROOTS OF INTIMACY: PSYCHOLOGICAL THEORIES

Sigmund Freud: Love and the Importance of Early Childhood

Love is so central to human experience that it has commanded the attention of many outside the realm of literature. All great philosophers and students of human behavior have had something to say about it. The views of certain thinkers have had an especially powerful influence on what we now expect of love and marriage. Foremost among the definers of love as an influence on human behavior is Sigmund Freud (1856–1939).

Freud, the founder of psychoanalysis, developed a theory about the effect of early childhood on an adult's capacity for intimacy and love later in life. Equating sex with love, Freud maintained that very young children had sexual feelings, which he called *infantile sexuality* (Freud 1905). In the earliest stages of development, the child is capable only of being "polymorphously perverse." That is, the child experiences a variety of unfocused sexual feelings, pleasurable sensations evoked regardless of which parts of the body are touched and which person does the touching.

These infantile sexual feelings eventually focus on a love object, the parent of the opposite sex. A girl's first affection is for the closest adult of the opposite sex—her father—and a boy's first childish desires are for his mother (Freud 1900). The *Oedipus complex* (male love for the mother) eventually is transferred to an appropriate heterosexual object—a mate or wife. The female's love for her father eventually shifts to love for a husband. But *libido*, or sexual energy, is the driving force in all varieties of human loving—love for parents as well as love for spouse. Thus, Freud postulated, all love has sex as its original base.

At first, Freud insisted that any close relationship was tinged with *eros*, or carnal love. Later he modified this view by broadening the notion of sex to include "all attitudes and tender feelings which originated in the primitive sexual drives." Some impulses, originally sexual in aim, become inhibited in individuals; the spontaneous expression of these impulses is discouraged by the individual's conscience or by society. Freud's broader concept of "sex" includes these impulses as well as those that have been exchanged or substituted for sexual ones. Freud did not deny that the psychological factor is important in sex. Indeed, his later concept of sex assumed it (Freud 1921). Although Freud refused to lessen the importance of sexual feelings, he did expand the meaning of "sexual." His concept of the word *eros* suggests more than the physical aspect of love.

Erik Erikson: Trust and the Developmental View of Love

Freud saw a progression in the individual's capacity for emotion, from self-involved, narcissistic love to a love that could go beyond mere drive satisfaction. It was Erikson who integrated Freud's idea of emotional progress into a theory of developmental stages, in which emotional development continues throughout life (as we examined in Chapter 1). The individual who, in adult life, seeks only pleasure for himself or herself has not developed fully. The person who must immediately gratify every urge—giving up whatever does not provide instant gratification, unable to postpone even for a brief time any desired thing—this person is unable to form deep, intimate, sharing relationships. The person is unable to love.

Yet most individuals are capable of loving. In Erikson's view, the capacity for love has its beginnings in infancy. It is rooted in trust. If the individual's needs are to be freely expressed, he or she must develop a sense of being able to count on others. Infancy and early childhood are crucial stages for the development of such trust. The infant cries. The parent responds, learning to distinguish cries of hunger from cries of distress, teaching the infant that the many needs it feels will be responded to with appropriate behavior, both physical and emotional. Gradually, the infant sees that the world, as epitomized by this parenting figure, will certainly respond to its call. An inner certainty develops as the result of these many predictable, nurturing responses. The infant trusts.

Incorporating this inner certainty of responsive love, building upon this

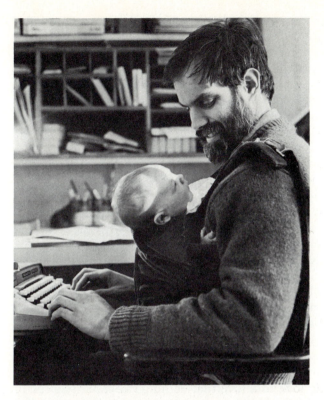

Without a nurturing relationship based on trust, a child's ability to love will be distorted. (Heleen Howard, Positive Images)

foundation of trust, the infant can gradually acquire self-trust. Trust becomes the foundation for the individual's capacity to cope with his or her own bodily urges, from urges to get rid of bodily wastes to later sexual urges. A sense of trust created by the continual communication between the infant and the nurturing person also serves as the basis for a much later development, a sense of one's own identity. Only by interacting with the environment can the infant gain a sense of self, a sense of the boundaries between the self and the world. If such interaction fails to take place, or is severely disturbed, the boundaries are not defined; the sense of self does not develop properly (Anderson and Carter 1978, pp. 143–144).

Developmental Disturbances in the Capacity for Love. If infants are kept in institutions where no provisions are made for substitute parenting, they will not get enough interaction with a nurturing or caring person. Infants in institutions where there is little or no physical interaction with a caring person may even die, as research by the psychoanalyst René Spitz has shown. Even if the child grows up with a parenting figure, this person may not provide enough interaction. She or he may be too busy caring for other children, or too poor to afford child care while earning a living. The child may be unable to interact because of previous deprivation, maturational deficiencies, or a variety of other internal or external deficits (Anderson and Carter 1978, p. 145).

A distorted relationship with the nurturing person may also blunt the child's ability to love and be intimate with others in later life. This can happen when the child doesn't learn to differentiate the self from the parent. This blurring of self and parent is especially likely to occur when parents do not distinguish the boundary between themselves and the child, as when the parenting figure wants the child to remain totally dependent. The relationship can also be distorted if the parent is unable to give emotionally—if, for example, he or she is cold and isolated, or vain, egotistical, or pathologically narcissistic. Involved only with the self, such a parent may not be able to provide the child with more than physical care. Or the parent's energy for caring may be exhausted by other demands in the family.

The formation of attachment bonds to at least one responsive, nurturing figure, as we shall discuss in Chapter 11, is a basis for normal development. Studies show that separation from the parenting figure after the age of three months can irreparably damage the child, who may come to have what Bowlby describes as an "affectionless character," a shallow and untrusting personality, "unable to enter into intimate emotional transactions with other persons." The underpinnings of self-esteem are secured in those countless early interchanges between parent and child (Bowlby 1969).

Psychoanalyst Heinz Kohut (1977) explains how such interchanges build self-esteem. The infant looks into the mother's face. She is smiling and accepting and pleased about the infant's presence. This reflection of self seen in the mother's face becomes the child's first experience of high self-esteem. The mother has reflected a "you-me." She is excited about that you-me. Through the mother's excitement, the child experiences a sense of being worthwhile.

A key ingredient of this interaction is the *empathy* of the parent. Empathy is the ability to feel how the other feels, the capacity to experience another's feelings vicariously. The parent's ability to take on the feelings of the child teaches the child that human understanding is possible. Later, we will discuss empathy as a quality to be cultivated on a give-and-take basis in a marital relationship. In the parenting situation, however, the parent must do most of the giving. Heinz Kohut sees the mother, for example, reaching out, merging with the child, experiencing or trying to experience what the child feels. But she also has her own, much calmer, feelings to contribute. In Kohut's words, the sequence is this: "The child is very anxious. The mother is just empathically anxious, just a tiny bit which allows her to understand. The child is wet or hungry—but for the child it is the end of the world. There are no buffers yet. The mother, with her overall aura of calmness and just enough empathic anxiety, picks up the child, this huge bundle of anxiety. The child merges and becomes a part of this whole body of the mother. He feels that she is calm and he becomes calm'' (Kohut 1977).

Thousands of such encounters between mother and child, father and child, mother and father and child gradually develop into the individual's feelings about the self. By the time of young adulthood, the kinds of relationships a person seeks are not usually the complete psychological mergers of the infant days. The person who has attained a reasonably high degree of self-esteem seeks intimacy not merely to lean and gain strength and sustenance, but also to share personal strengths.

Influence of the Individual on Early Experience.   The roots of intimacy in marriage or other adult relationships extend far back into one's earliest experiences. But even in infancy, the individual has an impact on these experiences. Under the influence of Freud, psychologists and other students of human behavior for many years attributed the temperament of the child wholly to its mother. If the child was "difficult" (fussy, eating poorly, crying, restless at night), the mother was assumed somehow to have failed. The Freudians sought the causes of an infant's behavior in the mother's attitude toward being a woman, her relationship with her own mother and father, the way she was nursed and toilet trained, and her early childhood experiences. But findings about genetics, prenatal influences, and the influence exerted on the mother or caretaker by the infant's style of behavior have now made it clear that the mother or caretaking person does not deal with totally malleable human clay.

Individual temperament is not totally dependent upon either mother or father. A major study by Thomas and Chess (1977), which followed hundreds of infants from birth to adulthood, showed that individuals have certain temperamental styles that are apparent from the first week of life. Parents do, of course, make a difference in the way these styles are expressed. The word "continuum" is useful here. At one extreme of the caretaking continuum might be the parent with endless patience, warmth, and supportiveness. At the other extreme is the abusive parent. But even an abusive parent may not abuse all the children in the family, and the most loving parent will have a slightly better rapport with one or another of several children in a family. Again, a particular child evokes a particular response.

People do have choices. At every stage of life, a range of possibilities exists. But the choices that exist in terms of relationships are influenced by a number of factors in the child and in the environment, notably the child's genetic endowment and temperamental style and the parents' capacities to nurture and guide that individual child. These elements, interacting at varying stages of childhood and adolescence, form our unique psychosocial histories. Each of us has our own personal history with intimacy long before we begin to think in terms of marriage.

Carl Jung: Parents as Models for Male and Female

It was Carl Jung (1875–1961), a student of Freud's and later a founder of his own school of analysis, who suggested that parents not only influence the child's later capacity for love and intimacy, but also provide the most influential models of male and female behavior. Jung thought that we carry these models with us throughout our adult lives and that they powerfully influence both our behavior and our expectations for ourselves and others in adulthood.

In Jung's view, masculine and feminine principles govern biology and social relations. Man was designed for woman and woman was designed for man, and this is the basis of their mutual attraction. Biologically, "the whole nature of man presupposes woman, both physically and spiritually. His system is tuned in to woman from the start, just as it is prepared for a quite definite world where there is water, light, air, salt, carbohydrates, etc." (Jung 1966, p. 188). The same is true of woman; her nature presupposes man.

According to Jung, our society defines generally masculine and generally feminine roles. "Father becomes the son's model for manhood, mother becomes the feminine ideal. Or mother becomes the daughter's feminine model and father her masculine ideal," says Jungian analyst June Singer (1973, p. 231).

As the most influential models of male and female behavior, the mother and father suggest what is possible in a relationship. They let the child know whether it is safe to show affection and tenderness. They convey attitudes about sexuality, characterizing it by their ongoing behavior, rather than a given "birds and bees" lecture. Because of what they show, parents may convey to their children the idea that sex is part of a loving relationship or the notion that sex is a means of exerting power and manipulating the opposite sex. Whether children emulate the pattern seen at home or seek to flee from the example, that model continues to influence their sexual behavior.

Interaction between a man and a woman can take place on at least three levels. The first is the surface level, at which the stereotype of a woman interacts with the stereotype of a man. This type of very superficial relationship can occur when adolescents date or when people first meet. At a second level, however, a man and woman relate to each other's unconscious expectations about the other. According to Singer:

A man has developed an unconscious image of an ideal woman, including her appearance and the way she will behave. When he meets a woman who seems to conform to this image, in part at least, he anticipates that she will conform to it in all particulars. She should understand his needs, conform to his schedule, make up his deficiencies, and even, by some miracle of intuition, instinctively know what turns him on in bed without ever having to be guided or informed by him. In other words, she should be this living doll who is his unconscious. . . . In the same way, a woman's unconscious designs the shape and function of her dream man and endows him with everything she needs and wants. (Singer 1973, p. 243)

Our models and expectations of "masculine" and "feminine" have a good deal to do with parental influence. But these unconscious expectations are also shaped by an individual's attributes and personal experience.

Finally, Jung believed a third level of interaction was possible. Men and women can get in touch with each other, relating not only to what they expect based on the models they have had, but to what is actually there. This is a crucial step in learning to love.

This is what is meant by truly identifying with someone: vicariously experiencing what happens to the other person as if it had happened to oneself, putting oneself in the shoes of the other person, seeing experience from his or her point of view. Identification seems to be something that happens when one person internalizes or makes his or her own the attitudes of another (Turner 1970, pp. 66–67). But such identification with another of the opposite sex requires access to our sometimes hidden opposite-sex traits: for men, their female side, or *anima;* for women, their male side, or *animus.* In a full male-female relationship there are four elements, man and woman, anima and animus. Jung called the relationship involving all four elements "the marriage quaternio" (Singer 1973, p. 242). (See Figure 2.1.) Jung's theories appear to be the first to use marriage as the setting for full disclosure of our male and female sides. At the highest level of interaction, Jung believed, men and women are able to understand one another sympathetically, by getting in touch with the full spectrum of their humanity. At this level a man can express his feminine side and a woman her masculine side. Some people believe that in today's freer society, men and women are more likely than they once were to achieve this type of full-spectrum intimacy.

Abraham Maslow: Deficiency-Love versus Love for the Being of Another Person

Abraham Maslow, a contemporary psychologist who died in 1970, saw a new concept of intimacy emerging. It is one that allows for greater independence and autonomy, less possessiveness and jealousy. Maslow, who is considered one of the founders of "humanistic" psychology, developed a

FIGURE 2.1 Jung's "Marriage Quaternio"

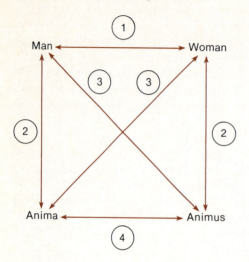

Source: Adapted from *The Collected Works of C. G. Jung*, trans. R.F.C. Hull, Bollingen Series XX, Vol. 16: *The Practice of Psychotherapy*. Copyright 1954, © 1966 by Princeton University Press. Reprinted by permission of Princeton University Press.

theory of self-actualization, proposing that self-actualized, independent individuals can form more richly rewarding relationships.

Maslow defined two kinds of love: "B-love (love for the being of another person, unneeding love, unselfish love) and D-love (deficiency-love, need love, selfish love)" (Maslow 1962, p. 42). D-love is concerned with self-gratification; the lover is an object that can be used, shown off, possessed. Because the loved one is regarded as an object, D-love carries with it the potential for anxiety and hostility: objects can be stolen by others; or the loved one may make changes that threaten the other. Thus, the D-lover may be jealous of the other's career or success, as well as fearing sexual infidelity. B-love, on the other hand, involves a genuine disinterested regard for the interests and well-being of the other person. Instead of limiting the growth of the other or surrounding the relationship with anxieties and jealousies, B-love has a creative and even therapeutic effect. While a person in B-love may be anxious for the welfare of the other person, he or she does not fear the other's outside relationships or development of personal qualities or abilities. B-love contributes to full human development.

B-love, as Maslow describes it, leads to the romantic ideal of love within marriage, but love carrying an element of freedom for the other person, which is distinctly modern. Autonomy and room to grow and change be-

Sympathetic understanding between women and men is possible when each recognizes the full spectrum of his or her humanity. (Cynthia Benjamins)

come paramount features of a relationship. Possession, jealousy, and ownership, which were once related to love and marriage, are cast aside. This concept of intimacy is very close to the ideal of love in marriage that many people seek today.

OBSTACLES TO LOVE

Lack of Identification and Response

An intimate relationship will not be established unless one begins to experience what happens to the other person as if it had happened to oneself, unless one begins to *identify* with the other person. Usually, people are attracted to other people who satisfy their ideals. When we see someone we admire, someone who has qualities we would like to have ourselves, we identify with that person. A bright young student may identify with an admired teacher, for by associating with that teacher, the student's own identity or self-image is enhanced.

It is hard to respond warmly to someone we don't admire or respect. Similarly, it is hard to identify with someone who never responds to us, no matter how much we may admire them. To return to our example, a mutual relationship between the student and teacher can be created only if the teacher responds to the student, in turn, with warmth and respect.

A loss of our own sense of self-worth can also be an obstacle to love. It is difficult to love someone we admire if being around that person reminds us only of our own inferiority (Turner 1970), pp. 66–68).

Unrealistic Expectations

Adult men and women come to relationships, as Jung and others have suggested, with models of an ideal man or woman. Young couples may idealize each other, supposing the other to have all the wonderful qualities they have imagined. The difficulty comes when the partner fails to live up to these unrealistic expectations or shows an unexpected failing. Disillusionment, perhaps even divorce, may follow.

Young couples are sometimes unaware of the set of expectations or scenarios that they have written for each other in their marriage. They are bitterly disappointed when their mates do not behave according to the "script." Such partners need to become aware of their unrealistic expectations and be willing to give them up when they do not fit reality.

Partners must get in touch with each other, relating not only to what they expect but to what is actually there. For Jung, the level at which partners get in touch with each other is the highest level of interaction between a man and a woman. In this phase, as June Singer puts it:

The woman may be able to put herself into his place and to understand his way of looking at her and, in a wider sense, his way of meeting the world. Because of her openness to his attitudes she is able to work with him, without expecting to be indulged for her own peculiarities. She is not ashamed or embarrassed to be forthright, to voice her views with conviction, to assert her values. This parallel development in man enables him to allow that side in him which has been repressed, to reemerge as a tender, nurturing quality, charged with sympathy and affectionate response. (Singer 1973, p. 244)

In this atmosphere of openness and empathy, intimacy becomes possible. It is this kind of relating that is most likely to produce a happy marriage.

Excessive Dependency—"Need Love"

Reliance on each other for psychological and physical needs is a necessary part of every marriage and one that binds couples to each other. But even the most stable, enduring relationships may suffer from excessive dependency. As we saw in Maslow's theory of self-actualization and B-love, dependency can be an obstacle to a creative, altruistic, and pleasurable love relationship. D-lovers are possessive and jealous of each other. Their love is a means to gratifying their own selfish desires and not an end in itself, not intrinsically enjoyable. D-lovers are anxious and hostile with one another, and so they cannot contribute to each other's growth and development. They would benefit by becoming more independent, more self-reliant and self-actualized. Perhaps each partner can benefit by focusing on his or her own personal development without expecting and demanding the other to contribute to it. Once they "let go" of each other, paradoxically, they may be able to experience a genuinely altruistic and compassionate love for one another. Each may then feel eager to contribute to the personal development of the other.

Lack of Intimacy, Failure of Communication

Playing games is one way of avoiding intimacy. Eric Berne elaborated a theory of human transactions that explained "the games people play" (Berne 1964). As Box 2.1 explains, game transactions can involve the use of stock responses to trap one's partner or defend one's ego. Whether we think of games as routinized transactions that couples fall into or occasional remarks and ploys, games set up obstacles to love. Being intimate carries with it certain risks. When an intimacy is betrayed, the person will not be inclined to risk betrayal again. A child who anticipates an angry response, or no response at all, from parents or siblings is not likely to express affection for them.

Certain responses weaken trust. If one person invites another to be intimate, for example, by asking, "Are you upset, Bill?" and the other does not respond to the invitation, this discourages the questioner from inviting intimacy in the future. Insensitivity is a failure to interpret what another person says empathically, with sympathy and understanding, when that person has invited us to do so. To persist in a face-value interpretation of what Mary says, when Mary is clearly upset about something, is to be insensitive to her feelings.

Secrets revealed in moments of intimacy can be used in ways that harm the intimacy and trust in a relationship. Jonathan reveals that things are not going well at work, that he has failed to complete an important assignment. Jane may use this revelation later in an argument to win a point, but in doing so she weakens the trust between them. Jonathan will be less likely to confide in her again. Such violations of intimacy may discourage love. Intimacy can also be violated when husbands or wives reveal privileged secrets about their spouse to someone beyond the family.

Every relationship has moments of frustrated love. A woman may not be able to respond to an offer of love by her husband for any number of incidental reasons—preoccupation with her job or with her children. A husband cannot be there whenever his wife needs him. Any relationship of genuine caring must be able to sustain a certain number of frustrated "love moments." These small refusals and denials will not devastate a

BOX 2.1   Communication and Transactional Analysis

Eric Berne, author of *Games People Play* and founder of a popular theory of human behavior called Transactional Analysis, demonstrates how games, in which we deal with only a partial aspect of the self and the other, can serve as barriers to intimacy. According to Berne, adults tend to interact in one of the following three states:

1. The *child* state is the adult's unique childhood experience preserved in its entirety.
2. The *adult* state allows the person to gather information about the world in order to function within it.
3. The *parent* state is essentially made up of behavior copied from parents or authority figures. It is taken whole without modification. (Steiner 1974, p. 29)

Each state has its positive and negative aspects. The child state of a person is the source of spontaneity, sexuality, and creative change. It is the "mainspring of joy" (Steiner 1974, p. 19). But the child state is also the source of fear, helplessness, shame, and intimidation. The adult state is both rational and emotionless. The parent state can be nurturing, but it can also be oppressive and prejudiced.

Let's take an example of how people interact in these states, or how, to use Berne's terminology, they carry out "transactions" in these states. A wife says to her husband, "Pick up your socks." Her husband responds, "I'm sorry, dear." The wife speaks to her husband as a parent would to a child; the husband responds to his wife as a child would to a parent. This transaction is diagrammed below.

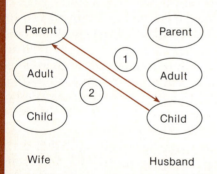

In transactions with each other people give and get "strokes." One of Berne's important insights was that people play marital and sexual games, which are a series of moves with a snare or "gimmick." Such games give strokes for the players, without the threat of intimacy (Steiner 1974, p. 38). People need strokes so desperately, claims Berne, that they willingly accept and give out negative strokes when they cannot get or give positive ones. Not all transactions fall into the game category. There are more honest and open operations, in which partners reveal and express what they actually feel. They ask for and give strokes freely, thus making intimacy possible.

continuing mature relationship, as long as most love acts initiated by either man or woman are returned and as long as their overall relationship is characterized by intimacy, compassion, and affection.

SUMMARY

1. The major purposes of this chapter are to present a historical perspective on the concept of love, especially on the changing views of the relationship between love and sex and love and marriage; to explore how several theorists explain the development and nurturance of human love; and to discuss some of the barriers that may inhibit or distort the development of love in intimate relationships.
2. Love has been discussed and analyzed by philosophers, poets, novelists, biologists, historians, and social scientists, but no agreement has been reached on an exact definition of this elusive concept.
3. Historically, two kinds of love have been recognized: *eros*, which is carnal or sexual love, and *agape*, or spiritual love. The relationship between love and sex has a varied history: at times the connection was seen as one between good (love) and evil (sex), while at other periods in history, especially in the Middle Ages, when courtly love was the ideal, love and sex were viewed as representing almost the same concept. The relationship between love and marriage has a similar history, moving from the belief that love in marriage was nearly impossible to the common theme in the United States today that values love as the basis for marriage.
4. Most major theories of human development recognize and attempt to explain the origins and importance of the capacity to give and receive love. Freud, Erikson, Jung, and Maslow all recognize the developmental nature of this capacity, as well as the importance of the family or primary caretakers in fostering the ability to love.
5. One key element in the early development of the ability to love is trust, which is nurtured by positive parental responses to the needs of the infant and young child. These parental responses depend in part on the parenting figure's ability to empathize or feel what the child is feeling. The child's identification with parental figures and significant others represents another important process in the development of a capacity for loving and being loved.
6. Maslow's concept of B-love as encompassing autonomy, growth, and change for each partner in an intimate relationship, without the elements of possession, jealousy, and ownership, may come close to describing the ideal marital love desired by many couples in American society.
7. Obstacles to the achievement of this ideal love are numerous. Some barriers are due to a lack of identification with one's partner, which

may be influenced by our own low levels of self-esteem. Other obstacles to love arise from unrealistic expectations of those whom we love, excessive dependency on the loved one to fulfill all our wants and needs, and communication failures that include a reliance on games to avoid intimacy and violations of trust.

KEY CONCEPTS

Eros Self-actualization
Agape B-love
Courtly love D-love
Empathy Identification
Anima Game transactions
Animus

QUESTIONS

1. How do you define love? Is love a reality; can it be described? How do you know when you love someone?
2. Assume you are interested in researching the question, "How do we know we love each other enough to marry?" What questions would you ask to investigate the meaning of love in marriage?
3. Considering the varied history of love, present and support the argument that love is *not* a proper basis for marriage.
4. How can the development of basic trust be short-circuited by parenting figures and by factors or influences outside the parent-child system?
5. How can parental models influence our patterns of expressing or withholding love? Is it possible for such models to influence our loving behavior even though we have chosen to live our lives differently than our parents?
6. Consider the various obstacles to love. Based on your experience and observations, what factors do you think represent the most serious threats to the continuing development of love in marriage?

SUGGESTED READINGS

- Goode, William J. "The Theoretical Importance of Love." *American Sociological Review* 24, no. 1 (February 1959): 38–47. A classic article that analyzes the way love relationships are controlled by societies, resulting in various patterns for defining love within specific social structures.
- Kelling, George W. *Blind Mazes: A Study of Love.* Chicago: Nelson-Hall, 1979. Discusses the concept of love in primary relationships, including people's unique definitions of this elusive concept and several processes

involved in the development of love relationships. The final chapter presents the results of a field study on love relationships conducted by the author.

- Lewis, C. S. *Four Loves*. New York: Harcourt Brace Jovanovich, Inc., 1971. An insightful exploration of the joys and pains of four kinds of human love: affection, friendship, erotic love, and love of God. Lewis discusses such elements as jealousy, possessiveness, laughter, and play as they relate to love and loving.

- Maslow, Abraham H. *The Farther Reaches of Human Nature*. New York: Viking Press, 1971. A collection of essays by Maslow that highlight his humanistic perspectives on Being, Self-Actualization, Creativity, and other aspects of living and loving.

- Orlofsky, Jacob L. "The Relationship Between Intimacy Status and Antecedent Personality Components." *Adolescence* 13, no. 51 (Fall 1978): 419–442. A study of how the ability to develop and maintain intimate, loving relationships in young adulthood is related to Erikson's earlier developmental stages of trust, autonomy and identity.

- Powell, John. *The Secret of Staying in Love*. Allen, Tex.: Argus Communications, 1974. An easy-to-read and practical book giving Powell's view that the major component for sustaining love over time is communication, especially the honest sharing of feelings and emotions.

- Viorst, Judith. "Just Because I'm Married, Does It Mean I'm Going Steady?" in Barry J. Wishart and Lewis C. Reichman (eds.). *Modern Sociological Issues* (2nd ed.). New York: Macmillan, 1979. A light-hearted discussion of the kind of love that provides intimacy and emotional support in marriage; focuses on everyday love, which fulfills the need for companionship and affection.

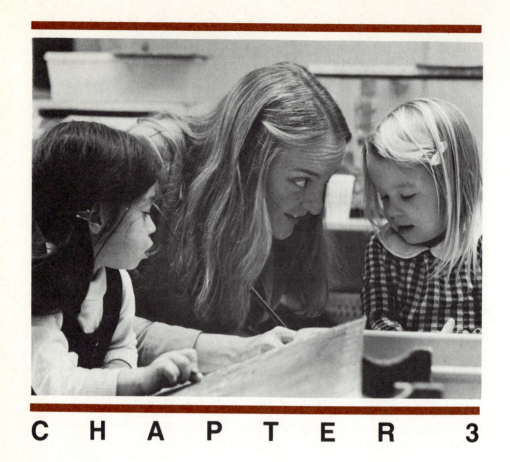

C H A P T E R 3

The Individual and the
Family in Society

SON: I don't want to go to school.

MOTHER: You've got to go to school.

SON: The kids laugh.

MOTHER: Why do they laugh?

SON: If I say a word, just one word in Spanish, they go around repeating it. *Amigo, amigo,* haha *amigo.* All day long.

MOTHER: I'm sorry it's hard for you. But you cannot run from this. School is your ticket out of the *barrio.*

SON: I like *el barrio.* I don't want to take that lousy bus and spend all day with the anglos and blacks.

MOTHER: You were picked to be in that special junior high school. It's an honor to the family. You will be the first Gomez to go to college.

SON: You could use the money for yourself, for Theresa.

MOTHER: No, every penny I make at the factory goes in that box and right to the bank for your college. Then you will help your sister.

SON: All right, today, I'll go to school. I don't know about tomorrow. *(MOTHER COUGHS)* You should see a doctor with that cough.

MOTHER: I'm taking the herbs *Abuela* gave me.

SON: It's not *Abuela.* In English it's Grandmother.

MOTHER: The herbs Grandmother gave me.

SON: Americans take pills, not herbs.

MOTHER: Americans have money for pills. Herbs and a few candles to Our Lady of Guadalupe will cure the cough.

SON: I'll bet you're inhaling some chemicals at the factory. You should complain about this to the government. Go to the free clinic, at least, over on Sheffield.

MOTHER: You wait in line there all day, crowded in with other sick people. You get sicker than before. Come out of the bed. I'll make you breakfast.

SON: Should I drop Theresa at the Head Start?

MOTHER: No, she's going to *Abuela*, to Grandmother's today.

SON: At Grandmother's she'll speak Spanish. At Head Start, they speak English. Mama, when are you going to become an American?

MOTHER: When my son goes to college.

INTRODUCTION

In the preceding chapters we have concentrated on individual and family stages and developmental tasks. We have also sought the roots of intimacy and the sources of our attitudes concerning love and marriage. We now turn to a consideration of the larger social world. What forces outside the immediate family affect the family and the individual? We know that the family attempts to modify the environment for its developing children, but here we shall see that the family's control over circumstances is only partial. The parents' own backgrounds affect their family structure and their child-rearing styles. When their children come into direct contact with the world outside the family—at school, through peer interaction, via television and books—the values that the family has been inculcating often come into conflict with other cultural values. Thus social forces somewhat beyond an individual's control play a role in developing a capacity for intimacy and in shaping an attitude toward marriage and family. As social scientist Kurt Lewin said, "The fish is in the sea and the sea is in the fish" (Lewin 1935); it is unnatural to separate the two. In our attempt to understand both the individual and the individual's environment, however, we shall look at the sea and ask what impact it has on the fish.

THE FAMILY IN ITS ENVIRONMENT

In extreme circumstances, the physical and social environment can have a direct, adverse impact on children. If there is no food, children starve. If there is disease in the air they breathe, the food they consume, or the objects they touch, or even if the dangers come to them in the womb via their mother or their genes, parents are unable to protect them. The developmental tasks we have been discussing assume a certain degree of safety and protection from severe threats to the child. We know that in many cultures families are unable to control the dangers of famine, drought, and disease that prevail in their environment.

In the United States and other developed countries, the family usually can modify the environment, or "mediate it." When we say the family mediates the environment, we mean the family filters it, reduces its dangers, and makes it palatable. The family mediates between the child and the physical environment in such ways as dressing the child in warm clothes when it is cold, purchasing food and reducing it to bite-sized pieces for the child's consumption, and sterilizing bottles when the infant is too young to fight off ordinary germs.

The family also mediates between the outside social environment and what the child actually learns as appropriate social behavior. In the United States, for example, most children learn to speak English and to eat with a knife and fork. Whether children speak English with a certain accent or sentence structure, whether they speak Spanish before learning English, whether they hold the fork in their fist or balance it delicately between thumb and index finger—such things depend upon the family in which they are raised.

Although the surrounding social world may have certain standards of behavior, these are mediated by the family, which suggests to the child how to respond in certain situations and even how to feel. For example, males in our culture are generally taught not to cry in public. A given family decides how to convey this message or whether to convey it at all.

The family is the first and most important socializing agent. (Andy Brilliant)

Some families will suggest to an eight-year-old boy that it is "braver" not to cry when his team loses the baseball game; others will react with such disapproval that the child will feel deeply ashamed; still others will accept crying as a healthy way of showing emotion. Moral values and political orientations, in addition to sex roles and social attitudes, are also transmitted through the family. Because of this mediating role, the family is often referred to as an *agent of socialization*, or a *socializing agent*.

The family is the first and most important socializing agent, but not the only one. Peers become increasingly important as a child matures. Other relatives and teachers play a role, as well as "leaders" of various types— gang leaders, political leaders, religious leaders, and cult figures; even those who achieve success, such as the superstars of film and the recording industry, can encourage a type of cultic worship. Television has also become a socializing agent, though its content varies and its effects differ according to how old children are, how much exposure they get, and what social tendencies they already have.

Three basic concepts are involved in the complex relationships between family and environment: *culture*, *society*, and *socialization*. These concepts have been defined in many ways. Here we offer simply a basic working definition of each.

1. Society. A society is a group of people living and working together (Anderson and Carter 1978). The way of life followed by this group who live and work together represents their culture.
2. Culture. Culture is a term that takes in those manners, morals, tools, and techniques binding a particular group or society together (Anderson and Carter 1978, p. 35). Jerome Bruner calls toolmaking, social organization, language, the management of prolonged human childhood, and the human urge to explain the world the "five great humanizing forces" (1968). These five forces can also be seen, as Anderson and Carter (1978) make clear, as the major dimensions of a culture. In the United States, then, we have a culture using advanced technology, organized into families along the political plan of a democracy and the economic plan of modified capitalism. We speak English, encourage individual achievement in our children, and try to explain the world primarily through scientific means, but also with the help of Judeo-Christian ideas. Naturally, this is an oversimplification, but these five dimensions provide a starting point for talking about our culture.

In a pluralistic society such as the United States, where many ethnic, racial, and religious groups coexist, the term *subculture* becomes necessary. It is used to designate a cluster of cultural differences usually stemming from a common country of origin, religion, language, and, initially, a similar socioeconomic base. If we refer to an individual, for instance, as belonging to the Hispanic subculture of New York, we know much more about the person than if we said simply "an American" or "a New Yorker." In addition to this cultural pluralism, there is also within American society today "a new pluralism evident in family forms and attitudes" that must be considered along with the influence of the subculture. For example, we have middle-class nuclear families with one worker and with two workers, single-parent families that are rather isolated, and some that are part of an extended family network (National Commission on Families 1978).

3. Socialization.   Socialization has been defined as "the process by which an individual acquires the mores, beliefs, skills, and other characteristics appropriate in his or her particular society" (Ferguson 1970, pp. 17–18). Through the socialization process, a given society transmits its shared institutions, beliefs, values, customs—its shared culture—from one generation to the next.

Linkages Between Families and the Dominant Culture

One concept that will be useful in trying to understand how the dominant culture affects specific families is "linkages" (Stolte-Heiskanen 1975).

Every society has some links between its economy and political structure, on the one hand, and its families and their needs, on the other. In preindustrial America there were few linkages. The economic unit was, in many cases, the same as the family unit. There were few taxes or government regulations. Citizens voted for public officials, but the areas of life controlled by the government were very few. Freedom from such controls had been a central motivation of those who founded this country and the millions of immigrant groups who fled to the United States in its formative decades.

Industrialization and the tendency to place the economic unit outside the family inevitably led to placing many aspects of family needs outside the direct control of the family unit. The dangers of work to the individual's health, especially the dangers to children in the work place, eventually led to some control of work conditions through federal legislation and through the growth of unions. It may have been the desire to exclude children from competition with adult workers that encouraged child-labor laws, as well as more humane considerations. Compulsory public education, begun in the late nineteenth century but not fully established until the twentieth century, meant that children, regardless of their native culture, were required to speak English and attend school until age 16. In school they would come in contact with other cultural values.

At first the notion of eliminating subcultural differences prevailed. More recently, there has been an emphasis on preserving ethnic and cultural differences while still transmitting the values of the dominant culture. The movement of women into the work force, which had once affected primarily industrial and farm workers, now involves middle-class, white-collar workers as well. With the work place distant from the home, women who are mothers must make provisions for the care of their young children, leaving the door open for other institutions to increase their influence over the family.

Government, business, industry, and labor unions have become involved in family life by regulating work schedules, salaries, employment opportunities, maternity and paternity leaves, and day-care allowances. One can see that the linkages between family needs and our institutions have increased in number and in strength. If we consider the many regulations that control the quality of the food we eat, the medicine we take, and the air we breathe, we can see that an almost paradoxical development has taken place. While families may appear to be atomized and disconnected from economic and political institutions, they are in fact more tightly linked to them than in the preindustrial period. While a sense of community may have weakened or disappeared, especially in urban areas, families are now more closely bound to government, industry, and technological change. Figure 3.1 illustrates some of the basic linkages between a culture and families. Below are a few examples of these linkages.

Linkages Between Technological Change and Families

Medical Advances. In this century alone, life expectancy has increased by 20 years. Medical advances have not only cured illness and prevented disease; they have led to the possibility of prolonging the lives of people who would otherwise have died, thus raising serious ethical and economic issues and changing family structures. Grandparents live long periods of married life apart from their children. When they are ill, a difficult dependency on children may ensue, creating problems of severe economic and psychological drain on adult children. How can outside intervention *support* families in such circumstances of caring for their aged, rather than supplant or replace families (National Commission on Families 1978)?

On the other end of the spectrum are the remarkable advances in genetics, fertility and birth control, and prenatal care. In the last 15 years, for example, we have learned the structure of DNA, the basic genetic substance. Knowing the way the chromosomal strands are replicated, the code by which DNA specifies the insertion of amino acids in proteins, seems remote from the daily lives of married couples and families, but ultimately such discoveries have profound effects (Mayer 1970; Goodfield 1977). Humans can now replicate DNA molecules, creating new forms of life. Is it ethical to control this basic genetic substance? If a synthetic virus can gobble up oil slicks, is it all right for one industry to produce and therefore control a substance that can affect the entire society? In 1980 such sanction was given by the Supreme Court when it handed down a 5–4 decision allowing Ananda Chakrabarty a patent for *Pseudomonas aereogi-*

FIGURE 3.1 Linkage Mechanisms Between the Culture and the Family

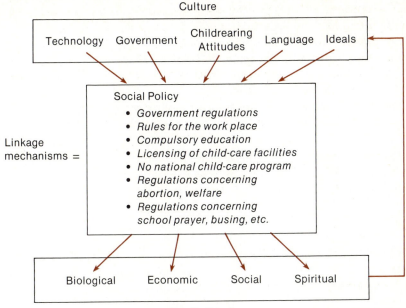

nosa, the oil-eating bacteria he had created while working for General Electric. Human intervention into the basic elements of life may advance the control of cancer, diabetes, and other illnesses, but it may also expose the population to harmful agents and give rise to new sources of power that will require some form of control.

In the area of reproduction and embryology, Dr. Jean Mayer (1970) singles out the development of effective hormonal contraception for females ("the pill") and the banking of frozen sperm as two of the most significant developments in the twentieth century. We shall discuss these and other advances relating to conception in Chapter 10, but for our purposes here we can at least recognize that medical technology allows families to control birth and makes fertility possible for married people, as well as unmarried adults, who want children. Other recent technological advances that directly affect the structure and the quality of family life include test-tube fertilization and implantation of the fertilized egg in the womb (the "test-tube baby"), the possibility of operating on a fetus still in the womb ("fetology"), the opportunity to detect chromosomal defects before birth, and the technology that permits a baby weighing only one pound to stand a chance for survival.

A new area, which Joshua Lederberg has called "euphenics," may one day engineer the development of a given embryo by modifying or inserting DNA, thus providing new instructions for the child's development. A potentially diabetic child, for example, would be operated on prenatally and given new genetic instructions for synthesizing sugars (Mayer 1970, p. 186). Such possibilities have enormous implications for families and for our society. "Playing God," as June Goodfield (1977) called this, means playing for enormously high stakes—the very future of our children. Should a scientific aristocracy decide the fate of future generations? These are some of the questions raised by the new technology.

Advances in Mass Transit. New modes of transportation influence the culture. The automobile has been a force in changing sexual behavior, allowing greater separation between work and home, influencing strict sex-role divisions, and enabling family members to engage in activities and socialize with a variety of groups. Airplane connections allow for commuter marriages in which couples work in different cities and see each other on weekends or even less frequently. These innovations also provide opportunity for travel, exposure to other subcultural social groups, and increased opportunities to meet, form relationships with, and marry people who are not similar to those of one's original family.

Mobility in the technical sense has increased mobility in the social sense, from one economic group to another. A construction worker with little formal education sends his son to a distant college where the boy meets the daughter of a wealthy businessman. They marry and live in a different city, their daughter becoming an elected official. Mobility may weaken the ties of the immediate family to the extended family, or it may make visiting possible and one's far-flung relatives more accessible.

Household Labor-Saving Devices. Housework is supposedly easier now, and its technical nature may make household chores doable by any member of the family, male or female, young or old. The possibility for everyone to share housework is there, although women have remained in charge of most of these responsibilities. Home computers are likely to become a common tool for family communication as well as a master control for household devices (Koff 1979).

Communications Advances. The telephone makes it possible to establish and maintain interpersonal relationships across great distances. Computers have already been used to aid in dating services and matchmaking. In *The Third Wave* (1980), futurist Alvin Toffler suggests that advances in communication systems may permit many more people to operate businesses and various services from their own homes, transforming the home into an "electronic cottage," a center for work and family affairs.

Linkages Between Government and Families

Governments in most Western countries regulate a good part of the individual's life, and the family's as well. Government health programs obviously affect the family's well-being. Economic policies, such as high interest rates, may determine whether a family is able to buy their own home or take a vacation. Tax policies and allocations by local and federal government for child-care funds may determine whether a mother is able to work. The family menu and children's nutrition are affected by the legislative subsidies that raise and lower the costs of beef and wheat.

The list goes on. The Consumer Product Safety Commission forbids the sale of toys with sharp detachable parts, which may be swallowed by small children, and requires that children's sleepwear be treated with a flame retardant. Daylight-saving time sets the time of day a schoolchild gets up, and the subsidized school lunch program provides carrots and peas for lunch. In addition to fire and police protection, public schools, and adult-education opportunities, the government provides parks and recreational facilities. Depending on a family's residence and economic and social status, its quality of life will be affected by such government projects as urban renewal, taxes, and zoning regulations. As it sleeps, eats, works, drives, shops, or plays, every family in the United States is affected by federal regulations made in Washington, D.C. (Jackson and Witt 1976, p. 195; Paolucci, Hall, and Axinn 1977, pp. 38–44.)

Some social scientists, such as Catherine Chilman (1976), argue for more comprehensive national planning of families and the things they depend upon for their well-being—income, housing, health care, education, employment, recreation, transportation, and community services. The lack of really effective social welfare programs to help families is often charged to the frugality of legislators and the incompetence of administrators. It is thought that if only we put more money into the programs, they would work. On the other hand, critics of government involvement in social welfare programs, nursing homes, juvenile courts, and foster-care systems point to the abuses of power sometimes evident in such institutions. They question whether a government-regulated system of social welfare is appropriate to solving the major problems confronting families today. As Ira Glasser (1978) has written, people who are taken care of by government may become "prisoners of benevolence." Their destiny is no longer in their own hands, and their status in society is diminished. Another matter decided by the government that has far-reaching implications for families is the question of how low a family's income should be before they are considered poor. In 1981, for example, some officials were urging that an income of $6,200 for a family of four, set as the poverty level in 1977, should be raised by at least $3,000; others were urging that the poverty line remain the same despite the fact that the cost of living had risen markedly during this period (Chambers 1981).

In the past, linkages between government and families have been "pathology-focused"—focused on serious disturbances such as drug abuse, child and spouse abuse, juvenile crime, and teenage pregnancy (National Commission on Families 1978). Can family needs be met in a more supportive way if social policy concentrates on prevention of social problems through supporting a variety of viable families, or will this simply extend government influence and open the door to excessive intervention and control? As we examine some of the existing linkages between families and government, we should keep this question in mind.

Welfare and Marital Stability. We have noted that developments following the Industrial Revolution brought government and our legal system into the province of child welfare. The welfare system was designed to help families with dependent children. In recent years the question has been raised as to whether welfare actually serves to increase divorce and prevent remarriage. One study of a sample of 4,322 females between the ages of 30 and 44 determined that low-income white women who received Aid to Families with Dependent Children, food stamps, and other public assistance dissolved their marriages more frequently than those low-income white women who were not receiving welfare (Bahr 1979). Of course, the possibility exists that certain individuals "are more prone to accept welfare and to dissolve their marriages" (Bahr 1979, p. 558). Bahr gives the example of the person with low self-esteem who lacks communication skills and feels powerless as a person; she may move toward divorce and welfare. He also suggests that welfare may represent a relief from marital misery, a way out of an unbearable marriage, the only viable alternative open to a very poor woman. Draper (1981) re-evaluated Bahr's data, using different statistical tools, and he did not find the same relationship between public assistance and marital instability. In fact, Draper concluded that divorce and separation may cause women to go on welfare, perhaps as a means of keeping the rest of the family together. The results of these two studies indicate that the effects of government support on family stability are subject to different interpretations. The research evidence to date is conflicting and does not clearly support one view or the other.

The Government as an Employer and Regulator of Work. Federal, state, and city governments, taken together, represent one of the largest single sources of employment in the country. Governments can pioneer new policies of employment that affect families, as well as control the employment practices in the private sector. Employment opportunities for women, blacks, and Hispanics have improved as a result of government policies and regulations. Flexible scheduling, which permits employees to have some control over their work schedules, is now used in varying degrees by more than 50 percent of the state governments and in 19 percent of the federal branches of government. Flex-time, which permits parents to start work earlier and return home earlier if they choose, has been shown to increase the amount of time parents spend with their children while increasing productivity and morale at the work place (Winett and Neale 1980).

Governmental Influence on Day Care. Even without a federal day-care program, direct federal expenditures on child care amounted to $2.5 billion in 1977 (Malone 1977). A projected 10.4 million children under age six will have mothers in the labor force by 1990 (Hofferth 1979). Public policy, as Hofferth makes clear, affects day-care demand and supply. She lists five ways this can occur: (1) lowering the cost and raising the quality of group day care will tend to increase its use; (2) welfare policies requiring women to work or providing less than a living allotment force women to work and increase day-care demand; (3) policies promoting extended pregnancy or parental leave, and those which encourage flexible work scheduling, decrease day-care need; (4) "policies that provide a public-service job to the principal earner in two-parent families (as in proposed welfare reform

Government policies affect the demand for and quality of day-care programs. (Martha Stewart, Picture Cube)

legislation), or that offer generous maternal work leave while children are young (as in some European countries), should reduce demand for all types of day care" (p. 655); and (5) tax policies can affect the type of day care by specifying which types will be deductible.

Legislative and Judicial Influences on Children's Rights. The question of the individual rights of minors has been decided largely in the courts. Legalization of abortion occurred through legislation that was tested in the courts and held constitutional, but the access of welfare recipients to abortion has been ruled a matter of state policy. In some states, then, abortion for welfare recipients will not be paid for, and this may have the effect of making abortion unavailable. In the most recent rulings, the rights of adolescents to obtain birth control, to have abortions, or to have children if they desire them—and even if parents object—has been supported by the courts (Paul et al. 1976). All too often the courts, when dealing with issues of juvenile rights, appear to be inconsistent, arbitrary, and capricious (Murphy 1974; Prescott 1981). In Chapter 11 we shall see in detail the way child neglect and abuse can be controlled by the manner in which states and the courts define these terms. Divorce hearings tend to consider the opinions of older children in terms of custody disputes, though the overriding consideration tends to be "the best interests of the child." That extremely broad phrase may cause children to be removed from the custody of a divorced woman who is living with a man (*Jarrett* vs. *Jarrett*, 1980), or it may remove a child from the custody of parents who seek to return him to another country against his will (*Palovchek* vs. *Palovchek*, 1980). To provide stability, some psychiatrists have argued that custody assignments should be absolutely final (Goldstein, Freud, and Solnit 1973), while others urge that custody be made a joint arrangement (Roman and Haddad 1978) to encourage co-parenting and equal influence of parents.

Divorce Proceedings as an Influence on the Family. The increase in the number of divorced persons in the United States means an increase in the number of families directly affected by the courts. One study that concentrated on 205 individuals divorcing in the state of Pennsylvania found dissatisfaction with the legal process in almost every case: "The data suggest that divorce statutes based on an adversary model encourage collusion and dishonesty" (Spanier and Anderson 1979). As we shall discuss further in Chapter 12, adversary divorce statutes, developed when divorce involved blame and punishment, no longer "reflect the reality of the divorce experience" (Spanier and Anderson 1979, p. 612). "Marriages rarely fail as a result of wrongdoings committed by one spouse," note Spanier and Anderson. "Furthermore there is serious doubt about whether the adversary system encourages reconciliation." In this Pennsylvania study and in other divorce studies, it appears that the process of finding grounds for divorce and the need to prove inadequacy of one parent in custody disputes tend to reduce the chance of reconciliation and even damage the future of the divorcing couple as co-parents of their children. Even individuals who live together for an extended period of time may find themselves under the influence of the courts through "palimony" suits and paternity suits.

Socioeconomic Class Influences on Families

The effects of the culture are not the same for rich families and poor families. Occupation, educational background, salary, gender, and ethnicity all figure into the status of a particular family. The social position and income of families headed by professionals differ from the status of families headed by white-collar workers or workers with primarily manual skills. Families headed by unskilled workers frequently find themselves in the ranks of the poor. They are more likely to receive welfare and be under the influence of government or institutional regulations.

Until recently, women have had fewer skills, less of a full-time attachment to the work force, and a lower economic status than men. In 1976, for example, the median income for full-time, year-round employed men was $13,455; for their female counterparts it was $8,099. As Figure 3.2 illustrates, mean annual income also varies according to the type of family, with two-worker households generally having the higher income and female-headed households having the lower income. In most divorces, women wind up both raising their children and holding jobs. Although employed mothers who are heads of households appear to work more hours per week at jobs, housework, and family tasks than all other groups of adults, their labors are not reflected in their economic circumstances (National Commission on Families 1978).

The terms "middle-class," "working-class," and "lower-class" are commonly used to express socioeconomic differences, yet they are not always adequate to explain status differences. A two-worker, working-class family may have a higher income than a one-worker, middle-class family. Social differences resulting from occupational or educational factors don't always coincide with economic differences. Sociologist Bert Adams has provided a useful model that emphasizes important features distinguishing the various classes in our society (see Table 3.1).

Socioeconomic status affects a given family in at least four basic ways: in their ability to provide food, clothing, and shelter; in the values they incorporate regarding money, which may affect the financial security of relationships and the future of their families; in attitudes and values about work that may affect their ambitions and life goals; and in the way sex roles are structured in their marriage and in the socialization of their

FIGURE 3.2 Types of Households and Employment with Mean Income in 1977

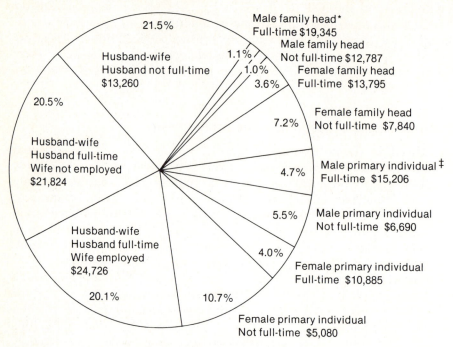

*Family head = unmarried individual living with and supporting children or other relatives.
†Primary individual = unmarried household head living alone or with unrelated individuals.
Source: George Masnick and Mary Jo Bane, *The Nation's Families: 1960–1990*, (Cambridge, Mass.: Joint Center for Urban Studies of MIT and Harvard University, 1980), p. 5.

children. To further refine our understanding of how a culture influences and accommodates to family needs, we must consider another intervening variable—ethnicity.

Ethnic Subcultures versus the Dominant Culture

In our pluralistic society there is often a discrepancy between the forces at work in one's ethnic subculture and the forces in the dominant culture. In some cases, as with the Amish, the subculture rejects the dominant culture, including its technological advances, and attempts to lead a life set apart. Within large urban areas there are neighborhoods in which certain subcultures predominate. Belonging to a subculture or minority group does not necessarily injure the self-esteem of the individual. In an Irish-Catholic neighborhood, for example, when a subculture is dominant, being Irish Catholic means being part of the "in group" (Rosenberg 1965). But in other cases, even when most of the people in the neighborhood belong to

TABLE 3.1 Social-Class Characteristics

	Occupations	Economic Condition	Marriage and Family Views	Values
Middle Class	Professionals, managers, salespeople, clerks	Well above subsistence level	Husband-wife relationship built on happiness, communication, and mutual gratification in all areas, including sex. Children encouraged to develop individuality and self-control	Upward mobility, education, equality, work, and success
Working Class	Varied manual and technical skills; plumbers, electricians, construction workers, factory workers, masons, carpenters	Adequate but more vulnerable to unemployment, economic cutbacks, factory shutdowns	Roles of husband and wife segregated, with wife tending to be responsible for children and kin, husband for breadwinning and discipline. Children encouraged to be obedient to authority and hard working. Extended family ties important, with female relatives as confidantes for wife, male relatives and friends as sources of companionship for husband	Order, freedom, and enjoyment after work, and the social network of immediate and extended family
Lower Class	Unemployment high; employment at unskilled work such as maintenance jobs, housecleaning, waitressing and waitering in less affluent eating establishments, piece work	Poverty level	Many broken homes, erratic child rearing involving harsh discipline at times, immediate gratification at others' expense	Survival with the help of kinship ties
Upper Class	Professionals, government officials, business executives	Extreme wealth	Kinship ties for inheritance and power, marriages to maintain or increase prestige and power	Perpetuation of wealth, domination of society's power and resources

Source: Adapted from Bert N. Adams, *The Family: A Sociological Interpretation*, Houghton Mifflin Company, 1980, pp. 120–124. Copyright © 1980 by Houghton Mifflin Company.

the same subculture, there is a sense of being "marginal," to use Lewin's (1948) term, on the fringe, not part of the accepted group. This was the case with Jews in Europe and in this country, and it is the experience of many black and Hispanic families. For these groups, low self-esteem is not an occasional or individual event, but an ongoing and inescapable message of the dominant culture.

Cultural Influences on Blacks. Describing the character development of blacks in a hostile environment, Leon Chestang suggests that the black experience of injustice, inconsistency, and impotence creates a special kind of split personality: "Impotence is the feeling of powerlessness to influence the environment. On a personal level, it is the feeling of the father unable to secure employment and therefore unable to support his family" (1980, p. 42). Ideally, our culture encourages individuals and families to influence government and other institutions. When large cities with substantial black populations have only a small percentage of blacks in major decision-making positions, the minority feels a negative reflection of its needs and powers, an invisibility, as Ralph Ellison once called it in his now classic novel of the black experience, *Invisible Man*, first published in 1947. Part of the black experience, in Chestang's opinion, has been the development of a depreciated character that "aggresses passively," that has a desperate and angry acceptance of negative attributions, as in this passage from Ellison's *Invisible Man:*

Oh, I'd yes them, but wouldn't I yes them! I'd yes them till they puked and rolled in it. All they wanted of me was one belch of affirmation and I'd bellow it out loud. Yes! Yes! Yes! That was all anyone wanted of us, that we should be heard and not seen, and then heard only in one big optimistic chorus of yassuh, yassuh, yassuh! All right, I'd yea, yea and oui, oui, and si, si and see, see them too; and I'd walk around in their guts with hobnailed boots. (1953, pp. 439–440)

There is another side of the invisible, yeah-saying black person that Chestang calls the transcendant side, the part of the personality that will not be squelched, that waits to fulfill a goal. The "up by your bootstraps" philosophy currently advocated by black economist Thomas Sowell and others has led to the upward mobility of blacks and a new black middle class (Sowell 1981). William Julius Wilson (1980) argues that race, as a historically significant negative factor, does not now play as important a role in upward mobility as does education: "The income discrepancies between black and white workers is basically a reflection of discrepancies in seniority" (p. xi). According to Wilson, the problem for the future, in the narrow sense, is the growing gap between poor blacks and middle-class blacks and, in the larger arena, the gap between the poor (regardless of race) and the middle class (regardless of race).

One of the most important things we can learn about a subculture is the fact that it is composed of individuals. Stereotypes eliminate individual differences, making it easier to categorize and diminish members of a group. Sensitizing people to individual differences in another ethnic group tends to reduce prejudice. One experimenter showed black and white children many pictures of the other race, each time altering one trait such as hair style or facial expression. Learning to distinguish between one face and another tended to sensitize children and reduce their racial bias (Katz 1973).

Black families have a higher percentage of single-parent households. The economic gap between husband-wife and single-parent households has widened. The trend for blacks to live in single-parent households has increased in recent years (see Figure 3.3), and remarriage rates are lower for black women than for white women (Bianchi and Farley 1979). On the other hand, "black families do not constitute a monolithic pattern of familial relationships" (Willie and Greenblatt 1978).

Even during the period of slavery, when one-third of black families were forcibly dissolved by white owners, substantial numbers of blacks maintained stable families. Looking at Nelson County, Virginia, in 1866, Gutman (1976) found that 55 percent of the marriages had existed for more than 10 years and 15 percent for more than 30 years. Using Gutman's data, Rodgers-Rose estimates that, two years after emancipation, no more than 25 percent of all black households were headed by females (Rodgers-Rose 1980, p. 20). Reviewing four classic studies of power relationships in black

FIGURE 3.3 Proportion of Children Under 18 Living with Both Parents or with Mothers Only, 1960–1977

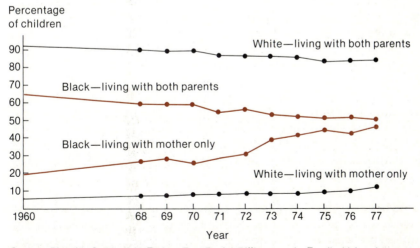

Source: Bianchi, S. M., and Farley, R., "Racial Differences in Family Living Arrangements and Economic Well-Being: An Analysis of Recent Trends," *Journal of Marriage and Family*, August 1979, Vol. 41, No. 3, p. 542. Copyright © 1979 by the National Council on Family Relations. Reprinted by permission.

families (Middleton and Putney 1960; Mack 1978; TenHouten 1970; Willie 1976), Willie and Greenblatt (1978) show that power relationships in black families vary. They are not necessarily matriarchal, as Moynihan (1965) had contended. "It is the black poor," these authors stress, "who have a high incidence of one-parent families" (p. 692), but the majority of black families have husband and wife present.

There appears to be a deepening schism in the black population. Female-headed families have increased significantly since publication of the Moynihan report—from 23.2 percent of all black families in 1962 to 28.0 percent in 1969, 37.0 percent in 1976, and 40.5 percent in 1979. "What has been happening is clear: the black underclass of the ghetto has been expanding at precisely the same time as the black middle class has also been expanding and moving ahead" (Gershman 1980).

When husband and wife are present, it appears that black families are no more likely to be matriarchal than white families. Socioeconomic class makes the difference in decision-making power, with middle-class black and white couples more likely to share in decision making and working-class husbands more likely to be the final arbiters. The lower-class black families in which husbands were present, far from being mother-dominant, actually tended to be patriarchal, or father-dominant. The studies reviewed, taken together, show a variety of adaptations. In some cases it appears that the black middle-class family may be more egalitarian than the white middle-class family.

Looking at the West African origins of many black families, Rodgers-Rose (1980) reports that working outside the home, living separately with one's children until they reached the age of three, and even practicing polygamy tended to give the black woman in West Africa a separate identity. Independence, a strong work orientation, and the importance of motherhood were not products of slavery but a heritage that survived slavery. Being forced to have children in rapid succession while continuing to work long hours caused black women, originally socialized to take care of themselves, to strengthen their independence and self-reliance (Rodgers-Rose 1980, p. 21). The experiences of persecuted minority groups prove that family bonds endure. The strength of marital and family ties is made clear in the case histories of black families documented by records of the period (Gutman 1976), and popularized in Alex Haley's *Roots*. Even the attempt to eliminate an entire ethnic group, as occurred in the Holocaust, cannot eradicate family bonds.

The Chicano Family. Spanish-speaking groups in the United States include Puerto Ricans, Cubans, and Mexican-Americans, or *Chicanos*. With a population of between 7 and 10 million, Chicanos are the largest Spanish-speaking group in the United States, and the second-largest minority group—only the black population is larger (Mindel and Habenstein 1981).

They are also the most cohesive of the Hispanic groups. They share a common language, religion, and set of family values within our society, and they often share a bitter experience because of the differences between their subculture and the dominant culture. Guadalupe Gibson (1980) emphasizes the importance of understanding ethnic values in order to interact effectively with a particular ethnic group. Here are two of the significant features of the Chicano family:

1. **Mutualism** *(carnalismo).*   Chicanos believe in a responsibility of human beings for one another, which extends beyond the immediate family to a network of relatives. This predominance of person orientation over goal orientation, of cooperation over competition, may induce a Chicano to leave work if a relative is in need. It may give Chicanos the appearance of being overly easygoing in school or at work and not very competitive. In one experiment comparing white Americans and Mexican-Americans, however, white children competed even when cooperation would have been more productive. The Mexican-Americans could compete, but their tendency was to be cooperative (Kagan and Madsen 1971).

2. *El Barrio.*   This term is often used interchangeably with the term "ghetto," yet *el barrio* for many Chicanos represents home, whether it

Children from the *barrio*, taught to value cooperation and mutualism, may experience cultural shock when they enter schools that stress competition and individualism. (Terry McKoy)

refers to their actual community or to a state of mind. The *barrio,* as Gibson stresses, reinforces the values of cooperation and family, and it encourages the children to speak Spanish instead of English. "It can very well be for most Mexican-American children that they spend the first five years of their lives with practically no contact with the community beyond the barrio" (Gibson 1980). It is the *barrio* and its residents then—rather than the dominant white culture—that supplies child care, home-remedy health care, and psychological support for the Chicano family. Even the medical advances affecting the majority of Americans have not reached many Chicanos. While life expectancy for the rest of the population has been extended to 72 years, Chicanos have a life expectancy of 57 years. Chicanos share a Roman Catholic belief that emphasizes the cult of the Virgin Mary, though it appears that an increasing number are not practicing Catholics, and some are anticlerical (Gibson 1980; Goodman et al. 1971).

Coming from the *barrio,* sharing a language, a common religion, and a common set of values, the Chicano child enters a school where English rather than Spanish is spoken, and competition and individualism are stressed rather than cooperation and mutualism. Efforts to provide bilingual classes may soften this cultural shock, but linkages between the dominant culture and citizens of the *barrio* are still very few.

We cannot possibly evaluate in detail all the many subcultures that exist in the United States. According to the *Harvard Encyclopedia of American Ethnic Groups* (1980), there are at least 100 ethnic groups in the United States. These necessarily sketchy examples simply illustrate that the linkages between families and our common culture differ due to ethnicity as well as social class and gender. The generalizations made concerning marriage and family life tend to be made on the basis of white, middle-class experience, but it should be clear at this point that the surrounding cultural sea is not the same for all.

PATHWAYS FOR SOCIALIZATION

How does the sea get into the fish? How does the culture with its particular values become part of the child's individual behavior? The process of socialization begins the moment the child is born and continues through countless interactions with parents and siblings. The values of the society are at first mediated through parents—the primary socializing agents. But as the child develops there are more and more opportunities for direct contact with the outside world or, at least, with agents of socialization outside the family—television, peers, teachers.

Two pathways for absorbing the culture have been studied extensively: *social cognition*—the understanding of the world of human interaction—

and *social learning*—the learning that takes place through observing and imitating other models of behavior.

Social Cognition

There is a relationship between intellectual (cognitive) growth and the development of social understanding. The study of social cognition, using Jean Piaget's model of developmental stages in cognitive growth, explores this relationship. In Piaget's view the individual adapts to the environment in stages, assimilating new information when there is an internal readiness. Social cognition, or social understanding, appears to proceed in a similar way. At first the child is egocentric, viewing the world as an extension of the self, unable to imagine the world from another point of view, unable to assume the perspective of another. At about the age that school begins (six or seven), the child develops an awareness of others and a greater sensitivity to others. As the child matures, sensitivity to the nonverbal language of others, such as facial expressions and gestures, increases. The child picks up dress codes and rules of the culture. During adolescence the child will be able to understand not only another perspective, but even the abstract notion of another culture. It is at this time that mental or cognitive growth and social understanding enable the individual to think in terms of a world view, to criticize such things as conformity or competitiveness, liberalism or conservatism. Table 3.2 gives the broad outlines of the progressive stages of social cognition.

Role taking is one area of social cognition that relates closely to marital interaction. By about eight years of age children begin to realize that others have their own values and goals and that these may be different from their own. They see that these different values affect the way people think and feel. They acquire the ability to see themselves and their behavior from another's point of view; they also see that another person can imagine how they feel, but they cannot yet get outside the two-person perspective (Selman and Byrne 1974). Mutual role taking is evident in eight- and ten-year-olds. At this level, children can imagine a disinterested spectator whose point of view they can distinguish from their own and that of the other person in a two-person situation. They discover, too, that each of two persons can consider the other's point of view simultaneously and mutually. They can put themselves in the other's place before deciding how to respond. Each can see the situation from the point of view of a disinterested observer. The ability to assume multiple perspectives develops even later, in late childhood or early adolescence.

This developing ability to comprehend another person's point of view will be crucial to the capacity for mutually satisfying intimate relationships. It also makes the individual vulnerable to messages from the culture—through peers, TV, teachers—concerning how others view them.

TABLE 3.2   Stages of Social Cognition

Age	Stage	Description
Prior to 6	Egocentricism	No distinction between child's view of social situation and the perspective of the other
6 to 9	Initial role taking	Child infers feelings, thoughts of others, recognizes his/her thoughts and inner feelings
10 to 11	Mutual role taking	Simultaneous taking of other's perspective
12 to 16	Recognition of generalized other	Adolescent recognizes that he/she and the other can examine the dynamics of a social situation; he/she can look at a social system
Postadolescent	Relativity of social facts	Individual appreciates influences of culture, history, and personal emotional state on the social situation

Source: Adapted from Robert L. Selman and Diane F. Byrne, "A Structural-Developmental Analysis of Levels of Role Taking in Middle Childhood," *Child Development* 45 (1974): 804–805. © The Society for Research in Child Development, Inc. Used by permission.

By school age, a young girl may begin to perceive that others define her future role choices based on gender. This new input may conflict with parental socialization. This is the time a Chicano boy of the *barrio* may begin to see himself from the perspective of a white middle-class child and notice the many things that make him different, and, in their eyes, even undesirable.

Agents of socialization modify the child's view. In class a teacher may stress positive contributions of minority groups, or she may neglect to regard them at all, making them feel invisible or demeaned. The teacher may encourage their aspirations, providing examples of minority people who have achieved goals. The child also encounters peers at this point, who may encourage bitterness, cynicism, or aggression. Or perhaps the child will be fortunate enough to have peers and group leaders who are doing constructive things in the neighborhood. What does it mean to be a man in this world? What is "manhood" for a certain Chicano boy? The boy has his father and his brothers as examples. Now how will peer attitudes influence him? How does one treat women? Role-taking abilities permit the boy to assume the role of the girl to some extent, but those tendencies can be curtailed by a peer group that promotes a macho ideal and rough values or insensitive treatment of women. The experience of role taking as modified by agents of socialization will influence attitudes about sex roles, racial differences, work, competition, and cooperation. Therefore, it will shape behavior that will influence marital interaction and parenting.

Social Learning

As the individual's powers of social cognition are gradually developing, as the individual's capacities for role taking and empathy are expanding, the individual is also accumulating observations. He or she is noticing who gets rewarded in the class, the neighborhood, the peer group, and why those persons receive rewards. The unique quality of each person's notion of woman/man, boyfriend/girlfriend, husband/wife will be largely determined by observing and imitating those around him or her, especially those who demonstrate power, those who receive rewards, and those who show warmth and acceptance.

Social learning theorists, such as Albert Bandura, stress the importance of observation and imitation (Bandura, Ross, and Ross 1963, pp. 3–11). They have found that children are likely to imitate and take as their models people who are perceived as powerful and capable of giving them

Social learning theory stresses the importance of imitation in the socialization experience. (Elizabeth Crews)

desired rewards. Parents are the supreme models in terms of social learning. Parents, at first, are all-powerful; they control all the resources. They dispense food, reduce discomfort, and offer smiles and caresses. Later, language is combined with these basic rewards. With language parents can promise rewards or threaten to remove them—"If there's any more shouting down here, you'll miss 'Sesame Street'!" Yet what parents do themselves is of even greater importance, according to social learning theory, than what they tell their children to do or not to do. A parent's effectiveness depends on whether they "model" the behavior they seem to be demanding, whether they demonstrate it themselves. As children grow older, they become more adept at recognizing what kind of models their parents are. So parents' effectiveness increases if they demonstrate what is wanted as well as giving rewards for desired behaviors.

Kagan and Moss (1962) suggest that the child has two powerful motivations for acquiring parents' behaviors. First, the child gains rewards by imitating the parent; second, the child feels more powerful, more in control of the environment, when imitating the behavior of someone who is obviously already in control of the environment. Powerful models encountered later on—teachers, other relatives, religious and political leaders, peers—may also be imitated for some of the same reasons.

Power is not the only reinforcement for imitation. Warmth and acceptance also figure in the child's social learning. Moreover, warm and accepting figures, especially parents, encourage independence, while lack of attention or very little attention encourages dependency (Sears, Rau, and Alpert 1965). This can be seen even in marriage, where a very critical husband or a very critical wife seems to cow his or her spouse and encourage dependency by undermining the other's confidence.

Social learning theory, with its stress on the importance of modeling desired behavior, is helpful in explaining how adults acquire tendencies to be either aggressive or "prosocial"—cooperative, giving, altruistic, empathic (Mussen and Eisenberg-Berg 1977). It also helps us to understand how models other than parents can influence a child's socialization. Watching hundreds of hours of aggressive behavior on television, mingling with peers who exert power by shows of force, engaging in sports that put the highest value on winning—these experiences can work to reinforce behavior that will not enhance intimate relationships.

Television as a Socializing Agent

Television occupies a unique position in our culture. On the one hand it is a technological advance, a tool of sorts; on the other it is a socializing agent, a teacher of behavior. Television provides a common ground that almost all of us share. Children in the United States watch between three and six hours of television each day, seven days a week. This means that by age 16, children in this country have spent more time watching TV than going to school. If trends continue with both parents working outside the home, it may be that television racks up more hours with the children than parents.

For many children television is the primary source of information about other races and ethnic groups, other social classes and occupational groups, sexuality, adults, the outside world, and the values of our culture. To many children, television is also a peer—"the electronic peer," as Ross Parke (1978) has called it. Ninety-eight percent of all homes in the United States have at least one television set, and more than half have two. Parents have some effect on the amount of television their children watch; parents who are heavy viewers are likely to have children who are heavy viewers. But parents seem to put few restrictions on the amount of time their children watch TV. With more two-worker and single-parent families, the departure of parents for work may create what Stein and Friedrich (1975) call a "socialization void," where no one is available to mediate TV's influence. Unlike the classroom situation in which the teacher can mediate the child's perceptions, the messages from TV— concerning women and men, ethnic groups, aggression—can be absorbed directly without modification.

What messages concerning our culture does TV convey?

Aggression.   The content of television programming has altered somewhat since the 1950s, with more women and blacks represented and a variety of family types shown, some of them facing realistic problems such as divorce, family violence, drugs, alcohol, and sexual decision making. In addition, we now have programs of educational value such as "Sesame Street" available. Yet aggression remains prevalent, especially on certain prime-time and "kids' shows." Defining *violence* as an actual act of physical force or as one causing pain, Gerbner (1972) found that 58 percent of the shows typically viewed by children featured a good deal of violence. Gerbner's findings during the 1970s aroused the public and pressured some stations into reducing aggressive content (McBroom 1980). But many of the programs made in the 1970s continue to be recycled on smaller channels, through cable TV and video cassettes.

Experimental studies have indicated that exposure to aggression on TV tends to increase aggressive behavior, but the findings of a ten-year longitudinal study (Lefkowitz et al. 1977) provide the most conclusive proof that TV, interacting with an attraction to aggression, can produce aggressive behavior later on. The study found that a boy in third grade who shows a preference for violent TV is likely to display aggressive behavior in adolescence. A preference for violent TV was a better predictor of later

aggression than social class, IQ, age, parental aggression, or parental puni-
tiveness. Aggressive children may *choose* violent TV, but exposure to aggression is one of the components in the formula that produces aggressive
acts: aggression-prone child + exposure to aggression on TV = aggressive
acts later. It is the one element in the formula that could, theoretically, be
controlled.

Sexism. A study of sex-role stereotypes on TV (Sternglanz and Serbin
1974) found that males outnumbered females on TV and were rewarded
for their assertive behavior. Females tended to be deferent and were even
punished for being very active. Today there are more active women—even
violent women—on TV, but many of the old stereotypes persist—the
dumb blonde, the wife dedicated to washing out collars and bathtub rings,
the helpless woman saved by the strong and capable man, the young and
old victims destroyed because the hero didn't know about them or didn't
arrive in time. In a recent interview (McBroom 1980), Gerbner reports that
heavy viewers of TV are more sexist than light viewers are, as well as being
more prejudiced about older people.

"Invisible" Groups. Elderly people are rarely seen on television. Though
older Americans constitute 11 percent of the population, they comprise
only 2 percent of the characters on TV. The majority of the older people
depicted are not held in high esteem or treated courteously. Consequently,
"heavy viewers believe, Gerbner has found, that the elderly are unhealthy,
in worse shape financially, not active sexually, close minded, and not good
at getting things done" (McBroom 1980, p. 6). Invisibility or distortion is
also the fate of many ethnic groups, including Asians and American Indians. As Stein and Friedrich (1975) have observed, TV is not a mirror
reflecting society in all its richness and diversity, but a prism refracting
our pluralism and projecting only certain facets—including sexism,
ageism, and commercialism.

Unlike other socializing agents, television has no capacity to respond to
an individual's needs. Children who have difficulty interacting with peers
may like the electronic peer for this reason: it can't hurt them. But this
state of affairs does nothing for their social development, nothing to improve their social skills or at least expose their problem so help can be
obtained. Television teaches what the culture at large is doing, but it often
distorts that information or neglects to inform us about existing groups.
Television has the capacity to expose children to prosocial behavior rather
than aggression, to new ways of seeing sex roles, other age groups, and
other cultures (Liebert and Poulos 1975). But as long as profit is the motive, this will happen only if altruism, empathy, and cooperation begin to
get higher ratings than aggression and sexism.

The greatest danger of television is that it will take the place of other socializing agents—parents, peers, teachers—causing people to prefer the safety of electronic relations to the risks and vulnerability demanded in real-life intimacy. In the last decades of the twentieth century, it appears that the government, technology, and other socializing agents beyond the family are having more impact on our attitudes concerning marriage and family. The control of these nonfamily socializing agents has become an increasing concern of couples young and old. How will they maintain control over their own lives? How will they transmit their values to their children? The contemporary fish fears being overwhelmed by a rising and seemingly indifferent sea.

SUMMARY

1. The purposes of this chapter are to consider how the environment beyond the family impacts upon attitudes, values, and behaviors related to intimacy; to examine how social class and ethnicity influence the family mediating function; and to describe the processes of social cognition and social learning as important developmental aspects in socialization.

2. The transmission of the values, modes of conduct or manners, social organization, language, and tools of a society or a particular social group (commonly referred to as culture) to the young is accomplished through the process of socialization. Parents and other family members are usually the first socializing agents. As the child matures, peers, teachers, religious leaders, club leaders, and even television become important elements in this transmitting and translating process.

3. The family usually serves as a mediating unit between the child and the greater environment, monitoring and filtering its impact upon the child and sometimes even modifying the environment. Various aspects of the greater environment have important, though sometimes not clearly recognized, influences on family relationships. For example, scientific and technological advances in medicine, transportation, and communication have produced dramatic changes in lifestyles and patterns of relating. Numerous government programs and policies affect many areas of family life. Environmental effects often have positive outcomes for families, such as the elimination of disease or protection from toxic substances. Negative effects—such as environmental pollution or jobs that are mechanized and impersonal—are also in evidence.

4. Socioeconomic class affects a family in several ways, including their ability to provide for physical needs such as food, clothing, and shelter; their attitudes and values about money and work; and the ways in which sex roles are structured in the marital and family systems. Socioeconomic class interacts with gender, rendering women's incomes in general significantly lower than those of men. This is a particularly

difficult situation for employed mothers who are single-parent heads of households.

5. Ethnic background is also a significant factor in how the family carries out its mediating function and in what aspects of culture are transmitted to children. These family functions become more difficult when a particular subculture is held in low regard by the dominant culture. Differences in language, values, and religion may set a particular ethnic family apart from the dominant cultural group and increase the problems of socialization and mediation.

6. Social cognition refers to the way in which we come to understand the responses of others and includes the component of role taking. The ability to understand social relationships and to view things from another's perspective are developmental processes that are related to cognitive functioning and opportunities for social interaction. Social learning is based on observation and imitation of rewarded behavior. Parents who demonstrate or model the desired behaviors are more likely to obtain results when they are perceived as powerful, warm, and accepting. Social cognition and social learning are both important processes in the transmission of cultural expectations and values.

7. Television has become a potent agent of socialization in American society. It gives numerous messages about cultural values, including many negative models involving aggression, sexism, and ageism. Like most other aspects of the greater environment, television also has abundant potential for education and the encouragement of such prosocial behaviors as altruism, empathy, and cooperation.

KEY CONCEPTS

Agent of socialization   Dominant culture
Society   Socialization
Culture   Social cognition
Subculture   Social learning
Socioeconomic class

QUESTIONS

1. Considering your personal family experiences and your observations of contemporary families, give some specific examples of how the physical or natural environment may influence family systems. Include examples of both positive and negative effects.

2. The United States is commonly called an "advanced technological" society. We also hear our contemporary times labeled "the age of technology." Discuss the meanings you attach to such terms, and indi-

cate how you think technology will have an impact on family life in the near future.

3. Interview a grandparent or great-grandparent about the changes they have seen in American society within their lifetime. Do they believe these changes have influenced the family? In what ways?

4. Think about your own socialization experiences and discuss how certain aspects of this process have influenced your attitudes and values about intimate relationships.

5. Review the material presented in this chapter on social cognition and devise some approaches that might be used to help individuals learn to take the role of the other. Discuss ways in which this process of role taking can enhance intimate relating.

6. Recall a recently viewed television program or a popular press article that you read. Discuss how the presentation you have selected could influence individual behavior in relationships.

7. Is it possible for children to be socializing agents for their parents? If not, why not? If so, give an example of how such a process might work.

SUGGESTED READINGS

- Boulding, Elise. "The Family as an Agent of Social Change." *The Futurist* (October 1972): 186–191. Though the family is usually seen as reacting, adapting, and adjusting to major changes within the greater social system, Boulding presents the intriguing view that it is quite possible to look at the family as a potential agent of revolutionary social change.

- Coleman, Thomas F. "Sex and the Law." *Humanist* 38, no. 2 (March/April 1978): 38–41. A summary article on how changing sexual behavior in the United States is influencing the legal system and prompting some rethinking and revision of laws regulating human sexual interaction.

- Erikson, Erik H. *Childhood and Society* (2nd ed.). New York: W. W. Norton, 1963. Another classic work by Erikson that details his developmental stages and focuses specifically on the role of the social environment in human development.

- Kamerman, Sheila B., and Kahn, Alfred J. (eds.). *Family Policy: Government and Families in Fourteen Countries*. New York: Columbia University Press, 1978. A number of leading scholars and experts in social policy analyze such areas as the costs and benefits of child-care programs, income-maintenance plans, housing, population policy, education, and social services as these impact upon families in 14 countries.

- Keniston, Kenneth, and The Carnegie Council on Children. *All Our Children: The American Family Under Pressure*. New York: Carnegie Corporation, 1977. A provocative analysis of the situation of American families today as they are pressured by economic and social forces over which they may have little or no control. Keniston argues that the ideal of the self-sufficient family is a myth.

- Kohn, Melvin. *Class and Conformity: A Study of Values*. Homewood, Ill.: Dorsey Press, 1969. A classic work that presents the results of three research studies on the relationship between social-class background and the values and methods of child rearing.

- Rice, Robert M. *American Family Policy: Content and Context*. New York: Family Service Association of America, 1977. A basic reading for understanding the influence of social policies on families and exploring the debate over whether the United States should adopt an explicit family policy.

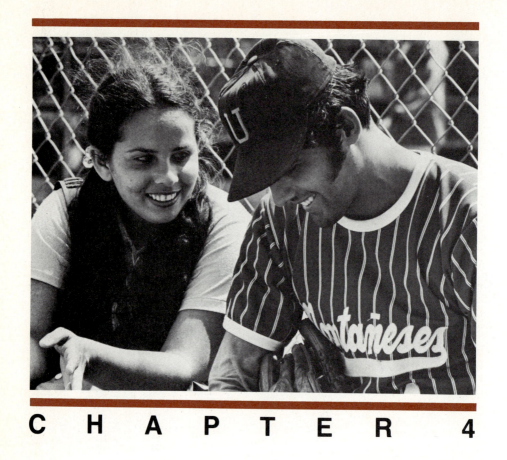

C H A P T E R 4

Sexual Behavior

HE: What do you mean you want to wait? We've been going together for three months.
SHE: I just want to wait.
HE: For what?
SHE: For marriage.
HE: You've got to be kidding!
SHE: No, I'm not kidding.
HE: That's like telling me you're going back to the Stone Age.
SHE: I always thought my forehead was a little low.

HE: It's like using oil lamps instead of electricity, sending smoke signals instead of using the telephone. Don't you believe in progress?

SHE: Not in all things.

HE: Seriously, you know I love you.

SHE: And I love you.

HE: But I'm only human.

SHE: It's a choice I've made. I can't force it on you.

HE: No, not much. I'll just tango with myself. O.K., I'll try to live with it.

SHE: It's the way I was brought up. I don't consider myself that religious, but somehow that was one message that stuck.

HE: Out of all the messages in the Bible, how about love thy neighbor? Did you ever read "The Song of Songs"? All right, don't explain. I'll run. I'll take cold showers, go to an ashram, meditate, learn to sleep on a bed of nails, wear a hair shirt . . .

SHE: How about kissing me before you become a monk?

INTRODUCTION

Sexual experience exists on many levels. On one level, sexual behavior is a sequence moving from pleasurable stimulation to accumulating tension and finally to gratifying release. Both men and women go through purely physiological changes, as pulse rate increases, nipples become erect, penis and clitoris become engorged with blood, muscles grow tense. But as this passage from Hemingway's *For Whom the Bell Tolls* shows, sexual behavior has other dimensions as well:

Then there was the smell of heather crushed and the roughness of the bent stalks under her head and the sun bright on her closed eyes and all his life he would remember the curve of her throat with her head pushed back into the heather roots and her lips that moved smally and by themselves and the fluttering of the lashes on the eyes tight closed against the sun and against everything and for her everything was red, oranged, gold-red from the sun on the closed eyes, and it all was that color, all in a blindness of that color. For him it was a dark passage which led to nowhere . . . beyond all bearing, up, up, up and into nowhere, suddenly, scaldingly, holdingly all nowhere gone and time absolutely still and they were both there, time having stopped, and he felt the earth move out and away from under them. (1940, p. 159)

Here is sexual experience on the mythical level—mythical because it is surrounded by the romantic aura of the old courtly love tales, which depicted passion as intense, outside of marriage, and short-lived, and mythical also because it perpetuates a male ideal of sexual experience, which was to become an impossible dream for many couples. The myth of the simultaneous orgasm—that the woman and the man would be sexually fulfilled by the same stimulation, at the same moment, and to the same degree—is one that seldom finds expression in real lovemaking.

An orgasm does not feel the same to everyone, not even for two people deeply in love. For each person, some orgasms are more memorable than others. Psychological factors can make the same physiological climax feel ordinary or seem like supreme fulfillment. Social factors can make sex seem normal or shameful.

The sexual experience exists, then, on at least four levels: a physiological level, a psychological level, a sociological level, and also on what we might call a mythological level, where sex serves as a symbol for True Love, Romance, Conquest, Power, or Adventure.

In this passage from Erica Jong's novel *Fear of Flying* (1973), the speaker fashions a sexual symbol of passion without commitment:

When you came together zippers fell away like rose petals, underwear blew off in one breath like dandelion fluff. Tongues intertwined and turned liquid. Your whole soul flowed out through your tongue and into the mouth of your lover. (pp. 11–12)

In a sense, the myth of sexual pleasure without commitment, guilt, or payment is a symbol of liberation. For women in our culture, sex has been anything but casual, so for a woman to utter such a wish, even in a novel, would have been inconceivable until the past decade.

Although sex is an intimate and private matter, and there is at any given time a wide variety of sexual behaviors, our sexual attitudes and behaviors tend to be influenced by shifts in the sexual climate, changes in what is regarded as acceptable. Between the 1940s and the 1970s, radical shifts occurred in America's sexual climate. We shall explore some of these changes in this chapter.

Overt heterosexual relations usually do not occur in our society until late adolescence or early adulthood. Yet a sexual self emerges gradually as the individual develops. There are certain psychological and sociological factors that tend to influence sexual identity, forces that affect individual sexual behavior before and long after a marriage takes place.

DEVELOPMENT OF A SEXUAL SELF

Childhood

The Freudian View.   Until the twentieth century, sexuality was not considered a proper subject for scientific inquiry. Sigmund Freud probably did more than any other individual to encourage interest and open discussion of this once taboo aspect of human behavior. Until recently, our thinking about sexuality has been dominated by Freudian concepts.

Freud recognized sexuality as an integral part of life from the beginning. He viewed psychosexual energies (which he termed *libido*) as a basic
force that fueled human behavior. Sexual development was seen as "a
continuous contest between biological drive and cultural restraint" (Simon and Gagnon 1977, p. 263). This contest takes different forms at different times in the individual's life. In infancy (the oral stage), libido is directed toward gratification through sucking and other oral pleasures. In
the toddler period (the anal stage), the child has the libidinous urge to
mess and generally overturn the rules. Toilet training and discipline of
other types constitute a general nay-saying to the child's drive to rampage
unrestrained. The early childhood phallic stage involves a discovery of the
penis and vagina, along with a rivalry with the parent of the same sex
for the favors of the parent of the opposite sex. Seeing the world from a
man's viewpoint, Freud called this the *Oedipus complex* after the king in
Greek mythology who unknowingly married his mother. After this period
of rivalry with the father for the favors of the mother, the young boy's
libidinous urges, in Freud's opinion, go underground. After this latency
period, however, puberty brings the libido to the fore with renewed force.
The Oedipus complex is finally resolved when the adolescent directs his
psychosexual energies away from his mother to a lover.

The whole scheme that Freud articulated was geared to male development. He believed that females experience the absence of a penis (resulting
in "penis envy") and that their adolescence is marked by an immature
sexual urge, much milder than that of males, that can mature into full
sexuality only after marriage. Despite the inherent bias in his view, Freud
was able to show sexuality as a continuous force. His scheme helped to
explain why experiences occurring long before puberty could affect sexual
behavior later in life. In many respects, sexual development is continuous.

Contemporary Views. Beginning at birth, and perhaps even before that,
humans have sensory feelings, feelings of pleasure that Freud considered
sexual. Erections occur in baby boys moments after birth, even before the
umbilical cord is cut. This observation, made by Dr. William Masters*
when he was a practicing obstetrician-gynecologist, made him realize
something he would later confirm in the laboratory: sex is a natural, normal part of human rhythms, occurring during both sleeping and waking
hours. For male and female, cycles of sexual excitement—erection and
lubrication—are part of being alive. These cycles begin at birth and continue into old age. Although adults may dismiss infantile erections as
simply reflexive and consider children's sexuality as mere play, certain
aspects of sexuality develop in a continuous, uninterrupted fashion from

*Personal communication

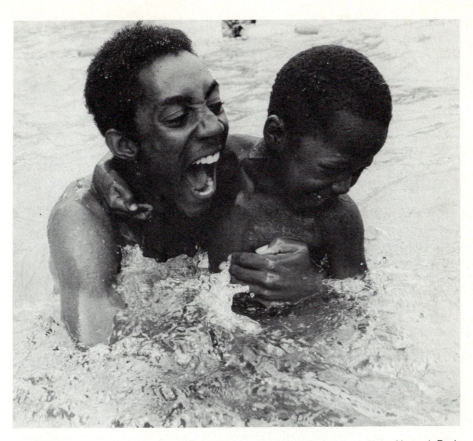

Affectionate contact between child and adult facilitates healthy development. (Jerry Howard, Positive Images)

infancy, along with other bodily functions. As sexuality develops, it is uniquely vulnerable to social and cultural control.

Some contemporary psychologists and sociologists question Freud's assumptions and disagree with his view about what constitutes sexual behavior. Simon and Gagnon, for example, argue that "continuity is not causality. . . . An infant or child engaged in genital play . . . can in no sense be seen as experiencing the complete set of feelings that accompanies adult or even adolescent masturbation" (Simon and Gagnon 1977, pp. 263–264). They contend that the individual learns sexual behavior and that some of this learning takes place before sexual feelings are present, even before secondary sexual characteristics develop. Little girls, imitating big girls, cover their chests long before they have developed breasts. In the view of these researchers, behavior is not always the masked expression of the primordial psychosexual drive or libido. This is especially true for children.

Although we do not become sexual all at once at adolescence, as the Victorians believed, we do move into a new realm of sexual possibilities at this time. In what we might call the "post-Freudian" view, early experiences of infancy and childhood create a potential for sexual experiences. If these first experiences include sufficient touching and emotional comfort, the infant's capacity for pleasure can eventually develop into a capacity for intimate sexual relations. But a lack of affectionate contact can stunt this growth process. Harry Harlow found that rhesus monkeys who were given a terry-cloth surrogate mother, instead of a monkey mother, were later incapable of normal monkey business. They didn't masturbate, didn't seek heterosexual contact, and were incapable of mothering (Harlow and Mears 1979). A degree of physical interaction, combined with emotional attention, seems to allow the individual to learn behavior that later will facilitate normal sexual activity.

Sexual preference, discussed in Box 4.1, is probably determined by a variety of factors, learned and inherited. The combination of biological, psychological, and sociological forces that determine sexual preference are apparently at work long before adolescence.

Adolescence and a New Sense of Sexual Identity

Exploration of bodies, "playing doctor," and other forms of sex play are quite common in childhood, but they seem to have more to do with curiosity about oneself and the parts adults regard as taboo than they do with satisfying a primordial urge. A good deal of behavior concerning sex roles is learned during childhood. But sexual experience as such begins at adolescence with the biological events of puberty. The timing of puberty varies, but girls generally undergo these changes between the ages of 12 and 14, and boys go through puberty about two years later. The complex changes of puberty begin in the brain with the signal to release certain hormones. Over a period of about two years, the reproductive organs mature, and adolescents develop sex characteristics which give them the physical attributes of men or women. Although the physical events and sexual experiences of adolescence are quite different for male and female, the sense of oneself as a sexual being—a *sexual identity*—is part of the overall sense of individual identity that develops during the teenage years. The experience of socializing with the opposite sex and feeling desirable or undesirable, the events that surround sexual arousal, and the combination of guilt, anxiety, and satisfaction that accompanies such feelings—these are some of the elements that shape this new sense of sexual identity.

For males, the first ejaculation is usually brought about by masturbation. For most boys, this form of gratification continues to be the major sexual activity during adolescence. Simon and Gagnon suggest that the "capacity for detached sexual activity . . . may be the hallmark of male

BOX 4.1 Sexual Preference

How is sexual preference established? What causes some boys and girls to become homosexual, while the majority of others become heterosexual? An important study comparing homosexual and heterosexual men and women has yielded findings that shed light on questions concerning sexual development. Based on extensive interviews conducted in 1969 to 1970 with 979 homosexual and 477 heterosexual men and women living in the San Francisco Bay area, *Sexual Preference* (Bell, Weinberg, and Hammersmith 1981) reveals that a strong inclination to be either heterosexual or homosexual exists *before* the actual onset of sexual activity. Sexual feelings for either the opposite sex or the same sex seem to precede adolescence.

This study suggests "a strong continuity between a person's childhood and adolescent sexual feelings . . . and his/her adult sexual preference" (p. 187). These researchers attribute sexual preference to early predispositions that may, at least in some cases, have a biological basis. Freud may have been correct in seeking early indicators of later sexual preference. But Freudian theory—which traces male sexual preference to the resolution of sexual feelings for the mother—is discredited by this study. The authors found that the importance of the role of parents in the development of their sons' sexual orientation has been "grossly exaggerated" by past researchers. Their sample indicated that "boys who grow up with dominant mothers and weak fathers have nearly the same chances of becoming homosexual as they would if they grew up in 'ideal' family settings" (p. 184).

It is not boys' relationships with their mothers that determine sexual preference. Although parental influence is generally overrated, according to this data, it is fathers who seem to have a greater influence on children's sexual preference. Cold, detached fathers seem to predispose children, particularly sons, toward homosexuality.

Homosexuality may cause poor peer relations, but it seems that poor peer relations do not cause homosexuality. Many homosexuals do not conform to gender expectations and so are isolated from their peers. Male homosexuals are especially likely to display what is called "gender nonconformity," or behavior not typical of their sex—in the case of males, behavior that is not typically masculine. Boys are also more likely to be ostracized for such deviation from peer norms. But peers do not, in the view of these researchers, cause either gender nonconformity or homosexuality. This study also questions the connection between homosexuality and traumatic experiences in childhood, such as a severe punishment for early sex play, a rape (in the case of lesbians), or a homosexual seduction. Such events figure in the sexual histories of certain homosexuals, but they are not the typical causes of same-sex preference. In addition, many lesbians and gay men have had heterosexual experiences, but have found them ungratifying.

Sexual preference is not usually a choice or conscious decision that one makes as an adult. Sexual orientation is "a pattern of feelings and reactions" ingrained in the individual. Although sexual preference cannot yet be traced back to a single social, biological, or psychological root, the tendency to be homosexual or heterosexual seems to emerge in childhood and early adolescence (p. 222).

The study concludes with two important reminders: (1) Sexual orientation is not usually reversible. "There is no reason to think it would be any easier for homosexual men or women to reverse their sexual orientation than it would for heterosexual[s] to become predominantly or exclusively homosexual." (2) "It is possible for homosexuals and heterosexuals to enjoy mature, constructive and rewarding lives" (p. 222).

sexuality in our society" (1977, p. 267). Males usually fantasize while they masturbate, casting much of their daily experience in an erotic light.

Females tend to develop sexual identity in a context of intimacy. For them, sexual activity seems more deeply embedded in a social context. Female friendships, from the preschool period on, are marked by more emotion and intensity than male friendships (Clarke-Stewart and Koch, in press; Selman 1981). During adolescence, heterosexual attraction occurs in an emotional and romantic context. Masturbation is less common among teenage girls. A national survey conducted by Sorensen (1973) reported that 49 percent of all adolescents say they have masturbated; 58 percent of all boys and 39 percent of all girls report masturbating at least once. Only 28 percent of all adolescents report masturbating regularly: 36 percent of the boys and 21 percent of the girls (Sorensen 1973, pp. 129–132). Although the age of first intercourse is earlier for many girls today than in previous generations, and the belief in sex only after marriage is not as prevalent as it was even a decade ago, most young women combine their first sexual experience with notions of love and an intense relationship. Their very reluctance to use birth control relates to this need for seeing themselves as swept away by romantic feelings (Sorensen 1973). Few adolescent girls can view sex as an end in itself, detached from emotional commitment.

Girls also differ from boys in viewing themselves and the opposite sex as prospective mates. Although they are not as sexually active as boys, they are trained to make themselves sexually attractive. Simon and Gagnon (1977) suggest that this conditioning to use sexual attractiveness for other purposes—getting a mate, raising a family—affects female sexuality throughout life.

Bringing with them these two different orientations toward sex—the male detached and pleasure-oriented, the female linking sex with love and romance or marriage—teenage boys and girls begin to date. In the process of dating, they teach each other. As Simon and Gagnon put it: "Dating and courtship may well be considered processes in which each sex trains the other in what each wants and expects" (1977, p. 269). This process begins very early in the United States; girls usually start to date at 14, on the average, and boys at 15. In Europe, dating begins about two years later. The dating experience has changed somewhat for high school and college students. Relationships begin in friendship groups from which boys and girls pair off, seeing each other casually. Less common now is the traditional "date," in which the male picks up the female at her house at an arranged time, wines and dines her at his expense, and returns her to her residence at an arranged time (Murstein 1980, p. 780).

Despite the trend toward less formality, dating still has a built-in difficulty: it has its own conventions and so dictates standards for acceptable behavior. Girls are afraid to sound too bright or too serious. Boys feel obligated to project a certain amount of "cool" or savoir-faire. The dating experience, as two major authorities on adolescent behavior tell us, cannot usually give an opportunity for full self-expression (Douvan and Adelson 1966). This may explain the common complaint of young people who marry their high school sweethearts: "We went together for years, but after we were married I realized we didn't know each other." Another reason that dating may be less than an intimate interchange in adolescence is that the individuals do not yet know themselves fully.

Despite the limitations of the dating experience, the years of high school and early college dating provide some opportunity to integrate physical impulse with social behavior. The detached sexual urge of the adolescent male becomes modified by romantic notions and perhaps the desire to marry. The romantic notions of the adolescent young woman may be eroticized and modified to focus on a real man rather than on a storybook character.

By later adolescence (age 18 or 19), young people have a clearer sense of their own sexual nature and a more realistic orientation to the opposite sex. After the adolescent period of experimentation and learning, a sense of the sexual self emerges. As Erik Erikson (1963) has explained, this sexual character becomes part of the larger notion of one's own identity. Many people go into marriages in order to find themselves, sexually and in other ways. But Erikson contends that intimacy, the appropriate challenge of the young adulthood stage, cannot be attained without first gaining an individual sense of identity. Without this firm sense of who one is, the essentials of an intimate relationship—the giving and sharing, the exposure of oneself, and the sexual and emotional union—are not possible. A firm sense of identity also helps the individual in a relationship benefit from periods of solitude or "distantiation" (Katchadourian and Lunde 1972, p. 209). Individuals who feel totally bereft when separated from a mate or lover often lack a firm sense of self.

Same-Sex Attractions Among Adolescents. Less than 4 percent of the men and 3 percent of the women in the United States make the exclusive choice of same-sex partners. However, feelings of attraction to people of one's own sex and sexual experimentation with individuals of the same sex are much more prevalent, especially during adolescence. Over one-third of all men and about 13 percent of all women have at least one homosexual experience in their lifetimes. Fantasies concerning people of the same sex are reported by many adult heterosexuals. Statistics vary, but there is general support from Kinsey's surveys to the present showing that many people who are heterosexuals have experimented with or been aroused by a person of the same sex, especially in their youth (Kinsey 1948; 1953; Bell, Weinberg, and Hammersmith 1981).

Since adolescents are especially anxious about sexually appropriate feelings and behavior, they often carry with them, as they mature, deep feelings of guilt and shame concerning homosexual impulses or behavior. Talking to a loving partner or a therapist, or simply reading the many books now available concerning sexuality, may relieve this burden of guilt. Understanding that it is not abnormal for a heterosexual to feel some same-sex attractions might diminish some of the pain and confusion of growing up. Exclusive feelings of attraction to the same sex present special problems for the adolescent, since there are few people to turn to at this stage of life for support and guidance. In Chapter 5 we shall discuss homosexuality as a lifetime pattern.

Each of us, then, has a personal psychosexual history that develops continuously from birth, but is given a definite shape and expression during adolescence and young adulthood. Yet this personal development is influenced by forces in one's environment. Cultural attitudes have a great impact on one's attitude about sex and one's actual sexual behavior. Proof of this emerges from such surveys as the Kinsey reports, which revealed social class differences, and from comparisons of contemporary attitudes about sex with markedly different attitudes and practices in the past. We shall examine some of these social class, cultural, and historical differences in sexual matters.

SOCIOECONOMIC AND CULTURAL DIFFERENCES IN SEXUALITY

Social Class

The first comprehensive studies of sexual mores in the United States were conducted by A. C. Kinsey and his associates in the late 1940s and early 1950s (*Sexual Behavior in the Human Male*, 1948; *Sexual Behavior in the Human Female*, 1953).

Males. The studies found that males from lower socioeconomic groups seem to put an earlier emphasis on heterosexuality than middle-class males and, as adolescents and young men, they are more likely to experience sex outside of a social context. Psychologists and sociologists speculate that this is partly because social life among poor and working-class families tends to be segregated by sex. Women tend to socialize with other women, men with other male friends, and this pattern persists long after marriage. A young man raised in a sex-segregated setting may find it easier to separate his own sexual activity from a social relationship. Casual sex then becomes an easier choice than masturbation.

Masculinity and sexual prowess are encouraged by lower-class adolescent groups. A boy from a poor family may feel more pressure to prove that he can "make it" at an early age. Even if he becomes sexually active as a teenager, however, he is likely to remain *homosocial,* in the sense that most of his friendships and social contacts will be with other boys, not girls.

The middle-class adolescent, on the other hand, tends to think of sexuality as part of a social relationship. Middle-class males, at least in Kinsey's sample of the 1940s, began having sexual involvements with women at a much later time. Like lower-class boys, their friendships with other boys were important in adolescence and early manhood, but they tended to socialize more with girls (Kinsey 1948).

In a recent article on the dilemma of blue-collar, middle-aged males, Shostak (1980) reports that blue-collar males "continue to be ambivalent about female sexuality and often retain a lingering covert distinction between the girls they marry and the girls they use." He notes that women in their forties are "wary about engaging in sexual behaviors that seem to threaten their traditional 'good girl' status" (p. 319). Yet the younger working-class men and women—as well as some of the middle-aged women who are spending more time outside the home—appear to be adopting more liberal sexual mores as well as new role definitions that stress warmth, equality, and companionship. Shostak's analysis of the traditional working-class male sex role and some of the changes now taking place emphasizes the links between sexual behavior and sex roles. Changing conceptions of sex roles influence the sexual behavior of men and women.

Since working-class couples are having fewer children and are increasingly moving toward the two-worker pattern, these changing role expectations and sexual patterns are likely to continue in the direction of valuing more warmth and equality.

Females.   Kinsey's report on female sexuality (1953) revealed less sexual activity among women, less sexual promiscuity—fewer partners and less extramarital sex—and also less of what Kinsey termed psychological responsiveness to erotic material or situations. Kinsey found fewer marked social-class differences in female sexual behavior, largely because all social classes at that time were moving in the same direction in relation to female sexuality: namely, trying to control it.

Kinsey's data on infant response suggested that males and females start with approximately the same degree of responsiveness and curiosity. A later study concentrating on male and female infants as they develop into young children indicates that their sexual responsiveness and curiosity are initially similar, but parents respond differently, curtailing the explorations of females but not males (Galenson 1979).

Even at the time of the Kinsey report on women, critics recognized that the data he had collected could be regarded not as proof of low sexual responsiveness among women, but as evidence of the incredible power of social conditioning to restrain sexual behavior. Kinsey's data suggested what more recent research has confirmed—that social conditioning plays an enormous part in sexual response.

At about the same time Kinsey was gathering his data of the sexual behavior of American males and females, Ford and Beach were gathering information on sexual behavior in other cultures.

Cross-Cultural Comparisons

Comparisons of different cultures reveal an extraordinary range of attitudes and practices concerning sexual behavior (see Table 4.1). Ford and Beach (1951) categorized preliterate cultures according to levels of adult permissiveness. Restrictive societies, at one end of the spectrum, insisted on female virginity at the time of marriage, prohibited preadolescent sexual behavior, and meted out severe punishments when prohibitions were breached. Among the Chagga of Tanzania, who are quite sexually active after marriage, an uninitiated boy caught in the sex act would be placed on top of his partner and staked to the ground. The United States was once included among the restrictive cultures. Now, with our greater permissiveness concerning masturbation and premarital coitus, we fall into the semirestrictive category, where codes for juveniles are different from those for adults but are not severely enforced (Katchadourian and Lunde 1972, p. 186). In some of Ford and Beach's permissive societies, children freely

TABLE 4.1 Cross-Cultural Comparisons of Sexual Practices

Tribe	Locale	Sexual Practice
Keraki (male)	New Guinea (seminomads)	Intercourse once a week
White Americans (male)	North America (housedwellers)	Three orgasms per week primarily through intercourse in marriage (also by masturbation, homosexual activity, intercourse outside marriage with prostitutes and companions)
Chagga	Tanzania (agriculturists)	Intercourse up to ten times a night
Mangaians	Polynesia (seafaring people)	High value on female sexual satisfaction: woman to have two or three orgasms to the man's one
Navajo	North America (Indians)	Three sexes recognized: male, female, and *nadle*

Sources: Data from Anna K. and Robert T. Francoeur, *Hot and Cool Sex: Cultures in Conflict*, Harcourt Brace Jovanovich, Inc., 1974; Alfred C. Kinsey, et al., *Sexual Behavior in the Human Male*, Saunders, 1948; and C. S. Ford and F. A. Beach, *Patterns of Sexual Behavior*, Harper & Row, 1951.

engaged in autoerotic activities and sex play, and girls and boys of 11 or 12 engaged in coitus. Adults in some cultures actually instructed children. Every society, even the most permissive, has some restrictions on sexual activities such as incest.

In terms of frequency of sexual contact, Kinsey had found with his sample of 6,000 white males between the ages of 14 and 85 an average frequency of three orgasms per week, primarily through sexual intercourse with spouse, but also through a variety of other means, including masturbation, homosexual activity, petting, and ejaculation during sleep. The Chagga have coitus up to ten times a night, while the Keraki have sex a moderate once a week. Even within the Kinsey sample, there were wide variations of frequency.

Certain non-European societies appear to have incorporated more flexibility into their sex categories. For example, the Navajo Indians have recognized three sexes: male, female, and a third sex called *nadle*, or hermaphrodite. The *nadle* may engage in either male or female work, dress as a male or female, and marry a spouse of either sex. The *nadle* is often called on to serve as a mediator in disputes between men and women and to preside at religious ceremonies (Francoeur and Francoeur 1974, p. 19). One is reminded of the wise Tiresias of Greek drama, said to possess male and female traits.

Attitudes toward female sexuality vary from culture to culture. Some cultures regard women as less sexual than men, an attitude that naturally affects sexual practices. Mary Jane Sherfey, a psychiatrist and psychoanalyst who developed a theory of female sexuality (1966), speculates that, in earlier ages, primitive women, like certain primates, were insatiable, capable of performing coitus from 20 to 50 times a day during the peak period of *estrus*, or fertility, and of "consorting with one male several days until he is exhausted, then taking up with another" (Seaman 1972, p. 40). The Mangaian culture of Polynesia places high value on female sexual satisfaction (Marshall and Suggs 1971). Anthropologist Donald S. Marshall notes that

The Mangaian male lover aims to have his partner achieve orgasm . . . two or three times to his once. His responsibility in this matter is so ingrained into the Mangaian male that upon hearing that some American or European women cannot or do not achieve a climax, the Mangaian immediately asks (with real concern) whether this inability will not injure the married woman's health. (Seaman 1972, pp. 34–35)

This attitude, as we shall find out shortly, has not characterized traditional American culture.

Women as Property. One way to recognize the vulnerability of sexual behavior to cultural influence is to compare contemporary attitudes with those that prevailed in earlier periods. That sex is not simply the private, purely personal experience it seems to be is shown in no better way than by its close historical link with property, ownership, and economics. Until the women's suffrage movement began in the latter part of the nineteenth century, laws and customs in many countries judged a woman to be her husband's property. An early seventeenth-century Kentish law read: "If a man forcibly carries off a maiden, he shall pay fifty shillings to her owner and afterwards buy from the owner his consent" (Francoeur and Francoeur 1974, p. 13). A husband, and he alone, was allowed sexual access to his wife. She was expected to be a virgin when she married and to remain sexually faithful to her husband, whereas he was free to have premarital and extramarital relations (Turner 1970, p. 329). A man's wife was regarded as his property, not only because he had exclusive sexual rights to her, but also because she was the mother of his children—and, more importantly, his heirs. The "civilization" of sex made sense to the man who needed to know which children were his rightful heirs. In this sexual *quid pro quo*, a woman was bound to reproduce for her husband alone and to nurture her children for many years, while her husband was bound to protect his wife and children from danger.

This rationale, which explained mating in prehistoric days, continued to hold sway down through the centuries. Women moved from the cave to the Victorian doll's house, protected and disenfranchised from political and sexual prerogatives. Men were to suppress emotions and passivity, to deny nurturant inclinations. From the survival needs of the species and the property needs of a patriarchal society came the familiar male and female stereotypes of Western culture. These male and female stereotypes still have a powerful hold on our society, especially in the sexual domain.

The male stereotype calls for an aggressive, competitive he-man, a "superstud" who is both athlete and breadwinner. His counterpart is the sentimental woman, submissive and in need of protection (Francoeur and Francoeur 1974, p. 12). The naive, virginal bride is supposed to love and cherish her strong, sophisticated husband, to whom she "belongs." At least as recently as 20 years ago, women were in fact likely to be sexually naive, men more experienced. The Kinsey study shows premarital and extramarital intercourse to be much more common among the white males sampled than among the women surveyed. Prior to the 1960s, men and women were entering marriage with widely different sexual backgrounds and experience (Katchadourian and Lunde 1972, pp. 159–160).

The Double Standard.   A *double standard* of sexual conduct is part of the sex-as-property legacy. The sexual standard for women restricts sex to marriage. The standard for men allows sex to be either "casual" (premarital or extramarital) or "serious" (marital). Sex, in either form, is "purchased," the serious kind with a marriage license, the casual type with cash.

As we discussed in our brief history of love, this double standard was strengthened by a religious dimension, which sharply separated the "good girls" who didn't from the "bad girls" who did. This dualism has not disappeared from Western culture. The imagery of purity and corruption is still a central symbolic dimension of male sexuality, according to John Gagnon (1972). Though the pattern is changing, the terms "easy lay" and "loose girl" are still extant. In the early years of adolescence, a small number of girls who become involved in sexual experience may still serve as the targets of male interest and contempt and of female rejection. People of rigid religious upbringing often enter marriage with deeply ambivalent feelings about sexuality. Men who have polarized women into virginal types, who are held in high esteem but infrequently held in passionate embrace, and "other" types, who arouse erotic feelings but are devalued as tramps or prostitutes, may have difficulty responding with sexual freedom to women who enjoy sex, but do not trade in it. Sexual enjoyment with their own wives can become a problem for men with such attitudes. The woman who has denied her sexual feelings for fear of falling into the disreputable and "unmarriageable" category may have trouble dispensing with the notion that sexuality is crude, unseemly, and ungodly.

Sexual messages from the media reflect changing societal mores and raise new questions. (Jerry Howard, Positive Images)

SEXUAL MORES IN THE EIGHTIES

Sexual mores in the United States are changing rapidly. Religious influence has waned, and the media's endorsement of sexual gratification is blatant and pervasive. Even the old association of sexual freedom with property and other forms of public power is serving to create a new type of sexually assertive woman. In his survey of current sexual practices, Gay Talese (1980) recognizes a new type of woman who does not wait for a man to court her and bring her sexual satisfaction, but goes out and finds it.

National surveys indicate that patterns of sexual behavior are different today than they were when Kinsey surveyed them (Zelnick and Kantner 1977; Sorensen 1973). By 19 years of age, half the young women surveyed have had sexual intercourse, the median age of first intercourse in this group being 16. Though sexual activity among blacks has tended to begin earlier, activity in the white population is accelerating faster. A large number of young women are becoming sexually active during adolescence. Another trend is the disconnection of sex and marriage. For the young women coming of age in the 1980s, sex is not firmly bonded to marriage or even the promise of marriage. Figure 4.1 shows the number of young men and young women in the United States who are sexually active, by age and marital status.

High school girls and boys surveyed by Shirley and Richard Jessor (1975) tended to regard sexual activity as something that should be part of a love relationship, including but not limited to marriage. At the college level, the Jessors found many young men and women who believed that sexual intercourse was all right even for two people who did not know each other—in short, sex at first sight, love later or not at all. The majority of adolescents and young adults, however, believe that sexual intercourse should be reserved for those relationships characterized by affection and caring.

Adolescent Contraception and Childbearing

Each shift in sexual mores brings with it its own particular problems. The increase in sexual activity among adolescents has not been accompanied by any comparable increase in early sex education or use of birth control. Sociologist Ira Reiss and his colleagues found "comfort with sexuality" to be a key factor in the use of contraceptives (1975). This kind of comfort may come at the college level after sexual identity has been consolidated into a firm sense of who one is. But it is not prevalent among female adolescents who are typically involved in romantic dreams of falling in love. And despite efforts on the part of such organizations as Planned Parenthood to heighten male responsibility for contraception, it is the woman who gets pregnant and therefore the woman who seems more

FIGURE 4.1 Number of Males Aged 13–21, and Females Aged 13–19, Who Are Sexually Active, by Age and Marital Status, United States, 1978

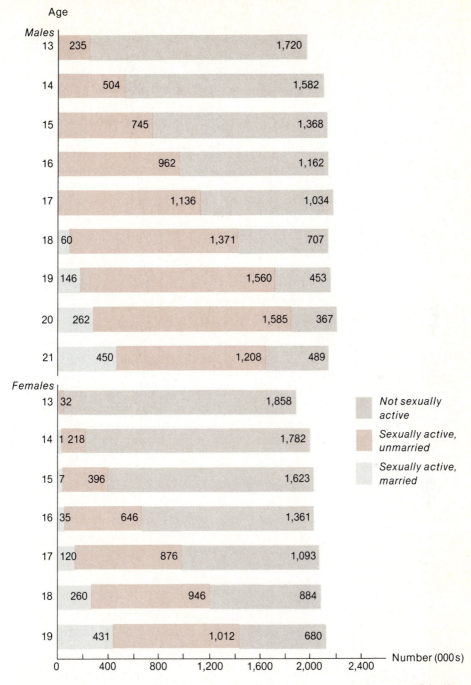

Souce: Adapted from *Teenage Pregnancy: The Problem That Hasn't Gone Away,* p. 7, published by The Alan Guttmacher Institute, New York, 1981, with permission of the publisher.

educable when it comes to contraception. These attitudes may change, especially if adults become more communicative with their children concerning sexuality and contraception. So far, adult society has not found sufficient comfort with sexuality to accept the fact that many adolescents will be sexually active and so will need information about and access to birth control. (A full discussion of methods of contraception appears in Chapter 10.)

More than half the adolescents who become pregnant give birth, and 94 percent of those young mothers keep their babies (Guttmacher Institute 1976). Some are helped by supportive families and special programs for teenage mothers. But others are not welcome at home and must be content with isolation and a drastically lower living standard. The frustration of being prematurely harnessed to the care and feeding of another totally dependent human being soon catches up with them. The result is a high incidence of child abuse among teenage parents, a variety of behavioral problems for their children, and an increasing number of children who themselves will have difficulty being adequate, self-sufficient people and loving parents.

Delay in becoming a parent is crucial to a teenager's future. Josefina Card and Lauress Wife have followed a nationwide sample of 375,000 students who attended junior and senior high school in 1960. The results of their study, called Project TALENT (1978), show that teenage parents suffer a downward slide regardless of academic ability, racial or socioeconomic background, or educational expectations. The single fact of having children during adolescence can stunt the lives of young people, turning prospects of stability or upward mobility into premature stress and responsibility, dead-end jobs, and low income, if not welfare and poverty:

Virtually all of the men and women who did not have children before age 20 received high school diplomas. The adolescent parents had the same level of academic ability, the same racial and socioeconomic background and even the same expectations regarding college. Yet a high proportion of the adolescent childbearers did not complete high school. . . . Almost none of the women who bore children before age 20 completed college compared to more than one fifth of those who did not have children by age 24. (Card and Wife 1978)

Sheppard Kellam (1980), who headed a ten-year study of low-income black youths, found delay of childbearing a key factor in decreasing the likelihood of both divorce and poverty for young women.

Venereal Disease

The term *venereal* comes from the Latin word "Venus"—the goddess of love. Such diseases are so named because they are usually transmitted through intimate sexual contact or lovemaking. Some authorities advocate the label *sexually transmitted diseases*, or *STD*, because this term has not yet acquired the stigma attached to the label venereal disease, or VD (Masters, Johnson, and Kolodny 1982; Victor 1980).

The three most serious of these diseases are *syphilis*, *gonorrhea*, and *genital herpes* (see Box 4.2). Penicillin treatment has helped to render syphilis the least prevalent of the three diseases, with estimates of between 100,000 and 150,000 new cases reported in 1977 (Jerrick 1978). Unreported cases, however, may run to several hundreds of thousands. The incidence of gonorrhea is almost as frequent as the common cold, with more than one million cases reported annually. Experts suggest that reported cases may represent only 25 percent of actual cases that occur each year (Masters, Johnson, and Kolodny 1982). The incidence of genital herpes is estimated at one million cases per year. Most authorities characterize venereal disease as having reached epidemic—even pandemic—proportions.

The majority of reported cases of venereal infection occur in young adults and are typically more prevalent in males than in females. The sex difference is usually attributed to the greater sexual activity of males. Numerous hypotheses have been suggested for the increasing rate of sexually transmitted diseases, including the increasing incidence of sexual contact among adolescents and young adults combined with lack of information about disease transmission, symptoms, and treatment. Even when people are well-informed, the stigma attached to VD may trigger guilt, shame, or denial, which can lead to postponement or neglect of treatment. The declining use of condoms and contraceptive jellies or creams in favor of the birth-control pill is also a factor in increasing rates of VD, since these former methods provided some protection from the spread of disease. According to Seaman and Seaman (1977), the pill creates a vaginal environment that makes women more susceptible to sexually transmitted diseases; pill users have twice the rate of VD infections as the general female population.

It is extremely important to be aware of the increasing incidence of sexually transmitted diseases and to recognize the possibility of infection as a risk of sexual contact. Preventive measures for males include the use of condoms and soap and water genital cleansing after intercourse. For females, douching and soap and water cleansing of the genital area are thought to be reasonably effective measures. Although these preventive measures are very helpful, they are *not* foolproof. Recognizing symptoms and seeking prompt medical treatment are imperative actions for curing venereal infections.

Beyond Adolescence

Changes in sexual behavior are not confined to adolescents in our culture. Female adults also are more likely today to have extramarital affairs.

BOX 4.2   Syphilis, Gonorrhea, and Genital Herpes: Causes, Symptoms, and Treatments

Syphilis

1. Cause.   A spiral-shaped form of bacteria that enters the body directly through the skin and thrives in warm, moist mucous tissues of the body—mouth, throat, vagina, cervix, urethra, and anal canal. Syphilis is usually transmitted through sexual contact, but an untreated syphilitic mother can pass the disease to her unborn child through her bloodstream when the bacteria penetrate the defenses of the placenta. Thus, an infant may be born with the disease *(congenital syphilis).* A blood test such as the Wassermann will detect the presence of this disease at all stages. Such tests early in pregnancy can prevent congenital syphilis if the expectant mother is subsequently treated.

2. Symptoms.   Syphilis has three distinct stages: primary, secondary, and tertiary. The *primary stage* is easy to recognize for males; a crusty sore, or *chancre,* appears at the place where the bacteria enter the skin. This painless sore is usually located on the external genitals, though it may also appear on the lips, mouth, or around the anus. In females the chancre usually appears on the inner labia, vagina, or cervix and is thus much more difficult to detect (Rome et al. 1976). The *secondary stage* of syphilis appears from two to four months after the initial infection and includes a reddish, non-itching rash over parts of the body. Additional symptoms include mouth sores, hair loss, low fever, headache, and sore throat—all symptoms of various other diseases, which complicates diagnosis and treatment. The *tertiary stage* of the disease follows a long latency period, which may last from five to fifty years. If untreated, the consequences of this final stage are severe, including lesions of the skin, central nervous system involvement, cardiovascular disease, blindness, and death.

3. Treatment.   Syphillis is very responsive to treatment with penicillin or other antibiotic drugs. If treated prior to the tertiary stage, there is usually no permanent physical damage.

Gonorrhea

1. Cause.   A form of bacteria, called *gonococcus,* which thrives in the warm, moist mucous tissues of the body. Gonorrhea is usually transmitted through sexual contact, but newborn babies may be born with this disease due to contact with the infected birth canal of the mother during delivery.

2. Symptoms.   For males, the early symptoms of gonorrhea include painful urination due to inflammation of the urethral canal and a discharge of pus from the penis. If untreated, these symptoms will usually recede in about two months, but the infection continues and may result in painful swelling of the testes and in sterility. For females, detection of gonorrhea is difficult because only about 20 percent of infected women experience early symptoms (Morton 1977). When such symptoms exist, they include painful inflammation of the vulva and occasionally a pus-like

BOX 4.2 (Continued)

discharge from the cervix. Serious complications involving infection of the Fallopian tubes and ovaries, which may result in sterility, are more common in females than in males due to the absence of early warning symptoms (Hart 1977).

3. Treatment. Injections of penicillin or other antibiotic drugs are effective in eliminating the infection. Early treatment prevents permanent physical damage.

Genital Herpes

1. Cause. A virus called *herpes simplex, type 2*, which is very similar to herpes virus, type 1, which causes common cold sores. This disease is usually transmitted through intimate sexual contact, but the unborn fetus may become infected through the mother and suffer severe consequences, including brain damage and death.

2. Symptoms. Small painful sores usually appear on the penis, in males, and in the vagina, external genitals, anus, and on the thighs of females; other symptoms resemble those of a low-grade flu infection. Although these initial symptoms disappear within a few weeks, the disease usually remains dormant and will recur throughout life, especially during periods of weakened body condition due to physical illness or emotional stress. For women, it appears that the virus that causes genital herpes can also cause cancer of the cervix (Reyner 1975; Kessler 1979). It is recommended that females who have had this disease have a pap smear every six months. Although research on genital herpes is inconclusive, indications are that the disease is highly contagious when symptoms are present. Most authorities recommend that sexual activity be avoided for two weeks after all sores have healed.

3. Treatment. There is no known cure for genital herpes at this time. Several measures have been tried with some success, such as the use of cold, wet compresses to relieve pain and the application of antibiotic ointments to contain the spread of the infection.

The rate among young women is particularly high, with at least one major survey indicating that 26 percent of married women engage in extramarital sex before the age of 35 (Bell and Peltz 1974). Another study of 1,500 married men and women, conducted in 1972 by the Playboy Foundation (Hunt 1974), shows that while only 8 percent of young married women in Kinsey's day reported extramarital affairs, 24 percent of married women under 25 reported extramarital experiences in 1972.

Women now are more likely to express dissatisfaction with their sex partners. The change appears to be in female expectations rather than in male effectiveness. In *The Hite Report,* based on 3,000 responses to detailed questionnaires sent to American women, approximately 30 percent of the women complained of insufficient clitoral stimulation (Hite 1976). In this report, it appeared that many American men were ignorant of or insensitive to the sexual needs of women. Many males seemed to be assuming that if, in Hemingway's idiom, "the earth moved" for him, it also moved for her. Between the Kinsey report and the Hite report a major breakthrough occurred in our knowledge of human sexuality. These findings, based on laboratory observations of human sexual response, make it somewhat easier for men and women to separate sexual myth from reality.

HUMAN SEXUAL RESPONSE

Even in the recent past, people have been uninformed about sexual response. Until William Masters and Virginia Johnson began their research, no one had attempted a direct scientific study of sexual response. The material in Masters and Johnson's first book, *Human Sexual Response* (1966), was based on direct observation of the physiological responses of about 600 men and women ranging in age from 18 to 89. These people were volunteers who had been carefully screened so that they represented a mentally and sexually "healthy" sample of people. The volunteers were videotaped in mirrored rooms as they had intercourse and masturbated so that such things as physiological response and the length of sexual response could be directly observed and recorded. The female volunteers used a camera-equipped plastic penis during masturbation so that the researchers would have a filmed record of their physiological sexual response. The researchers observed that sexual response in both women and men has four phases (see Figures 4.2 and 4.3). The following summary of the four phases of sexual response was developed by Joann DeLora et al. (1981, pp. 84, 86–88, 90–92), based on Masters and Johnson's 1966 work:

Four Phases of Female Sexual Response

Excitement Phase

- Vagina. Lubrication within ten to thirty seconds of effective stimulation. Barrel lengthens, inner two-thirds distends. Irregular expansive movements of walls late in phase; wall color changes to darker, purplish hue.
- Labia majora. Thin and flatten against perineum (the area between the anus and the vulva) in women who have not had children; become markedly distended with blood in women who have had children.
- Labia minora. Expand markedly in diameter.
- Clitoris. Increases in diameter through vasocongestion, elongates in some women (less rapidly than vaginal lubrication occurs; vaginal lubrication, not clitoral erection, is the "neurophysiological parallel" to male penile erection) (p. 181). Vasocongestion varies from barely discernible to twofold expansion, depending on whether stimulation is direct or indirect and on individual variations in anatomy.

FIGURE 4.2   Changes in the Female Anatomy During the Sexual Response Cycle

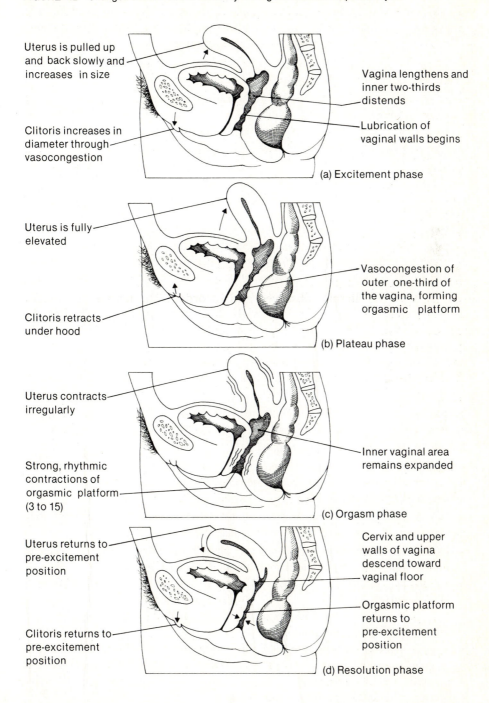

Uterus is pulled up and back slowly and increases in size

Vagina lengthens and inner two-thirds distends

Clitoris increases in diameter through vasocongestion

Lubrication of vaginal walls begins

(a) Excitement phase

Uterus is fully elevated

Vasocongestion of outer one-third of the vagina, forming orgasmic platform

Clitoris retracts under hood

(b) Plateau phase

Uterus contracts irregularly

Inner vaginal area remains expanded

Strong, rhythmic contractions of orgasmic platform (3 to 15)

(c) Orgasm phase

Uterus returns to pre-excitement position

Cervix and upper walls of vagina descend toward vaginal floor

Orgasmic platform returns to pre-excitement position

Clitoris returns to pre-excitement position

(d) Resolution phase

- Uterus.   Pulled slowly up and back if initially in normal anterior position.
- Breasts.   Nipple erection due to involuntary contracting of nipple muscle fibers. Vein patterns in breast extend and stand out. Actual breast size increases and areolae (areas surrounding the nipples) markedly engorge toward end of phase.
- Sex flush.   In some women a rash appears between the breastbone and navel late in this phase or early in the plateau phase.
- Myotonia (muscular rigidity).   Initial total-body responses include increasing restlessness, irritability, and rapidity of voluntary and involuntary movement. Myotonia increases in long muscles of arms and legs; abdominal muscles involuntarily tense; involuntary contractile rate of muscles between ribs increases, increasing respiratory rate.
- Other.   Heart rate and blood pressure increase.

Plateau Phase

- Vagina.   Marked vasocongestion further reduces central opening of the outer third by at least one-third. Base of vasocongestion encompassing outer third of vagina and engorged labia minora, called the *orgasmic platform*, "provides the anatomic foundation for the vagina's physiological expression of the orgasmic experience," and is regarded as a sign that plateau stage has been reached (p. 76).

    Further increase in inner width and depth of vagina during this phase is negligible. Production of lubrication slows, especially if phase is prolonged.
- Labia majora.   No further changes.
- Labia minora.   Vivid color changes; varies from pink to bright red to deep wine. Orgasm invariably follows if stimulation continues once this "sex skin" color change occurs.
- Clitoris.   Retracts from normal position late in phase; withdraws; at least 50 percent overall reduction in length of total clitoral body by immediate preorgasmic period.
- Uterus.   Full elevation is reached.
- Breasts.   Markedly increased areolar engorgement. Unsuckled breast increases one-fifth to one-fourth over unstimulated size by end of phase; little or no increase in breast that has been suckled.
- Sex flush.   Spreads over breasts in some women; may have widespread body distribution by late plateau stage on those affected.
- Myotonia.   Overall increase. Involuntary facial contractions, grimaces, clutching movements; involuntary pelvic thrusts late in phase near orgasm.
- Other.   Hyperventilation develops late in phase. Further increase in heart rate and blood pressure.

Orgasm Phase

- Vagina.   Strong, rhythmic contractions of orgasmic platform (three to fifteen), beginning at intervals of eight-tenths of a second and gradually diminishing in strength and duration; may be preceded by spastic contraction lasting two to four seconds. Inner vaginal area remains essentially expanded.

- Labia.   No changes.
- Clitoris.   Retracted and not observed.
- Uterus.   Contracts irregularly.
- Breasts.   No specific reaction.
- Sex flush.   Peaks.
- Myotonia.   Muscle spasms and involuntary contraction throughout the body. Loss of voluntary control.
- Other.   Hyperventilation, heart rate, and blood pressure peak. Urinary opening will occasionally slightly dilate, returning to usual state before orgasmic platform contractions have ceased. Rectal sphincter sometimes rhythmically contracts involuntarily.

Resolution

- Vagina.   Central opening of orgasmic platform rapidly increases in diameter by one-third. Cervix and upper walls of vagina descend toward vaginal floor in minimum of three to four minutes. Vaginal color returns to pre-excitement state, usually in about ten to fifteen minutes. Occasionally production of lubrication continues into resolution phase; suggests remaining or renewed sexual tension.
- Labia majora.   Rapidly back to pre-excitement levels if orgasm; slowly if only plateau levels were reached.
- Labia minora.   Sex-skin color returns to light pink within five to fifteen seconds after orgasm. Further color loss is rapid.
- Clitoris.   Returned to pre-excitement position within five to fifteen seconds after cessation of orgasmic platform contractions. Vasocongestion usually disappears five to ten minutes after orgasm, ten to thirty minutes in some women; may take several hours if there was no orgasm.
- Uterus.   Cervical opening dilates early in phase; observable in women who have not borne children.
- Breasts.   Nipples rapidly return to normal size. Nonsuckled breasts lose size increase in about five to ten minutes. Superficial vein patterns may last longer.
- Sex flush.   Rapidly disappears from body sites in almost opposite sequence of appearance.
- Myotonia.   Obvious muscle tension usually disappears within five minutes of orgasm. Overall myotonia resolves less rapidly than superficial or deep vasocongestion.
- Other.   Heart rate and blood pressure return to normal. Hyperventilation ends early in stage. A sheen of perspiration appears over the bodies of some women.

Four Phases of Male Sexual Response

Excitement Phase

- Penis.   First physiologic response to effective stimulation is erection, within three to eight seconds; erection may wax and wane throughout excitement phase.

FIGURE 4.3 Changes in the Male Anatomy During the Sexual Response Cycle

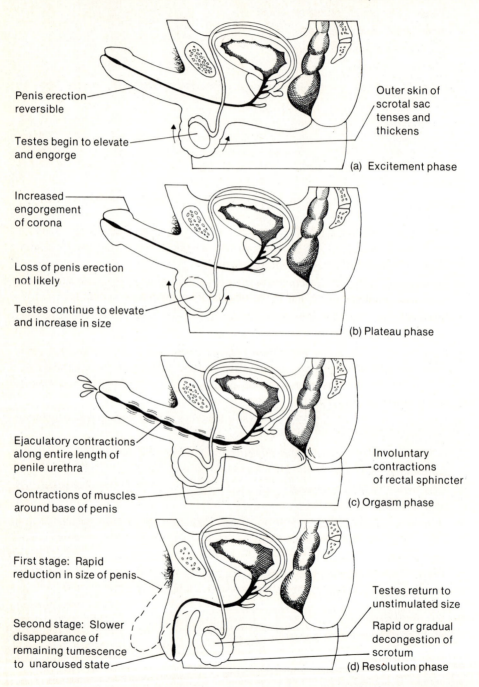

Penis erection reversible

Outer skin of scrotal sac tenses and thickens

Testes begin to elevate and engorge

(a) Excitement phase

Increased engorgement of corona

Loss of penis erection not likely

Testes continue to elevate and increase in size

(b) Plateau phase

Ejaculatory contractions along entire length of penile urethra

Involuntary contractions of rectal sphincter

Contractions of muscles around base of penis

(c) Orgasm phase

First stage: Rapid reduction in size of penis

Testes return to unstimulated size

Second stage: Slower disappearance of remaining tumescence to unaroused state

Rapid or gradual decongestion of scrotum

(d) Resolution phase

- Scrotal sac.   Decreases in internal diameter; outer skin tenses and thickens; muscle fibers contract. Localized vasocongestion.
- Testes.   Elevate toward perineum (the area between the anus and the testes); if phase is prolonged, may redescend and re-elevate several times.
- Breasts.   Nipple erection and swelling develop in some men late in phase; remain throughout rest of sex cycle.
- Sex flush.   Sometimes appears late in phase. Occurs or fails to occur with wide variation in same individual and between individuals.
- Myotonia.   Observed late in phase. Similar to female pattern. Both voluntary muscle tension and some involuntary.
- Other.   Heart rate, blood pressure, and respiration increase as sexual tension increases. Rectal sphincter contracts irregularly after direct stimulation.

Plateau Phase

- Penis.   Increase in coronal area of glans due to increased vasocongestion. Glans deepens in color in some men.
- Scrotum.   No further reactions.
- Testes.   Continue to increase in size until about 50 percent larger than in unstimulated state. Further elevate until in pre-ejaculatory position against perineum.
- Sex flush.   First appears late in plateau more frequently than in excitement phase. Indicates high levels of sexual tension.
- Myotonia.   Voluntary and involuntary tensions increase. Pelvic thrusting becomes involuntary late in phase. Total body reactions of male and female quite similar.
- Other.   Further increases in heart rate and blood pressure. Hyperventilation appears late in phase.

Orgasmic (Ejaculatory) Phase

- Penis.   Ejaculatory contractions along entire length of penile urethra. Expulsive contractions start at intervals of eight-tenths of a second and after three or four reduce in frequency and expulsive force. Final contractions are several seconds apart.
- Scrotum.   No specific reactions.
- Testes.   No reactions observed.
- Myotonia.   Loss of voluntary control. Involuntary contractions and spasms.
- Other.   Heart rate, blood pressure, and hyperventilation peak. Degree of sexual tension is frequently indicated by physiological intensity and duration of hyperventilation. Involuntary contractions of rectal sphincter.

Resolution Phase

- Penis.   Two stages: Rapid reduction in size to about 50 percent larger than in unstimulated state; less rapid if excitement or plateau stages have been intentionally prolonged. Slower disappearance of remaining swelling, especially if sexual stimulation continues to take place.

- Scrotum.   One of two patterns: Rapid decongestion, or decongestion occurring over one or two hours. Typically, but not always, individuals consistently follow one pattern or the other. In general, within the individual pattern, the more the prior stimulation, the longer the resolution process.
- Testes.   Rapid or slow resolution relative to scrotal pattern.
- Breasts.   Loss of nipple erection if present; may occur slowly.
- Sex flush.   Disappears rapidly in reverse order of appearance.
- Myotonia.   As in female, rarely lasts more than five minutes, but not lost as rapidly as many of the signs of vasocongestion.
- Other.   Heart rate and blood pressure return to normal. Perspiration sometimes appears on soles of feet and palms of hands. Hyperventilation resolves during refractory period. Ejaculation cannot again occur until this refractory period has passed.

Sexual Differences

The human male and the human female, like the rest of the animal kingdom, have complementary functions expressed by distinctly different apparatus (see Figures 4.4, 4.5, 4.6, and 4.7). They have analogous parts: the male penis is analogous to the female clitoris; the male scrotum to the female labia. But there are some significant differences, listed below:

1. The female sexual cycle—the time it takes to go from excitement to orgasm—is several seconds longer and somewhat more complex than the male sexual cycle. A typical male, once aroused and making no attempt to restrain himself, can go from erection to ejaculation more quickly than a typical unrestrained female can go from lubrication to orgasm.
2. The clitoris is a small organ, compared to the penis. One cannot hold on to the clitoris as one can hold a penis. The erection of the clitoris, which looks very similar to a penile erection when seen on film at close range, is almost impossible for the male to see or feel. In fact, when this "erection" (actually a combination of muscle tension and blood congestion) occurs, the clitoris is hidden from view under the clitoral hood. As the clitoris is the erotic center of the female orgasm, the male is almost entirely dependent upon the female to *tell* him what is happening, how much stimulation she needs, if he is to satisfy her.
3. The female has the potential to experience a number of orgasms in a relatively short period of time. After ejaculation, the male requires a longer recovery period before he can move toward another orgasm. The male is satiated after he ejaculates; the female may require a number of orgasms before she feels totally satisfied.

FIGURE 4.4   Female Internal Sexual Anatomy

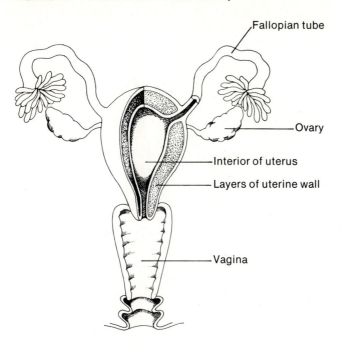

Fallopian tube

Ovary

Interior of uterus

Layers of uterine wall

Vagina

FIGURE 4.5   Female External Genitals

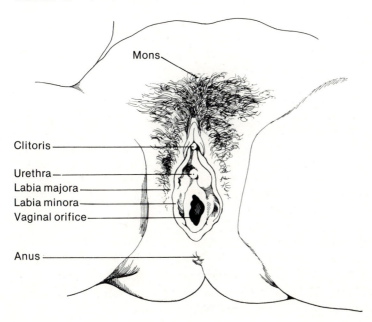

Mons

Clitoris

Urethra

Labia majora

Labia minora

Vaginal orifice

Anus

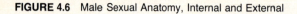

FIGURE 4.6   Male Sexual Anatomy, Internal and External

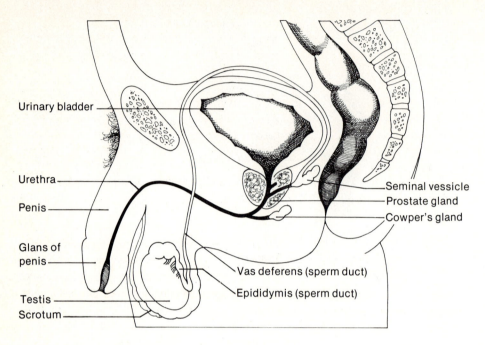

Urinary bladder

Urethra

Penis

Glans of penis

Testis
Scrotum

Seminal vessicle
Prostate gland
Cowper's gland

Vas deferens (sperm duct)
Epididymis (sperm duct)

FIGURE 4.7   Male External Genitals

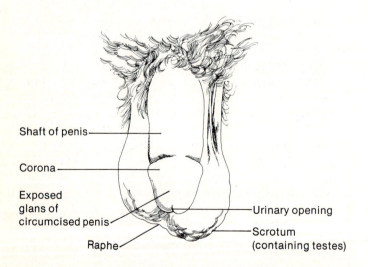

Shaft of penis

Corona

Exposed
glans of
circumcised penis

Raphe

Urinary opening

Scrotum
(containing testes)

4. The male ejaculates with the same organ that erects, the same organ that is his erotic center. But the female's center of eroticism is the clitoris, while her center of orgasmic contractions (and the opening to the place of conception) is the vagina. The male must ejaculate if reproduction is to occur; the female need not have an orgasm for conception to take place.

While a woman may suffer from pressures to suppress her sexuality, or at least express it only in ways to serve the male and the reproduction of the race, men suffer from pressures to express their sexuality quickly, frequently, and incontestably. For men the stress on size, speed, and performance creates emotional stress. The male is beset with what Masters and Johnson have called "phallic fallacies" (1966, p. 188), the most common of which is the notion that the size of a penis, flaccid or erect, reflects sexual prowess:

There is no organ about which more misinformation has been perpetrated. The penis constantly has been viewed but rarely seen. The organ has been venerated, reviled, and misrepresented with intent in art, literature, and legend through the centuries. These intentional misrepresentations have varied in magnitude with the culture. Our culture has been influenced by and has contributed to manifold misconceptions of the functional role of the penis. These "phallic fallacies" have colored our arts and, possibly of even more import to our culture, influenced our behavioral and biologic sciences. (1966, p. 188)

The men in the Masters and Johnson sample whose penises were smaller in the flaccid state were frequently those whose penis size doubled during erection, while some men with large penises did not experience such a radical increase. Sexual stimulation serves as the great equalizer. Nothing in Masters and Johnson's findings suggest that sexual satisfaction is related to the size of a penis in its resting state. Myths and centerfolds notwithstanding, the build of a man and the size of his penis have nothing to do with what kind of lover he will be.

All this attention to size and appearance overlooks a major factor of intercourse that was substantiated by the Masters and Johnson research: the vagina expands to accommodate the penis that enters it, if the proper stimulation has occurred. Thus, a man who enters a woman before she has been stimulated causes the woman pain and deprives both of them of pleasure. Her vagina is not lubricated and has not extended to receive him; the outer third is not ready to produce the hugging effect that would occur with proper stimulation. Some women with exceptionally small vaginas may require a high degree of excitement before penetration can be tolerated. More common is a sensation many women experience during the excitement phase: that the fully erect penis, regardless of size, is lost in the vagina. This is especially true of women who have given birth to many children. So the man whose partner reports that she can't feel his penis need not feel a sense of inadequacy any more than she need feel that there is something wrong with her vagina. Fortunately, anatomy is not destiny when it comes to sexual fulfillment.

The key to any mutuality of sexual pleasuring between male and female is communication. Both man and woman must convey, verbally or non-verbally, what they require to achieve satisfaction. And each must be open to receiving the other's message and acting upon it.

We are just beginning to realize that typical or "normal" American attitudes toward sex roles and sexual behavior have been unhealthy. Realizing where the sexual differences between men and women lie and what the key to sexual pleasure is, we look at what has been a typical sexual agenda for American couples and wonder how any of them found gratification (see Box 4.3).

Mutual sexual satisfaction requires communication. (Andy Brilliant)

The worst of all possible schemes somehow became the core of our Western sexual mores, the very definition of civilized relations between men and women. In a society with such admittedly unhealthy notions about sexuality, what is sexual adjustment? It is easy enough to fire off a list of common sexual dysfunctions—impotence, orgasmic difficulties, premature ejaculation—but not so easy to separate these complaints from ignorance, negative conditioning, double standards of sexuality—all of which we could call the "social dysfunctions" affecting sexuality.

COMMON SEXUAL MYTHS AND PROBLEMS

Clitoral Stimulation

The Hite Report (discussed previously on pages 113–114) revealed a great variety of sexual preferences and sensations among women, but a common complaint of insufficient clitoral stimulation during lovemaking. While some women reported a need or desire for an extended period of arousal, approximately 30 percent of the women surveyed felt that they were not getting enough clitoral stimulation.

This is not surprising. Ask which positions have been emphasized in our culture's view of lovemaking—those that facilitate clitoral stimulation or those that make it highly unlikely that the penis will come in contact with the clitoris or the area surrounding it. The most common position, with the male superior (sometimes known as the "missionary position"), allows for little contact between penis and clitoris or the surrounding *mons* area. Yet this position is the one we see in movies and read about in novels, the

---

BOX 4.3 The Worst Possible Program for Mutual Sexual Satisfaction

1. Convince men that they must perform as quickly as possible. That way they cannot possibly pleasure the female, who requires a longer period of stimulation.
2. Teach men that the vagina is the site of female sexual excitement. That way they will never bother with the real source of erotic pleasure—the clitoris.
3. Teach women that sex is only for reproduction. That way they'll never be satisfied because they will feel guilty about attending to the organ that has nothing to do with reproduction and everything to do with sexual pleasure—again, the clitoris.
4. Teach women not to talk about sex—never to say, "Would you stroke my breasts a little longer?" or "I find it very arousing when you lick my armpits," or "Would you spend time stimulating my clitoris before you enter my vagina?"
5. Teach men not to ask if they are pleasing women. Teach them that they should know automatically if women are pleased, and so should never have to ask. And in case a woman talks despite all those proscriptions against making sexual demands, teach the man that "nice" women don't talk about such things. This will assure that the woman who is the mother of his children will never be the same one who makes sexual demands and achieves satisfaction.

one that always makes the earth move. The others are at best thought to be departures from the norm, at worst (and the law often supports the worst view of sexual differences), thought deviant and illegal.

But in Masters and Johnson's *Human Sexual Response,* one finds the summary of 11 years of direct observation and reports by hundreds of women: "Unless the male partner makes a specific effort to bring the shaft of the penis in direct apposition to the total mons area, the clitoris is not stimulated directly by penile thrust with the female in the usual supine position" (1966, p. 60). In short, the standard position for sexual intercourse is almost a certain guarantee that the woman will *not* achieve orgasm.

Sex therapist Helen Singer Kaplan confirms this view: "There are millions of women who are sexually responsive, and often multiply orgastic, but who cannot have an orgasm during intercourse unless they receive simultaneous clitoral stimulation. Most of these women enjoy intercourse and the pleasure of reaching orgasm with the penis contained in their vagina, but coitus in itself is not sufficiently stimulating to enable them to reach a climax" (1974, p. 398). A substantial number of "normal" women with reasonably healthy marriages don't climax during *coitus* (intercourse) simply because they need more than the relatively mild clitoral stimulation provided by that activity.

Clitoral versus Vaginal Orgasm.

Why is there an argument about clitoral orgasms and vaginal orgasms? What part does intercourse play in this process of achieving orgasm?

Freud, lacking the data that Masters and Johnson accumulated and living in a society that gave women no opportunity to express sexual feelings in a direct manner, developed a theory of two types of orgasm: the immature "clitoral" orgasm and the mature "vaginal" orgasm. Sex during the teenage years may well be sex without actual coitus—either through masturbation, mutual masturbation, or oral sex. Women who engage in lovemaking that includes intercourse are likely to value coitus as an important part, a finale or conclusion to their lovemaking. But this progression does not indicate that one leaves the clitoris behind when one grows up, as one might abandon a teddy bear. Until recently, however, most people did not question whether Freud's notion was true or false.

There is no doubt now that, physiologically, there are not two different types of orgasm. A woman who reaches orgasm during intercourse is not healthier or more mature than one who requires additional clitoral stimulation. Clitoral stimulation, direct or indirect, is the initial source of erotic pleasure for all women. Contractions take place in the vagina no matter how the orgasm has been stimulated. But the pleasure of those contractions is usually enhanced by the presence and thrusting of the penis; many women find the sense of fullness and completeness that intercourse provides exquisite.

Masturbation

Our ignorance concerning sexuality has produced many myths and superstitious beliefs. Nowhere do we see the psychological impact on sexuality more clearly than in the area of masturbation. The word carries connotations of something unnatural and deviant, particularly in the case of women. Although all babies, in the process of exploring their bodies, discover their genitals as a source of pleasure, girl babies are so consistently discouraged from touching themselves that, in the past, they have either masturbated with guilt and conflict or have become conditioned not to touch themselves "down there." (Perhaps it is feared that women would learn to do without men if they realized they could achieve orgasm without them.)

But men have also been urged to forego masturbation, particularly those who came from religious homes. Until recently, boys commonly were warned that masturbation could grow hair on their palms or cause blindness or mental illness. A noted disciple of Freud, Alfred Adler, reports the case of a boy whose hands were tied to the bed sides every night to prevent him from "abusing himself." These proscriptions against masturbation are a common source of male humor, as in Philip Roth's novel *Portnoy's Complaint*. Women, however, were expected not to masturbate because it was assumed that they didn't have those sexual needs.

Though both males and females are fully capable of bringing themselves to orgasm through self-stimulation, there is no indication in the course of human history that either men or women will choose this form of pleasuring over interpersonal contact and mutual pleasuring. And there is evidence from Harry Harlow's studies of monkeys (Harlow and Mears 1979) that masturbation while one is maturing is related to normal sexual behavior in adulthood. In Harlow's studies, monkeys who did not masturbate in their youth were not interested in sexual activity later. Most monkeys—and most humans—masturbate at some time before they begin to have sexual relations. The Sorensen survey of adolescent sexuality (1973) indicates that, despite the reticence of parents (83 percent had not discussed masturbation with their adolescent children), adolescents are aware of masturbation and no longer have superstitious beliefs about its consequences. Despite this more enlightened attitude, many adolescents still regard it as socially unacceptable and even deviant (Sorensen 1973, pp. 143–144).

One of the most instructive things a woman can do for her partner is to masturbate in front of him. According to Masters and Johnson, "No two women have been observed to masturbate in identical fashion," (1966, p. 63) but most stimulate the entire mons area, and others concentrate on the clitoral shaft. The clitoral glans is rarely stimulated directly, as it is very sensitive to the touch. A man could be aided in his efforts to give pleasure to a woman if he knew what type of movements pleased her, how gentle or brusque to be, and where to touch her. But women who can barely bring themselves to masturbate in private find it virtually impossible even to admit that they masturbate and out of the question to demonstrate this self-stimulation in front of their partners.

Those who have gathered information concerning masturbation have added proof to the theory that females—far from being less interested in sex or less capable of arousal and orgasm—are capable, physiologically, of far more sexual activity than males. Masters and Johnson observed the multiorgasmic nature of most women. They found that during masturbation, with no psychosocial distractions to repress sexual tensions, many women whom they described as "well adjusted" enjoyed a minimum of three or four orgasmic experiences before they reached apparent satiation (1966, p. 131).

Not only is the female capable of a rapid return to orgasm if she is restimulated, but she is also capable of maintaining the orgasmic experience longer than the male does—20 to 60 seconds. Masters and Johnson call this state of ongoing orgasmic experience "status orgasmus." "This physiologic state of stress is created either by a series of rapidly recurrent orgasmic experiences between which no recordable plateau-phase intervals can be demonstrated, or by a single, long-continued orgasmic episode" (1966, p. 131). They note that in their experiments, women achieved the maximum physiological intensity of orgasmic response by self-regulated mechanical or automanipulative techniques (that is, masturbation with hand or vibrator). The second most intense orgasms occurred with a partner orally or manually manipulating the clitoral area. The lowest intensity occurred during intercourse (1966, p. 133). Lest new myths of female sexuality be perpetuated, note that the women who volunteered for the Masters and Johnson study may have differed from average women in some way. Because Masters and Johnson employed neither a control group nor a national survey, such results as these may still be questioned.

When men, most of whom were brought up to believe that women have lower levels of sexuality than they, are confronted with sexual expectations of more (or at least some) and better orgasms, they can become angry, intimidated, or confused. Some of them are actually rendered impotent by these unexpected demands. They have not gone through the consciousness-raising process that many women have experienced through books and magazines and groups that confirmed their self-knowledge. Many men may need a period of re-education. Sex therapy, as we shall see later, is primarily sex education or re-education.

Sex and Pregnancy

Myths about sex before and after pregnancy are another source of confusion and possible sexual dysfunction. Physiologically, pregnancy makes a woman more sensitive to sexual stimuli. Except for the time just before delivery, when physical exhaustion intervenes, and the time after birth, when painful uterine contractions and unhealed episiotomies prevent or overshadow erotic enjoyment, pregnancy and birth should heighten erotic activity. Nowhere do we see more clearly the decisive impact of psychological factors on sex than during pregnancy and after birth.

Masters and Johnson discovered that psychological factors—both the fear of hurting the unborn child and the complex adjustment to feeling oneself as a mother—made women who had never given birth feel ambivalent toward sex or definitely opposed to it in the first three months (*trimester*) of pregnancy. In the second trimester, however, all the women, according to Masters and Johnson, report an increase in eroticism. They become interested in fantasies and sex dreams, and their demands for effective sexual performance increase.

The third trimester presents many complications in attitudes about sex, one of which may be caused by the medical profession. Obstetricians commonly recommend a period of continence (which in this case means abstention from intercourse) both before and after delivery. A three-month period of continence—six weeks before delivery and six weeks after—seems to be the general rule today. Masters and Johnson believe that such a long period of time without intercourse puts an enormous strain on the couple, which, in many cases, is unnecessary, and they urge doctors to decide the question of continence on an individual basis.

Since pregnancy is usually a time of marital stress (see Chapter 10), doctors could be helpful to couples during this period if they would emphasize the possibility of sexual activity other than intercourse, encourage husbands to take on more responsibility for the home and other children during this time, and urge couples to communicate their feelings during this period. One husband admitted that his pregnant wife reminded him of the time when his mother was pregnant, a time when he had felt excluded and jealous of the forthcoming rival. He waited seven years to reveal these feelings. Becoming a parent is so intimately involved with our early feelings toward our own parents and toward ourselves as children that the prospect is bound to uncover many sensitive areas that influence our sexual feelings.

Sex and Menopause

In menopause, even more than in pregnancy, the decisive importance of psychological factors gives them precedence over the physiological ones.

Masters and Johnson state that, despite the physiological changes women experience during menopause, "there is no reason why the milestone of the menopause should be expected to blunt the human female's sexual capacity, performance, or drive. The healthy aging woman normally has sex drives that demand resolution. . . . There is no time limit

Psychological factors combined with sexual myths may increase marital stress during pregnancy, and couples can benefit from expressing their feelings during this period. (Susan Lapides)

drawn by the advancing years to female sexuality" (1966, pp. 246–247). While the clitoris receives and reacts to sex stimuli as effectively in an older woman, her clitoral area is more sensitive to irritation or trauma from an uncontrolled or thoughtless male approach than is that of a younger woman (1966, p. 240).

Changes in hormones that reduce sex steroids and other processes of aging may also affect a woman's lubrication and sexual performance. But having intercourse regularly seems to help women maintain their sexual capacity:

If opportunity for regularity of coital exposure is created or maintained, the elderly woman suffering from all of the vaginal stigmas of sex-steroid starvation still will retain a far higher capacity for sexual performance than her female counterpart who does not have similar coital opportunities. (1966, pp. 241–242)

Women react in many different ways to the biological changes of menopause. With fears of pregnancy and responsibilities for young children no longer issues, some women discover a renewed interest in sex. Others respond with alarm to signs of diminished capacity. Masters and

Johnson suggest that if counseling could take place before menopause occurs, tensions of the postmenopausal period could be greatly reduced (1966, p. 246). Such preventive counseling would also serve to allay men's fears about sexual performance.

"Phallic Fallacies"

Fears about their "performance" have plagued men of all ages. Just as women were not able to express sexual needs, men have been unable to express fears of sexual inadequacy. Masters and Johnson report that members of the under-40 group worry primarily about premature ejaculation. Their early sexual experiences frequently had been brief encounters with prostitutes. The sad and often cruel situation of such sexual pressure is depicted in Jacques Brel's song "Next," in which the man's first and only relationships have been hurried encounters with prostitutes while the next man waited in line. For some men, sexual initiation may have been stolen back-seat copulations, where climaxing quickly was essential to avoid discovery or to keep the woman from changing her mind. Still other men experienced their earliest sexual activity in a masturbation contest, with honors going to the boy who could ejaculate first.

In the United States, sex therapists report that premature ejaculation is one of the most common complaints, one that often leads to *secondary impotence*—the man is afraid he will ejaculate too quickly and as a result begins to find he can't achieve an erection (see page 132). Masters and Johnson found that the better-educated men in their group worried more about being able to delay long enough to satisfy their female partners. Once the men passed the age of 40, however, all of them, regardless of education or economic differences, began to worry about achieving erections. This fear intensified with age. Masters and Johnson later learned that there was a sharp upswing in male impotence after the age of 50. They came to believe that fear is 80 percent of impotence. And the fear of being unable to achieve an erection rests on another firmly entrenched "phallic fallacy"—the notion that impotence is an inevitable result of aging. What are the real sexual changes caused by aging, and which are the inadequacies caused by fear or stress?

The young male can erect immediately, enter early, and ejaculate rapidly; the male over 60 is slower to erect, slower to penetrate, slower to ejaculate. The male over 60 is likely to be satisfied with fewer ejaculations, one or two a week, regardless of the number of opportunities or demands. Fear of diminished sexual capability, combined with a normal decrease in the speed and frequency of erection and ejaculation, seems to be the most common cause of secondary impotence. Because the condition is based primarily on fear, it is usually a transitory one. Research by Masters and Johnson supports their claim that "in most instances, secondary impotence is a reversible process for all men regardless of age, unless there is a background of specific surgery or physical trauma" (1966, p. 203).

In addition to his increased vulnerability to rejection, the older male's sexual responsiveness, according to Masters and Johnson, is affected by a number of factors, including boredom with a monotonous sexual relationship that lacks variety, worry about success at work, and physical or mental illness (1966, p. 264).

SEXUAL DYSFUNCTION

After their direct observations and interviews were compiled in *Human Sexual Response* (1966), Masters and Johnson turned their attention to the treatment of sexual dysfunction, explaining the therapy program they developed at their clinic in St. Louis. Their findings, published in 1970 as *Human Sexual Inadequacy*, influenced many other sex therapists, a number of them developing programs that differed from Masters and Johnson's two-week treatment regimen (Kaplan 1974; Barbach 1975).

Recent criticism of the Masters and Johnson treatment findings (Zilbergeld and Evans 1980) does not dismiss the contribution of these pioneers. The critics do remind us that some sexual problems are deeply rooted; they are not always easily overcome by brief treatment programs such as the one offered at the Masters and Johnson clinic. Masters and Johnson may have been most helpful in demonstrating that sexual problems are common in our culture. In this section we shall discuss some of the most common sexual dysfunctions and suggest a few of the typical treatments recommended. Since sexual behavior is tied to a unique individual with a unique psychosexual and physiological history, dysfunctions in sexual behavior require individual attention. Self-help books may give individuals the confidence they need to deal with problems, but they also tend to make the solution of sexual problems appear overly simple and general.

Sexual Dysfunctions of the Male

We can see now that sexual dysfunctions may be influenced by sexual myths and social conditioning.

Primary Impotence.   Some men have never been potent with a woman, although they may attain good erections by masturbating and have spontaneous erections in other situations. If we assume that the male in question is not a homosexual, this condition is called *primary impotence*. Primary impotence may be associated with disturbing experiences from the past or endocrine disorders, but this is not always the case. Helen Kaplan notes: "While potency problems may be associated with serious psychopathology in some cases, many men who suffer from this condition appear to be otherwise psychologically healthy" (1974, p. 257). Because there are many possible causes of this condition, a man who suffers from primary impotence should look for a sex therapist who is a psychiatrist or is part of a team with a medical doctor or psychiatrist.

Secondary Impotence.   A man may have functioned well for some time, but now finds himself unable to achieve or maintain an erection. If the problem is not ignored, it can usually be treated and resolved. If, for a period of a month, a man finds he cannot achieve an erection—and he is not aware of a strong reason for this change (such as illness, a sudden tragedy or period of great stress, an increased intake of alcohol or other drug)—he would do well to find a competent therapist quickly. The longer he waits, the more likely he is to develop feelings of depression, humiliation, and anger as a result of his frustration. Such feelings may lead the temporarily impotent man to a distorted expression of "masculinity" through excessive drinking, physical violence, and hostile domination of his wife, children, or employees.

Premature Ejaculation.   A man suffering with this complaint is unable to control his ejaculatory reflex. Once he is sexually aroused, he reaches orgasm very quickly. There are a number of different scientific definitions of premature ejaculation, ranging from 30 seconds to two minutes after vaginal entry. The actual time or number of thrusts does not matter as much as whether the man feels he has control over his ejaculatory reflex and whether he usually reaches orgasm before his partner does. Treatment of premature ejaculation involves a new orientation for the man. He specifically concentrates on his erotic sensations, relishing the gradual build-up rather than rushing to a conclusion. His wife or lover can help him in this by using the "squeeze technique," gripping the erect penis and exerting pressure that prevents him from proceeding to ejaculation. According to Masters and Johnson (1970), a couple needs to practice this technique until the man gradually gains a sense of control over his ejaculatory response. The man cannot, in their opinion, use this technique by himself.

A man who ejaculates prematurely leaves his partner unsatisfied. Her dissatisfaction, which may be shown in anger or outward hostility, may discourage him from making any more sexual advances for fear that he will lose control again and only increase her hostility. She in turn may begin to withdraw from sexual encounters. Some men try anesthetics on the penis, masturbation before coitus, sedatives, alcohol, even jogging. But none of these actually improves control; it only decreases the erotic pleasure of sexual contact. Ironically, the result of these attempts to dull sensation may be impotence.

Retarded Ejaculation.   In this case, a man responds to sexual stimuli with erotic feelings and a firm erection, but he is unable to ejaculate or can ejaculate only under very special circumstances—by receiving oral or manual stimulation from his partner, by masturbating after his partner has reached orgasm, by leaving the room and masturbating alone.

Even individuals who have always had problems with premature or retarded ejaculation stand an excellent chance of reversing the complaint and gaining control. The longer couples wait to treat these difficulties, the more likely it is that other complaints will develop.

Sexual Dysfunctions of the Female

At one time there was only one description for a woman who had any type of sexual dysfunction: she was "frigid." As female sexual response has become better understood, this insulting label is being replaced by more accurate categories.

General Sexual Dysfunction.   A woman may think of herself as the classic frigid woman because she is simply not aroused; she seems to have no erotic feelings; she doesn't lubricate; she doesn't seem to feel any physical or psychological sexual response. The causes for such a general dysfunction range from insensitivity on the part of her partner, to failure or inability to communicate to him what she wants, to early experiences that have distorted some aspect of her sexual identity, making her feel that responding sexually might be dangerous or "dirty." Although the majority of such general dysfunctions are not medically caused, a physical checkup followed by sessions with a qualified sex therapist in whom the woman can easily confide may cure this dysfunction. Ideally, both male and female should be treated, at least initially.

Primary Orgasmic Dysfunction.   A woman may have never experienced an orgasm, although she has had some erotic feelings: she has become aroused, lubricated, perhaps sensed other sexual responses such as the erection of the nipples, but she has never experienced the release of those sexual tensions. The reason may be that she has never been effectively stimulated, either by herself or by her partner. If the need is for effective stimulation, she and her partner may well benefit from available self-help literature and illustrated manuals. Her first step may be an orgasm achieved through masturbation, or it may be a process of making the acquaintance of sensual feelings that she has never before accepted in herself.

Secondary Orgasmic Dysfunction.   In this case, a woman has had orgasms, either by masturbation, or by oral or manual stimulation from a partner, or during intercourse. But lately she hasn't been able to achieve an orgasm by these means. This might relate to some major event in her life such as taking on or losing a full-time job, becoming pregnant, or approaching menopause. Some relatively minor experience might have triggered an old prohibition from her childhood or adolescence—and women usually have plenty of old prohibitions to choose from. A change of partners or a change in the behavior of one's partner may also contribute to temporary dysfunction.

Situational Orgasmic Dysfunction. This phrase is used in the case of a woman who achieves orgasm only in certain situations, when tension and anxiety are low. For example, she may be able to climax through masturbation, but not with her partner.

Failure to Achieve Orgasm During Coitus. We have noted that the need for clitoral stimulation may make orgasm during coitus an impossibility for many healthy normal women. But there are some cases in which women wish to have an orgasm during intercourse, but the act of coitus inhibits them, no matter how much clitoral stimulation they receive.

Therapists are just beginning to understand the causes and treatment of sexual dysfunctions, particularly those that occur in women. Some behavior that may have been classified as abnormal or dysfunctional in the past, such as inability to achieve orgasm during coitus, now appears to be simply a normal variation of female sexual response. Other complaints may have been misdiagnosed; the report of painful intercourse (dyspareunia), for instance, has been attributed to an intact hymen, but in many cases the complaint persists after the hymenal tissue is removed. Some doctors have put too much emphasis on the physical causes of sexual complaints. Some psychologists, on the other hand, have stressed the psychological causes and ignored legitimate physical complaints. Most practitioners have not understood the effect of psychological and social pressures on a woman's sexual functioning. Almost all those who have treated individuals with sexual complaints in the past have been unaware of the *couple dimension* of the sexual dysfunction—both the ways in which dysfunction results from a particular pairing of two individuals and the ways in which male and female can cooperate to overcome dysfunction.

SEX, LOVE, AND MARRIAGE

How is sex related to love? To marriage? Love and the feelings of intimacy and security that occur within marriage can greatly enhance the pleasure and satisfaction of the sexual experience for both partners. We have already noticed how important it is for both partners to communicate with each other while engaging in foreplay and sexual intercourse. The woman especially must feel free to tell her partner what stimulates and excites her. Trust facilitates this kind of intimate communication and relieves either partner from the pressure to "perform" and to compete with rivals for sexual favors. When marriage is based on trust and love, it provides a unique opportunity for mutual sexual satisfaction.

As the double standard that subordinates the female to the male gives way to more equitable norms, women are becoming freer to feel and to express their sexuality both within and outside of marriage. The traditional code that restricted sex for women absolutely to marriage is being replaced by a looser code that allows sex outside of marriage, while stressing the primary importance of love in all sexual relationships. Casual sex for women carries all the risks it has always had for men, with the added ones that a woman may not feel free and trusting enough to express her sexual needs to her partner and that she may become pregnant if she is careless about birth control. Casual intercourse can intensify rather than compensate for the sense of loneliness and isolation that motivates it.

In our society, selective premarital experience still seems to be preferred to indiscriminate sexual activity before or outside of marriage, and the social code that is emerging finds sexual intercourse acceptable to the degree that it takes place in a relationship of tender feeling and intimacy (Turner 1970, pp. 330–331). The combination of sex, love, and marriage is still the most frequently chosen setting for intimate relations. In the next chapter we shall explore some recent and some age-old alternatives to the traditional linking of sex and marriage.

SUMMARY

1. The major objectives of this chapter are to discuss development of the sexual self as a continuous process throughout life; to review the impact of selected factors, such as culture, social class, and changing social norms on sexual behavior; to explore the nature of human sexual response in women and men; to correct some misinterpretations about sexual behavior; and to discuss common problems in sexual functioning and their treatment.

2. The recognition that human sexual development is a continuous process beginning at birth is usually viewed as an important contribution of Freudian theory. Several contemporary theories of sexual development differ from Freud's view. Yet it is generally agreed that the sexual self that emerges as an element of adult identity owes its content in part to the socialization experiences of growing up within a specific family or kinship system in a particular culture and social group during a certain time in history. Adult sexual functioning cannot be explained solely on the basis of biology: psychological and sociological forces have a profound impact on sexual attitudes and behavior.

3. Variation in male and female expression of the sexual self reflects not only the obvious physiological differences, but also the expectations

and values of the social group concerning appropriate sex-role behavior in adult life. In the United States, girls are generally less sexually active than boys and tend to view sex more in the social or romantic context of love and marriage. Boys, in general, bring a more detached and pleasure-oriented sexual view to the relationship. In a certain sense, the dating and courtship processes in American society may represent a training period for working out these two different orientations toward sexuality.

4. The early Kinsey studies in the 1940s and early 1950s highlighted the differences in sexual experience between females and males, indicating a substantial degree of conformity to the double standard. The Kinsey surveys also indicated social-class variations in sexual behavior. Research on current sexual attitudes and behavior in American society indicates some significant changes, notably an increasing amount of sexual activity among both adolescent and adult females. Changing sexual mores also bring particular problems. The United States is currently confronted with an increasing birth rate for adolescent females and a seriously accelerating rate of venereal disease.

5. The pioneering research efforts of Masters and Johnson (published in 1966) provided the first scientific data on human sexual response. Male and female sexual response is typically divided into four phases: excitement, plateau, orgasm, and recovery. The observations of similarities and differences between males and females made by Masters and Johnson have provided the first balanced and scientific explanation of human sexual response. Their findings have been particularly useful in the enhancement of sexual pleasure for intimate couples and for designing treatment programs for sexual dysfunctions.

6. One of the most significant findings of the Masters and Johnson research involves the importance of clitoral stimulation as the initial source of erotic pleasure for women. Knowledge about one's sexual self and open communication between intimate partners about sexual needs and wants are primary avenues for enhancing sexual pleasure.

7. Sexual dysfunctions may be part of an ongoing psychological or interpersonal problem. But a number of common dysfunctions seem amenable to education and treatment. Most sexual problems can be resolved, though appropriate therapy may be necessary.

KEY CONCEPTS

Libido
Sexual identity
Double standard
Venereal disease

Sexual response
Clitoral stimulation
Masturbation
Sexual dysfunctions

QUESTIONS

1. Consider the statement: "Sexuality is a continuous process throughout life, beginning at birth." Discuss its meaning, drawing upon the theoretical and research data presented in this chapter. Include some examples from your personal experiences or observations to illustrate your presentation.
2. Considering the many factors that can influence an individual's perception and experience of sexual interaction, discuss when, how, and from whom children should receive information and education about human sexuality.
3. Using the information presented in this chapter, describe what you think are the primary problems or conflicts related to sex in adolescence, young adulthood, the middle years, and the later years of adulthood.
4. Describe the value position that you think the majority of college students hold related to premarital sexual intercourse. Describe the value position that you think the majority of the same population hold regarding extramarital sexual intercourse. Is the double standard alive and well in contemporary American society in relation to establishing one's sexual self? Discuss the reasons for your answer.
5. Changes in social attitudes and values related to the expression of human sexuality can precipitate certain social problems. Describe one such area related to sexuality that seems to present difficulty for contemporary American society. Discuss your proposals for preventing or treating the selected problem.

SUGGESTED READINGS

- Bullough, Vern, ed. *The Frontiers of Sex Research*. Buffalo, N.Y.: Prometheus Books, 1979. Focuses on numerous topics in the field of human sexuality. The many contributors are experts in the areas presented and offer the latest findings about sexuality from such fields as medicine, biology, sociology, psychology, and other disciplines.
- Hite, Shere. *The Hite Report: A National Study of Female Sexuality*. New York: Macmillan, 1976. A unique and contemporary book that reports the findings of a national survey of women on various aspects of sexuality. Numerous excerpts from the actual survey data are included, which can provide valuable understanding of the pleasures and problems of defining the female sexual self.
- Masters, William H., and Johnson, Virginia E. *Human Sexual Response*. Boston: Little, Brown, 1966. A comprehensive and detailed report on several years of laboratory research investigating human sexual behavior. This pioneering book provides the basis for much of the current work in the treatment of sexual dysfunctions.

- Masters, William H., and Johnson, Virginia E., in association with R. J. Levin. *The Pleasure Bond: A New Look at Sexuality and Commitment*. Boston: Little, Brown, 1974. In-depth discussion of growth and development in sexual relationships over time. The book includes interviews with men and women concerning sexual satisfaction in marriage, their approach to problems, and the process of sexual enhancement.
- Morrison, Eleanor S.; Starks, Kay; Hyndman, Cynda; and Ronsie, Nina. *Growing Up Sexual*. New York: Van Nostrand, 1980. A unique view of sexual development and experience based on anonymous excerpts from autobiographical papers by university students in a human sexuality course, providing an excellent stimulus for exploring and reflecting upon personal sexual experiences and for considering various aspects of human sexuality in serious discussions.
- Pierson, Elaine C., and D'Antonio, William V. *Female and Male: Dimensions of Human Sexuality*. New York: Lippincott, 1974. This book is a good source of basic information on human sexual functioning. The biological aspects of sexual intercourse and reproduction are factually presented. Discussions of the psychological and sociological components of sexual experience and major value issues related to such areas as sexual standards, abortion, and sexual violence are sensitive and realistic.
- Spanier, Graham B. *Human Sexuality in a Changing Society*. Minneapolis, Minn.: Burgess, 1979. A textbook that is focused on the developmental model and includes topics from a multidisciplinary perspective. Research findings are presented and discussed in an easily understood format. A number of nonresearch selections that contribute to understanding human sexual functioning are also included.

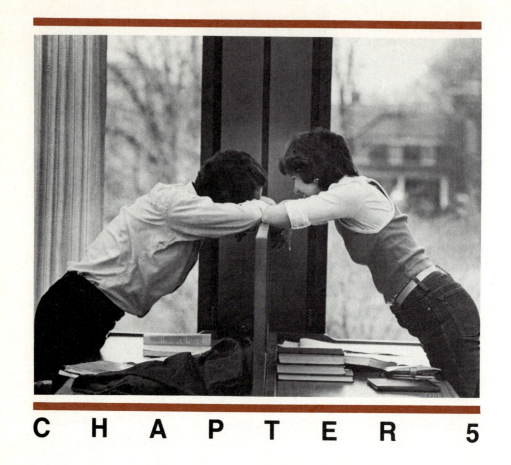

C H A P T E R 5

Varieties of Intimate
Relationships

SHE: I guess that's everything.

HE: It looks like enough.

SHE: A person accumulates a lot of stuff in three years.

HE: We're going to be a little short of closet space.

SHE: We can add some racks and shelves. An engineering major and a biochem student ought to be able to think of something.

HE: I told my mom last night.

SHE: What did she say?

HE: You know she likes you. And she said it's better to find out if you can live together before you get married than the way she did.

SHE: I wish my mother felt that way—and dad is even more strait-laced than she is.

HE: What are you going to tell them?

SHE: I'm telling them that I'm moving, which is true, and that I have a new roommate. . . .

HE: Which is true.

SHE: But I haven't mentioned the gender of the roommate.

HE: But you've got to tell them sometime.

SHE: I don't want to be hassled by them before my lab practical.

HE: What if they call and I answer the phone?

SHE: They already know we're going together.

HE: In the middle of the night?

SHE: They never call in the middle of the night.
HE: I don't want them to find out that way. Why don't we just get it over with and tell them straight out?

INTRODUCTION

Penelope waits patiently for Odysseus, putting off attractive suitors for decades until her husband finally returns. Romeo and Juliet, aged 14 and 16, can barely wait even a day after they meet to marry. Nineteenth-century female novelist George Sand leaves her husband, has a series of lovers, and then settles down with composer Frederic Chopin for a relatively conventional stretch of living together. During the same period, American writer Henry David Thoreau chooses to leave all attachments and possessions for a spell of solitude and simplicity at Walden Pond. The impulse for love and intimacy finds expression in a lifelong marriage or a brief affair, in clandestine adultery or celibate life, and in innumerable other variations. An atmosphere of greater sexual freedom has evolved during the twentieth century, making it possible for homosexuals, as well as heterosexuals involved in a variety of types of unconventional relationships, to live more openly.

Why does a person choose one lifestyle or relationship pattern over another? And what factors influence changes in intimate patterns over the course of a lifetime? In this chapter we shall explore some of the elements involved in our decisions about primary relationships. We shall also explore various styles or patterns of relating that exist in the United States today.

THE NEED FOR INTIMACY

The individual cannot exist apart from his or her relations with other people. This is the central theme of Harry Stack Sullivan's theory of interpersonal relations (1953). It is also a central theme of this chapter. A person's identity and self-concept are bound up with a set of relationships that the person has—with mother, father, brother, child, cousin, teacher, lover, mate—each of whom can be a "significant other." Like the modern existential philosophers Martin Buber and Gabriel Marcel, Sullivan believed that the fundamental requirement of being human is a relationship. "I-You" or "I-Thou" has meaning; "I" by itself does not.

In most theories of human development, we find a similar theme related to the need that humans have for close, personal interaction with other human beings. We also find numerous references to the difficulties and conflicts that can arise from our attempts to fulfill these needs. As we recall the developmental stages and tasks discussed in Chapter 1, it is evident that much of life has to do with attachment, identification, and interdependence within the human family. Humans have *survival needs* for food and shelter, but they also have *relationship needs* for physical and emotional affection. Etzkowitz and Stein note that once the material survival needs are satisfied, the second level of human relationship needs becomes central. These needs include work, intimacy, avocational activities, and social communality (1978, p. 438). Etzkowitz and Stein also indicate that such second-level needs are not resolved during one stage of life or one age period, but appear as issues to be dealt with throughout the adult years.

By the time a woman is 21, for example, the need for intimacy has typically taken her through an intense attachment to mother and father, several close friendships with girlfriends, dating and going steady with at least one young man, and perhaps an admiring "mentor" relationship with an older adult. Once an individual reaches young adulthood, the options in terms of seeking intimacy multiply. In the United States today, this is true for both women and men. So if we follow four young women graduating from the same high school class, we may find that one gets a college education, marries, and has children, while her classmate marries, divorces, remains single for a time, lives with another man, and then marries him. Still another classmate moves into a commune, lives with a series of different men, and then marries and remains with the same man. The fourth classmate never marries, although she has some intimate relationships and later decides to adopt a child and raise that child herself.

These four hypothetical women represent four different patterns of intimacy that Etzkowitz and Stein have identified in contemporary American society.

The first pattern represents the traditional middle-class expectations related to love and work in the typical sequence: education, career, marriage, parenthood, and retirement. The authors indicate that while this pattern probably still is followed by the majority of adult women and men, many other adults are freely choosing to live their lives in different ways. They identify a second pattern that involves shifts back and forth between traditional and alternative arrangements. Examples of this pattern might include marriage, divorce, and singlehood; married parenthood and then single parenthood; or marriage, divorce, singlehood, and remarriage.

A third pattern involves moving from early experimentation with alternative or nontraditional patterns to traditional patterns later on. For instance, early experimentation with communal living may lead to cohabitation with a partner of the opposite sex and eventually to marriage. Finally, a fourth pattern seems to be emerging in which individuals choose singlehood as a permanent lifestyle, perhaps incorporating single parenthood (Etzkowitz and Stein 1978).

It is not only the young who deviate from the traditional sequence of dating, mate selection, marriage, and parenthood. And such deviations are no longer only temporary choices prior to "settling down" with a permanent mate. The four patterns outlined above suggest that, at least for some individuals, styles of intimate relating may fluctuate throughout life. Even for those who initially choose a traditional pattern, such unpredictable events as divorce or death of a spouse may thrust them into a nontraditional style at some point in their lives. We shall now look at some of the forces that influence one's style of relating.

Changes and Choices

We have already discussed at some length in earlier chapters the developmental changes and tasks that occur during adolescence. Adolescence is seen as a period of time when some independence from childhood ties with parents becomes necessary, when the achievement of intimate relationships outside the family unit is a part of normative growth, and when finding one's place within one's self and within one's society is a primary focus. Complete resolution or "working through" of such important and global tasks is not restricted to adolescence. The process continues in other forms during the adult years.

The teenage years represent the first significant period of experimentation in the realm of social relationships, though not the last. After experiencing physiological changes, cognitive transformations, and new perceptions in terms of social role taking, adolescents may want to experiment with new styles of relating. Some of this experimentation may be a form of rebelling against parental authority. It is not accurate, however, to suggest that adolescents or young adults who cohabit with a partner of the opposite sex or become involved in same-sex relationships are doing so solely as a means of rebelling against adult authority.

Relationship decisions are not always motivated by the wish to rebel. The selection of nontraditional styles may be influenced by the norms and values of one's peers, who represent a potent force during adolescence. Members of the extended family system and other significant adults likewise provide powerful role models. Changing attitudes and values of the greater society as presented repeatedly by the popular media may also influence choices. Before dating even begins, young people have already seen such alternatives as divorce, living together without marriage, single parenthood, homosexuality, affairs, and casual sexual encounters portrayed on television and film, if not by living examples in their own families or neighborhoods.

Exploring nontraditional ways to fulfill intimacy needs is not unique to the younger generation. Alternative lifestyles are chosen by middle-aged persons, especially those engaged in collectivist living arrangements (Dressel and Avant 1978). Alternative living patterns among the elderly are also coming to light. In this regard, it is interesting to note that more than a decade ago, in the 1970 census, over 18,000 couples aged 65 and above listed themselves as unmarried and living together (Dressel and Avant 1978, p. 14).

An adult's motivations for selecting nontraditional living arrangements may be at least as numerous as those of an adolescent, if not more so. Pooling resources and extending support systems are not uncommon reasons for experimenting with different patterns of living. Older adults sometimes substitute cohabitation for marriage so that they can maintain maximum social security benefits and widows' pensions (Dressel and Avant 1978, p. 23). Incorporating or combining nuclear families into modified communal systems can expand the number of adults available to care for children and, theoretically, can enhance the basis of both physical and emotional support. Feelings of loneliness or boredom within a relationship prompt people to try new approaches. An oppressive sense that a relationship is stifling one's personal growth also leads individuals to experiment with alternatives. Sometimes alternative patterns are forced upon individuals, as when singlehood and single parenthood are a result of the death of a spouse or divorce. For some, a variation in living patterns may represent a way of trying to make the promises of an idealized romantic vision finally come true—if not within marriage, then outside of it.

Before we examine some of these nontraditional living patterns, it might be well to recall the origins of what we now regard as the traditional view of marriage and family. We shall see that the United States has always encompassed a number of living styles, and even those ideals concerning marriage that we identify as the most widely accepted have never been fully realized in practice.

THE FAMILY: TRADITIONAL AND CONTEMPORARY PERSPECTIVES

Some kind of "family" seems to exist in all known human societies—whether it consists of a husband, a wife, and children; a group of kinsfolk who cooperate economically and share a common dwelling; or some other grouping. Traditionally, families seem to have had several apparently universal characteristics. Kathleen Gough (1977, p. 24) cites these qualities as typical of traditional families:

- Sexual relations and marriage are forbidden between close relatives.
- Men and women cooperate through a division of labor assigned by sex roles.
- Marriage is a "socially recognized, durable, although not necessarily lifelong, relationship," from which arises "social fatherhood," a special bond between a man and his children.
- Men, in general, have higher status and authority in their families than women do, although older women may have some authority over younger men.

In Western culture, the traditional nuclear family is thought to include a lifelong, legal, sexually exclusive relationship between a man and a woman, with children, where the male is the primary provider and ultimate authority (Macklin 1980, p. 905). In the United States today, there are numerous variations on this theme. As the 1979 census indicates, there has been a gradual increase in the percentage of persons residing in single-parent or dual-career families, as well as an increase in those living alone or in households composed of unrelated individuals (Bureau of the Census 1979, Table A). Today, sexual exclusivity and the ultimate authority of the male are values that many families have rejected. Even before the twentieth century, however, notions concerning sexual behavior and the roles of husband and wife underwent many variations.

Family historians are not in complete agreement, but they generally believe that variations in family ideals and in actual husband-wife behavior have not been unusual in the United States. John Demos (1977) characterizes the changing nature of families from colonial America to the twentieth century as a complex interaction between the family unit and the greater society. Changing economic and political circumstances have always had a powerful influence on individual families. According to Demos, in colonial times there were strong bonds between the family and the community at large. The family was a microcosm of the larger society, producing and exchanging goods, providing vocational education and training, and occasionally supplying social services, such as when an elderly person, an orphan, or even a criminal would be placed with a family. Contrary to popular belief, colonial families were nuclear, rather than extended. The newly married couple were expected to leave the family home and set up a new household. They did not typically live with parents and other relatives.

Throughout the history of the United States, the pendulum has taken some significant swings between individual freedom and community control. The 1700s were dominated by a spirit of adventure and freedom in the settling of the frontier. Since women had no legal or property rights at this time, they needed men to support and protect them. But the men needed capable wives to clothe and feed them and to produce and rear children who would help them on the land. As Morton Hunt suggests, marriage was a thoroughly functional mechanism during this period (1972, p. 401). Yet during this same period, women managed taverns, inns, stores, and shops and occasionally had careers in publishing, journalism, or medicine (Demos 1976). Women interacted easily and informally with men in all sorts of everyday encounters.

The 1800s and early 1900s represented a swing away from the expansionist, adventurous mood of the country (Demos 1976, p. 18). The status of women declined, children were subject to strong discipline, and sexual mores became more restrictive. It was not until the twentieth century that changing social conditions were once again propitious for greater equality between the sexes and experimentation in patterns of intimate relationships.

The types of lifestyles that are emerging in the United States today are the result of numerous forces set in motion much earlier. The decline in *familism*, or family solidarity, and an increase in individualism began when the United States industrialized. Industrialization exerted a centrifugal force, pulling family members outside the home. Compulsory education drew children away from home for longer periods of time and instilled values that were sometimes contrary to those of the family of origin. The authoritative father was not around to provide discipline or deliberate on family matters. In the twentieth century, technological advances and improved contraceptive methods have combined with relative affluence to further alter the status and structure of the family. Women and children have slowly gained more power to control their own lives, and this shift in the exercise of power has enabled men to be less rigidly tied to a work ethic and a breadwinning role. With less energy required to meet physical and security needs, greater resources are now being devoted to personal development and even the pursuit of pleasure (Macklin 1980, pp. 905–906).

The power of the social control that once existed in rural America has weakened or vanished in today's urban society. While some groups seek to reassert those controls and small numbers of individuals choose to join cults and other tightly controlled communities, there is widespread support for personal change and growth—within marriage and outside of it. Those boundaries that now exist seem to be imposed *not* by the community at large, but by couples themselves.

EXTRAMARITAL RELATIONSHIPS

A significant percentage of couples who marry do not "forsake all others." Kinsey's data made this fact clear. He found that about 50 percent of married men had engaged in extramarital sexual relations, and about 42 percent of married women had either petted or had coitus with partners other than their husbands (1948, 1953). More recent research tends to put the figure somewhat lower for men, but about the same for women (Hunt 1974).

Cuber and Harroff (1966), in their study of sexual behavior among the "affluent," found that husbands and wives reported about the same incidence of involvement in extramarital affairs. Francoeur and Francoeur (1974) argue that the college generation is in the vanguard of the sexual revolution. Their study of unmarried students added this nuance concerning college students: A sample of 566 unmarried students at the University of South Carolina were asked if they thought they would engage in extramarital sex after they were married. The researchers found that the more sexually active students were before marriage, the greater the likelihood that they believed they would engage in extramarital sex after marriage. Those who said they would probably engage in extramarital sex said they believed they would find it more rewarding, more emotionally and sexually satisfying, than sexual relations with their marital partner. The authors noted, however, that "this tendency to rationalize projected EMS [extramarital sexual] behavior may be due largely to a lack of foresight about the possible negative outcomes" (Bukstel, Roeder, Killmann, Laughlin, and Sotile 1978, p. 339).

Even though many individuals do not engage in extramarital sex, societal attitudes toward extramarital relations have changed to accept it as an option. Our society no longer appears locked into the concept that adultery is an inexcusable act. The term "adultery" itself has been replaced by synonyms such as "infidelity," "an affair," or "playing around." In the past, a spouse might view adultery as automatic grounds for divorce. Today, an extramarital relationship need not end the marital relationship, and in some cases, spouses report that such extramarital relationships have indeed enriched the marriage.

Fantasies and flirtations involving people outside the marriage are also more widely accepted now. If we look at the several forms of "infidelity" suggested by sociologist Jessie Bernard (1977), it appears that all married people may be "unfaithful" at some point in their marriage. Bernard defines the forms of infidelity as follows:

1. Flirtation, a kind of nonserious behavior that does not compromise the sexually monogamous marital relationship
2. Occasional, unplanned, or irregular sexual relations outside marriage that the participants view as not threatening the marital relationship and that may only trigger a residue of guilt
3. A regular, nonserious "playful relationship which arises between working men and women who use the lunch hour for their relationship at her apartment" (p. 134). The relationship has the potential for becoming serious, thus straining or perhaps ending the extramarital relationship.
4. A semiserious relationship that, while not threatening the marriage of the male partner (with the female usually being single), remains a stable, ongoing extramarital relationship
5. The affair, a relationship involving a serious degree of "monogamous" commitment by each partner, which begins with a high degree of erotic activity but which, over time, moves to a comfortable arrangement
6. "Fantasied infidelity"—the imagined sexual relations with another partner. With the sexual imagery present in movies, television advertising and programming, as well as the overt sexuality in many magazines, it is difficult to believe that there exists a man or a woman who has not had a fleeting "fantasied infidelity."

7. A deep, noncoital, but nevertheless intimate relationship between a man and a woman that involves "a profound sharing of the self" (p. 136)

Recognizing that the emphasis in interpersonal relations was shifting away from strict fidelity toward individual growth, George and Nena O'Neill outlined a new model for marriage that they called "open marriage." They conceived of the model as a design for personal growth within the marital arrangement that eliminated some of the restrictions previously considered an integral part of monogamy (1972, p. 43). In reviewing the O'Neills' theories, Dale Wachowiak and Hannelore Bragg (1980) listed eight key characteristics that the O'Neills used to define an open marriage:

1. Here-and-now living combined with realistic expectations
2. A greater emphasis on the personal privacy of the mates
3. Open and honest communications including fantasy sharing, self-disclosure, and productive fighting
4. Role flexibility
5. Open companionship, which permits each partner to become involved in deep, personal, even sexual relationships with other individuals
6. Equality for both partners in terms of power as well as responsibility
7. A value on the identity or uniqueness of the individual
8. An assumption of mutual trust

The O'Neills had not ruled out the possibility of sexual companionship outside the marriage. They viewed this as a matter for a couple to decide after they have achieved and experienced "mature love, have real trust, and are able to expand themselves, to love and enjoy others and to bring that love and pleasure back into their marriage without jealousy" (1972, p. 257). Although the vast majority of the book *Open Marriage* deals with matters other than extramarital relationships, the focus of public attention was directed at the O'Neills' idea that open marriage, under certain circumstances, could logically lead to sexually open marriage.

Sexually open marriage (SOM) requires full disclosure of extramarital relationships and full acceptance by the respective spouses. Although this type of arrangement has not yet been thoroughly researched, preliminary accounts indicate that a sexually open marriage is even more difficult to maintain than a marriage in which extramarital affairs are kept clandestine. Most of the data on extramarital behavior refers to affairs that are kept secret from one's spouse. Regardless of their behavior, most couples seem to like the new ideal of having room in the marriage for personal growth, but they do not usually condone extramarital sex.

Wachowiak and Bragg (1980) conducted a study of upper-middle-class couples. They found that the more "open" a marriage was (in the terms described above), the greater the satisfaction with the marriage. This was true especially among those women who were older, had children, and had been married longer. But openness was not construed by this group as freedom to have affairs: fully 96 percent of the people interviewed said that "extramarital sex would never be tolerated in our marriage" (p. 59).

We are still faced with the disparity between what people *say* and what people *do*. Does "never be tolerated" mean that extramarital sexual relations would automatically cause the marriage to fail, or are these people being hypocritical? Hunt offers us a particularly insightful explanation:

A . . . thoughtful answer might be that the majority of people have always experienced extramarital desires, at least from time to time, and kept them hidden; in today's climate of open discussion these desires are being manifested in the form of discussion and of an unconcealed appetite for vicarious experience. At the same time most people continue to disapprove of such behavior because they believe that when it becomes a reality rather than a fantasy, it undermines and endangers the most important human relationship in their lives. (1974, p. 256)

Swinging

Swinging (sometimes referred to as "wife swapping") is the term used to define an exchange of sexual partners by married couples for casual sexual encounters. Researchers estimate that approximately two percent of the U.S. population has engaged in swinging (Hunt 1974), although about 75 percent of the couples who experiment with this variation of sexually open marriage drop out within one year (Murstein 1978). It should be noted that many couples engaged in swinging do not define this activity as extramarital sex, since they share the experience as a married pair.

Gilmartin (1977), in a comparison of 200 swinging and nonswinging couples, concluded that swingers interact more frequently with friends but have less contact with kin and neighbors, are more detached from religious and political activities, report more frequent intercourse with spouses, and rate their marital happiness higher than nonswingers. In gathering data on personal history, Gilmartin found that swingers report less gratifying relationships with their parents, begin heterosexual activities at an earlier age, go steady more often, marry at an earlier age, and are more likely to have been previously divorced. According to Gilmartin (1977) and Henschel (1973), it is husbands who typically introduce their wives to the idea of swinging. Actual participation in this activity may be the culmination of the gradual decision-making process beginning with negative responses to the idea, which change over time and under pressure from the spouse, to partial acceptance of swinging on a limited trial basis.

If the first experiences are traumatic, further participation is not likely. If the initial experiments with this lifestyle are gratifying, however, the couple is likely to include swinging activities in their relationship to a greater degree.

While it is difficult to assess the effects of swinging on the relationship of a particular couple, one major factor that seems to influence the outcome of the activity is the extent to which spouses come to agree on the appropriateness of this lifestyle (Macklin 1980; Gilmartin 1977). Some therapists have reported negative consequences of swinging, especially when one spouse (usually the wife) feels coerced into the activity by the other spouse under threat of terminating their marriage if acceptance of the swinging idea is not forthcoming (Holtzer 1980).

Denfield (1974), in a survey of marriage and family counselors, found that ex-swinging clients report such problems as jealousy, guilt, competing emotional attachments, and fear of discovery by children and neighbors as reasons for dropping out. It was also found that while swinging may lead to an initial improvement in the marital relationship, such positive outcomes are often only temporary.

COMMUTER MARRIAGES

Professional men and women who have their own careers in different locations sometimes choose to maintain separate households after marriage. Such couples are content to be together on weekends or for several weeks at a time after a long separation. This kind of arrangement, like living together, is not entirely new. Consider sea captains, traveling salesmen, truck drivers, and airline pilots, who had to spend a good part of the year away from their families. In those cases the woman kept the home fires burning. The difference in the new commuter marriages is the presence and pulls of *two* careers. Both the wife and the husband are required by their jobs to be in different geographical locations. Rather than having one spouse sacrifice a career, both agree to spend briefer periods of time together. The number of people who have the economic means and the emotional stamina to conduct this type of marriage may be small, but the entry of women into high-level jobs and demanding careers is making commuter marriages less rare. (Some of the problems and satisfactions of dual-career marriages are covered in Box 7.3, pages 216–218.)

SINGLEHOOD

When Manfred Kuhn conducted a study of unmarried people in the 1950s, he concluded that for much of his sample, failure to marry reflected a high rate of personal and social problems, including hostility toward marriage

Singlehood represents an increasingly chosen life pattern. (Terry McKoy)

and members of the opposite sex, emotional fixation on one or both parents, and unwillingness to assume responsibility. Other factors were less psychological and more social and environmental: poor health, poverty, physical unattractiveness, and geographical, educational, or occupational isolation (Stein 1978, p. 385). More recently, however, sociologists have reported more positive motivations among people committed to singlehood. The single men and women studied by Peter Stein (1978), for example, commonly reported that they rejected marriage because it restricts personal growth and creates a confining, unrealistic social identity. Other voluntarily single people interviewed by Stein perceived a sense of isolation and loneliness in the exclusive relationship of marriage and complained that married couples don't have close friends. In Chapter 14 we shall explore the life cycle of singles.

A larger percentage of people are choosing singlehood now than in previous decades. Current predictions indicate that eight to nine percent of those now in their twenties will experience a lifetime of singlehood, as opposed to four to five percent of those now 50 years old (Glick 1976). There are more singles now, and the status of the single person is viewed more positively. Contributing to the increase in singlehood are at least three factors: (1) new vistas for women, including opportunities for higher education and an expanding range of lifestyle and employment options; (2) more women than men of marrigeable age; and (3) the increasing ease with which singles can enjoy active social and sexual lives (Macklin 1980).

Singlehood is likely to have differing effects for those who choose it than for those who want to marry but don't find a suitable mate. As singles become a larger segment of the population, we should have more information on its effects. Currently, the research suggests that long-term singlehood is often a more positive state for women than for men. Women who remain single tend to be superior to single men in terms of education, occupation, and mental health (Macklin 1980, p. 907).

COHABITATION

Variations and adaptations of traditional marriage—such as open marriage, swinging, and commuter marriage—have been proposed and are being tried by some couples as means of enhancing marriage and family life, as possibilities, perhaps, for reaching the contemporary goals of personal growth and the growth and enhancement of relationships. We have little evidence so far about either the effectiveness or the harmfulness of

Cohabitation is often a premarital or postmarital interim arrangement rather than a substitute for marriage. (Jean-Claude Lejeune)

such variations. For the most part, however, such possibilities are intended not to destroy or replace the marital and family system, but rather to add openness and make its boundaries more flexible, in the hope of developing more viable, satisfying relationships.

Cohabitation, more popularly known as "living together," is more difficult to categorize in its relation to marriage and family models. According to Yllo, additional terms—including "quasi-marriage," "trial marriage," and the older phrase "shacking up"—are also used to refer to a more or less permanent relationship in which two unmarried persons of the opposite sex share a living facility and a sexual relationship without a legal contract (1978, p. 40).

Living together is a practice that cuts across the generations, but it is more common among the young. In a comprehensive review of the demographic data, Glick and Spanier (1980) chart a sharp upswing in cohabitation. There were an estimated 1.1 million unmarried men-women couples living together in 1978. This represented a substantial 19-percent increase between March 1977 and March 1978. About 50 percent of the unmarried men and 60 percent of the unmarried women had been previously married. Divorce accounted for some of the rise in cohabitation. But of the never-married women and men living together, 85 percent were under 35 years of age. The under-35 never-married women "tended to be employed and better educated than their married or previously married counterparts. Blacks constituted a disproportionately large share of the number of couples living together outside of marriage, although a large majority of all cohabiting couples are white" (p. 30).

Why is there this increase in the number of couples living together? Glick and Spanier offer this explanation:

Increasing feedom in adult behavior, less pressure to marry at traditional normative ages, and a greater acceptance of unmarried cohabitation as a life style are evidently providing a context in which this way of living is becoming increasingly accepted. . . . (1980, p. 30)

The research on cohabitation is quite recent and often involves only small regional samples (most notably college student populations). Studies comparing cohabiting and married couples show that individuals who live together tend to see themselves as more liberal, particularly concerning sex roles and sexual equality. They are also less likely to have religious affiliations. But few other differences have been found. Cohabitation prior to marriage does not seem to make a significant difference in the stability or success of a marriage. Rather than being a substitute for marriage, living together generally appears to be an alternative that precedes marriage or follows the breakup of an existing marriage. It is, according to sociologist Bert Adams, premarital or postmarital rather than antimarital (1980, p. 396). In a regional study of university students, Bower and Christopherson (1977) found that about the same proportion of those who had cohabited intended to marry as did those who had not. For some couples, then, living together is viewed as almost a step or stage in the process of mate selection or courtship, a sort of testing period to check compatibility and readiness for marriage (1977, p. 452). In a national study of 2,510 males, Clayton and Voss found that many of the men saw their cohabitation arrangements as preludes to marriage, or as interim arrangements after a divorce, not as substitutes for marriage (1977, p. 283).

When cohabitation is viewed as a prelude to marriage or a step in the courtship process, it resembles a trial marriage, what Margaret Mead has called "marriage in two steps." Mead distinguishes two kinds of marriage: The first allows for experimentation with the couple relationship—a trial period—designed for individual and couple growth within a time-limited commitment period, through a two- or three-year renewable contract. The second step is the "parental marriage," which is entered into if the couple decide to have a child. Parental marriage requires a more permanent commitment and closely resembles the nuclear family system as we currently know it (1966, pp. 48–49). These two types of marriages can become two steps in the same marriage, step one being experimental, step two being parental.

Living together is an increasingly commonplace arrangement for Americans, but many young people still find their parents upset about cohabitation and sometimes unwilling to accept the arrangement. "Trouble with parents" is a problem, especially for younger cohabiting couples, as Macklin has documented in regard to college populations (1972, p. 468). Some have suggested that trial marriage proposals that require a form of contract or license might reduce the opposition from parents, from other family members, and from those in society with a more traditional bias.

So far there is no widely used legal or social sanction for cohabitation, although a few "palimony" cases have been won that awarded sums of money to women who had lived with men, usually celebrities, for an extended period. Ordinary people who live together need to be aware of difficulties that may arise from their status, especially when the question of dividing up joint property arises. In her book *Living Together: A Guide to the Law for Unmarried Couples* (1976), attorney Barbara Hirsch explores the many legal ramifications of extended cohabitation—what she calls "consortium." She proposes a 14-page legal contract that specifies financial obligations and privileges, payments of taxes, rent, medical bills, food, and clothing. The contract makes clear what happens if the consorts split up, or if one dies, or if conception occurs, or if one wants a child and the other doesn't. While such a contract is just a hypothetical document, it proves that parties who live together take on many of the problems and responsibilities that face a married couple, but they enjoy none of the legal protections of marriage.

COMMUNES

Today's communes may seem to be a radical departure from the American family traditions we have traced, but communes do have precedents in the utopian communities of the eighteenth and nineteenth centuries. These early communities proposed radical alterations in family structure, ranging from the celibacy practiced by the Shakers to the polygamy of the early Mormons to the complex marital structure of the Oneida community.

Rosabeth Moss Kanter studied some 30 nineteenth-century American communes, including Brook Farm, where American writer Nathaniel Hawthorne lived and which he fictionalized in *The Blithedale Romance*. Nine of the communities—the successful ones—lasted 33 years or more, while the other 21 (counted as "failures") lasted less than 16 years and averaged only 4 years. The profile of a typical successful community differed from that of the unsuccessful ones. In successful communities the key was homogeneity, or similarity in status, attitude, purpose, and most other aspects of life. Geographical isolation heightened the community's sense of its own territory and discouraged friendships with people outside the group, people whose attitudes and goals would be different.

Romantic love or close friendships between two persons were discouraged in favor of a more impartial, diffuse affection spread throughout the community. This was made easier by the fact that the group was fairly homogenous (they had similar backgrounds and viewpoints), by regular group contact, and by rituals emphasizing the communion of the whole group. The group's homogeneity was further intensified by an underlying ideological or utopian political or moral basis that the community shared. That is, most successful communities had an elaborate system of beliefs, rather like a religion, that provided purpose, justification, and meaning, as well as an ultimate guide for decisions and disagreements. Successful communities also had strong, charismatic leaders, who symbolized the community's values. When a member showed disagreement or deviance or lack of commitment, he or she would be criticized in sessions of mutual criticism.

Conformity to a nonconformist ideology was one characteristic of the more successful early communes; commitment through sacrifice and investments was another in many successful, long-lived communities. Because participants invested all their money and property in the community, they had a high stake in its fate. To join the group, a person had to

Shared ritual at Findhorn commune (Jerry Howard, Positive Images)

undergo a strenuous process of conversion to the community's values, just as full-fledged members of a church or religious group are sometimes required to be confirmed. There was communistic sharing of property and labor (Kanter 1977, pp. 566–567).

Kanter has studied not only the early communes in American history, but also their recent descendants. She concludes that today's communes "seek to recreate a romanticized version of the extended family" (p. 565), in which interpersonal relationships are intimate, participatory, and meaningful, rather than isolating, meaningless, fragmented, and machinelike. Most communes today are small, with 6 to 40 people. Most lack any kind of political or religious platform or even mundane daily routines. Their motto is "Do your own thing." Child rearing in most is collective, so that all children can say that all adults in the community are their parents. Most seek, and perhaps succeed in creating, a family-style intimacy and warmth. As a member of a Taos, New Mexico, commune commented: "It's really groovy waking up and knowing that forty-eight people love you." Although most communes today do not demand strict conformity to an ideology or routine, they typically do reject other ways of life. Commune members find a common purpose and a sense of cohesion in shared values, symbols, and rituals.

The number and duration of communes vary, with some springing up to meet a certain political or social need and then disappearing. Conover (1975) has estimated the existence of 45,000 such communities, with approximately 755,000 residents. Some communes—notably the kibbutzim in Israel—are stable and long-lived. "The failure rate of communes is high," Kanter tells us, "but so is the failure rate of small businesses. And no one is suggesting that small business is not a viable organizational form" (1977, p. 577).

SAME-SEX INTIMATE RELATIONSHIPS

Cultural attitudes toward homosexuality have varied widely across history and national boundaries. The Greeks romanticized homosexuality; Plato and Sappho idealized it. The Romans were less romantic about homosexuality, regarding it as a purely physical attraction (Hunt 1959). When the survival of the culture is threatened, reproduction becomes a prime concern and homosexuality is condemned. This was the case with Biblical Jews. Old Testament injunctions against homosexuality became part of Christian tradition (Rowse 1977). It is only in recent decades, when overpopulation has become a serious concern, that many Western cultures have adopted more liberal attitudes toward homosexual choices.

Until very recently homosexuality in the United States was almost universally viewed as "deviant behavior"—and still is regarded that way by a substantial portion of American society. The first significant change in that attitude toward homosexuality came with the research into the sexual practices of American men and women conducted by Kinsey and his associates, first on men in 1948, then on women in 1953.

Kinsey, Pomeroy, and Martin (1948, p. 638) devised what they called a heterosexual-homosexual scale. It was a zero-to-six rating system:

0. Exclusively heterosexual with no homosexual experience
1. Predominantly heterosexual, only incidental homosexual experience
2. Predominantly heterosexual, but more than incidental homosexual experience
3. Equal heterosexual and homosexual experience
4. Predominantly homosexual, but more than incidental heterosexual experience
5. Predominantly homosexual, but incidental heterosexual experience
6. Exclusively homosexual

The research findings caused a furor (Pomeroy 1972). Among the many findings that shocked people was the percentage of men who had had at least one overt homosexual experience that included orgasm: 37 percent. Thirteen percent of males had more homosexual than heterosexual experiences, and 18 percent of males had about equal homosexual and

Same-sex intimate relationships are becoming more visible in the United States today. (Susan Lapides)

heterosexual experiences; 4 percent were exclusively homosexual. The incidence of homosexual experience in women was found to be less than that of men. Twenty-eight percent of the women said they had a homosexual arousal or orgasm by the age of 45, but only 13 percent actually achieved orgasm through same-sex activity. Less than 3 percent of the women were exclusively homosexual.

The implication was obvious—if such a significant proportion of the population had homosexual experiences, could such sexual behavior be labeled deviant? Sociologist Howard Becker insisted that the deviant label told us nothing about the individual's behavior:

Deviance is not a quality of the act a person commits, but rather a consequence of the application by others of rules and sanctions to an "offender." The deviant is one to whom that label has successfully been applied; deviant behavior is behavior that people so label. (1963, p. 9)

Another question that seemed to trouble psychologists and sociologists was the degree of deviation. Kinsey had recognized a wide range of homosexual involvement, but the label "homosexual" did not indicate whether a person was exclusively homosexual or only occasionally preferred same-sex partners. Other research dispelled the notion that homosexuality was necessarily linked to psychological abnormality. Psychologist Evelyn Hooker studied a sample of 30 male homosexuals; except for their sexual preferences, Hooker argued that these men would be seen as normal (1957).

Although Kinsey may have brought the subject of homosexuality "out of the closet," few of his adherents followed his example. For the most part, the subject of homosexuality remained taboo. In 1951, "Donald Cory Webster" (a pseudonym) wrote *The Homosexual in America*, an autobiographical study that portrayed the homosexual as one more member of a minority, not that different from Jews in Nazi Germany, Catholics in Ulster, Protestants in Italy, or blacks in the United States or South Africa. Webster sought to describe what it was like to live as a member of a sexual minority—"the blind alleys and the dead-ends . . . the discrimination . . . the sneer, the joke, the abusive language . . . the humiliation and self-doubt . . . the struggle to maintain self-respect and group pride" (p. 4).

Almost 30 years later, the subject of homosexuality is coming out of the closet and homosexuals are openly demanding equal rights. The majority of the nation's homosexuals may still be afraid to admit who they are; perhaps only one percent of the homosexuals in this country are public about their sexual preference (*Time*, April 23, 1979). But homosexuals are more visible in our culture today.

An event that helped homosexuals to emerge as a social and political force occurred in June 1969. New York City police had conducted several raids on the Stonewall Inn, a Greenwich Village bar that catered to homosexuals. Taking a cue from the ongoing protests against the war in Vietnam, as well as public confrontations initiated by the civil rights movement, homosexuals clashed with police on the streets of New York City. This was the first time that avowed homosexuals protested what had been an ongoing policy of police harassment. The "gay rights" movement was born.

Today, persons who are obviously homosexual are portrayed on television and in movies. Historians, such as A. L. Rowse (1977), offer portraits of such prominent homosexuals as Leonardo da Vinci, Michelangelo, Tchaikovsky, Oscar Wilde, Marcel Proust, Somerset Maugham, Walt Whitman, and countless other artists, writers, economists, kings, and noblemen. The lives of Gertrude Stein and Virginia Woolf are dramatized, including their central lesbian relationships. Edmund White, traveling across the country, found homosexual communities in every major American city. In his book *States of Desire* (1980), White describes homosexual

communities from Portland to Miami Beach. In Chicago, New York, San
Francisco, Los Angeles, Houston, Boston, Kansas City, and Washington,
D.C., gay rights have become active political issues, with voters passing or
rejecting gay-rights measures. White suggests that regional characteristics
are reflected in the many different types of homosexual communities.

The diversity of homosexual life is confirmed by the studies of
homosexuals in the San Francisco Bay area (Bell and Weinberg 1979; Bell,
Weinberg, and Hammersmith 1981). In their 1979 work, *Homosexualities:
A Study of Diversities Among Men and Women*, Bell and Weinberg were
concerned with the variety of intimate same-sex relationships. (Findings
concerning sexual preference are discussed in Box 4.1, p. 99.) These researchers found that homosexual preference was not automatically tied to
one set of attitudes, values, or characteristics. The world of the homosexual, as sampled from one of the largest homosexual communities in the
United States, is not monolithic.

Based on their interviews and questionnaire reports from 979 men and
women, both black and white, Bell and Weinberg (1979) formulated five
categories of homosexuals.

1. "Closed-Coupled."   These were homosexual couples who were "closely
   bound together" and who looked to each other "rather than outsiders
   for sexual and interpersonal satisfactions." These couples, some of
   whom described themselves as "happily married," were found to have
   "superior adjustment," reported higher levels of sexual satisfaction,
   were "less tense . . . and more exuberant than the average respondent,"
   more self-accepting, and less depressed or lonely than the other respondents; in fact, they were "the happiest of all" (pp. 219–220).
2. "Open-Coupled."   Although these couples were living with a special sexual partner, they were "not happy with their circumstances and
   tended (despite spending a fair amount of time at home) to seek satisfactions with people outside their partnership." Sexual satisfaction was
   not as great as in the closed-couple arrangement. Both the men and the
   women sought a high degree of outside sexual contacts—behavior that
   concerned them because it put them in greater jeopardy of being arrested or publicly exposed. "Psychologically, they were about as happy,
   exuberant, depressed, tense, paranoid, or worrisome as the average
   homosexual respondent." Lesbians in the open-coupled group were
   found to have less self-acceptance than open-coupled heterosexuals or
   male homosexuals (pp. 221–222).
3. "Functionals."   "These men and women seem to organize their lives
   around their sexual experience." They had few sexual problems and
   engaged in a wide variety of sexual activities. "Of all the groups, they
   were the most interested in sex, the most exuberant, and the most
   involved with their friends." The men were "the most likely ever to

have been arrested, booked, or convicted for a 'homosexual' offense" because of their high degree of sexual activity. Bell and Weinberg do not single out the "Functionals" as an ideal type; they note that these men "are more tense, unhappy, and lonely than their Closed-Coupled counterparts" (pp. 223–224).

4. "Dysfunctionals." This was the group that conformed to the stereotype of the "tormented homosexual." Not only did they have trouble functioning sexually, but they were also more likely to have been robbed, beaten, and subjected to extortion; they reported more work problems due to their sexual orientation. "The Dysfunctional lesbians were the least exuberant and the most likely to have needed long-term professional help for an emotional problem, and their male counterparts were more lonely, worrisome, paranoid, depressed, tense, and unhappy than any of the other men" (p. 225).

5. "Asexuals." These men and women had little or no sexual activity with others. They were "less overt about their homosexuality," had fewer friends, and were lonely. "The asexual lesbians were most apt to have sought professional help concerning their sexual orientation but also to have given up counseling quickly, and they had the highest incidence of suicidal thoughts (not necessarily related to their homosexuality)" (pp. 226–227).

Bell and Weinberg stress that almost half of the white homosexuals have no regret over being homosexual. However, a closer look at their statistics shows that regret is expressed by the other half of the subjects surveyed, although in only 6 percent of those questioned was it described as severe (McCracken 1979). There are no comparable statistics offered for heterosexuals, but we do have comparative data on suicide rates. The suicide rate among homosexuals is markedly higher: 18 percent of white homosexual males report at least one suicide attempt, while white heterosexual males report a 3-percent suicide-attempt rate; 25 percent of white lesbians had tried suicide at least once, as compared to 10 percent of white female heterosexuals (Bell and Weinberg 1979, p. 453). Promiscuity is also more prevalent among male homosexuals than among male heterosexuals, with the majority of white homosexual males (79 percent) surveyed by Bell and Weinberg reporting that more than half of their homosexual contacts were with strangers. Contact with strangers is rare (6 percent) among lesbians. We need additional research to indicate to what extent public attitudes toward homosexuality and promiscuity may have a bearing on regret and suicide rates.

Until recently, most research focused on male homosexuals. The 1970s, however, brought a growing interest in lesbians, including descriptions of how one acknowledges a lesbian identity and the implications of assuming such an identity in our society (Tanner 1978; Lewis 1979). Bell and Weinberg noticed marked differences between male homosexuals and lesbians. Sexual contact with strangers is prevalent for the majority of male homosexuals, but it is rare among lesbians. There is also greater sexual fidelity among lesbian partners. Although male homosexuals and lesbians continue to encounter restrictive legislation and other forms of discrimination, their status has improved markedly in the past decade.

In the early 1970s, the American Psychiatric Association voted to remove homosexuality from its list of mental disorders. Today, gay rights organizations exist to champion the rights of homosexuals. In some areas, the homosexual vote is actively courted by politicians. Increasingly, nonjudgmental reports on male homosexuality and lesbianism are being disseminated. In 1980, Masters and Johnson reported on sexual response among homosexuals, confirming the fact that homosexuals were physiologically the same as heterosexuals in their sexual response. Thus, the stages of orgasm we described in Chapter 4 also describe orgasmic response for male homosexuals and lesbians. Masters and Johnson compared homosexual activity with that of heterosexuals and found homosexuals more understanding of their partners' sexual needs, perhaps because they have more knowledge of the same sex (1980).

Controversy continues to rage concerning the causes of homosexuality and the extent to which homosexuals should be accorded equal rights. Information gathered in the past decade, particularly the studies conducted by Bell and colleagues, suggest that homosexuality is a pattern of feelings and behavior established before adolescence. Orientation toward same-sex relations is not a decision made in adulthood, although that preference may not be openly admitted until adulthood.

Sexual preference appears to be less vulnerable to peer influence and other experiences than Kinsey and others had believed. Despite the fact that Masters and Johnson (1980) reported that the homosexuals they treated who wished to turn to heterosexuality had a 50-percent chance of making this change, most therapists and much of the important recent research suggest that sexual orientation is not likely to be reversed. Although some homosexuals have occasional heterosexual experiences and some heterosexuals have occasional homosexual experiences, the basic preference does not represent a conscious or changeable decision, such as a decision to live in a commune for a period of time. A preference for same-sex relations is therefore unlike other types of choices we have discussed in this chapter. Homosexuality represents "a statement from and about the deepest aspects of one's self and the conscious or unconscious attempt to honor them" (Bell et al. 1981, p. 222). (See Box 4.1 for a more detailed discussion of sexual preference.)

Careful, unbiased investigations of same-sex relations are helping to dispel misconceptions concerning homosexuality and alleviating certain injustices that homosexuals have experienced in our predominantly heterosexual society.

CONCLUSIONS

There are those who argue that our society has gone too far, become too permissive, self-indulgent, or decadent. It may well be that these excesses (if, indeed, they are excesses) are a product of our political-economic system. As social critic George Will (1980) has put it, "Capitalism undermines traditional social structures and values; it is a relentless engine of change, a revolutionary inflamer of appetites, enlarger of expectations, diminisher of patience." A system that encourages freedom in the economic marketplace cannot expect its citizens to reject freedom in the social marketplace. The history of totalitarian governments shows us that they restrict freedom in the social as well as economic marketplace. It was no mere accident that Nazi Germany chose homosexuals as one of a number of groups singled out for extermination.

Yet the existence of so many other lifestyles and life choices places the family composed of husband, wife, and children in a new and more relativistic position. They are practically a minority group. Mom and Dad cannot insist that theirs is the only choice—or even the only choice that can bring happiness. The existence of all these options may seem to undermine the family as we have traditionally defined it. Looked at in another way, however, communes and cohabitation, open marriage, and the many same-sex couples who form long-lasting relationships are examples of people trying to make families work. Each of us, in his or her own way, tries to meet the universal challenge of finding human connections, sharing vulnerability, and experiencing intimacy. We have this yearning in common.

SUMMARY

1. The main purposes of this chapter are to discuss factors that influence the styles or patterns of intimate relating; to explore the traditional marriage and family arrangement and some contemporary variations; and to focus on lifestyle patterns whose structures or goals differ significantly from those of traditional or contemporary marriage and family relationships.

2. Human beings have a need for close, personal interaction with other humans—for intimacy, belonging, affection. The patterns of relationships for fulfilling this need are strongly influenced by cultural values, available role models, and social institutions that support and promote certain patterns and restrict or prohibit others. Changes in society and in one's personal life, combined with the desire to improve or enhance

intimate relationships, may encourage experimentation with different lifestyle alternatives at various times during the life cycle.

3. The concept of family seems to exist in all known human societies, although its structure and functions vary. An analysis of the American family from colonial times to the present illustrates how family relationships and roles have varied according to changing social and economic conditions. The small nuclear family of contemporary America, with its emphasis on emotional and physical intimacy, nurturance, and support of individual development, is largely a response to industrialization, affluence, and the relaxation of community control.

4. Some proposed contemporary variations in marriage and family patterns are intended to increase the fulfillment of intimacy needs, to motivate greater achievement of the ideals of the nuclear family. Proposals such as open marriage and swinging are designed to modify, but not replace, more traditional marital and family patterns.

5. Research on cohabitation arrangements suggests that this lifestyle pattern is viewed by most proponents as a stage in the courtship process or as an interim living situation rather than as a replacement for marriage. Although various trial marriage models have been proposed with the goal of obtaining societal approval and some legal protection for living-together partners, these attempts to formalize the cohabitation alternative have not been implemented in the United States.

6. Other lifestyle patterns, such as communes and singlehood, differ significantly in structure and goals from traditional and contemporary concepts of marriage and family. These patterns may provide viable alternatives for some individuals.

7. Until recently, homosexuality was a choice that involved social stigma and ostracism. Attitudes concerning homosexuality are in a state of change, with a general improvement in the status of male homosexuals and lesbians and a greater appreciation for individual differences among homosexuals.

KEY CONCEPTS

Relationship needs	Commuter marriage
Traditional nuclear family	Singlehood
Open marriage	Cohabitation
Sexually open marriage	Homosexuality

QUESTIONS

1. Discuss your view of the ideal pattern or patterns for fulfilling intimacy needs during the life cycle. What factors in your background most strongly influenced your selection of this pattern as ideal?

2. Based on the information presented in this chapter, discuss the strengths and weaknesses of the traditional marriage and family systems in the United States.

3. Which contemporary proposals for modifying the traditional nuclear family, such as open marriage, sexually open marriage, or swinging, do you think have the most likelihood of success in terms of greater achievement of intimacy? Explain the reasons for your answer.

4. What are the primary benefits and problems you have experienced or observed in cohabitation arrangements? Do you think that a more formalized approach, such as a relationship contract, would help resolve the problems of this pattern?

5. On the basis of the information presented in this chapter, defend the argument that communes provide a more viable means than the contemporary nuclear family for satisfying human needs for nurturance, belonging, and affection.

6. Do you think that greater numbers of Americans are choosing to remain single? Interview some of your peers about their views on this question. What are the advantages and disadvantages of singlehood as a long-term lifestyle alternative?

7. In your perception, are homosexual relationships becoming more accepted or tolerated in the United States? What do you think is the prevailing attitude toward homosexuality among college students? What is your attitude toward homosexuality?

SUGGESTED READINGS

- Delora, Joann S., and Delora, Jack R., eds. *Intimate Life Styles: Marriage and Its Alternatives*. Pacific Palisades, Calif.: Goodyear Publishing Company, 1972. An important collection of articles that focus on the contemporary family, current alternatives, and future possibilities for intimate relating. In addition to several selections on the changing American family, this work also includes articles on mate-swapping, swinging, cohabitation, communes, singlehood, and lesbian relationships.

- Hart, Harold H., ed. *Marriage: For & Against*. New York: Hart Publishing Company, 1972. An easy-to-read collection of papers by a number of experts on the family who present their views on the benefits and problems of marriage in contemporary American society. Most contributors predict that marriage is likely to endure, though not without some important changes.

- Houriet, Robert. *Getting Back Together*. New York: Avon Books, 1972. This is a personal account of the author's travels to a number of communes and collectives in the late 1960s. In an interesting style and format, this book describes the ideals, structures, and functions of various communes across the United States during that time period. A good source for understanding the modern commune movement.

- Lewis, Sasha G. *Sunday's Women: A Report on Lesbian Life Today.* Boston: Beacon Press, 1979 (hardcover), 1981 (paper). An interesting and informative book that explores what it means to grow up lesbian in a heterosexual society. Lewis discusses issues in identity, presents various patterns of lesbian relationships, and explores lesbian perspectives on a changing societal and political environment.
- Mead, Margaret. "Marriage in Two Stages." *Redbook Magazine,* July 1966. A classic article by Mead that outlines her proposal of the trial marriage model. Provides good background information for considering a more formal definition of cohabitation arrangements that are viewed as part of the courtship process.
- National Council on Family Relations. *The Family Coordinator* 24, no. 4 (October 1975). The entire issue of this journal focuses on the exploration and analysis of variant family forms and lifestyles. Of particular interest are the articles on egalitarian relationships, communes, singlehood, and alternative family forms and the law.
- Stein, Peter J. *Single Life: Unmarried Adults in Social Context.* New York: St. Martin's Press, Inc., 1981. This work presents discussions about some of the major issues facing those who choose not to marry and those who are single as a result of divorce or death of a partner. Some of the areas covered are friendships, intimacy, work, and living arrangements.
- Weinberg, George. *Society and the Healthy Homosexual.* New York: Anchor Books, 1973. A revolutionary and humane book that discusses the prejudice against homosexuals prevalent in society today. Dr. Weinberg's goal is to help educate the public on the issue of homosexuality.

Part Two
Intimacy in Marriage

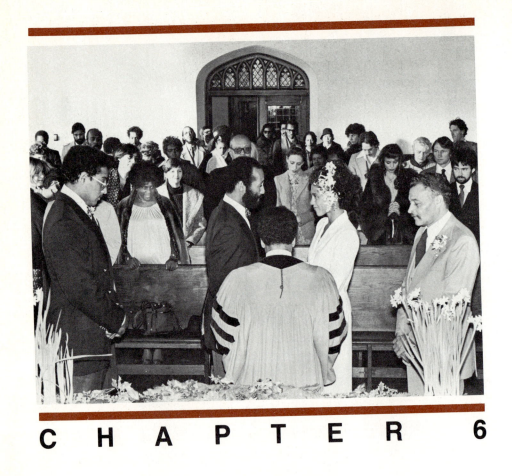

C H A P T E R 6

Mate Selection

SHE: I can't hear you—the music's too loud.

HE: Let's step outside. I don't care much for this music anyway.

SHE: Fine, neither do I.

HE: That's better. You look even prettier out here.

SHE: Flattery will get you everywhere. I swore I wouldn't come to another fraternity mixer and here I am.

HE: I can think of better ways to get to know someone, but I'm glad you didn't skip this one. Are you a freshman—freshwoman, freshperson?

SHE: First year home ec.

HE: That's refreshing. Everyone I meet nowadays is planning on going into business.

SHE: I've got plans, but mine are in the field of nutrition. I think we can do a lot to keep healthy by eating the right things. *(WITH A NERVOUS LAUGH)* Now I sound like my mother trying to get me to eat oatmeal.

HE: I agree with you and your mother. I like oatmeal and granola—also hot fudge sundaes. That's what I miss. We had a place back in Muskegon that had the best hot fudge you ever tasted.

SHE: Was it called Ricky's?

HE: How did you know?

SHE: I had a friend at camp who lived in Muskegon. I visited her one summer. Jenny Clifton was the best volleyball player and frog finder at Camp Wauconda.

HE: Jenny Clifton! I don't believe it. She was my first date.

SHE: Do you still see her?

HE: No—we lost touch when she went out East to school. Where are you from?

SHE: Akron, Ohio. Not much bigger than Muskegon, but I like smaller cities.

HE: Me, too. In fact, my dream is to become a psychiatric social worker and go back to Muskegon. The hospital there has an adolescent psychiatric unit.

SHE: That's nice. It's a pleasure to meet someone who's still interested in people, in helping and healing them.

HE: Instead of in becoming well-heeled.

SHE: . . . or rich heels.

HE: Can I take you for some frozen yogurt, with a little fudge on top? Just kidding. I'll go on the wagon—granola all the way.

SHE: I'd really like to have mine with fudge. Let's go.

INTRODUCTION

When two people marry, they are making one of the most important decisions of their lives. Yet how do such decisions get made? Take a woman who decides to marry a certain six-foot-tall, blue-eyed male. He likes tennis, Bach, the poems of Keats, and the novels of Mark Twain. He also earns his living as a lawyer in a prestigious law firm. Which one of these attributes caused her to choose him? Is it his good looks? His professional situation, which guarantees her wealth and status? Was this a culturally rooted recognition that he would share with her common attitudes and values? Or was the choice prompted by accidental circumstances—the fact that she met him at an all-Bach concert on a spring evening, and he quoted her favorite line from "Ode to a Nightingale"? Or is it a certain combination of personal and social attributes that makes one person believe the other is the right one? If similarity of backgrounds plays a part, why does one woman make an exotic match with a man of a different race and culture while her sister marries the boy next door?

Marital choice seems to be a unique blend of chance and destiny, of momentary feeling and weighty considerations involving far-reaching

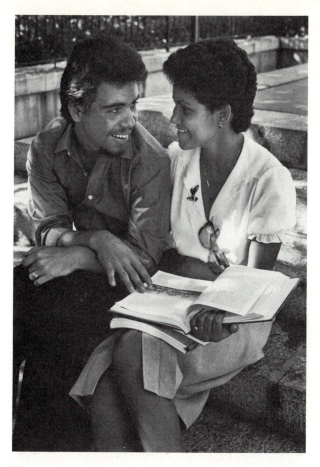

Mate selection is a choice that expresses one's deepest being.
(Janice Fullman, Picture Cube)

aims. Whether the selection of a mate is based more on chance or on careful reflection, the choice will have lifelong consequences; that is true even if the marriage does not last a lifetime. A person's mate becomes the most significant "other" in his or her life, the individual who most profoundly affects one's psychological state and one's social and economic status. Like career choice, mate selection is a choice that expresses one's deepest being.

It may also be the choice that most fully expresses the values and social organization of one's society. In some societies, social pressures against marriages across traditional class and racial lines are so great that only the most independent or rebellious spirits form such unions. Indeed, the very process by which mates are selected reflects in microcosm the larger social organization. As we shall see when we look at courtship practices in other cultures, the choice is not always simply a personal one. The world of English novelist Jane Austen was full of aunts and anxious parents eagerly arranging "suitable" marriages for charming heroines—"suitable" in terms of social class and wealth. Yet even in a closed society, personal factors—what Jane Austen called "sentiment"—play a part in marital arrangements. In this chaper we explore the balance of *social factors*— religion, race, ethnic group, and social class —and sentimental or *personal factors*—personality and physical attractiveness—in courtship and mate selection.

ENDOGAMY AND INTERMARRIAGE

The marriages in Jane Austen's novels, like most proper marriages of the eighteenth and nineteenth centuries, were *endogamous* marriages. "Endogamy" comes from the Greek *endo*, meaning "within," and *gamia*, meaning "act of marrying" or "to marry." Endogamy, then, is marriage within a specific tribe or similar social unit. The endogamous group is one bounded by socially significant lines of distinction, such as religion, and by values to which the group is deeply committed. *Intermarriage* is marriage between members of two such distinctive societies or subcultures (Cavan and Cavan 1975, p. 164). It can occur only when there are clear endogamous boundaries between different groups, subcultures, or societies.

There are various patterns of endogamy—cultural, religious, racial, and socioeconomic. We shall see how the various lines of distinction overlap and intersect as, for instance, religious endogamy results in ethnic endogamy or social class endogamy, and as some forms of intermarriage are allowed while others are not.

In-Groups and Out-Groups

Endogamy may be seen as the tendency of people, whether or not they are aware of social or group pressure, to marry within their own group. This tendency is based on what sociologists and psychologists sometimes call "in-group" feelings. An in-group in this sense is any group with which people feel identified, the group to which they belong, the one they long for when they are away from it. The in-group inspires attitudes and feelings of loyalty, devotion, sympathy, respect, and cooperation. Outsiders are generally regarded with indifference, repulsion, or antipathy (Cavan and Cavan 1975, p. 169). Recalling the concept of "significant others" described in Chapter 5, we can say that, at the very least, each person belongs to an in-group consisting of the significant others in his or her life. Most people, though, whether they are conscious of it or not, have in-group feelings about a broader group of persons.

The values defining an in-group can be religious, national, ethnic, professional, educational, or social. In the United States, identities are formed primarily by race, religion, ethnicity, and generation. Most groups with strong religious, ethnic, national, or class values tend to be endogamous: they marry within their own group and encourage or even require their children to do so as well. This not only preserves the group for future generations, but also strengthens the group's identity in the present. Marriage in these situations is as important to an individual's family and group as it is to the individual (Fullerton 1977, p. 250).

Societies vary in their degree of endogamy. Some groups demand or require that a member marry within the group, with a penalty of expulsion, rejection, or "disinheritance" for those who do not. Some groups or societies are permissive or indifferent to the marital partners of their members. Most religious and ethnic groups in the United States today simply *prefer* that members marry within the group and express disapproval of those who do not. In American society, innumerable groups coexist and interact, sometimes harmoniously, sometimes with tensions and conflict—Catholics, Protestants, Jews, Italians, Poles, blacks, whites, Chicanos, Cubans, wealthy and working-class people, young and old.

Intermarriage

Unless the endogamous society is physically isolated, intermarriage does, in fact, occur. Racial intermarriages occur everywhere in the world.

Endogamy is divisive; it encloses each person within the confines of its culture. Intermarriage is a breaching of these constraining boundaries. (Cavan and Cavan 1975, p. 165)

Throughout the history of the United States, large numbers of peaceful peoples of many races, nationalities, and religious and ethnic backgrounds have immigrated and frequently intermarried with the earlier, more settled inhabitants. These waves of immigration into a settled society with its own strong social organization often brought about intermarriages of a permanent, stable sort. However, the frequently forced sexual relations between whites and blacks resulted in interracial offspring who usually had the benefit of only one parent. Children of mixed unions may also be deprived of group support. Sometimes, as in the case of children born in Vietnam of GI fathers and Vietnamese mothers, the mixed-blood child is ostracized.

Intermarriage, when it occurs, must be approved by some group if it is to be considered a form of marriage with the commitment of husband and wife to the roles and responsibilities of marriage. In the United States, it is now unconstitutional for a state to deny a marriage license to a couple simply on the grounds that they are of different races, religions, or ethnic backgrounds. Interracial marriages may not be accepted or acknowledged by the family of either bride or groom, but so long as some third group with authority (in our society, the state issuing the license) recognizes the union, it is valid. In earlier times and in other cultures, relationships of couples with different religions and racial backgrounds have been forbidden by law. In some cultures even today, certain kinds of intermarriage are given a less-than-legal status, as quasi-marriages or semipermanent unions.

EXOGAMY

We have noted the tendency of human beings to be endogamous. But there is also a strong *exogamous* force at work in most societies. Exogamy and intermarriage are not the same. Unlike intermarriage, exogamy is not a *chance* marriage outside some group, but rather the *requirement* that members of a society marry outside their kinship group. While the rules of endogamy set boundaries on the pool of eligible mates on one side, the rules of exogamy set boundaries on the other side (Fullerton 1977, p. 251). This almost universal concept is ideally shown in the traditional Indian village, where a person marries within the same Hindu caste—rule of endogamy—but outside the home village—rule of exogamy (Cavan and Cavan 1975, p. 167).

Incest and Other Taboos

The most universal rules of exogamy involve incest and homosexuality. Even in societies that condoned homosexuality, such as classical Greek culture, marriages were allowed only between heterosexuals because of the important link between marriage and childbearing. Incest taboos are almost, but not quite, universal. In ancient China, people were forbidden to marry anyone with the same surname, even though the common relative may have lived several thousand years before (Udry 1974, p. 153). Yet in ancient Egypt, sibling marriage was a common practice, apparently as a means of keeping aristocratic estates in the family and consolidating property that would otherwise pass to outsiders by the laws of inheritance. Various theories have been put forward to explain the rule against incest, the most common being that incest increases the risk of congenital disease and defects. However, incest taboos existed long before knowledge about genetics, so it is likely that other factors were involved. Anthropologist Claude Lévi-Strauss, who views marriage as the most profound trade relation, conceives of the incest taboo as one of many rules of exchange or trade that exist in any society:

I will give up my daughter or my sister if my neighbor will give up his also. . . . The fact that I can obtain a wife is, in the last analysis, the consequence of the fact that a brother or a father has given up a woman. (1957, p. 94)

In the United States, laws against incest forbid a man or woman to marry close relatives: sister/brother, mother/father, daughter/son, niece/nephew, grandmother/grandfather, grandchild. Most states also forbid marriages to half-siblings and sometimes first cousins, as well as unions that are not strictly incestuous, such as marriage between a man and his father's former wife, his son's former wife, his former wife's mother, and so on. In some states there are laws against marriage to one's stepfather, stepdaughter, and so on, even where the relationship implies no blood ties.

As remarriage becomes more common, the problem of the legal definition of incest is likely to become even more complicated. Divorces and remarriages bring about a higher incidence of what Virginia Satir (1972) calls "blended families": situations in which divorced people with children from a prior marriage marry and move into the same household. This blending may occur when the children on either side are already approaching or into their adolescence. The incest taboo may need to be either reinforced or redefined to take into account the large number of new family relationships created by divorce, remarriage, and the blending of families.

CROSS-CULTURAL COMPARISONS

Methods of mate selection are related to the whole structure of a society's way of life. As a general rule, those who determine mate selection in a given society are those who have the most to gain or to lose by the selection. In societies where extended families are still common, and where young married couples usually live with their parents or in some larger kinship unit, parents often control mate selection. Until the twentieth century, matches in Europe and England commonly were arranged by the parents. Mates sometimes did not know each other before marriage; sometimes they were betrothed in childhood (Udry 1974, p. 169). Even in societies such as ours, where young married couples typically set up their own households, parents may still have a large amount of control if substantial exchanges of property are involved—if, for example, either mate has a large trust fund that will become the joint property of the new-lyweds. But when the young people are not bound to complicated financial legacies, as is true for most people in the United States, they are likely to select their own mates without much parental interference (Udry 1974, p. 169). Of course, no marriage affects *only* the couple involved, and even in the most open, individualistic society, marital choices are not entirely personal. To the extent that groups within our society resist alliances with people regarded as "outsiders," they will seek to control mate selection.

The world as a whole seems to be moving gradually toward greater freedom of choice in selecting marriage partners. Data from Africa, India, Israel, and Malaya indicate conditions arising that tend to enhance freedom of mate choice: later age at marriage, higher educational levels, higher socioeconomic levels, and a shift from rural to urban living (Matras 1973; Strange 1976).

Data from communist countries are scarce, but information from China shows that the marriage age has risen significantly, with the average Chinese couple marrying in their late twenties. Political compatibility is considered a very important criterion for choice of a mate. Marriages arranged by parents still exist, though they are much less common than in precommunist days. Couples in the Soviet Union are also urged to consider political compatibility as the prime reason for marriage, but "marriage for love" is accepted (Huange 1972; Salaff 1973).

In societies such as Sweden where cohabitation is accepted and children born out of wedlock are supported by the state or by parents, there has been a steep decline in the marriage rate (Trost 1975). The possibility of economic independence for women has had a worldwide impact, giving women in many cultures greater freedom of choice in mate selection. In countries where women still lack economic opportunities, there is little individual freedom in mate selection, and early marriage prevails.

FACTORS IN MATE SELECTION

Social Class

Although Americans pride themselves on the individualism and freedom of their society, social classes do exist in the United States. We have already discussed some general social-class influences on marriage and family life (Chapter 3), as well as class influences on attitudes toward sexual behavior (Chapter 4). In subsequent chapters, we shall see how class differences make for important differences in family structure, marital-role expectations, sex roles, family goals, and child rearing. Marriage across social-class lines is also a way of enhancing one's own social status, especially in an open society where such marriages are condoned. Thus we can expect social class to continue influencing people's mate choices.

Social class influences one's expectations about how men and women should relate as husbands and wives, fathers and mothers. These expectations, in turn, influence our perceptions of others—and so our mate choices. A person from the middle class (of which there are numerous subclasses, from self-employed professionals to small business owners) will expect his or her spouse to be a companion; they will share a relationship that is independent of their relationship with their shared children. The middle-class person will want to share activities with this companion and to develop similar skills—say, tennis or music. He or she will expect their friends to form a loose-knit social network appropriate for people who are upwardly mobile. Settling into a neighborhood of family and old friends might hold them back in their upwardly mobile careers.

A young person raised in a working-class family is likely to have another set of expectations. A traditional working-class woman, for instance, might not expect a great deal of interpersonal interaction or companionship with her husband. She might expect that he will have skills and responsibilities—maintaining the home and earning money—that will complement her very different skills and responsibilities—raising children, housekeeping. She may expect to remain in the same neighborhood, partly to be near her female relatives, who provide most of her emotional support. The segregated conjugal roles that she expects in marriage will be supported by a close-knit social network of relatives, friends, and neighbors who know one another.

These differences in outlook and expectations make cross-class marriages unlikely to occur in the first place and perhaps difficult to sustain when they do occur (Fullerton 1977, pp. 498–503). Working-class people marry at an earlier age than their middle-class counterparts, so they are simply removed from the marriage market of the typical middle-class adult. In the past, young people from the two classes have not lived in the same neighborhoods or attended the same schools. All these factors once came together dramatically to lower the likelihood that men and women from the working class and the middle class would get together or see each other as prospective mates. This situation appears to be changing in several respects.

The expectations of young working-class women and men seem to be more similar to those of the middle class, even though their work experience and occupational choices remain different. Shostak (1980) notes that blue-collar women are out in the world far more than before. They are expecting more companionship, emotional support, and personal attention—expectations that used to be associated with the middle class. Along with certain new and more liberal attitudes about sexual behavior (noted in Chapter 4), young "blue collarites" are adopting a new value framework that includes "a lessening of automatic obedience to and respect for established authority" (p. 320). These changes are accompanied by integration efforts in schools that make use of busing or attractive programs that bring together children and adolescents from divergent backgrounds. There is now more *propinquity*, or proximity, between the middle class and the working class in urban areas, as well as fewer rigid distinctions between the two in several areas that relate to marriage expectations. Whether these shifts have the effect of increasing interclass marriages may depend on the presence of other shared features—such as educational background and goals, religion, ethnicity, and race.

Education

Education and occupation are important indicators of social class and status. Many middle-class occupations and all the professions require high levels of education. Sharing a common educational background seems to be an important factor in mate selection. Because education and socioeconomic status are so tightly linked, similar educational level often means similar socioeconomic status.

The U.S. Census Bureau revealed that in the 1950s most people married someone with a similar education, although usually men had a few more months of education than the women they married. College-graduate males tended overwhelmingly to choose women on their own educational level, even though they outnumbered female college graduates two to one. There is some suggestion, however, that college men pick college women as wives because they are more available socially, not because these men intrinsically prefer educated women (Fullerton 1977; Udry 1974).

The woman who marries a man with less education than she has is said to have married "down." Such marriages are still less socially acceptable than marriages in which the husband has more education than his wife, as long as the discrepancy in the latter marriage is not embarrassingly wide.

Religion

According to J. R. Udry (1974), there are more studies available on the influence of religious convictions on marital choice than on any other social factors. Social scientists agree that people tend to marry within their own religion, but few agree on the extent to which this is true.

If a woman does not identify with her Lutheran upbringing, for example, she will not restrict her dating to Lutherans. If she lives in a religiously mixed area, her chances of meeting—and falling in love with—someone of a different religious background are good. People of certain groups, how-ever, identify deeply with the religion of their parents. This is especially true of Catholics, Mormons, and Jews. Children raised in strongly religious families feel insulated from other religious groups, even if these faiths prevail in their neighborhoods:

Only slowly does such a child grasp what the [religious] label means, and what it might be like to be a member of some other faith remains one of the mysteries of his childhood. ("I wonder what they do in there?" is the half-curious, half-fearful question that floats through his mind when he passes the temple of another faith.) Such a child becomes an adult for whom religious community is a highly significant in-group. (Fullerton 1977, p. 257)

Such people might find it difficult to live in emotional comfort with a husband or wife of a different religion. On the other hand, for some people, belonging to a church is simply part of being raised in a certain neighbor-hood or town, not a part of their personal identity. Some Protestants re-gard their religious being not as something they *are* (whether they like it or not), but rather as something they can consciously *choose* to be. This atti-tude lends itself to changing religious affiliation (though usually within the various Protestant denominations), which is just what many rural Protestants of earlier generations did when they moved to the city (Fuller-ton 1977, p. 256).

Evaluating the importance of religion as a factor in mate selection is complicated, first, by the intermingling of religion with other forces; sec-ond, by the possibility of changing one's religion. Religious background is often inextricably tied to other factors that also are important influences on mate selection:

Being Italian and being Catholic . . . are so entwined in the self-image of a small child growing up in an Italian-Catholic neighborhood that it will never be entirely possible for that person to separate these two group affiliations. (Fullerton 1977, p. 258)

We have already noted that 90 percent of Chicanos are also, at least nomi-nally, Roman Catholics. Religious background is often linked to social class as well as to ethnic background. Fundamentalists often are members of the working class, while Episcopalians—in the tidelands South, for example—are members of the established elite, as are Congregationalists in Massachusetts (Fullerton 1977, p. 256). Because ethnicity and social class are often bound up with a particular religious denomination, the tendency to marry someone with the same ethnic and social-class background usually propels mates into the same church or synagogue. This interbreeding in the same religious group is called *religious homogamy* (Udry 1974, pp. 164–165).

Second, although it is impossible to change the social class or ethnic background from which one comes, religion is to some extent voluntary. Many people convert to the religion of their future spouse. A study in the Midwest showed that three out of four marriages of persons raised in different faiths became homogamous because one spouse converted to the religion of the other (Udry 1974, p. 163). Are we to count such marriages as homogamous from the point of view of religion?

The religious training and ambiance of the earliest childhood years inculcate values and attitudes toward the world that may not be matters of religious dogma or doctrine per se. These broadly cultural values—for example, the value put on education and learning in most Jewish families—may not be shared by someone who is not of the same religion. A marriage between a convert and someone brought up in a religion may still be an intermarriage to the extent that the two people do not share important cultural values associated with the religion of their childhood. If we calculate intermarriage based on *early* childhood religious preference or affiliation, the rates of intermarriage will be much higher. Furthermore, if statistics on intermarriage took into account all the varieties of Protestant denominations, the rates of intermarriage would again be much higher. But two people nominally affiliated with different denominations of Protestantism may well share the same cultural values and so be intermarried only nominally (Cavan and Cavan 1975, p. 167).

Religion, in some instances, is tightly tied to sex-role division, attitudes about child rearing, and ethical values. But there has been a tendency for these ties to weaken. Reviewing the trends in religious intermarriage, Adams (1980) and Kerckhoff (1976) report an increase in intermarriage between the 1940s and 1960s, then a stabilizing trend. During the 1970s there seemed to be a tendency for intermarriage between different religious groups to increase.

An early study of divorce rates (Landis 1949) indicated that Catholic-Protestant intermarriages were more likely to end in divorce than marriages of two Catholics or of two Protestants. But the increase in divorce during the 1970s was not confined to one religious group. An extensive marriage and family counseling study (Beck and Jones 1973) showed mixed-marriage couples only slightly more likely to report marital problems than those of similar backgrounds (70 percent versus 66 percent) and just a bit more likely to have a problem with childen (71 percent versus 68 percent); problems experienced by mixed-marriage couples, however, were more likely to be rated as severe (p. 151). A common religious background, with its frequent ties to cultural attitudes concerning roles and child rearing, may help couples deal with marital stress, though it is no absolute insurance against divorce. An absence of this common background, while it may not be a source of basic conflict, may serve to heighten conflict when it does occur.

Clustering and Salience

Intermarriage or outmarriage depends upon two principal factors: (1) the *clustering* of important variables around religions, race, or ethnicity, and (2) the *salience*—or importance the individual attributes to—ethnic, religious, racial, or other values. The clustering that produces homogamy, such as the Mexican-American-Catholic-working-class combination, may decrease, especially after a group lives in this country for several generations. Salience may also change over time.

Burr (1973) indicates that salience is a tempering factor in mate selection, telling us whether any given background factor is important enough to the individual to actually influence mate selection. Bert Adams provides the diagram in Figure 6.1 to show how salience stands between background factors.

Race

Race is likely to have salience, and this is especially true of mate selection involving blacks and whites. These marriages are uncommon and, for the most part, resisted by both black and white groups. Since 1967, when the Supreme Court declared laws against interracial marriage (antimiscegenation laws) unconstitutional, intermarriage has increased somewhat, from 1.4 percent racially mixed marriages in 1963–1966 to 2.6 percent in the period 1967–1970 (Monahan 1976, p. 225). Monahan also found a difference in the pattern of interracial marriages. The typical interracial pair had been a low-status white female married to a black of higher status, but

FIGURE 6.1   Salience: Importance of Background Factors in Mate Selection

Source: Bert N. Adams. *The Family: A Sociological Interpretation* (3rd ed.), Houghton Mifflin Co., Boston, 1980, p. 238.

Monahan saw more socioeconomic similarity between black and white partners emerging. For example, in Philadelphia he found professional and white-collar groups represented in intermarriages, as well as working-class and lower-class groups (p. 188).

Another review of the statistics indicates that interracial marriages have higher divorce rates than racially homogamous marriages. Interracial marriages between a white male and a black female are less frequent than those between a black male and a white female, and the former are also less likely to endure (Heer 1974); after ten years Heer found 63 percent of black husband–white wife marriages still intact, versus 47 percent of white husband–black wife marriages. There is now somewhat more propinquity for blacks and whites at schools and colleges and at the work place, but there has also been an increase in racial pride among blacks, which has tended to discourage mixed dating and marriage. Single blacks entering occupations and professions previously dominated by whites may face a particularly limited number of prospective dates—and ultimately, mates—of their own race. Stein (1978), in his review of the literature on singles, notes that there are very few opportunities for middle-class single blacks to meet other black singles. This situation may cause a slight increase in interracial marriages in the future, but the barriers to such marriages are still formidable.

Though black-white marriages are not likely to become commonplace, marriages between Japanese-Americans and those of other racial groups are already typical. This development represents a radical departure from the strict proscriptions against intermarriage in Japan before World War II. Fifty percent of the marriages of Japanese-Americans are to people outside their racial group, a marked increase from the 1950s, when the outmarriage rate was 30 percent (Tinker 1973; Kikumura and Kitano 1973). Intermarriage, as Cavan (1969) has suggested, can be a sign that the individual has actually withdrawn from his or her own social group or that the individual may be in conflict with some aspect of the group's values—such as sex roles or child rearing. In the case of the Japanese-American woman, it may be the submissive sex role dictated by the culture that causes defections, or it could be a gradual change in the two factors we have discussed—salience and clustering. Postwar shifts in both American and Japanese-American cultures, particularly changes in the past 20 years, may have brought these two races from a point of war, hatred, and vast differences to a place where many values are shared.

Age

Since the early 1900s, the average age difference between mates has steadily grown smaller, as has the proportion of marriages in which the husband is older. Men and women are choosing mates of about their own age, and more men are marrying women the same age or older than they are. This trend was identified and reported by the 1970 census, which surveyed husbands of all ages; the older husbands reflected the trends in marital choice of earlier generations, while younger husbands reflected more recent trends. More than 80 percent of husbands who were 70 years and older had married younger women, with a median age difference of 3.8 years. But men aged 35 or younger had married women whose median age was only 1.7 years less than theirs. Among these younger men, only 71.7 percent were older than their wives. Men who have been married more than once, but whose wives have not been married before, tend to marry younger women more often than any other age group. But even for those who had been married before, the census reported the same general tendency for younger couples to be closer in age (Fullerton 1977, pp. 258–259).

The tendency for younger couples to be near the same age may reflect the value placed on companionship and equality in marriage. Fullerton (1977) believes, however, that age-group endogamy is a sign of increasing age-group segregation, as people come more and more to identify with their own age group and to feel alienated from those in other generations, whether younger or older. This stratification by age is reflected in recreational facilities and communities that exclude children (or older people), generation-specific vocabularies and slang, fashions and styles, as well as a noticeable age snobbery that encourages divisiveness and the breaking down of traditional responsibilities and lines of authority between young and old.

Not only do couples tend to be closer in age, but they also are marrying at an earlier age. In 1890 the average age of men at their first marriage was 26.1 years, and that of women, 22 years (Udry 1974, p. 155). In the 1970s, the average age of men at first marriage was 23, and that of women, 21. And a substantial segment of the single population is choosing to delay marriage until the late twenties. While the majority of couples marry in their early twenties, approximately one quarter of men and women are remaining single until the age of 30 (Stein 1978).

PERSONAL INFLUENCES ON MATE SELECTION

In societies where parents have primary control over mate selection, they specifically consider such factors as social class and religious, ethnic, or racial background when arranging a suitable—that is, endogamous—marriage for their son or daughter. But in most Western cultures, where marriages are no longer "arranged," mate selection depends on a variety of factors, including proximity, personal attraction, and similar interests

People tend to marry those with similar interests and values. (Barbara Alper)

and values. Some of these factors go into the feeling of being in love. The individuals about to marry will probably say they are marrying because they love each other. In the following pages we shall examine the answers of social scientists to these questions: What is this thing called love, and how does it lead to marriage?

Minimal Condition: Propinquity

In a society where marriages are arranged for social and financial convenience, a couple may not even see each other before the wedding. But in the United States, where participants usually select their own mates, proximity becomes an important factor. In such a system, the condition of being close to another serves as a more significant limit to mate selection (Adams 1979). In fact, one sociologist has suggested this mate selection equation: "The probability of marriage decreases as the distances between premarital residences increases" (Catton 1964, p. 526).

Numerous studies show that the likelihood of two people getting married is directly related to the physical distance they must cover—and hence the energy they must expend—to see and interact with each other (Udry 1974, p. 156). *Propinquity*, or physical nearness, is conducive to endogamous marriages, since people of similar social, economic, and racial backgrounds tend to dwell in the same neighborhoods and work in similar places. Among people living in heterogeneous urban settings, propinquity may not imply similar social or religious backgrounds. On a university campus, for example, the girl next door may be of a different race, religion, age, and social class.

Initial Attraction

Once "boy meets girl" or "girl meets boy," the question becomes "Will boy be attracted to girl—and vice versa?" What are the elements of early attraction—"love at first sight," or at second and third sight? That romantic feeling drawing two strangers across a crowded room is likely to result from physical attraction (Murstein 1976). College people who meet at a dance, for example, will go on a subsequent date if they find each other physically attractive.

This beauty is not just in the eye of the beholder (Walster 1966). More than 300 studies have been done on mate selection and physical characteristics, and at least 105 characteristics have been studied, including age, weight, stature, forearm length, hair color, general health, basal metabolism, and even pulse rate before exercise. There is overwhelming evidence that physical attractiveness is a factor in mate selection. Further, not only do persons who marry tend to rate each other as having the same degree of attractiveness, but by objective standards they *do* have the same degree of attractiveness (Udry 1974, p. 177).

Physical attractiveness is especially important in determining initial reactions. Young women have also been influenced by empathy and eligibility. The traditional explanation for this is offered by Rubin:

> Since the woman rather than the man typically takes on the social and economic status of her spouse, she has more practical concerns to keep in mind in selecting a mate. In addition, the woman is often in a greater rush to get married than the man because her years of "marriageability" tend to be more limited. Thus, she cannot as easily afford to be strongly attracted to a date who is not also a potentially eligible spouse. (1973, p. 205)

This picture may change for a number of reasons. Women are relying more on themselves for social and economic status. Many of them are having a number of intimate relationships before they marry, and substantial numbers are remaining unmarried. Finally, with the two-worker family becoming the norm, it may be that "eligibility" begins to figure in men's reactions to women, with a woman's potential as a breadwinner becoming a factor in mate selection. But these considerations are likely to come later. Across a crowded room, it's apt to be physical attraction that draws two people together and brings them to the next date.

Once the initial attraction is present, the relationship actually begins. We might call this the period of "early relating." During this stage, the two people disclose information and feelings. He talks about his home town, says his parents are divorced, shares his fears of not making the grades for medical school. She talks about her shy adolescence, her passion for chocolates, her dream of being an architect, her fear of heights. This kind of self-disclosure results in what Lewis (1973) calls *pair rapport*—comfort in each other's presence, a sense of affinity, a discovery of common interests or backgrounds. This development of pair rapport, which results in intimacy and commitment, may be thought of as a spiraling process:

When one person reveals himself to another, it has a subtle effect on the way each of them defines the relationship. Bit by bit the partners open themselves to one another, and step by step they construct their mutual bond. The process only rarely moves ahead in great leaps. . . . And inasmuch as no one can ever disclose himself totally to another person, continuing acts of self-revelation remain an important part of the developmental process. (Rubin 1973, pp. 180–181)

Thus the couple moves into a phase of "deeper attraction." This phase, Bert Adams notes (1979), is hastened by the couple's discovery that they have similar values, ideas, and goals, or at least ones that are not in conflict. They find together what Adams calls a "coorientation" or "value consensus." For example, she discovers that he thinks, as she does, that people should return to an emphasis on hard work and tough, traditional education in the "three R's" for children, yet should keep advancing in terms of male-female equality. This kind of discovery of similar values, according to Byrne's work (Byrne 1971; Byrne and Clone 1967), tends to confirm her conception of reality. It validates her interpretation of society, making her feel more competent and bolstering her self-esteem. This mutual reinforcement may be especially significant for relationships in a society that tends to present many versions of reality, many notions about the good life. This evidence seems to suggest that similarities would be a stronger basis for attraction than opposing or complementary traits.

Do Opposites Attract?　Are similar personalities also more likely to be attracted to each other than opposite types? Is attraction a matter of finding the missing piece in your personality, the complement, the person who compensates for your weaknesses and requires your particular strengths?

The philosopher Arthur Schopenhauer (1928) eloquently presented a nine-teenth-century version of this view:

Every one will decidedly prefer and eagerly desire the most beautiful individuals . . . but, secondly, each one will specially regard as beautiful in another individual those perfections which he himself lacks, nay, even those imperfections which are the opposite of his own. Hence, for example, little men love big women, fair persons like dark. (Quoted in Udry 1974, p. 171)

Theodor Reik and other psychoanalysts have suggested that we choose mates who compensate for what we see as our psychological deficiencies, a shy person choosing an assertive mate, for example. In the 1950s and 1960s, Robert Winch attempted to formulate this view in a way that could be tested scientifically. Using this formulation to compare the personalities of engaged and married couples, he concluded that "persons whose need patterns provide mutual gratification will tend to choose each other as marriage partners." In other words, "people fall in love with someone who satisfies them." Winch claimed to find evidence that couples' personality traits and needs complemented each other in two ways. If one spouse had a high need for, say, achievement, the other would be low in that need. At the same time, their personality traits, Winch claimed, would complement each other, so that if one spouse was domineering, the other would be submissive (Winch 1958).

But other researchers following Winch have not confirmed his theory of complementary needs and traits. Indeed, the hundreds of studies that have been done to test this view indicate that mates are more alike in physical, social, and psychological characteristics than they are different and that even before marriage, they were more alike than chance would allow (Udry 1974, p. 172). Winch's theory has been criticized on several grounds. It has been pointed out that spouses often are not aware of having complementary traits, and these traits really have nothing to do with the reasons they married. There has not been much empirical support for the notion that perceptions of complementary traits result in attraction. For example, dominant males do *not* tend to pick females they perceive as submissive, and submissive males do not tend to pick females they perceive as dominant. Since we have been finding social and psychological differences in males and females throughout their development, it is not surprising that young men and women have somewhat different notions of what they perceive as attractive in the opposite sex. But the sociological and psychological literature to date does not support the notion that mates, like Jack Sprat and his wife, have to mesh by virtue of opposite yet complementary differences.

When dealing with the complex issue of human personality, we would be foolish to oversimplify, suggesting that a man and woman must share all values, all psychological strengths and weaknesses. Napier (1971) suggests that attraction involves a mixture of the comforting familiar qualities and the intriguing unfamiliar ones: "You are like me; you remind me of myself, but you are also strange and different" (p. 393). And Murstein (1976) indicates that a strong feeling of insufficiency in some area can cause a person to seek a partner "whose personality makeup is as different as possible from the unacceptable or unfulfilled aspects of oneself" (Murstein 1976, p. 304). (As we shall see in subsequent chapters, it is an illusion that a mate can compensate for a severe psychological deficit—an illusion often dispelled by divorce.) Finally, we might consider the possibility that a change in attitude about sex roles—from complementary male and female traits being valued to *similar* traits being valued—may be contributing to the current emphasis on the attraction of similar types. Contemporary marriages probably involve a mixture of similar and complementary traits with the emphasis on the similar aspects of the partners. Jack Spratt may like his meat lean, but chances are that he and his wife both prefer country music to disco.

The social similarities we have already discussed in terms of in-groups and endogamy figure in the process of deepening attraction that results in intimacy. Yet as we have pointed out, these racial, ethnic, and religious values must be salient categories. Individuals may wind up rejecting some of their own group's values: Catholicism may no longer be a salient factor in mate selection for a particular Catholic young man; sharing a Polish heritage may no longer be salient to a particular Polish young woman. But chances are that some of those categories will be personally important to each of the potential mates, which in turn increases their sense of intimacy.

Ideal Images

Another impetus to intimacy is the feeling that the other matches an ideal image. Carl Jung believed that each person carries within an image of an ideal mate. The ideal may derive from the parent of the opposite sex (Napier 1971), but in our society, where mothers have been the primary source of affection for children, both male and female may be trying to duplicate relations with the mother (Aron 1974). The family constellation of birth order and the role an individual has played may also influence the image of the ideal mate. Personal ideals of mates are also influenced by cultural ideals. As these cultural images change, so, too, do some of our personal images concerning ideal husbands and wives.

In the dominant (white Anglo-Saxon) American culture, the ideal man used to be tall, handsome, silent, and strong—masculine and macho. This ideal may be changing in the face of women's liberation and the move toward personal fulfillment; the new ideal is a man who, while strong, is caring as well as courageous, sensitive, and capable of expressing his personal feelings, including feelings of vulnerability.

Such cultural ideals influence personal choices in two ways. They make having a certain mate a status or prestige symbol. A woman influenced by the cultural ideal of the macho man will naturally seek a man who fits that ideal. But even if she does not find him, she may *idealize* the mate she does choose by attributing to him features of the ideal.

PREMARITAL STAGE OF MATE SELECTION

During the later stages of mate selection, the individual tends to ask: Is she right for me? Is he right for me? The answer may depend somewhat on the individual's self-esteem or personal appraisal. They are asking whether

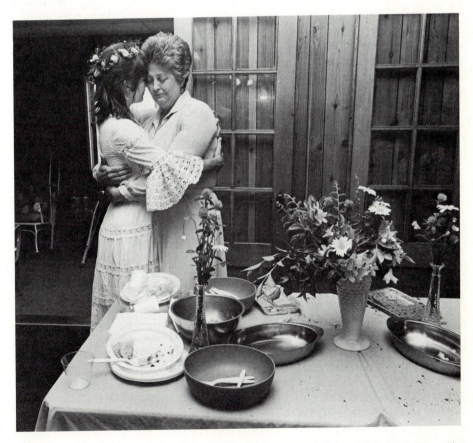

Parents and other kin are emotionally involved in mate choice, and their reactions can influence the outcome. (Abigail Heyman, Archive Pictures, Inc.)

the prospective mate is as good as they can get. Is the other a good bargain? Klemer (1971) found that low self-esteem tended to cause an individual to marry someone met prior to college. Such people may believe that they can't afford to let go of a sure thing. People who feel they will have very few other opportunities, such as those who believe they are past the "marriageable" age, may feel they can't afford to be choosy, because this may be their last chance (Adams 1979).

Throughout the process of mate selection, relatives and friends can hasten or impede the growth of the relationship. In the early stages, parental influences can lend an aura of romance. In the popular musical *The Fantasticks*, the neighboring families purposely try to create this "Romeo and Juliet effect" by pretending to oppose the match and even building a wall between their two houses. But such opposition, if genuine and deep-seated, eventually will probably undermine the relationship. When there is approval, or at least acceptance, among friends and relatives, the man and woman come to be regarded as a couple, and the relationship can be put on what Murstein (1976) calls a "conveyor belt" that moves the couple along to the altar. The relationship has become "more than the sum total of the categorical influences, personalities, and values of the two people who constitute the couple" (Adams 1979, p. 263). Marriage is now a distinct possibility. The giving of a ring and formal engagement are signs of the "escalators," which move the couple to the final stage of mate selection. At this point, only the discovery of legal barriers (see Box 6.1) or of a prior deception (such as one partner's having misrepresented an element of his or her background) is likely to keep the pair from finalizing the choice by marriage. A summary of the factors that influence mate selection appears in Figure 6.2.

BOX 6.1 Legal Barriers to Marriage

There is a profound consensus in Western society that the state should interfere as little as possible with the most intimate and personal contract its citizens can form: marriage. In keeping with this view, most countries have only minimal regulations for such contracts. In addition to the laws against incest mentioned earlier, most states, for reasons of public health, refuse marriage licenses to those who are mentally ill, mentally retarded, addicted to drugs or alcohol (Fullerton 1977, p. 265). All states require a premarital test for venereal disease (Drinan 1975, p. 258).

Although they are not usually enforced, laws in many states also refuse marriage licenses to those suffering from epilepsy or tuberculosis. Other laws, concerning age and marital status, are based on social norms. Although the age of majority varies from 18 to 21, depending on the state, most states have laws forbidding minors to marry without their parents' consent. All states have laws forbidding persons who are already married to marry someone else without becoming legally divorced (Fullerton 1977, p. 265).

FIGURE 6.2   The Mate Selection Process in the United States

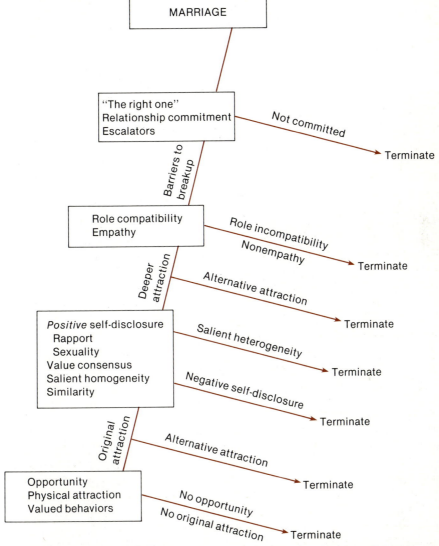

Source: Reprinted with permission of Macmillan Publishing Co., Inc., from *Contemporary Theories About the Family, Vol. I, Research Based Theories*, by W. R. Burr, R. Hill, F. I. Nye, and I. L. Reiss, copyright © 1979 by the Free Press, a division of Macmillan Publishing Co., Inc.

SUMMARY

1. The primary purposes of this chapter are, first, to discuss the control of mate selection exerted by culture and social group within selected societies, including the United States; second, to explore the influence of social class, religion, education, race, and age on mate choice; and, third, to review the more personal variables in choosing an intimate, that is, physical attraction, complementarity, and ideal images.

2. All cultures exert some control over the selection of marital partners, although such control sometimes is implicit or informal and not readily acknowledged. In other situations, societal control may be quite well defined (as with laws that prohibit marriage between certain categories of individuals). Marriage among members of the same social group is referred to as an endogamous union. Intermarriage defines a union between members of two distinct societies or subcultures. In the United States, endogamous boundaries tend to be formed primarily by race, religion, ethnicity, and generation.

3. Most societies, in addition to rules of endogamy, also have stipulations against marriage between certain social group members. These rules of exogamy commonly (in the United States) involve homosexual unions and incestuous relationships. Considerable variation exists between cultures in the specifying and enforcement of endogamy and exogamy considerations. The United States is usually seen as a culture that encourages relatively free choice in the selection of a marriage partner.

4. In contemporary America, social-class placement is increasingly being defined by occupation rather than family name or family wealth. Even so, the majority of individuals tend to select mates from similar social and occupational backgrounds. Marriages between partners from widely divergent social backgrounds are more the exception than the rule.

5. The tendency toward endogamy—marrying within one's own social group—is also evident in the areas of religion, education, race, and age. Research on these variables indicates that the majority of marriages in the United States reflect spouse similarities in religious orientation, level of education, race, and age. While a significant number of studies have investigated the effects of intermarriage, particularly interfaith unions, the results of such research as related to marital happiness or satisfaction are inconclusive. Effects seem to depend on the meaning and significance each couple attaches to such differences.

6. In cultures where choice of a marriage partner is in large part an individual matter, the influence of personal factors becomes an important consideration. One important, but often overlooked factor is propinquity or physical nearness. We are more likely to meet, interact with, and perhaps marry people with whom we are in close proximity.

Another important variable in the initial stages of a relationship is physical attractiveness. It has been proposed that the mate selection process involves a stage or steplike progression from propinquity to physical attraction, self-disclosure, and, finally, value consensus.

KEY CONCEPTS

Endogamy   Religious homogamy
Intermarriage   Propinquity
Exogamy   Pair rapport
Incest taboo

QUESTIONS

1. Define and give examples of the concepts of endogamy, intermarriage, and exogamy as these situations exist in American society today.
2. In view of the numerous factors reviewed in this chapter indicating that individuals tend to marry someone quite similar to themselves, how do you explain the popular idea that "opposites attract"?
3. Explore and discuss your own views on the selection of a marital partner or close intimate. What factors do you think have influenced you most in your standards or ideals about primary relationship partners?
4. Describe what you perceive to be the cultural ideal in physical attractiveness for males and females in the United States today. Where do these ideals originate? What brings about changes in standards for evaluating physical attractiveness or beauty?
5. Select one dimension where intermarriage occurs—religion, race, age, social class, or educational level—and explain the potential strengths and stresses of marital unions that cross this boundary.
6. Discuss the influence that self-esteem may have on the selection of intimate partners.

SUGGESTED READINGS

- Berscheid, Ellen, and Walster, Elaine H. *Interpersonal Attraction*. 2nd ed. Reading, Mass.: Addison-Wesley, 1978. The focus of this book is on attraction and rejection among human beings. Various factors influencing attraction, such as similarity between individuals and need fulfillment or rewards provided by each partner in a relationship, are discussed. Processes and problems in evaluating potential intimates are also considered.
- Davis, Murray S. *Intimate Relations*. New York: Free Press, 1973. A fascinating book that explores the relationship process of how strangers become friends, friends become lovers, and lovers become spouses. The

author describes not only how initial encounters move into long-term relationships, but also how intimate unions may unravel or regress and how spouses become strangers.

- Eckland, Bruce K. "Theories of Mate Selection." *Eugenics Quarterly* 15 (1968). A capsule review of the numerous theories that have been proposed to explain mate choice. A unique feature of this article is the attention given to biological views on mate selection.
- Murstein, Bernard I. *Who Will Marry Whom? Theory and Research in Marital Choice.* New York: Springer, 1976. A contemporary analysis of theory and research in mate selection and development of the author's theoretical view of mate choice as a dynamic process. Murstein's work is highly regarded in current social science explanations of marital partner selection.
- Sager, Clifford J., and Hunt, Bernice. *Intimate Partners: Hidden Patterns in Love Relationships.* New York: McGraw-Hill, 1979. An analysis of the hidden or unconscious factors that people bring with them to love relationships, which often precipitate problems and lead to relationship failure. The authors present seven different profiles of relationships and explain how these profiles interact to create different kinds of partnerships.
- Snyder, Eloise C. "Attitudes: A Study of Homogamy and Marital Selectivity." *Journal of Marriage and the Family* 36, no. 3 (August 1964). An interesting study that investigates whether the degree of attitude similarity frequently noted in marital pairs is present prior to the partners' initial meeting and dating experience or whether this similarity develops as a result of what is labeled "adjustive interaction." Indications from this preliminary work suggest that increasing interactions between partners during the courtship process may be the primary factor in shaping attitude similarity.
- Winch, Robert F. *Mate Selection.* New York: Harper, 1958. This classic work by Winch represents the author's development of the theory of complementary needs as a major component in mate selection. Though subsequent research and analysis has not fully supported this view, it was for several years regarded as a major explanation of mate choice.

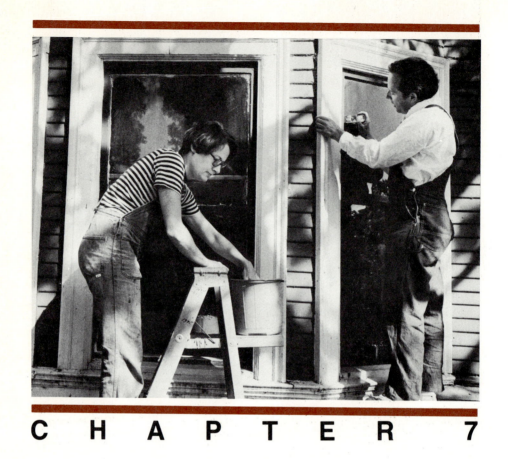

C H A P T E R   7

Interactive Processes:
Role Patterns

SHE: I got the job.

HE: That's wonderful, honey. When do you start?

SHE: In three days.

HE: Three days! What about the kids?

SHE: I thought we could work that out together.

HE: You know more about that stuff. It's always been your responsibility.

SHE: But I'm going to be working full time, just like you.

HE: Wait just a minute! Being a full-time secretary is not the same as being a full-time comptroller.

SHE: No—you get more pay, but the hours are the same. We'll have to do more sharing.

HE: Look, I haven't got any ideas about day care. Lori isn't going to like it. And what about Jim's Scout meetings?

SHE: Lori's over three. I think she'll do fine. You call the "Y" and I'll check out that kiddie college. Don't look so glum. Think of the extra money.

HE: Yeah, maybe we could plan for a vacation this winter.

SHE: Sure, maybe even the Bahamas. Oh—Mondays and Thursdays will be

a little tough. I have to work late those nights, so you'll have to pick up
the kids.

HE: What if I have to work late, too?

SHE: Look, we need my salary. Other couples manage when both of them
work.

HE: I guess I can take the kids for burgers those nights.

SHE: Well, it won't be just those nights. I mean, I'll be home at six every
night, so we really ought to share the cooking.

HE: Last time I made dinner, you told me to stick to mixing paint.

SHE: That's why I picked up this terrific paperback, *First Time Cook*. It
takes you step-by-step from refrigerator to stove.

INTRODUCTION

Role—the word calls to mind a part in a play, the traits assumed by an
actor or actress. Roles are assumed by husband and wife when they marry,
but men and women practice or rehearse these roles all their lives. They
watch their own mothers and fathers. If Mom and Dad work and share the
household duties, they think of these things as part of the roles they will
assume. If the jobs are sex-segregrated, they learn that some tasks are part
of a woman's role, some suitable only for a man. As children, they play at
these roles, influenced by their peers and teachers, as well as by the approval or disapproval of their parents. Television conveys other role models, as do books, plays, and movies.

By the time two people marry, they have had years of rehearsal for their
roles—in play, in school, at work. Most people assume the roles they have
learned and practiced. But what happens when the roles one has rehearsed
no longer serve the needs of reality? What happens when a married
woman who has rehearsed the role of woman as homemaker, complementing man as breadwinner, finds that she needs to or wants to go to work?
She hasn't rehearsed the role of the assertive, competitive wage earner.
She still finds herself concerned about the welfare of her children, often
feeling anxious about them, and sometimes she feels guilty after she has
spent a day intensely involved in her work role. When a man who has
never nurtured and fed the family is thrust into sharing the home-
making/child-rearing role, he may feel underrehearsed and inadequate. He
may also worry about getting behind in his competitive breadwinning
role. The single parent faces the full range of these dual-role problems and
faces them alone.

In this chapter we shall discuss the concept of roles, the different roles
one may assume in marriage, the way roles have been defined in this
culture and in others, and the changes brought about in role definition by

women in the labor force. We turn now to roles in marriage and family—the established territory and the new frontiers.

THE CONCEPT OF *ROLE*

Whenever we discuss interpersonal behavior, and especially when we discuss marriage and family, two concepts are very important: *role* and *social position*. These two key concepts are defined in terms of each other. A role is a cluster of traits and tasks tied to a particular social position. A social position is a particular location within a social group to which rights and duties are assigned (Aldous 1978, p. 10; Scanzoni and Scanzoni 1976, p. 16).

In any small group engaging in an activity, roles develop quickly. A group getting together for a spontaneous volleyball game, for instance, will soon see the skills and temperaments of players as fitting with their positions. The woman who plays the net is soon seen as "the net player" and becomes established in this role. She is expected to guard the net and not intrude on other players' ground. Her role is functional: it contributes to the goals of the group, and other players count on her to play it. Her role, like theirs, is a system of duties to others, demanding corresponding rights from them.

The position of husband/father or wife/mother may include the roles of breadwinner, sexual partner, disciplinarian, teacher, chef, nurse, companion, therapist, student . . . one could go on. Each culture has a set of expectations concerning husband/father or wife/mother. These expectations may change as the culture changes, and a given family often adapts personal needs to role expectations and changing circumstances. In social units as small and intimate as the family, unique roles are bound to develop that never match the cultural ideals of the wife role or husband role.

SEX ROLES

Every society has roles based on sex, a set of expectations based on one's maleness or femaleness. Yet these expectations vary from culture to culture. Margaret Mead, in her book *Male and Female*, observes that the biological differences between the sexes have given rise to vastly different definitions of sex roles from culture to culture: "Upon the contrast in bodily form and function, men have built analogies between sun and moon, night and day, goodness and evil, strength and tenderness, steadfastness and fickleness, endurance and vulnerability. Sometimes one quality has been assigned to one sex, sometimes to the other" (1973, p. 38).

Every society, then, has sex roles. Every culture divides the array of possible human traits between the sexes, rather than recognizing the full potential of all human beings. Mead observed that men and women differ in "the way they contribute to the creation of the next generation; that otherwise in all respects they are simply human beings with varying gifts, no one of which can be exclusively assigned to either sex" (Mead 1973, p. 39). In recent years our culture has begun to consider that the differences between male and female may be much less significant than we had assumed. Yet even those who advocate flexibility in sex roles have been influenced by the traditional conceptions of male and female.

In American culture, the traditional masculine role carries with it the following trait expectations: strength, dominance, aggression, competition, and rationality. A masculine person is expected to control personal feelings and to refrain from expressing emotion spontaneously, except perhaps for anger and other feelings associated with aggression. Social scientists call traits that are related to work and mastery *instrumental* characteristics.

Mead notes that the need for evidence of achievement, which seems to be required for males in all cultures, may arise from the fact that women in every culture have the obvious achievement of giving birth to a new human being. Men seem to need a sure sign of their own achievement. In many cases, when the area of male achievement has been designated, it automatically becomes an area that women cannot enter:

There seems no evidence that it is necessary for men to surpass women in any specific way, but rather that men do need to find reassurance in achievement, and because of this connection, cultures frequently phrase achievement as something that women do not or cannot do, rather than directly as something which men do well. (Mead 1973, p. 168)

So in our culture, instrumental traits, which tend to include competition and aggression at the work place and on the playing field, were designated as the masculine sphere of achievement. We came to believe that women could not compete and achieve at the work place or on the playing field.

In the traditional feminine role, a woman demonstrates *expressive* characteristics. This is the term used by social scientists for qualities relating to emotions, expressions of feeling, and an emotional involvement with other people. A woman is expected to be passive—or at least non-aggressive—nurturant, and affectionate. She is supposed to be gentle, romantic, and dependent. She is expected to facilitate social relationships and to show love and understanding rather than aggression and competition.

These expressive and instrumental qualities are the basis of social roles for husband and wife in many marriages and, until recently, supplied the cultural ideals for marriages. Such a marriage is a stable collaboration based on separate but related "male" and "female" skills and interests. The woman's passive, nurturant temperament is complemented by the man's aggressive daring. Roles are assigned to husband and wife on the basis of these "masculine" and "feminine" traits. Thus, the aggressive male makes decisions dealing with the world, while the understanding female covers the home front, cares for the personal needs of her husband, and rears their children. The male initiates change and takes risks; the female conserves the old and provides a safe retreat for her husband (Koos 1946).

Mead and other social scientists stress the variability of sex roles—the changes in the meaning of masculine and feminine from one period of history to another and from one culture to another. But men and women do have different sexual organs, different reproductive functions, and different hormone levels, which seem related to aggression and passivity. Does this mean, as Sigmund Freud thought, that "anatomy is destiny," that male babies are predisposed to be competitive and female babies to be nurturant? Do biological traits cause men "to act like men"—instrumental and achieving—and women to "act like women"—expressive and supportive? Or is it possible that what we have defined as masculine or feminine behaviors could be purely the result of socialization and arbitrary cultural conditioning?

These questions continue to be controversial and may never be conclusively answered, but we now have a great deal of empirical data on sex roles. When Maccoby and Jacklin (1974) reviewed the research on sex differences, they concluded that many differences have more to do with cultural conditioning than with biological predestination. None of the qualities observed by social scientists is found only in members of one sex and not in the other. Although men tend to be more aggressive than women, and this characteristic does have some biological underpinning in terms of hormone levels, one can find in any given culture some aggressive women and some passive men. Cross-cultural work conducted by Gutmann (1975) demonstrates that aggressiveness and passivity vary even within a certain male or female over the life cycle. There is a good deal of overlap in characteristics, with a significant proportion of both men and women sharing any given trait. Other research on roles (Bem 1975) indicates that *androgynous* behavior, which exhibits a range of instrumental and expressive capacities, may be more useful for solving a variety of problems than either of the traditionally masculine or feminine behavior divisions. Men and women are being called upon to be androgynous, to combine assertiveness and nurturance, to have the role flexibility that allows them to use the appropriate trait as they move from intimate relationships to work relationships.

Changes in the nature of work are hastening sex-role changes. Work in postindustrial America has become detached, to a great extent, from physical strength and stamina. Few paid tasks require more exertion than the lifting of a 30-pound child—something women have done for centuries. Given the wide range of physical capabilities within each sex, it turns out that women at the far end of the strength spectrum are capable of handling even the most arduous jobs. Society is now more willing to recognize qualities in women—qualities of strength and intelligence—that it virtually denied before.

The sociological research on sex roles can be divided into three levels (Scanzoni and Fox 1980). The first level analyzes the big picture of social divisions according to dominant and subordinate groups. When researchers look at large population samples, they find that men, as a group, tend to enjoy greater amounts of valued rewards than women, as a group. A second level of analysis looks at the division of labor by sex (Nielsen 1978), seeking to learn how such divisions come about. In most preindustrial societies, men become attached to roles in the public sphere and women to roles in the private sphere, especially in the family. Thus, men gain public rewards and status. Since women produce goods and services for immediate use by family or clan—rather than for use by the society at large—women gain recognition or power in the private sphere. In modern societies, more women work in both public and private spheres. As we have noted, work is now less likely to require physical strength. Yet men continue to dominate the public sphere. The overall division of power, or *stratification pattern*, has not yet changed.

A third level of research asks what roles men and women choose when they have options. By and large, the findings indicate that more women than men prefer egalitarian norms. Men tend to prefer a traditional division of sex roles. The preference for equality is more marked among educated adults. An education gap may intensify conflicts over equality. The potential for serious conflict is most probable in households where women change their sex-role norms over time, becoming more egalitarian than their husbands. At the age of 21, a woman may have been content to assume a traditional homemaking role. At 38, with more education and experience under her belt and her children in school, she may opt for much greater equality. Even in households where both husband and wife are traditional, the assumptions of husband and wife differ. The traditional woman operates on the assumption that "if the family does well, I do, too," while the traditional man operates on the assumption that "if I do well, the family does, too" (Scanzoni 1978, p. 116). If the woman becomes egalitarian, she may change her "doing well" definition, seeing her own fulfillment as crucial to the family's well-being. Such shifts will clearly require negotiation. Women accurately perceive that pushing for equality will involve risks—greater potential for serious conflict and even a possible termination of the relationship. Many women may harbor preferences for greater equality, but never act on them because they fear the relationship will be jeopardized.

Sex Roles among Black Families

Black people in the United States were enslaved from the country's inception through most of the nineteenth century, and they suffered the aftereffects of slavery for decades following the Civil War. With survival determining their behavior, black families have had to develop sex roles that are more open than those of mainstream families. "Black women have often had to share the roles designated by society as male roles, just as Black men have had to share some of the traditionally designated female roles" (Hill 1972, p. 17).

Black women, as McCray points out, have often had to take on the role that carries out the instrumental function of the family. But there has been flexibility on both sides, with men and women interchanging roles when necessity required it. While some white families are becoming more flexible in role divisions, this is a departure from the past; "for most Black families this clear-cut distinction never existed" (McCray 1980, p. 74). "The highly functional role that the Black female has historically played has caused her to be erroneously stereotyped as a matriarch, and this label has been quite injurious to Black women and men" (Lardner 1972, p. 41). "Matriarchy" is not a suitable term for the single-parent situation. It implies that the female is head of a household in which a male is present. Where no male is present, or where the male is unable to find employment, the woman takes on an instrumental and expressive role. This matrifocal shift during unemployment has occurred among white families as well as black ones. Elder's (1974) studies tracing the effects of unemployment on families during the Great Depression suggest that, in a society that has assigned breadwinning exclusively to men, the loss of that role causes a lowering of self-esteem, for both fathers and sons. More recent studies on the effects of unemployment suggest a change in its significance as sex roles and work attitudes change (see Box 7.1).

A high incidence of single-parent families occurs primarily among the black poor. For those with incomes below the poverty line, more than half of the black families were headed by females in 1974 (Peters and deFord 1978). The majority of black families have both spouses present (Willie and Greenblatt 1978). When males are present, the black family seems as egalitarian as the white—perhaps more so since role flexibility is part of the black family's heritage (Middleton and Putney 1960). In middle-class black families, females do not dominate the decision-making process. Surveying sex-role research for black families, Willie and Greenblatt conclude

> ## BOX 7.1   The Changing Effects of Father's Job Loss
>
> Glen Elder, Jr. (1974) has studied Berkeley, California, families that had infant children in 1929, the year the Great Depression started. Looking at those families who lost a third or more in income, Elder found a dramatic difference in the effects of deprivation on mothers and fathers, boys and girls. He found that mothers grew in importance as a source of both income and emotional support, while fathers became estranged and peripheral. Ties between fathers and sons weakened. Ties between mothers and daughters grew stronger. Elder also reports that boys in these deprived families wound up feeling incompetent and powerless. At adolescence they tended to meet life with indecision and withdrawal. Girls, on the other hand, were self-confident, goal-oriented, and assertive. The results for the boys were most serious during adolescence, but even in later life they were more troubled than men from nondeprived homes.
>
> Recently, Detroit-area men who had been unemployed for two years were interviewed by Louis Ferman, Research Director of the Institute of Labor and Industrial Relations at the University of Michigan (Ferman 1979). He found a wide range of reactions to job loss, from extreme anguish to nonchalance or even enjoyment of the nonworker status. Many men suffered because their self-image as breadwinner was diminished, particularly if they were afraid that they could not get another job. A related finding was that older men tended to suffer more shame over job loss than younger men. There are implications that men in their early thirties are finding self-worth to be less tied to their work and more to their families. In fact, in looking at these two male roles—work and family—psychologist Joseph Pleck of the Center for Research on Women, Wellesley College, found that most men now get more satisfaction from their families than from their jobs (Pleck 1979).

that "black families with both spouses present are not matriarchies and may differ very little from white families of similar socioeconomic rankings" (1978, p. 19).

A final feature of sex roles in black families is the historic and current role of the extended kin network as a significant source of support. In the past and today, grandmothers and other relatives have often helped in the care of children, as well as informally adopting children whose parents were unable to care for them (Hill 1977, pp. 54–55). This network relieves the isolation that other families, especially single-parent families, have experienced. It serves to reduce some of the strain of the single-parent role.

Sex-Role Socialization

When two people marry, they may not be conscious of forming role divisions. Newlyweds have not customarily set forth assignments as to who will do which task. She prepares a meal, he mows the lawn, and these become established tasks for each. Why, do so many women wind up preparing the meals and so many men mowing the lawn? Traditional cultural ideals of male and female permeate family life. There is also the tendency of like to choose like, the inclination in mate selection for men and women to choose partners of similar backgrounds and values, as we have discussed in Chapter 6. This tendency makes it likely that people who marry will have similar role expectations. The woman is more likely to continue preparing those meals and the man to mow those lawns because of what they have learned in childhood. Both have spent hours observing, practicing, and preparing for roles they will assume in adult life.

Many explanations have been offered as to how the sex roles of mother and father become part of children's behavior. Psychoanalysts use the term "introjection," suggesting that children identify with and ultimately incorporate the roles of their parents. Behavior modification theory stresses the importance of rewards and punishments as the way parents teach roles to their children. Social learning theory emphasizes the impact of observation and modeling. These mechanisms are the pathways of socialization, the means by which children assume sex roles similar to

Children learn by observing and imitating adults. (Jerry Howard, Positive Images)

those of their parents. Children learn by identifying with parents, observing parents and other adults, and being rewarded or punished. As adult sex-role behavior changes, so, too, will children's.

Children of parents who subscribe to the traditional notion that some behaviors are appropriate for girls and some for boys will quickly become aware of the approved behaviors and practice them. Take the little boy who hurts himself and then runs crying to his parents for sympathy. If they warn him not to be a "crybaby" or a "sissy" or label his plea for sympathy "feminine" and tell him only girls cry, then he will be discouraged from engaging in such behavior again. If the boy also sees that his father doesn't cry when he is hurt, but does show anger, he learns that sadness and crying are not part of his role, but anger is acceptable. Applause from parents for a daring tree climb adds the component of risk taking to his concept of masculinity. What children see around them is ultimately more powerful than what they are simply told. When they see certain role behavior modeled and then are rewarded when they behave in the same way (or are punished when they don't), the social learning becomes firmly rooted.

Girls have traditionally been socialized to show the expressive side of their nature, to be gentle and conciliatory. In the past their mothers have modeled these traits. But if a girl's mother is herself independent and assertive, she will encourage these more instrumental qualities in her daughter—both directly through rewarding the daughter's assertiveness and indirectly by the example or model her behavior provides. This connection has been proved in the research on working mothers we discuss later in this chapter. Maternal employment is associated with assertiveness and accomplishment in daughters.

Influence of Social Status and Religion.   The nature of the sex role to which a child is socialized depends partly on the social status and religious background of the child's parents, teachers, and other significant role models. Racial and ethnic heritage, as we have suggested, also exert a special influence. Currently, there is an ethos of equality between the sexes. The more educated and secular the parents are, the less likely they are to draw sharp distinctions between male and female roles. Working-class parents tend to socialize their children to sex-typed behaviors and encourage gender differentiation. Both working- and middle-class parents stress instrumental qualities in their sons, but some middle-class parents tend to encourage their daughters and their sons to develop both instrumentally and expressively.

There are several reasons for this difference between working-class and middle-class views of sex roles. According to sociologist Melvin Kohn (1963; Kohn and Carroll 1960), working-class people tend to view social reality as fixed, as something over which they have little control. This sense of powerlessness contrasts with the sense of freedom that usually prevails in the middle class. Middle-class children are more likely to be educated to view change as both possible and desirable for themselves and society. They are educated to humanistic values that emphasize qualities men and women share, such as intellectual and artistic capacities (Scanzoni and Scanzoni 1976, p. 32). These differences in social realities and education make for differences in sex-role socialization.

There are several ways of interpreting data of working- and middle-class patterns of sex-role socialization. Janet Saltzman Chafetz (1974), for example, has argued that instrumentality means different things in these two social groups. Working-class boys tend to denigrate school achievement as "feminine," while middle-class boys learn to aspire to academic excellence as an important form of masculine mastery and competence.

Though older working-class men may resist role changes, many middle-aged and large numbers of younger men and women are changing their role definitions to what Yankelovich (1974) has called the "New Morality." This includes the liberalization of sexual mores, reduction of obedience to authority, lessening of respect for authority figures, a belief that one has the right to more of one's wants. These attitudes, according to Shostak, are being embraced by many young "blue collarites"; ironically, TV, which Shostak calls "the most powerful cultural equalizer of all," has speeded the process. By middle-class standards, TV may be sexist; by working-class standards it may have a liberalizing influence. Blue-collar women, however, appear to be the most significant source of sex-role change:

Large numbers of blue-collar women, for example, have been newly freed by their use of effective contraceptives from their historic bondage to unwanted pregnancies (or induced miscarriages and abortions, legal or otherwise). As they have gained, for the first time in history, the power to conceive at will, many are drawing their husbands into earnest family planning discussions and family well-being reviews. Choosing to have fewer children than ever before, these blue-collar mothers are advising their husbands to invest more heavily than ever in parenting—for there will be less of it in their lifespan than true of all previous blue-collar generations. More companionship, more emotional support, and more personal attention are sought by these women from their men than ever before. (Shostak 1980, p. 322)

Religion is a factor in determining sex roles for working-class as well as middle-class families. The child who learns that sex roles are "divinely ordained" will have highly differentiated sex-role expectations for males and females. A study of American college women showed that Mormons and Catholics regard marriage and childbearing as sacred callings. In a random regional sample of 3,100 married men and women, Scanzoni and Scanzoni found that persons who viewed motherhood as sacred ("Marriage and family were established by God") also held more traditional views of the wife's role, believing that a woman's greatest responsibility is to her family and that women are naturally suited to certain tasks. Studies indicate that Catholics hold a less egalitarian view of sex roles than other religious groups. For example, Catholics surveyed tended to believe that a husband's interests are predominant and more important than the wife's, that he has a right to be bothered if his wife is away from home, and that he shouldn't be as willing as his wife to stay home with a sick child (Scanzoni and Scanzoni 1976, pp. 35–37).

THE CHANGING STRUCTURE OF MARRIAGE

Scanzoni and Scanzoni (1976) have examined the structure of marriages, the way sex roles interact in family life, and the relative power of husband and wife. They have identified a number of different marital structures: the "owner" model, the "head-complement" or "directorship" model, the senior-junior partnership, and the equal partnership.

Marriage as Ownership

From Biblical times until the twentieth century, husbands have been regarded as owners and wives as property. The ownership model is still common in many parts of the world. But, as we have discussed in Chapter 2, (pages 44–45), views of women have changed gradually over the centuries. In the United States, the values of companionship and individual equality eventually enhanced the status of women, changed the roles of husband and wife, and altered the structure of marriage.

Marriage as a Hierarchy

Gradually the ownership structure gave way to the head-complement model of marriage. The husband no longer "owns" his wife, but he is definitely the "director" or head of the family. She demands more rights from him, however, and he has more duties to her. Her role is still to please him, to bear and rear his children, and to find meaning through him and reflect credit on him. The primary difference is the question of obedience. Final decisions in most matters are still his, but she is free to discuss her views, to try to influence his decisions. She is expected to show deference to him, but not necessarily obedience. Since she is now his friend and lover, not simply his property, there is more room in the marriage for empathy, affection, and companionship. This structure continues to prevail in many marriages today, especially when the husband provides the only source of income.

In either the ownership or directorship structures, the wife, as subordinate to a dominant husband, will try to establish a viable role for herself, one that gives her a sense of identity and is also functional. She can do this in any number of ways. She may establish her own special sphere of influence: parenting and meal preparation make up the traditional sphere. One still hears many women say, when they are preparing a meal, "I don't allow anyone in my kitchen." The woman may assume a role of moral perfection or play the role of an invalid, weak and needing protection. Or, as often happens, she may establish a viable role for herself as the mediator in family conflicts. She may assume a negative role as the resentful critic who, having no opportunity for input into decisions, feels free to criticize constantly those who make the decisions (Turner, 1970, pp. 188–191). Thus emerges the stereotype of the nagging wife. Whichever role she chooses, she must not encroach on the man's sphere of influence.

In both these structures, marriage is a stable collaboration based on skills and interests that are specialized—some male, others female—and interdependent. His role is to support the family and to make a living in a competitive world, a role that calls for risk taking and aggressiveness. Hers is to bring up the children and support his work efforts and confidence, creating a safe haven for him when he retreats from the pressures of work.

Marriage as a Partnership

Money isn't everything in a marriage, but the ability to make money has a powerful effect on the structure of a marriage and the roles husband and wife assume. Earning power influences the decision-making process and—as we shall see in Chapter 9—the management of conflict. As women have entered the public sphere of paid employment, the structure of marriage has shifted to a partnership arrangement.

The working woman is not a new phenomenon. Throughout history, most women in most societies have been employed in economic production. It is simply that we did not choose to call it "employment" and that it usually took place at home, where women could also supervise small children. It was only with the Industrial Revolution and the development of factories that both women and men began working outside the home. Even then, it was usually single women who went out to work rather than working at home. Only after World War I did married women become a significant part of the American labor force. Until World War II, the consensus was still that "a woman's place is in the home," where much of the family production—clothing, baking, laundry—remained. By 1978, however, the labor force included half of the women with children from the ages of six to seventeen, over one-third of the women with children from the ages of three to five, and somewhat under one-third of the women with children under three years of age (Masnick and Bane 1980). Box 7.2 discusses some trends for working mothers.

Women seem to be moving in the direction of greater attachment to their work, but they are still more likely than men to move in and out of the job market. One common pattern is working full-time before having children, stopping for a while when the children are infants, working part-time when the children are young, and working full-time again when the children are in school. Other factors in the life cycle contribute to the shifting power base in marriage. The birth of a child tends to move couples to a more traditional, male-dominant role pattern, partially because, as Rapoport and Rapoport have found, women often become less active in the labor force and less ambitious immediately after their children are born (1971, p. 20). Middle age, with children less dependent or out of the home, usually brings the couple to a more egalitarian arrangement.

When a married woman becomes a wage earner, the structure of the marriage changes significantly, as she is no longer totally dependent on her husband for survival. Part of the family's income comes from her resources. Assuming this new role of breadwinner gives women more power in marital decisions, especially decisions about financial arrangements and how money is used. Continuing the business metaphor, we can think of such structures as partnerships, either *junior-senior partnerships*, or—in those marriages (still a minority) in which the woman's career is regarded by both as equal in importance to her husband's—*equal partnerships*.

Senior Partner and Junior Partner.   Paralleling the change in women's paid employment has been a change in sex roles and decision-making power. The wife who works is no longer obligated to remain in her separate sphere of influence. She may continue to exhibit expressive traits, but her work encourages instrumental traits as well. She now has options concerning her role.

While marriage is not simply an economic arrangement, shifts in work style and earning power tend to change the structure of a marriage and the power the woman has in it. The fact that the wife is no longer totally dependent on her husband for survival removes her, as Scanzoni and Scanzoni put it, "from the position of being an adjunct to a benevolent head whose ultimate jurisdiction is undisputed" (1976, p. 216). In terms of decision-making power, the wife, no longer merely receiving an allowance but now making a real contribution (as a "junior partner") to family resources, is likely to become more significantly involved in decisions involving money. The wife's work involvement may also bring the husband into some of her traditional spheres. He may take a greater role in child

> **BOX 7.2   Trends for Working Mothers**
> A report from the Harvard-MIT Joint Center for Urban Studies (Masnick and Bane 1980) provides a clear picture of the changes in women's participation in the labor force, as well as projections concerning the future (see Figure 1.2, p. 6). Since 1960 there has been a marked increase in both part-time and full-time employment of married women with children. The proportion of wives with school-age children working full-time year-round increased from about 16 percent in 1960 to about 26 percent in 1978. The proportion of wives with children under age three working full-time year-round increased from about 3 percent in 1960 to about 10 percent in 1978. Women with children under age three are still unwilling, for the most part, to take on full-time jobs, while women with school-age children (ages six to seventeen) are far more likely to work full-time. Women currently earn only about 60 percent of what men earn for comparable work, and many women work at low wages on part-time jobs. The trend, however, is toward more full-time work for women with childen of all ages, and Masnick and Bane predict that by 1990 wives will contribute up to 40 percent of family income.

rearing, meal preparation, and other tasks that were once exclusively hers. With this greater flexibility comes a greater challenge to the marriage; many more decisions are open to negotiation.

Equal Partners.   In the majority of two-worker families, the woman's earnings, and in many cases her commitment to work outside the home, are not as great as her husband's. But in some cases a married woman has a position and a career roughly equal to her husband's, and they both recognize this equality. Scanzoni and Scanzoni call this an equal-partnership marriage. Rapoport and Rapoport (1971), who have conducted extensive research on sex roles as they relate to work, call these marriages "dual-career families." This new structure requires both heads of household to be involved in maintaining the family, while both pursue "careers"—that is, "jobs which require a high degree of commitment and which have a continuous developmental character" (Rapoport and Rapoport 1971, p. 18).

With this equality on the job front, a more equal division of household chores and child-rearing tasks becomes possible. Now almost everything connected to roles is open to negotiation; there are few assumptions. Neither automatically assumes that they will have children. If they do have children, it is not automatically assumed that she has primary responsibility for child care. Rather, they will make explicit arrangements to share child-care responsibilities. An equal-partner marriage means that the wife, like her husband, has the option to travel for her work. It is not automatically assumed that the couple will live where the husband's work is, or even that they will live in the same house, since their separate careers may require that they live separately part of the week and commute to alternate locations on weekends (Scanzoni and Scanzoni 1976, pp. 235–237).

Couples in equal-partner marriages must relinquish at least some of their traditional sex-role expectations of "masculine" and "feminine" behavior and personality. As Turner (1970) has noted, the traditional equation of "masculine" with instrumental qualities and "feminine" with expressive qualities creates a situation of female subordination and male dominance. Unless this strict dichotomy between "masculine" and "feminine" is renounced, an equal partnership is not possible without enormous role strain and unhappiness. Some of the advantages and disadvantages of the equal-partner or dual-career marriage are discussed in Box 7.3.

ROLES OF THE SINGLE PARENT

Divorce is the primary event that thrusts a parent—usually the mother—into assuming all the traits and tasks associated with the roles of breadwinner and homemaker. Desertion, the death of a spouse, the birth of children out of wedlock, and the chronic unemployment of a husband may also place a woman in a situation where she is the sole head of the household. Over 14 percent of all households in the United States are now headed by women. This figure is likely to increase as divorce rates continue to rise and remarriages among divorced women fail to keep pace. Not since 1940, when the single-parent family was likely to be led by a middle-aged widow, have such a large number of American families been headed by women. The majority of single-parent families today are headed by a divorced woman between the ages of 25 and 44. Over 75 percent of these women are working. They may receive child support, but the bulk of their income (over 60 percent) derives from their own earnings (Masnick and Bane 1980).

Working wives suffer role strain, but the situation is much more severe for working single parents. They must assume all the traits and tasks—instrumental and expressive, breadwinning and homemaking, car maintenance and meal preparation, budgeting and housecleaning. They must make all the decisions alone. Women who have been socialized to perform only the expressive functions, and women who have no work experience, may find this new, all-encompassing role staggering. The situation for divorced women is made more stressful, especially during the year or two immediately following the divorce, when children may react negatively to their changed circumstances (Hetherington, Cox, and Cox 1978).

Whether a woman feels intolerable role strain after a divorce and whether her children will show severe deficits appear to depend on the degree of psychological, social, and economic support she can muster after the divorce. Divorced fathers who continue to take a parenting role improve effects for both mother and children, as research demonstrates (Hess and Camera 1979). Stepfathers and surrogate fathers (other men who take the role of father) also ameliorate the situation (Oshman and Manosevits 1976).

Fathers who have custody of children appear to receive more support from friends and relatives than mothers with custody do (Warshak and Santrok 1979). Perhaps fathers feel fewer qualms about asking for help; in addition, they probably receive more voluntary offers of help because their social position (father/breadwinner) traditionally does not include the role of full-time, nurturing parent. Ironically, single fathers, because their incomes have not dropped, are also better able to afford to hire outside help.

Divorce is now both more common and more acceptable in American society, as such popular TV characters as "Alice" and Ann Romano of "One Day at a Time" suggest. This relatively recent acceptance is likely to reduce the role strain on single parents. Research on the effects of father absence indicates that the reaction of the community to the father-absent family is crucial in determining the effects of his absence on the mother and children. When a community supports the single parent in the breadwinner, disciplinarian, and nurturing-parent roles, the children do not seem to suffer serious deficits. When the single parent is isolated and ostracized, however, children tend to have problems with maturity, peer adjustment, and a secure sense of their own sex role (Herzog and Sudia 1973).

A number of factors affect the ability of single parents to cope with their complex role: the extent of financial loss; the social position of the family in the community; the degree of support offered by the community and the social policies of the culture at large; availability of child care; job possibilities and work schedules that allow the single parent to meet parenting needs; and whether or not the single parent is already employed or at least trained for paid employment. Also significant is the extent to which a single mother's many roles are shared by ex-husband, male friends, surrogate parents, women friends, or relatives. All these variables will figure into the roles played by divorced parents, their effectiveness as parents, and the outcome for their children. Chapter 12 provides a detailed discussion of the causes of divorce and its effects on husband, wife, and children.

WORKING WIVES AND MOTHERS

During the past three decades, labor-force participation rates for women have increased significantly. The greatest increase in employment rate has been for married women with husbands present and children under 18. Between 1950 and 1978, the employment rate for this group of women rose from about 18 percent to about 52 percent (Masnick and Bane 1980).

BOX 7.3 Dual-Career/Equal-Partner Marriages

The pattern of wives whose commitments to careers are equal to those of their husbands is a relatively new one, and much more research will be needed to assess what has been called "the strains and gains" of the dual-career marriage. In their case studies of five such marriages, supplemented by prior research on sex roles and working, Rapoport and Rapoport (1971) found these features:

1. Management of Competitiveness and Envy.   Husbands in these marriages regarded their wives' work as important. The wives needed this approval and found that their husbands' cooperation facilitated their careers in many ways. With wives who were highly motivated to work—women who considered work as an integral part of their identity—and husbands who did not resent achieving women, competition was not a serious problem.

2. Overload.   Strain and, at times, sheer exhaustion from trying to sustain career and family were serious problems. Children were called upon to take on more responsibility in these families, but generally these couples had less free time and had to make more deliberate efforts to achieve family leisure; otherwise, work swallowed up all their time. On the other hand, this dual-career family could afford a holiday when it was needed. Because of the customary overload, the vacations these families chose were ones in which they could be pampered.

3. Handling Child Rearing.   These couples were established in their occupations before they began to have children. Husbands participated more in domestic life, but these couples had to hire help of various types to aid in child rearing. With two substantial incomes this was not a financial problem, but wives still experienced some guilt and ambivalence; husbands still reported occasional resentment at modifying their own careers to accommodate the wife's career needs and the demands of house and children.

4. Problem Solving.   These couples were unusually adept at communicating their feelings and working out problems they encountered. Though they faced conflicts and anxieties that one-worker families might not have experienced, both husband and wife felt that they needed the dual-career structure to satisfy their personal requirements for self-expression at home and at work.

5. Satisfaction Levels.   The dual-career marriages had as many very happy levels as those in the more conventional—what we have called head-complement—variety. None of the couples interviewed by Rapoport and Rapoport placed their careers ahead of their families, though in some couples one partner was more oriented toward work. In other research reported by Rapoport and Rapoport (1971), couples who were intensely and equally bent on career advancement as a priority ahead of families experienced low levels of satisfaction.

In other studies, job seeking for young dual-career couples was found to be a problem. There is little support available to dual-career couples while they are both seeking jobs. And when two spouses are both undergoing the same stresses and strains, it is difficult for them to seek support from each other, since in some cases that means siding with one's spouse against oneself (Berger et al. 1978, p. 26).

Children may take on more household responsibilities when both parents work. (Carol Palmer, Picture Cube)

A questionnaire survey of 160 dual-career couples and interviews with 15 such couples found that only a little over half of the couples agreed to an egalitarian procedure for job seeking before they began the process. That is, only half of them agreed to look for jobs independently of each other and then accept the best joint offer, or agreed to look in the same geographical area (Berger et al. 1978, p. 27). Among couples who didn't adopt a procedure for equality, women were much more likely to follow men to their job locations. But because of the situational pressures and the extra difficulties that the women faced in finding suitable jobs, only one-quarter of the final decisions were egalitarian. One husband reported that although he initially agreed to follow his wife, in the end he was unwilling to do so (p. 25).

Most couples reported satisfaction as well as stress in seeking jobs together. Couples were pleased and proud when they located two acceptable positions in the same area. They also reported getting more satisfaction from their marriage when they both had jobs they liked (Berger 1978, p. 32). In evaluating dual-career marriages, we should remember that such couples choose to accept the strains caused by such a relationship. They both take on these difficulties "as part of their fashioning a lifestyle that most fully satisfies their fundamental needs and values" (Douvan and Pleck 1978, p. 146).

Sometimes a dual-career marriage means that a couple must live separately during part of the week or year. A common warning to married people who make such

BOX 7.3 (Continued)

arrangements is that separation inevitably weakens the marital relationship. In one sense, of course, this is true. Any important relationship depends on two people's spending time together. And there is no doubt that a couple's time together suffers when they are living in different places. As social scientists point out, however, the "balance between separation and togetherness is a critical, complex issue" (Douvan and Pleck 1978, p. 138). Some case studies show that temporary separation can actually improve a dual-career marriage by allowing partners to become more involved in society outside the family. Separation, in fact, is common in many traditional forms of marriage: upper-class families in which women spend part of the year in summer homes or resorts, Asian or European families in which the husband leaves his family while he goes abroad for a job or training, military families, and so on (Douvan and Pleck 1978, pp. 138–139). What makes these arrangements acceptable in traditional terms is that it is the husband—not the wife—who, for business or professional reasons, is separated from the family.

In dual-career marriages, a wife's separation for business or professional reasons may help her deal with an ambivalence that she may have at the start of her career, an ambivalence that comes from her own early socialization to the feminine ideal of a woman who devotes herself entirely to her family. For a woman who is still considered an extension of her husband by her peers and colleagues, separation may help her in getting a job or in establishing her own professional identity (Douvan and Pleck 1978, p. 139).

For decades, researchers have been raising certain questions about working mothers:

- Does a woman's working role conflict with her role as a mother and homemaker?
- Do the personality traits needed in the working world undermine her nurturant role?
- What effect does a woman's working have on the stability of her family and the health and welfare of her children?

Working is bound to create some role strain if the woman is still expected to fulfill her role as *sole* nurturer and homemaker. Although the husbands and children of working women take on more household responsibilities than those of nonworking women, the working wife usually continues to assume most of the responsibility for the home and children (Rallings and Nye 1979). Pressures on working wives are not yet offset by help and general role adjustment on the part of husbands (see Box 7.4). Husbands do spend more time with their children when they are allowed to start and finish work earlier (Winett and Neale 1979). Cultural support in the form of government and business policies can reduce some of the strains on working parents.

BOX 7.4   **Pressures on Working Wives**

Laura Lein, a social anthropologist at Wellesley College, has produced an NIMH-funded study that seems to substantiate the conventional assumption that working wives with children experience an overload. She found that *both* husbands and wives feel that care of home and children is the woman's responsibility. Men are willing to assist their wives, but they resist such domestic tasks as washing dishes.

Women, on the other hand, are willing and even eager to assume a breadwinner role in addition to their homemaker role. Lein also found that working mothers refuse to lower their standards concerning the care of children and home. Women report great stress in coping with demands of job and family and are "rushed, constantly under pressure, never able to consider a task properly finished," Lein says.

Women usually choose jobs that allow them to be close to home and accessible to their children. Men, however, seek jobs that offer security even at the expense of advancement, stimulation, and proximity to their children (Lein 1979). As this and other studies indicate, the fact remains that unless both partners recognize the need for a more equitable distribution of responsibility, working mothers will continue to bend under the strain.

The government has provided some funds for day care, as noted in Chapter 3, even though there is no national day-care program. Schools are offering more extended afternoon activities. Approximately ten percent of government and industry employees are now on flexible work schedules that allow for earlier starting and finishing times. But social policy and the private sector have not yet caught up with the rise in maternal employment: employment does not automatically bring about changes in role expectations. Even in countries such as the Soviet Union where extensive day-care facilities are available, women are expected to be responsible for after-hours child care, as well as housework and shopping.

Attitudes of Men and Women

The ambivalence of American men concerning working wives was documented by Mirra Komarovsky (1973) when she tested 53 young men attending an Ivy League college. One-third of the men in her sample were troubled by the problem of dealing with women as intellectual equals. Many of them wanted an intellectual companion, but were anxious about looking bad next to a smarter woman—what has been called "sociological ambivalence" (Merton and Barber 1963). For example, one of Komarovsky's subjects stated: "I want a girl who has some defined crystal of her own personality and does not merely echo my thoughts." But later, when he found such a girl, he felt "nervous and humble."

The majority of the men in this sample (70 percent), however, were not suffering from the companionship/need-for-superiority conflict. Some did not find intellectual accomplishments a threat; others didn't feel the need for intellectual superiority. In the past, women themselves have tended to "play dumb" (Komarovsky 1946; Wallen 1950). But when Komarovsky compared the responses of college women in the early 1970s with those of women in 1946 and 1950, she found that women were becoming much less likely to play down their own intellectual abilities (Komarovsky 1973).

The college men in Komarovsky's sample expressed a preference for women who were intelligent, as well as being sexually attractive, loving, and displaying social amenities. Yet when they were asked how they would feel if their future wife chose to work, their sociological ambivalence emerged again. Here is a typical response:

I believe that it is good for mothers to return to full time work when the children are grown, provided the work is important and worthwhile. Otherwise, housewives get hung up with tranquilizers, because they have no outlet for their abilities. . . . Of course, it may be difficult if a wife becomes successful in her own right. A woman should want her husband's success more than he should want hers. Her work shouldn't interfere with or hurt his career in any way. He should not sacrifice his career to hers. For example, if he is transferred, his wife should follow—and not vice versa. (1973, p. 881)

Komarovsky states that "The ideological support for the belief in sharp sex role differentiation in marriage has weakened, but the belief itself has not been relinquished" (1973, p. 879). She cites these as some of the inconsistencies revealed by men during lengthy interviews (1973, pp. 873–884):

- the right of an able woman to a career of her choice
- the admiration for women who measure up in terms of the dominant values of our society
- the lure such women present and the threat they pose
- the conviction that there is no substitute for the mother's care of young children
- the deeply internalized norm of male occupational superiority
- the principle of equal opportunity irrespective of sex.

Though American men may be ambivalent about work, American women seem to be incorporating a work component in their role expectations. Adolescent girls, in the process of consolidating their identity, now expect to combine work outside the home with marriage and family (Konopka 1976). With more women being socialized to instrumental as well as expressive qualities, with job opportunities increasing and inflation continuing, the old question of whether a woman works for enjoyment or for money is becoming irrelevant. Though there may be pleasure in earning money and in experiencing social contacts at work, most women work because they have to work, because they've been trained to work, and, increasingly, because "paid worker" is a new aspect of their role

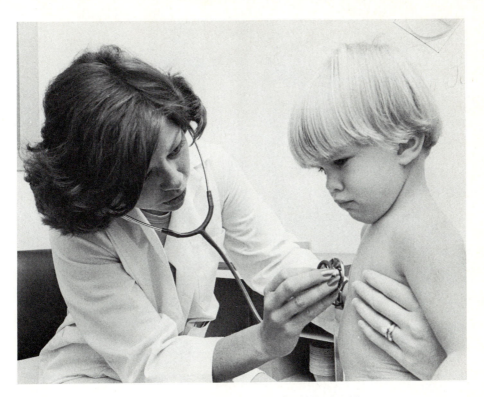

Work has become an important aspect of women's role. (David Krathwohl)

before and after marriage. At the same time, the majority of women continue to see their role as parent as a primary one, particularly during the years when their children are very young.

Effects on Children

A woman's satisfaction with her work outside the home may be the single most important factor in determining the effects of working on her children. Research studies have not always examined husbands' attitudes, but their support, encouragement, and cooperation undoubtedly affect mothers and, through them, children. In their sample of dual-career families, Rapoport and Rapoport (1971) found that husbands urged their wives to develop their work careers and actively shared in child-care responsibilities.

The effects of maternal employment also vary according to the age of her child or children and the attitudes of her socioeconomic class and community toward working mothers. The mother of an infant or a toddler

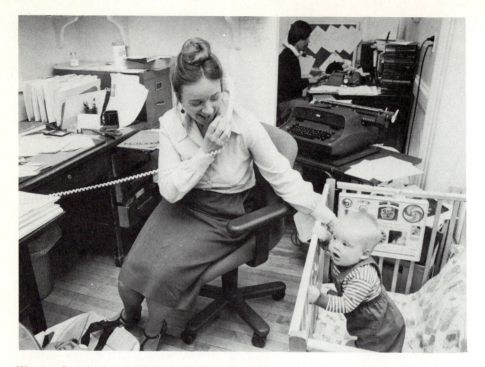

Women often choose jobs that allow them to be close to home and accessible to their children. (Martha Stewart, Picture Cube)

is likely to feel more anxiety about working than the mother of a school-age child. Infants and very young children require a consistent loving care-giver. In our mobile society, relatives are not always available to provide care. Day care for children under three is rarely available. Having both parents at work may be detrimental to infants unless a qualified and caring substitute parent is available.

School-age children, with their greater independence, are better able to deal with their mother's working if cultural attitudes are positive. This is particularly significant for school-age boys, who show signs of problems when their mother's employment seems to diminish their father's self-esteem and, by association, their own. At adolescence, girls may benefit from enhanced self-esteem when mothers work. Lack of supervision or negative cultural attitudes may result in some negative effects for adolescents, though delinquency does not appear to be one of them (Woods 1972; Etaugh 1974). Generally, maternal employment seems to have both a more powerful impact and a more positive effect on daughters than on sons.

Keeping in mind that a child's development depends upon role models provided by both mother and father, and also remembering that the child's age is significant, we can recognize the fact that a mother who works models a different sex role than one who doesn't. This, of course, has effects on her children. Evidence suggests that the children of a working woman have a more egalitarian view of the division of household tasks, perceive maternal employment as nonthreatening to marital relations, favor social equality, and have a more positive view of maternal employment and of female competence. Such a child, whether boy or girl, tends to express a higher estimate of his or her own sex (Hoffman 1974).

Working-class children whose mothers are employed, however, may be affected differently than middle-class children. The working-class woman is less likely to have an equal-partnership marital structure. The job she is able to get is less likely to be a well-paying and satisfying one. Her employment will probably bring more role strain because her social position continues to be more traditional; she is still expected to be responsible for home and child care. The very fact that she has to work may indicate some failure on the part of her husband in terms of his role as breadwinner (McCord, McCord, and Thurber 1963). Early research indicated that maternal employment in a working-class family hurt a son's image of his father, making him less apt to name his father as the person he admired most (Hartley 1960) and more likely to evaluate his father lower than his mother (McCord, McCord, and Thurber 1963). More recent Canadian studies report the same pattern among school-age children (Kappel and Lambert 1972) and adolescents (Propper 1972). But when the sample was taken from a community in which most mothers were employed, children of mothers who worked full-time were better adjusted than those whose mothers didn't work or worked part-time (Woods 1972). Changes in community attitudes, increases in the number of mothers working, and changes in marital structure and role division may eventually alter the somewhat detrimental effects of maternal employment on sons of working-class families.

In the middle class, where marital structures are more likely to be egalitarian and husbands more likely to share the home responsibilities, maternal employment gives sons a different and possibly more positive image of their fathers. The son of a middle-class working mother is more likely to see his father as a nurturing, warm, and expressive parent than is the son of a middle-class mother who stays home (Vogel et al. 1970).

In both lower and middle classes, girls seem to gain in self-esteem when their mothers work. A girl whose mother works, studies suggest, will be more independent than the daughter of a nonworking mother. Following her working mother's example, she will probably begin working as an adolescent (Douvan 1963; Roy 1963) and will want to work when she is a mother (Hartley 1960; Banducci 1967). Her image of women and traditional femininity also will probably differ from that of girls whose mothers do not work. She will not see herself as traditionally feminine, but will tend to see women as competent, effective, more active in the outside world, and less restricted to the home. Daughters of working mothers tend to admire and want to emulate their mothers more than do daughters of nonworking mothers (Rallings and Nye 1979, p. 216). Having a working mother is a significant background factor for career-oriented women and highly educated professional women (Hoffman 1974).

Working mothers seem to have a positive effect on children's images of female sex roles; their working does not seem to adversely affect children, especially when the culture supports their social position. As with the absence of the father, cultural acceptance of the mother's situation increases her satisfaction and thereby helps her cope with the demands of her double role as breadwinner/parent. With these supports, she is better able to be effective both as a mother and a worker.

Effects on Husbands

The effects of women's employment on their husbands seem to vary primarily according to socioeconomic status. Some studies indicate that the marital satisfaction of working-class husbands is decreased by their wife's employment, perhaps because they are forced to become more involved in housekeeping and other traditionally feminine roles. Marital satisfaction of middle- and upper-class husbands actually increased when their wives went to work (Rallings and Nye 1979, p. 215). Lois Hoffman, concluding a major review of maternal employment studies, gives us the best last word on the subject: "The context within which maternal employment takes place—the meaning it has for the family and the social setting—determines its effects" (1974, p. 218).

ROLES AND MARITAL SATISFACTION

Role expectations are beliefs or rules people have about what people (ourselves or others) ought to do in a certain role. *Role behavior,* on the other hand, is the way a person actually behaves in a role. When people's role behavior does not match their own or another's expectations for that role, there is stress and conflict. A woman's husband masks his private thoughts; she is irked by his aloofness. His behavior does not match her role expectations: she expects more sharing of thoughts and feelings. Perhaps he does not conform to the role expectation of intimacy and sharing because he is unable to or afraid of doing so. His natural temperament may not be suited to it, or he may feel the demand is excessive. Perhaps he does not share her role expectations, so that his role as her companion and friend does not give him a sense of worth or accomplishment.

Whatever the reason, both will feel dissatisfied—he because he fails to meet her role expectation (especially if he shares it, but is unable to match it in his behavior), she because she experiences his failure as a failure to reciprocate. She has performed her role as a wife adequately, but her role is given meaning and support only by his reciprocating role. He is not cuing her to continue her role (Turner 1970, p. 292).

Role Strain

A variety of studies show that the more *congruence*, or matching, there is between role expectations and role behavior, the more satisfied individuals tend to be with their marriages (Burr 1976, pp. 297–298). No preconceived notion concerning sex roles can perfectly fit the unique temperaments and interests of family members. So all couples will experience some gap between role expectations and role behavior. This gap or discrepancy between what one expects of a mate and what the mate actually does is called *role strain*. A flexible definition of sex roles tends to reduce role strain. If a husband or wife defines sex roles narrowly, however, or if one is unable to adjust one's original role expectations to the other's changing needs, there is likely to be tension and conflict (Turner 1970, pp. 293–294). Each person will be either straining to fit personal behavior into an inappropriate mold or resisting the imposition of another's unrealistic expectations. Either way, there will be resentment, frustration, and anger.

Most women (and most men) work out of economic necessity. Yet many working wives have entered marriage with traditional expectations that did not include the role of wage-earner. Traditional roles must change to adapt to changed circumstances. Unless such couples are also able to change their role expectations, their ideals of "feminine" and "masculine," both partners will feel inadequate: he as a provider, she as a homemaker and mother. Even the most "liberated," egalitarian couple can experience role strain as they balance work against family and reach a consensus on just how independent they should be of each other at different stages in the life cycle.

If a couple can change either their role expectations or their role behaviors, the marriage may be strengthened. Some role expectations and behaviors are so deeply ingrained that it may be impossible to change them. In such cases, it may be helpful either to change the importance attached to the discrepancy or to look for the compensatory aspects of the relationship. For example, by focusing on the aspects of her husband's character and personality that she likes, a wife may be able to overlook the gap between what she expected and what her husband can actually do. Or, by realizing that he is not diminishing his masculinity by sharing the breadwinning task, a husband reduces the strain caused by his wife's working outside the home. The role gap needs to be acknowledged, at least, by both partners; when role gaps are unresolved, ignored, or simply repressed, both partners will carry around negative feelings. The resentment is bound to come out in unexpected ways, such as occasional aloofness or secrecy (Burr 1976, p. 301).

Because marriage is a relationship that involves many aspects of the lives of two distinct individuals, even the best of marriages will have some incongruencies. Dealing openly with discrepancies between expectations and behavior does more than simply take away undesirable effects. It adds to the desirable aspects of marriage, by creating deeply satisfying feelings such as closeness, importance, and caring (Burr 1976, p. 300).

The ability to discuss and negotiate expectations allows partners to satisfy new personal needs and helps them adapt to changes brought about by personal growth or unexpected crises. Successful negotiation enables couples to reach agreement about role expectations and a better match between their expectations and behaviors. But successful negotiation calls for the skill of good communication, which we will examine in Chapter 8. Like any effective communication, negotiation depends on the two people's confidence, esteem, and trust for each other and for themselves. Unlike business negotiating, it is best in marriage to share more information rather than less, so that each partner understands the other (Scoresby 1977, p. 94).

In traditional marriages, there may appear to be less reason to discuss role expectations explicitly, for both spouses have come to the relationship with an unspoken agreement about conventional sex roles. (Even in these cases, one spouse's definition of "conventional" may differ from the other's, so expressing expectations is helpful.) But when spouses begin taking unconventional roles, as in equal-partner marriages, then lack of explicit agreement about roles creates confusion and dissatisfaction. Couples also need to re-evaluate their roles to fit changing circumstances or new phases of family development. The birth of children, changes in career or job, retirement—all these changes call for a re-evaluation of role expectations. By being made explicit, role expectations become more acceptable to those involved. They also become negotiable (Gowler and Legge 1978, pp. 52–58).

Over the life cycle, as we shall see in subsequent chapters, the roles of wife and husband undergo many changes. In the course of their marriage, husband and wife may move from traditional roles to egalitarian roles to various arrangements in between. Some degree of role flexibility will help married people as they go through the many fluctuations in role requirements and expectations that age, parenting, the economy, and social change are bound to create.

SUMMARY

1. The central objectives of this chapter are, first, to define and discuss the origin and meaning of sex roles; second, to explore various types of family structures and circumstances in relation to role interaction; and,

third, to indicate the need for congruence between role expectations and behavior in the marriage relationship.

2. *Role* is defined as a cluster of traits and tasks tied to a particular social position, while *social position* represents a specific location within a social group to which rights and duties are assigned. How one fulfills a given role such as wife or husband is influenced in part by cultural ideals and expectations of self and partner.

3. *Sex roles* represent those expectations assigned to us by our culture on the basis of having been born male or female. Traditional sex-role definitions linked the masculine ideal with *instrumental* characteristics—traits associated with accomplishment, work, and mastery. The feminine role, as traditionally defined, focused on *expressive* characteristics—traits associated with nurturing, understanding, and fulfilling the needs of husband and children.

4. The traits and tasks assigned at birth on the basis of sex are now recognized as reflecting the beliefs, attitudes, and values of a particular culture or social group at a given period in history. Research indicates that sex roles vary significantly between and within cultures, thus raising serious questions about the influence of biological sex differences in determining sex-role expectations. Once again, the process of socialization is an important tool in transmitting cultural definitions of sex-role behavior.

5. Changing cultural expectations related to sex roles are illustrated by the various marital and family structures discussed in this chapter. The ownership model, which persisted through the nineteenth century, has gradually given way to more egalitarian relationship forms. The head-complement and senior partner–junior partner models, while still preserving the traditional emphasis on instrumental and expressive characteristics, grant more rights to the wife and assign more duties to the husband. The equal-partnership model rejects the traditional sex-role divisions based on instrumental and expressive characteristics and emphasizes the interchangeability of functions between partners.

6. An increasingly frequent family structure in contemporary American society is one in which the female is the sole parent. Most often this particular family form is the result of divorce, which transfers the responsibility for both the instrumental and expressive functions of parenting to the ex-wife/mother. Though a number of negative effects have been discussed in relation to this family structure, these are not automatic. Various factors can prevent or lessen negative outcomes, such as a stable and adequate financial situation, community support, and role sharing by the ex-spouse, relatives, and friends.

7. Greater numbers of women than ever before are entering the work force; the most dramatic increase is among married women whose husbands are present and who have children under 18. The stress of too many duties and too little time is a frequent problem for women who

share the provider role with their husbands and are still expected to carry out all or most of the traditional child-care and homemaker functions. The effects of maternal employment on children depend on such factors as job satisfaction, age and sex of children, socioeconomic class, and community attitudes toward working mothers.

8. Studies have shown that higher levels of marital satisfaction are related to a greater congruence, or matching, of role expectations and behavior. Conflicts and tension result when spouses hold differing role expectations and are unable to resist conforming to narrowly defined patterns. The ability to discuss and negotiate discrepancies between expectations and behavior can reduce role strain and lead to personal and relationship growth.

KEY CONCEPTS

Role
Social position
Sex role
Instrumental characteristics

Expressive characteristics
Marital structure
Role strain
Negotiation

QUESTIONS

1. Recall your growing-up years and list some of the instructions you remember your parents giving you about how to be a girl or boy. Discuss whether your parents presented role models consistent with these instructions. Did you ever experience any conflict over what you were told was appropriate behavior and what you actually observed in your family or social group?

2. What does the statement "Anatomy is destiny" mean to you? Do you agree or disagree with this view? Support your position with research evidence and personal observations.

3. In considering the four marital structures presented in this chapter (owner-property, head-complement, junior partner–senior partner, and equal partners), which pattern do you think is most prevalent in the United States today? Why? Do you foresee any change from this pattern in the near future?

4. Consider the example of a young married couple who have both completed their college educations and have been offered desirable jobs in two locations separated by several hundreds of miles. Discuss the three factors that you think will have the most influence on this couple's decision about accepting or rejecting one or both of these career opportunities.

5. Define the concept of *role strain* and illustrate your definition with a

hypothetical example involving the husband or wife role. Discuss some guidelines that can help couples recognize and resolve the effects of role strain.

SUGGESTED READINGS

- De Riencourt, Amaury. *Sex and Power in History*. New York: Delta Books, 1974. A unique interpretation of history that emphasizes the changing roles of women throughout the centuries, from tribal and feudal cultures to the Renaissance and industrial societies. The author traces how sexual differences have shaped the influence, social position, and economic status of the female sex through the ages.

- Janeway, Elizabeth. *Man's World, Woman's Place: A Study in Social Mythology*. New York: Dell Publishing, 1971. A reasoned approach to the exploration of the traits and attitudes as well as the obligations and restrictions that are assigned to women on the basis of having been born female. Much of this work centers on the potentials and problems that such role expectations bring to marriage and family relationships.

- Kanter, Rosabeth Moss. *Work and Family in the United States: A Critical Review and Agenda for Research and Policy*. New York: Russell Sage Foundation, 1977. An excellent survey of the interaction between family roles and occupational roles. Attention is given to the effects of occupational structure and organization on family life and to family influences on the world of work. The particular situation of working women and the effects of both work and family on individual well-being are also discussed.

- Komarovsky, Mirra. *Dilemmas of Masculinity: A Study of College Youth*. New York: Norton, 1976. A fascinating study of Ivy League male college seniors using in-depth personal interviews to explore views and values about changing sex roles. The results indicate ambivalence and inconsistency about the question of working wives, as well as an intellectual commitment to sexual equality that is sometimes dominated by a strong emotional attachment to traditional marital and family roles.

- Maccoby, Eleanor E., and Jacklin, Carol N. *The Psychology of Sex Differences*. Stanford: Stanford University Press, 1974. A comprehensive review and analysis of research and theory related to real and assumed differences between females and males. An excellent resource work for those interested in exploring questions concerning sex differences in a number of areas such as achievement motivation and aggression.

- Tolson, Andrew. *The Limits of Masculinity*. New York: Harper & Row, 1979. This book investigates the limitations of traditional masculine role expectations. The author presents an analysis of how traditional role expectations are supported in the broader social system and relates his experiences in a men's group that attempted to change the pressures of the masculine role.

- Weitzman, Lenore J. *Sex Role Socialization: A Focus on Women.* Palo Alto, Calif.: Mayfield Publishing, 1979. This work examines how "sex-appropriate" behavior is usually established at an early age and how sex-role socialization affects females as they mature. The author also explores ethnic variations in female sex roles and ways to help women overcome stereotyped sex-role behavior.

- Wilkinson, Doris Y., and Taylor, Ronald L. (eds.). *The Black Male in America: Perspectives on His Status in Contemporary Society.* Chicago: Nelson-Hall, 1977. A collection of articles by 15 authors that describe the black male experience from an interdisciplinary view. Issues discussed include fatherhood, impotence, and dating between blacks and whites.

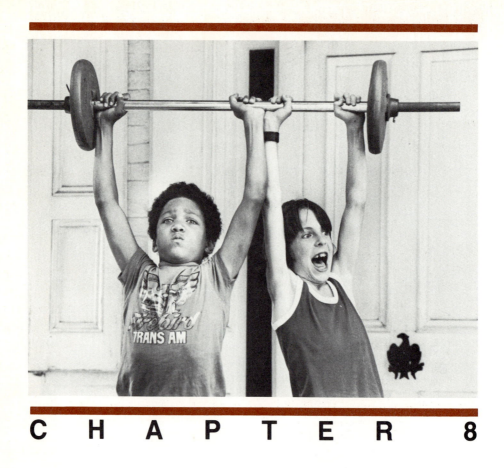

C H A P T E R   8

Interactive Processes:
Communication

SHE: Who's there?
HE: Just me.
SHE: Hi, honey. Rough day?
HE: Fair.
SHE: Just fair?
HE: Just fair.
SHE: No cost-of-living increase, then?
HE: Nope, not this year.
SHE: Hmm . . .
HE: Do you want a pizza?

SHE: I thought I'd make a salad, with turkey and hard-boiled eggs in it. That's what they have for day three of the diet.

HE: To hell with the diet.

SHE: You said you wanted to lose weight.

HE: Not today.

SHE: Well then, *you* have a pizza. I'm having the salad.

HE: Is Scott eating with us?

SHE: He's studying at his friend's.

HE: He'll have some pizza when he gets back. He's always hungry.

SHE: No, he's sticking to the diet, too. He asked me not to bring in any fattening food.

HE: Well, now I guess the whole house is going to be run by a 15-year-old punk.

SHE: Oh, go ahead. Order your pizza. Make it a large with extra cheese. Have a few beers and a cigarette with it. Then we can all be rich with your insurance policy.

HE: I'm going out.

SHE: Where?

HE: Just out.

INTRODUCTION

Within our own families, most of us seek and expect intimacy. There are some who have found the desire for solitude stronger than the need for intimacy. The nineteenth-century American writer Henry David Thoreau, famous for his solitary retreat to Walden Pond, said: "I never found the companion that was so companionable as solitude." Indeed, solitude is conducive to reflection and flights of imagination. All of us need a degree of apartness, the opportunity to examine feelings or thoughts that we do not care to share with others. But Thoreau returned, finally, from the solitude of Walden Pond, communicating through the writing of *Walden*. Even those of us who are most reserved need to communicate thoughts and feelings, preferably to a person who cares. Communications, verbal and nonverbal, can be a couple's most powerful means of creating greater intimacy. When those communications become distorted, intimacy can be violated and even destroyed.

In this chapter we shall ask some questions about the nature of language and communication. *Communication*, which we shall define as the exchange of common meanings with another through both verbal and nonverbal means, is an area that has been the center of intense interest and research in recent decades. Advances in linguistics, *kinesics* (the study of communication through body movement and gesture), and communications technology have opened new vistas. Researchers have been able to apply tape recorder, film, and videotape to the study of ethnic differences in communication, family styles of communication, and interaction between married couples. This research reveals different patterns of communication and various barriers to communication. We shall discuss some of these findings, examining the conditions favorable to intimate communication.

LANGUAGE AND COMMUNICATION

In the animal kingdom, everything that a creature perceives has some significance or meaning for its actions and ultimately for its survival. Existence is saturated with meaning: Clouds mean rain, a rustle in the underbrush means danger. Just as animals and human beings read signs in natural events, so we read or interpret the gestures and behaviors of other human beings: A man trembles and we interpret his trembling as a sign of fear. He is communicating his fear to us. At this unsophisticated level, even silence communicates. Freud has suggested that it may be impossible *not* to communicate:

He that has eyes to see and ears to hear may convince himself that no mortal can keep a secret. If his lips are silent, he chatters with his fingertips; betrayal oozes out of him at every pore. (Quoted in Davis 1974, p.97)

Although silence or a simple gesture may eloquently express some feelings, such a communication is not efficient for expressing our more complex ideas and emotions. For this and other purposes, verbal languages are necessary. Such languages are *symbolic*—that is, made up of signs or symbols that refer to or denote things in our experience. But unlike nature's signals, human signals or languages do not have universal meaning. Our verbal signals or words are arbitrary. In the United States, the word "dog" refers to a member of a certain canine species because, by culture and common experience, we as English speakers use this symbol (written or spoken) to refer to this animal. In other places, societies have evolved other sets of sounds or written marks—other languages (Samovar and Rintye 1974, p. 139; Schramm 1974, p. 9). An individual could make up private symbols to refer to things in his or her experience, but unless there were other persons who could share their meaning, this person would not be communicating by using these signs—he or she would not be using language. In this sense, language is a socially institutionalized, public system of symbols.

The use of these public sign systems—languages—is a complex symbolic activity. Animals use certain sounds to communicate, such as mating calls. Dolphins and chimpanzees have been taught certain specific human sounds or words. But human beings have the most complex public sign system. They have many words and also many ways to use a given word—many "meanings." The same bit of language can have one meaning in one context and an entirely different meaning if used in another context, or spoken in another tone of voice, or accompanied with a different gesture. "I hate you," said in a certain context and tone of voice, can mean "I love you." Speakers of English must understand more than simply the *denotations*, or explicit meanings, of words. For instance, "gal," "girl," "young lady," and "woman" are all words that refer to a female person, but each term has different *connotations*, or associations, to skilled speakers of the language. In addition, people often attach their own personal association to words. Language is inherently public, but two people who speak the same language may not understand each other.

Meaning, as distinct from language, is a complex relationship among the language, the object referred to, the speaker, and the listener. *Communications* (or information) *theory*, which was developed originally in response to problems in the transfer of telephonic signals across space, has provided new terms for the basic elements of communication: message, source, receiver, channel, decoding or interpretation, and feedback. Consider, for example, the State of the Union message delivered annually by the President to Congress. Whatever its content, it has certain elements in common with all speech communication: the President's *message* has a certain *source* (the President); it is *encoded* by the President in language (English in this case). It is delivered through a certain *channel* (spoken words in this case), although it will also be communicated by another *channel* (the printed word) when it is reprinted in the *New York Times* the following day. The message is heard by *receivers* (members of Congress) who must interpret or *decode* it, and who, by their silence or applause, yawns or laughter, offer *feedback* as the message is being communicated. In this sequence, we can identify certain common elements that would be present in any human speech communication: source of the message; the way the message is encoded, expressed, or symbolized; the message itself; the channel or medium used to send it; the receiver; the way the receiver decodes or "reads" the message; and the feedback the receiver gives (Samovar and Rintye 1974, p. 136).

Some recent research has focused on formal aspects of communication: how long one person speaks before letting the other speak, whether a person is silent before speaking, who interrupts whom. This research has shown that in communication, each partner adjusts his or her speech to the other's, each partner's speech patterns are influenced by what the other says and how it is said. For example, if he speaks for two minutes, she will respond for roughly two minutes, but if she begins the conversation with a much shorter comment, he will pace his speech accordingly. There is also a correlation between the two speakers' pauses before speaking: if she waits before speaking, he is likely to do so as well; and if he interrupts, she will also. Relational or formal characteristics of this kind seem to be found in conversations regardless of the topic being discussed (Thomas 1977, pp. 13–14). Patterns of communication—who interrupts, who talks first and last, who talks most—can be detected in most two-person relationships.

LEARNED STYLES OF COMMUNICATION

Verbal behavior is only a part of an integral complex of behavior learned in childhood. Family culture, sex-role identification, racial and ethnic background, and social class all influence individuals' styles of verbal and nonverbal communication.

The Family Communication System

Each family, being a small unit that is both isolated and subject to diverse influences, tends to develop its own communication system. In many families, communication is largely unstructured. Most topics can be discussed at almost any time. She reads in the newspaper that Chase Manhattan is raising its prime interest rate again, and this sparks a discussion of family budgeting. He complains of a backache at breakfast, so she begins chiding the children for not helping their father in the yard. Since the family is a small unit, if one person does all the talking and does not allow others to speak, that person can single-handedly control family communication.

Because a family is also relatively isolated from outsiders, skewed patterns of communication can be maintained for long periods of time. Unfortunately, most people are reluctant to seek outside help in the form of counseling, which might teach them how to communicate effectively. When a family lacks an open system of direct communication, family members do not say what they mean or reveal what actually is troubling them. The father, who is upset about pressures at work and even fears the loss of his job, remains silent through dinner and then blows up when his five-year-old son spills a glass of milk. The mother, who has returned to school but feels guilty about neglecting her family, keeps her personal conflict to herself. But when her husband says, "Gee, honey, this chicken is awfully dry," she bursts into tears. Family members commonly bring home grievances from school or work and vent their frustrations on one another or on their pets (Thomas 1977, pp. 16–18).

The style of communicating we have witnessed in our own families as children—our parents' manner of making decisions, resolving or not resolving conflicts—makes a deep impression on us. Many of us internalize this pattern. Later, as adults, we repeat or recreate in our own families the style of communication we witnessed as children.

Ethnic Identification

Some aspects of communication, such as talkativeness or reticence, emotionalism or stoicism, may be influenced by a family's membership in a particular ethnic group. A common cultural and religious history can combine to give members of an ethnic group a distinctive style that others easily recognize. Not every member of a group has this style, of course. According to some stereotypes, however, the English are reserved; the Italians, gregarious and voluble; the Chinese, reticent and subtle; the Mexicans, easy-going and cooperative. Certain ethnic styles have been recognized informally in literature and folk humor and more formally by anthropologists using audio and videotapes. Anthropologist Ruth Benedict documented a unique tribal style of communication among the Dobu tribe of New Guinea. The Dobu reveal very little to one another because of their extreme fear that any information imparted to another will be used against them. Among the Dobu this style is considered the norm (Benedict 1934). In our culture, such suspicion might be considered abnormal or even paranoid. Students of human behavior need to understand the context in which communication (or any other behavior) takes place, in order to evaluate its significance.

Intimacy in Modern Times

Norms of communication change with the historical tides. In the Victorian era, discussing certain kinds of feelings was not the norm. To reveal personal information to strangers, without a proper introduction, or to members of the lower class was simply "not done."

Georg Simmel (1950), a nineteenth-century German sociologist, speculated that "modern" men and women had become so individualized that, unlike the people of other eras, they could not have close intimate friendships with other human beings. Superficially, at least, twentieth-century Americans seem to be more open about their feelings. Yet we tend to have few friendships that allow us to reveal all aspects of ourselves. Our friendships often speak to only one facet of ourselves: we have tennis friends, school friends, drinking buddies, work friends, bridge friends. Whether out of our need for privacy or our fear of being vulnerable, we tend to compartmentalize our relationships. (Derlega and Chaikin 1975, pp. 22–23). A couple can have backyard barbecues with their neighbors every week in the summer without discovering they are on the verge of divorce. Neighbors, colleagues, and business associates may see each other every day, yet

Our friendships often express only one aspect of ourselves. (Cynthia Benjamins)

never know that the acquaintance is suffering physical or emotional pain. Our tendency to share our happiness and success with friends while hiding our sadness and failure limits the possibility of friendships that are truly intimate.

Mobility also impedes intimacy. Intimacy is based on trust, and trust is established only gradually over time. Many Americans simply do not live in one place long enough to form deep, trusting, and intimate friendships. The average American moves 14 times in a lifetime. Forty million Americans change their home address at least once a year. This extreme mobility is bound to affect the formation of intimate friendships (Derlega and Chaikin 1975, p. 5).

Sex-Role Influences

In Chapter 7, we traced differences in sex roles that affect styles of communication, friendship patterns, and ultimately behavior in the marriage context. Some of these influences result in the stereotypes of the strong, silent male and the talkative, emotional female. Even in early childhood, girls tend to form more intense and intimate relationships, whereas boys associate with large groups and orient their friendships to a particular activity or game. Mothers seem to talk more to their daughters than to their sons, and girls seem to talk more than boys (Clarke-Stewart and Koch, in press). In traditional modes of child rearing, girls are encouraged to show their feelings, while boys are praised for suppressing feelings in the service of achievement—first, mastery of games and sports, then mastery in work. In our culture, as well as in many other Western societies, traditional sex-role expectations for men require that they hide their feelings. This proscription against public display of certain emotions tends to put many men out of touch with their own feelings. Some men reach adulthood without being able to recognize or discuss many of their emotions. In an essay written for *Ms.* magazine, called "Men: Why Aren't We Talking?", Marc Fasteau wondered how it would be if men talked as women do:

Can you imagine men talking to each other saying: "Are you sure you're not angry at me?" . . . "I'm not as assertive as I would like to be." . . . "I feel so competitive that I can't get close to anyone." . . . "I just learned something important about myself that I've got to tell you." (Fasteau 1972, p.16)

When women wish to express aspects of themselves that are not consistent with role expectations, they, too, may "cover up" or remain silent. In surveys conducted in the late 1960s and early 1970s, psychologist Matina Horner (1972) discovered that college women have been inhibited in seeking and enjoying success. They have actually avoided success because of its unfeminine associations. Although women in the 1970s and 1980s appear to be becoming more open about their achievements, many women may be apprehensive about discussing their career aspirations or other traditionally "unfeminine" attitudes with their male friends or husbands.

Yet women still tend to emerge from their sex-role socialization feeling freer to talk and express their emotions. Psychologists observing the interaction of their married clients in a clinical setting do note that wives tend to express feelings more eagerly and easily than their husbands and that husbands seem less interested, even indifferent, to their wives' talk. This can create problems if wives interpret their husbands' lack of communication as an absence of affection or perceive an inequality in the relationship because they are disclosing more than their husbands (Derlega and Chaikin 1975, pp. 80–81).

In videotapes taken of couples who had come to a clinic for mar-

Women usually emerge from their socialization experience feeling freer to talk and express emotions. (Melissa Shook, Picture Cube)

riage counseling, Gottman (1979) found sex-role influences evident in communication problems. The husbands at the clinic tended to be negative listeners. They were more likely than wives (and more likely than happily married couples) to hear negative feelings when statements made by their wives were not necessarily negative. If a wife said, "Look at those beautiful pictures of the Eiffel Tower," the husband, listening negatively, might hear: "She's nagging me about a vacation again. She knows we can't afford Paris, but she's got to keep harping on it." Wives who came for counseling were more likely to speak negatively and even agree negatively than were happily married wives. The husband would say, "Mother gets very blue when she's alone on Labor Day. It used to be the time of our annual family picnic." The unhappily married wife might reply sarcastically, "Sure she does, so I have to cancel our plans to go away for the weekend so she won't be lonely. That's great!"

Gottman found husbands more prone to either tuning out or expressing anger, wives more likely to suppress negative emotions concerning the marriage. Women apparently are more likely to "sit on their anger," allowing resentment to build until there is no chance for a productive interchange. The women interviewed for *The Marriage Savers* (Koch and Koch 1976) tended to feel guilty and responsible for marital difficulties. Instead of sharing this burden, they often turned the anger against themselves and became depressed. Marriages can be one place where man and woman may express the full range of their personalities, regardless of sex-role dictums. But lack of trust can cause couples to revert to stereotyped behavior. To some extent, couples seeking to improve communications need to overcome sex-role limitations.

What husband and wife hear in the spouse's communications, as well as the way they respond, is influenced by their general level of satisfaction with the marriage as well as their sex-role conditioning. Social-class factors play a part in communication style by providing different sex-role socialization—the working-class orientation stressing more traditional, sex-segregated styles of social interaction—and in a number of other ways we shall look at now.

Social Class and Intimacy

Certain social class differences in communication styles seem to show up in childhood. Gottman et al. (1975) observed differences in the behavior preferences of third- and fourth-graders from middle-income and low-income schools. In the middle-income schools, popularity was associated with verbal reinforcement. But in the low-income schools, children preferred those who gave nonverbal reinforcement. We see such a contrast in styles in the early episodes of the "Happy Days" TV series with the Fonz providing more of the thumbs-up and backslapping type of nonverbal support and Richie Cunningham leaning toward verbal reinforcement, such as "Gee, that was great, Fonz."

We have already discussed different role expectations in the middle and working classes, as well as different attitudes toward marriage and family life. Some of these differences in expectations are related to educational and occupational disparities. Working-class employees are more likely to be using their hands and somewhat less likely to be using verbal skills. Lack of verbal interchange between husband and wife seems to be viewed differently by couples with different educational backgrounds. Mirra Komarovsky, gauging attitudes towards marital intimacy, asked couples to respond to this story:

A couple has been married for seven years. The wife says that her husband is a good provider and a good man, but she still complains to her mother about her marriage. She says he comes home, reads the paper, watches T.V., but doesn't talk to her. He says he "doesn't like to gab just for the sake of talking." But she says he is not companionable and has nothing to say to her. *What do you think of this couple?* (Komarovsky 1967, quoted in Derlega and Chaikin, p. 78)

Better-educated couples in Komarovsky's sample—those with at least a high school education—believed that the wife has a legitimate grievance, while less-educated couples said that if the husband wants to be left alone, that is his business.

The working-class style of child rearing and marriage has tended to follow a pattern of male-female division (Kohn 1963). This may reinforce the stereotypical "strong, silent male" sex role, making men reluctant to share problems with their wives. Men of the working class tend to have less autonomy in their jobs than middle-class men. They may actually have a greater need for solitude, a need to have some respite from rules, regulations, and grievances. The solidarity experienced in the company of other men may seem more acceptable an answer, in light of their work and upbringing, than crying on a wife's shoulder. Working-class women, accustomed to turning to other women or female family members for intimate and social communication, may be more accustomed to men who say little and need solitude.

NONVERBAL LANGUAGE

The characters in a good novel or film speak as eloquently with gesture, facial expression, and body movement as they do with their voices. The dockworker played by Marlon Brando in *On the Waterfront* conveys as much emotion toward his girlfriend with his gestures and facial expressions as the most articulate courtier. Nonverbal language is used by all men and women in all social classes. The most astute linguist will misread volumes unless he or she also understands the nonverbal signs and expressions—the "body language"—of others. This is the language used when Henry Tilney in Jane Austen's novel *Northanger Abbey* calls on Catherine Morlan after a long unexplained absence:

Catherine . . . said not a word: but her glowing cheek and brightened eye made her mother trust that this good-natured visit would, at least, set her heart at ease for a time. (Austen 1965, p. 203 [originally published in 1818])

Our gestures and facial expressions can communicate as much as our words. (Jerry Howard, Positive Images)

Wordless communication is limited and often unconscious, but, as this scene from Henry James's *Portrait of a Lady* shows, it expresses emotion very efficiently. Novels—and life—are full of scenes in which few words are spoken but much is said:

"You like me then, Pansy?" . . . "Yes—I like you." . . . The tone in which she had said these four words seemed to him the very breath of nature, and his only answer could be to take her hand and hold it a moment. (James 1956, p. 307 [originally published in 1881])

Early psychoanalysts may have been correct in speculating that non-verbal behavior is more reliable than verbal behavior in measuring a person's true feelings. If Catherine in *Northanger Abbey* or Pansy in *Portrait of a Lady* had verbally denied caring for their suitors, we would—given the nonverbal clues to their feelings—surely have ignored them. The new field of *kinesics*, the study of communication through body movement and gesture, confirms this intuition. One recent study tested this idea clinically. Using an electronic filter, researchers eliminated the higher frequencies of a certain recorded speech so that the words were unintelligible, but the vocal qualities remained: intonation, tone, stress, frequency and length of pauses. Though more limited in range than the verbal message, these qualities still communicated the speaker's feelings or attitude about the subject. One group was asked to judge the vocal qualities of the tape; a second group, the written transcription of what was said in the speech; and a third group, the tape and transcription together. Sometimes the vocal information reinforced or added a new dimension to the verbal message, but sometimes it contradicted the words. When this happened, most people in the study gave credence to the vocal, not the verbal, message (Mehrabian 1974, p. 89; Davis 1974, p. 94).

Nonverbal clues reinforce or add meaning to our verbal utterances. Certain forms of speech suggest eagerness, dislike, or boredom. Compare the distant statement, "Those people need help," with the more intimate, warmer version, "These people need our help." Interruption, silences, facial expressions, gestures, and posture indicate attitude toward the listener or audience (Mehrabian 1974, p. 90). Posture can express discomfort, boredom, impatience, arrogance, or contempt. Excessive bodily movement of hands or feet expresses restlessness, insecurity, or a sense of immaturity. Hands and arms can express openness and self-confidence if they are given free and spontaneous movement, or inner tension or rejection if the arms are clasped across the chest or held stiffly to the sides. Stooped shoulders express low self-esteem, while a backward tilt suggests pride and self-confidence. A person's walk, whether a strut or a stroll, is expressive, as is one's manner of eating and drinking, which can communicate coarseness, gentility, good or bad manners, education, social status, timidity, or sexuality. Observing two Americans out of earshot we can usually tell when one speaker has finished speaking by the drop of the head or hands and the lowering of the eyes. We might even be able to judge when one speaker was making a prediction about the future (a forward movement of the torso) or commenting with hindsight on some past event (a slight backward movement) (Davis 1974, pp. 98–99).

The face is a rich source of nonverbal messages. Kinesicians have identified 23 different expressive positions of the eyebrows alone. Tightly pursed lips or a grimace express determination or anger, while a gentle grin expresses agreement, and open-mouthed laughter, joy. Eyes can express hatred or lust, fear or incrimination (Davis 1974, pp. 95–96; Zunin and Zunin 1972, pp. 78–88).

Because people often hide feelings behind words, nonverbal behavior may be a better discriminator of feelings than verbal behavior. Ray Birdwhistell (1970) has devised a series of signs or "kinegraphs" for observers to use in recording and accurately describing nonverbal behavior. Some of these are shown in Figure 8.1. Gottman (1979) has attempted to apply the findings from the vast research literature on nonverbal behavior to the study of marital interaction, associating facial features, expressions, and emotions (see Table 8.1). We may never become as adept and accurate

FIGURE 8.1 Kinegraphs

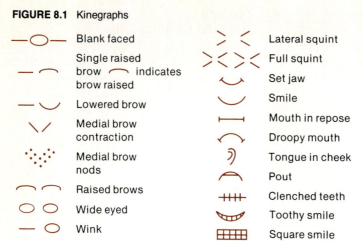

Source: Adapted from Birdwhistell, Ray, *Kinesics and Context: Essays on Body Motion Communication*, University of Pennsylvania Press, Philadelphia, Pa., 1970, p. 329.

at reading faces and bodies as we are at reading words, but increased awareness of body language can facilitate communication.

One reason we can never be absolutely sure that a body movement has universal significance is the existence of cultural differences in nonverbal styles. Every culture and ethnic group has its own body language as well as its own style of communicating. The English cross their legs in a different way than Americans do (Davis 1974, p. 93). Certain gestures and body language are characteristic of Americans, at least of Anglo-Saxon and white middle-class Americans. For example, Americans tend to be careful about how and when they use eye contact, so as to avoid any sexual implications, while people from other cultures do not hesitate to stare at strangers. Business negotiations have been disrupted by cultural misunderstandings of body language. Americans are distressed when a Brazilian invades their personal space by standing just inches away while they are talking. To the Brazilian, greater distance would indicate hostility.

In societies such as ours, in which several cultures coexist, these differences in body language can result in unfortunate misunderstandings. Turning one's back to the speaker, for instance, which seems to suggest disavowal or disapproval in white American culture, is a friendly, intimate gesture among black Americans. Meeting the glance of a person in a position of authority is a sign of respect in white culture, but an expression of disrespect in black culture. If black youths drop their eyes in a confrontation with an authority figure, this may be interpreted by whites as shiftiness and the desire to hide something; in fact, black children are often taught to show respect by lowering their eyes (Johnson 1974, pp. 106–108). These are the broad outlines of verbal and nonverbal communications.

TABLE 8.1 Emotions and the Three Areas of the Face

Emotions and Subtypes	Brow	Eyes	Lower Face
Surprise 1. Questioning surprise (has neutral mouth) 2. Astonished surprise (has neutral brow) 3. Dazed surprise (has neutral eyes)	Eyebrows curved and high; brow furrowed horizontally	Wide; white of eye showing below the iris	Jaw drops; relaxed open mouth
Fear 1. Only fear brow or mouth connotes worry or apprehension 2. Apprehensive fear differs from horrified, frozen fear—Shock	Raised and straightened corners of brow drawn together	Upper eyelid raised, lower eyelid tense; eyes opened and tense	Mouth open but lips not relaxed; tension in upper lip; corners of lips may be drawn back
Disgust 1. Disgust 2. Contempt	Eyebrows are down	The opening of the eye is narrowed, producing lines and folds below the eye	Upper lip is raised; tip of nose changes; lower lip slightly forward; nose wrinkled; cheeks are raised
Anger	Eyebrows drawn down and together; brow lowered; no horizontal wrinkles unless they are permanent	Lids are tensed; eye seems to stare out; upper eyelid is lowered	Two types of mouth: lips pressed together or open, square mouth depends on whether person is speaking or trying to gain control
Happiness	Not necessarily involved in this expression	Cheek is raised; crowsfeet wrinkling; eyes not important; lower eyelid has wrinkles below it	Corners of lips drawn back and slightly up; intensity related to amount of teeth showing; nasolabial grooves visible
Sadness	Inner corners of the eyebrows are raised and may be drawn together; sadness triangle between eyebrow and upper eyelid	Raised lower lid increases sadness expression; gaze is often down	Corners of lips down; lips will be loose and trembling if person is near crying or trying to hold it back

Source: John M. Gottman, *Marital Interaction*, Academic Press, 1979, p. 60. Reprinted by permission.

Now we shall move in for a closer look at the way communication is conducted—or avoided—between intimates.

UNDERSTANDING COMMUNICATION PATTERNS

Intimacy and Self-Disclosure

Social scientists call the activity of revealing things about oneself *self-disclosure*. The ability to disclose information about oneself, especially personal and sometimes painful information, is a valuable social skill when used appropriately. Most of us know instinctively when and how much to reveal about ourselves. We do not usually tell secrets to strangers or to persons who show no interest in us. In normal two-person interaction, when one person discloses personal information, the other reciprocates with personal disclosures. The failure to reciprocate personal information is one way of signaling that intimacy is not desired. Failure to recognize such signals or cues can lead to rejection.

For example, if a young man fails to notice that a classmate does not reciprocate and continues to reveal the details of his parents' recent divorce, he is not taking situational clues into account. His classmate may avoid or ignore him in the future. Some contexts or situations are not appropriate for intimate disclosures. The woman who uses a creative writing workshop to talk about her traumatic childhood may be disclosing her feelings at an inappropriate time. On the other hand, reserve may be equally inappropriate in certain situations. Someone who always holds back personal disclosures, even when a friend has disclosed personal information, may find that he or she has no close friends. At least one study indicates that persons who have been rated as neurotic by an independent standard (the Maudsley Personality Inventory) do not adapt their self-disclosures to the situation and ignore situational clues (Derlega and Chaikin 1975, pp. 33–34). Sensitivity to situational clues and the ability to provide reinforcing statements or supportive gestures are social skills that become evident in childhood. Many of these skills are learned in one's family.

Family Influences on Communication Patterns

In recent years, many marriage and family therapists have become convinced that families must be viewed as systems rather than as collections of individuals. The family system, without using formal orders or memos, nevertheless dictates a particular style of communication as it assigns various functions or roles to its members. The whole is far greater than the sum of its parts; in fact, the parts cannot be understood without comprehending the whole. A person's manner of communicating his or her feelings and personal problems cannot be understood by simply hearing that individual's story or past experiences. One must see the whole family to figure out what function those unique problems or communication quirks may have played in the family system.

An apparently disturbed child is brought in for therapy. The therapist asks to see the whole family and discovers, first, that the mother is a secret alcoholic whose problem is never revealed. Aided by the rest of the family, she keeps up her role of competent, active club woman. The father is sullen and disappointed in his marriage and in his career, though he never expresses this directly. The daughter is acting out the problems that the family refuses to acknowledge. She plays the role of "sick child," so the cover-up can continue, though she is no sicker than the other family members. It is not the girl who needs "fixing," but the whole system, with its covert style of communication, that needs changing.

Psychiatrist R. D. Laing has come across many examples of disturbed family systems. His collection of poems, *knots*, conveys the strange, convoluted communication style that such families may adopt.

JILL: I'm upset you are upset
JACK: I'm not upset
JILL: I'm upset that you're not upset that I'm upset you're upset.
JACK: I'm upset that you're upset that I'm not upset that you're upset that I'm upset, when I'm not.
JILL: You put me in the wrong
JACK: I am not putting you in the wrong
JILL: You put me in the wrong for thinking you put me in the wrong.
JACK: Forgive me
JILL: No
JACK: I'll never forgive you for not forgiving me.

(Laing 1972, p. 21)

Reciprocity, Symmetry, Complementarity

The Laing poem is jarring because most of us expect positive remarks to be reciprocated with positive messages and negative remarks to be countered with negative messages. A clinical study conducted in 1974 (Thomas 1977, pp. 14–15) indicated that this kind of *reciprocity*, or reciprocal communication, is characteristic of marital communication. Analyzing communication patterns of marital partners in conflict situations, Thomas found that behaviors initiated by one partner tended to elicit a similar response from the other. For example, when one offers an objective, analytical comment ("We seem to be engaging in defensive communication."), the other tends to respond with another remark in the same tone. When one says, "I've had a rough day. I'm sorry if I'm not listening to what you say," or some other conciliatory remark, the other tends to respond in kind (Thomas 1977, p. 14).

When messages are reciprocal, the interaction in such a balanced style of interchange can be described as *symmetrical:* partners mirror each other's behavior, and status differences are minimized. It has been found that distressed couples engage in more negative interchanges; fewer positive interactions; more nagging, criticizing, and rejecting; less praise, sympathy, and approval (Thomas 1977, pp. 14–15).

In Chapter 7, we discussed various role divisions in marriage. The *complementary* style of communication tends to prevail in more traditional relationships, a partnership that assigns the husband the breadwinner role, the wife the homemaker role. He is then permitted the stern or angry mode, the communications that convey orders, while she gives the gentler, more nurturant messages. Egalitarian marriages or equal partnerships tend to generate symmetrical communication. She can be angry and stern, intellectual, or nurturant and supportive, and he has the same freedom in their interchanges. Either communication style has its dangers: The husband and wife who must respond in kind to every subject, every issue, may wind up in a state of continual competition, sparring, and conflict. Complementarity may put the spouses in a communications straitjacket. He must always initiate; she must always follow. He is always stern; she always calms him down with a soothing remark. In healthy relationships, there are patterns of both complementary and symmetrical interaction. In some areas, she initiates and he follows; in others, he initiates and she follows.

Communication problems have been cited as the number-one cause of marital difficulties (Beck and Jones 1973). One way for couples to deal with a communication problem is to become aware of their own patterns of interaction. Psychiatrist Robert Ravich (1971) designed a game to reveal a couple's communication patterns. It is played with trains and allows the therapist and the couple to see how they communicate. The couple may avoid a collision by one always traveling a direct route, the other taking the longer indirect route, thus indicating an inflexible role division or distorted complementarity. Or they may have a symmetrical pattern, each taking the shortest way, colliding, and then negotiating the question of who will proceed first. The "train game" suggests that effective marital interaction requires some flexibility in communication style, just as marital needs over the life cycle require some flexibility in the role each spouse plays.

Bonding

When a child is born, the sight and touch of the infant arouse a strong emotional response in the mother and father. As they fulfill the infant's needs, bonds of love are formed. The child, trusting the parents to feed her when she is hungry, clean her when she is messy and supply her with the pleasure and comfort of their touch, forms a bond with her parents—a bond that causes her to feel a need for them even when she is not hungry or messy.

Bonding also occurs between husband and wife as they attempt to fulfill each other's needs, communicating their feelings and dealing with the many big and little issues that arise throughout their marriage. The bonds may be pleasant and predictable: He displays loving, romantic feelings; she reciprocates. She conveys anxiety and distress; he comforts her. When both partners are willing to listen to each other and find out what the other needs, their bonds are based on effective interaction: love that is reciprocated, fears that are allayed, anxieties that are overcome.

CONFLICTED COMMUNICATION

Discrepant Bonding

Of course, not all behavior is reciprocated. Not all bonds forged between husband and wife promote love or even encourage problem solving. She nags, he withdraws; he withdraws, she nags. She thinks she nags *because* he withdraws—*if* only he would not withdraw, she would not nag. He thinks he withdraws because she nags—*if* only she would not nag. In fact the causality is circular (Burr 1976). His wishes to be alone have become bonded to her desire for interaction. Such bonding of conflicting emotional states or feelings is called *discrepant bonding*. This leads to the kind of convoluted communication that R. D. Laing depicted in *knots*.

Games

Another way of explaining discrepant bonding emerges from the work of Eric Berne (1964), who called such interactions "games." In Berne's scheme, games can take the place of genuine communication if people do not recognize their partner's state of mind. Remember (see page 56) that Berne saw the adult psyche as having three divisions: parent, child, and adult. Communications emerging from the parent state could be nurturing and supportive in tone or scolding and punitive. When adults speak from their child state, they can express emotion, playfulness, and desire. The adult state of mind gives rise to information in the form of questions, answers, or statements. Two people cannot always synchronize their states of mind, but they can become adept at figuring out what state of mind the other is in from the kind of expression the other uses. When a spouse becomes affectionate and indicates the wish to make love, the need is for another equally playful and, in that sense, childlike response. A lecture or a scolding would not be in order.

In Berne's scheme, discrepancies occur when one partner's *child* communications always result in the other's *parent* communications. If both are in a childlike mode—wanting to play cards, indulge in a hot fudge sundae, make love—then they are not playing a game. Or if one wanted a hot fudge sundae and the other recognized the partner's state of mind—"I'd love to take a break with you, but I've got to prepare this speech tonight"—they would not be playing games. But if every time he expresses a yen for a sundae or an hour of lovemaking, she reminds him that he is overweight or oversexed, then they are playing games instead of communicating. Whether we call the repeated discrepant patterns "games" or "discrepant bonding," we can see that such patterns prevent the spontaneous expression of feeling in a relationship.

Theories of language and communication acknowledge the importance of self-esteem and saving face. Every act of communication is, at the most abstract level, a request for validation: "Agree with me." "Be on my side." Making such a request means risking the rejection, ridicule, or indifference of the audience. Communication involves risk. People sometimes are afraid to risk a negative response, afraid to expose themselves to rejection, so they avoid direct communication: She wants to go to a movie with him, but instead of asking him directly, she says, "It would do you good to see a movie," or "If you want to see a movie, we'll see one" (Satir 1974, p. 22). Or he wants her sympathy, but instead of asking for it directly, he complains about various symptoms: "My left shoulder aches, I have a shooting pain in my eye, and this report is due Monday morning." People make most statements in an attempt to influence the listener; they hope that the listener will respond with support, if not total agreement. If we are unsure of how our requests will be received, if we fear rejection or ridicule or simply indifference, we may disguise our requests through indirect communication (Satir 1974, pp. 18, 22). People who are generally more self-confident believe that their messages will be well received and will, therefore, risk more direct communication.

Low Self-Esteem

Self-esteem—our feelings about ourselves—influences our verbal style and effectiveness. Each person has a concept of self and an evaluation of this self-concept. A person's self-esteem is measured not by that concept of self, but by how that concept is evaluated (Burr 1976, p. 81). If a man thinks of himself as sensitive and kind-hearted, but holds these virtues as unmanly and feminine, he may suffer from low self-esteem. If a woman thinks of herself as astute and aggressive, her self-esteem will be boosted if she values these qualities. But if she considers them unfeminine, her self-esteem is lowered.

When a person's self-esteem falls below a certain level, he or she becomes anxious and defensive. Based on observations of their clients, many family counselors speculate that this anxiety and defensiveness interfere with and inhibit communication (Burr 1976, pp. 84–87). We cannot attempt to give a technical explanation of the variety of defense mechanisms observed by therapists, but a few of them are familiar to all of us: *fantasy* is the attempt to satisfy desires through imaginary achievements; *projection* is the placing of blame for a problem on others; *compensation* is the covering up of a weakness by emphasizing a strength; *repression* consists of keeping uncomfortable or threatening thoughts from becoming conscious thoughts. Defense mechanisms are not always dangerous to one's mental health; they become a problem only when they distort reality enough to interfere with living one's life and attaining one's goals (Burr 1976, p. 87). Intimate communication requires a minimum of defensiveness. Yet parents teach us whether or not it is safe to let down our defenses. When parents make openness unsafe, they teach a distorted style of communication.

Double Messages and Double Binds

When a child's mother asks for a hug, yet stiffens and withdraws when the child approaches, the child is receiving a *double message*: two contradictory injunctions or commands issued through two different channels. On the verbal level, the mother is saying, "Come here." On the nonverbal level, she seems to be saying, "Go away." How should the child respond? Perplexed, the child may respond with another double message, hugging the mother and at the same time pulling away. If the child frequently receives such messages, he or she may be in what psychologists call a *double bind* (Burr 1976, pp. 473–474; Satir 1974, p. 19).

Double binds occur in intense, long-lasting relationships. Two elements make the situation *binding:* first, the need for acceptance and, second, the presence of an unspoken law against commenting on the double message. Conflict and misunderstanding result. Consider another common situation: He asks her what the matter is. She replies, "Nothing," but her tone of voice and posture clearly suggest that *something* is the matter. This situation by itself does not create a double bind. But if it occurs frequently, and the couple has an unspoken rule against talking about the double message, then they are both in a double bind. With the help of a psychotherapist or counselor, couples or individuals in double binds may learn to recognize the problem and begin to break the unspoken law against commenting about the double message. Schizophrenia is sometimes traced to childhoods marked by double binds, for schizophrenic communication, a kind of double message, may be the only appropriate response to a double bind (Bateson, Jackson, Haley, and Weak-land 1956).

Validating versus Invalidating Communication

Communication can be a way of validating other people, enhancing their self-esteem, endorsing their right to feel whatever is being expressed. Validating other people encourages more openness, more communication. We have seen that talk can also *invalidate* others, undermine their self-esteem, "disqualify" the importance of what they are saying.

There are many verbal and nonverbal ways to disqualify the other or even oneself. People who start a sentence and then trail off disqualify the importance of their own thought: "I really want to get out tomorrow and look for a new job, but I guess it will rain, so, oh, never mind. . . ." Indirection or obscuring serves to disqualify statements. He is thinking: "I'd like to go out to dinner with you, just the two of us." He might gear his statement to the merits of the food instead of the merits of his mate—"I hear there's a terrific rib place that's just opened. Why don't we go?"—or he might deprecate someone else instead of expressing appreciation for her—"It might not be unpleasant to find ourselves dining out together, unaccompanied by friends less stimulating than ourselves."

Satir gives an example of how disqualification works to obscure communication: She wants to go to a concert with him and asks if he would like to go. But because she fears his rejection, she defends herself by denying all or part of her message: "No, I don't necessarily want to go. I thought *you* wanted to go." Such conversations can escalate into arguments if he or she engages in further denial by announcing, "You can go or not. I don't care," or, worse, "If you want to be a stay-at-home, that's your business" (Satir 1974, pp. 23–24).

Another means of obstructing communication and invalidating the other is to deny what the other person says, to *disconfirm*. Disconfirming or denying what another person says about her or his own thoughts and feelings tends to lower the other's self-esteem and to increase anxiety and confusion in the communication. She says, "I'm worried about becoming pregnant." If he says, "You think you don't want to become pregnant, but you really do," he is disconfirming her statement. If he adds, "All normal women want to be mothers," he further depletes her self-esteem. The possibility that she will discuss her anxieties about having children is diminished. And the trust in the relationship is reduced. The unhealthy habit of disconfirming is common in schizophrenic families, in which parents seem to ignore their child's feelings, describing as happy the child who openly describes himself or herself as depressed (Bateson et al. 1956).

A personal feeling cannot be denied. One may not feel the same as the other, but recognizing the right of the other to "own" his or her feelings is a basic element of an intimate relationship. Disconfirming the personal feelings of another is a way of saying, "You have no right to feelings that are different from mine or disturbing to me." It is a severe invalidation that cuts off intimacy.

IMPROVING INTIMATE COMMUNICATION

Metacommunications

A couple straitjacketed by conflicted communication may be liberated if they become aware of their ineffective pattern of communication. Using *metacommunications*, or talking about the way they are communicating, is one way of bringing about this awareness (Scoresby 1977, pp. 109–110). Metacommunications indicate a person's awareness of all the nonverbal and emotional aspects of a particular message, an awareness of the context (Gottman 1979). In a paper on the double-bind hypothesis, four of the most noted researchers in the fields of communications, interpersonal relations, and psychology—Gregory Bateson, Don D. Jackson, Jay Haley, and John Weakland—explained the importance of metacommunications:

The ability to communicate about communication, to comment upon the meaningful actions of oneself and others, is essential for successful social intercourse. In any normal relationship, there is a constant interchange of metacommunications messages such as "What do you mean?" or "Why did you do that?" or "Are you kidding me?" and so on. To discriminate accurately what people are really expressing, we must be able to comment directly or indirectly on that expression. (1956, p. 258)

Using metacommunications, couples clarify messages and feelings by talking about them. Skills related to this ability include asking for the literal meaning of words spoken, discussing nonverbal communication, labeling messages, or explaining why messages have been sent. Messages can be explained in terms of what the other person did: "You washed the dishes, and I wanted to thank you"; in terms of the other's feelings: "You look depressed, and I wanted to show you I sympathize"; or in terms of the other's request: "You asked me to say what I thought." Messages can also be explained in terms of the response the speaker was trying to elicit or evoke in the listener: "I wanted you to sympathize with me." Or they can be explained in terms of what the speaker was trying to get the other to do or say: "I wanted you to help me clean the house." Sometimes metacommunications can be about nonverbal messages: "You say nothing is the matter, but you won't look at me and your tone of voice is angry" (Satir 1974, pp. 14–15; Scoresby 1977, p. 111).

It is important in such delicate conversations to describe what one observes without evaluating or labeling the other. It is one thing to say, "You don't look happy, though you say you are"; to couch this description in evaluative or labeling terms—"You are such a sourface"—is threatening and will certainly interfere with objective discussion. Labels of people in families sometimes become fixed, so that one may be labeled "the dominant one" within the family, and the other "the dependent one." Such labels are almost always misleading, since we all possess a variety of traits. Sometimes such labels become self-fulfilling prophecies, as when a wife behaves as the dependent partner because that is her assigned role. It is also wise to avoid making ungrounded inferences. For example, it would be unwise for a wife to infer, without inquiring, that because her husband looks unhappy, he is upset with her or somehow holds her responsible for his unhappiness (Scoresby 1977, p. 116; Burr 1976, p. 475).

In a healthy, spontaneous relationship, each partner may be so in tune with the language and expressions of the other that they rarely need to talk about how they are communicating. John Gottman's video study of problem solving (see Box 8.1) indicates that couples expressing great satisfaction with their marriages do very little metacommunicating when they solve problems, while distressed couples use metacommunicating as a way to avoid problem solving. Most couples fall between the extremes of great satisfaction and severe distress. They need metacommunications to help them make adjustments in their ongoing interaction. By verifying their mutual perceptions of each other, partners gain confidence and resolve differences.

Venting Emotions

Intense emotion can interfere with communication. One technique for calming emotion is to interrupt the discussion in progress and vent the feelings in a way that neither threatens the other nor makes the other responsible for the emotion. She might say, "I might feel differently later, but right now I am upset and threatened by what you are saying." By expressing her feelings in a nonthreatening way, she lessens their intensity and thus may be able to continue the discussion in a reasonable, controlled manner (Burr 1976, pp. 50–58). Distressed couples have difficulty expressing feelings in a nonthreatening way, however, and thus their venting often leads to anger and upset.

Decision Making

Communication and metacommunication facilitate decision making. In many families, decision making is as unstructured as other forms of discussion and interaction. Decisions are made as situations arise, while family members are eating, playing, getting dressed, going to work. In the midst of normal family hubbub, decisions may not be final. But eventually disagreements must be resolved, decisions made. One sign of a successful marriage is a couple's ability to make decisions, create solutions, and fulfill goals (Thomas 1977, p. 17; Scoresby 1977, pp. 67–68).

Some couples avoid or postpone decisions. They put off deciding whether to go to his parents or hers for the holiday until it is too late to get plane reservations, and the decision—to stay home—makes itself. Such decisions are made by default. There are many reasons to postpone decisions. We may fear commitment to something definite without a guarantee that we can get it; we may believe "the best-laid plans" can be upset by unforeseen events (Burr 1976, p. 73). Some people value a fulfilling present and believe that planning for the future interferes with spontaneity. But there can be no doubt that careful decisions and planning help us see alternatives we might otherwise ignore. Decisions made with care and communication on both sides are more creative and ultimately more satisfying for both people involved.

How a couple goes about making a decision may be as important as the decision itself. In healthy relationships, important decisions reflect the values of *both* partners and are made jointly so that both partners will be motivated to carry them out.

When families make decisions together, the worth of each family member is enhanced and the family unit is solidified. (Sylvia Johnson, Woodfin Camp & Associates)

BOX 8.1 Two Styles of Decision Making

HUSBAND: Well, we've got another budget problem.
WIFE: Even with my salary?
HUSBAND: We're going to be short about $75.00 next month.

This could be the beginning of a major battle, or it could be the first step in solving a problem. All couples must deal with problems regularly, be they financial difficulties, conflicts about whether to have children, disagreements over how to discipline them, or personal issues concerning sexual or emotional dissatisfaction. Psychologist John Gottman of the University of Illinois (Champaign-Urbana) has been videotaping the problem-solving patterns of married couples. He finds distinct differences in the way problems are solved by happily married pairs and the way they are tackled by couples who are not satisfied with their marriages (1979, pp. 105–123).

Dealing with couples aged 25 and 26 who had been married about three years, Gottman found there were three phases to resolving a marital problem. First the couple "builds an agenda"; they get out a statement of the problem that validates their feelings. With happily married couples, this phase might go this way: She says, "Bob, I can see you're really upset about this." He says, "I know you've been trying to save for a vacation this summer, so I hate to even bring it up."

The unhappy couple, on the other hand, does not engage in validating feelings. They don't acknowledge and endorse each other's emotional states. When they do agree, the agreement has a sarcastic edge: "Yeah, sure, not enough money again, so I guess I give up the beauty parlor and my pottery class and you give up nothing— right?" Or the exchange may start off with a direct personal attack: "You always lose your temper when the bills come in. You're such a skinflint, just like your mother. . . ." The issue is surrounded by hostility even before it is examined.

Phase two of solving a problem, for both happily and unhappily married couples, is arguing. Here Gottman found the two groups of couples to be similar. They each disagree, and the partners in each group summarize their positions. "I haven't bought myself a new piece of clothing in months. I don't see how I can cut down any further." Or: "I'd be happy to wear jeans to court, but I don't think the judge would approve."

Phase three, the negotiation phase, separates the satisfied from the dissatisfied couples. The satisfied ones are more likely to propose "contracts": "How about this? I buy my next suit at that huge discount store out in the suburbs. And you bowl once a week instead of twice." Unhappy couples do a lot of negative talking about how they communicate: "We never can agree on this money issue. You're always calling me stingy, and I always see you letting money slip through your fingers." These unhappy couples seem to get stuck expressing lots of negative feelings and assuming that something negative is going on, even when it's not verbalized. Gottman calls this "mind-reading with negative affect."

All couples engage in mind-reading. They look at the expressions on each other's faces, and they speculate about what those expressions mean. The happily married spouses are more likely to remain neutral. For example, the husband notices that his wife's face is drawn and frowning. He mind-reads: "She looks exhausted and un- happy. I wonder if it's her boss, or did one of the kids call her with bad news?"

BOX 8.1 (Continued)

The dissatisfied spouse also mind-reads. But instead of questioning and probing feelings while remaining neutral, he or she suspects the worst: "She looks tired again—damn! Now she's going to say she has a headache and she can't take in the movie we were going to see. Naturally, there'll be no sex either." This is mind-reading with negative affect. Gottman suggests that the problem in unhappy marriages is not that the couple hides their feelings. It's that they constantly rake angry feelings over the coals—their own angry feelings. They seem unable to endorse or validate the feelings of the other with empathy and concern. They don't know how to stop the series of complaints and countercomplaints that characterize their arguments. They rarely propose contracts that could lead them to a solution, such as: "I can't give up bowling now. I'm already signed up with the league. But I will walk to the station and take the subway to work. That should save the same amount on gas."

Most couples who are married or living together are neither perfectly happy nor dissatisfied enough to seek marriage counseling. They could benefit from Gottman's findings by mirroring what they perceive in their partner, validating his or her feelings—"You really do look anxious tonight"—rather than assuming something negative. They could curtail those endless sessions of exchanging criticism and anger by proposing something that requires each person to give a little.

Source: John M. Gottman, *Marital Interaction: Experimental Investigations.* New York: Academic Press, 1979. Used by permission.

The perceived importance and complexity of the decision affects how it is made. Some decisions—to accept a job in another city or to have children—are full of implications for other goals and decisions. One may decide impulsively to see a new movie, but the decision to have a child or buy a house calls for more careful deliberation (Scoresby 1977, pp. 68–70).

Good decisions are made in stages. First, the persons affected should agree on what needs to be decided. Opening statements of the problem should be made tentatively. Tentativeness or neutrality is an important communication skill for good decision making, as a show of power can evoke defensiveness and insecurity. The next step is to consider various alternatives. While the decision is being made, couples should avoid confusion by not introducing irrelevant issues. They must be able to integrate their divergent points of view, compromising if necessary (Scoresby 1977, pp. 75–76).

Ideal methods of decision making do not always work out in practice, especially when each partner has something personally important at stake. All couples, for example, seem to go through an arguing phase as they examine alternatives. Box 8.1 compares the intimate communications of happily and unhappily married couples during the decision-making process.

Being adept at communicating may help spouses to manage conflict.

Chapter 9 will deal more fully with the inevitable problem of managing conflict. By now, however, we should understand that intimate communication involves the willingness to be vulnerable. To do this we need to know that the other person is sensitive to our feelings, cares about those feelings, and is willing to try to bring those feelings to a more positive place. Tools and techniques cannot create this trust. They can only help us to reassure our partner: "Yes, you can trust me."

SUMMARY

1. The purposes of this chapter are to explain communication processes and explore the influencing effects of selected factors such as sex, ethnicity, and social class; to discuss several common patterns of communication in intimate two-person relationships; to illustrate conflicted and problematic communication; and to suggest procedures for improving interaction in primary relationships.
2. Communication is a complex process involving both verbal and nonverbal signs and symbols called language. Language is a public or shared system, meaning that there is an intricate process among the words spoken, the object referred to, the speaker, and the listener. Information theory describes the basic elements of communication as message, source, receiver, channel, interpretation, and feedback.
3. Verbal and nonverbal ways of communicating are learned in childhood in the context of a particular culture, family system, sex, ethnic and racial identification, and social class. These socialized differences often underlie misinterpretation and conflict in intimate communication.
4. Kinesics is the study of communication through body movement and gesture, commonly known as nonverbal or body language. Nonverbal signals can reinforce or add additional meaning to our spoken word. They may also contradict our verbal language, thus confusing the message.
5. Studies of two-person communication have identified a variety of patterns that can be useful tools in understanding positive and negative components of marital interaction. Differences in expectations related to self-disclosure are frequently a result of sex-role learning, which encourages a greater expression of personal feelings for females than for males. Understanding and identifying symmetrical (reciprocal), complementary, and bonded communication sequences can also provide useful insights for clarifying and enhancing intimate interaction.
6. Common barriers to positive communication include low self-esteem, double messages, double binds, and the use of verbal and nonverbal behaviors to disqualify or disconfirm one's own or one's partner's messages.
7. Positive communication in intimate relationships may be enhanced through the use of metacommunications: communications about how

we communicate. The ability to vent emotions in an appropriate, non-threatening manner and to develop a rational approach to decision making within an intimate relationship also increases the chances of quality communication.

QUESTIONS

1. On the basis of your experiences and observations, what topics are most likely not to be discussed around the family dinner table? What do you think are the most important areas for couples planning long-term relationships such as marriage to discuss?
2. Give examples of how you think your verbal and nonverbal behaviors have been influenced by your sex, racial and ethnic identity, and social class.
3. Indicate some nonverbal behaviors that you consider typically male and typically female. How important is it for children to learn these behaviors? Why?
4. Consider an important primary relationship in which you are currently engaged and illustrate a symmetrical, or complementary, or bonded sequence of communication that has recently occurred in your communication in this relationship.
5. On the basis of information presented in this chapter, and from personal experience, discuss how self-esteem relates to communication.
6. Describe a common situation that you have observed in marital or other intimate relationships that illustrates the concept of disqualifying through verbal or nonverbal communication.
7. Define metacommunication and discuss how this technique can be used to enhance communication between intimate partners.

KEY CONCEPTS

Communication	Double message
Nonverbal language	Double bind
Self-disclosure	Disqualification
Bonding	Metacommunications

SUGGESTED READINGS

- Allred, G. Hugh. *On the Level: With Self, Family, Society.* Provo, Utah: Brigham Young University Press, 1974. This is a practical self-help guide for improving interpersonal interaction. The author draws heavily from communication theory, includes numerous examples, and discusses many problems that occur frequently in primary relationships.
- Doty, Betty. *Marriage Insurance.* Redding, Calif.: The Bookery, 1978. A step-by-step guide focused on teaching communication skills to married

couples. This guide includes numerous examples, methods to evaluate communication skills, and exercises for couples to practice.

- Hawkins, James L., Weisberg, Carol, and Ray, Dixie L. "Marital Communication Style and Social Class." *Journal of Marriage and Family* 39, no. 3 (August 1977): 479–492. An investigation into the influence of social class on the style of communication between marital partners. Four interactional styles are described, and the relationship between style and social class is evaluated by several different measures of communication.

- Jourard, Sidney M. *The Transparent Self,* 2nd ed. New York: Van Nostrand Reinhold, 1971. A classic work by Jourard, exploring the concept of self-disclosure. Some important chapters focus on self-disclosure and the healthy personality, the male role, and disclosure in love and marriage.

- Narcisco, John, and Burkett, David. *Declare Yourself: Discovering Me in Relationships*. Englewood Cliffs, N.J.: Prentice-Hall, 1975. A practical discussion of self-defeating and ineffectual behaviors and how these can be changed to more effective actions with a new language of interpersonal relationships, which the authors call "declaring behavior."

- Powell, John. *Why Am I Afraid to Tell You Who I Am?* Chicago: Argus Communications Co., 1969. A very easy-to-read little book that offers numerous ways to grow through improved communication, especially in the area of self-disclosure.

- Scorseby, Lynn A. *The Marriage Dialogue*. Reading, Mass.: Addison-Wesley, 1977. An informative analysis of the role of communication in establishing and maintaining marriage relationships. Several processes are presented that can be applied by couples to improve their communication skills. Emphasis is placed on decision making and conflict management.

- Zunin, Leonard, and Zunin, Natalie. *Contact: The First Four Minutes*. New York: Ballantine Books, 1973. An intriguing examination of the significance of the first four minutes of human encounters. Emphasizes communication possibilities for the initial minutes of interaction with strangers, friends, and family members.

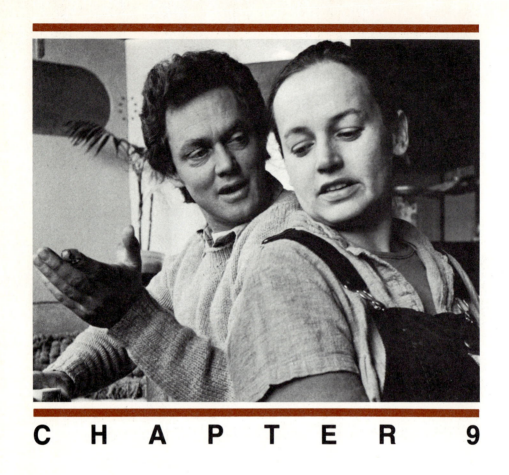

C H A P T E R 9

Conflict Management

SHE: Where's Sue?

HE: I sent her to her room.

SHE: Why?

HE: No shoes on, short shorts.

SHE: It's hot.

HE: It's also Sunday dinner. I've barbequed. You've baked a pie. Mother's coming. Sue can at least put on a skirt and a pair of shoes.

SHE: You used to let Mike come down without shoes.

HE: We made a lot of mistakes with Mike. Sometimes I think they ought to give you a test kid, a robot programmed to look like a kid and act like a kid, so you can make all your mistakes before you have a real one.

SHE: I don't think Mike turned out so badly.

HE: No, he's doing great—a year and a half of college and two years as a handyman in California. Really great.

SHE: He's finding himself.

HE: He's lost. I'm not going to have another shoeless wonder at the table.

SHE: It's your Mother, isn't it? She's written Mike off and now she's working on Sue.

HE: She'll pay for Sue's first-year tuition if Sue just gets three As this year.

SHE: I think that's too much pressure for Sue.

HE: Sue considers waking up in the morning too much pressure. I think it's time we stopped worrying about pressure. Living is pressure. What's she going to do in college?

SHE: She'll do the best she can.

HE: If you were harder on the kids, they'd be able to take more pressure.

SHE: Sure, they'd be like us, punching clocks and never having time to enjoy themselves.

HE: We go out.

SHE: But we do it on the same day each week with the same people. It's never spontaneous. It's never free.

HE: Your son's free, oh yeah, real free, a free *loader*. *(CALLING UPSTAIRS)* Sue, have you got those shoes on?

INTRODUCTION

Conflict, power, negotiation, bargaining—what do these concepts have to do with marriage? The storybook depiction of marital progress shows a couple meeting, falling in love, marrying after a period of courtship, and living happily ever after. Yet other novels and plays, to say nothing of police blotters and legal records, make it clear that family life is full of conflict. As Tolstoy tells us in the beginning of the novel *Anna Karenina:* "All happy families are like one another; each unhappy family is unhappy in its own way" (p. 17). It might be more accurate, if less poetic, to say that each family has periods of happiness and periods of unhappiness. Which one predominates may depend to a great extent on how the family manages conflict.

Social scientists are beginning to realize that adjustment and negotiation in response to conflict go on continually in family life. Conflict in families can be managed so it does not result in violence. Family violence, although it affects a substantial number of wives, husbands, and children, is deviant; family conflict is not.

In this chapter we shall explore the special nature of family conflict, noting the rules and strategies that can lead to peaceful resolution, as well as the processes that appear to end in greater tensions. We shall examine the effects of conflict on family stability and the sources of conflict between spouses, suggesting effective ways to resolve inevitable clashes. Once we accept conflict as normal rather than deviant, we begin to see that the important question is not how to end all conflict, but how to manage it successfully.

THE CONCEPT OF CONFLICT

The term *conflict* has been defined in two ways. The first definition refers to an intense struggle that occurs when one person tries to injure another. The struggle may concern claims to status, power, or scarce resources, or it may be a dispute over values, but the conflict is not resolved unless the rival is neutralized, eliminated, or defeated (Coser 1968, p. 232). According to Ralph Turner, the injury done to one's opponent in conflict is what distinguishes conflict from disagreement or rivalry. The injury need not be palpable, but there must be a clear "winner." In discussions of differences of opinion or interest, one person's view may be subordinated to the task of reaching agreement. In conflict, as Turner defines it, disagreement can be resolved satisfactorily only by "forcedly imposing one's viewpoint on the other" (Turner 1970, pp. 135–136).

Other social scientists conceive of conflict more broadly, as a type of interaction that may begin with disagreement, but can end with compromise and resolution. From this perspective, conflict is a complex process that includes not only the more unpleasant aspects of conflict—name calling and coercion—but also the stages by which it is resolved through communication, role taking, compromise, and bargaining. Viewed in this way, conflict has positive value. Indeed, according to the "conflict theory" articulated in the nineteenth century by Georg Simmel (1959), family life is an ongoing confrontation between individuals with conflicting interests within a common situation. Though the individual needs of family members may be contradictory, they are also interrelated; each has some stake in sustaining the family unit. So instead of quitting the family, the individual members negotiate. They are always negotiating among themselves. Even when an arrangement satisfactory to all has been reached, it is open to continuous negotiation and renegotiation.

Conflict, then, is a more or less normal part of family life. Conflict, not harmony and stable equilibrium, is bound to ensue when two or more individuals with many differences live together as closely as a family does. Family stability cannot simply be equated with harmony, equilibrium, or adjustment. Indeed, stability is not incompatible with conflict and disorder. Families continue in the face of problems and disharmony (Sprey 1969, pp. 699–702). Later in this chapter, we shall examine the reasons why families survive despite conflict.

Conflict need not interrupt cooperative functioning in families, since cooperation requires only shared procedural rules about how tasks should be completed, not consensus or agreement on other values. It is useless to hope for complete agreement among family members; rather, we should seek an effective way of dealing with the differences.

If conflict is normal in family life, then the key question becomes "How is cooperation possible?" Horowitz (1967) defines cooperation as "the settlement of problems in terms which make possible the continuation of differences and even fundamental disagreements." Two or more people can cooperate in a task without sharing the same attitudes or values. They do not necessarily cooperate better when they share more values. Unhappily married spouses may not be unhappy about their differences, but about their inability to live with these differences. If we wish to retain the notion of harmony as a key to understanding successful marriage, then it should be redefined as the management of conflict, not its elimination (Sprey 1969, pp. 703–704).

Positive Conflict

Not only is conflict inherent in families and marriages; it may even have positive benefits. It does seem that the closer and more intimate two people are, the more intense their conflicts can be (Turner 1970, p. 136). In this sense, conflict may "go with the territory" of intimate relations. It may be a requisite of self-disclosure that one fully discloses areas of difference without backing down or covering up. A total lack of conflict may indicate a lack of openness in the marriage. Conflict in marriage is similar to discipline in parenting in that both are positive and valuable when they occur in the context of love and basic acceptance. Both, however, can also serve as an expression of rejection. In Chapter 8 we saw how discrepant bonding and other problems of communication can prevent conflicts from being resolved. As with communication techniques, the management of conflict can be learned if the basic desire to further the relationship exists. When conflicts are left unresolved, they erode trust and love. As Sprey points out (1969, p. 700), when conflict is effectively managed, it can reinforce solidarity, help maintain an equitable division of labor, and even reduce the boredom of too much consensus.

Constructive conflict brings issues out into the open, where they can be bargained over and resolved in a way satisfactory to both people. Conflict that focuses on issues, problems, and conditions and defines its source may enhance stability by leading to change—change that removes the source of that particular conflict. This does not mean that any kind of conflict is beneficial per se. As we shall see in the section on verbal and physical aggression, venting anger and aggression without regard for its effects on others has no long-term benefits for family members. But couples who do not know how to present grievances and negotiate conflicts effectively may

Conflict may have positive benefits. (Sybil Shelton, Peter Arnold, Inc.)

vent their resentment and hostility in destructive ways, or they may suffer needlessly in silence for years. Failure to manage conflict can ultimately result in the dissolution of the relationship.

Basic and Nonbasic Conflict

Whether conflict threatens a marriage depends partly on what sort of conflict it is. John Scanzoni (1972) distinguishes between *basic conflicts*—those that concern the very basis of the relationship—and *nonbasic conflicts*. One way to understand the difference is by analogy with a game. Basic conflicts concern the very rules of the game. Without consensus or agreement on these rules, the game cannot continue. The game itself consists of conflicts and rivalry between two opponents; but these conflicts, which occur within the context of the game, are not basic. They do not threaten the game's existence or continuance.

Couples disagree about all sorts of things, some of which seem trivial and mundane to outsiders. Many disagreements are not basic to the marriage. She likes to dine at a Japanese restaurant; he prefers Greek food. He prefers a modern decor; she likes French provincial. But other conflicts that center on apparently superficial matters betray a basic conflict between husband and wife. Take this mundane issue: how to spend the weekend. She wants friends over; he wants to be alone. If they have a fundamental agreement that each person's needs must be considered in this marriage, that when they are in diametrical opposition they must each negotiate and compromise, then their conflict can be resolved. Every couple has certain unwritten rules of this sort. If, despite this unwritten rule, this original understanding, one spouse insists that the other capitulate completely, their conflict has become a basic one and their marriage is threatened (Scanzoni 1972, pp. 72–73).

In most marriages basic conflicts tend to emerge from two interdependent areas: the economic and the expressive. When expectations in either of these areas are disappointed, conflict often results. In traditional marriages where the husband is expected to bear primary financial responsibility for his family (even if his wife works), a basic conflict arises when he fails to fulfill his provider role. Given the expressive function of marriage in satisfying affectional and sexual needs, a wife's decision not to have any sexual relations with her husband strikes at the very core of their relationship (Scanzoni 1972, pp. 73–74). In an egalitarian, two-worker marriage, sexual withdrawal and failure to provide a share of earnings may be equally damaging, equally conflict-producing, coming from husband or wife. The basic agreement underlying these partnerships is sharing of financial responsibility and expressive functions.

Personality and Situational Conflict

Some conflicts are based on personality needs; others are rooted in specific situations. *Personality conflict*, which is based on one or both spouses' need to vent hostilities, is destructive; it is best dealt with, perhaps, by therapeutic treatment of the hostile personality. *Situational conflict*, in contrast, is based on specific demands, and it aims at a specific result (Scanzoni 1972, p. 76).

The notion that anger in marriage should be dealt with by resocializing one or both partners tended to prevail in the popular marriage literature until the 1960s. Advice columns in newspapers and magazines stressed "adjustment," usually on the part of the wife, and discouraged the venting of hostilities (Koch and Koch 1976). This trend began to change, parallel to changes in attitudes about sex roles. As husband and wife came to be regarded as equals, as instrumental and expressive functions began to be shared, the idea that couples needed bargaining sessions became popular.

George Bach insisted that regular bouts of conflict could benefit the relationship if couples followed certain rules. He tried to make couples understand that anger is a perfectly normal emotion in marriage. When that anger is expressed according to certain rules—such as, "We'll fight for 50 minutes, and we won't bring up anything that happened prior to this year."—fighting can be a means of finding greater intimacy. "Fair fighting," in Bach's opinion, is so healthy for marriage that he has said, "A fight a day keeps the doctor away" (Bach and Wyden 1968, p. 26).

Whether fighting can actually be conducted fairly depends on many factors in the marriage—the partners' personal degree of impulse and aggression control and the degree to which disagreement requires change. Conflict over issues that demand profound changes in the marriage are not likely to be handled by facile "rules of the game." When anger runs deep, fair fighting can too easily become verbal abuse. Later on in this chapter we shall see that it is often difficult to prevent verbal abuse from turning into physical abuse.

Settling a basic conflict is likely to require changes in both partners—and may even require changes in the family system or in the network of friends, relatives, and neighbors who affect that system. Family therapy and "network therapy" (in which the entire network of family and friends of an individual is seen at once) are efforts to bring about such necessary change in the system rather than just in the individual.

An individual's anger and frustrations may also be linked to broader social problems that go beyond the immediate family or friendship network. These can be issues that affect an entire race or sex and call for some recognition of a social inequity. Such issues can cause situational conflicts. Looking at the high divorce rate among low-income black families, for example, it is not appropriate to view narrowly the problem in these families as calling for individual therapy with each black spouse to bring about his or her alignment with middle-class ideals of marital harmony. The problems of such families can be addressed only by looking at the broader social and economic structure of society, which has in the past denied economic power to black males, making it difficult or impossible for them to fulfill the provider role within their families.

Social change rather than individual therapy is clearly what is wanted by feminists and others who would like to alter the traditional marriage structure in a more egalitarian direction. Adjusting to the status quo, swallowing their anger, will no longer do for women who feel oppressed. Women may spark conflict in their families because they require more equal distribution of household tasks and child-rearing responsibilities (Scanzoni 1972, pp. 78–79). There are conflicts that cannot be resolved by socialization of a maladjusted personality. These require bargaining and negotiation, during which all concerned make some changes. If the changes required are profound, a third party may help to resolve the conflicts, but a resolution may be unattainable without social changes.

CONFLICT ISSUES

Communication problems, children, sex, and money seem to be the four most common sources of family conflict.

Communication Problems

Data based on a large sample of families seeking help from family service agencies in the United States and Canada reveals communication problems to be the most frequent catalyst for marital conflict (see Figure 9.1). Nine out of ten couples with marital problems reported difficulties in communication. Clients told counselors: "We can't talk to each other"; "I can't reach him"; "She doesn't understand me"; or "Every time we talk to each other it ends in an argument" (Beck and Jones 1973, p. 148). As we have made clear in Chapter 8, communication difficulties can cover a multitude of problems, including lack of sociability, failure to express tenderness or endearment, unwillingness to disclose information or personal feelings, and a basic lack of trust in each other.

Children

Almost half the families coming for marital counseling reported conflicts over children. (In Chapter 11 we shall see that these problems with children may relate to other issues in the marriage.) Conflicts over children may cover a number of areas, from disagreement about discipline and child-rearing practices, to fears that children will expose marital or personal problems, to anxieties over aging and potency, which the presence of teenagers can aggravate. Certain children, despite dedicated parenting, have difficulty with school or friendships. Children with physical, mental, or emotional handicaps can put great strains on the marriage relationship.

The Family Service Association study reveals that marital and children's problems tend to occur in combination (see Figure 9.2). When children reach adolescence, conflict levels are typically high. Teenagers need to establish their own identities, and this process often involves tension and disagreements between parents and children. In their search for identity, adolescents may break rules and test limits. Their behavior may be more extreme if they are aware of their parents' marital problems. Equally important is the timing of teenage years, coming as it usually does when parents face their own identity crises. Marital problems in combination with children's problems thus reach their peak when children are teen-

FIGURE 9.1   Areas of Marital Conflict or Difficulty*

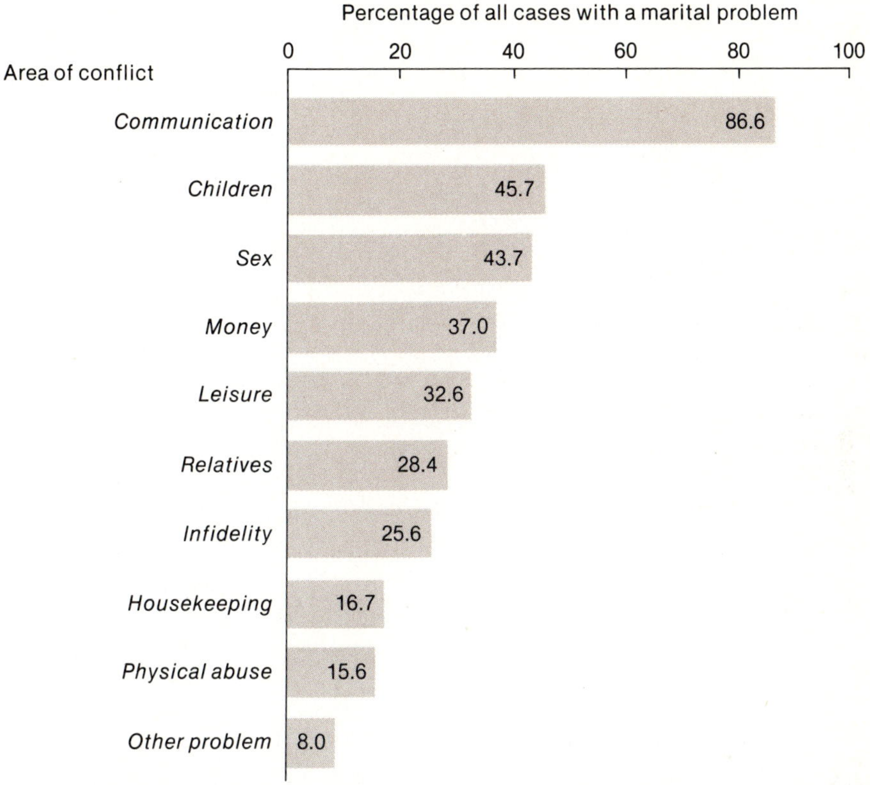

Percentage of all cases with a marital problem

Area of conflict	
Communication	86.6
Children	45.7
Sex	43.7
Money	37.0
Leisure	32.6
Relatives	28.4
Infidelity	25.6
Housekeeping	16.7
Physical abuse	15.6
Other problem	8.0

*Data based on 1,579 intact families with marital problems seeking help from family service agencies during a sample week. The areas of conflict reported were identified by the counselors at the time of case closing and are based on information shared with the counselor during the counseling process.

Source: Adapted from *Progress on Family Problems: A Nationwide Study of Clients' and Counselors' Views on Family Agency Services,* by Dorothy Fahs Beck and Mary Ann Jones, p. 148, by permission of the publisher. Copyright 1973 by Family Service Association of America, New York.

agers (Beck and Jones 1973). As we shall see in Chapter 14, marital satisfaction tends to dip during the years when children are teenagers and then rises again when children are launched on their own lives.

Sexual Problems

Sexual dissatisfaction was reported by four couples in ten. Here, too, a lack of trust makes sexual relations problematic. We have also noted in our discussion of specific sexual problems (see Chapter 4) that people today

FIGURE 9.2 Marital and Children's Problems by Years Married*

Percentage of cases*

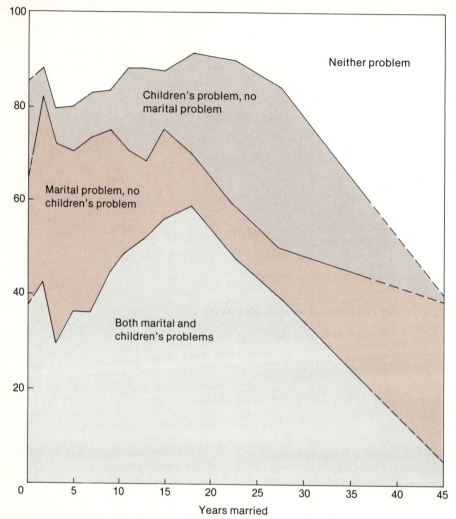

Years married

*Data based on counselors' reports of the problems presented and years married for 2,204 married couples seeking help from family service agencies during a sample week.

†Percentages at lower and upper extremes of years married represent projections of trends prevailing at midpoints of top and bottom categories.

Source: Adapted from *Progress on Family Problems: A Nationwide Study of Clients' and Counselors' Views on Family Agency Services,* by Dorothy Fahs Beck and Mary Ann Jones, p. 150, by permission of the publisher. Copyright 1973 by Family Service Association of America, New York.

are more apt to expect satisfying sexual relationships and to seek help (or other partners) when sexual fulfillment does not occur.

Money

Money was a primary source of conflict for one in three couples. In our chapter on the economics of the family (Chapter 13), we shall discuss certain practical aspects of family money management. Here we can examine some factors that make money a common source of marital conflict.

Money stands for much more than hard cash. It has powerful symbolic value in our culture, being associated with love, power, and self-control. Money can symbolize a parent's protection and a child's need for love. Some parents try to buy their children's love or use money and "things" as substitutes for time spent with their children. One early study of middle-class high school students indicated that a satisfactory emotional relationship in childhood was related to the ability to manage money later (Prevey 1945).

Money management and financial success are related in American culture to prestige, self-respect, power, competition, and love-worthiness. Traditionally, men have gained in emotional strength as they demonstrated skill and success in business. Conversely, the lack of money or employment tends to make men feel impotent and may cause them to turn to violence as a sign of their power and control. Women, too, are moving into this power arena, and their new economic independence has an impact on their sense of personal power, their willingness to put up with dissatisfaction, and even their willingness to retaliate with physical force when they are abused.

Efforts to earn money may be used as simply one more way of showing love and affection—parents work overtime and weekends to provide a higher standard of living for their family and prove their love. But sometimes the work and the salary become a substitute for love and affection—the husband or the wife may become so completely wrapped up in breadwinning that they have little time for each other or their children. In her interpretation of the King Midas fairy tale, Nancy Datan finds parallels to contemporary work compulsions. Midas wished for and was granted the ability to turn everything he touched into gold. "Before long he touched his lunch and deprived himself of the sustenance of food, and touched his beloved daughter and deprived himself of the sustenance of love." Datan sees a parallel between the Midas legend and today's "workaholics," those men and women who substitute success and rewards in the world of work for the rewards "of the inner self and its needs" (Datan 1980).

Even religion, which tends to stress spiritual over material values, can become contaminated with money, creating family tension. The "Protes-

Conflicts often arise over the demands of work—earning money—and the demands of family. (Charles Gatewood)

tant ethic" stressed the value of hard work, thrift, frugality—all values essential to the frontier culture of the United States in the eighteenth and nineteenth centuries. But it also came to put a high value on the accumulation of capital and became an engine of capitalism by somehow implying that those who failed to accumulate capital were spiritually lacking (Tawney 1937). Organized religion inevitably requires dues (or tithes or donations), lending special prominence to large fund raisers and donors, regardless of their spiritual purity. Even religions cannot completely dissociate themselves from money.

Within a family, subtle struggles for power and dominance may be carried out through money. The husband who refuses his wife's request for an increase in the household allowance or who gambles away a part of his earnings may be using money as a way to refuse love or as a weapon to retaliate for past hurts. Conflict over money may also be a safety valve for releasing other potentially dangerous animosities (Neisser 1960, p. 345).

THE STAGES OF CONFLICT

Any given episode of marital conflict can be broken down into steps or stages, with the general form of a minidrama. Ralph Turner has sketched the stages of conflict as follows (1970, p. 137):

1. Gesture Exchange.   Transformation of interaction into conflict.
2. Period of Conflict.   The exchange of symbolic blows.
3. a. Accommodation.   The cessation of overt conflict, or
   b. Conciliation.   Activation of the counterprocess of harmony.
4. Reassessment.   Typically a period following the end or interruption of overt conflict during which the participants re-enact the conflict in imagination.
5. Aftermath.   Either a reactivation of the conflict, avoidance of the conflict source, or conciliation, depending on the results of the reassessment stage.

We shall use some scenes from Leo Tolstoy's novel *Anna Karenina* (translated by Magarshack 1964) to illustrate these five stages of marital conflict.

Gesture Exchange: Transforming Interaction into Conflict

The transformation of an interaction into conflict may occur by words or gestures. Such transformation typically depends on some doubt or anxiety or some expectation of love or acceptance that is disappointed by the other's response. Here's the way it starts at the Oblonsky household:

Everything was in confusion in the Oblonsky household. The wife had found out that the husband had had an affair with their French governess and had told him that she could not go on living in the same house with him. (p. 17)

Thus the novelist introduces a major family conflict. How will it be resolved? What are the various stages of conflict and its resolution? This particular conflict begins when Dolly Oblonsky discovers the letter that reveals her husband's infidelity: "She . . . was sitting perfectly still with the letter in her hand, looking at him with an expression of horror, despair, and indignation." Marital conflicts often begin with gestures that express tension or resentment: She is moody and silent; he complains about trifles.

Period of Conflict: The Exchange of Symbolic Blows

This is the stage at which verbal, and sometimes physical, abuse occurs. One party, as Turner puts it, perceives an unfavorable self-image in a situation (Turner 1970, p. 138). Oblonsky has done something that seriously threatens Dolly's identity as his wife, as the woman he loves exclusively. His infidelity has cast her in a most unfavorable role as the wife who is no longer sexually attractive to her husband, as a person whose interests and feelings can be disregarded even after nine years of marriage.

Dolly retaliates with symbolic blows: She "shuddered as though in physical pain, broke out with her characteristic heat into a flood of cruel words, and rushed out of the room."

Dolly is also morally outraged by an act that in the nineteenth century was a serious transgression of conventional morality. As his wife, Dolly has come to identify intensely with Oblonsky by taking on his qualities, including his prestige and standing in the community, as if they were her own. Oblonsky's failure to live up to her moral standards now threatens that long-standing identification with her husband. Outraged, she feels certain that she cannot continue to identify with a man who has done such a thing. In retaliation for these hurts, she hurls at him "a flood of cruel words" to hurt *his* self-esteem and thereby protect her own. Only later does Oblonsky have a chance to defend himself:

"My God, what have I done? Dolly, for heaven's sake! . . . Dolly, what can I say? . . . Just one thing: I'm sorry, I'm sorry. Think . . . Cannot nine years of our life make up for a moment, a moment . . ." (p. 27)

Dolly, at this point, is beginning to soften, but Oblonsky makes the mistake in the course of his defense of bringing up the one issue that is driving her from him: he admits to "a moment of infatuation." At this admission her fury rises again:

"Go away!" she screamed more piercingly than before, "get out of here and don't talk to me of your infatuations." (p. 27)

Accommodation: Cessation of Overt Conflict

The scene ends only when Dolly succeeds in sending her husband from the room. This scene is perhaps melodramatic from today's point of view, but it serves to illustrate how conflicts are ended. In this particular episode, as Dolly sends her husband away, separation ends the encounter.

Reassessment

In the fourth stage of conflict, participants typically replay the conflict as if they were running a movie in their heads. They also examine their options (Turner 1970). Dolly, for example, re-evaluates her position as the mother of a brood of children. She is helped in her reassessment by Anna Karenina, who persuades her that Oblonsky really loves her and that Dolly would be better off if she forgave him and took him back. In the reassessment stage, both Dolly and Oblonsky review the conflict, remembering details that might improve the outcome.

"Dear, oh dear!" he groaned, remembering what had happened. And in his mind's eye he saw again all the details of the quarrel with his wife; he realized the utter hopelessness of his position and, most tormenting fact of all, that it was all his own fault. (p. 18)

Dolly, too, reassesses her situation; first dwelling on the other woman and the wrong that her husband has done, then remembering that she still loves him:

She . . . began going over in her mind the conversation they had had. "He has gone! But what has he done about *her*?" she thought. "He isn't still seeing her, is he? Why did I not ask him? No, no, it will never work. . . . And how I loved! Good Lord, how I loved him! . . . And don't I love him even now? Don't I love him even more than ever now?" (p. 29)

Aftermath

In this stage, the couple can begin fighting again. They can try to avoid each other and the divisive issue, or they can conciliate. The aftermath stage depends on the result of their reassessment (Turner 1970, pp. 152–153). As a result of going over her situation and listening to her sister-in-law, Dolly forms a new goal of harmonization and gives up her original conflict aim to hurt Oblonsky by leaving him. In the aftermath of their conflict, Oblonsky and Dolly continue as husband and wife, but with a lingering sense of hurt (on Dolly's part) and contrition (on Oblonsky's part) that inhibits relaxed interaction, at least for a time. Dolly tries to forget, while Oblonsky gives up his affair and is especially solicitous toward his wife. A conciliation, or at least an accommodation, is achieved, with each partner making a contribution. When the conflict is resolved, disrupted household activities will resume their former order, but Dolly's ability to respond affectionately to her husband, her trust in him, has been impaired.

Intense as this conflict is, it is an example of a conflict more easily resolved than many, because Oblonsky agrees with his wife that he is in the wrong. Their situation calls for his reassurance and sympathy, and he is willing to provide both. In many conflicts, however, both partners have grievances, and both feel they are in the right. In such a case, neither partner may be willing to placate or accommodate the other without assurances that his or her grievances are also answered.

The Oblonsky example does illustrate the special nature of family conflict. In another relationship, a disagreement can sometimes be dealt with simply by terminating the relationship or minimizing contact. Indeed, Dolly's initial strategy is to minimize contact with her husband until she has had time to assess the situation.

During the reassessment phase, some couples contemplate separation or divorce. (We shall discuss this option in detail in Chapter 12.) But family conflicts are unlike other interpersonal conflicts because there is usually a very strong reluctance either to walk away from the situation, on the one hand, or to win at all costs, on the other.

Permanent or even temporary separation may be costly to husband and wife financially as well as psychologically. In terms of finances, if the wife does not have her own income from an independent source, she may be forced—even temporarily—to depend on her husband for funds to support herself and their children. The payment may come through funds for alimony or child support. Even if the husband agrees to provide money, he may be hard pressed to do so because two households are more expensive to maintain than one.

Quite apart from the economic difficulties of temporary or permanent separations, there is the tremendous emotional cost of dissolving a family. The desire to keep the family intact gives conflict in families its special character. As long as both partners have the desire to keep their marriage together, there will be an unspoken rule against serious hurt. This reluctance to inflict serious damage distinguishes conflict between allies from conflict between enemies (Straus 1974, p. 15).

Turner's description of the process of conflict, which we have outlined above, is fairly complex. A somewhat simpler explanation of the conflict process is offered by Duvall and Hill (1975, p. 360). First, there is the *build-up* of tension or discord. Second, there is the *climax* of tension. In this stage, partners engage in a variety of techniques for dealing with conflict, including coercing, coaxing, name calling, accusing, arguing, masking their real feelings, and pretending. In the final stage of *resolution* or accommodation, one or both begin to communicate understanding of what the other is saying.

CONFLICT MANAGEMENT

Constructive conflict can leave a marriage stronger than before, but it calls for special skills in handling conflict so that it does not become violent or painful (Duvall and Hill 1975, p. 362). John Scanzoni discusses a framework for describing conflict management skills that focuses on sex roles. There are, he maintains, two kinds of techniques for dealing with conflict—role induction and role modification. *Role induction* involves one partner's changing while the other does not. Using role induction, one partner employs a variety of techniques aimed at *inducing* the other to change, without the acting partner undergoing any change. Some of these techniques may be used not primarily to induce change, but only to wound the other partner and thereby protect one's own self-image. For some social scientists, such as Turner, the aim to hurt or damage the other as a way of bolstering one's depleted self-image is the essence of conflict. Even when role-inductive strategies are aimed at changing the other partner, they are usually only temporary. Real change, if it occurs at all, comes about as a result of *role modification,* when *both* partners change their attitudes and behaviors (Scanzoni 1972, pp. 86, 92). We shall look at the familiar methods of role induction first and then examine the more constructive role-modification methods.

Role Induction

The techniques of role induction include the following:

1. Coercion. Coercion consists of overt attacks, threats, verbal or physical force such as hitting, shoving, or giving orders. Overt verbal attacks are often made from a morally protected position and almost always evoke temporary retreat or defensiveness. Dolly Oblonsky attacks from such a position of moral righteousness. It is difficult for Oblonsky to attack her because, in his behavior toward her, he has violated even his own standard of good conduct. In general, one partner is in a stronger position if his or her grievance stems from moral indignation or outrage.

2. Coaxing. Coaxing consists of asking, promising, pleading, begging, tempting—all techniques to bring the spouse to one's position without bargaining or exchanging. One partner may give in to such tactics for a while, but usually the basic conflict is merely submerged or put aside for a time, only to re-emerge later.

3. Masking and Unmasking. Another technique for trying to bring someone around without bargaining is to engage in pretense, deception, or distraction. *Masking* includes a range of behaviors, from outright lying to evading and censoring or selectively telling the facts. He complains that she is too involved in her career and doesn't spend time with him; she placates him, smoothing over the conflict with deceits and lies about extra assignments at work.

Unmasking is also a technique used in conflicts. All people harbor some dreams or illusions about themselves or about significant others. Such illusions can be functional defenses, best left undisturbed so long as they do not interfere with a person's ability to deal with reality. But at the height of an intense episode of conflict, one partner may unmask painful truths, destroying illusions and damaging the other's ego, thus bolstering his or her own ego. Such revelations are often only half-truths, but the grain of truth in them is enough to inflict lasting pain. A jealous wife, suspicious of her husband's extramarital activities, may suddenly announce that he is not the great lover he thinks he is, a jab that can only leave lingering hurt, no matter how much she denies it later. Or a husband, upset with his wife's spending habits, reminds her that she herself once admitted to using clothes to cover up what she believes is an unattractive figure. As this argument proceeds, he tells her she *does* have an unattractive figure and expensive clothes can't hide it. Such unmasking only exacerbates the basic conflict. Even when the conflict is resolved, both partners may carry lingering doubts about the truth of remarks made to inflict pain in the heat of conflict (Scanzoni 1972, pp. 88–91).

4. Postponement.   Another technique for inducing someone else to take one's view is simply to postpone the conflict, in the expectation that the other person will change his or her mind. By using this technique, one can let a conflict drag on, unresolved, for weeks, months, or even years. For example, a wife has been complaining about her husband's gambling. His habit has depleted their resources. She now demands that he change. The husband agrees to give up gambling altogether, "just as soon" as he has broken even or made a little fortune. By postponing his final renunciation of a habit that his wife finds disagreeable, he can agreeably continue that habit. In fact, he is not changing at all, but he induces his wife to go on adapting to his destructive behavior. By accepting the postponement, she accepts the role of the one who adapts and changes.

Role Modification: Constructive Quarreling

Destructive quarreling uses many of the techniques of role induction. Remarks are directed at the other person rather than at the issues, in an attempt to hurt the other's ego by destroying illusions (unmasking) or belittling and punishing (name calling). Such quarrels succeed only in alienating the other person. Their one value, note Duvall and Hill, is that they "succeed in alienating incompatible couples" (1975, p. 359).

Even when such strategies succeed in changing the behavior of one partner, the change is usually temporary. Emotions run high in such quarrels and often interfere with clear communication. Arguments are heated, perhaps with one or the other partner yelling or stomping out of the room. Such behaviors may be temporarily useful in venting anger or releasing tension, but they do not settle a conflict finally in a way that both partners can accept.

Quarreling and conflict *can* be constructive if both partners avoid each other's sensitive spots (which means letting the other know what those spots are) and are not distracted by irrelevant issues, barbs about relatives, or gripes that have been left to fester (Duvall and Hill 1975, pp. 360,

362). Genuine settlements are possible in an atmosphere of calm discussion, when partners listen to each other and bring in relevant facts or even a disinterested person to help resolve the conflict.

Conflicts can be *ended* without being resolved in a way that satisfies all concerned. The techniques of coercion or coaxing can be used to end a conflict, so that one person submissively accepts the other's will. Genuine resolutions occur, however, only when both partners change their attitudes and behaviors through role modification, which includes the variety of strategies discussed below.

Role Taking.   Role taking occurs when one partner begins to see things through the eyes of the other, and vice versa. Each partner begins to see the other's grievance in terms of its roots and meanings within that person (Duvall and Hill 1975, p. 362). He complains that he always has to make the first move as the prelude to lovemaking. While he may not be able or willing to express his complaint forthrightly, she begins to understand that he would like to feel sexually desirable and sought-after because she recognizes those same feelings in herself. She also vicariously experiences what it must be like always to pursue but never to be pursued.

Role taking is no magical guarantee of improved relationships. A conflict may be so deep, so basic that the relationship has to be dissolved. If, for example, she contends that he is an uncultured bore who will never make a living, and he knows she comes from a family of vastly different means and education, he may decide that, from her point of view, this will never work out: "We must separate."

Joking and Banter.   Once two people have insights into each other's feelings and perceptions, they gain some distance from the conflict. They can see the absurdity in some of their behavior and laugh at themselves and with each other. Joking relieves the tension of many conflicts. It may even help resolve nonbasic conflicts. When good will is restored, partners may engage in banter, light, playful, teasing remarks, and good-natured raillery. Such joking and banter does more than release tension; it may also restore bonds by reminding each partner that the degree of intimacy between them is great. In joking and bantering, each agrees not to take the other's remarks at face value. Partners are able to laugh at remarks that would be insulting or disparaging between less intimate friends. These "jokes" are symbols of the intimacy between them (Turner 1970, p. 93). In short, the couple laughs *with* each other, not *at* each other.

Exploration.   At some point, partners must agree to abandon their indignation and hurt and to direct their argument toward a cooperative examination of the problem. Each partner probes and tests the ability of the other to establish a creative solution.

If Dolly Oblonsky were merely suspicious of her husband's infidelity, without having any concrete evidence, she might explore the situation by an ambiguous gesture or remark: "You're spending a lot of time away from home these days." If he retaliates and betrays no guilt, she can always say she has been misunderstood: "I only meant that I missed having you around." Or the attack can be made in front of others, so that only the other, who cannot retaliate in public, recognizes the jibe or insult.

At the exploration stage of role modification, questions of legitimate power, resources, and bargaining become important. There are, as Thomas C. Shelling puts it, "situations that ultimately involve an element of pure bargaining—bargaining in which each party is guided mainly by his [or her] expectations of what the other will accept" (1960, p. 21). Husbands and wives have *power* over each other, in the sense of being able to impose their wills. She wants to spend the summer in town so she can continue taking night courses toward her degree in business administration, while he wants to take advantage of a sabbatical to go to Europe. They talk, looking for alternatives that will satisfy both their needs. If he is the chief provider, he has more power in deciding how money will be spent. But she can argue that if she stays and finishes her degree, her income potential will be greater. Or she may simply stress her personal need for a career that promises fulfillment. In marriage, power is not determined only by economics, but economic issues do have a way of influencing power, even in a relationship where loving concern for the other should be paramount.

At least one test, used repeatedly in the United States and abroad, shows that husbands have more power than wives and that the higher a husband's job status, the more power he has (Scanzoni 1972, pp. 67–68). In this test, husbands and wives are asked who actually makes the *final* decision about such issues as (1) what car to get; (2) whether or not to buy life insurance; (3) what house or apartment to rent or buy; and (4) what job the husband should take. The responses are combined into an index as a measure of family decision making.

Since power and authority rest on resources, and husbands traditionally have more resources than their wives, men are usually in a better bargaining position. They are also in a position to abuse power. As we shall discuss shortly, sex-segregated decision making—he decides about money; she decides about meal preparation—seems to be a factor in family violence.

Changes in sex roles, as we explained in Chapter 7, also involve changes in the division of power. When a wife is working, she has more leverage in marital decision making. When she has a career rather than a "job," studies show that her power also increases (Scanzoni 1972, p. 69). The wife's economic position changes the nature of conflict management. Take this example involving a dispute over money: The husband has purchased an expensive video tape recorder. If the wife is contributing to their income, she may be more likely to complain about this expenditure and even to insist they cannot afford it. If the dispute is handled constructively, the two may decide, as Scanzoni suggests (p. 216), on separate bank accounts or on a plan in which each contributes a portion to family support and household needs, but each keeps a certain amount for personal use.

Power relationships do influence the nature of conflict management, but economic shifts do not ensure a peaceful resolution. When she earns a living rather than being given an allowance, her bargaining position improves. Ultimately, however, conflict resolution requires deep mutual concern for the other—not just a balance of power.

Compromise. At this stage, spouses discover what each will actually accept for the reality of their daily lives. In the case of the husband who wanted to spend the summer in Europe and the wife who wanted to go to summer school, a compromise could be reached if he agreed to spend a few weeks in Europe without her while she finished her summer courses, and she agreed to take courses that would allow her to finish early so she could join him abroad.

Consolidation. Once a couple has agreed to a compromise, they must make that compromise work. Where the compromise involves ongoing behavior—he will stop nit-picking, she will be more supportive—rather than action performed only once, the new behavior must become part of their daily interaction (Scanzoni 1972, pp. 96–97).

Each stage of conflict calls for certain skills and rituals, especially the beginning and ending of conflict episodes. At the outset, the partner with the grievance should assure the other that his or her love is not conditional or dependent on the other's agreement with the complaint. This statement of loyalty to the relationship can set boundaries for the dispute. It is important that the partners begin by trying to define and agree on the problem, to discover together the areas of their disagreement. Artistry—as well as restraint—is called for in ending an episode of conflict, to ease the resumption of normal interaction and dispel lingering hurt and doubt (Duvall and Hill 1975, pp. 360, 362). If the discussion has been tense or heated, and especially if hurtful things have been said, one partner cannot simply offer to end the conflict. The hurtful remarks must somehow be discounted as exaggerations, denied as untrue, or reinterpreted as banter or raillery (Turner 1970, p. 149). These guidelines assume mutual trust between the partners and conflicts that are not basic. When conflicts are basic and trust has already been undermined, couples are likely to require outside help.

Seeking Professional Advice

Couples in conflict can turn to a friend, member of the clergy, or professional therapist for advice and counseling. A professional therapist or counselor can often help a troubled couple by discussing some of the techniques of conflict management outlined here or by uncovering basic problems that need to be tackled. Because the therapist has emotional distance from the problems, as well as experience in talking to couples with similar problems, he or she may guide husband and wife to creative compromises and solutions or help them with role modification.

Qualified therapists use a variety of techniques to help couples improve communication and manage conflict. Videotaping interactions, teaching couples to take turns "griping" and feeding back the gripe, family "sculpt-

A qualified therapist or counselor can often help a couple to improve their communication and manage conflict. (Bohdan Hrynewich)

ing" (expressing one's view of the family conflict by posing family members as if one were sculpting)—these are only a few techniques currently in use by marriage counselors (Koch and Koch 1976).

But most couples appear to wait until conflict has become severe or unendurable before seeking the help of a marriage counselor. At this point they are in a poor position to locate and evaluate the numerous possibilities for professional help. Even if the pair finds a well-qualified therapist, the situation may have reached a point of cumulative pain and anger that even the most adept therapist would find difficult to change.

Analyzing the results of a conflict-tactics test given to a nationally representative sample of 2,143 couples, Murray Straus noticed a strong reluctance among American couples to seek outside help in order to settle conflicts:

Given the privacy norms of the contemporary American nuclear family, it takes a conflict involving violent acts to make the partners desperate enough to be willing to (or to be forced to) breach this privacy by bringing in an outsider to help mediate the conflict. (1979, p. 82)

Cumulative Conflict

Some couples have a very low tolerance for conflict, while others accept it much more easily as a part of their relationship. Harmony is created when conflicts are *resolved*, but what feels like resolution for one partner or couple may not feel "settled" to another. How people handle conflict and what they accept as a genuine resolution are influenced by previous experiences in one's parental family. Success in handling conflict also seems to be dependent on the conviction that problems can be *solved* or resolved by consensus. Whether conflict or communication needs to be dealt with, interpersonal trust remains the bottom line of family life (Duvall and Hill 1975, p. 362). Not all conflicts are resolved or ended by compromise, consolidation, or coercion. Some are ended only by the dissolution of the relationship in divorce or separation.

A couple can haggle over the same problems year in and year out. Such chronic conflicts—traceable to the partners' personalities or their divisions of labor—need not be cumulative. But "if neither discussion, mediation, nor accommodation succeeds in settling family conflict, the last resort is separation" (Sprey 1969, p. 705). Dissolution also occurs if either partner ceases being gratified by the relationship or re-evaluates alternatives to the relationship. Chronic conflict can then become cumulative, ending in divorce (Turner 1970, p. 160).

Economic or parenting considerations still prevent some dissatisfied couples from divorcing. But today the prevailing attitude seems to be that it is better to divorce than remain unhappily married. Divorce, as we shall see in Chapter 12, is not a simple solution to marital unhappiness. Yet after a period of ongoing conflict, it may be the only solution.

VERBAL AND PHYSICAL VIOLENCE

Family violence has become the subject of intense concern and widespread investigation in recent years. As Box 9.1 indicates, estimates concerning the extent of spouse abuse range widely from one million to more than seven million cases of regular, weekly abuse (Straus 1978, pp. 85–86; Walker 1978, pp. 145–146). Spousal violence depends on the interaction of

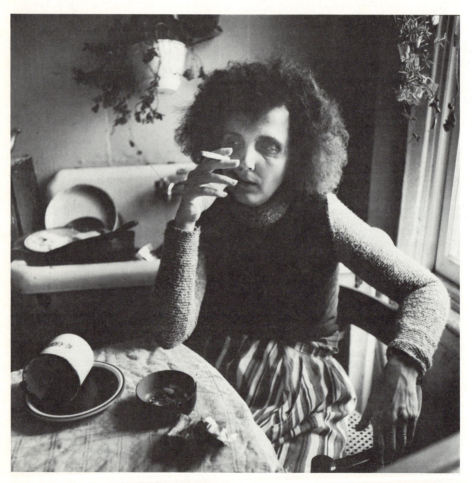

Chronic conflict and physical abuse in families is very prevalent. (Arthur Tress, Woodfin Camp & Associates)

BOX 9.1   The Incidence of Spouse Abuse

Murray A. Straus estimates that 7½ million couples have had at least one violent episode that went beyond what he calls the "ordinary pushing, slapping and shoving." Speaking at a congressional committee hearing, Straus said that about "1.8 million wives are beaten by their husbands each year" and that "for a third of those 1.8 million couples such beatings occur five or more times during the year, with a sizable number just about every week" (1978, pp. 85–86).

Suzanne Steinmetz's data from her national survey suggests that about "3½ million women are battered by their spouses in a given year," while about 250,000 men each year are "battered by their wives" (1978, p. 164). It is usually the stronger family member who abuses the weaker: husbands beat wives, parents batter children. Steinmetz complains that unscrupulous individuals have inflated and sensationalized the figures of spouse abuse. Yet she acknowledges that other researchers might find a higher incidence of domestic violence using a different definition of violence as well as by studying different populations (1978, p. 172). Lenore Walker estimates that "one out of two women will become battered at some time during their lifetime." Walker defines violence widely, however, including those situations in which "a woman . . . really lives under such psychological or physical harrassment that she feels she is powerless within a situation she cannot control" (1978, pp. 145–146).

a number of factors: attitude toward violence, socioeconomic circumstances, the behavior of one's partner, as well as one's sex and one's idea of appropriate role behavior. There is some suggestion that inequitable distribution of tasks can also be a factor in mothers' abusing their children.

Family violence has existed since Cain slew Abel. A Talmudic law from the year 1000 specifies rules for punishing wife beaters and providing the injured spouse with a separate dwelling. But the recording of data concerning family violence and the establishment of government programs to combat it are new developments. Sheltered homes for battered women, programs of therapy for victims of abuse, as well as for abusers, and educational programs to prevent family violence have sprung up in the past decade. In this section we shall examine some of the evidence on family violence, especially spouse abuse. (Child abuse is discussed further in Chapter 11, pp. 365–369.)

The institution of marriage has changed significantly over the last century or so, and part of the change is in styles of conflict. The image we have of a typical middle-class couple of the Victorian era is one of restraint, refinement, civility. A wife politely defers to her husband's wishes; a husband courteously chides and corrects his wife. The rational approach to conflict has been, and remains, one of calm discussion of issues, bringing in relevant facts or disinterested outsiders to help settle the dispute.

Today such intellectualizing may seem to lack the genuineness of "gut-level" responses. Some couples prefer to "let it all hang out," by expressing even their most negative feelings of hostility and aggression without sparing the feelings of their partners (Straus 1974, p. 21). Some therapists and marriage counselors emphasize the importance of "leveling" with one's partner, by saying what is really on one's mind, even if such revelations are painful. They advocate brutally honest, gut-level communication, arguing that "hurting is a necessary part of a [marriage] relationship" (quoted in Straus 1974, p. 13). Straus compares this practice of brutal honesty to the old medical practice of bloodletting: it may be harmless in some cases, but disastrous in others. Such therapists encourage their clients to drop their inhibitions and "outmoded notions of etiquette" and civility, by expressing their sexual and aggressive fantasies or engaging in acts of symbolic aggression such as whacking a towel down on a mattress or even hitting each other with foam rubber bats (Koch and Koch 1976).

Such ideas represent what Straus calls the "catharsis theory," which assumes that "all of us have built into our nature a greater or lesser tendency toward aggression which cannot be bottled up." Fundamental to this theory of human behavior is the belief that aggression is a deep, biologically based motivation that cannot be ignored but must be released in minor "explosions." The biological determinism of thinkers such as Konrad Lorenz (1966) and Edward O. Wilson (1978) bolsters the catharsis theory by postulating a basic innate drive of aggressiveness in human beings. This innate-drive theory is related to the psychoanalytic doctrine, derived from Freud, of an "instinct for aggression" (Straus 1974, pp. 13–14).

In the 1970s, new approaches to psychotherapy emphasized the value of physical and emotional nonverbal communication. Verbal communication and rational discussion were deprecated as mere rationalization. Couples were encouraged to express anger, as well as all other emotions.

Spouses who level with each other, even at the cost of incivility and pain, may temporarily release tension and frustration, but (Straus argues) they may also intensify their aggressiveness even to the point of physical abuse. Rather than warding off physical aggressiveness by relieving tensions, "leveling" and other forms of verbal aggressiveness may actually contribute to physical abuse. To test his hypothesis, Straus constructed a questionnaire for college students designed to discover correlations between verbal and physical aggression. The questionnaire was given to students, who were asked to report on conflicts in their families during the previous year.

Of the student group, 16 percent reported that their parents had used physical violence against each other during that year. Throwing something at the other person, pushing, grabbing, shoving, and hitting (or trying to hit) the other person were all combined as examples of physical aggression. Expressions of emotion, anger, and verbal aggressiveness were measured by such indicators as arguing heatedly, yelling, insulting, sulking, refusing to talk about it, and stamping out of the room. Throwing an object (but not at the other person) or smashing something were also included because they are so important for the catharsis theory, even though they are acts of symbolic violence and not of verbal aggression per se. Such expressions of verbal and symbolic aggression contrast markedly with more rational methods of solving disputes, such as trying to discuss issues calmly, getting information to support arguments, or bringing in someone else to help settle things (Straus 1974, pp. 16, 20–21).

Straus found a correlation between verbal and physical aggressiveness. The therapeutic aggression advocated by certain marriage counselors may not really be therapeutic (1974, p. 13). Straus's research directly contradicts the catharsis theory by suggesting that

opportunities to observe or give vent to anger, hostility, and violence tend to produce greater subsequent levels of aggression and violence. (1974, p. 14)

The greater the "ventilation" of aggressive feelings in the course of a dispute between husband and wife, the greater the amount of physical aggression. (1974, p. 20)

The husband who yells at his wife or breaks furniture when he is angry is not simply venting anger that he would otherwise take out by physically assaulting her. In households where yelling and shouting occur more than rational discussion, physical abuse is more common than in households where spouses intellectualize their differences, repress them, or try to discuss them calmly.

The results of the student survey do not support a "catharsis theory." They do support the more widely accepted "social learning theory," which holds that the more frequently an act is performed, the greater the likelihood that it will become a standard part both of the behavioral repertoire of the individual and of others' expectations of that person's behavior. A person who learns to hurt a spouse verbally has also learned or practiced part of what is involved in physical abuse, namely, deliberate hurting. Verbal and physical abuse have important elements in common, which may explain why they often occur in the same families (Straus 1974, pp. 14, 21).

The notion of "threshold of aggression" also helps explain the correlation between verbal and physical aggression. According to this idea, a human being's system of impulse control operates like locks in a canal, with the locks rising or falling to permit certain "vessels"—certain behaviors—through. Social circumstances are important in defining when we allow ourselves to engage in physical aggression; that is, what the threshold is for such behaviors. It may be that this threshold is lowered by engaging in insults and other forms of verbal aggression, causing disagreements to lead more easily to physical aggression (Straus 1974, p. 21).

Whatever theory or notion we use to explain the correlation between verbal and physical abuse, it follows that the long-term effects of verbal aggression may be harmful, even though the immediate effect of such behavior may be a beneficial release of tension. Furthermore, the catharsis theory is based on observations of couples and individuals who have sought therapy, but whose needs are not necessarily those of the general population. Therapists report that many couples who come to them have always avoided all conflict. Releasing inhibitions may be good advice for these atypical couples, but it does not follow that symbolic aggression and verbal abuse are therapeutic for most couples (Straus 1974, pp. 25–26).

Straus used the information gathered in his research to develop what he calls the "Conflict Tactic (or C-T) Scales." These scales are designed to measure the use of reasoning, verbal aggression, and violence within a given family. When the C-T Scales were administered to 2,143 couples, the results indicated that for about a quarter of married couples, "the marriage license is a hitting license " providing the violence is not "excessive" (Straus 1979, p. 82); 27.6 percent of the respondents indicated that slapping a spouse is either necessary, normal, or good. (Only 5 percent of the total sample believed that all three were true of slapping.) Most couples regard a beating as excessive. Wives are more likely than husbands to distinguish between the use of a gun or knife and the "ordinary" violence of marriage. The survey also revealed that rates of domestic violence are related to three main factors (Dibble and Straus 1980, pp. 71–80):

1. Prior beliefs are related to the incidence of domestic violence. Couples who express a belief that slapping a 12-year-old child is normal are more likely to abuse their own children. Of those who expressed this belief, 72 percent actually used violence against their children. Of the respondents who believed that slapping one's spouse is necessary, normal, and good, 33 percent reported an actual act of violence against their spouses.

2. Whether spouse abuse actually occurs is influenced by circumstances such as income, employment status, and sex. As Table 9.1 shows, a low level of income generally increases the likelihood that a person will slap his or her spouse. (An exception to this rule is the spouse whose partner is violent and who believes that slapping a spouse is normal. Among this group, those with a *higher* level of income were more likely to abuse their spouses.) Low income also makes it more likely that a woman who believes slapping is not normal will wind up hitting, especially hitting back (Straus and Dibble 1980, p. 78). Wealthier husbands may use their money as a means of punishing wives; and the poor man who cannot achieve the leadership role in his family by breadwinning or gaining prestige may turn to violence to obtain what he sees as a socially approved role in the family. The low-income woman is more likely to be hit by her husband and more likely to hit back. Middle-class wives are less likely to be hit by their husbands. They are also less likely to retaliate.

TABLE 9.1 Percentage of Respondents Who Were Violent to Their Spouses, by Belief Regarding the Normality of Slapping a Spouse, by Marital Partner's Violence, and by Total Family Income

Total Family Income	Percentage Violent Among Those Whose Partner is Nonviolent and Who Believe Couple Slapping is:			Percentage Violent Among Those Whose Partner is Violent and Who Believe Couple Slapping Is:		
	Not Normal	Normal	Q	Not Normal	Normal	Q
0–$11,999	5% (414)	10% (122)	.34	67% (39)	71% (63)	.11
$12,000 or more	4% (854)	7% (254)	.24	49% (59)	78% (49)	.56

Source: Ursula Dibble and Murray A. Straus, "Some Social Structure Determinants of Inconsistency Between Attitudes and Behavior: The Case of Family Violence," *Journal of Marriage and Family* 42, no. 1 (February 1980): 78. Copyrighted 1980 by the National Council on Family Relations. Reprinted by permission.

3. People who believe slapping is normal and also have violent partners are very likely to actually abuse their own spouse (see Table 9.2). Both fathers and mothers are much more likely to be violent toward their children if their partners also have used physical punishment against the children (see Table 9.3). In fact, Dibble and Straus conclude that "violent behavior by the spouse has a much greater impact on the respondents' violence than the respondents' own attitudes about violence. This applies to both hitting one's child and hitting one's spouse" (1980, p. 79). Studies of women who have committed murder indicate that abuse by husbands is a prime motive for homicide (Jones 1980).

There may be ways in which our society foments violence, as Merton suggested over 40 years ago (1938, pp. 672–682). Some jobless and poverty-stricken men are led to family violence when they are unable to find legitimate means for demonstrating leadership in their families. Certain aspects of women's socialization, such as the belief that they do

TABLE 9.2 Percentage of Respondents Who Were Violent to Their Spouses, by Belief Regarding the Normality of Slapping a Spouse and by Marital Partner's Violence

Was Marital Partner Violent?	Percentage of *Husbands* Who Hit Spouse Among Husbands Who Believe Slapping a Spouse Is:			Percentage of *Wives* Who Hit Spouse Among Wives Who Believe Slapping a Spouse Is:		
	Not Normal	Normal	Q	Not Normal	Normal	Q
No	5% (607)	9% (196)	.31	4% (794)	6% (202)	.23
Yes	57% (42)	76% (58)	.40	52% (62)	74% (61)	.45

Source: Ursula Dibble and Murray A. Straus, "Some Social Structure Determinants of Inconsistency Between Attitudes and Behavior: The Case of Family Violence," *Journal of Marriage and Family* 42, no. 1 (February 1980): 77. Copyrighted 1980 by the National Council on Family Relations. Reprinted by permission.

TABLE 9.3 Percentage of Fathers and Mothers Who Were Violent to Their Children, by Belief Regarding the Normality of Slapping a 12-Year-Old and by Actual Physical Punishment of Child by Partner

Partner Physically Punished Child	Percentage Violent Among *Fathers* Who Believe Slapping Is:			Percentage Violent Among *Mothers* Who Believe Slapping Is:		
	Not Normal	Normal	Q	Not Normal	Normal	Q
No	18% (79)	34% (143)	.40	26% (81)	53% (184)	.53
Yes	61% (36)	83% (234)	.52	81% (32)	88% (286)	.25

Source: Ursula Dibble and Murray A. Straus, "Some Social Structure Determinants of Inconsistency Between Attitudes and Behavior: The Case of Family Violence," *Journal of Marriage and Family* 42, no. 1 (February 1980): 75. Copyrighted 1980 by the National Council on Family Relations. Reprinted by permission.

not control their destiny—sometimes called "learned helplessness"— may contribute to the aggressor-victim pattern in relationships (Walker 1977–1978, pp. 525, 534).

With our new awareness of the prevalence of family violence, we must find ways in which society can reinforce attitudes that discourage spouse abuse, child abuse, parent abuse, and other forms of conflict that employ violence as a means of resolution.

SUMMARY

1. The objectives of this chapter are, first, to define and describe the concept of conflict, especially in the context of two-person intimate relationships; second, to indicate some common conflict issues in marriage and family relationships; third, to discuss and apply information about the conflict process and conflict management; and fourth, to present information about verbal and physical violence in primary relationships.

2. Conflict, as used in this chapter, refers to the entire process of initiating and resolving, or at least ending, disagreements or confrontations that occur in intimate relationships over differing interests. Broadly defined, conflict is viewed as a normal part of life for marriage partners and family members, whose positions and needs may be contradictory but interrelated. When managed constructively, conflict can lead to positive relationship growth.

3. Conflict may be categorized as basic when it threatens the very existence of the relationship. Nonbasic conflict usually concerns less important issues, disagreements that the partners know will not lead to relationship termination if left unresolved. Conflict may also be related to personality needs (that is, the need to vent hostilities) or to the specific, and sometimes changing, demands of the situation.

4. Issues that cause marital conflict vary from couple to couple, but the most common sources of conflict are communication problems, money disputes, sexual dissatisfaction, and disagreements concerning the children.

5. According to one theoretical view, all conflicts, regardless of the issue involved, follow the same basic process: a beginning or initial gesture exchange that triggers the actual period of conflict; accommodation or reconciliation ending the conflict; a period of reassessing the conflict situation; and, finally, the aftermath stage.

6. Conflicts can be managed, or mismanaged, in several ways. Two major methods include role induction and role modification. The aim of role induction techniques is to motivate one's partner to change without changing oneself, that is, getting the partner to admit that you are right and he or she is wrong. Role modification techniques require some change or adjustment in both partners for the good of the relationship. Power, especially breadwinning power, may influence conflict management, though satisfaction with the marriage ultimately determines the outcome of conflict.

7. The use of coercive methods involving verbal or physical violence is a destructive approach to conflict resolution. A growing body of research evidence links the verbal ventilation of hostile or aggressive feelings with higher rates of actual physical abuse. Though venting anger may be an appropriate technique for some couples in a controlled therapeutic setting, there is evidence to indicate that verbal and physical abuse have important elements in common and frequently occur together.

8. Family violence relates to the attitudes of husband and wife, the behavior of both marital partners, and the socioeconomic level of the family. High rates of child abuse and spouse abuse in all segments of our society underscore the importance of teaching conflict control and providing parents with healthy means of exerting family leadership.

KEY CONCEPTS

Conflict	Situational conflict
Basic conflict	Processes of conflict
Nonbasic conflict	Role induction
Personality conflict	Role modification

QUESTIONS

1. On the basis of the information presented in this chapter and your experience and observations, present a definition of conflict that you

think best applies to intimate relationships. Do you agree that conflict is a normal part of family life? Why or why not?

2. Outline the advice you would give a couple who are involved in a serious relationship and have a basic conflict that they are unable to resolve.

3. Describe a recent conflict that you had with a close friend, sibling, parent, lover, or spouse, or a conflict that you witnessed. Was the conflict basic or nonbasic? Why? Identify the stages of the conflict according to Turner's model presented in this chapter. What role-induction or role-modification techniques were employed in the course of the conflict?

4. On the basis of your experience and observations, what issues seem to be the most frequent sources of conflict between parents and adolescent or young adult children? Between siblings?

5. What methods of conflict resolution do you think are the most constructive? What methods do you think most intimate partners actually use?

6. The United States is often characterized as a violent society, with statistics on child abuse and spouse abuse frequently used as evidence to support this view. Considering the greater social system, describe your proposal for a program to prevent or decrease family violence.

SUGGESTED READINGS

- Beckman-Brindley, S. and Tavormina, J. B. "Power Relationships in Families: A Social-Exchange Perspective." *Family Process* 17, no. 4 (December 1978): 423–436. A theoretical approach to the analysis of power in family relationships that centers on power interactions as fluid and situation specific. The authors maintain that power should be viewed as a fluctuating process that is dynamic and reciprocal across decision-making areas, rather than as a stable, nonchanging factor dominated by one family member.

- Berne, Eric. *Games People Play*. New York: Grove Press, 1964. A fascinating book that introduces various "games" people play in interpersonal relationships. These games are described and interpreted in the language of transactional analysis.

- Justice, Blair, and Justice, Rita. *The Broken Taboo: Sex in the Family*. New York: Human Sciences Press, 1979 (hardcover), 1981 (paperback). A frank look at incest in the family, based on a review of the research literature and on over one hundred case studies. The authors explode some of the harmful myths that surround the subject of incest, look at possible causes, and attempt to assess what can be done to help those involved in such relationships.

- Kammeyer, Kenneth, ed. *Confronting the Issues: Sex Roles, Marriage, and the Family*, 2nd ed. Boston: Allyn and Bacon, 1980. A series of articles that focus on controversial issues in primary relationships. Topics include alternatives to marriage, marriage contracts, parenthood choices, parent-child relationships, and open-marriage possibilities.

- Lederer, William J., and Jackson, Don D. *Mirages of Marriage.* New York: Norton, 1968. An interesting, easy-to-read, yet comprehensive discussion of the problems of married couples. Particular attention is given to the numerous myths about marital relationships and how to make marriage work.

- Rosner, Stanley, and Hobe, Laura. *The Marriage Gap.* New York: McGraw-Hill, 1978. A practical analysis of several major issues in marital relationships, including readiness for marriage, vital dimensions of a good marriage, ways to save a marriage that is breaking up, and the time to uncouple.

- Steinmetz, Suzanne K., and Straus, Murray A., eds. *Violence in the Family.* New York: Dodd Mead & Co., 1974. A basic collection of articles about violence in the family system. Readings emphasize the circumstances surrounding violent behavior, reasons for violence, and ways to help control and reduce this kind of interaction. Both spouse and child abuse are considered.

- Wahlroos, Sven. *Family Communication.* New York: Signet Books, 1974. A clinical psychologist's guidelines for improving family relationships and emotional health. The author's major concern is quality communication, and many helpful suggestions are included for resolving conflicts constructively.

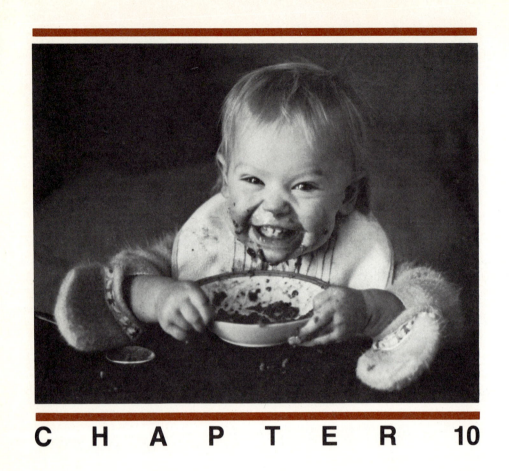

C H A P T E R   10

Decisions About Children

SHE: Look at that baby. Isn't she adorable?

HE: Yeah, she is cute.

SHE: It almost makes you want to have one, doesn't it?

HE: You know I've always wanted kids.

SHE: But you always wanted me to stay home with them.

HE: If we have a baby, maybe we could get some help. Your aunt offered.

SHE: Aunt Fran, five of her own and she wants to take on another. It makes me feel guilty.

HE: Look, if you want to keep on working, why not let Fran help out? We'll have enough to pay her, and I know she could use the money.

SHE: I do have the summers off . . .

HE: I can take my three weeks when it's time for the baby, as long as it's not the tax season.

SHE: We can plan around that.

HE: Nine months from now would be perfect.

SHE: We may not hit the jackpot the first time.

HE: Are you sure it would be right for you? Last time we talked about it you said you wanted to wait until you got tenure.

SHE: Tenure is at least three years away.

HE: I don't want to let a baby picture make you do something you'll regret.

SHE: It's not just the picture. I've been feeling so good about you and me, I'm sort of overflowing. I'm ready to share us.

HE: Wouldn't you want to be home with the baby, just that first year? Could you miss just one year of work?

SHE: Could you?

HE: We're going to need my salary more than ever, but that first year, a full-time mother is really important for the baby.

INTRODUCTION

To become a parent or not to become a parent: That is the question. It is a complicated question for many contemporary couples and one that is distinctly modern. Before 1968, childlessness was listed in many reference books under "sterility"—the assumption being that only a sterile person would face a life barren of children. Although childless couples are still in the minority, the trend toward marriage without children is on the upswing. An increasing number of women remain childless throughout their twenties. Delayed childbearing results in fewer children per family and more childless couples. Veevers (1979) estimates that five percent of married couples are now choosing not to have children—while only a decade ago, only one percent chose to remain childless. According to the U.S. Bureau of the Census (1979c, p. 65), ten percent of all married couples today are childless; thus, about half of all couples without children are childless by choice, and the other half are childless due to sterility.

In this chapter we shall discuss the choice to have children as a difficult one that should be weighed carefully by husband and wife. We shall present information on the psychological costs of having children, as well as some of the rewards. (In Chapter 13 we shall discuss the dollars-and-cents aspect of parenting.) We shall also discuss some unsuitable reasons for having children, motivations that are likely to extract a heavy price both from the marriage and from the well-being of the children.

Most couples who want to have children are still interested in controlling conception. Many couples are delaying childbearing until their thirties. Among those who do raise children, the trend is toward fewer children—an average of two per family rather than three or four. Because families are having fewer children, and also because more couples are divorcing, the average size of the American family has shrunk from 3.7 persons in the 1960s to 3.4 persons in the 1970s, with an expected drop to

3.0 persons by 1990 (U.S. Bureau of the Census, 1977). Married couples are carefully weighing the questions of how many children to have or whether to have children at all.

MAKING THE CHOICE

Reasons for Having Children

"Be fruitful and multiply" was God's injunction to Noah, according to the Old Testament. But it was given at a time when the human race needed to replenish itself. We live in an era when overpopulation is more of a threat than is extinction through underpopulation. Some couples today choose not to have children as a means of helping the human race move toward Zero Population Growth (ZPG), while a small number of Jewish couples try to be more fruitful to replace the millions of Jews exterminated in World War II. But most American couples consider parenthood with more personal motives in mind.

Here are three basic questions concerning parenthood that can help couples separate positive reasons for having children from those that are not likely to increase satisfaction for the couple or produce happiness for the child. (Additional pros and cons of having children are included in Box 10.1.)

1. Do we have the resources in our marriage for parenting?   In addition to the desire to have children, people need to have the necessary energy, as well as the emotional and material assets required of parents. Elizabeth Whelan, in her book *A Baby . . . Maybe*, suggests that the question, "Do we want to have children?" should be changed to "Do we have the sincere desire to welcome a child into our life for its own sake and a readiness to share our time, love and attention . . . ?" (1975, p. 59). Children do not increase the family resources except in the sense of possible long-term satisfactions, and these are by no means predictable.

In some respects, as Nancy Datan (1977) points out, the infant is a competitor for the couple's resources. Although childless couples who decide to keep their time, energy, and finances for themselves are often labeled selfish, Datan suggests that these couples are guilty of nothing more than "accuracy at arithmetic":

Any quantity divided by two yields greater portions than the same quantity divided by three or more. Parents who fail to make this calculation in advance learn it soon enough after the fact of parenthood and some respond by abuse or abandonment. (p.10)

BOX 10.1   The Pros and Cons of Having Children

In a six-country study, Fred Arnold et al. (1975) examined the positive and negative values people assigned to having children. Arnold acknowledges that the study does not represent all the pros and cons of parenting—some of the values of childbearing and child rearing (both positive and negative) are described less fully than others. Yet the categories are explicit enough to begin an examination of the question: What are the values of having children?

Positive General Values

1. Emotional Benefits.   Happiness, love, companionship, fun; also viewed in reverse as relief from strain and avoidance of boredom or loneliness.

2. Economic Benefits and Security. Benefits from children's help in the house, business, or farm, from care of siblings, and from sharing of income; old-age security for the parents, including economic support, physical care, and psychological security.

3. Self-enrichment and Development. Learning from the experience of child rearing; becoming more responsible and mature; incentive and goals in life; being viewed as an adult, a grown woman or man; self-fulfillment; feeling of competence as a parent.

4. Identification with Children. Pleasure from watching growth and development of children; pride in children's accomplishments; reflection of self in children.

5. Family Cohesiveness and Continuity.
Children as a bond between husband and wife; fulfillment of marriage; completeness of family life; continuity of family name and traditions; producing heirs; having future grandchildren.

Negative General Values

1. Emotional Costs.   General emotional strain; concern about discipline and moral behavior of children; worry over health; noise and disorder in household; children as nuisance.

2. Economic Costs.   Expenses of child rearing; educational costs.

3. Restrictions or Opportunity Costs. Lack of flexibility and freedom; restrictions on social life, recreation, travel; lack of privacy; restrictions on career or occupational mobility; no time for personal needs and desires.

4. Physical Demands.   Extra housework; caring for children; loss of sleep; general weariness.

5. Family Costs.   Less time with spouse; disagreements over rearing of children; loss of spouse's affection.

BOX 10.1 (Continued)

Large-Family Values

1. Sibling Relationships.   Desire for another child to provide companionship for existing children; enriching the lives of children; avoiding an only child.

2. Sex Preferences.   Specific desire for a son or daughter; desire for a certain combination of sexes among children.

3. Child Survival.   Concern that existing children may die; need for more children to have enough survive to adulthood.

Small-Family Values

1. Maternal Health.   Concern that too many pregnancies, or pregnancy when the mother is beyond a certain age, is bad for the mother's health.

2. Societal Costs.   Concern about overpopulation, belief that another child would be a burden to society.

Source: Fred Arnold et al., *The Value of Children: A Cross-National Study, Introduction and Comparative Analysis*, the East-West Population Institute, East-West Center, Honolulu, Hawaii, 1975, pp. 9–10. Reprinted by permission.

Child-abuse rates are particularly high among unmarried teenage mothers, those who have the most limited personal, social, and economic resources. Divorce rates are also much higher than national averages for people who marry because of a pregnancy (Guttmacher Institute 1976). A couple must have sufficient personal resources—maturity, psychological stability, marital stability—before they can share their resources with a demanding infant: "It is only fair, after all, that when we bear children, we must stop being children" (Jaffe and Viertel 1979, p. 32). They must also have the skills to communicate and manage conflict if they are to deal with the inevitable stresses that parenthood brings.

Having a baby to help stabilize a less than happy or satisfying marital relationship is an inadequate reason to bring a new human being into the world. Babies do not heighten marital satisfaction. As we shall see in Chapter 14, satisfaction over the life cycle decreases when the first child arrives. Couples followed during the stages of pregnancy showed signs of strain as the pregnancy progressed, with many couples requiring counseling before the child was born (Shereshefsky and Yarrow 1973).

2. Is parenting the best way for us to satisfy our needs for "generativity"?   Many influential psychological theories have insisted that there is an "instinct" for parenthood. Sigmund Freud saw pregnancy as the only healthy resolution of "penis envy"—the wish to incorporate and retain the male symbol of power, a wish he believed was shared by all females. Karen Horney, on the other hand, believed in "womb envy"—the notion that men were motivated to creativity and accomplishment to compensate for their inability to conceive and give birth.

Many factors influence the decision to have children. (Jean Shapiro)

Erik Erikson's scheme of developmental stages presents *generativity* as a crucial challenge of adulthood. The choice between generativity and stagnation, he suggests, is usually and most successfully met by a choice to have children.

Generativity . . . is primarily the concern in establishing and guiding the next generation, although there are individuals who, through misfortune or because of special and genuine gifts in other directions, do not apply this drive to their own offspring. And indeed the concept of generativity is meant to include such more popular synonyms as productivity and creativity which, however, cannot replace it. (Erikson 1968, p. 138)

Yet even in Erikson's opinion, generativity can be satisfied by assuming a role that serves future generations in a broader sense, such as teaching, helping younger siblings, creating works of art or original ideas that generate new life for society in a symbolic way. One can think of many childless people who have made such contributions, including Emily Dickinson with her poetry, Jane Austen and George Eliot with their novels. More recently Anna Freud, Katherine Hepburn, Lillian Hellman, and Gloria Steinem come to mind. There are also innumerable examples of people who were generative for society but much less successful as parents, including Bertrand Russell, Winston Churchill, and Franklin D. Roosevelt.

There are many ways to contribute to future generations. Procreation is one of them. But the satisfactions that parenthood may bring depend on the personal resources the couple has and the need they share for parenting. Those who depend totally on parenting for generativity may feel stagnant when their children begin to grow up and "leave the nest." In today's world, generativity is only partially satisfied by procreation, and then only if the couple has other sound reasons for desiring children.

3. Are we having children simply to relieve social pressures or to satisfy personal inadequacies? "Antinatalists" claim that most people have children simply because of social pressures, not to satisfy any deep, instinctive need. They suggest that pronatalist forces tend to push people into becoming parents against their will. Religious movements want to perpetuate themselves; in some faiths, notably the Catholic religion, preventing conception and aborting a fetus are sins. To many people in our society, children indicate stability; political candidates and ambitious executives often flaunt family pictures, whether or not they symbolize real family happiness. The older generation is often anxious to have grandchildren, and friends who already have children may encourage childless couples to join them. Whether instinct or social pressures are responsible, most Americans hold strong pronatalist attitudes, and couples who choose to be childless are likely to experience some social disapproval (Cooper et al. 1978).

Many subconscious forces are at work creating both positive and negative feelings about parenthood. On the positive side may be the many loving experiences we have had with our own parents, the pleasure they demonstrated at our achievements, the comforts they supplied when we failed. On the negative side may be the ambivalent or even negative feelings we have about our own childhood and our parents. These may have created a desire to get back, to retaliate by manipulating our children or by using them as a means of controlling our spouse or parents. Fecundity or fertility may also appear to be a means of resolving doubts about one's masculinity or femininity. Parenting, as we have indicated in discussing sexuality, does not cure sexual dysfunction. If anything, it tends to intensify doubts and fears in this area. At some point in their pregnancy, pregnant women may feel unattractive. Pregnancy brings some periods of forced sexual inactivity; many couples display sexual ambivalence and practice abstention long before the baby's birth is imminent.

Needs to control or possess another human being or to enhance one's status are common reasons for becoming parents—and foolish ones. Those who calculate genetic odds remind us that the "egg toss" is the most costly and risky gamble of one's life. Each couple who conceive a baby can produce any one of about 144 billion distinct human beings (Rugh and Shettles 1971, p. 18). If one needs a final, sobering thought, there is the inescapable fact that parenting is for life. It binds parents to children: "You can have an ex-wife, ex-husband, ex-job, but you cannot have an ex-child" (Whelan 1975, p. 14).

The choice to have children also binds husband and wife. Even after divorce, fathers and mothers have to continue to be parents to their children, if the children are to avoid some of the more serious psychological consequences of marital dissolution. Couples who become parents may find new depths of sorrow and joy that test their relationship in many ways, at times enhancing it, but definitely altering it. Their relationship, which from its beginnings was one between lovers, partners, sometimes adversaries, and often friends, expands to include the new roles of mother and father.

Voluntary Childlessness

Although the number of couples who remain childless by *choice* appears to be small—about 1 in 20—we know very little about how or why this decision is made. Still, this decision is made by about 5 percent of the married couples in this country and thus is worth investigating for what it tells us about that 5 percent—and what it tells us about the other 95 percent.

In reviewing the still scant and incomplete data about voluntary childlessness, Veevers (1979) found that couples who make this decision come from all walks of life but usually live in large urban areas, have married at a later age (and married more than once), are nonreligious, college-educated, and financially well-off, with "both husband and wife employed in relatively high-income positions" (p. 10).

Are these couples happier or unhappier than couples with children? Veevers concluded that "overall, the presence or absence of children seems to make remarkably little difference to the probability of divorce or to the levels of marital satisfaction" (p. 14). An extensive survey of satisfaction over the life cycle (Campbell, Converse, and Rodgers 1976), which we shall review thoroughly in Chapter 14, suggests that a group of childless couples in fact expressed more satisfaction than a comparable group of married couples with children. Most of the childless couples in this study were "pre-parents"—they were planning to have children eventually. Childless couples, however, do not appear to have higher divorce rates than couples with children (Whelan 1975). But we don't know whether older childless couples will feel any less satisfaction as they age than other couples who are parents and then grandparents.

Although about one-third of the couples decide before marriage not to have children, "the majority of childless couples enter marriage apparently intending to have children but remain childless as a consequence of a series of postponements which follow four definite stages" (Veevers 1979, p. 16):

1. Obtaining a marriage objective (that is, being out of debt)
2. Indecision about when to have a child
3. Discussion about the pros and cons of parenthood
4. A final decision not to have children

About half the childless couples "more or less spontaneously" agree not to have children. Couples who remain childless fall into typical categories, says Veevers—"repudiators" and "aficionados."

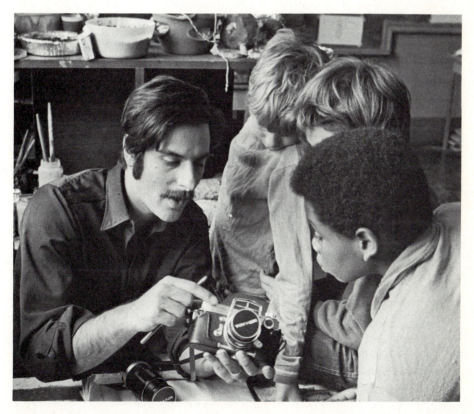

Adults who choose not to become biological parents can still show concern and caring for children. (Charles Gatewood)

308 INTIMACY IN MARRIAGE

Repudiators tend to defend their nonparenthood rather publicly, proclaiming their independence from (and sometimes abhorrence for) procreating. Ellen Peck, author of *The Baby Trap* (1971) and one of the founders of The National Organization for Non-Parents, can be seen as one such example.

Aficionados may choose not to be involved in biological reproduction, but manifest their caring for children by their involvement with other young members of their family, the children of friends, or community programs concerned with the quality of life and the future of young people. Those who like children but give up parenthood because of other interests seem to make up the larger segment of voluntarily childless couples (Cooper et al. 1978).

PLANNING FOR CHILDREN

To have children or not to have children? Couples will answer this question with a mixture of conscious and unconscious responses. If they possess self-awareness and a reasonable degree of self-esteem, if they have sufficient economic resources and physical health, if their marriage is stable and their relationship is not burdened by excessive conflict, and if their own childhood experiences have produced relatively positive feelings about parenthood, then raising children is likely to be a comparatively easy task. The decision, however, is theirs.

Timing of Parenthood

One of the great paradoxes of human development is that we are required to make crucial choices before we have the knowledge, judgment and self-understanding to choose wisely. Yet, if we put off those choices until we feel truly ready, the delay may produce other and greater costs. This is especially true of two great choices of early adulthood: occupation and marriage. (Levinson 1978, p. 102)

The ideal time to become parents would be when a couple have resolved certain previous conflicts, achieved the emotional maturity and marital satisfaction that bring about true intimacy, and confronted any basic conflict in the marriage.

Some couples are not prepared to make what has been called the "trade that parenting requires":

Becoming parents involves loss or, more accurately, trade. We lose a powerful and thrilling selfishness. We lose the right to be unpredictable, irresponsible, spontaneous. Most parents feel, at the end of the first year of parenting, that they have traded these attributes for something just as valuable—a deep understanding of what it is to be part of the ongoing human race. (Jaffe and Viertel 1979, p. 207)

Others choose not to have children because of career considerations. Some of the tensions surrounding the question of career versus children may be due to one's stage of life. People marry at the average ages of 21 for women and 23 for men, when their careers are just being launched. Levinson (1978) calls the period of time between ages 22 and 28 "Entering the Adult World." The vast majority of couples who decide to have children do so during this period. Even those who postpone parenting may consider the possibilities at this time. While Levinson was describing this stage for men, we can see its applicability for women:

The distinctive character of this developmental period lies in the co-existence of two tasks: to explore, to expand one's horizons and put off making firmer commitments until the options are clearer; and to create an initial adult life structure, to have roots, stability, and continuity. (Levinson 1978, p. 80)

Note that the two tasks are in fact contradictory. How can one "put off making firmer commitments" while at the same time setting down "roots, stability, and continuity"? These conflicting developmental tasks surround this period with a certain tension and confusion. Men and women often feel torn between the wish to develop further as an individual and the desire for a nest and a family.

In terms of biological fitness, the ideal time for a woman to have children is the decade between ages 20 and 30 (Montagu 1962). Yet births during the teenage years and births after age 30 are both on the upswing.

Teenage pregnancy accounts for 1.1 million conceptions and 554,000 births per year (Guttmacher Institute 1981). Many of these births either occur out of wedlock or are the cause of hasty marriages that are likely to end in desertion or divorce. The fetus that develops in an immature maternal body is at a disadvantage. Teenagers are more likely to have premature and low-birth-weight babies; mortality rates for both infants and mothers are higher in the teen years. Social and economic support is generally less adequate for these teenage mothers, many of whom fail to have proper prenatal care and sufficient postnatal support (Guttmacher Institute 1981).

Delayed Childbearing.   Although the majority of women have children between the ages of 18 and 30, many women over 30 are now choosing to have their first child (Glick 1977). Between 1972 and 1982, childbearing in the 30-to-44 age group rose an estimated 15.2 percent (*Time* 1982). Many of these women delayed marriage and postponed having children in order to finish college or advance in their jobs. The choice to delay childbearing may have advantages for a couple, allowing them a chance to enhance their own relationship and improve their economic position. But women who have children between the ages of 35 and 45 have an increased risk of health complications in themselves and their babies. A mother over 35 is more likely than a younger mother to bear a child with Down's syndrome (mongolism). The chance that a woman will have a second Down's child also increases with age (see Table 10.1). Miscarriage is also more likely later on. Advances in prenatal and obstetrical care have reduced some of the risks. One of the most significant advances is the *amniocentesis* test. After the exact position of the fetus is charted by a technique using ultrasound, the doctor extracts a small amount of the amniotic fluid that surrounds the fetus. The fluid contains fetal cells, which are grown and analyzed for problems, such as the chromosomal abnormality that causes Down's syndrome. If the test reveals a serious disorder, the parents then have the option of terminating the pregnancy. Some critics believe women have been oversold on the potential dangers of waiting to conceive after 30 and the health advantages of starting families early (Seaman 1975). If women plan to have only one or two children and if they have taken the precaution of the amniocentesis test and provided for good pre-natal and obstetrical care, they can usually begin childbearing in their early thirties without grave inherent dangers. The majority of births, even to women who are older than 35, are normal.

The "Motherhood" Ideal

Motherhood has become idealized beyond recognition in our society. But in deciding when to have children, one needs to deal with the realities of motherhood. A classic example of the idealized version can be seen in TV advertisements for diapers. A baby wets, either while lying in his crib or while being held in the arms of an embarrassed neighbor. A new, more absorbent diaper makes its appearance, and the result is a pair of happy,

TABLE 10.1 Recurrence Risks for Down's Syndrome at Different Maternal Ages

Maternal Age	Risk per Pregnancy	Percent Recurrence Risk (Approximate)	Chance of a Normal* Baby (Percent)
15–19	1 in 2,000	0.05	99.95
20–24	1 in 1,000	0.1	99.9
25–29	1 in 1,000	0.1	99.9
30–34	1 in 600	0.17	99.8
35–39	1 in 280	0.4	99.6
40–44	1 in 70	1.3	98.7
45 plus	1 in 40	1.9–2.5	97.5
All mothers in the population	1 in 665		

* Normal here = absence of Down's syndrome.
Source: From *Textbook of Human Genetics* by Max Levitan and Ashley Montagu. Copyright © 1971 Oxford University Press, Inc. Reprinted by permission.

smiling individuals—mother and (dry) infant. Infants in television commercials never have bowel movements, never suffer from diarrhea. At no time do we see a drawn, exhausted mother once more laboring to keep her infant clean. Instead we are bombarded by portraits of totally satisfied mothers. Another typical depiction of parenthood can be seen in commercials for cameras: Happy families do make good pictures, but people who buy into these fantasies of a happy, untroubled family life are in for a rude awakening.

Feminist sociologist Jessie Bernard (1974, p. 14) believes that some women are beginning to reject this romanticized, idealistic portrait of motherhood. They no longer are willing to accept sole responsibility for child care, nor to make child care their primary activity. And they are demanding an end to the isolation that mothers have experienced in the past, as they performed their role separated from one another and from the larger society.

Although American society has a strong bias in favor of children, it provides few services or accommodations that would actually support parents in their efforts to combine work and child rearing. The question of child care is so controversial that even efforts to address this need (as attempted by the 1980 White House Conference on Families) have bogged down in heated debate and political cross-fighting.

Unlike Sweden, the Soviet Union, and China, the United States has no nationally supported, comprehensive day-care program. Many have raised serious questions whether such a national program should even be attempted. Companies and labor unions are just beginning to address this issue. A few companies have established day-care centers on the premises; others provide vouchers or reduced rates at local community facilities. Still others allow "flex-time" schedules, which let employees choose a work shift that suits their needs.

But child-care facilities, especially for infants, are scarce and uneven in quality. There are questions about whether even a good facility can provide adequate care for infants. Older children, however, may actually benefit from a good day-care program (Clarke-Stewart and Koch, in press). Women with infants who continue full-time work usually choose to have a single babysitter, housekeeper, or relative as the child's caretaker if possible. The majority of new mothers choose to work part-time or take a leave of absence from their jobs until their children are about three years old (Masnick and Bane 1980), but more women are continuing to work full-time even when their children are very young.

We have already considered the likelihood of role strain for working mothers since they tend to assume—or to have left to them—most of the responsibilities of child rearing and housekeeping. New parents, especially new mothers, feel some ambivalence whether they are working away from home or staying at home with the children. According to Cowan and

Cowan's study of new parents (Koch and Koch 1980), new mothers who are at home feel some yearning to be at work, while mothers who are working feel some anxiety about their children's well-being. Many women still feel qualms about working outside the home instead of doing full-time mothering, yet women whose identity includes work as a major component can't feel total satisfaction at home with an infant all day; if they do, then they experience guilt feelings about their lack of ambition. As the authors of *Becoming Parents* have expressed it:

Traditional views of society, contrasted with the early view expressed by the women's movement, have created a Catch-22 that tightens like a vise around many new mothers. No matter what they choose to do a little voice chirps into their ears that it is the wrong decision. (Jaffe and Viertel 1979, p. 39)

Perhaps new mothers socialized to a dual work/parenting role must live with a certain amount of ambivalence, at least in their early years of parenting. A support network of other new parents, according to Cowan and Cowan and other researchers, provides a place for airing conflicting feelings and gaining the assurance that this sense of unrest is almost universal.

BIRTH CONTROL: PREVENTING UNWANTED PREGNANCY

The choice to have children should stem from a conscious mutual commitment. Ideally, prospective parents should have mature reasons for wanting children, the necessary psychological and material resources for sharing their future with another human being, and a realistic view of how parenting will affect their lives. Unwanted pregnancy resulting from failure to practice birth control forces a couple to face a difficult decision: having an abortion or having a child that one or both of them don't want or can't yet support.

A large number of births in the United States are unintended—including many to married women. Between 1970 and 1972, married women had an annual average of 3,041,000 births. It is estimated that one-third of these were unintended—either mistimed or simply not wanted at any time (Tietze 1979). Giving birth to an unwanted child may place an intolerable stress on a marriage. No one would choose to begin life unwanted. Birth control is the safest and least traumatic way of preventing forced parenting and unwelcome children. As Table 10.2 demonstrates, the use of contraception definitely reduces the chances of unwanted pregnancies, abortions, and unwanted births. Approximately two-thirds (67.7 percent) of unintended pregnancies occur in women who have not used contraception (Tietze 1979).

TABLE 10.2   Estimated Annual Number of Unintended Pregnancies With and Without the Use of Contraception

Marital Status and Outcome	Total	With Use of Contraception	Without Use of Contraception
Total	2,041,000	660,000	1,381,000
Married			
Live birth	981,000	396,000	585,000
Legal abortion	140,000	56,000	84,000
Illegal abortion	100,000	40,000	60,000
Unmarried			
Live birth	340,000	68,000	272,000
Legal abortion	280,000	58,000	222,000
Illegal abortion	200,000	42,000	158,000

Note: Estimates, by pregnancy outcome, for 1970–72, based on annual averages during a three-year period.
Source: Christopher Tietze, "Unintended Pregnancies in the United States, 1970–1972." Reprinted with permission from *Family Planning Perspectives*, Volume 11, Number 3, 1979.

Most sexually active couples (86 percent) in the United States, married or not, practice some kind of birth control. But even today, when contraception has become relatively safe and reliable, there are millions of people who simply cross their fingers and hope for the best!

When a man and a woman have intercourse, sperm is ejaculated through the man's penis into the woman's vagina. If no contraceptive precaution is taken, some of the sperm swim through the cervical opening into the uterus and finally into the Fallopian tubes. If a sperm unites with an egg (ovum) from the woman (usually at the outer third of a Fallopian tube, nearest the ovaries), fertilization occurs (see Figure 10.1).

Contraception interrupts that process.

Choosing a method of controlling conception is a matter of serious consideration for both women and men. Nevertheless, it is the woman who risks pregnancy if no birth control is used, and it is she who will probably shoulder much (or all) of the parenting responsibility. Although research efforts have been devoted to developing a male birth-control pill, most methods of birth control are geared for use by women; most of the dangers are also theirs.

Methods of Birth Control

The Pill.   The birth-control pill, marketed under a variety of brand names, is the contraceptive device most widely used by married women (see Table 10.3). It is believed to be the most effective contraceptive, but is also the

FIGURE 10.1   The Pathway of Sperm from the Vagina to a Fallopian Tube to Fertilize an Egg

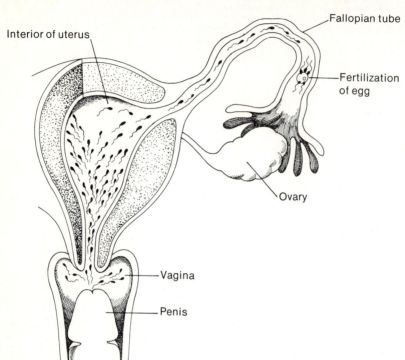

most controversial in terms of safety. The most common type of birth control pills in use are those that combine the hormones progesterone and estrogen. These *combination* pills are taken regularly, beginning on the fifth day after the start of menstruation, whether or not one plans to have intercourse that day. They are "aesthetic" in that they don't require the woman to handle jellies, foams, or her own genitals (which appear to be drawbacks of other methods for many young women). They allow sex to be spontaneous. The rate of the pill's effectiveness is close to 100 percent—better than any other method (Katchadourian and Lunde 1975).

The pill works to prevent conception by inhibiting egg (ovum) matura-tion. The estrogen inhibits the pituitary gland from producing FSH, the hormone that normally triggers the maturing of an egg. In one sense, the estrogen sends a false signal to the ovaries not to develop the egg (not unlike what happens normally if a woman becomes pregnant). Without a ripened and released egg, there can be no fertilization. The progesterone also acts as a contraceptive agent. It increases the thickness of the mucus in the cervix so that sperm have a difficult time penetrating the cervical opening, and it also keeps the lining of the uterus from developing fully

TABLE 10.3   Percentage Distribution of Contraceptive Use Among Married Women in the United States (1976)

Contraceptive Status	Percentage of Married Women (Aged 15–44)
Total using contraception	89.8
Pill	29.5
IUD	8.1
Female sterilization	12.7
Male sterilization	12.8
Condom	9.5
Withdrawal	2.6
Diaphragm/cervical cap	3.8
Other	10.6
Total not using contraception	10.2

Note: Percentages do not add up to 100 because some women were using more than one method.
Source: Kathleen Ford, "Widespread Contraceptive Use Found in Britain: Condom Popular." Reprinted with permission from *Family Planning Perspectives*, Volume 12, Number 2, 1980.

enough to allow a fertilized egg to implant. Although the combination pill is most widely used, there are actually two other kinds: the *progestin-only* pill, which contains synthetically made progesterone, and the *sequential* pill. The latter is no longer used because of its links to cancer.

Some writers and researchers, notably Barbara and Gideon Seaman (1977), have vigorously objected to physicians, student health centers, and other organizations prescribing the pill without providing its users with an understandable and detailed breakdown of its dangers. Seaman and Seaman list more than 16 known side effects of birth-control pills, including blood-clotting disorders, stroke, heart attack, and blood clots.

On the other hand, Savitri Ramcharan, who conducted a study funded by the National Institute of Health, extending over a 12-year period and involving 16,000 women, argues that "the risks of the pill, if they exist at all, are negligible" (*Time* 1980, p. 40). The study involved women enrolled at the Kaiser-Permanente Medical Center in Walnut Creek, California, who ranged in age between 18 and 54 years. One-quarter of the sample took oral contraceptives regularly. These are some of the findings:

Pill users did not have higher mortality rates than non-users, if they did not smoke, and ran no greater risk of developing circulatory problems or cancer of the breast, ovaries or lining of the uterus. Though the researchers did note a slight increase in lung cancer, they said that it was probably caused by the women's heavy cigarette smoking. Similarly, they said, a significant increase in cervical cancer could be attributed not to the Pill, but to sexual habits, including sex at an early age and multiple partners. (*Time* 1980, p. 40)

Despite this optimistic report, women should have a thorough checkup before taking any oral contraceptive. They should report any adverse side effects to their physicians, and they should consider the merits of other methods of contraception, some of which have no side effects.

The IUD (Intrauterine Device).   For women who can wear it, the IUD is an effective (94–99 percent) method of birth control. (Some women cannot tolerate the insertion of the small device inside the uterus.) Various intrauterine devices have been used for centuries to prevent pregnancy in animals. Since the first IUDs were designed for humans in the 1920s, millions of women throughout the world have used them, but physicians are still unable to explain exactly why the presence of this foreign object in the uterus prevents the fertilized egg from implanting itself on the uterine wall. They suspect the device produces an inflammation that alters the chemical balance of the uterus and thus prevents implantation (McCraven 1980). Figure 10.2 shows several types of IUDs that are used.

The IUD must be inserted in the uterus by a physician. Once in place, it provides ongoing protection. There is no need to take a pill each day, altering body chemistry, and no need to insert anything before sexual activity, so sex can be spontaneous. But using an IUD involves complications that the use of barrier-type birth control—such as the diaphragm, condom, or foam—does not. All IUDs have one or two strings extending into the upper vagina so that the physician or wearer can check to see if the IUD is present. This is important, since approximately 10 percent of IUD wearers spontaneously expel the device (Katchadourian and Lunde 1975).

There are other complications connected with IUDs that are causing some of the two to three million American women who use them to consider other methods (McCraven 1980). An estimated 10 percent of the women wearing IUDs ask that they be removed because of bleeding, cramping, or pain associated with the device. Becoming pregnant while wearing the IUD is a problem, because the miscarriage rate for wearers is about 50 percent, as compared with an overall 15-percent miscarriage rate for nonwearers. One IUD was removed from the market in 1974 after being associated with the deaths of pregnant women who were wearing it. The IUD also seems to increase the possibility of infection in the uterus, ovaries, and Fallopian tubes. If such infection is not treated, the tubes may become scarred and future fertility may be jeopardized. Though serious side effects with IUDs seem to be rare, even the remote risk of infection or infertility may be enough to deter a woman from choosing this device.

The Diaphragm.   The diaphragm is a rubber disk that fits over the cervix. Diaphragms come in different sizes. They must be prescribed by a doctor,

FIGURE 10.2   Several Types of IUDs

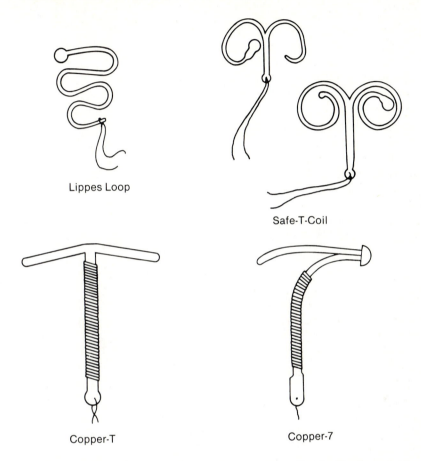

Lippes Loop

Safe-T-Coil

Copper-T

Copper-7

who measures the woman to assure proper fit. A diaphragm involves no discomfort or physical interference with sexual pleasure, but it must be inserted shortly before intercourse in order to prevent conception. Spermicidal foam, cream, or jelly, which can be purchased without a prescription, must be placed on the diaphragm in order for it to be effective. Figure 10.3 shows how to use a diaphragm.

A woman who uses a diaphragm must be conscientious about using it correctly. Being comfortable with one's body is a prerequisite for conscientious usage. Insertion is quick and simple, but some women are uncomfortable handling their genitals and may be better off using another method. The effectiveness rate of the diaphragm is lower than that of the pill, but this is apparently due to failure to use the diaphragm rather than failure of the device itself. Seaman and Seaman cite research from the

FIGURE 10.3 Using a Diaphragm

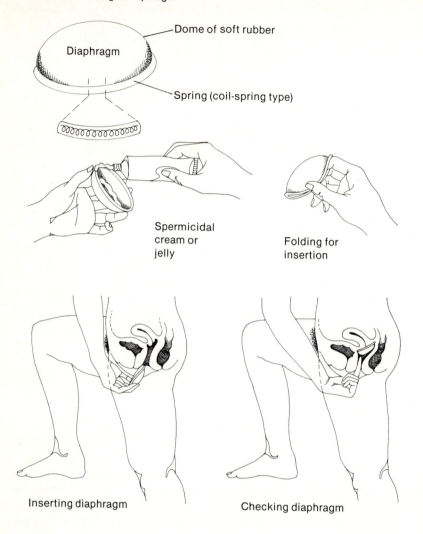

Dome of soft rubber

Diaphragm

Spring (coil-spring type)

Spermicidal
cream or
jelly

Folding for
insertion

Inserting diaphragm

Checking diaphragm

Margaret Sanger Research Bureau showing that two percent (37 out of 2,168) of the women using diaphragms became pregnant. But of those 37 women, 22 were found to have used the diaphragm inconsistently or not at all. The Sanger research, along with other studies, points to the conclusion that the diaphragm, *if properly fitted and properly used,* can be considered more than 99 percent reliable (Seaman and Seaman 1977, p. 176).

The Cervical Cap. Though not readily available in the United States, the cervical cap, or pessary, is similar to the diaphragm. It is a small device that fits over the cervix and is kept in place by suction. The cap is made of plastic, metal, or rubber and can be left in place for days or weeks. The estimated failure (pregnancy) rate is about eight percent, although this figure is not documented by United States statistics because of the small number of American women who use the cap.

Spermicidal Foams, Creams, and Jellies.   Spermicidal agents, like the diaphragm, must be inserted into the vagina shortly before intercourse. They have the advantage of being easily available without a prescription, but the fact that they must be used each time intercourse takes place tends to reduce their actual effectiveness. The failure rate with foams is close to 25 percent.

The Rhythm Method.   Despite calls by American Catholics for the Roman Catholic Church to modify its stand against contraceptive methods, each Pope has continued to reaffirm the church's traditional ban on all methods of contraception except for the rhythm method. Increasing numbers of Catholic women, however, do use some form of birth control. According to Westoff: "By 1970 two-thirds of all Catholic women were using methods disapproved by the Church; this figure reached three-quarters for women under 30 years of age" (1973, p. 80).

The idea behind the rhythm method is to identify those days during a woman's menstrual cycle when fertilization will not occur. Using the calendar chart (Table 10.4), we can determine that if a woman's cycle is 22

TABLE 10.4   The Fertile Period

Shortest Cycle (Days)	Day Fertile Period Begins	Longest Cycle (Days)	Day Fertile Period Ends
22	4	22	12
23	5	23	13
24	6	24	14
25	7	25	15
26	8	26	16
27	9	27	17
28	10	28	18
29	11	29	19
30	12	30	20
31	13	31	21
32	14	32	22
33	15	33	23
34	16	34	24

Source: From *Fundamentals of Human Sexuality*, by Herant Katchadourian and Donald T. Lunde, p. 143. Copyright © 1972 by Holt, Rinehart and Winston, Inc. Reprinted by permission of Holt, Rinehart and Winston, CBS College Publishing.

days, then she will be most likely to be fertile from the fourth through the twelfth day of the cycle. For pregnancy prevention, 2 days are added to either end of the fertile period. Using this method, then, one would refrain from intercourse from the second through the fourteenth day of the cycle. That means 13 days of abstinence or sexual activity other than coitus.

The problem with rhythm is that only a minority of women have menstrual periods regular enough to practice this method with any degree of reliability. It is complicated by the fact that a woman's fertile period may vary from month to month. The other unknown is the longevity of sperm. Sperm live up to 72 hours or longer after being deposited in the vagina—another 3 days in which the possibility of fertilization is dramatically increased.

A variation on rhythm is the "temperature" method (see Figure 10.4). A rise in a woman's temperature usually means she is ovulating. By taking her temperature every morning (before arising, eating, drinking, or smoking), by avoiding sexual intercourse until three days following the rise in temperature, and then having intercourse only for the days remaining in her cycle, the woman has a reasonably good chance of preventing pregnancy. But these elaborate precautions must be followed carefully in order for the temperature method to work. Even so, the method can fail because some women do not display any changes in body temperature when they are ovulating, and temperature also changes because of colds, sore throats, and minor infections.

The efficacy of the rhythm method depends on how highly motivated the man and the woman are to keep to their calendar or thermometer. Estimates of failure (pregnancy) range from 15 to 31 percent. Because it

FIGURE 10.4   The "Temperature" Method of Birth Control. The slight rise in basal body temperature (BBT) after ovulation can be used to help determine the "safe days" for sexual intercourse.

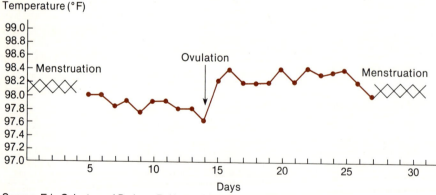

Source: Eric Golanty and Barbara B. Harris, *Marriage and Family Life,* Houghton Mifflin Company, Boston, p. 313.

requires many days of abstinence and an ongoing curtailment of sexual spontaneity, the rhythm method is one of the least effective methods of birth control.

The Condom.   The condom is the only contraceptive device for men (see Figure 10.5). Condoms are the most widely used and conveniently obtainable contraceptives. A condom can be purchased over-the-counter at almost any drugstore and even from dispensers in washrooms. There is no reason, aside from momentary embarrassment, that women cannot purchase condoms. The condom, if used as directed, can be between 97 and 99 percent effective in preventing pregnancy. Although many men say the condom interferes with pleasurable sensations during intercourse, both partners must consider the consequences of not using one if no other means of birth control is available.

The more expensive condoms are made from natural animal tissue; less expensive ones are made from a latex material. The man or the woman unrolls the condom onto the erect penis before intercourse. After intercourse, when the man withdraws his now flaccid penis from the vagina, one of the partners must take care that the condom does not slip off and allow sperm to come in contact with the vagina.

Withdrawal.   Some people believe that if the man doesn't ejaculate while the penis is in the vagina, there is no possibility of conception. This misconception has caused many an unwanted pregnancy. Masters and Johnson call the stage when ejaculation is bound to occur the period of

FIGURE 10.5   Condoms

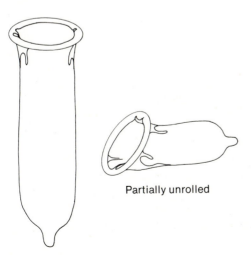

Partially unrolled

"ejaculatory inevitability"—of all times during lovemaking, this is probably the most difficult for the man to control. Even if he is able to pull out moments before orgasm, he must ejaculate somewhere. If his semen is deposited near the vaginal lips, the sperm have an opportunity to swim all the way up into the Fallopian tubes and fertilize the egg. A man also may secrete some sperm from his penis before ejaculation, once again increasing the possibility of conception. The pregnancy rate for couples who practice withdrawal as a method of avoiding pregnancy is about 20 to 30 percent.

Abstinence. A mother was discussing birth control with her daughter: "My child," the mother said, "of all the methods of birth control, the most effective is drinking orange juice." "Orange juice?" the daughter replied, incredulously. "How can drinking orange juice be used? Do you drink it before, during, or after intercourse?" "Instead of" was her mother's reply.

There are some techniques for sexual satisfaction that do not include intercourse. Sex play that includes mutual masturbation or oral stimulation until both partners achieve orgasm (taking care the sperm does not come near the vagina) can be highly pleasurable for both partners. (These techniques can be accompanied by orange juice.)

Surgical Sterilization

Sterilization has become the most popular means of avoiding pregnancy for couples over 30. Over "one-quarter of all older couples practicing contraception had been surgically sterilized [in 1972]; the operations were almost equally divided between men and women" (Westhoff 1973, p. 21). The trend accelerated during the 1970s and 1980s, especially for women. Sterilization has attracted well-deserved negative publicity in those cases where it has been performed without consent of the subject—women, in most cases, who were either poor or labeled as retarded. This forced sterilization has been judged illegal. Voluntary sterilization, in the legal sense, has been considered a matter of personal choice. As with any operation, sterilization involves some medical risks.

The most usual operation for sterilization of the female is the *tubal ligation* (more commonly called "tying the tubes"). The Fallopian tubes are severed, which prevents the egg from reaching the uterus. There are various techniques for surgically severing tubes. Other operations for sterilizing females include panhysterectomy (removal of the internal reproductive organs), hysterectomy (surgical removal of the uterus), oopherectomy (removal of the ovaries), and the salpingectomy (removal of the Fallopian tubes). These are medical procedures intended to deal with other physical disorders, measures that are not indicated when the only concern is birth control.

The *vasectomy* is the principal method for sterilizing a male. This operation is a relatively simple procedure: A physician anesthetizes each side of the scrotum and makes one or two small incisions; a small piece is cut out of each vas deferens (the tubes that carry sperm from the testes to the penis), and the ends are tied off. Semen is still ejaculated by the man, but after the vasectomy, it contains no sperm.

Sterilization is thought to be 100 percent effective. There are unusual circumstances, however, in which a pregnancy can still occur. A woman, for example, might be already pregnant at the time of the operation; or sometimes the severed tubes can grow back. After a vasectomy, sperm may remain in the vas deferens for a few days or for months, depending on the number of ejaculations the man has.

In the case of women, there are some potential dangers: "For conventional tubal ligation, the estimated mortality rate is 25 per 100,000. . . . Serious complications short of death occur in about 5 percent of female sterilizations" (Seaman and Seaman 1977, pp. 226–228). In the case of men, the side effects of sterilization are minimal.

While the vasectomy is a simpler procedure than the tubal ligation, neither operation should be undertaken lightly. A tubal ligation is not reversible; a vasectomy can be reversed in some cases, but not all. Sterilization should be preceded by thorough discussion among the spouses, the physician, and perhaps even a trained therapist.

Abortion

Abortion is a means of terminating an unwanted pregnancy that is generally chosen when other birth-control methods have been neglected or have failed. In 1977 there were 1.32 million legal abortions, 25 percent of which were obtained by married women (Tietze 1979). The Roman Catholic Church and other religious and secular groups condemn some abortion; with equal force and numbers, a variety of organizations and individuals defend the right of a woman to choose abortion over bringing an unwanted pregnancy to term. One issue that makes an objective discussion of abortion so difficult is the moral implication of this choice. Which is more "immoral"—to deny a legal, medically safe abortion to a woman or teenager who does not want to give birth, or to abort a fetus that, potentially at least, could develop into a human being?

The move to legalize abortion received its impetus from changing attitudes about the rights of women. Bumpass and Presser cite four major sources for the changing attitudes and practices with regard to abortion. First, the pill, along with other contraceptive devices, allowed couples to manage the act of conception more effectively at a time of their own choosing. Second, society is slowly removing the barriers placed in the path of women, allowing them growing equality of opportunity. Third, the

Supreme Court ruled in 1973 that state laws prohibiting or limiting abortion were unconstitutional. Fourth, "the increasing employment of suction procedures for abortion has decreased the risk involved and made abortion on an ambulatory basis both safe and feasible" (1973, p. 41).

Yet because abortion relates to the emotionally charged possibility of motherhood, it is not a simple procedure psychologically. For most women, young or old, having an abortion produces some inner conflict, some sense of loss. Linda Franke (1978), documenting the abortion experience, calls these conflicting feelings "the ambivalence of abortion." On the other hand, unwanted motherhood can have its own serious and long-lasting destructive effects on mother and child. Faced with a very difficult decision, many unmarried and married women choose abortion.

Before proceeding with an abortion, one must be certain that one is pregnant. On the surface, this would seem obvious to the point of being ridiculous. But newspapers still report "abortion mills" that will tell a woman she is pregnant (and thus in need of an abortion) when in fact she is not. Most women assume they are pregnant if they miss a menstrual period. This is the most common sign of pregnancy, but there may be numerous reasons other than pregnancy for a woman to have missed her period. If one is tested for pregnancy and the result is positive, a woman should see a trained medical person and have the test verified before undergoing an abortion. Being informed about the procedure is helpful in maintaining a consumerist attitude.

Several different methods for abortion are used, depending on the stage of pregnancy. The three major procedures are dilation and evacuation, dilation and curettage, and the saline method.

Dilation and evacuation is a relatively low-risk, low-cost procedure in which a tube connected to a vacuum pump is inserted into the uterus. All the tissues in the uterus related to conception are removed by suction. This procedure can be used up to about 12 weeks of pregnancy and is often done on an out-patient basis in a clinic or hospital.

Dilation and curettage (D and C) is a more complicated procedure, usually performed in a hospital when the woman is between 7 and 12 weeks pregnant. The procedure basically calls for the scraping or loosening of tissues from the inner walls of the uterus. (It is also used for medical reasons other than abortion.)

The *saline method* is commonly used during the second trimester of pregnancy (three to six months). It is a more complicated operation because, by this time, the fetus has become too large to be removed by other methods. A needle is inserted into the uterus and an abortion-inducing fluid is introduced into the amniotic sac that surrounds the fetus. Usually within 12 to 24 hours, the woman will experience contractions and deliver the fetus and the placenta. This method can result in medical complications and, because the fetus is well developed at this point, there may be heightened emotional and ethical conflicts for the mother and the physician.

Finally, a woman should be prepared to deal with the ambivalence that abortion can arouse. As Linda Franke puts it:

Everyone should know that, in spite of the rhetoric from the right, claiming that women who abort are murderers, and from the left, claiming that abortion is an instant panacea for an unwanted pregnancy, the abortion experience is actually a period of great stress for every person involved. There is indecision; there is pain. There is regret, and there is relief. And all persons entering or leaving the abortion experience without recognizing the probability of these emotions are simply fooling themselves. (1978, p. 21)

FERTILITY/INFERTILITY

Once a couple decide to have a child, they tend to expect conception to occur right away. In fact, few couples who want children conceive on their first try, or even after several months of regular intercourse without birth control. Generally, intercourse at a time when conception is likely to occur helps to ensure fertility. The thermometer indicating ovulation can be used in the service of conception as well as in the interests of prevention. Coitus that occurs within 3 days of ovulation, approximately in the middle of the mature woman's 28-day menstrual cycle (or when there is the relative rise in temperature), increases the likelihood that the ripened ovum released from the ovary into the Fallopian tube will meet one of the millions of sperm propelled by ejaculation. Fertilization actually occurs when the nucleus of one successful sperm combines with the nucleus of the ovum. Within half an hour, the merger is complete (Flanagan 1962; Rugh and Shettles 1971).

The most common cause of *not* conceiving is anxiety. Jaffe and Viertel (1979) report the experience of one couple who attempted to conceive, became anxious, stepped up sexual activity, felt obligated to have sex repeatedly yet found no satisfaction in it, underwent fertility tests, became convinced of their sterility, and then finally arrived at the office of a sensible obstetrician. He gave them this simple report:

1. Fully 50 percent of all couples have enough trouble getting pregnant that they end up consulting a professional.
2. Any couple that has *any* difficulty getting pregnant goes through a period of really rotten sex. This may be God's best joke on mankind, since sex is supposedly there only to make procreation possible.
3. Psychological distress is the most frequent cause of conception failure.
4. There was no reason that . . . [this couple] had not conceived except that panic had become a way of life for them. (p. 272)

The doctor advised them to begin again, forgetting all about the past testing, temperature taking, and measuring; he suggested that they just have intercourse as many times as they comfortably could, beginning 12 days after the wife's next period. With the pressure off and the relief of knowing they were not freaks of nature, the couple relaxed and tried again. The wife missed her next period (Jaffe and Viertel 1979, pp. 271–272).

Yet there are other couples who have fertility problems that are not so easily solved. Approximately one in five couples of childbearing age— about six million couples—are not fertile. In 40 percent of these cases, the problem is determined to be the man's (Fleming 1980). He may not produce enough sperm, or his sperm may not be viable. If efforts to increase sperm count (by having less frequent intercourse or by storing sperm) do not work, the couple may consider the possibility of artificial insemination. Artificial insemination now accounts for 20,000 babies a year. The sperm of donors are stored in one of 17 frozen-sperm banks in the country; these *cryobanks* now contain over 100,000 sperm samples. The identity of the sperm donor is not revealed to husband or wife, but the doctor who picks the sperm knows the physical and ethnic characteristics of the donor so that suitability can be considered. Some doctors try to "involve" the husband by having him present during the insemination, having him perform the insemination, or mixing the father's sperm with the donor's sperm. One woman who assists in the laboratory procedure described her method of involving the father this way:

I load the donor in the syringe first. . . . Then I put the husband in, just a few drops, maybe 15 percent of the total 1.2 cc.'s. That way, he comes out first, and the donor is behind pushing. It only takes one; maybe it's the husband's that gets in. I like to think so. (Fleming 1980, p. 20)

In 60 percent of the reported cases of infertility, the problem turns out to be the woman's. A woman may have difficulty maintaining the fertilized egg; there may be some blockage of her Fallopian tubes that prevents egg and sperm from meeting and implanting; or there may be other difficulties relating to hormones or egg production. Fertility drugs have been developed that tend to enhance the possibility of conceiving and carrying pregnancy to term. DES (diethylstilbestrol), once thought to help prevent miscarriage, was later found to increase the incidence of cancer in the daughters of women who used it and to have other side effects. Yet other fertility drugs have proven to be safe and effective, though they may increase the likelihood of multiple births. In 1977, a new method introduced for women with infertility caused by Fallopian-tube problems resulted in the first so-called test-tube baby. In this method, an egg is extracted from the mother and placed in a solution to which the father has contributed sperm. Then, after the egg has been fertilized *in vitro*, it is replaced in the uterus. The only test-tube portion is the period of fertilization and very early cell division; after that, prenatal development proceeds normally inside the mother. The process is not yet a widespread one, but the first test-tube babies have been normal at delivery and are developing in a healthy manner. Even more recently, a few women have volunteered to be surrogate mothers or gestators, agreeing to conceive and carry to term the babies of men whose wives are infertile. The fertility of the majority of couples, aided by medical advances in conception, now allows most couples who want to become parents to do so.

AFTER CONCEPTION: PREGNANCY AND BIRTH

The Prenatal Period

From the moment of conception, when the fertilized egg is microscopic in size, to the moment of birth, when the full-term neonate is ready to be delivered, there is a sheer increase in size of two million percent (Hetherington and Parke 1975, p. 54). Other aspects of the prenatal transformation are equally dramatic. The more scientific knowledge we acquire, the more miraculous the process of prenatal development seems to be. Accompanying the marvelous changes taking place as new life grows within the mother are psychological and interpersonal changes that the expectant mother and father undergo as they prepare for parenthood.

The nine-month period of life from conception to birth—the prenatal period—is usually divided into three *trimesters* or three-month segments. The highlights of each trimester are simply suggested here, along with some characteristic changes in the expectant parents' relationship.

The First Trimester (Conception Through Third Month). One of several hundred million active spermatozoa has managed the journey from vagina to Fallopian tube, where the egg is penetrated and fertilized. The 23 chromosomes of the male's sperm (it originally had 23 *pairs*) combine with the 23 chromosomes of the female's egg (it, too, used to have 23 *pairs*) to form a *zygote* with 23 pairs of chromosomes—half from the father and half from the mother. These chromosomes carry the genes that encode the child's genetic heritage.

The fertilized egg, or zygote, divides first into two separate, complete cells. More and more cells are formed; some cells form the embryo, others form the placenta. The mother's body secretes additional amounts of progesterone and estrogen, balanced in a way that prevents the occurrence of additional conceptions while readying the uterus for implantation. By the time implantation occurs, the zygote has divided and changed shape.

From the second week through the seventh week of pregnancy, the embryo is susceptible to defects. Defects may result from the chromosomal combination between mother and father or from environmental factors such as drugs, disease, drinking, smoking, or poor nutrition. During the embryonic period, the central nervous system is developing, and the blood vessels and stomach are forming. The brain begins to operate, and the reproductive and genital structures are evolving. This so-called embryonic period is a time of great vulnerability.

The woman's body is also changing, though these alterations are not as dramatic as the transformation taking place inside her uterus. Her uterus enlarges, she gains weight, and she may suffer from nausea. Her breasts swell; the nipples darken and become tender. She produces additional hormones. Her caloric intake increases—she is feeding herself as well as the unborn baby.

Her emotional state is in flux as well. She is experiencing physical and hormonal changes in herself, and she is increasingly conscious of the child growing inside her. She reflects on this phenomenon, for while the process is as old as humankind, it is unique for her. She may be quiet and withdrawn, expectant, fearful, anxious, joyous, threatened, passionate, cautious, reflective, and spontaneous. She may experience herself one moment as lustful and filled with abandon, and the next as disinterested in sex and wary. She may be alternately energetic and exhausted.

The father-to-be is also on an emotional rollercoaster. He is proud, but also concerned. He is uncommonly sensitive to the changes in his wife, but often unable to anticipate her moods. When she withdraws emotionally, he often finds he is unable to enter her world. He has helped initiate a new life, but now, as her body nurtures the fetus, he seems unneeded. He may feel abandoned: "He may become overly sensitive to the changes in his wife and may perceive her emotional and sexual withdrawal as a personal rejection of him. His response can vary anywhere from an oversolicitous attempt to gratify her wishes to a complete withdrawal from the overwhelming demands of the situation. For some, this may involve a retreat into work, sports, or even sexual affairs" (Hittelman and Simons 1977, p. 23).

Both husband and wife may spend long periods of time reckoning with their new identity of parents-to-be, contrasting this state with their old but continuing identity as children of their parents. Some of the emotions they experience come from the realization that *bearing* children means they must stop *being* children (Jaffe and Viertel 1979). Any leftover business from their own childhoods may surface now, as they prepare to become parents.

Despite periods of anxiety and withdrawal, the prospect of parenthood can strengthen a marriage. Introspective moments and self-discovery can be shared with one's partner during quiet times of conversation and reflec-

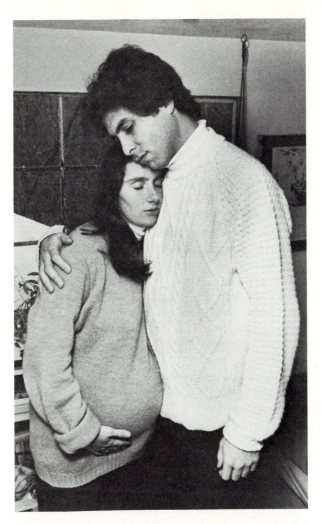

Moments of sharing and reflection during pregnancy can reveal untapped strengths in a relationship. (Jerry Howard, Positive Images)

tion. Husband and wife may find a reservoir of untapped strength in their marriage. Sharing personal discoveries, as well as hopes and fears for their unborn child, can create a profound sense of trust and affection between husband and wife.

The Second Trimester (Fourth Through Sixth Months).   By the beginning of the fourth month of pregnancy, the sex of the fetus can be determined and the skeleton is forming. Because the nervous system has connected to the muscles, the fetus moves, though, at first, these movements are not felt by the mother. The fetus has eyelids and fingernails. Soon there will be eyebrows and eyelashes, and by the beginning of the fifth month, the fetal heartbeat can be heard.

The mother looks in the mirror and acknowledges that, yes, she is visibly pregnant. "During this period . . . the majority of women experience heightened sexual tension and an increased desire for sexual intercourse" (Hittelman and Simons 1977, p. 26). Now the mother begins to detect the baby's movements. Although this may reassure the mother and father that the baby is alive and may cause them joy, many questions will remain until the birth. Above all, the parents are wondering, "Will our baby be normal?"

Most American mothers do not have to fear the tragic effects of a malnourished fetus or a deprived infant, but even if the mother's physical needs are taken care of, prospective parents may worry about the child's intelligence, health, and personality. A thousand imagined ills can cross their minds.

While the mother often may have mixed feelings about the changes in her physical and mental state, her husband may also be confused: "Some men react to their wives' fertility with envy and jealousy, feeling their own lives are empty and sterile in comparison. Others, identifying with their wives' creative energy, develop new creative interests for themselves. Some so closely identify with their wives that they show a weight gain comparable to their wives' and experience nausea, stomach distress, abdominal bloating and even 'sympathy pains'" (Hittelman and Simons 1977, p. 28).

The Third Trimester (Seventh Through Ninth Months). By the sixth month, the fetus has developed sufficiently so that in rare cases it can survive outside the mother's womb with the help of modern prenatal incubators and other equipment. By the seventh month, the various organs have developed, as well as the ability to breathe; at this stage the fetus has about a one-in-ten chance of surviving birth. By the eighth month the fetus's chances of survival outside the mother have increased dramatically to three out of four. By the ninth month, the mother almost seems to be working overtime to ensure the healthy birth of the child. Hormones are being produced to aid the mother's milk production. The weight of the head causes the fetus to shift into a head-down position. Ultimately, other hormones will urge the fetus out of the womb and into the birth canal. During the last days before birth, the mother's blood will produce antibodies to temporarily protect the newborn from measles, mumps, whooping cough, and other diseases.

No wonder that the mother-to-be often feels tired at this time. She is now concerned about the birth of her child, dependent upon what she may consider outside forces. Her husband may perform more of the duties that she had assumed prior to pregnancy. Sex, which may have been glorious for the couple during the second trimester, now may become infrequent because of the woman's size or because of largely unwarranted fears of "hurting" the child. Physicians often tell couples to refrain from intercourse for as much as six weeks before as well as six weeks after the birth of the child. These precautions are designed to give the mother a sexual moratorium. Although some doctors (Masters and Johnson 1966) question a lengthy abstinence during pregnancy, they agree that after birth the new mother needs a month to regain her normal hormone balance as well as her emotional equilibrium. In the ninth month, the husband and wife often eagerly await the end of pregnancy and the real-life addition to their family.

Birth

More and more American parents are determining the conditions in which their babies will be born. Although approximately 95 percent of hospital deliveries still take place under some type of anesthetic (Brackbill 1979), research into the negative effects of giving medication to the mother, as well as findings that support the positive aspects of unmedicated or "natural childbirth," are turning more and more women away from the use of drugs during childbirth (Henig 1978). (Figure 10.6 illustrates the process of birth.)

Drugs affect the infant as well as the mother. Anesthesia increases the mother's risk of death. The infant is affected through the mother's blood stream. Anesthetics and analgesics lower the mother's blood pressure and oxygen intake, thus reducing the supply of oxygen in the fetal blood stream and sometimes causing *anoxia,* or oxygen deficiency. Some studies indicate that the consequences of oxygen deprivation during delivery and childbirth can have long-range effects on the child. For example, the infant's muscular, visual, and brain development may be affected. But the most significant consequences of mild anoxia appear to be the impairment of the newborn's responsiveness, which in turn impairs the early days of mother-child interaction (Gluck 1977).

Preparing for childbirth and having the support of their partners help many women go through the rigors of labor without medication. The Lamaze prepared-childbirth method is one of the most popular approaches. The Lamaze course consists of six to eight weeks of classes that involve expectant mothers and fathers in learning about the experience of childbirth. Films are shown, discussions are held, and the couple learn the details of labor and delivery. The mother learns a variety of exercises for relaxation, breathing, and muscle control. The father functions as coach during the practice sessions. During labor and delivery, the father times contractions, reminds the laboring mother about the proper method of

FIGURE 10.6 The Birth Process: *a* and *b*, as the baby starts to emerge from the uterus, its head bends forward, causing the chin to touch the upper chest; *c* and *d*, the baby's head rotates from a sideways to a forward-facing position; *e*, the head extends upward to permit an easier exit from the vagina; *f*, after the head emerges, it rotates back toward the side to facilitate the birth of the shoulders.

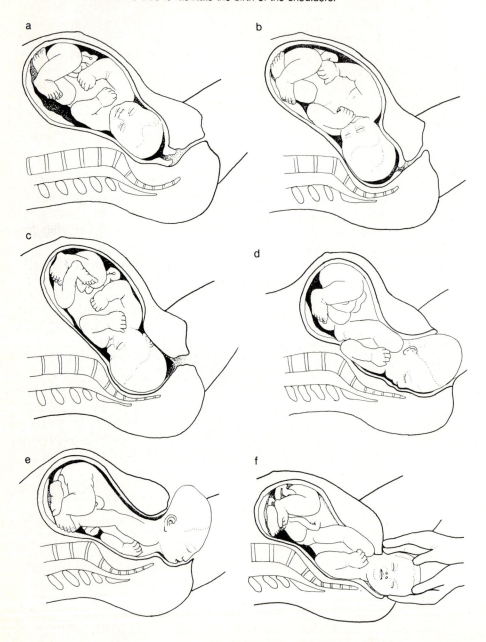

breathing, wards off intrusive hospital personnel, and offers support and encouragement. The mother may choose another person to be her coach if the father is not available or chooses not to be involved. Though some hospitals may resist any intrusion, thousands of hospitals permit and even encourage methods such as Lamaze.

A large and careful study was made of pregnant women at Evanston Hospital in Illinois who used the Lamaze method of childbirth. This study compared 500 women who took the Lamaze courses with 500 women who were not prepared by this method; the two groups were not otherwise markedly different. The Lamaze-prepared women in the study "had only one-fourth the number of Caesarean sections and one-fifth the amount of fetal distress. The death rate for fetuses and newborns . . . was one-fourth [that of those women who had not taken Lamaze training]. Postpartum infection in the Lamaze-prepared mothers was one-third less." These women also had fewer and less serious perineal lacerations. The findings also reveal that "the control group had 3 times as much toxemia of pregnancy and twice as many premature infants" (Hughey, McElin, and Young 1978).

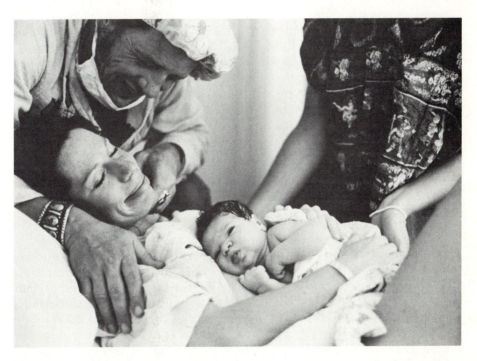

Parent-infant bonding immediately following a home birth shared by both parents (© Suzanne Arms, Jeroboam, Inc.)

The emotional rewards of childbirth that is prepared for and unmedicated are equally impressive. Klaus and Kennell (1976) coined the word *ekstasis* to refer to the emotions that the mother and·father experience when both are conscious, active participants in the birth of their child. Deborah Tanzer, chief author of *Why Natural Childbirth?*, noted the feelings of "rapture or near-mystical bliss" when mothers and fathers participated in the "natural" birth of their child (Tanzer and Block, 1976). Many research studies indicate that the first few minutes after the birth of the infant offer mothers and fathers a unique opportunity to bond themselves to their infant.

Home deliveries by a nurse-midwife or an obstetrician offer the couple a chance to experience birth in familiar surroundings while also saving the enormously high costs of a hospital delivery. Although complications that require hospital care may occur during childbirth (estimates of such complications are one in ten births), good prenatal care and accessibility to a hospital, as well as careful monitoring during delivery, can make home births a viable option for many couples.

New devices for monitoring the fetal heartbeat and the mother's contractions have been developed, warning physicians with early signs of impending trouble. This may account, in part, for the rising number of babies delivered by Caesarean section. Once the attending physician knows there is a risk, it is difficult to proceed with a normal delivery.

Even if medication is necessary because of delivery complications, preparing for childbirth through Lamaze or other available childbirth courses gives expectant parents a sense of solidarity before and during the birth experience—a time when fathers and even mothers can feel that the hospital has virtually supplanted them. It gives couples a chance to learn about parenting together, increasing the likelihood that parenting will continue to be a shared experience after they are home with their baby.

AFTER THE BABY IS BORN

Three individuals are developing during a first pregnancy: a baby, a mother, and a father. This new triad must exist harmoniously—no easy task for all three: "Pregnancy is an intense period of rapid and uncontrollable changes—in terms of physical development, fluctuating emotional states, the formation of new identities for husband and wife, and the shifting of marital relationships" (Hittelman and Simons 1977, p. 22).

Lois W. Hoffman and Jean D. Manis studied 1,569 wives and 456 husbands to determine what effects, if any, a child had on the marital relationship. They note that their findings are "suggestive" and not "definitive," but the results deserve attention. Most of the husbands and wives they interviewed felt that "children brought them closer together." They saw the birth of a child as changing them "into an adult"—something they saw as a positive change—they became "more responsible," and their life now had more meaning.

Even in very diverse families the first child meant adulthood, new responsibilities, a new status in the community and with relatives and friends, a readjustment of tasks, a transformation from "couple" to "family." A dependent, irrational, highly demanding, important person enters the scene and his[her] future depends on his[her] parents. (1977, p. 16)

At the same time, most couples reported that their relationship with each other seemed to change. The marriage appeared to swing in a more "traditional" direction, with the husband as the dominant figure in the relationship. This may account for Hoffman and Manis's finding that the higher their educational level, the less positive was the couple's view of parenthood. Wives who have high educational and career goals may find themselves torn between mothering responsibilities and some traditional pulls, on the one hand, and their commitment to sharing and equality in the marriage, on the other. Despite the role strain that a contemporary couple may experience, despite the stress that the new child brings with it, couples tend to regard parenthood as a source of pleasure that outweighs the sometimes frustrating and negative aspects of becoming parents.

SUMMARY

1. The major objectives of this chapter are to discuss decisions related to parenthood, including the benefits and drawbacks of having children; to provide accurate information about the various methods of birth control; and to describe the process of pregnancy and birth, considering the development and birth of the infant as well as the joys and stresses of these events for the intimate partners.
2. Most developmental theories, whether concerned with individual or family growth, view parenthood as a natural progression or stage of adulthood. In Erikson's view parenthood is considered a part of the stage of "generativity" occurring after the resolution of the identity and intimacy stages of development. Other theorists agree that the parenting role requires maturity related to life goals and developmental conflicts (for the individuals and for the couple). These positions represent theoretical values about ideal family development, and obviously many people become parents without resolving either the identity or the intimacy aspects of growth.
3. Research indicates a number of reasons that children are valued or

desired—for example, love, companionship, old-age security for parents, self-fulfillment, and family continuity. Children also bring certain drawbacks, such as worry, financial expense, physical strain, and conflicts between parents over child rearing. Regardless of costs, the majority of married couples both desire and produce offspring, though the actual number of children considered desirable is decreasing.

4. Though the United States is usually categorized as a strongly pronatal society, approximately 5 percent of all married couples choose to remain childless. This childless lifestyle is most popular among college-educated, dual-career couples. The limited research to date on such couples suggests that the presence or absence of children seems to make little or no difference in their marital happiness or stability. Since voluntary childlessness as a significant life pattern is relatively new to society, little is known about its effects on couples in their later years.

5. Methods of preventing conception are not modern inventions, though factual knowledge about the details of reproduction and improved technology have combined to produce more effective means of birth control and more comprehensive sources of information about available choices. None of the current contraceptive possibilities has been proven completely effective or without disadvantages, some more serious than others. When other contraceptive methods have been unsuccessful, abortion is a method of terminating the unwanted pregnancy that results. Ideally, decisions about method of birth control should be shared by the sexually intimate couple. Realistically, the traditional view that pregnancy and childbirth are a woman's responsibility is still a strongly held value position in the United States. Accurate information for decision making in this important area of life is imperative.

6. The nine months of pregnancy are generally divided into three time periods of three months each (trimesters). Significant changes occur during these times in the development of the fetus as well as in the expectant parent or parents. Pregnancy and childbirth are termed crisis events by most married couples, especially the birth of the first child. The stresses of reproduction can be minimized through such measures as good couple communication, especially the ability to share both positive and negative feelings; accurate information about pregnancy and childbirth; and participation of both expectant parents in the birth process.

KEY CONCEPTS

Generativity
Voluntary childlessness
Pronatalist attitudes

Methods of birth control
Trimesters of pregnancy

QUESTIONS

1. Based on your reading of this chapter and your experiences and observations, why do you think most people who marry also have children? Discuss what you think are the reasons that the birth rate in the United States is declining.
2. In a sexually intimate nonmarital relationship where children are not desired, which partner should be primarily responsible for contraception? Why? Does this contraceptive responsibility change in any way if the couple is married? If so, how?
3. Do you agree with the view that assigning the responsibility for contraception to females is yet another example of the double standard? Why or why not?
4. Summarize the conditions that you perceive in the greater social system to support the description of the United States as a "pronatalist" society. Are there any contemporary indications that this view is changing? What effects do cultural values related to procreation have on individual couples?
5. In reviewing the physical, psychological, and social changes that occur for expectant parents during pregnancy and childbirth, propose an educational program designed to help reduce the sense of crisis that frequently accompanies these events.
6. Why do you think that issues related to decisions about whether or not to have children and what methods (if any) of birth control to use are often not resolved or perhaps not even discussed by sexually intimate couples?

SUGGESTED READINGS

- Boston Women's Health Book Collective. *Our Bodies, Ourselves: A Book By and For Women.* New York: Simon and Schuster, 1976. A contemporary perspective on the roles, rights, and challenges of women in the United States. Fundamental information is provided on the physiology of sex, reproduction, birth control, and health care for women.
- Hawke, Sharryl, and Knox, David. *One Child by Choice.* Englewood Cliffs, N.J.: Prentice-Hall, 1977. A unique book that explores the situation of couples who choose to have one child only and discusses the strengths and stresses that accompany being an only child.
- McCary, James L. *Human Sexuality.* New York: Van Nostrand Reinhold, 1973. A comprehensive text on human sexual functioning, which includes information on contraceptive methods, pregnancy, and childbirth. The major focus of this work is on the physiological aspects of human sexuality.
- Rossi, Alice S. "Transition to Parenthood." *Journal of Marriage and the*

Family 30 (February 1968): 26–39. A now classic article that describes the role transitions and unique features of parenthood. Particular attention is given to social pressures toward becoming parents, the irreversibility of the role, and the lack of preparation for assuming the responsibilities of parenting.

- Sarvis, Betty, and Rodman, Hyman. *The Abortion Controversy*. New York: Columbia University Press, 1973. A reasoned and comprehensive approach to the controversial topic of abortion. Issues are clarified with helpful information and discussion. This work presents a serious analysis of this difficult question.

- Veevers, Jean E. *Childless by Choice*. Scarborough, Ontario: Butterworths, 1980. A comprehensive exploration of the lives of those who choose not to have children. The author draws upon the findings from her numerous research studies on the question of voluntary childlessness to present an overall view of this lifestyle.

- Well, J. Gibson, ed. *Current Issues in Marriage and the Family*. New York: Macmillan, 1975. A collection that includes good articles on the question of whether or not to have children. Information provided is useful for those considering the option of voluntary childlessness.

- Whelan, Elizabeth. *A Baby . . . Maybe*. New York: Bobbs Merrill, 1975. A highly readable book that spells out the pros and cons of parenthood, leaving the decision up to the reader. Whelan includes some of the wrong reasons for choosing to have children and some good reasons for remaining childless.

Part Three
Marital and Family Intimacy Over Time

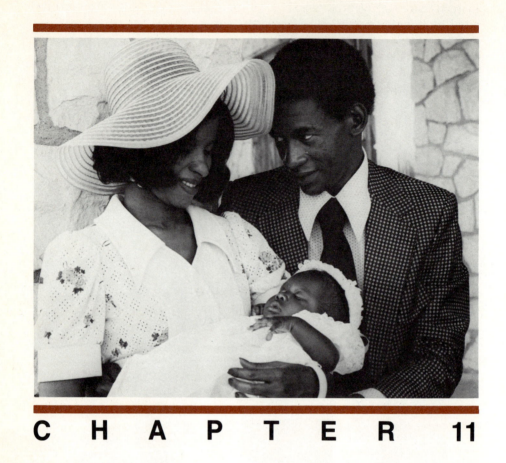

C H A P T E R 11

The Effects of Parenthood

HE: I'm home. Honey?

SHE: Oh, hi. I must have dozed off.

HE: Anything wrong? How's the baby?

SHE: The doctor said 100 degrees is nothing unusual for a nine-month-old with a cold. He said just to keep her in. I hope hot dogs are all right for dinner. I don't even have the right buns. We'll have to use hamburger buns.

HE: Sure. You sound depressed.

SHE: Let's face it. I'm a lousy mother.

HE: Hey, you're a great mother. The baby'll get over her cold in a day or two and you'll be fine.

SHE: It's not the cold. She's too much for me, and yet she's not enough for me.

HE: You miss your work—that's normal. How can a bright, active adult feel perfectly satisfied spending all her time with a nine-month-old. I mean, how far can you go on a goo and a smile?

SHE: I miss the work, but I miss being a person, too, being noticed, getting paid, not just giving, giving all day long. But see, if I were a good mother, I'd be paid enough with the little things she does. She drank with her cup today. I couldn't handle the old job now. I can hardly get up in the morning. I'm supposed to feel fulfilled, and I love her so much, but half the time I'm just ... *frustrated.*

HE: You want to know something—so am I. I spend half the time worrying about the bills and the other half wondering if I'm moving up fast enough, or moving at all.

SHE: I think the baby got her cold because I didn't put her snowsuit on yesterday. I thought the heavy jacket would be enough, but it got windy. What if she gets another earache?

HE: We need to go away together.

SHE: With her cold?

HE: She's staying. We're going. I'm making reservations for next weekend, one of those get-away packages, Friday night to Sunday.

SHE: She's teething. She'll hate it. We've never been away from her overnight.

HE: Both grandmas have been begging for her. It's our turn to be pampered; we need a nice dinner, a show, breakfast in bed, the museums, a new dress for you ...

SHE: You're talking $200. We can't afford that ...

HE: We can't afford this, either.

INTRODUCTION

Parenting appears to come naturally. Biologically, we are endowed with parenting potential. We can reproduce. Mothers automatically manufacture milk, and their bodies spontaneously respond to the needs of their infants for sustenance. Fathers, and other adults who are present at a birth or within earshot of a baby's cry or smile, will be drawn to meeting the infant's needs.

Yet, most of what we do as parents is learned—from our own parents, from other parents, and from the child. This learning process requires parents to be responsive and empathic with their child. In order to have the energy to meet this constant demand, parents must nurture and encourage each other. With this mutual support, parents can respond to the many cues the child offers.

The newborn is not a blank sheet (or *tabula rasa*) on which parents inscribe their teachings. Even at birth, an infant has individual tendencies and some basic skills. Despite their helpless appearance, newborns have an amazing ability to enchant parents and others. This ability to enchant is crucial to the infant's healthy physical and psychological survival, for it attracts adults and encourages them to feed, comfort, and attend to the baby's needs. A baby's power to intrigue and charm adults guarantees this new individual a role in the socialization process, which ultimately transforms the infant into an accepted member of human society.

CREATIVE PARENTING

We are just beginning to discover, through the filming and recording of infant-parent behavior, just how adept infants are at cooperating with and even initiating the process of socialization. Parents, too, are much more competent than they realize. Changes in sex roles, isolation from other parents, and a confusing and constant stream of "expert" advice often undermine the confidence of parents, particularly new ones. In fact, parenting requires just the ordinary, everyday creativity that most of us possess. We shall use the concept of ordinary "creative parenting," put forth by psychoanalyst E. James Anthony (1980), and discuss a few of its basic ingredients, including response to the infant's attachment needs, empathy, teaching of impulse control, encouragement of prosocial behavior, and ongoing responsiveness to a child's individual endowments.

Instinct versus Learning in Parenting

For a cat there seems to be no problem about being a cat. It is easy; cats seem to have no complexes or ambivalences or conflicts, and show no signs of yearning to be dogs instead. Their instincts are very clear. . . . Our instinct-remnants are weak and subtle, and they are hard to get at. Learning of the extrinsic sort is more powerful than our deepest impulses. (Maslow 1967)

Commenting on this observation by Abraham Maslow, Anthony (1980) suggests that creativity is the human substitute for instinct. He believes that creative aspects to parenting can be developed to compensate for our "attenuated instincts."

The question is still raised, however, whether women actually have more of a predisposition to parenting than men and, if they do, whether their tendency toward parenting is learned or instinctive. Jessie Bernard contends that "all women are socialized into the nurturant or 'stroking' function" (1975, p. 158). Sociobiologists, on the other hand, led by Edward O. Wilson (1978), stress the notion that parenting behavior is biologically rooted and thus more instinctive with the female. Despite such differences of opinion, most human behavior specialists would agree that parenting behavior seems to be a product of social learning, aided and abetted by some biological readiness. Women undergo biological changes during pregnancy that heighten their feelings of attachment to their children even before birth. Along with the physical acts of nursing and cuddling the infant, this readiness facilitates the nurturing function. As with other aspects of sex roles, however, these biologically based functions are minimal compared with the socially learned behaviors that make one act like a parent.

Harry Harlow's (1974) experiments with surrogate terry-cloth mothers for newborn monkeys showed that monkeys deprived of live mothers did not develop normally; they were not interested in sexual relations and they were totally inadequate as parents. For most higher primates, parenting is primarily a learned set of behaviors. Male chimpanzees and females other than the mother have been known to adopt and nurture a motherless chimp (Lawick-Goodall 1971). There are many human examples of individuals who were not the biological parents—women and men—who supplied the nurturing functions typically attributed to the biological mother.

Learning can also be negative. Studies of child abuse indicate that abusive parenting is learned during childhood (Kempe and Helfer 1972). Abusive parents usually have been treated harshly by their own parents. The evidence from these and other sources indicates that extraordinary stress and negative learning can teach parents to harm their own children. But given just the usual care and concern that most humans receive, ordinary people can learn to be good parents, regardless of sex and actual biological ties to a child.

The Current Parenting Dilemma

The problems in parenting today stem from at least three sources: changing role expectations, lack of parenting education, and the isolation of parents from support networks. Women's dual membership in the worlds of work and child rearing has spawned new "advice" to answer the already confusing question of "how to be a good parent." Contemporary young mothers are given a series of contradictory messages: To be a good mother, you must stay at home with your children and be a full-time parent. If you stay at home with your children, you will be an incomplete and unfulfilled woman. You can do it all—raise your children and have an extraordinary career.

Trying to be a supermother, superworker, and all-around superwoman is frustrating and impossible. Women and men are perplexed by such changing expectations. LeMasters claims:

It is impossible to interview modern parents without concluding that large numbers of them are confused, frustrated, and discouraged. They have been robbed of the traditional ways of rearing children without having an adequate substitute; they feel that they cannot achieve what they are expected to achieve; the standards for child rearing are too high; the authority of parents has been undermined by mass media, school officials, courts, social workers, and the adolescent peer group. (1977, p. 53)

Fathers are hearing that they should share the role of caretaker, but their experience with parenting is even more limited than their wives'. How will they know what to do?

An ongoing study of 128 couples becoming parents for the first time (Cowan and Cowan 1980) reveals that many new parents share similar problems: no training in how to care for children, their own parents living far away, isolation from other new parents in the community. Psychologists Carolyn and Philip Cowan, conducting this study at the University of California at Berkeley, note that once a child appears on the scene, certain aspects of married life are "up for grabs." Even couples who had an egalitarian arrangement, spouses who had the cooking, cleaning, and shopping divided up between them, find that everything is open for renegotiation: Do we both get up for the 3 A.M. feeding? Who changes the diapers?

A swing toward traditionalism often occurs at this time (Hoffman and Manis 1977). A wife may want to assume primary responsibility for the child, focusing a good deal of her attention on the infant. A husband who thought he was an equal partner may feel that he now must take a back seat, both as parent and as the emotional center of his wife's world. After a few months, a wife who has devoted every waking moment to her newborn infant may begin to feel restless and thwarted at home and may at the same time feel guilty for not being satisfied with full-time mothering. A woman who has gone right back to work after the birth of her baby may experience terrible pangs of regret and longing when she leaves her infant in the morning or when she thinks of the infant during the day. She and her husband may try to juggle the baby chores, but they suffer severe exhaustion after being up with the baby during the nights and then facing the unrelenting demands of their careers in the mornings.

Mixed feelings about new parenthood seem normal for husbands and wives, whether they have traditional or egalitarian marriages. Some Berkeley wives interviewed by the Cowans didn't like being home with the child; others resented being at work, away from the child. The Cowans found that a certain amount of frustration and failure seemed to go with the new parenting territory. What made the difference for the couples in this study was having a support network, being able to share their feelings with others who could confirm that all this was normal. In groups established by the Cowans, but often operating on their own, couples could talk openly about being exhausted after caring for an infant. They could discover that other couples, too, felt they had almost forgotten how to make love. Feelings of inadequacy or anger, which create guilt when bottled up, could be shared in such groups.

Isolation.   Isolation during child rearing is a phenomenon of modern Western culture. Psychologist John Bowlby (1980) has attributed the unusually high rates of depression and alcoholism among English urban housewives to isolation. And Alice S. Rossi (1968) has observed that the United States has become to a large extent a system of "isolated households." Parents who are divorced, widowed, or remarried with a "second family" tend to be even more isolated from support networks in our society (see Box 11.1).

Men and women are forced to parent as if they were the first parents on earth. In more primitive societies, new mothers would typically have the companionship and encouragement of other women who are mothers themselves, as well as the kin network of people who care about this particular mother and child. Instead, American mothers find themselves cut off from adult society. Rossi (1968, p. 27) points out that just when the infant is neediest, the young mother finds herself distant from kinswomen who could assist her in mothering.

The job of mothering is, in fact, overwhelming: "The new mother starts out immediately on 24-hour duty, with responsibility for a fragile and mysterious infant totally dependent upon her care" (Rossi 1968, p. 35). The new mother, as it turns out, has had little preparation for what is an enormously taxing job. While it is true that opportunities for learning about the process of childbirth have grown during the last decade, and special groups such as the LaLeche League offer opportunities for nursing mothers to exchange information, anecdotes, and questions, the vast majority of mothers face their new task alone.

The Experts.   Because of their isolation from sources of guidance and support, families have come to rely on impersonal "experts" for insights into child care and parenting, making people in the media their substitute kinfolk. But television and books can't quite take the place of people who know a family; the televised advice of experts is not adapted to the family's personal needs. All new ideas, regardless of merit, have a slot in the media marketplace. The result is often confusing. It is possible to turn on a television talk show in the morning and hear a child guidance expert insist that parents should never raise their voices or hands to a child, and later in the day hear another expert argue that children have a basic need to understand clearly the boundaries of right and wrong, even if parents must resort to occasional yelling or a firm spank on the bottom. With all this contradictory information, parents can spend many sleepless nights wondering if they are too strict or too permissive with their child. Their confidence is undermined.

"How-to" books on child rearing are equally ubiquitous and unsettling. Almost every parent has read at least one such book, and a substantial number have read more than five! Clarke-Stewart calculated that 23 million child-care books were sold in the United States from 1972 to 1977. She wondered if it were mere coincidence that the number of families in the United States with children under 13 years of age was also 23 million (Clarke-Stewart 1978, pp. 359–360).

BOX 11.1 Reconstituted Families

Within five years of divorce, three-quarters of all divorced people are remarried (Duberman 1975, p. 3). Many of these so-called reconstituted or blended families resulting from remarriage involve children. Duberman sampled 88 reconstituted families, 70 of which had children from a previous marriage. Child rearing was the greatest single problem for these families. But if the couple remarried at a younger age, the integration was better, especially if the remarried couple had a child together.

Stepfathers tended to have better relations with their stepchildren than stepmothers did, but when children were under 13 and when the stepmother gave the children a chance to initiate contact, they were also able to form strong ties with their stepchildren. Duberman found the biggest single problem to be the absent parent's undermining the new stepparent-stepchild relationship. The majority of stepparent-stepchild relations in Duberman's sample were relatively good. And the divorce statistics for second marriages indicate that they are almost as stable as first marriages.

Remarried parents do suffer even more than others from isolation and lack of guidance and support. Paul Bohannan finds their situation chaotic, "with each individual set of families having to work out its own destiny without any realistic guidelines" (1971, p. 137). As with other phenomena we have studied, such as single parenting, parenting in a reconstituted family is likely to become easier as these families increase in number and become another accepted type of homestead on America's diversified family landscape.

Clarke-Stewart reviewed 200 of the most popular child-rearing books and found they had two major themes or goals:

The experts want to increase parents' *confidence.* They start out with deliberate efforts to reassure parents: Parents are capable; they know more than they think they do; they should relax and enjoy their kids. . . . On the other hand, such reassurances must be carefully balanced with the other aim of these books, which is to increase parents' *competence.* (1978, p. 367)

One source of confidence for new parents is the discovery that the infant will help them in their parenting role. The infant has the competence to lead the way. Important new research on infants, reviewed by Clarke-Stewart and Koch (in press), supports the biblical prophecy, "A child shall lead them."

THE COMPETENT INFANT

Thanks to this flood of research, most of which was accomplished in the 1970s, we know that from the moment of birth, the infant exhibits many kinds of highly complex behavior, all of which are designed to prepare him or her for survival and growth in a social world. Evidence gathered by researchers who have studied the formation of parent-infant bonds has established these findings:

From the moment of birth, infants demonstrate highly competent interactive behavior. (Elizabeth Crews)

1. The infant at birth is able to capture and enchant its mother as well as other individuals present at the birth.
2. The infant not only displays the capacity to interact with the caretaker on a primitive but identifiable social level, but also possesses the ability to *initiate* that interaction.
3. The infant has the ability to behave in partnership with its caretaker, to form relationships and relationship behavior that will carry through the entire life span of the infant.

All this from a newborn!

The Moment of Birth

Pediatricians Marshall Klaus and John Kennell (1976) observed how mothers and others present during home births behaved toward the newborn infants. The doctors were struck by the highly emotional behavior shown by those who were present immediately before and after birth. They noted that mothers, fathers, and bystanders present during those home deliveries reported feelings of "ecstasy," an exaltation, a rapture never before experienced. Klaus and Kennell contrasted these emotions with those displayed by mothers in hospital delivery situations where, for various reasons, infants were immediately separated from their mothers. Klaus and Kennell found that infants who were allowed to be with their mothers immediately after birth appeared to thrive and grow, while their counterparts who had been taken from their mothers were less likely to flourish. Although they had no organic disease, these infants did not gain weight at the normal rate or show the normal advances in behavior.

The reactions of the two groups of mothers were also significant. Mothers who cared for their infants immediately after birth gently caressed infants and often spent long periods of time just staring at them. These mothers reported strong positive feelings about their children and themselves. Mothers who were separated from their infants reported being fearful for their infants' welfare and anxious about themselves (Klaus and Kennell 1976).

Evidence is still being gathered about the "bonding" process that exists from the moment of birth, a phenomenon that links infant to mother. Although the early moments with the newborn help the bonding process, both mother and father have thousands of opportunities to form attachments to their infant after the delivery. Observations of parents and infants reveal that the infant is preprogrammed to attract and interact with adult human partners so as to maximize his or her survival.

The resources the infant possesses to insure survival include (1) sound, (2) facial expressions, and (3) an acute sense of timing (Clarke-Stewart and Koch in press). The infant's repertoire of behavior in turn produces extraordinary behavior in adults: (1) adults' voices become exaggeratedly high-pitched; (2) their facial expressions are exaggerated; and (3) they speak a language called "baby talk."

Early Interaction Between Mother and Child

Interestingly, it is the infant who will lead the mother in what has been called their "dance."

The mother enters the room and picks up her child. The baby will begin its greeting of the mother, the "words" consisting of facial expressions, excited movements of the arms and legs, sounds, perhaps the cessation of crying and the substitution of cooing or gurgling. The mother in turn speaks in soft, high-pitched tones, her eyes open wide. She has exchanged greetings with her child.

The dance is also evident while the child eats. It will be the infant who chooses to

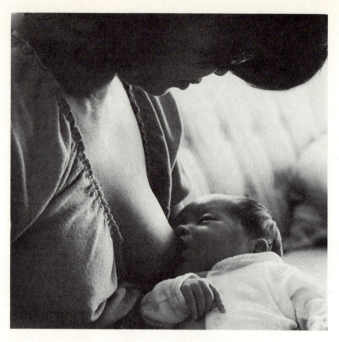

↑ The mother-infant "dance" (Florence Sharp)

← Parents and children share a sense of joy and security in their mutual attachment. (Florence Sharp)

↓ One of the most difficult challenges of parenthood is to provide a base that is secure, yet allows the child room to venture out and explore. (Jim Caldwell)

Children need time to be alone. (Elizabeth Crews) ↑

The need for attachment is never completely outgrown. (Paul Conklin) →

The infant forms separate bonds with the mother and with the father. (Charles Gatewood) ↓

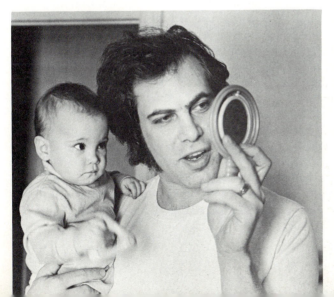

suck. As it does so, the mother is generally quiet and inactive. The baby pauses, and the mother strokes, caresses, and talks to the infant. It is enough for the time being, and the infant will resume sucking while the mother, taking her cue from her child, becomes quiet.

Or the infant looks at something. The mother's gaze will follow the infant's eyes, and an object will be identified. The baby will look away and so will the mother.

The infant gazes at the mother's face, and the mother looks into her child's face. They stare at one another until the infant breaks off. They will not resume their mutual gazing until the infant chooses. (Clarke-Stewart and Koch in press)

The infant's crying is a superb mechanism to signal distress. Not only does it attract the attention of its mother, but it also alerts all adults within earshot. At the moment when the child is most vulnerable, its resources are marshalled into long, loud cries that the parents or other adults hear and recognize. These cries mobilize the adults into action, insuring that the child's needs will be met. Sometimes the cries persist after the baby's needs are met, infringing on the needs of husband and wife for a few intimate moments of their own. The pull created by the infant is so strong that many new parents find a day or weekend away from home necessary to escape the constant and undeniable demands of a new baby.

ATTACHMENT BEHAVIOR

John Bowlby and others who have observed the social competence of infants describe the early tendencies of infants to engage parents as *attachment behavior*. Attachment behavior is a preprogrammed, biologically rooted ability on the part of the infant. Although it is most significant in infancy and early childhood, the need for attachment, unlike the infant's need for dependency, is never completely outgrown.

Although attachment behavior is critical to the infant's well-being, it is also important for the mother. If that attachment is firmly based, mother and infant will share a sense of joy as well as a sense of security and satisfaction. If that attachment behavior is disrupted, either inadvertently or deliberately, if it is threatened or thwarted, the result will be anxiety and anger on the part of the infant as well as the adult. If the attachment behavior is severely disrupted, the result will be grief and depression (Bowlby 1980).

Most of the research on attachment has centered on mother-child bonds. But work is now being conducted by researchers Main and Westoff that examines the child's attachment bonds to both mother and father (Bowlby 1980). Even during the first year of life, the infant forms different attachments, separate relationships or bonds with the mother and with the father. One child may have a secure relationship with the father but not the mother. Children who turned out to be most competent and confident had secure relationships with both parents. This current work would support findings reported on divorce that stress the formation of separate relationships to each parent and the need for those parenting functions to be fulfilled by father and mother, even if they no longer live together as a family (see Chapter 12).

Once having established an intimate attachment relationship with its parents, the infant feels secure enough to venture out and explore. At first these explorations are very limited. But as the infant grows into a toddler, with the ability to get about physically and express thoughts and feelings verbally, these explorations take the child outside the home. Contact is established with others. The child's circle of contacts continues to expand, especially when the child is secure in the knowledge that he or she can return and receive sustenance from that secure attachment base. When the outside world proves temporarily confusing or hostile, the attachment figures will provide love and care, encouraging the child to venture forth once more. This is one of the most difficult challenges of parenting—providing a base that is secure but not too inhibiting, teaching children to do without us, yet assuring them that if they should need the nurturing and love we once provided, it will be there for them.

Continuing Attachment Needs

Attachment behavior does not end with childhood; individuals continue to need reassurance that they will receive nurturance from others. We can see instances of emotion-laden attachment behavior exhibited when an adolescent girl expresses concern over her ability to attract boys of her own age. We can see this kind of behavior manifest itself when a middle-aged man seriously questions the years he has devoted to a certain career. We can see attachment behavior when an expectant mother wonders whether she will be able to care for her child in the best possible manner. The adolescent, the expectant mother, the new father, the man of 40 who has lost his job or doubts his virility, the woman who faces menopause and the adolescent rebellion of her children—all need nurturing. All need to touch a secure base; all have ongoing attachment needs. In many ways, marriage serves to fulfill these ongoing attachment needs that were first experienced and satisfied in childhood.

Adults whose early attachment needs were not satisfied tend to have difficulty fulfilling the needs of their own children. Mothers who have had a troubled infancy and childhood tend to spend less time with their own infants. When they are with their babies, they do not hold them as long or look at them as much as mothers who report that they had happy childhoods (Frommer and Shea 1973; Wolkind, Hall, and Pawlby 1977). Yet the majority of women and men have the ordinary, everyday creativity to help their infants do what they are prepared to do—form an attachment to their parents.

PARENTAL EMPATHY

To apprehend who our children are and what they need at the various stages of their development, we must employ *empathy*. We have stressed the need for empathy in understanding one's spouse, in communicating effectively. It is equally essential in the parenting role. Empathy is the ability to feel how another feels. It depends upon some basic skills of social cognition that develop during childhood and allow us to take the role of another. One must recognize what the other is feeling before one can feel it vicariously (Feshbach and Roe 1968). Recognizing anger, sadness, or fear does not mean one will feel that way, too. Yet we can experience the feelings of others vicariously; we can be empathic. Both boys and girls exhibit this skill beginning at ages eight, nine, or ten (Maccoby and Jacklin 1974). Social role training, however, tends to encourage female expression of emotion and to discourage male emotional expressivity. This training encourages girls to be empathic to a greater degree than boys. The social activity of girls and their more intimate friendship pattern enhance this social sensitivity.

If we imagine a boy and girl going to see a movie such as *The Black Stallion*, the differences become obvious. Both children watch as the boy in the movie is shipwrecked: his father has been drowned, and he is on an island utterly alone; he begins to cry. The children reflect these same feelings on their faces as they watch the shipwrecked boy. But the boy spectator is much more likely to cover his tears, especially if he is a preteen or adolescent, and especially if he is in the company of his peers. Boys are equally capable of recognizing the emotions of others and feeling vicariously what the other feels, but they usually have not been encouraged to demonstrate this empathy. Later, as parents, many men find it easier to teach their sons baseball than to share emotions with them. Although sex-role training may limit us, we all have the capacity to understand and respond to our children's feelings.

Parental empathy goes beyond ordinary understanding of what the other feels. It is the ability to merge temporarily with the child and then to emerge from that sharing experience, guiding the child to a new place.

Heinz Kohut (1977) has described the process of empathy between mother and infant in which the mother takes on the feelings of the child as if she were the child (see pp. 48–49). In marriage and other intimate adult relationships, we expect empathy to be returned: "I understand and feel to some extent what you are feeling; you endorse my feelings in the same way." But the infant or very young child does not yet possess the ability to be empathic with his or her parents. At this stage of life, empathy is a one-way street.

Parents can feel drained by trying continually to be empathic. In fact, this is one source of stress on the marriage. If both parents are empathic, they can share this nurturing function and at the same time support each other's needs for understanding. The child needs empathy, as we all do, "to feel we are not alone in our progress through life" (Paul 1970, p. 340). But children also need empathy as a bridge to independence. Empathy reassures them that they have the ability to deal with feelings, to survive an experience and even enjoy or learn something from it. Those monsters in the dark are real; so are the sense that one will die of excitement before a birthday party and the despair of having lost a game, or a new bracelet, or an important friend. It is empathy that can prevent children, and at some stressful moments even adults, from feeling overwhelmed by intense emotions.

No other writer has so vividly portrayed the desolation of life without empathy as Franz Kafka. In *The Metamorphosis*, Gregor Samsa awakens one morning to find himself transformed into a gigantic insect. His mother screams in terror; his father shoos him away. Though his parents are frightened of the change at first, a more terrible period begins for Gregor when they become indifferent to him, regarding him as a nuisance, something to be put up with until he dies. In a contemporary children's book, a boy named Treehorn finds himself getting smaller and smaller, but his parents don't even notice that he is shrinking. Indifference—especially if chronic and continual—is devastating to a child. There is evidence to suggest that a child would rather be scolded, criticized, punished, even abused, than ignored.

The parent whose child feels at times as if he or she also has been transformed into a repulsive creature must first endorse those feelings. But somewhere in that endorsement, the parent needs to plant the belief that those feelings will change, that the metamorphosis of growing up will have a hopeful outcome. The example in Box 11.2 illustrates only one of the thousands of opportunities parents have to supply this vital need for empathy.

Parents cannot be continually empathic, nor should they be. A parent who finds a child has broken a friend's toy, punched her little sister, gorged himself on candy, or run across the street without looking for traffic—a parent who makes such discoveries shouldn't immediately repress all anger and try to assume the role of the child, experiencing vicariously the child's envy, jealousy, craving, or careless yearning to be across the street at the park. Warmth and affection, though essential to children, must be

BOX 11.2   An Example of Empathy

A mother takes her four-year-old boy to the playground during the summer. Several other youngsters are splashing around in the wading pool, appearing to be having a good time. The mother urges her child to go into the pool: "Look at all the other children your age who are having a fine time, splashing and cooling off." The mother perceives the play to be an enjoyable experience. But for the child it verges on being terrifying. The child does not know the other children. They seem to be playing very roughly, splashing water, pushing, and shoving. "What if I get water in my eyes?" the child thinks. "What happens if I fall and my head goes under water?" The mother leads the child by the hand to the strange pool, a place the child does not wish to go. He is afraid. It is all too strange.

The mother now has two choices. She can continue to take her child to the pool, lead him into the water, and tell him to have a happy time as she turns and leaves. But if the mother is empathic, she will recognize the child's fears. She will talk with him, explain the process of play in the pool, reassure him that she will remain nearby and in sight, and watch to see that he is safe. She may walk into the pool with him, holding him by the hand as he adjusts to the temperature of the water.

Perhaps the experience will trigger some distant memory in the mother, a time when she was a child and was frightened by a strange situation. Then she may be able to verbalize what her child may now be feeling, saying: "I remember when I was your age, when I was just as scared." Now the child is reassured. His mother does know how he is feeling. He is comforted by learning that he is not alone with his fears and that the very feelings he was ashamed to admit have been experienced by other people who now seem strong and able. This gives him hope that he will overcome these fears just as his mother has.

But if the mother is plagued by her own insecurities and worries about the child—perhaps he does not play as "boyishly" as the other children—or if her parents forced her to deny fear, then she may propel him into the pool where he must face this fearful situation alone.

combined with guidance and discipline. The way parents combine affection and control accounts for a number of different styles in parenting, which we shall discuss next.

STYLES OF PARENTING

Children whose parents express affection for them are more likely to be secure and affectionate themselves. Children whose parents are rejecting tend to be irritable and aggressive, and they are more likely to have emotional problems (Clarke-Stewart and Koch in press). Warmth and affection alone are not enough, however; parents must also teach their children a certain amount of impulse control. The type of discipline parents use will be particularly apparent in children's behavior outside the home.

Assertiveness and social responsibility reflect disciplinary practices. The combination of fondness and firmness seems to produce the healthiest children.

Discipline

Diana Baumrind (1967, 1971, 1973, 1977, 1979), using questions and observations of parents and children, has defined three major patterns of parenting: (1) authoritarian, (2) permissive, and (3) authoritative.

Authoritarian parents are neither affectionate nor sympathetic. They insist on obedience, requiring children to assume responsibility but giving them few rights.

Permissive parents are just the opposite. They give their children rights equal to adults', but they do not require them to assume responsibility. Though they are loving parents, they have relinquished control of their children.

Authoritative parents exert control, but they are also loving. As the child matures, they gradually allow her or him to assume more and more responsibility.

Observed at nursery-school age, children of authoritarian parents tended to be withdrawn and discontented. Children of permissive parents showed immature and dependent behavior. Children who had received warmth and consistent discipline from authoritative parents were friendly, happy, and self-reliant. The authoritative pattern is not only the most salutary, but also the most commonly practiced and advocated style. It requires loving parents to set limits and to enforce them.

Effective Punishment. Once the child learns to walk and talk, the parent is confronted with the question of how to enforce limits, how to demonstrate to the child that exceeding limits will have unpleasant consequences. Reviewing a variety of studies conducted in laboratories and homes, Parke (1977) found the effectiveness of punishment to be dependent on five factors:

1. Timing. The closer the punishment comes to the act, the greater its effectiveness.

2. Intensity. An intense punishment—a loud scolding, loss of an important privilege or toy, an extreme withdrawal of affection or company—is effective. But punishments that are too intense may cause anxiety. Those that are accompanied by humiliation, such as being publicly ridiculed in the classroom, are counterproductive, producing resentment and perhaps aggression.

3. Relationship. If the child values and loves the punisher, the punishment is more effective.

4. Justification.   Reasoning geared to the child's level of understanding increases the effectiveness of the punishment. The three-year-old who has dumped his food on his sister's lap is firmly removed from the table *and* told that food must be eaten. The child is told that tomorrow he will help wash his sister's jeans, but for now he must go to his room without the rest of dinner or dessert.

5. Consistency.   Punishment should be consistent rather than occasional. Ideally, parents should agree on punishments. But given personality differences between husband and wife, as well as the fact that parents don't witness every misbehavior, there are bound to be inconsistencies. Every parent has lashed out in anger with an unrealistic punishment—"No dessert for a year!" Husbands and wives who discuss punishments and settle on a few simple ones that can be carried out realistically have the best chance of succeeding as effective disciplinarians.

Even when carried out effectively by loving parents, discipline can produce some anger. One of the difficult jobs parents have is to teach their children how to express feelings in an appropriate way and control those aggressive or hostile impulses that are inappropriate. Those who have looked at the kinds of parental behavior that seem to lead to aggression in children find these parents have failed to give their children loving attention—either by being very permissive and failing to provide positive guidelines or by neglecting to provide any guidelines (Feshbach and Feshbach 1972).

One study of families of highly aggressive boys identified a particularly detrimental situation in which the parents contradicted or undermined each other. One might lay down a punishment; the other would quickly withdraw it (Patterson and Cobb 1971). Seeing anger in the home between mother and father or seeing or receiving physical punishments can also give the child training in aggression.

Modeling Appropriate Behaviors.   Parents who show empathy, who demonstrate that they can put themselves in the place of the child or in the place of others, are "modeling" a prosocial behavior. Bandura and others who contend that social behavior is largely learned by observation have stressed the importance of models for children (Bandura 1977; Bandura and Walters 1963). Parents are the most significant models. Laboratory tests suggest that other models tend to be imitated if they are warm, if they are similar to the child, if they are powerful, if children are rewarded for imitating their actions, and if the child who observes the model clearly understands the behavior being witnessed (Mussen and Eisenberg-Berg 1977).

Social-learning advocates, such as Bandura, encourage parents to look at their deeds as well as their words and to consider the total environment, not just their own homes. Parents who preach good acts but spend their days exploiting others will not succeed in teaching prosocial behavior. Bandura also suggests that peers, television, and other adults whom the children encounter frequently can be powerful influences. For example, the TV hero who gets the woman, the money, and the acclaim by using force teaches that aggression brings rewards. Children in our society tend to receive a high degree of training in competition and less training for cooperation. On television, children witness aggression far more frequently than they witness prosocial acts such as sharing, altruism, and empathy.

Children can learn to share, to cooperate, and to give time and material things to others. They can be trained in empathy by parents who feel for others and remind their children to do the same: "When you took that girl's toy, did you notice how her eyes got watery and her smile turned to a frown? If you give it back, I'll bet she smiles again."

Social-Class Influences on Parenting Styles

Parents appear to have a choice of child-rearing methods, but they are influenced by their own upbringing and their membership in a particular socioeconomic group. We have touched on some of these influences in previous chapters. Here we shall try to understand some sources of these differences as they affect parenting.

In his classic paper, "Social Class and Parent-Child Relationships," Melvin Kohn (1963) found a direct correlation between the social class of the parents and the various techniques they use to raise their children. These techniques for child rearing are directly related to the parents' personal values, which in turn are related to educational level, occupation, racial or ethnic heritage, and numerous other variables that contribute to the personal history of the mother and father. The parents' history thus colors the way they see the world; it conditions their dreams (or nightmares) for themselves and their children.

We can only describe the ways in which the middle and working classes *tend* to parent. The word "tend" is stressed because there are wide variations within such categories as "middle" and "working" class. Nevertheless, social science is able to describe certain characteristics that generally hold true.

Working-Class Parents/Middle-Class Parents.   Kohn, building on the work of Evelyn Mills Duval, believes that working-class parents value tradition. *The American Heritage Dictionary* (1969) defines *tradition* as: "The passing down of elements of a culture from generation to generation, especially by oral communication." In its most overt form, the parent passing on tradition is saying to the child: "If it was good enough for me, it's good enough for you." According to Kohn, working-class parents believe they have worked for, "and partially achieved, an American dream" (1977, p. 274). He (more often than she, because working-class families tend to be more stereotyped in sex roles) has cut out a piece of the American dream by following the "rules." Thus, he thinks, if his sons and daughters follow the "rules," they too will be able to obtain a piece of the American dream.

Middle-class parents, too, have achieved part of the American dream, but their methods are different; their rules are more flexible, permitting a "more substantial degree of independence of action" for parent as well as child (Kohn 1977, p. 275). Even if middle-class parents were once poor, as is the case with many first- and second-generation Americans, their own children need not worry about necessities. They are able to encourage their children to pursue their wishes regardless of the cost. The individualism of middle-class children tends to be valued more than their adherence to traditional mores.

As we suggested in Chapter 3, socioeconomic status is often defined by occupation. A sanitary worker is working class; an advertising copywriter is automatically middle class. Yet the contribution of the working-class individual may be more essential to the good of society than that of the middle-class person; even the money earned by the working-class individual may be more than the earnings of the middle-class individual, as would be the case with a working-class, blue-collar steelworker of some seniority as compared to a middle-class, white-collar sales clerk in a department store. And within the bounds of each social class, there are some parents who are loving and affectionate and others who are not.

The generalities about middle-class and working-class occupations, if we recognize their limitations, are still useful in gaining further insight as to how each class will parent. Kohn (1977) offers us three refinements of work in differentiating middle class from working class:

1. Middle-class occupations deal more with the manipulation of interpersonal relations, ideas, and symbols, while working-class occupations deal more with the manipulation of things.
2. Middle-class occupations are more subject to self-direction, while working-class occupations are more subject to standardization and direct supervision.
3. Getting ahead in middle-class occupations is more dependent upon one's actions, while in working-class occupations it is more dependent on collective action, particularly in unionized industries.

Kohn summarizes by stating: "Middle-class occupations require a greater degree of self-direction; working-class occupations, in large measure, require that one follow explicit rules set down by someone in authority" (p. 274).

Using these insights, together with evidence gained through research, we can begin to see how these class differences will tend to affect child-rearing practices.

Class Differences in Discipline and Punishment.   Perhaps the most relevant data on the different styles of parenting are in the area of physical punishment as a method of discipline: "Working class parents are apt to resort to physical punishment when the direct and immediate consequences of their children's disobedient acts are most extreme, and to refrain from punishing when this might provoke an even greater disturbance" (Kohn 1977, p. 275). Janey is doing cartwheels in the living room. She lands on the corner of a coffee table, breaking one of the legs. Janey will receive a spanking—she broke the table, and so she gets spanked. But if Janey is doing cartwheels in the living room, making a great deal of noise but being careful not to bang into the furniture, Janey's working-class parents will not spank her.

Middle-class parents are not so much concerned with the deed as with the intention behind it: "Middle-class parents . . . seem to punish or refrain from punishing on the basis of their interpretation of the child's intent in acting as he does. Thus, they will punish a furious outburst when the context is such that they interpret it to be a loss of self-control, but will ignore an equally extreme outburst when the context is such that they interpret it to be merely an emotional release" (Kohn 1977, p. 275). John is at the dinner table, stuffing chocolate cake into his mouth with his hand. He is told repeatedly to use his fork, but ignores his parents and is finally told to leave the table. John howls in anger, the cake spewing from his mouth. John gets spanked. But if after John has told his parents that he was teased in school that day, he sits at the table and stuffs cake in his mouth morosely, he is simply told to stop. He howls in outrage, saying, "Everybody is picking on me." John is not spanked.

The working-class parent is concerned with the consequence—the broken coffee table—while the middle-class parent is concerned with the intent—what motivated the child to be morose and explode in a temper tantrum. Working-class parents generally live out their lives following external rules. To help their children survive and prosper in society, they see their role as imposing restraints and rules in order to prepare their children for what they will encounter in the outside world. Kohn sees middle-class parents as acting in a manner that promotes flexibility and independence. Such flexibility and independence might not serve the child who must assume a job that requires rigid obedience.

Middle-class parents are deeply concerned with their child's education. The greater the education, parents believe, the greater the opportunity for choice. The greater the choice, the greater the child's opportunity for personal fulfillment—something middle-class parents can afford to encourage. Of course, they expect their children to find personal fulfillment in

high-status and high-paying careers. If personal fulfillment results in social slippage, the middle-class parent is severely disappointed; maintaining or improving status is a value cherished by the middle class—as much
as or more than personal freedom.

Fathers play a particularly crucial role in defining class structures for
their children. Mothers in both the middle and the working class act as
facilitators for their children's growth and development, while fathers are
called upon to demonstrate the values held by a particular class. In
middle-class families, mothers call upon fathers primarily to be supportive of children (boys in particular) and, secondarily, to set down rules
and regulations. In working-class families, fathers are called upon to be
more "directive," to announce what the child may or may not do (Kohn
1977, p. 276). In middle-class families, fathers generally accept their supportive role; in working-class families, fathers tend to resist this role,
claiming it is the responsibility of mothers to nurture the children. We
have already noted that men and women in working-class families tend to
be more divided into same-sex groups before and after marriage. The notion that child rearing is "woman's work" is more likely to prevail in the
working class. We have been indicating a change in working-class values, a
loosening of these once rigid sex-role boundaries, as women of the working
class share economic burdens and spend more time outside the home and
as men begin to experience the satisfactions of nurturing their children
and of expressing the full range of their feelings, rather than only those
defined as obviously masculine. When the younger generation of the working class marry and become parents, we may see a change in their child-
rearing practices, with less emphasis on strict obedience and more stress
on individual expression for boys and girls.

Some Ethnic Differences in Parenting Styles

Child-rearing practices in general now tend to be similar for black and
white parents, as does the level of children's self-esteem (Silverstein and
Krate 1975). But class differences combined with ethnic differences make
for marked departures in terms of fertility rate and numbers of children
born out of wedlock. College-educated black women continue to have the
lowest fertility rate of all married women. But more than half of all black
births now occur outside of marriage to black women on the lower end of
the income and educational scale (Bianchi and Farley 1979). This means
that black children are much more likely than white children to grow up in
single-parent homes.

Chicano families were once assumed to be headed by aloof and authoritarian fathers and subservient mothers. But recent research suggests
that parent-child relationships in Chicano families are warm and nurturing. Burrows (1980) found Chicano fathers to be playful and companion-

able with children. Goodman and Beman (1971) also noted the strength and warmth of affection demonstrated in the Chicano family, especially the intensity of family affection expressed by *barrio* children, compared to responses by both black and white children.

Among Native Americans, family life is likely to be affected by poverty. In a study of 120 urban Native-American families, researchers found that one-third of the families were headed by females; 27 percent were receiving public welfare. Only one-third of these families had an adequate income, and the limited income had to accommodate an average of three children in each family. Native-American children continue to be trained for independence at significantly earlier ages than either white or black urban children (Miller 1980). Native-American children also have to contend with the negative image presented in cowboy-and-Indian films and stories. Native Americans are rarely seen on contemporary television programs or commercials.

As we discussed in Chapter 3 (see page 76), children need to see themselves depicted favorably. Failure to be acknowledged—what Ralph Ellison called "invisibility" (1972, pp. 497–498)—can create anger and despair. Parents require encouragement and endorsement from their own communities and from the society at large in order to help their children to become productive individuals.

INFLUENCES OF THE CHILD ON THE PARENT

Parenting is an interactive process, even though some aspects of early parenting, such as empathy and physical care, require an enormous one-way output of energy by the parents. The research of the 1970s tended to put greater emphasis on the child as an influence on its parents. We have stressed the competence of the infant who is a partner in the "dance" of socialization. Each child brings to that dance certain traits—physical appearance, health or frailty, activity or lethargy. Parents do not respond in the same way to each partner—each child. Some infants are actually more responsive to cuddling; they gurgle, coo, and move close when being held, thereby "rewarding" the parent, encouraging more affection and ultimately receiving it. Other infants stiffen and fuss when they are held, discouraging parents from displaying affection; they are likely to be cuddled and petted less. Through the child's own uniqueness, the child changes the dance.

Among those early traits that influence parent-child interaction is a constellation of behavioral tendencies that can be called "temperament." Thomas and Chess (1977) conducted a longitudinal study of children, following their development from infancy through adolescence. From the beginning, each child showed definite temperamental patterns. Some children, for example, were "difficult" from birth—harder to please, more prone to fussing and crying, highly active, resistant to cuddling. The outcome for the difficult children depended, in part, on something Thomas and Chess have called "goodness of fit," the way in which the child's temperament fits with the temperaments of its parents. Some parents welcome an active and demanding child; others find such pressures wearing and at times unbearable. Even parents with a record of child abuse do not abuse all their children. The unfortunate pairing of an abusive parent with a child who inadvertently triggers abuse is further evidence that each parent-child dyad (or pair) has its own pattern of interaction.

In addition to temperamental compatibility, researchers have found that birth order affects parent-child relationships. Parents tend to be more demanding of their first-born children, usually giving them more responsibility. They are more relaxed, as a rule, with second-born children. First-borns and siblings spaced widely apart tend to be subject to greater parental influence (and later to general adult authority). Second-borns, especially if they are close in age to the oldest, are less likely to conform to adult authority, more likely to conform to peer influence.

Siblings have an important influence on a child's development and on the way the child relates to parents. An opposite-sex sibling creates more stimulation and anxiety for the first-born than a same-sex sibling. A same-sex older sibling tends to reinforce traditional sex roles, so that, for instance, a second-born girl with an older sister is less likely to be assertive (H. Koch 1955, 1956; Sutton-Smith and Rosenberg 1969). Siblings of the opposite sex are sometimes more likely to be imitated than parents. The overall constellation of the family, the way the child fits into the family grouping, also influences parent-child behaviors.

A child's sex influences his or her upbringing from the moment of birth. As we have discussed in previous chapters, many of the differences attributed to male and female relate to their socialization. This socialization may begin when female newborns are described as "dainty" and "delicate," while male newborns are described as "sturdy" and "tough" (Scanzoni and Fox 1980). Small physiological differences between the sexes in levels of aggression or verbal fluency are maximized when males are socialized for competition in the marketplace and females are socialized for nurturing the next generation.

Some aspects of this socialization appear to be changing. Mothers and other women continue to be the primary caretakers of children, but fathers are gradually taking a more active role. Psychologists and sociologists are now giving more recognition to the importance of the father's role in child development. Children are more apt to see flexibility in role models as their mothers work outside the home and their fathers take on certain nurturing functions. There is no evidence to suggest that teaching children some role flexibility will produce effeminate sons or masculine daughters. Both men and women will have to work and rear children in the future.

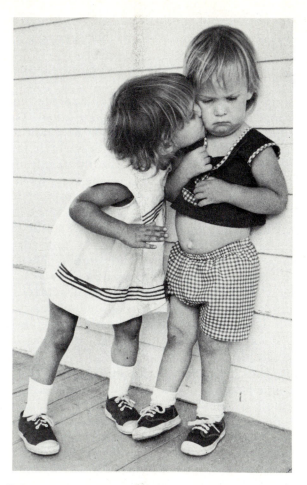

Siblings have an important influence on a child's development.
(David Strickler, Picture Cube)

More parents are adopting a single standard of emotional expressiveness and high achievement as they rear sons and daughters who will come of age in the next century.

WHEN PARENTS FAIL

American society considers a family to be the best place to rear a child. Usually this is the family into which the child is born. The family performs several functions: Biologically, the family reproduces, thus assuring the perpetuation of the species. Psychologically, the family helps construct and shape the personalities of its members. The family also socializes its new members by inculcating in them the cultural, racial, and religious heritage of the family, as well as helping the new members perceive its moral and ethical standards.

For centuries, common law has held that only in the most extreme, provable cases may a child be taken from his or her natural parents. Courts and judges have historically rejected societal attempts to interfere with the privacy of the home and the sanctity of parent-child relations. Yet under the doctrine of *parens patriae*, the state permits itself the power to intervene into the privacy of parent-child relations if it is deemed "in the best interests of the child." The history of intrusion into the family by government is complex, yet many legal experts believe the state (or its agents) is becoming more and more directly involved with parent-child relationships. In the United States, however, the state is not monolithic. It does not represent one distinctive policy or point of view. It is not at all unusual for one agent of the state, say, a child welfare worker, to participate actively in separating a child from its parents, while another agency of the state, the court, orders the child returned to its parents.

The state charges the parents with providing for the financial security of the child, maintaining the child's health and education, and giving the child a moral environment in which he or she may know the difference between right and wrong. Theoretically, these guidelines are clear; in practice, they are not.

When a family fails to meet these guidelines, it is accused of neglecting the child. There is general agreement as to what constitutes child abuse, though the guidelines for neglect are subject to many different interpretations. Child abuse involves physical injury that is not accidental; the injury (or injuries) result from intentional acts on the part of parents or guardians. Omissions, including failure to provide obvious safeguards that would prevent physical injury, are also considered abuse (Kempe and Helfer 1972, p. xi). Abusive parents have typically had abusive or unreasonable parents themselves, as Box 11.3 explains. Our discussion of family violence in Chapter 9 showed that abuse also tends to be encouraged by an abusive partner, by the parent's belief that abuse is "normal" and, for women, by an unrelieved burden of child-care responsibility.

But neglect is more difficult to define. People who judge these matters are more likely to perceive neglect in a poor family than in a rich one. This used to be true of child abuse, before stricter procedures were instituted for reporting unexplained or repeated physical injuries to children. With neglect, socioeconomic class continues to play a role. For example, middle- and upper-class families are rarely charged with neglect, not because they always treat their children well—some of them do neglect their children—rather, "because our society does not, as a practical matter, have the same standards for the middle- and upper-class parents that it tries to enforce on the lower classes" (Katz 1971, p. 24).

In fact, the vast preponderance of child neglect proceedings are insti-

BOX 11.3   Abusive Parents—Abusive Children

Abusive parents seem to share a style of child rearing as well as a similar upbringing. Here are some of those common features found by Kempe and Helfer (1972, pp. 4–5):

1. A high demand for the child to perform so as to gratify the parents
2. The use of severe physical punishment to ensure proper behavior
3. A high vulnerability in their marital relationship to criticism, disinterest, abandonment by the spouse
4. A sense of personal inadequacy and low self-esteem
5. Dependency on the child for emotional support
6. Unrealistic expectations as to what a child can do
7. Attributing the child's failure to perform to "deliberate stubbornness," willful disobedience, or a malicious desire to thwart the parents' wishes. With this assumption and with their child-rearing style, such willful disobedience must receive severe punishment.
8. Abusive parents were treated this way by their own parents when they were children. They were "expected to perform well, to gratify parental needs very early in life, and then were criticized, punished and often abused for failure to do so."

Abusive parents may have a variety of individual problems, but they share the common background features of poor parental models and low self-esteem. In order to break the vicious cycle of abusive parents producing children who then become abusive parents, Kempe and Helfer, as well as others treating abusive parents, suggest that these parents receive therapy that supports their self-image. At the same time, these parents need training in parenting, which they did not receive from their own parents, so that they learn what they should realistically expect from children at various ages. These specialists believe that with the proper training, the majority of abusive parents can learn to overcome their problem. In recent years, self-help organizations such as Parents Anonymous have formed a network of support groups that allow child abusers to admit what they have done and gain knowledge and encouragement to change from others who have had the same problem.

Source: C. Henry Kempe and Ray E. Helfer (eds.), *Helping the Battered Child and His Family*, 1972, pp. 4–5. Used by permission of J. B. Lippincott Company.

tuted against lower-class parents. Lower-class parents are also more likely to fit the profile of the neglectful parent. They are more likely to be poor, more likely to have single-parent households, and less likely to be able to afford supervision for their children while they are at work. Since their access to care is limited, lower-class parents are also more likely to have emotional and personality difficulties that go untreated. Lacking access to care or the funds to obtain it, they are more likely to have children with medical or psychiatric needs that have gone unmet. These are prime ingredients for neglect charges. The situation is further complicated by the great variations from one state to another in neglect statutes, some of which are stated in Box 11.4.

BOX 11.4 What Constitutes Neglect

Stanford N. Katz, in his book *When Parents Fail* (1971), reviewed neglect statutes in the various states and found enormous variations in stipulations as to when and under what circumstances a child can be considered neglected and thus in need of being removed from his or her natural parents. Below are 18 of the many different specifications. Neglect can be charged when:

1. a child lacks parental care because of the parent's fault or the parent's mental or physical disability.
2. a parent refuses or neglects to provide for a child's needs.
3. a parent has abandoned a child.
4. a child's home, by reason of neglect, cruelty, or depravity of the parent, is unfit.
5. a parent refuses to provide for a child's moral needs.
6. a parent refuses to provide for a child's mental needs.
7. a child's best interests are not being met.
8. a child's environment, behavior, or associations are injurious to him or her.
9. a child begs, receives alms, or sings in the street for money.
10. a child associates with disreputable or immoral people or lives in a house of ill repute.
11. a child is found or employed in a bar.
12. a child's occupation is dangerous or when the child is working contrary to the child labor laws.
13. a child is living in an unlicensed foster home or has been placed by its parents in a way detrimental to the child or contrary to law.
14. a child's conduct is delinquent as a result of parental neglect.
15. a child is in danger of being brought up to lead an idle, dissolute, or immoral life.
16. a mother is unmarried and without adequate provision for the care and support of her child.
17. a parent, or another with the parent's consent, performs an immoral or illegal act before a child.
18. a parent habitually uses profane language in front of a child. (pp. 57–58)

Source: From *When Parents Fail: The Law's Response to Family Breakdown* by Stanford N. Katz. Copyright © 1971 by Stanford N. Katz. Reprinted by permission of Beacon Press.

As the list shows, the problem with child-neglect statutes is that they contain vague, ill-defined language that is open to wide interpretation. For example, Kathy's father smokes marijuana at home in the evenings. Is Kathy being neglected? Is she, as statute #15 puts it, "in danger of being brought up to lead an idle, dissolute, or immoral life?" Could Kathy be removed from her home on the grounds that she is being neglected? Perhaps. But a closer look at Kathy's home life reveals that her father is a physician, her mother writes articles for the local newspaper, and Kathy herself is in the upper 10 percent of her class and attends Sunday school. Kathy knows her father smokes marijuana in the evenings; she also knows he does not drink hard liquor. Does Kathy feel she is being neglected? No.

We can be certain that if charges of neglect were brought against Kathy's father, a battery of lawyers would be hired to fight the charge. But if her father were a part-time auto mechanic with an eighth-grade education, perhaps a member of a minority group or someone unaware of his legal rights, the possibility that his daughter might be taken from him for the same behavior is far greater, at least in the lower courts. The higher courts have displayed a different attitude: "Appellate judges appear increasingly unwilling to employ neglect laws to impose their middle-class mores upon families and to punish a parent's undesirable conduct unless [it] can be shown to result in damage to the child" (Katz 1971, p. 69).

Questions of parental versus children's rights remain, even though the law is tending to rule on the side of the child. For example, some parents bitterly protest the idea that, according to laws in their state, their 15-year-old daughter has to have parental consent to have her ears pierced, but she has the legal right to obtain birth-control devices, and even abortion, without her parents' knowledge or consent. Some parents strongly disapprove of the education their children are receiving in the public schools, finding it inadequate and devoid of intellectual content. They wish to take their children out of school and educate them at home. The state very often refuses to permit such actions by the parents, no matter how well qualified they may be to teach their children at home. The trend in this century has been for the state to assume more power in matters of neglect, abuse, and children's rights. While disagreement exists concerning parents, children's, and states' rights, it is important to keep in mind those situations of serious child abuse or neglect that require outside intervention to protect the child.

Despite the fact that children's rights and parents' rights sometimes come into conflict, parents are usually able to contribute to the best interests of their children. This is most likely to happen when parents have learned what those interests are, when society supports them in their parenting task, and when the individual parents continue to be responsive to individual traits and developmental changes in their children as they move from infancy to adulthood.

Our increasing understanding of genetic influence, prenatal influence, and the many individual differences caused by the interaction of social class and heredity may help to relieve parents of the feeling that everything that happens is "their fault." Given a reasonably positive set of environmental circumstances and at least a moderate degree of hopefulness about living, the ordinary sensitive mother and the ordinary sensitive father have the capability to raise a healthy child.

SUMMARY

1. The primary objectives of this chapter include an investigation of the strengths and stresses of the parenthood role in the United States; a

presentation of current research and theory related to attachment behaviors and needs; an exploration of the outcome of differing child-rearing practices; and a review of the concept of children's rights, particularly the right to freedom from abuse and neglect.

2. The parenthood role in contemporary American society is often described as overwhelming and confusing. Several factors combine to produce stress, especially for new parents. These factors include changing social perspectives on the roles of mother and father, extremely high standards for child rearing, social isolation, especially of mothers, and conflicting advice from experts about child rearing.

3. Recent research on infant behavior indicates a series of complex behaviors evident at birth that allow the newborn to interact in a socially cooperative manner with adult caregivers in order to insure survival. These complex abilities are referred to as attachment behaviors and seem to play a part in the bonding process between infant and parents. Attachment needs continue throughout life as human beings seek the nurturance and support necessary for their physical and emotional well-being.

4. Empathy, or the ability to understand what another person is feeling, is an extremely important ability in parenting. As discussed in earlier chapters, empathy is also an important component in establishing and maintaining intimate relationships such as marriage.

5. Contemporary research on child-rearing patterns indicates that parenting according to a model that combines fondness and firmness, termed the authoritative approach, seems to produce the healthiest children. The effectiveness of punishment as a means of setting limits depends upon appropriate timing and intensity. Punishment works best in the context of love and consistency, tempered with the giving of reasons appropriate to the child's developmental level.

6. Prosocial behaviors such as cooperation and empathy are strongly encouraged by parental models who engage in such behaviors themselves. On television, and perhaps in real life, children witness numerous examples of aggression, violence, and antisocial acts. Awareness of how children learn through the observation of models should alert parents to the need to monitor TV viewing and to provide counterbalancing examples of prosocial interaction.

7. The socioeconomic status of parents, the ethnic background of the family, and personal qualities of the child all influence the upbringing of children. Class differences in parenting style seem to relate to occupational differences, with middle-class children more apt to be trained for self-directed work, while working-class children tend to be reared for work that is supervised and cooperative.

8. Questions concerning the rights of children, particularly the right to freedom from abuse and neglect, raise complex problems in relation to the rights of parents and the role of the state. Traditionally the United

States has maintained that the family, especially the family of birth, is the most appropriate environment for the child. The courts have been reluctant, except in extreme cases, to remove a child from his or her parents. Issues related to changing family patterns and social attitudes will continue to raise questions about the appropriate balance between the rights of children and the rights of parents.

KEY CONCEPTS

Attachment behavior   Abuse
Parental empathy   Neglect
Styles of parenting   Children's rights
Discipline

QUESTIONS

1. Consider your own experiences as a parent or a child and describe what you think are the most difficult aspects of parenthood. Do you agree that most parents find their role confusing and lack preparation for this undertaking? Why or why not?
2. Observe adults in interaction with infants. Do adults respond to babies in the same way as they do to older children or other adults? If not, what differences in behavior were noted? Where do you think adults learn how to interact with infants?
3. Based on the information presented in this chapter, discuss and give examples of how attachment and empathy needs begin at birth and continue throughout life. Why are these two needs important to intimate partnerships between adults?
4. Do you think that spanking a young child is ever justified? If so, under what conditions? Would you place any conditions on spanking as a form of punishment?
5. Define a program for parents suggesting procedures for the encouragement of prosocial behaviors such as cooperation, kindness, and empathy in children of various ages.
6. Investigate how child abuse and neglect are defined in your community. How are such cases usually handled? What is the most common outcome? What programs would you institute to prevent child abuse and neglect?

SUGGESTED READINGS

- Chilman, Catherine S. "Parent Satisfactions-Dissatisfactions and Their Correlates." *Social Service Review* 53, no. 2 (June 1979): 195–213. An investigation of the satisfactions and dissatisfactions of mothers and fathers with family life, especially the role of parenthood. One important finding indicates that feelings of competence as a parent and high marital satisfaction are positively correlated with satisfaction in the parenting role.

- Clarke-Stewart, Alison, and Koch, Joanne. *Children: Development Through Adolescence*. New York: Wiley, 1983. A lively presentation of child and adolescent development, with many applications to contemporary life. The book pays special attention to individual differences among children in terms of temperament, intellectual styles and levels, and creativity.
- Eiduson, Bernice T. "Child Development in Emergent Family Styles." *Children Today* (March–April 1978), pp. 24–31. An interim report of a long-term study to investigate the effects of different life patterns on child development. Two hundred children growing up in various family situations, such as single-mother households, communes, and traditional two-parent families, are being compared in relation to environment, socialization practices, and physical and mental development.
- Friday, Nancy. *My Mother/My Self*. New York: Dell Publishing, 1977. An intriguing personal account of the emotional condition of women, based on a daughter's search for identity. The author recognizes the crucial tie between mothers and daughters, which lasts throughout a lifetime and affects all other significant relationships.
- Gallas, Howard B., ed. "Teenage Parenting: Social Determinants and Consequences." *Journal of Social Issues* 36 (Winter 1980). All of the articles in this journal issue focus on topics related to teenage childbearing and child rearing. Content includes socialization for childbearing, the father's impact on the mother-child system, coping with unmarried motherhood, and related topics.
- Hersh, Stephen P., and Levin, Karen. "How Love Begins Between Parent and Child." *Children Today* 7, no. 2 (1978): 2–6. A capsule view of recent research on the initial encounters between newborn infants and their parents. The article touches on much of the work that documents the first interactions between infants and adults moments after birth.
- Klein, Carole. *The Single Parent Experience*. New York: Avon Books, 1973. An interesting book exploring single parenthood as a lifestyle pattern in a realistic manner, with frank attention to the problems and stresses of this family form. The author includes a liberal number of interviews with single parents.
- Lynn, David B. *The Father: His Role in Child Development*. Monterey, Calif.: Brooks/Cole Publishing, 1974. A comprehensive review of research and theory related to fathering. Attention is given to the role of fathers in history and across cultures, as well as the father's influence on child development in such areas as sex roles, aggression, and mental health.
- Mirandé, Alfredo, and Enriquez, Evangelina. *La Chicana: The Mexican-*

American Woman. Chicago: The University of Chicago Press, 1981 (paperback). A review of the history and current status of Chicana women in the United States. A particularly relevant chapter on women in the family discusses values, characteristics, and roles involved in parenting and socialization.

- National Council on Family Relations. *The Family Coordinator* 28, no. 4 (October 1979). The entire issue of this journal focuses on men's roles in the family. Several articles include discussions of the father-child relationship: fathers as caregivers for newborn infants, single fathers, and homosexual fathers.

- Rodgers-Rose, LaFrances, ed. *The Black Woman*. Beverly Hills, Calif.: Sage Publications, 1980. Several articles in this collection focus on the role of parenthood for black women. Relevant topics include black family roles, child rearing, and socialization goals.

C H A P T E R 12

Relationship Termination

MOTHER: Annie, Scott—Dad and I have something to tell you.

FATHER: You know that your mother and I haven't been getting along too well, right?

ANNIE: Like the big fight over who should do the dishes last night?

SCOTT: Or the one about Mom's two-hundred-dollar suit. Boy, that lasted for three days.

FATHER: Yes, well, there have been lots of disagreements. Mom and I don't seem to agree on very much of anything, anymore.

SCOTT: Can I watch "The Incredible Hulk" now?

ANNIE: You're getting a divorce, aren't you?

MOTHER: Well . . . yes, yes, we are, but it has nothing to do with you or your brother. I mean we're not doing this in any way because of you kids.

SCOTT: A divorce?

FATHER: It's not because of any naughty thing you ever did, Scott, or any rules you've broken.

SCOTT: Why can't you just make up, like you always tell us to do after we fight?

MOTHER: We've tried. In fact, Dad and I have been going to a marriage counselor, a special person who helps you to get along.

ANNIE: You must have really picked a dumb marriage counselor.

SCOTT: Get another one.

FATHER: No, Scott, we've decided, Mom and I. We just can't make each other happy.

ANNIE: Patty's father moved away. She only sees him at Christmas and the Fourth of July.

FATHER: I'm not moving away. I'll be taking an apartment nearby. You can call me any time. I promise I won't leave you kids.

ANNIE: When you got married, you promised, you promised to love each other "till death do us part." Well, Mom isn't dead, is she?

FATHER: We've tried, Annie. We just can't make it together.

MOTHER: Annie, we know it's hard, but try to understand; what Dad and I once had, *that* is dead.

INTRODUCTION

Why do couples remain married? Is the stability of a marriage the product of happy spouses or an indication of strong religious or social pressures against divorce? The causes of divorce are diverse and complex. One cannot separate the social factors that contribute to divorce from the economic ones, nor can these be separated from psychological factors.

Those who study population trends and the statistics of marriage and divorce can tell us something about those who divorce: age, race, social and economic status. These indicators supply information with which one can make an educated guess as to which couples are most likely to divorce. In some ways, it is like handicapping a horse race. You can find out about who the horse's mother and father were; you know how old the horse is, what the name of the jockey is and how much he or she weighs, as well as where the horse finished in previous races. You take all this information and develop the odds for or against the horse's winning. For certain couples, like certain horses, the odds are good; for others, the odds are poor.

In this chapter we shall try to get a clear picture from the statistics about the trends in divorce and remarriage. We shall look at those who are getting divorced and then, using some of the approaches to psychological and social development we have already explored, offer some suggestions as to why people divorce. As divorce becomes more commonplace, involving millions of Americans, the *why* becomes more complex. One couple may divorce because they (or one of them) lacked a positive model for family life during their childhood; one couple may divorce because the husband is abusive (that was *his* distorted model), while another couple may divorce when one of them finds a more attractive and compatible partner.

The sheer increase in the number of divorces has affected the way spouses and children feel about themselves after a divorce. Divorce was once considered a sign of failure, carrying a stigma for both husband and wife. Divorced persons felt a degree of alienation from "married" society. Somehow they had "failed" in their effort to achieve what so many others had—marital happiness. We now see that "so many others" have not had successful marriages. Children, too, once felt stigmatized by divorce. They were the only ones in their class whose father wasn't living at home. Now the child has numerous companions who are living in single-parent homes. Though children still bear a psychological burden when divorce occurs, they are often relieved by reassurance from parents and others that they are not the cause of the divorce.

Changed attitudes about divorce and more effective research now indicate that the psychological impact of divorce, while often severe and stressful, can be mitigated over time by the handling of the divorce and the strengths of the parents and children involved.

FACTS ABOUT DIVORCE

Understanding Divorce Statistics

Looking at divorce statistics is like looking at an eight-ounce glass that contains four ounces: is the glass half empty or half full? Nearly half of all marriages will end in divorce; more than half of all marriages will remain intact. One difficulty with divorce rates is finding an accurate figure. Three easy-to-understand methods of looking at the divorce rate are offered below by Andrew Hacker:

If the present pattern continues, 40 percent of all women in their late twenties currently getting married will end up being divorced. As follows:

Among every 100 first marriages, 38 will result in divorce. Among those 38 divorced women, 29 will remarry. And 13 of those 29 will get divorced again.

So the original 100 women will have 51 divorces (38 plus 13) out of their 129 marriages (100 plus 29). And 51 out of 129 makes a rate of 40 percent.

(The divorce rate for first marriages is 38 per 100, as noted. For second marriages, it is 45 per 100.)

Another way to compute the divorce "rate" is by comparing the annual ratio of marriages to divorces. In 1976 there were 50 divorces for every 100 marriages in the country as a whole. Oregon and California led the list with 83 and 89 per 100. South Carolina and South Dakota were at the bottom with 21 and 22 per 100.

A third method simply records the number of divorces per 1,000 people in the population. In 1915, the national rate was one per 1,000. By 1966, it was 2.5 per 1,000. The latest figure, for 1977, is 5.1 per 1,000.

[Sources: Paul C. Glick and Arthur J. Norton, *Marrying, Divorcing and Living Together in the U.S. Today* (Population Reference Bureau, 1977), pp. 36–37; *Statistical Abstract of the United States* (U.S. Government Printing Office, 1978), Tables 114, 118, 119.] (Hacker 1979, p. 26)

For our purposes, we will say that four out of every ten marriages will end in divorce—the 40 percent calculated by Hacker's first method.

Who divorces? The median age for men is 29; the median age for women is 27. Fully two-thirds of first divorces involve women in their twenties. And 72 percent of those divorced women will have children at the time of their divorce. This circumstance vastly complicates the effects of the divorce. It also reduces divorced women's chances of remarriage, though age is a more significant predictor of remarriage for women than the presence of children. (We shall discuss remarriage statistics later in this chapter.)

Factors Associated with Divorce

Marital surveys taken by the U.S. Census Bureau have found some statistical correlations that suggest that certain factors—such as age, educational level, race, and socioeconomic status—relate to divorce. Such correlations say nothing about underlying psychological causes of divorce, but they do indicate which groups of people are more likely to divorce. (The census figures are for divorce ending a *first* marriage.)

Age and Education. Divorce seems to be most common among young people and those with less education. "Teenage marriages are twice as likely to end in divorce as marriages that occur in the twenties" (Norton and Glick 1979, p. 15). Youth and lack of education typically occur together. For example, women who marry at 17 probably have at best a high-school education. When researchers examined the relative influence of age versus education, they found the influence of education by itself to be minimal. Age is the key variable.

Youthful marriages fail more frequently than more mature marriages regardless of educational levels of the partners. The immature person has limited social resources because he or she has had less experience in social interaction. She or he may not have integrated the various aspects of identity into a firm and positive self-image. The possibility that the marriage was a way to escape from home is greater, and if one or both of the pair bring social immaturity to the marriage, the relationship may degenerate into a parent-child type of dependency (Lewis and Spanier 1979).

Race.   Probably for economic reasons, black couples divorce more frequently than whites. In 1975 the divorce rate among black couples between 35 and 44 years of age was as high as 25 percent; in the same year, divorce rates in the same age group were 19 percent for white men and 21 percent for white women. In addition, the percentage of couples separated but not divorced was higher for blacks than for whites. Another major difference in marriage patterns for blacks and whites was that white divorced women remarried much sooner than black divorced women (Norton and Glick 1979, p. 15). When income levels for blacks and whites are controlled, however, divorce rate differences for those in similar income brackets are less dramatic (Cutright 1971).

Socioeconomic Status.   The greater likelihood that blacks will divorce and their reluctance or inability to remarry are due in part to the social and economic disadvantages of this group in the United States. Poor people of all races and ethnic identifications tend to divorce more readily than economically advantaged people, at least in this century, when divorces have been fairly easy to obtain. (In earlier times, only the rich and powerful could divorce legally, and even then very few did.) Environmental conditions associated with marital and family problems are indicated in Figure 12.1; "inadequate income" leads the list.

The gap between rich and poor, especially among males, narrowed somewhat in the social upheaval of the 1960s. This apparently permanent change was reflected in the 1970 census report on divorce rates of males from the ages of 35 to 44. This age group was old enough to contract and break marriages and still young enough to reflect the impact of the important social changes of the 1960s. The census showed that these changes affected middle- and upper-class males more than any other social or economic group. The higher-status males continued to be relatively unlikely to divorce, but the gap between upper- and lower-status males narrowed in this period. The steadily rising divorce rate increased *more* rapidly among males who had high status in terms of education, occupation, and income than it did for more disadvantaged males (Norton and Glick 1979, pp. 13–14). In fact, the proportion of divorced men with one or more years of college rose to the level for all other men, according to a 1975 survey by the Census Bureau. It is still true, however, that men and women with a full four years of college have the lowest divorce rates.

In short, socioeconomic differences in divorce rates are now smaller

FIGURE 12.1 Environmental Conditions Presenting Serious Problems for Clients*

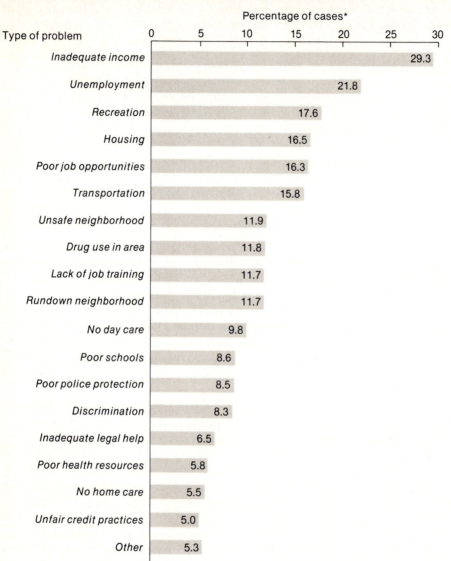

* Data based on reports from 1,543 cases served by family service agencies during a sample week for which judgments were available from both counselors and clients on environmental problems presenting serious problems for the families of these clients. Problems were counted as present if reported by either counselor, client, or both as serious.

† Sample limited to cases with client follow-up report.

Source: Adapted from *Progress on Family Problems: A Nationwide Study of Clients' and Counselors' Views on Family Agency Services*, by Dorothy Fahs Beck and Mary Ann Jones, p. 43, by permission of the publisher. Copyright 1973 by Family Service Association of America, New York.

than they used to be. Relaxed divorce laws and changing social norms have created a climate in which people of all social and economic levels view divorce as an acceptable alternative to an unhappy or boring marriage.

Factors Influencing the Rise in the Divorce Rate

The dramatic rise in divorce in the last few decades can be traced to a variety of factors, including more liberal divorce laws and changing sex roles. As we saw in Chapter 7, dramatic changes in sex roles have created strains that can affect marriages. Most married women are now working. For nearly half of the married women, work is interrupted only briefly for the birth of a child. Roles of husbands and wives are no longer simply complementary and clearly defined, with the husband acting as chief provider and the wife as mother and homemaker. Because she, too, contributes to the family's income, a married woman may expect more power in decision making and a more equitable distribution of household responsibilities. Such role changes call for major adjustments on the part of both spouses—adjustments that can be disruptive to a marriage (Norton and Glick 1979, p. 12).

Another factor in rising divorce rates is the growing acceptance of divorce as a reasonable alternative to an unhappy marriage. This acceptance has found legal recognition in divorce-law reforms that have lowered the costs of divorce, made free legal services available to poor families, and simplified divorce procedures. In some states, the period of state residence as well as the period of separation required to obtain a divorce has been shortened. No-fault divorce has been introduced in many states. No-fault does away with the concept that one party is responsible for the dissolution of the marriage.

Divorce-law reforms reflect a major change in society's view of divorce. Divorce was once considered to be a sign of immorality and a source of public censure. Divorce was granted only if one spouse badly misbehaved, by committing adultery, for instance, or through cruelty or desertion. In eighteenth-century America, a judge granted divorce only to a wife or husband whose spouse had failed to meet minimal conjugal standards. Divorce was a punishment, not a right (Bohannan 1970, pp. 43–44). The new attitude regards divorce as a right of citizens, not unlike their right to marry; divorce is now within the bounds of morality.

MARITAL STABILITY VERSUS DIVORCE

There are two central questions about marriage and divorce. One is "Why do some marriages end in divorce, while others remain intact?" This question refers to *marital stability*, to marriages terminated only by the natural death of one spouse, not by the will of one or both spouses. The other central question is "What makes a marriage happy?" This is a question about *marital quality*, the role satisfaction, management of conflict, effectiveness of communication, integration, and overall happiness of the married pair. The questions are different, but related in a crucial way. Two different couples may be equally unhappy, yet one couple may separate and the other may not. Many unsatisfactory marriages do not dissolve; a few good marriages may end in divorce (Lewis and Spanier 1979, p. 271). Yet, for the most part, couples who are happy remain together, and those who are not find divorce an increasingly acceptable alternative. Thus, stability and quality are now more likely to occur together in marriages.

Remember the first time you played with magnets? First you found that the magnet could actually pull pieces of metal. Then you placed two magnets on either side of a batch of metal filings. When you moved the magnets in opposite directions, the batch of filings in the middle was dispersed. George Levinger (1979) developed a theory of marital stability that reminds one of the magnets and the pieces of metal. Think of the magnets on either side as husband and wife, and the metal filings as their marriage. There are the pulls that bring two people together, such as status, money, and affection; Levinger calls these *attractions to marriage*. There are also *barriers to divorce* that reduce the pull away from marriage: fear of being lonely or alienated from friends and family, concerns over the effects of the divorce on children. Finally, there are forces that pull the two people apart—away from the marriage—such as economic independence or sexual and affectional appeals exerted by others.

Attractions to Marriage

Being married has certain economic, symbolic, and affectional rewards or attractions. Women have been an economically disadvantaged group; for them marriage has had substantial material rewards. To some extent, this continues to be true. In marrying, a woman traditionally chooses not only a husband, but also a standard of living. A man's standard of living also is often raised through marriage. It may take the combined incomes of *two* working adults to make home ownership feasible, for instance.

Symbolic rewards involve the status of partners in a marriage. A woman who marries a man whose educational and occupational status she perceives as high gets gratification from identifying with him: his status enhances hers. The reverse is sometimes true: men gain symbolic rewards by identifying with their wives' educational attainments or career successes.

Given the traditional male and female stereotypes that demand male independence and accomplishment, this pattern is still less common.

Affectional rewards of marriage include companionship, mutual esteem, and sexual enjoyment (Levinger 1979, pp. 44–50). As women achieve more economic independence and gain status based on their own individual accomplishments, the symbolic attractions of marriage are likely to diminish, while the affectional attractions gain more prominence.

Barriers to Divorce

Sanctions against divorce are both internal, dictated by conscience and feelings of guilt, and external, prescribed by legal, economic, or social considerations.

Even if it is never openly discussed, most couples consider divorce during moments of intense marital conflict or hurt. Barriers can inhibit such a drastic measure. For example, if either has strong religious beliefs concerning the sanctity and importance of the marriage bond, he or she probably will not seek a divorce. Obligation to the marital bond is influenced by a variety of factors in addition to religious belief. Both the length of a couple's acquaintance before marriage and the length of the actual marriage strengthen their feelings of obligation to the marriage bond. Studies have found that the longer an existing marriage has lasted, the less likely it is to dissolve. Not surprisingly, each partner's personal and family experience with marriage also influences his or her feelings of obligation. Has the person been divorced before? Is there a history of divorce between parents of either partner? Both these factors are correlated with a somewhat higher divorce rate and may tend to lessen the symbolic cost of divorce for that partner (Levinger 1979, pp. 51–52).

Community pressures also may attach a stigma to divorce. Community pressures are more intense in small or rural communities than in large or urban areas. People from small towns and farming families (other than migrant laborers, who make up a different group) have divorce rates that are substantially lower than those for city dwellers. This suggests that the stigma attached to divorce remains greater in small communities (Levinger 1979, p. 54).

Children present another barrier to divorce. A couple with children may be less inclined to get a divorce, in spite of serious difficulties. Staying together "for the sake of the children" was once a cliché among unhappily married couples. It is less so today when more and more couples are proceeding with divorces even when they have children. It still remains true, however, that children are a barrier to divorce for many couples. Childless couples have higher separation rates than child-rearing couples, although children can serve to decrease marital satisfaction at certain periods. Indirectly, children can exacerbate marital difficulties. In terms of the immediate decision to divorce, however, children may delay or prevent the decision (Levinger 1979, pp. 54–55).

Pushes and Pulls of the Primary Group

Pressures from primary groups and family, friends, religious and other community members can act as external barriers to divorce. A *primary group* is a network of friends and relatives who can act as a barrier against divorce, because a divorce between husband and wife would also destroy the cohesiveness of the primary group. But primary groups can also hasten a divorce if they compete for the loyalty and affection of the two spouses.

Extended family and friends can act as a barrier to divorce. (Jerry Howard, Positive Images)

In *Romeo and Juliet,* the Capulets and the Montagues attempted to divide the lovers by their rivalry and dissension. As explained in Chapter 6 on mate selection, when a relationship is new, as in the early stages of courtship, resistance to the couple or family differences can lend a certain attraction. It satisfies the taste for daring and defiance, the need to set ourselves apart from our parents. However, once a marriage is established, and especially when the spouses are well into their adult years, hostility on the part of the kinship network can undermine the relationship.

Primary group affiliations are more likely to conflict when there are marked religious differences, as when a Catholic marries a Protestant or an Orthodox Jew. In such interfaith marriages, when each spouse maintains an allegiance to the family and religion of his or her origin, the kinship networks of the two spouses may conflict and compete for their married children's affections. Religious differences also create conflicts of obligation within the marriage. A wife who is nominally Protestant but received no religious training may not understand her Jewish husband's insistence on spending Jewish holidays with his parental kin; such strong religious and family pressures are not part of her predominantly secular experience. It is perhaps not surprising, in view of the potentially conflicting obligations of interfaith marriages, that such marriages have a divorce rate higher than same-faith (or *intra*faith) marriages (Levinger 1979, p. 53).

Alternative Attractions

Whether they are conscious of it or not, most spouses occasionally compare their married state with alternative life situations. Levinger calls these "sources of alternative attraction." A typical case of this is the man who has an affair with another woman and eventually, preferring this second attachment, leaves his wife. This case is not as common, Levinger believes, as movies and novels would suggest. Levinger estimates that in 15 to 35 percent of divorces, sexual incompatibility and infidelity play a part. This motive for divorce—finding "someone else"—diminishes as couples grow older and the possibilities of remarriage decrease, especially for women (Levinger 1979, p. 57).

Economic rewards, such as the wife's opportunity for independent income if she divorces her husband, may be an alternative source of attraction. Although divorce usually brings economic hardships, sometimes one spouse can improve his or her financial well-being by divorcing. The new opportunities opening for women mean that many of them can hope to have a comparable economic status after divorce, especially if they have a high degree of education or training.

In many cultures, divorce rates vary directly with the status of women. The easier it is for women to achieve economic independence, the higher the divorce rate. A woman can leave the marriage more readily if she can support herself outside the relationship, as is becoming increasingly true in Western countries. In all of these cases, the distraught spouse who seeks a divorce must expect to find not only a comparable income, but also a more pleasant existence outside marriage (Levinger 1979, pp. 55–57; Lewis and Spanier 1979, pp. 272–273).

Marital Quality

Lewis and Spanier argue that "the quality of most American marriages is the primary determinant of whether a marriage will remain intact" (1979, p. 268). Quality develops over time and requires commitment. The willingness of a couple to work at their marriage depends on the many factors that we have discussed in this and previous chapters. These include the kind of parental models and childhood experiences each spouse has had, mutual regard, ability to communicate and manage conflict, sexual satisfaction and affection, a sharing of values and goals, and some flexibility in role expectations.

Initially, most couples bring some false expectations or unsuitable motivations to a marriage. Expectations of constant and intense love, inflexible attitudes concerning sex roles, hopes that marriage will cure loneliness or that children will solve marital problems—these are some common "mirages of marriage" (Lederer and Jackson 1968). Almost all couples are surprised when they find out what married life is really like. As one newly married young woman put it:

Marriage is not what I had assumed it would be. One premarital assumption after another has crashed down on my head. I am going to make my marriage work, but it's going to take a lot of hard work and readjusting. Marriage is like taking an airplane to Florida for a relaxing vacation in January, and when you get off the plane you find you're in the Swiss Alps. There is cold and snow instead of swimming and sunshine. Well, after you buy winter clothes and learn how to ski and learn how to talk a new foreign language, I guess you can have just as good a vacation in the Swiss Alps as you can in Florida. But I can tell you, . . . it's one hell of a surprise when you get off that marital airplane and find that everything is far different from what one had assumed. (Lederer and Jackson 1968, p. 39)

Simply recognizing that some of one's expectations concerning marriage are false, or even acknowledging the areas of difficulty in the marriage, does not necessarily prevent divorce from occurring. Marriages may be unstable or lacking in quality for a number of reasons, including inadequate resources, unbridgeable gaps due to differences in social, economic, or intellectual backgrounds, poor parent models, lack of mutual regard, ineffective communication, lack of companionship, inability to manage conflict, having been pressured into marriage, and sexual incompatibility. Some of the initial notions leading to marriage may turn out to be false or inflated. Considering the many false expectations concerning marriage and the numerous areas of potential difficulty, it is surprising that divorce occurs in only four out of ten marriages.

ENDING THE RELATIONSHIP: THE PROCESS OF "BREAKING UP"

To understand the dynamics of divorce, it may be helpful to look at the phenomenon of "breaking up" among couples who are not married. A study of breakups among unmarried couples in college sheds some light on the dissolution of relationships (Hill, Rubin, and Peplau 1979).

Anyone who has discussed a divorce with both partners realizes that the subjective experience of breaking up is quite different for each partner. Among unmarried couples we should not speak of *the* breakup, but of *his* breakup and *her* breakup; among divorcing couples, *his* divorce and *her* divorce.

The relationship that is being dissolved tends to have a "rejecting" party and a "rejected" party. In the affairs studied by Hill and his colleagues, partners experience the breakup very differently. The one who is anxious to leave—the rejecting lover—sees the breakup as rapid; the rejected lover sees it as slow. Estranged lovers rarely agree on the personal or internal causes, though they might agree about certain external circumstances: "He spent all his time studying"; "She went home for vacation." The rejected lover usually cites reasons that would shore up injured self-esteem: "We broke up because I needed more freedom," rather than, "He said we had to end the relationship because I was becoming too possessive." Whether one was the rejecting or the rejected party, former partners (in Hill's study) both claimed they wanted the relationship to end. They would not attribute the breakup to the other. A person generally can cope with change more easily when the change is perceived as something desired, not something imposed by others or by circumstances.

Women in the study of breakups tended to be more sensitive than men to problem areas in the relationship. Their retrospective reports may be somewhat distorted or biased, but if there is any truth in them, they indicate that women found differences in intelligence, conflicting ideas about marriage, desire to be independent, and an interest in someone else to be problem areas in the relationship. In contrast, men were more likely to cite only "living too far apart" as a problem.

Studies on satisfaction over the life cycle also reveal women to be more critical of marital relationships than men (Campbell, Converse, and Rogers 1976). Men and women tend to differ in their emotional responses to breaking up as well. Men leaving an affair suffer greater emotional upset as a result of breaking up. More commonly than women, they reported feelings of depression, loneliness, unhappiness, guilt, and "not being free" (Hill et al. 1979, p. 78). Interviewers for Hill's study were struck by a particular reaction found in men but not in women: their difficulty in reconciling themselves to the fact that they were no longer loved and that the relationship was over. Women were less likely to retain the illusion that the men really loved them after all.

Hill and his coworkers put forward two possible interpretations of the male-female differences they observed in breaking up. On one hand, they offered the more traditional explanation based on economics: Women must be more practical than men in their mate selection for economic reasons. A woman cannot allow herself to fall in love too quickly or afford to stay in love too long with the wrong person, because her years of marriageability are more limited than a man's. "Men . . . can afford the luxury of being romantic." Waller has written:

There is this difference between the man and the woman in the pattern of bourgeois family life: A man, when he marries, chooses a companion and perhaps a helpmate, but a woman chooses a companion and at the same time a standard of living. It is necessary for a woman to be mercenary. (1938, p. 243)

The other interpretation involves women's greater interpersonal sensitivity. The woman is more sensitive than the man to the quality of their interpersonal relationship. Traditionally, one of a woman's roles is to be sensitive, to create harmony, to conciliate. Often men are less sensitive because they have been socialized to view action and accomplishment as more important than sensitivity to others' feelings. This important difference in male and female socialization continues to affect relationships and their dissolution in adult life.

Premarital relationships and breakups can prevent marriages that would otherwise end in divorce from ever taking place. Yet some couples who are incompatible proceed to marry each other and *then* get a divorce. Why doesn't their relationship break up before marriage? A common explanation is that romantic love blinds lovers to the practical considerations of their marriage. But many people in love manage to seek partners who are similar to themselves in age, education, intelligence, social attitudes, and values, so this cannot be the whole explanation. The Hill study suggests that couples who can find external excuses may be more inclined to terminate a relationship. These people can make a graceful exit. Those who have no external excuse sometimes get caught up in the momentum of wedding plans and go through with a marriage that never should have taken place.

Premarital breakups can provide an interesting comparison with marital breakups and divorce, and can possibly be useful in preventing marital breakups. But there are crucial differences between breaking up a relationship and breaking up a marriage. The breakups we have been discussing in this section are more casual and much less stressful than divorce. There is more social disapproval attached to divorce. And it is more difficult for people to meet and become involved with new partners after a divorce than after a breakup. When the breakup of a marriage is imminent, couples may want to seek help from a marriage counselor. The outcome of such counseling ultimately depends on the wishes of the couple. As Box 12.1 suggests, saving a marriage is not the only value of marriage counseling.

THE AFTERMATH OF DIVORCE

Divorce causes a host of major changes in the lives of at least two people. Any change of such magnitude brings stress. At least one person must set up a new household, perhaps move to a new place. Everyday tasks, including chores and child care, must be completely reorganized. The economic structure of the former partners' lives changes. Existing property must be divided between them. Their social networks change as certain friends become "his" and others "hers." Perhaps the most stressful change is from being a spouse to being an autonomous individual; the divorced person must think in terms of "I" instead of "we." Divorced people must establish a new social network that recognizes and accepts this singlehood. In this section we shall look more closely at some of the effects produced by the stress of divorce.

Emotional Reactions to Separation and Divorce

Novelists, essayists, scholars, and filmmakers have noted the various kinds of "craziness" exhibited by the newly separated or just divorced. In Elia Kazan's *The Arrangement*, Eddie Anderson episodically goes "out of his mind" at age 43 when he starts an affair and ends his career as well as his marriage. Although most first divorces occur while the couple are in their twenties, separation and divorce can come at certain crisis points in the life cycle.

In his book, *Divorced in America* (1974), Joseph Epstein captures many of the emotional upheavals that men and women experience during this particularly stressful period in their lives.

Feelings of loneliness, of lostness, and of worthlessness are common among divorced men, and most common of all are thoughts (fantasies?) of returning to the old marriage, of picking up the pieces and putting everyone's life back together again. Frequently, men freshly divorced turn to heavy drinking, or frantic womanizing, or, at the other extreme, hermiting themselves away from any form of social life whatever. Extreme behavior of one kind or another more often than not appears to be the rule, and that a small minority of divorced men, by overdosing themselves, placing their heads in the oven, or firing a

BOX 12.1   Marriage Counseling and Divorce

Marriage counseling does not necessarily "save" a marriage. Couples going for marriage counseling at Family Service Association agencies (Beck and Jones 1973) tended to use therapy to help themselves to do what they wanted to do: couples who intended to stay together usually did, but only a small number of couples who wanted to separate when counseling began decided to reunite after therapy. Even when marriage counseling becomes divorce counseling, the process can be worthwhile. Breaking up a marriage is an emotionally draining and very complicated psychological experience. The presence of a qualified therapist may help husband and wife deal with the loss of the relationship and with their ongoing roles as parents. Effective counseling can explode certain myths concerning marriage and help individuals to avoid making the same mistakes in future relationships (Koch and Koch 1976).

Both the Family Service Association survey (Beck and Jones 1973) and a more recent study of people who filed for divorce but failed to go through with the action (Kitson 1980) suggest that wives who initially want a divorce, then decide to remain married, tend to be making greater emotional sacrifices than husbands in this category. Financial and parenting considerations, rather than real hopes of rebuilding the marriage, are the most typical reasons that some women have a change of heart after filing for divorce.

Finally, a comparative study of couples who benefited from marriage counseling and those who did not (Gottman 1979) suggests that men who are not overtly dominant and who have an emotional investment in the relationship equal to their wives' are most likely to benefit, while women who benefit tend to be those who can openly express their dissatisfaction with the relationship.

Marriages in which conflicts are of long standing are very difficult to help because hostility, role inflexibility, ineffective communication, and general disenchantment tend to increase over time. Unhappy marriages of less than 12 years' duration were more likely to be helped by counseling than those of longer duration (see Table 12.1). Wives seemed to be more responsive to counseling than husbands (Beck and Jones 1973, p. 153).

A variety of studies, then, suggest that some marriages cannot be saved and others perhaps should not be. They are fraught with severe difficulties and no longer have the potential for providing intimacy.

pistol into the backs of their mouths, choose the most extreme act of all, while sad and sickening, is not so surprising. (p. 232)

Women have their own set of often special problems: . . . there is much in the life of a divorced woman that cannot be other than deeply disheartening. A common experience among reasonably attractive women who have recently divorced, for example, seems to be the surprise telephone call from the husband of a friend or from the friend of an ex-husband suggesting a drink, date, or an afternoon at a motel—an incident scarcely calculated to remind one of the great dignity of the race.

In the realm of loneliness divorced women are further disadvantaged in not being able to seek out pleasure so openly or with so clear a conscience as divorced men. . . . Should a newly divorced woman indulge herself in a binge of emotional dishevelment similar to

TABLE 12.1   Couples Helped by Counseling, by Years Married*

	Married Under 12 Years	Married 12 Years or More
Counselor's ratings:		
Husband better	49.7%	38.9%
Wife better	69.3%	61.2%
Clients' ratings:		
Husband better	63.8%	54.2%
Wife better	73.1%	61.7%

* Based on 1,258 couples (served by family agencies) who were living together and whose most important problem was marital. Improvement rates relate only to improvement on the marital problem and not to improvement on other problems dealt with in counseling. Source: Reprinted from *Progress on Family Problems: A Nationwide Study of Clients' and Counselors' Views on Family Agency Services*, by Dorothy Fahs Beck and Mary Ann Jones, by permission of the publisher. Copyright 1973 by Family Service Association of America, New York.

that allowed the newly divorced man, including a period of cynical and destructive feeling toward men, she, too, would be in a tradition of sorts, though one for which no sympathy exists—the tradition, that is, of the manhater, the bitch, the ball-buster.

Yet if a divorced woman has children still at home she is, to some extent, spared some of the problems of divorce loneliness. . . . Children force one to keep up a façade. Even though the façade might initially be put up for the children, it can serve as well to protect the parent . . . from her own most destructive impulses. (pp. 235–237)

Divorce is a complex experience involving emotional, legal, and economic changes. In his book *Divorce and After* (1970), Paul Bohannan describes six "stations" or stages of divorce; each is a difficult process.

1. The Emotional Divorce and the Problem of Grief.   In essence, this is the issue of coming to terms with the "death" of a marriage for which all the parties concerned must, one way or another, mourn.

2. The Legal Divorce and the Problem of Grounds.   The idea that one of the partners in a marriage is responsible for the breakup and therefore should be punished has given way to the more enlightened notion that a relationship can dissolve through irreconcilable differences or "no fault." Still, in some instances where, for example, one spouse has not "forsaken all others" but has become involved with another person, divorce court judges may take that factor into consideration when deciding issues relating to economics and child custody. Though the judicial divorce provides what Bohannan calls "a legal post-mortem on the demise of an intimate relationship" (p. 43), it does not provide the nonlegal supports that might help the couple express the emotions inherent in the divorce process.

In Chapter 3 we suggested that the adversary system of handling divorce, which still prevails in certain states, often adds fuel to the fire. A study of 205 individuals separated from their spouses no longer than 26 months (Spanier and Anderson 1979) revealed that 85 percent of the people desired a change in the adversary legal process as it relates to divorce. "The data suggest that divorce statutes based on an adversary model encourage collusion and dishonesty" (p. 612). The people in the study said they "lied in hearings" and "agreed to trumped-up statements"—many of which were suggested by their attorneys.

3. The Economic Divorce and the Problem of Property. Here the issues will be both financial and emotional. The property must be divided (typically, one-third to one-half goes to the wife). The division of assets can be affected by the desire for revenge, the degree to which the spouses wish to "hurt" each other. A husband may seek to "hide" his financial holdings, allowing his wife the barest necessities, while a wife, on the other hand, may seek to "take" her husband "for everything he's got."

4. The Coparental Divorce and the Problem of Custody. Here again, the issue may be decided by a mixture of what the court wants and what the spouses want for themselves and their ex-spouses. The issues of child custody, child-support payments, and visitation rights may be decided "in the best interests" of the child or as a means of inflicting pain on each other. In both "stations" 3 and 4, divorce lawyers can exert a strong influence—for good or for ill. They wield strong emotional as well as legal influence on their divorcing clients (Koch 1975).

5. The Community Divorce and the Problems of Loneliness. No longer is the couple known as "the Smiths" or "the Joneses." Now each ex-spouse must find his or her own way from the society of marrieds (to which they generally belonged) to the unfamiliar social systems of what Morton M. Hunt (1966) has called "the world of the formerly married"—an often confusing mixture of former relatives, former friends, and a new world of divorced and single people.

6. The Psychic Divorce and the Problems of Autonomy. Now both spouses must sever that part of the other that they had previously internalized. Both spouses must now deal with individual guilt, anger, confusion, pain, and loss in such a way that they re-establish their own societal and emotional identity separate from their former spouse—a task that can often take years (Bohannan 1970, p. 34).

The Effects of Divorce on Children

Throughout the twentieth century, the proportion of children affected by divorce has increased, while the proportion of children affected by the death of a parent has decreased (due to the decline in the death rate).

Overall, the proportion of children whose lives are disrupted due to either divorce or the loss of a parent through death has climbed.

After a careful analysis of census figures, Mary Jo Bane (1979) concluded that an average of 45 to 50 percent of children in the United States suffer a disruption due to death or divorce. An extensive discussion of divorce in *Newsweek* magazine (February 11, 1980) stated that "there are currently 12 million children under the age of 18 whose parents are divorced—and all in all, around one million children a year suffer through the dissolution of their families."

Bane estimates that 23.4 percent of all children born in the United States in 1970, and 30.6 percent of all those born in 1976, will experience the divorce of their parents before they reach their eighteenth birthdays. Another 15 to 20 percent of children born in the 1970s will undergo a period of disruption due to death, long-term separation, or their having been born to an unmarried mother (1979, pp. 281–282).

A *Survey of Economic Opportunity* conducted in 1967 by the U.S. Bureau of the Census interviewed members of 26,500 households to create a picture of each family, using social, economic, and historical information, as well as information about the birthdates of each child. This survey has been used by Bane and others to estimate the incidence and duration of the disruptive effects of divorce on children.

A period of disruption follows the death of a parent, divorce, or separation. The average period of disruption in family life of the families studied was five or six years, but this figure has decreased over the century. This means that spouses are remarrying sooner.

In the vast majority of cases, mothers are awarded custody of children after divorce. Fathers are seeking custody in increasing numbers, but in 1979, at least 95 percent of divorces involving children ended in custody's being granted to the mother (see Box 12.2). Although many divorced fathers see less of their children, and some use divorce as an excuse for desertion, other fathers continue to parent after the divorce, and their continued involvement makes a crucial difference. When this continued father involvement occurs, sons are less likely to behave either aggressively or in a more "feminine" passive fashion. Daughters might show lower academic performance after the divorce, or have difficulties with their relationships with boys later on *if* the father ceases to be a parent. But fathers who continue to parent mitigate the long-range problems of divorce (Hess and Camara 1979).

Children of divorced parents typically show different psychological and behavioral problems than children whose fathers have died. Children of divorced parents may have greater difficulties with aggression and antisocial behavior, while children of widows are more likely to express their difficulties with the loss through anxiety and moodiness.

Hetherington (1972) studied the impact of father absence on lower- and

BOX 12.2 Child Custody: Parenting after Divorce

What happens to American men and their increasingly important role in the family when divorce strikes? Important research on the role of fathers in divorced families gives credence to the *Kramer vs. Kramer* syndrome. The days of the "disposable" father are over.

It was a rare event in the England of 1817 when poet Percy Bysshe Shelley was denied custody of his children because of his "vicious and immoral atheistic beliefs." In those days English law granted fathers nearly absolute right to custody of their children. It was not until the twentieth century that the "tender years" doctrine turned the custodial tide. The notion that children suffer irreparable damage if separated from their mothers in their formative years was supported by Sigmund Freud and a host of child psychologists who followed in his path. Until recently, a father was awarded custody only if the mother could be proved grossly unfit.

In the past decade more fathers have been suing for custody, and many have been granted it. A number of the decisions did not rely on the mother's "losing" in an adversary procedure; as in *Kramer vs. Kramer,* the mothers agreed to give custody—not because they were unfit, but because they wanted to try other things. In a few instances they simply recognized that their husbands would be more suitable parents for one or more of their children.

Psychologists Richard Warshak and John W. Santrock of the University of Texas in Dallas completed a study comparing father custody and mother custody (1979). They used only cases in which the father had gained custody by the mother's agreement—not by a court battle that proved the mother unfit.

Using psychological testing and videotapes of family interaction, the Dallas team found that children aged six to eleven did best with the parent of the same sex—daughters with mothers, sons with fathers. The study also showed that girls living with their fathers were less cooperative, less honest, more demanding, less independent, and less "feminine" than girls living with their mothers. Boys living with their fathers were more mature, social, and self-assured than those living with their mothers. They were also more honest and more cooperative, the team found. The 72 families in the Dallas sample—24 intact, 24 mother-custody, 24 father-custody—were all middle class. But mother-custody families suffered a drastic cut in income following divorce. Father-custody families did not. Add to this the stress of full-time employment for these divorced mothers, some of whom had not worked before, and we see strains on the custodial mother that don't always bear on custodial fathers.

Fathers also tended to have more support from friends, relatives, and various paid helpers—sitters, day-care services, housekeepers. Support systems, both formal and informal, may be more responsive to fathers because their situation as single parents is still relatively rare in our culture. Fathers may also experience less conflict and guilt when taking advantage of available help and day care. After all, they had not stayed home with the children before the divorce, nor had they had the primary caretaking responsibility, so using helpers did not represent a dramatic change for them.

Even when fathers do not have custody of their children—and 95 percent of divorced fathers don't—they play a major role in the psychological health of their

BOX 12.2 (Continued)

offspring. So says a study of family relationships after divorce, conducted by Robert Hess and Kathleen Camara of Stanford University (1979).

Fathers who had a strong, caring relationship with their children and continued to treat them as responsible individuals, rather than guests to be indulged and pampered, had better-adjusted children. "Disneyland fathers"—the term coined by one of the families in the Stanford sample—saw their children infrequently. They picked them up and took them out for expensive excursions, but rarely involved their children in such everyday activities as preparing meals, mowing the lawn, repairing a bike. Their children were markedly less confident and emotionally mature. The outcome for the children—ages nine to eleven in this sample—depended less on the frequency of visits and more on the quality of the interaction that took place when they did meet with Dad.

By comparing these different types of post-divorce situations with intact families, Hess and Camara found that at ages nine to eleven, at least, the sure sense of involvement with both parents was more important to the children than whether parents were "happily" or unhappily divorced or even whether they were divorced at all.

The Dallas and Stanford studies suggest that children growing up with divorced parents do not automatically show more maladjusted behavior than children growing up in intact families. The immediate effects of divorce may be severe, but the long-range effects depend largely on the concern of both parents (Koch and Koch 1980).

middle-class white adolescent girls. She found that daughters of divorced couples show significantly more "acting out" in their sexual behavior; daughters of widows tend to be shy, withdrawn, and nervous compared to other adolescent girls from divorced or intact families. Daughters of widows were less likely to engage in heterosexual activity than the other adolescent girls in the sample.

Telling Children about Divorce and Death.   As we find out more about the effects of divorce, we also learn certain ways of reducing the long-term deficits that divorce can produce. Telling children about an impending divorce is one of the most significant ways of reducing later problems. Judith Wallerstein, principal investigator on the "Children of Divorce" project (see p. 397), advises parents to tell their children about divorce and to gear the explanation to their children's age level. This will not prevent them from experiencing pain and sadness when they hear the news and for many months afterward. Children, like adults, need to mourn the end of one kind of family if they are to become able to deal with the new kind of family. Still, children who are not told about the divorce tend to have more severe, protracted problems later on. They are more likely to blame themselves for the breakup of the family (Wallerstein, interviewed by Koch and Koch 1974).

Telling children about the death of a parent and giving them permission

Fathers who continue strong, caring relationships with their children after divorce have better-adjusted children. (Barbara Alper)

to grieve and mourn are equally important, as many psychoanalysts have documented (Furman 1974). "Deceased loved ones can become ghosts that haunt the mind and make growing up a scary and precarious process. If we can gradually make mourning a conscious, acceptable part of life, we may ultimately diminish the awesome power of death over ourselves and our children" (Koch 1977, p. 80).

Single Parenthood and Its Effects on the Child. The effects of divorce on the child are both direct and indirect. The child is directly affected by the absence or limited availability of the noncustodial parent. If the child must move to a different neighborhood or must change schools, the loss of peers is another direct effect, one that is more serious for school-age and adolescent children.

But many other effects of divorce are indirect: They depend upon the mother's circumstances and attitude (assuming she has custody). In many cases the mother must enter the job market for the first time or increase her commitment of time and energy to work. She is less available than before. When children become older and more self-sufficient, the absence of the mother during the day may not be traumatic. But how does the mother feel about her changed circumstances? One woman may have wanted to be free of the marriage for years. Perhaps she enjoys the challenges of work. Another divorced woman may find the anxiety about her children and the new pressures of work overwhelming. Their different attitudes will be significant in determining the long-range impact of the divorce on the children. The question of dealing with the many roles of the single parent has been explored on pages 214–215. Most single parents suffer, at least temporarily, from role strain.

The multiple stresses of divorce can have an adverse effect on parent-child relationships. Because the mother tends to suffer the most stress, the mother-child relationship is often strained, at least initially. In their study of the immediate and one-year-after effects of divorce on preschoolers, Wallerstein and Kelly (1975) identified 15 lower-middle- and middle-class preschool children who still showed serious psychological problems one year after the divorce. (Wallerstein and Kelly found it normal for children to be extremely upset right after they learn of a divorce.) In 10 of the 15 cases of long-term upset, the children were those whose relationship with their mothers had deteriorated after the divorce. Their mothers had become less nurturant, less supportive, more anxious and tense following the divorce. Evidence shows that if the divorced mother continues to have the support of her ex-husband, the parent-child relationship is least threatened; mothers lacking this support may have difficulty controlling their preschool children (Hetherington, Cox, and Cox 1976).

Effects of Divorce at Different Stages of a Child's Development.   A child's level of development is important in the way he or she experiences and copes with divorce. Each child's response to divorce is unique, depending on individual personality, tolerance for stress, adaptive behaviors, and areas of competence. But children tend to proceed along similar lines of physical, emotional, and cognitive development, and at each stage they will have different skills for coping with their parents' divorce.

In the "Children of Divorce" project, children of 60 middle-class, well-educated families were interviewed intensively at the time of the divorce and one year later (Kelly and Wallerstein 1976; Wallerstein and Kelly 1974, 1975, 1976). The children were asked about their feelings and reactions to the divorce. Preschool children (ages three and one-half to six)

were confused about families and relationships and had no real understanding of what they meant. They also had difficulty in expressing their
feelings, but the predominant feeling among them was self-blame, probably because at this stage of their development they think largely in an
egocentric way. They see the difficulty in their parents' marriage not as an
issue between their parents, but as something that has gone wrong between them and their parents. Divorce is traumatic for them partly
because they lack a firm sense of the continuity of family relationships
following divorce and tend to think that a family is people living in the
same house. If the mother or father moves out, it seems to the child that
the absent parent is no longer part of the family.

Seven- and eight-year-olds are more aware of their feelings and more
open in admitting their sadness. But they are not able to admit their anger
openly. Perhaps this is because at this stage of subjective social reasoning,
children do not understand how someone can simultaneously hold two
opposing feelings of love and anger. As we have explained in our discussion
of social cognition (Chapter 2), children do show increasing awareness of
the inner motives for acts, so that, unlike younger children, they do not
blame themselves for the divorce. Yet seven- and eight-year-olds still have
strong feelings of being abandoned by their parents; some may believe, at
first, that mother was angry at father and drove him from the house. They
may fear antagonizing mother and consequently risking her abandonment
or even being driven away by her. Parents can reduce such anxieties by
reassuring children that the divorce does not mean they will abandon or
expel their children, that they will, in fact, continue to love and cherish
them.

Among nine- and ten-year-olds, the tendency was to hide consciously
feelings of suffering and present a more courageous front to the world.
They realized the difference between feeling a certain thing and acting on
it. With their greater ability to see themselves from others' points of view,
they were sometimes ashamed of their parents' behavior. Youngsters of
this age were also torn by their feelings of loyalty to their family and anger
that such a thing could happen. They experienced a good deal of loneliness
as their parents withdrew their emotional support in the period of crisis.
Quite naturally, they were afraid of not being loved.

Adolescents (from 13 to 18 years of age) were increasingly conscious and
expressive of their feelings of anger, sadness, loss, betrayal, shame, and
embarrassment. They were able to stand outside the family and see things
from a third-person perspective. They had a more realistic view of their
parents and of the significance of divorce than did the younger children.
Just as the preschoolers' inability to take an objective view inhibited their
adjustment to divorce, the adolescents' ability to stand at some distance
from the problem helped them in adjusting. Sensitivity to these develop-

mental differences can help divorcing parents to deal more effectively with the needs of their children. At all ages, the outcome of divorce for children depends on many factors, including the post-divorce behavior of parents, the presence of support networks for both parents and children, and the child's individual resources.

Effects of Unhappy Marriages.   While divorce can have many adverse effects on children, the effects of an ongoing unhappy marriage may be even worse. Nye (1957) questioned a random sample of high school students and then compared responses of students from single-parent homes with those from unhappy and conflict-ridden two-parent homes. Children from single-parent homes showed a lower incidence of psychosomatic illness and delinquent behavior than those from unhappy two-parent homes. Nye found this to be true even when he controlled for socioeconomic status. Adjustment was worse for the children of unhappy, though intact, homes at all socioeconomic levels. Reviewing previous research on separation from a parent against findings concerning the effects of conflict, Rutter (1971) found that conflict had consistently negative effects on children, while separation did not. Finally, a survey of over 2,000 children in need of psychiatric help found children of unhappily married and divorced homes predominating in the ranks of those requiring therapy (Zill 1978). Yet, those whose parents were separated or divorced did not have so great a need for help as those who were still witnessing marital conflict.

Without underestimating the serious effects divorce can have on children, it seems clear that "living with two parents whose relationship is conflict-ridden is much more damaging to the child's adjustment than simply living with a single parent" (Longfellow 1979, pp. 293–294).

Economic Effects of Divorce

Marriage is an economic institution in Western countries. In some states in the United States, husband and wife must own property as a single "legal person"—a unit that has many of the characteristics of a corporation, although technically it is not. Consequently, when a divorce settlement is made, the assets of the "corporation" are separated into two sets. At this stage of divorce, spouses often feel cheated because, as Bohannan notes, there is never enough money (Bohannan 1970, pp. 372–373).

In many cases the economic well-being of a family suffers as a result of divorce. Only half of the time do departing fathers continue giving financial support to their ex-wives and children. Even when mothers receive alimony, most of them must still work full- or part-time. Mothers with custody of their children are especially hurt by divorce. In 1975 the median family income of families with husband and wife was $15,534. But in the same year the median family income for families headed by women was $5,501 (Bane 1979, p. 282). Among families earning less than $5,000 per year, there are more than four times as many female-headed families as male-headed families. But among families earning $10,000 or more per year, there are almost 2.5 times as many male-headed families (Stein 1978, p. 10).

One partial explanation for this figure is that divorce is more common among families who are poor to begin with. Women in these poor families live on a combination of alimony, child support, and public assistance. But whatever a family's economic status, divorce usually does not improve it. Among middle-class families, it is estimated that the woman with custody of her children suffers a drop in income of one-third when the marriage is dissolved (Warshak and Santrok 1979). Figure 12.2 shows the dramatic decline in income for divorced mothers at every economic level. Women with children, without husbands, find themselves in such desperate economic straits partly because it is much more expensive to maintain two households than it is to maintain one. The combined incomes of husband and wife go much further when they are both living in the same house than when they divorce and set up separate households. And single working parents of younger children also face additional expenses in paying for outside help such as child care.

A father's ability to support his first family may be stretched to the limits if he remarries; his income may have been too low in the first place to share with another household. This means that the single mother's earning potential is crucial. Unfortunately, she is likely to suffer the ill-effects of wage discrimination and lack of training. Single mothers are concentrated in low-paying occupational groups, the clerical and operative jobs.

The economic and emotional problems created by divorce are not easily managed. No one can say how long it takes to "get over" a failed marriage. Bohannan's estimate is two or three years. Couples with children and those whose marriages were of long standing require more time to mourn the lost marriage and finally feel reintegrated and whole again.

REMARRIAGE

The majority of couples who divorce will eventually remarry. Men are more likely to remarry than women, and younger women, especially those under 40, are more likely to remarry than older women. Five-sixths of all divorced men remarry, compared with three-fourths of divorced women (Glick 1975, p. 19). According to Levinger's (1979, p. 57) analysis, the re-

FIGURE 12.2   Mean Family Income of Mothers Before and After Divorce or Separation, by
Income Thirds During Marriage

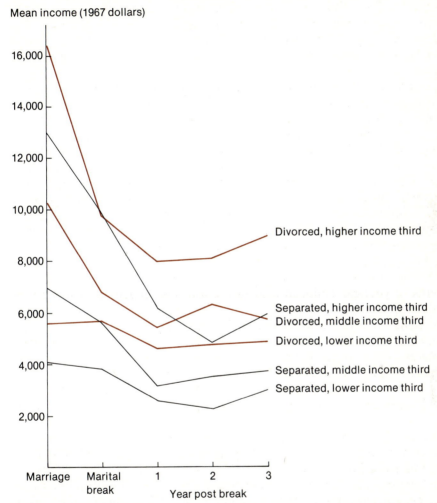

Mean income (1967 dollars)

Divorced, higher income third

Separated, higher income third
Divorced, middle income third

Divorced, lower income third

Separated, middle income third

Separated, lower income third

Marriage   Marital break   Year post break

Source: George Masnick and Mary Jo Bane, *The Nation's Families: 1960–1990* (Cambridge,
Mass.: Joint Center of Urban Studies of M.I.T. and Harvard University, 1980), p. 97.

marriage probabilities for women are 97 percent for 20-year-olds, 80 percent for 30-year-olds, but only 50 percent for 40-year-olds. Male chances
for remarriage also decrease with age, but much less drastically than for
women.

The pool of "eligible" partners, as determined by American dating patterns, increases with age for men and decreases for women. While a 45-year-old man might consider women from the ages of 20 to 45 as eligible partners, very few women of 45 would consider dating or marrying a man 20 years younger than they (Hunt and Hunt 1977; Glick 1976). Take the "typical" divorce: the man 29, the woman 27. When he looks for a second wife, the probabilities are that he will choose a woman five years younger than he. If he remarries fairly soon after his divorce, his second wife will be closer to his own age, but if he waits until he is in his forties, he is more likely to pick a wife who is 10 years younger than he. In contrast, only 14 percent of previously divorced women marry men who are, on an average, five years younger than they (Glick 1975, p. 19).

Divorced women with children are less likely to remarry than childless divorced women, and the odds of remarrying drop as the number of children increases. However, age seems to be a more critical factor than children. A woman in her twenties with three children has a better chance (72 percent) of remarriage than a childless woman in her thirties (60 percent).

In the final chapter of his book *The World of the Formerly Married* (1966), Morton M. Hunt notes that the courtship rules for second marriages are different from first marriages. Formerly marrieds, or "FMs," do not follow the

well-established route . . . [of] . . . dating and necking, petting, going steady, talking about marriage, heavy petting or intercourse, formal engagement and, finally, marriage. FMs ignore this orderly progression: they rarely linger for any time at the dating and necking stage, but proceed swiftly to full sexual relations—in advance of most of the development of feelings of love. (p. 269)

Each potential spouse must get to know the other's children, if there are any. There is little likelihood of a "formal" or celebrated engagement. And if the couple should decide to marry, each partner exchanges vows with the mental reservation, "I hope it works out this time" (Hunt 1966, p. 274).

Will it work out? Perhaps. According to the remarriage rates discussed at the opening of this chapter, slightly more than half of second marriages remain intact. But the complexities of a second marriage are very great. The once-married carry with them the baggage from the previous marriage. If, prior to the second marriage, the divorced person has spent a serious amount of time searching for reasons why the first marriage ended, examining the "mirages of marriage" that he or she once clearly saw as reality, then a second marriage can be a second, fresh start. But if the divorced person has learned little or nothing from the first marriage, if the unrealistic expectations are still deeply held, if the person has failed to grow and mature, then there seems to be little reason to believe that such a person's second marriage will be very different from the first.

Remarriage with children results in a "reconstituted" or "blended" family. (Elizabeth Crews)

One problem unique to second marriages with children is the "reconstituted" or "blended" nature of the new family. The children now have a mother and stepmother, father and stepfather, as well as a plethora of grandparents. This expanded kin network has the potential to provide a large extended family if the parents and stepparents encourage contact with the new relatives. (The special kind of parenting required for the blended family was discussed in Chapter 11, p. 347.)

While a second marriage may indeed be more complicated, the basic ingredients for success are essentially the same as those required in a first marriage. Above all, the couple must have a loving and enduring commitment to work on behalf of themselves, their mates, and their marriage.

SUMMARY

1. The purposes of this chapter are, first, to analyze data on trends in marriage, divorce, and remarriage based on demographic and social-change factors; second, to provide a model of marital stability that considers attractions within and outside the relationship and barriers

to termination; third, to discuss nonmarital breakups; and, fourth, to explore the effects of divorce on the partners in a marriage and on their children.

2. Current statistics on first marriage, divorce, and remarriage show recent increases in divorce and remarriage rates coupled with a declining rate of first marriage. Specific figures on the frequency of divorce are influenced by the method used to calculate divorce rates. It is estimated that nearly two of every three marriages will remain intact "until death do them part."

3. Data on the ending of first marriages through divorce indicate a greater incidence of divorce among those who marry younger, those who have less education, blacks, and economically disadvantaged couples. Changing social attitudes combined with liberalized divorce laws also contribute to the increasing divorce rate.

4. In attempting to understand the numerous factors involved in marital stability and marital dissolution, Levinger has proposed a comprehensive model that includes consideration of *attractions* within the marriage—such as economic and social status positions, mutual esteem, affection, and sexual enjoyment—as well as attractions outside the marriage, such as a more attractive or desirable partner or greater opportunities for economic or personal growth. Another set of factors involves barriers to divorce such as pressure from family and friends to remain married, social and religious sanctions against divorce, and the presence of children.

5. Breakups of unmarried couples are both like and unlike divorce. The person who decides to terminate the relationship (the rejecting partner) tends to experience less emotional trauma than the rejected partner. Breaking up is also less difficult when it is a mutual decision between partners. Several differences between men and women have been found in patterns of breaking up and its aftereffects. There is reason to believe that similar emotional responses are experienced by married and unmarried couples who are breaking up, but divorce involves social, legal, and longevity aspects not likely to be a part of nonmarital breakups. So stressful is divorce that it has been compared to the death of a loved one.

6. The effects that follow a divorce commonly include a reduced standard of living, social isolation, and child-custody and child-rearing difficulties. Although mothers traditionally have been awarded custody of the children in divorce cases, there is a growing recognition that ability to parent is not tied to sex. In addition, the continuing involvement of both parents with the children, even though they are no longer husband and wife, seems a positive contribution to the child's emotional and physical well-being. Children of divorced parents need to understand

that they are not the cause of the marriage dissolution. They also need the continued support and love of both parents.

KEY CONCEPTS

Divorce

Marital stability

Marital quality

Attractions to marriage

Barriers to divorce

Alternative attractions

Stages of divorce

Children and divorce

QUESTIONS

1. Discuss the major changes in contemporary American society that you think have the most impact on the increasing divorce rate. Indicate your reasons for selecting these particular social changes.
2. How do you explain the fact that intimate nonmarital relationships and marriages that seem stable and vital to the relative, friend, or casual observer sometimes end in breakup and divorce?
3. According to your experiences and observations, discuss the reasons why unhappily married couples sometimes remain together "for the sake of the children." Do you think this is a good idea?
4. List the differences found between females and males regarding nonmarital breakups. Assuming these sex differences are generally true for the majority of couples, discuss possible reasons for each difference.
5. Compare and contrast the breakup of serious nonmarital relationships with the termination of marriages through divorce. In what ways are these two situations similar? In what ways are they different?
6. Based on the material presented in this chapter, what kinds of social service and educational programs could be helpful for divorcing spouses? For children of newly divorced parents?

SUGGESTED READINGS

- Bohannan, Paul. *Divorce and After.* New York: Doubleday, 1970. A comprehensive discussion of divorce as a process that generally occurs over a substantial period of time. A significant portion of this work details what the author refers to as the "six stations" of divorce: the different stages and aspects of the process of termination.
- Cuber, John F., and Harroff, Peggy B. "Five Types of Marriage." In *The Significant American*, ed. J. B. Cuber and P. B. Harroff. New York: Hawthorn Books, 1965. A widely quoted work based on the authors' interviews with 211 men and women whose marriages had lasted 10 years or more and who said that they had never seriously considered

divorce or separation. The results of this study provide insights related to the issues of marital stability and marital quality.

- Epstein, Joseph. *Divorced in America*. New York: Dutton, 1974. A practical and personal book that describes and defines divorce in the United States as a social institution and as an individual crisis. Epstein explores the feelings and problems of the divorce experience, such as weekend parenthood, loneliness, a sense of failure, and the struggle of interacting socially and sexually as a formerly married person.

- Glenn, Norval D. "The Well-Being of Persons Remarried After Divorce." *Journal of Family Issues* 2, no. 1 (March 1981): 61–75. A summary of the findings from seven recent national surveys is used to examine the reported happiness of persons who remarry after a divorce. The effects of age, race, and socioeconomic status are considered.

- LeMasters, E. E. *Parents in Modern America*. Homewood, Ill.: Dorsey Press, 1974. The chapter "Parents Without Partners" discusses the situation of the one-parent family, including the particular problems of this life pattern as a result of divorce. Effects such as economic stress, social isolation, and child-rearing difficulties are explored.

- Raschke, Helen J., ed. "Ending Intimate Relationships." *Alternative Lifestyles* 2 (November 1979). This entire journal issue is devoted to articles about the process of relationship termination. Topics covered include divorce, separation, and uncoupling in primary relationships.

- Roman, Mel, and Haddad, William. *The Disposable Parent*. New York: Holt, Rinehart and Winston, 1978. A contemporary work presenting many of the current research findings on the effects of divorce on mothers, fathers, and children. The primary objective of this book is to argue the position for joint custody of children between divorced parents.

- Turow, Rita. *Daddy Doesn't Live Here Anymore*. Garden City, N.Y.: Doubleday, 1978. A practical guide for parents on how to handle children's concerns and questions about marital dissolution. Other common problems confronted by divorcing parents, such as competing for a child's affection, adjusting to a different standard of living, and preparing children for remarriage, are also discussed.

- Women in Transition, Inc. *Women in Transition: A Feminist Handbook on Separation and Divorce*. New York: Charles Scribner's Sons, 1975. A resource guide of information, techniques, materials, and advice compiled by an organization of women from various economic, ethnic, and educational backgrounds who have been through the divorce experience. It offers help to women for many divorce-related problems, from finding a lawyer, apartment, or job to maintaining good health and starting a counseling program for other women facing the difficulties of separation and divorce.

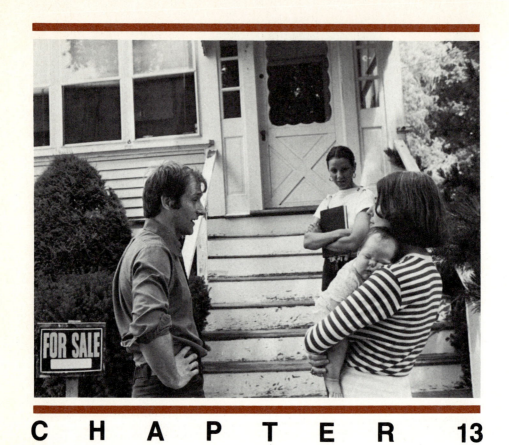

C H A P T E R 13

Achieving Economic
Life Goals in a Family

SHE: I love it.

HE: It's nice.

SHE: But?

HE: But we're not ready for a house.

SHE: This would be the perfect time, just before Mike starts kindergarten.

HE: We don't even have enough for the down payment. And the mortgage payments will be more than our rent now.

SHE: It's an investment. Houses are just going to keep getting more expensive.

HE: Next year I'll be making a little more.

SHE: And they'll be costing a little more. Look at this family room.

HE: It's not just the house. It will mean carpeting and new furniture. We're already overextended. I can't handle it.

SHE: But you won't have to handle it alone. The folks will help a little on the down payment.

HE: I can't take money from them.

SHE: You and your pride. This is not just your decision. I'm bringing in some money.

HE: Do you want to know exactly how much?

SHE: It's enough to give me a vote in this. I don't want it for myself. I want a home for the kids, for us. The schools are better here. It's safer.

HE: Kindergarten isn't that important. Maybe we can swing it next year. Besides, I'd like to get a little closer to the city. This is an hour commute each way.

SHE: But think of the weekends. It's so nice out here. You'll really relax. And I'll be much closer to work.

HE: Would you be able to work another ten hours a week?

SHE: Well, maybe later, after the kids are established at school.

HE: But we need the money now. The bank won't wait till later.

INTRODUCTION

Much of this chapter will focus on the family as an economic unit. The family provides the necessities of physical survival, as well as important insurance for the survival and economic improvement of future generations. We shall look at family "resources" in financial or economic terms. But before we turn to these issues, we should recall that people's needs for physical security and material goods are matched by equally powerful needs for love, respect, and a sense of belonging. Success may be defined by our culture as economic success, but success in terms of marriage and family relations cannot be measured in dollars and cents. The economic model that will be used in this chapter does not really encompass the contributions of parents to their children. Parents are responsible for ensuring and enhancing their children's self-esteem, and the economic model does not take into account the value of the parents' contributions of time, concern, information, education, and love. In the previous chapters we have outlined possibilities for improving or enhancing the exchanges of noneconomic resources in the family by means of communication, problem-solving, and conflict management.

A picture of the family that stresses economic resources must now take into account the contributions of working wives and mothers. Working women supply a portion of the family income in many cases (see Table 13.1). Working women in intact families contributed about one-quarter of family income in 1977. Women who were single heads of household contributed an average of 60 to 70 percent of their family's income. The percentage of family earnings contributed by women is likely to increase in the future, particularly if women begin to receive wages comparable to those received by men who do similar work.

Even when they are not supplying cash to the family, women contribute substantial noneconomic resources by managing a household and raising

TABLE 13.1 Proportion of Women Earning Greater than 20 and 33 Percent of Family Income for Specific Lengths of Time

	Years with Earnings Greater than 20 Percent				
Age in 1968	0	1–3	4–6	7–9	10
18–27	35.2	28.4	15.3	16.2	4.8
28–37	45.8	20.2	14.2	12.0	7.8
38–47	51.7	15.5	9.5	15.5	7.8
Total	45.0	20.7	12.8	14.4	7.0
	Years with Earnings Greater than 33 Percent				
Age in 1968	0	1–3	4–6	7–9	10
18–27	51.7	27.3	11.3	8.9	0.9
28–37	64.0	19.0	7.9	6.2	3.0
38–47	69.0	16.5	7.1	5.1	2.2
Total	62.4	20.4	8.6	6.5	2.1

Source: George Masnick and Mary Jo Bane, *The Nation's Families: 1960–1990*, Boston, Auburn House, 1980, p. 93. Reprinted by permission.

children; this is the area most often undervalued. One can try to place a dollar value on the many services women perform without pay: child care, housekeeping, interior decorating, family therapy, family nursing, cooking, meal planning, shopping, pet care, and so on. If every one of these services were paid for, the bill would range from $20,000 to $40,000 per year (Pogrebin 1975).

With an economic model of resources, both women and children suffer by definition, since they are not viewed in the stereotypical economic sense as either "productive" or "successful." The extent and amount of married women's economic contribution are closely tied to their childbearing role and to their husbands' economic status. Children keep many women from employment, although more women (more than 40 percent, an increase of over 18 percent since 1950) now combine paid employment and child rearing. Many do this when their children have reached school age, and some women manage to work outside the home while their children are preschoolers (see Figure 1.2, p. 6; and Box 7.2, p. 213). Children affect married women's employment patterns regardless of racial, social, or economic background, but differing backgrounds also affect employment patterns. For example, as we have already noted, black wives are more likely to work than white wives. In minority families the wife's income is particularly significant (Scanzoni and Scanzoni 1976, p. 220).

In families headed by women, women's work and earnings "make the difference between poverty and an adequate standard of living . . . between independence or dependence on alimony, help from relatives or public welfare" (Masnick and Bane 1980, p. 86). As a result of the historical pattern of economic discrimination against black males, employment for

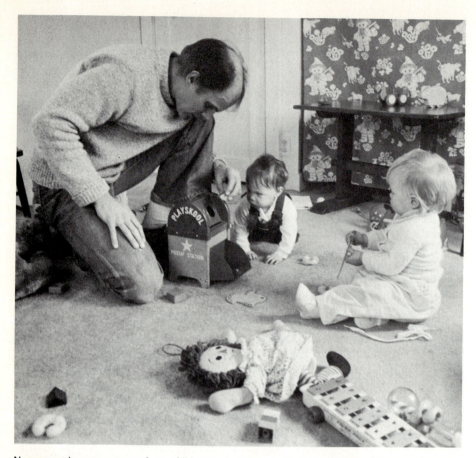

Noneconomic resources such as child care contribute to family well-being. (Margarite Bradley, Positive Images)

black women has been more accepted and respected by black men and by society in general. Attitudes in the white middle class are gradually changing. Women are being accorded some of the professional prestige given men (see Table 13.2). They are also having to meet demands for economic independence and self-reliance that have traditionally been made only on men. However, the gap between wages paid for work done by men and work done by women has not yet closed, as Table 13.3 illustrates.

Finally, we must point out that there is a bias in the subject of family finance, as presented both in this chapter and throughout the literature on marriage and the family. This analysis reflects a middle-class standard: it assumes a two-partner, intact family that has expectations concerning college for the children and a comfortable retirement for the parents.

TABLE 13.2   The Jobs Women Hold: Percent of Women Working in Occupations

Occupation	1970	1980
Professional-technical	14.5%	16.8%
Managerial-administrative	4.5	6.9
Sales	7.0	6.8
Clerical	34.5	35.1
Craft	1.1	1.8
Operatives including transport	14.5	10.7
Nonfarm laborers	0.5	1.2
Service, not private household	16.5	17.0
Private household	5.1	2.5
Farm	1.8	1.2

Source: *Chicago Tribune*, January 31, 1982, Sec. 12, p. 4. Used by permission.

Budgeting and principles of finance do have a wide application; however, people who choose other life patterns, such as singlehood or communal living, as well as families living at or near the poverty level, are likely to have different economic problems and goals.

ATTITUDES TOWARD MONEY

Economic issues pervade many apparently noneconomic aspects of life. The need to make a living may lead young people to pursue professions that carry with them a certain lifestyle, a particular circle of friends and social acquaintances, a standard of living that influences the food they eat, the books they read. A choice made originally only as a means of making a living can set the tone and character of a person's entire life. On the other hand, economic issues, especially the way a person manages money, are

TABLE 13.3   How Salaries Compare: Earnings of Full-time Workers, 1979

Salary	Percent of Women	Percent of Men
Less than $3,000	3.1%	2.1%
3,000–4,999	3.8	1.8
5,000–6,999	13.0	3.7
7,000–9,999	28.6	9.3
10,000–14,999	33.0	22.9
15,000–24,999	16.3	38.8
25,000–49,999	2.0	18.4
50,000–74,999	Less than 0.1	2.0
75,000 +	Less than 0.1	1.0

Source: *Chicago Tribune*, January 31, 1982, Sec. 12, p. 4. Used by permission.

influenced by many noneconomic factors. Money management is related to one's sense of one's own importance and to feelings of independence, responsibility, and control over one's life. Some people never learn to manage their money: they spend on things that they don't need, without planning for the future.

There are many reasons for mismanaging money, including the obvious one—ignorance. Many people never have learned how, because no one bothered to teach them. Others mismanage funds because they feel they have no control over their lives, and, in fact, have had no opportunity to manage money.

The symbolic value of money gives it psychological as well as economic significance, making it a potential source of conflict in families. People may mismanage money out of a desire to hurt those who are close to them; money serves as a means of revenge. Others use money to control or demean those who are economically dependent on them. We have already noted, for instance, that abuse and manipulation of a spouse by means of money is more common than physical abuse in the middle class.

Some people define their own self-worth in monetary terms. They suppose that the more money or material goods they possess, the more valuable they become. But this view ignores a truth that religious thinkers and philosophers have recognized—that human life has an intrinsic, nonrelative value. If individuals have a definite place in the scheme of things, then their value cannot be determined by comparing their material assets with the assets of other individuals. Nor can we assign worth to an individual based on the extent to which his or her skills or talents are in demand.

The law of supply and demand governs the cost of goods and services: high-priced items are those that are both scarce and wanted by many. The value of individual persons, unlike that of goods and services, should not be determined by the law of supply and demand. Nevertheless, an unemployed person, or one who has been demoted or is unable to land commissions or clients or accounts, is bound to feel some sense of diminished worth. In fact, one transcendent value of the family is to convince and reassure its members that they do indeed have intrinsic worth even if the outside world seems not to recognize it.

Some people come from families who have not stressed the individual's intrinsic worth. People from such materialistic families may follow suit by placing a price tag on everything that they and others do; or they may rebel against their family's materialistic lifestyle by retreating from the marketplace values, wearing unconventional clothes, disregarding appearances, working against the establishment. Frugality, carried to an extreme, can also have the effect of placing money over all else in importance. In the play *Long Day's Journey Into Night*, Eugene O'Neill portrays a family, based on his own, which is destroyed by distorted values. The father's stinginess was a major cause of the breakdown in family relationships, the son's alcoholism, the wife's drug addiction. In the play, it is charged that the father's unwillingness to hire a good doctor led him to bring his wife a quack who offered her morphine instead of proper medical care. For his son, whiskey was offered for childhood nightmares or stomachaches. But the miserly father could not be entirely blamed, for he, too, was addicted—to holding on to his money, spending it only on property or schemes that might multiply his wealth.

Although most people are not subject to such tragic imbalances when it comes to handling money, there are many different attitudes about money, many psychological and practical factors that lead a person to a particular style of money management or mismanagement. A couple just starting out would do well to explore each other's attitudes and feelings about money. Some couples may decide to make money and a higher standard of living a top priority; others may wind up choosing less lucrative but, in their opinion, more satisfying, goals—careers in the arts, education, or farming. They may agree that, in the long run, one partner or the other should go back to school and try a different occupation so that earning potential later on will be greater. Some couples will decide to spend money—for instance, to travel extensively—rather than to save or invest it.

These are fundamental decisions that two people should explore, preferably before they marry. Another potentially explosive issue that every couple must confront is that of "mine" and "yours," "his" and "hers" and "ours." It is probably best that each spouse have some money for personal use, which doesn't have to be accounted for to the other. Each couple will have their own way of resolving this issue.

PRINCIPLES OF PERSONAL FINANCE

There are three generally accepted principles of sound personal finance. The first is to be aware of how you spend your money in relationship to your actual earnings; the second is to use credit properly; and the third is to buy wisely. Let us focus on the first principle, which is really a question of careful budgeting.

Budgeting

Some people regard a budget as too contrived and self-conscious for their spontaneous and simple style of living. But keeping a budget is only a way of becoming more aware of how one's money is spent. It need not be a straitjacket, but should be used as a means of achieving the kind of lifestyle that one wants.

If people could buy absolutely everything they wanted, they would not need a budget. A budget is for those of us whose spendable income is finite, limited. Our purchases represent personal choices of one thing over another, and we must always choose among alternatives. A budget is a good way of becoming aware of these choices. It makes very clear what our options are: we know that if we buy an expensive stereo, we cannot buy a car or take a trip. Sound money management is not possible without a budget. Box 13.1 offers some very specific points on budgeting from Sally Campbell's five-step program.

Using Credit Effectively

From their first bank card to the purchase of a home or car and on to the choice of a retirement retreat or condominium, a couple will be using credit. People can use credit effectively or they can let credit use (and abuse) them, depleting their resources without offering them assets that can grow in value. Credit sounds complicated, but it is actually very similar to money. Both money and credit are used to buy goods and services; the difference is simply that credit is a less direct method of exchange than cash. *Credit* is a temporary loan of money. The kinds of credit available differ in the amount of the loan, its purpose, the length of time within which it must be repaid, its source (the type of lender), and the terms of repayment (interest charged and penalties imposed). The different types of credit vary widely in their cost, so you should choose your source of credit carefully.

Charge Accounts.   Retail stores are one source of credit. If you have a charge account at a retail store, the seller (the retailer) is also the creditor. Usually the store asks for no down payment and no interest if the amount is paid within 30 days. This is a very simple form of credit; the store does not take back the goods if they are not paid for, but may begin to charge interest or a penalty (McGowan 1978, p. 63). Such *open credit* (as some call it) is convenient. From the consumer's point of view, it is also a real bargain, especially if it is used properly. Proper use requires paying the bill in full at the end of 30 days.

Credit Cards.   You can also use credit cards to purchase goods. In some cases, as with a Sears credit card, an independent business is the creditor. In other cases, a bank or finance company is the creditor; for example, Chase Manhattan Bank is the creditor for Visa. Some credit-card companies, such as American Express and Visa, charge their customers an annual fee. The credit-card company usually gives the seller, such as a restaurant or department store, five to eight percent *less* than the purchase price of the goods. The seller, who expects to sell more as a result of offering credit, often passes the cost on to consumers (McGowan 1978, p. 64).

If properly used, credit cards have the advantages of retail credit—they

BOX 13.1   How to Create Your Own Financial Master Plan, by *Sally R. Campbell*

Step One: **Explore Your Attitudes About Spending.**   . . . Take a look at your spending patterns: do you find it easy or difficult to part with your money?

Next, discuss what is important to you both. Can you agree on what will come first when you have to decide between several desirable alternatives? . . . Determine now where your spending priorities are similar, where they are different, and where you will need to compromise when you merge your financial affairs.

Consider, too, how you will share income as a couple. To what extent will money be "mine," "yours," and "ours"? While too much emphasis on "mine" and "yours" can cause problems, each of you should keep some money for personal use. . . . The important thing is to recognize and discuss your attitudes about money and sharing, and from this, begin to work out a money management philosophy you can both live with—now and in the years ahead.

Step Two: **Set Up Specific Financial Goals.**   Decide what you want your money to do for you—now and through your lifetime. . . . Here's one way to organize your specific financial goals: (1) Make separate lists of goals that are important to each of you. Write them down in order of importance, and include the estimated cost of each item on the list. (2) Put your lists together and make whatever adjustments and compromises are necessary. (3) Divide the combined list according to when you wish to achieve each objective—in the immediate, near, or distant future. Now, with your goals firmly in mind, you are on your way to making your money do what you want it to do for you.

Step Three: **Examine Your Current Financial Position.**   . . . As individuals, each of you may have had an income and expenses of your own. When you combine these two incomes, and two sets of expenses, your financial situation will change, perhaps dramatically. . . . Look first at your income. How much do you each bring home monthly? What other income do you receive from interest and dividends, commissions, bonuses, moonlighting? How long can you expect your present income picture to last? If you both work, will this be temporary or permanent? If temporary, how long can you count on two incomes? Next, determine your assets and liabilities. Put together a net worth statement so that you know where you stand individually and as a couple. You may use Chart 1 or make up your own format for listing assets and liabilities. . . . If you have a minus net worth, paying off your liabilities and building up your assets may be one of your first financial goals as a couple. . . . Digging your way out of a financial hole will become increasingly difficult unless you can expect dramatic increases in income.

Step Four: **Estimate Living Costs and Other Expenses.**   . . . Start with the monthly expenses you know you must pay. Put down the fixed or definite expenses first, such as rent or mortgage payments, car payments, transportation costs. Next, estimate the amount you will need for flexible expenses that vary from month to month—such as food, clothing, entertainment. Make an estimate of monthly living costs and check it against actual expenses for two or three months. Then adjust your estimates to conform to reality—particularly if you are spending more than you are

BOX 13.1 (Continued)

CHART 1 Net Worth System

Assets	Description	Current Value
Cash in checking accounts	_____	_____
Savings	_____	_____
Investments—bonds	_____	_____
stocks	_____	_____
mutual funds	_____	_____
Insurance	_____	_____
Real estate	_____	_____
Ownership in a business	_____	_____
Other assets	_____	_____
Total assets		_____

Liabilities	Description	Amount Owed
Charge accounts & credit cards	_____	_____
Installment purchases	_____	_____
Personal loans	_____	_____
Real estate mortgage	_____	_____
Taxes	_____	_____
Other liabilities	_____	_____
Total liabilities		_____
Net worth (assets less liabilities)		_____

earning. Use Chart 2 or your own form to estimate and adjust monthly expenses.

In addition to regular monthly expenses, certain items come up periodically. One way to prepare for periodic expenses is to make a list of expected items and the estimated amount for each. Total these expenditures and divide the total by 12 to arrive at the amount you need to set aside each month to cover those expenses as they arise. Chart 3 may help you anticipate periodic expenses.

Step Five: **Create a Master Plan.**   With your income and expenses firmly in mind, you are ready to make up a master money management plan. . . . The purpose of a

BOX 13.1 (Continued)
CHART 2   Estimated Monthly Living Costs

Item	Estimated Amount	Actual Spending	Adjusted Estimate
Rent or mortgage payment			
Utilities—phone			
electricity			
gas			
water			
Installment payments			
Transportation			
Personal allowances			
Contributions			
Savings			
Food			
Clothing			
Entertainment			
Household furnishings			
Miscellaneous			
Savings for nonmonthly expenses			
Other expenses			
Totals			

master plan is to help you direct your dollars, control your spending, and reach your important goals—not to make you a slave to keeping a budget.

The essential steps in making a master plan are: (1) total your income; (2) total your expenses; and (3) measure one against the other, aiming at a balance to use for important goals. Use Chart 4 to make your master plan.

As you work with your master plan, the important thing is to maintain or increase the amount you set aside for your goals. If expenses exceed income or if you are not saving enough to reach important goals:

• Check your list of monthly and periodic expenses item by item to see where you

BOX 13.1 (Continued)

CHART 3 Estimated Periodic Expenses

Item	Estimated Cost	Payment Date
Taxes	_____	_____
Insurance	_____	_____
Vacation	_____	_____
Home improvements	_____	_____
Christmas	_____	_____
Major purchases	_____	_____
Other	_____	_____
Total	_____	

Monthly Savings for Nonmonthly Expenses
(total divided by 12) = $ _____

CHART 4 Money Master Plan

Item	Monthly	Annual
Income—earnings and other income	_____	_____
Expenses—living costs and periodic expenses	_____	_____
Balance—to save for important goals	_____	_____

could spend less and save more. Try to eliminate unnecessary spending that brings no lasting satisfaction.

• Look at installment payments to see when you can pay off these debts and thereby save the amount you are now spending on them.

• Reconsider anticipated purchases. Can anything be eliminated, postponed, or substituted with a less costly item?

• Investigate ways of increasing your income by moonlighting, working overtime, or getting additional training.

Keep working with your income and expenses until your money is buying the most satisfaction possible for you both.

Source: Reprinted by permission from the 1976/77 issue of *New Marriage*. © 1976, by Sally R. Campbell.

can be both convenient and cheap. In fact, if you pay the credit-card company in 30 days, most companies will not charge you interest; after 30 days, however, there is a high interest rate. There is also, perhaps, a psychological danger of being seduced by the urgings of these credit companies ("Buy now! Charge it! Pay later!") into buying more than you can afford.

Installment Credit.   If you want to buy a fairly large or expensive item, such as a new color television set, a videotape recorder, or a washer-dryer, you may have to buy it on installment credit. With this form of credit, you pay immediately 10 to 40 percent of the purchase price. This is your down payment. The contract is a legal agreement between you, the consumer or purchaser, and the dealer or seller. You take home the item, but the creditor keeps the certificate of ownership, the title to the item.

Installment buying usually is not a bargain from the consumer's point of view. The interest charges will be higher than for any other sort of financing. There are, in addition, service and insurance charges. It is usually better for the consumer to borrow the money elsewhere and pay cash to the dealer.

Consumers are also warned against certain "add-on" clauses that are common in installment-plan contracts, such as "set up" charges and credit life insurance. In some installment-plan contracts, all the items you purchase from one dealer over a period of time are written on the same contract. The payments and charges are then distributed proportionally over all your debts. This sounds fine until you realize what it means: Suppose you have almost completely paid for your color television when you decide to buy a video recorder from the same dealer. If, for some reason, you are not able to keep up the payments on the second item, *both* the television and the videotape recorder will be repossessed.

Borrowing Money.   For single, one-payment loans (or credit), consumers can turn to a variety of sources: commercial banks, retail stores, even some service businesses such as hospitals, doctors, and law firms (McGowan 1978, p. 66). The most costly sources of loans are the pawnbroker and the small loan company. Pawnbrokers charge a very high interest rate, sometimes as high as 50 percent. Similarly, small loan companies are often a poor source of credit. The careful consumer will always be on the lookout for shoddy but legal lending practices that make the true interest rate— already high enough—even higher. For example, "easy credit," touted as only a few dollars a week, may amount to a high 20-to-21 percent interest rate.

Bank credit cards, such as Visa, offer a cash-advance service, which is a quick, convenient source of cash. This kind of instant credit is similar to and about as costly as a revolving charge at a store.

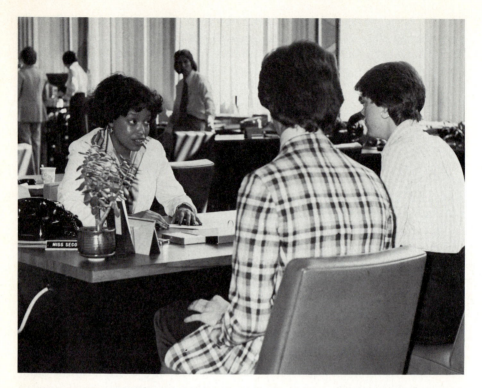

Establishing a good credit rating and taking advantage of the least expensive loans are important. (Read D. Brugger, Picture Cube)

Commercial banks and credit unions are both excellent sources of personal loans. Banks will give a loan only if you have *collateral*, such as stocks and bonds or a car, that you can put up as security for the loan; or a good credit rating; or a relative or business colleague who can cosign the loan. Couples who are already well established, and who have amassed substantial assets, such as investments, life-insurance policies, or savings, can borrow on any of these, using them as collateral. The interest rates for such loans are low compared with other kinds of loans. The advantage is that a family can continue to earn interest on the savings or to receive dividends from the stocks while they are serving as collateral.

Credit unions have different requirements. They are "owned" by the same people who borrow from them, usually employees of a company or members of another organization, such as a labor union. Access to a credit union is limited to those who founded it or who have been admitted subsequently. Eligibility for membership in the credit union is in a sense the member's collateral, and no other is needed. Interest rates are usually low because they are fixed by credit union policies. The fact that finance charges are not lost to "outsiders" fosters a spirit of "cooperative security" (McGowan 1978, p. 66).

Credit Rights and Ratings.   To get the least expensive loans, you must show that you are a good risk, and having a good credit rating is one way to do this. You establish a good credit rating *not* by paying cash for everything, but by using credit properly, by borrowing money and showing you are able to repay it.

Today women have credit rights equal to those of men, but as recently as the early 1970s, a married woman could not obtain credit in her own name, but only in the name of her husband. This meant that if the couple separated or divorced, or if the husband died, she was left without a credit rating and would have some difficulty in establishing one. The Equal Credit Opportunity Act of 1974, however, makes it illegal for a bank or lender to deny a woman personal or commercial credit simply because she is a woman. Married women who are not working still can establish their own credit by placing charge accounts, bank accounts, and bank credit cards in their own names, as well as in their husbands' names.

Both men and women can acquire bad credit rating without knowing it, through misrepresentation or misinformation. For example, suppose you delay payment for an item because, due to a computer error, you have been billed incorrectly. Your file with a given credit agency may say only that you delayed payment, not giving the appropriate explanation. You have a right to make inquiries about your credit rating if you suspect that you are being denied a loan because of a bad credit rating. If you are refused credit, the lender is legally obligated to tell you the name of the credit agency making the negative report. This agency must in turn tell you what is in your file. You can demand that any incorrect information be removed or enter your own explanatory statement if you believe an entry is misleading.

Money borrowed with the promise of a good financial return is probably a sound use of credit. If you are taking out a loan to pay for professional or vocational training, or to buy tools needed to produce income or save money, then your use of credit is profit-making and sound. For example, taking out a *mortgage* (a loan secured by a piece of real estate) on a house is often an excellent use of credit, especially if you live in an area where real estate values are appreciating rapidly. When you take out a loan from a bank to buy a house, the loan is secured by the house, which will be repossessed by the bank if the loan is not repaid on a certain mutually agreed upon repayment schedule. Usually the debt is paid off in equal installments, which include both interest on the loan and a payment toward the amount borrowed. Such debts typically are paid off very slowly, over a period of 20 or 30 years. This means that a family has to pay, overall, more interest, because they are in debt for a longer period of time. For almost all couples, however, it is the only way they can afford to make the monthly payments on a house. The interest rate on a mortgage loan does not increase unless one has taken out a special type of mortgage that remains low for the first few years and then goes up. These "balloon" mortgages came into use in the early 1980s, when standard mortgage rates became prohibitive for many buyers.

Not all loans are taken out with the hope of some future financial gain. People use credit or take out loans to satisfy immediate needs that have nothing to do with making money. Loans undertaken for hobbies or esthetic interests—to buy a piano or finance a trip down the Colorado River—are of this sort. While such use of credit does not promise financial gain, the personal satisfaction of the need may well be worth the finance charge. Such loans should not be taken out on emotional impulse alone. You should know the cost of the credit and weigh it carefully against the subjective value of the need it will be used to satisfy.

Wise Buying

Dealing with Inflation. Long-range projections or predictions about inflation are startling. For example, it is estimated that in the year 2000, the 1976 dollar will be worth 30¢, the minimum annual income will be $19,800, and to live as a family lived in 1976 on a $25,000 salary will require a salary of $112,500 (*Nation's Business* 1978, pp. 6–8; Gitman 1978, p. 62). A survey of consumer attitudes by General Mills (1976) found that the average American family is intensely concerned about inflation and unemployment and feels uncertain about the economic future of its members.

Inflation affects those who are least well-off, including the elderly poor, the most; wealthy people are least affected. Poor families are vulnerable to inflation because they typically have no savings and no flexibility in managing their resources. Heads of such families are especially susceptible to unemployment, and, because they cannot save money and have no collateral, they are unable to borrow or use credit. The wealthy, on the other hand, have the resources to cope with problems caused by inflation. It is true that their assets—bank deposits, notes, mortgages, insurance bonds—are susceptible to inflation because of fixed rates of return. But the wealthy are able to protect themselves in inflationary times by benefiting from higher interest rates on savings; they also find it easier to secure credit.

Inflation affects the spending habits of both rich and poor by encouraging people to buy "now" because the prices for the same goods will be even higher "later." In such an economic climate, it is more important than ever to get the most for one's money. It is probably worth your time to shop around, compare prices and products, and become well informed about the products you buy. (*Consumer Reports* magazine is a reliable source for ratings on major appliances and other household items.)

Avoiding Impulse Buying.   Some consumers are vulnerable to the psychological ploys of salespeople and advertising. Furniture discount houses, for example, lure people into their shops by advertising enormous discounts on whole roomfuls of furniture. Once the customers are there, they are easily persuaded to buy the more attractive, higher-priced items. (This practice is known as "bait and switch.") Others let themselves be rushed into buying something by salespeople who offer a "once-in-a-lifetime" deal. Some believe they must impress the salesperson by buying the more expensive items.

Planning purchases before going shopping helps avoid impulse buying. Even in shopping for such essentials as food, it is best to shop from pre-planned menus based on economic as well as nutritional factors. The wise shopper weighs economic considerations against those of quality. Lower prices do not necessarily mean lower value, but sometimes it is better to pay more for an item, such as furniture, that will last a long time than to pay less for something that will have to be replaced quickly. It is always advisable to take advantage of seasonal reductions in clothing and linens; but when shopping at sales, never buy something *only* because it is on sale.

Major Family Purchases

Major purchases such as an automobile or a house call for special consideration.

Buying a Car.   Next to a house, an automobile is, for most families, the single most expensive purchase. "The most economical way to buy a car is to pay cash, since you save the interest on the loan and you may get a better deal" (Gordon and Lee 1977, p. 326). Yet few people are able to walk into a car dealership and turn over $6,000 to $10,000 in cash.

Most family budgets include the cost of maintaining and operating a car. The purchase price of the car itself is only part of the cost of family transportation. Related costs include: (1) depreciation; (2) license, taxes, and other fees; (3) insurance; (4) interest on the automobile loan; (5) fuel and oil; (6) repairs, maintenance, and tires; (7) parking, garaging, tolls, and tickets. If all these items are added up and the total divided by the number of miles driven per year, you will have the true per-mile operating cost of your car. Calculated in 1979 for a new Chevrolet Malibu Classic, driven 15,000 miles per year, this figure was almost 18¢ per mile (and the figure has gone up every year). A 1978 study by the Bureau of Labor found that a family of four with a moderate income of $19,000 spent, on the average, $1,900 on transportation. Only food and housing were more expensive (*The Family Banker*, July/August 1979).

Families can economize on transportation by buying a car that is economical to maintain and operate and by relying more on alternative modes of travel, including car pools and public transportation. The Federal Highway Administration estimates that the average person can save over $500 by pooling with another person, and even more as the number of those in the car pool increases (*The Family Banker*, July/August 1979).

Buying a House.   Most families have a mental image of a "dream house," but the economic conditions of the late 1970s and early 1980s have made the actualization of that dream difficult for many and impossible for others. The following steps will help you to ascertain whether you can afford to buy a house.

First, you must estimate the amount of *dependable* income available for at least "the first third of the mortgage payments due on a house" (Miller 1975, p. 228). Extra money—such as from an unexpected pay raise, an inheritance, a lottery—doesn't count, as those extra sums cannot be depended upon.

Second, you have to realistically estimate your monthly housing expenses. This not only includes your payments on a mortgage (which may be consistent or may fluctuate, depending on the type of mortgage), but also includes insurance premiums (which should cover not only the physical structure of the home but also the valuable contents within the home). Then you'll need to add on the cost of maintenance (is a new roof necessary?), heating (remember that vicious winter of 1976?), air conditioning (that miserable summer of 1979?), electricity, telephone, water, sewerage, and property taxes. As of this writing, the interest on mortgage payments is tax deductible; however, this provision of the law could change (Miller 1975, p. 228).

Unfortunately, more and more American families are finding home ownership out of their reach. The median price of a house tripled between 1965 and 1980. Interest rates of 18 to 20 percent were common in 1980 and 1981 on mortgages for houses costing an average of $60,000 to $70,000.

It is generally true that a home of one's own is a good financial investment, since the price of housing seems to be rising. However, this is not always the case. A neighborhood could deteriorate, lessening the value of a house in a certain location. And while one's house might indeed appreciate, the cost of buying another house in another neighborhood might have appreciated far beyond the present value of your original house.

Miller (1975, pp. 231–233) suggests that before you think about what kind of house you want to buy, you should consider where you want to live. How far or distant is the neighborhood from work? What kinds of public transportation are available, and how reliable is that transportation? A freeway at noon on Sunday is far less congested than at 7:30 A.M. on Monday morning. Then, consider the property tax rate. Taxes may vary within a city, just as one suburb's tax rate may be twice that of a neighboring suburb. Find out about the schools. Talk with parents, teachers, principals. Examine not only what the schools are like now, but also where they might be headed five or ten years from now. (The cost of a private school education is not tax deductible.) How about the shopping situation? Are the stores close by and conveniently located? How about the air quality? Is the air clean or polluted? Is your home close to or far from industry? Crime is an important factor. While no home or neighborhood can possibly be crime free, it is a good idea to visit the local police station and ask to see the crime statistics from their annual report. Perhaps you can talk with a police officer, or even the chief of police. Walk around the neighborhood and take a look at your potential neighbors. Are these the kind of people you're comfortable with? Visit the local city hall and ask what zoning and developments are planned for the neighborhood. You need to consider all of these factors before you decide to buy a house in a certain area.

Taxes

The way our society is organized, taxes pay for public schools, public transportation, military defense, criminal justice systems, and various social welfare programs. Without taxes, we would not have these or many other goods and services. There are all kinds of taxes, levied by all levels of government—federal, state, local—and affecting different items—sales, property, inheritance. Income tax, probably the most significant tax, does not tax inheritance, gifts, consumption, or property—it taxes income. This includes earned income such as wages, salaries, tips, and income from farms and small businesses. It also includes unearned incomes: rents paid to landlords, interests and dividends earned by investors, the capital gains a homeowner earns when he or she sells a house for more than its purchase price, the royalties authors get on the sale of their books, alimony received from ex-spouses, and other miscellaneous sources.

Gauging one's taxable income is no simple matter. Standard exemptions—one for the taxpayer and one for each dependent—are straightforward. But then come the adjustments and deductions that can make a great difference in the amount of taxes a family pays.

The taxpayer must first decide whether to take the standard deduction or itemize deductions. The standard deduction is simpler, but it can cost you money in the long run. There are certain maximum standard deductions for married couples filing jointly, couples filing separately, and unmarried heads of households. It is not worthwhile to itemize deductions unless they will amount to more than these standard deductions. The only way to find this out is to figure the deductions you can take: medical expenses, state and local income taxes, real-estate and personal-property taxes, interest paid on a mortgage, contributions, and perhaps others.

Once you have adjusted your taxable income, computed your deductions, and subtracted your personal exemptions, you can figure your taxable income. The next step is to find or compute your tax and write out your check to the IRS! (Of course, you may be due a refund from them.)

What is the principle behind the tax table? How does the government decide how much of your income should be paid in federal income taxes? Federal income tax in the United States is supposed to be *progressive*, in the sense that it takes a larger and larger fraction of income as income rises. That is, the more money people make as income, the larger the percentage that goes toward their federal income taxes. A *proportional* tax would take the same percentage of income, regardless of how much that income is. Some states have a proportional tax system; some have a progressive system.

Many people are not informed enough about tax laws to take advantage of the legal exemptions, adjustments, and deductions open to them. Tax law seems to them to be such a bewildering labyrinth of details and procedures that they stay away from it altogether. These people either pay an accountant or consultant to figure taxes for them, or they may end up paying more money in taxes than they need to. Many people do not realize that the Internal Revenue Service itself is a good source of free information and help about filling out tax forms and maximizing deductions.

LONG-RANGE FINANCIAL PLANNING

Savings and investments

When inflation is high, the long-term planning represented by savings and investments is advisable, even though rising costs may make it more difficult to save. Saving money is putting money aside, usually where it will gain interest, for future use or for emergencies; investing it is putting it to use, using it to make more money. Savings should be thought of not as self-denial, as removing money from spendable income, but rather as the deferment of spending. People who save now can buy goods and services later, without having to pay costly finance charges. Savings also protect people against emergencies and unexpected expenses. Experts advise saving ten percent of your spendable income, at an interest rate that will not let you slip hopelessly behind inflation.

But a regular savings account is usually not enough. Wise families also put aside part of their spendable income for an investment or a bank certificate that will yield higher returns. They probably purchase their house not simply as a place to live, but also as a good investment, something that will grow in value over time. Consider a typical investment: The Jones family invests a certain amount each month for 12 years into an account paying ten percent interest. If the interest is compounded annually—and it will be if the investment is a good one—this means that, at the end of a year, the interest earned by that invested money itself begins earning interest. After 12 years, the Joneses will have accumulated a capital fund. They can withdraw a limited amount of money from the fund forever, without touching the principal or depositing more money, so long as the account continues to pay compounded interest.

Financial advisers always encourage taking advantage of the interest or dividends such capital funds yield. But to accumulate capital and take advantage of compound interest—the principle of growth on growth—you must start investing as soon as you are earning a regular income. As we have already noted, regular investment should be an item in your family budget.

Tax-deferred retirement plans, called Individual Retirement Accounts [IRAs], represent another avenue of saving for later years. An IRA allows a person to set aside, each year, a sum that will accumulate interest, but will not be taxed. Box 13.2 elaborates on the uses of the IRA.

Life Insurance

A couple with children will usually want life insurance to provide income for the family in case of the unexpected death of the chief income-earner or, sometimes, of either parent. A life insurance policy will protect the family financially by ensuring that they will have money to substitute partially for the loss of income. Theoretically, any kind of insurance can be thought of as a claim on money that is conditional on the probability of a certain event's happening—accident, fire, illness, theft. *Life insurance*, then, is a person's claim on money subject to the person's death. If the person dies while he or she has the policy, the beneficiaries can claim the money. Otherwise, the policy is just another consumer good (McGowan 1978, p. 111).

Many kinds of life insurance also include a financial investment on savings accounts. Such "insurance-plus-investment" or "whole-life" policies have the advantage of not needing to be renewed every five years or so. They guarantee payment throughout the person's lifetime. If you have such a policy, you do not lose it when you turn 65. Premiums, or the cost of the policy, do not increase over the years. It is questionable whether such premiums are really less expensive than "term insurance," a type of insurance that does not have cumulative benefits. It is less expensive than the cumulative type, but the cost of term insurance increases as the insured individual ages. Most people find that a plan that combines some term insurance with some whole-life insurance is the most prudent.

BOX 13.2 Money: IRA on My Mind, by *James T. Yenckel*

As of Jan. 1, 1982, for the first time, every one of the estimated 107 million workers in this country is eligible to set up an IRA—an Individual Retirement Account. For those under 40—with at least 30 working years ahead—an IRA, say some ads, could provide a retirement nest egg of as much as a half-million dollars.

If, for example, you contributed the maximum allowed of $2,000 each year for 30 years at 12 percent interest compounded each year, estimates Nina Gross, counsel for the American Bankers Association, you could expect $540,585.20 ready and waiting when you retire [see Table 1]. "That," she says, "is very, very nice."

For working couples, where both husband and wife sign up for an IRA, the family figure doubles to $1 million or more—before taxes.

"You'll be a millionaire only for a short time," notes Peter Elinsky, a tax partner in the Washington office of the accounting firm of Peat Marwick Mitchell and Co. And there is no assurance your money will consistently earn at 12 percent or that a half-million bucks will buy what it does today. Nevertheless, he considers IRAs an "excellent" investment.

IRAs are "a very, very big thing," says Reg Green, vice president of Investment Company Institute, an association representing 90 percent of the nation's 600 mutual funds, who are looking for a major share of IRA accounts. "We calculate $20 billion will be invested in each of the next few years."

. . .

Under a new tax law passed this year, each worker can establish his or her own retirement plan and contribute up to $2,000 annually. For working couples, each may pay in $2,000. If one spouse has no income, a spousal account can be established,

TABLE 1 Future Value of Annual Investments of $2,000*

| | Years | | |
Return	Ten	Twenty	Thirty
8 Percent Interest			
Tax exempt	$31,291	$98,846	$244,692
Tax rate of 30%	27,320	74,432	155,671
Tax rate of 40%	26,118	67,859	134,566
Tax rate of 50%	24,973	61,938	116,657
10 Percent Interest			
Tax exempt	$35,062	$126,004	$361,887
Tax rate of 30%	29,567	87,730	202,146
Tax rate of 40%	27,943	77,985	167,603
Tax rate of 50%	26,414	69,439	139,521
12 Percent Interest			
Tax exempt	$39,309	$161,397	$540,585
Tax rate of 30%	32,010	103,719	264,364
Tax rate of 40%	29,904	89,838	209,960
Tax rate of 50%	27,943	77,985	167,603

* Comparison of earnings in a tax-exempt IRA vs. a nonexempt investment in varying tax brackets.
Source: Courtesy, Investment Company Institute

BOX 13.2 (Continued)

with a total family contribution of $2,250 yearly (divided between wife and husband in separate accounts as they see fit).

Among the benefits making IRA so popular:

• The amount invested each year can be deducted from your income tax. For example, says the Investment Company Institute: "If you're in the 33 percent tax bracket and put away $2,000 a year . . . you'll save $660 in taxes immediately." The higher your tax bracket, the more you'll save each year you invest.

• The interest, dividends and capital gains the investment earns are not taxed immediately. That means the same amount of money invested in an IRA will grow more rapidly than non-IRA investments, which are subject to taxes. By the institute's calculations:

"Let's say you're in the 33 percent tax bracket and invest $2,000 annually in a regular investment that returns, on average, 10 percent yearly. At the end of 20 years, the value of your investment would be $84,372." In an IRA, under the same conditions, the amount is $126,005, "because you didn't pay taxes on the earnings . . ."

(You eventually do pay taxes on your IRA investment and earnings, but only as you withdraw them. The earliest you can take them out without penalty is age 59½ — or if you become disabled — though you may want to wait until you actually retire. They are then taxed as ordinary income. Presumably, retirement will have dropped you to a lower tax bracket, reducing the taxes you owe. You must begin to withdraw funds by age 70½.)

• The job-hopper who doesn't remain long enough to collect pension benefits can continue to build a retirement fund wherever he or she is employed. Or, if you quit a job and are eligible for a lump-sum payment of retirement benefits, the money can be put into a tax-deferred IRA account.

• With Social Security shaky and employer-funded retirement plans often inadequate, you are systematically providing a supplemental source of income.

Nevertheless, IRAs are not for everyone, warn financial advisers. If you do invest in such a program, plan on seeing it through until you reach 59½ because the penalty for early withdrawal is severe.

"I see a lot of people coming in on Jan. 4" to invest, says Glenn Schickler, vice president of Madison National Bank, "then in July saying, 'I've got $700 here I could use for something else. I lost my job or I'm going on vacation.'

"An IRA is not a substitute for saving for an emergency in the family. This is not a savings program for short-term goals."

To get back the $700, he says, you would be nailed with a 10 percent penalty ($70, in this case) to the government plus regular income tax. Additionally, if you've invested in something like an 18-month certificate of deposit, you could lose six months' interest.

As with any investment, says the institute, "You should think carefully before committing your money."

IRAs are being offered in a variety of forms by banks, savings and loan offices,

BOX 13.2 (Continued)

credit unions, stockbrokers, mutual funds, insurance companies and employers' payroll deductions. The plans differ in degrees of risk, administrative fees and other charges, flexibility, the rate of return and the minimum amount you must invest to get started (some will accept as little as $25 a month).

To determine what suits you and your goals best may take some shopping around. Once you've chosen a plan, you are not committed until you retire, but can switch to another option at least once a year without penalty.

. . .

There is no requirement that you must contribute the full $2,000 annually—that's the maximum. And in lean years, if you choose, you can skip the contribution altogether. You can even split the $2,000 between different investments.

The institute's Reg Green expects that about 20 to 25 percent of American workers in the $20,000 to $50,000 income range will sign up for some form of IRA in the next couple of years. Maybe as many as half of those who make over $50,000 will do so. As for the rest in the middle-income brackets:

"Lethargy," he suggests. "We all know we should be doing something that we aren't."

Source: Adapted from James T. Yenkel, "Money: IRA on My Mind," *The Washington Post,* December 23, 1981, p. C5. Reprinted by permission of *The Washington Post.* © *The Washington Post.*

CHANGING WORK ROLES

We have already discussed (Chapter 7) the close connection between earning power and decision-making power within the family. Over the family life cycle, earning power may vary considerably, with women's earning power more likely to begin or increase after children are in school. The wife's salary in a two-worker family provides, on the average, a quarter of family income. Wives' contributions to family income are likely to increase as their participation in full-time work increases. In 1977 only about half of working wives worked full-time all year. Even at the current relatively low levels, a wife's income can make the difference between poverty and getting along, between getting along and being comfortable, or between being comfortable and actually being prosperous (Masnick and Bane 1980, pp. 93–96). (See Figure 3.2, page 74.)

These economic facts of married life may hasten mutual decision making and eventually bring about a more equitable distribution of household tasks. Such a change in family roles is a slow process, but work accelerates role change in other areas. One study of over a thousand families in northern New York State conducted in 1976 revealed that men spent an average of 1.6 hours per day on housework, full-time homemakers spent 8.1 hours, and employed wives spent 4.8 hours (Pleck 1979, p. 284). Clearly the employed wife is still carrying more of the household burden, although she is doing fewer household chores than the full-time homemaker. Recent studies on flexible work scheduling indicate that husbands who are able to leave work earlier will spend more time with their children, if not more time on domestic chores (Winett and Neale 1979). Whether a man's greater involvement in family life and household tasks can ease his adjustment to retirement remains to be seen. It does seem that investing time in one's family as well as one's career can lessen the sense of stagnation in mid-life when one passes the peak of economic earning power. Our discussion of life-cycle satisfaction in the next chapter will take up this issue in greater detail.

UNEMPLOYMENT AND UNDEREMPLOYMENT

Traditionally, men have been the ones who were fired, laid off, or forced to work less than full-time. Today, both men and women are likely to suffer a period of unemployment or underemployment at some time during their lives. Many conditions in the larger social system affect unemployment rates, including instability in the economy, a phasing out of certain jobs, and an oversupply of employees in a particular field at a specific point in time.

In 1982, for example, the national unemployment rate passed ten percent. Teenagers and women were more likely to experience unemployment than men; black men were more likely to be unemployed than white men. Yet high rates of unemployment have pervasive effects on all segments of the population.

Personal or family circumstances may also be related to a nonworker status. Ill health may bring about a temporary layoff. Reaching a certain age may bring about retirement. Childbearing and the demands of young children, complicated by difficulties in finding appropriate child-care alternatives, may cause women to experience periods of unemployment.

Work-related changes such as unemployment are typically perceived as stressful events, as indicated by the Holmes and Rahe Social Readjustment Rating Scale. This scale was compiled by asking a sample of respondents how stressful they thought a particular life event would be. "Being fired," "retirement," and "change to a different line of work" were all rated as highly stressful. "Change in responsibilities at work," "trouble with boss," and "change in work hours and conditions" were ranked as medium-range stressful events (Holmes and Rahe 1967, pp. 213–218).

In addition to planning for retirement, married couples must prepare for the economic and psychological effects of a period of unemployment at some point in their married lives. The impact of unemployment or underemployment on the marital and family system will be influenced in a direct way by the decline in income. This will typically be most serious in the single-earner family with low financial resources.

A job carries with it much more than financial rewards. Most workers recognize and value a job as a sign of social position, as one source of identity, and as a means for obtaining a sense of achievement and satisfaction. When Studs Terkel interviewed hundreds of people for his book *Working* (1974), he found that a large majority of employed persons said that they would continue to work even if they inherited enough money to live comfortably. The loss of a job may thus mean at least a temporary decrease in self-esteem. The unemployed man or woman may experience feelings of inadequacy—and even worthlessness.

Being able to weather periods of unemployment involves financial planning and interpersonal skills. For a married couple, sufficient savings give the unemployed partner time to retrain or to select a new position without undue pressure. The support of a loving partner is crucial when one's work role is undermined. The ability to put into practice some of the information and skills discussed in the earlier chapters on communication and conflict management can be helpful in dealing with stress related to unemployment and other changes in work status. Women and men need to share feelings of frustration and anxiety concerning work or unemployment. If either husband or wife is seeking a job, both need to engage actively in the task of solving the occupational problem. Men who feel ashamed to admit they are out of work, or women who feel they have no right to be depressed about job loss, need to be reminded that they are loved and valued for their own worth. They need the opportunity to express their upset, but they also need to be reminded of past accomplishments and their ongoing merits. Chronic unemployment may be related to serious family discord, but a period of unemployment is a challenge to the family system that may ultimately bring husband and wife closer together.

ECONOMIC STAGES AND CYCLES OF THE FAMILY

The Establishment Stage

The financial problems of families will differ with the stages of the family life cycle and with the socioeconomic status of the family. This section is based on the economic stages of middle-class families. In the establishment years, young married people form their major goals and make decisions about occupations and a desirable level of living. A typical couple marry in their twenties. They are finishing college or just beginning to hold full-time jobs. They have no children, and their parents can still be counted on to help out if an unexpected financial crisis occurs. These are the halcyon days of relative financial ease. Since both partners may be working, their incomes are good. While inflation does affect them, it has little of the corrosive psychological effect it has on older couples who have seen their dollars dwindle in purchasing power. The young couple probably have few, if any, major financial commitments: no house payments to meet, no car payments or medical bills, no monthly payments for expensive furniture. New couples probably have more discretionary income at this time than at any other time in their lives, yet few appreciate their (usually short-lived) financial ease. The realities of most family careers should encourage young couples to begin saving and investing from the start, while both are working full-time and before their obligations accumulate.

This is not to say that couples at this stage should never rely on credit for major purchases such as a car or a house. Repayments on a mortgage or loan will, as a result of inflation, decrease in value over time. Meanwhile the couple enjoy the product they have purchased. Credit has been made more costly, however, as part of the effort to control inflation. Overdependency on credit can lead to overwhelming debt and bankruptcy.

The Child-Rearing Years

The Coming of the First Child.   The arrival of the first infant marks an important stage in the family's economic career. The decision to have a child will have radical economic consequences over the next 15 or 16 years. In families where children require long periods of advanced education, financial obligation to children can continue for 25 years. Even in the early years, there are many expenses that children bring. Owning a house with a yard or choosing a town with good schools becomes more important. Even while their first child is in the cradle, a couple must begin to think about her or his college tuition. As a result, most of a couple's income in these child-rearing years is absorbed by fixed expenditures such as rent or mortgage payments, costs of day care, or school tuition. Estimates of the cost of child rearing vary, but they are all high. According to Metropolitan Life Insurance Company, child-rearing costs will consume three years of the primary wage earner's salary for each child. The U.S. Department of Agriculture estimates that families will spend an average of $134,414 to raise a child born in 1979 to the age of 18 (see Table 13.4).

These are the long-term economic effects of the first child. But the infant's arrival has more immediate consequences as well. Although childbirth at home has increased somewhat in recent years, the majority of mothers no longer give birth to their babies in Grandma's four-poster bed. Most mothers give birth in hospitals—and hospitals and doctors cost money. Depending on the kind of insurance coverage a couple have, they will have to pay for part of the expense of childbirth. Even more important, most women stop working after their first child is born, at least for a time, and so the family's income is reduced just when family expenses are increasing. The transition to being a single-income family—even for a relatively short while—can be a difficult one if a couple have not prepared for it.

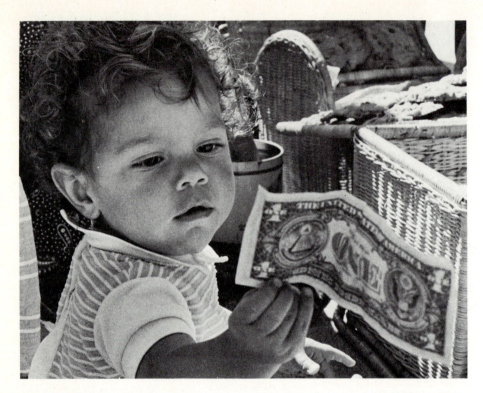

The arrival of the first infant marks an important stage in the family's economic career. (Rose Skytta, Jeroboam)

School-Age and Adolescent Children. Many women choose to remain at home when their children are small. Often it is not possible or practical to hire a substitute mother to care for small children while the mother is working; even if parents can afford day care or some other arrangement, they may feel that it is not in the child's best interests to be cared for by surrogates. When children start school, many mothers go back to work—but this does not mean that they immediately regain their old earning power. After six or more years out of the labor market, they may need to be retrained. At this time, many women decide to change career goals or complete their formal education in order to ensure greater earning power later on. The majority of women with school-age children return to work. One income is usually not enough to pay the soaring costs of sending children to college.

Most professional jobs today require more training and education than ever. The U.S. Bureau of the Census tells us that a college graduate's average lifetime earnings (in 1978 dollars) will be $1,800,413. For high school graduates the figure is $1,574,280; for grammar school graduates the figure is $1,241,361. Thus, a college graduate can expect to earn over $200,000 more than a high school graduate and over $500,000 more than a

TABLE 13.4   Cost of Raising a Child Born in 1960 or in 1979 to the Age of 18 at a Moderate Cost Level in the Urban North Central Region

	Child Born in 1960	Child Born in 1979*
Food	$ 8,766	$36,645
Clothing	3,662	12,129
Housing	10,467	41,121
Medical care	1,602	6,703
Education	520	2,288
Transportation	5,267	20,355
Other costs	3,990	15,173
Totals	$34,274	$134,414

*Figures inflated from 1979 constant dollar estimates at annual rate of 8%.
Source: Carolyn S. Edwards, "USDA Estimates of the Cost of Raising a Child: A Guide to Their Use and Interpretation," Misc. Pub. 1411, pp. 20–21, Hyattsville, Md.: U.S. Department of Agriculture, 1981.

grammar school graduate (U.S. Bureau of the Census, Department of Commerce, September 1978). The cost of such an education, however, can put severe strains on family finances. It is estimated that by 1985, the cost of four years at a private college will be $80,000, while the cost of four years at a public college will be $40,000. Students can help defray expenses; some may also be able to receive at least partial scholarships, but only one in five will receive significant financial assistance from sources other than the family.

The Middle Years

When the last child goes off to college, couples enter the "empty nest" phase. A new period begins. Usually about this time, or within the next decade, many men reach the peak of their careers, and the family reaches its maximum level of financial achievement. This pattern is changing, however, in dual-career families, where the wife's career usually peaks somewhat later than the husband's. The couple's lifestyle, including housing and financial security, is fairly well settled by this time. This is also a time when quarrels over money management may intensify. If financial and professional expectations have not been fully realized by this stage, the couple realize that they may never be, since there is little time left to advance or improve in terms of one's career. Retirement begins to loom on the horizon. Couples may want to accelerate their investments and savings, to prepare further for the coming period of fixed income and diminishing economic productivity. But these middle years can also bring a second period of relative affluence. This is especially true if the couple's home, furniture, appliances, and the children's college education have been paid for.

The Retirement Years

Most elderly people live on fixed incomes, determined by their private pension plans and supplemented by Social Security. Social Security, deducted from one's paycheck, is compulsory government insurance; it takes up almost seven percent of the worker's gross pay. It provides retired and disabled people with some income. Medicare and Medicaid pay the cost of medical care in old age. If you are self-employed or work for a nonfederal agency or company, then you are probably already paying for your Social Security insurance through deductions. Only those who have made contributions into the Social Security fund by working for a certain number of years are protected by it.

Although Social Security payments have increased over the last few decades twice as rapidly as inflation, they still aren't enough to keep many elderly people above the poverty level. Social Security, of course, may

Planning for financial security in the later years begins early in life. (Florence Sharp)

supply only a part of a retired person's income. A large part of his or her income may come from private pension plans, savings, or investments such as the tax-free Individual Retirement Account. The income of the elderly often fails to keep pace with the rate of inflation. The elderly person's economic and social plight is exacerbated by inflation, which increases the cost of food and clothing while income remains fixed.

The retirement years are again years of major decisions about housing and lifestyle; in addition, new problems of health and use of spare time appear. It is a time when a person's sense of self-worth is tested. If one's self-esteem rests primarily on marketplace values, retirement may be accompanied by feelings of diminished self-worth and usefulness, a sense of disengagement, and a loss of vitality. If one has not made plans for these years, or if one has been overly invested in material values, the normal crises of aging may be heightened. Couples should plan for retirement before it begins by asking:

- How much money will we need to live comfortably?
- How much money will we get each month from combined Social Security and retirement plans?

Since this will almost certainly not be enough to live on, couples must also ask:

- What additional money will we need to live comfortably?
- How will we get that additional money?

The economic challenge to husband and wife is formidable, but it can be tackled when decisions concerning money are not loaded with other issues in the marriage. Conflicts over money, as we have demonstrated in Chapter 9, can actually be conflicts over power and signs of frustration over unmet needs for affection. Couples who find themselves always arguing about money would do well to look beyond the obvious amount of assets, or lack of them, and ask themselves if they are really facing a scarcity of love.

SUMMARY

1. The major purposes of this chapter include the recognition of various noneconomic resources that families possess and exchange; presentation of basic information on managing economic resources related to budgeting, use of credit, and long-range financial planning; and discussion of the changing economic circumstances associated with different stages of the family life cycle.
2. The concept of resources is most often interpreted in economic terms as the amount of money or financial assets available to the family. This

model ignores the valuable contributions that nonworking women and children provide, while emphasizing the traditional male role as breadwinner. A definition of "resources" to include noneconomic as well as economic contributions offers a more comprehensive model for viewing the complex exchanges that constantly occur in family systems.

3. Inadequate financial management may be the result of several factors, including lack of knowledge, feelings of helplessness or insufficient control over one's life situation, or the desire to use money as a form of revenge. The first step to managing money more effectively is becoming aware of how one's money is spent. Developing a budget is one helpful approach to discovering the details of the economic exchange process.

4. Another major aspect of good financial management involves the appropriate use of credit. There are various kinds of credit, which differ according to the amount of the loan, its purpose, the length of time within which it must be repaid, the type of lender, and the terms of repayment. Understanding these differences and using them to advantage, plus establishing a good credit record, can result in significant savings.

5. Major expenditures such as housing, transportation, insurance, and education, as well as decisions about savings and investments, require careful consideration and analysis in most families. Objective, factual information and guidance are important resources in aiding the process of effective financial management.

6. Economic resources vary with the family life-cycle stage. Major considerations in the early years of marriage usually include job or career decisions, planning for large expenditures in such areas as housing and transportation, and setting goals to lessen the financial strain of later years. Families in the middle years of development are likely to find a substantial amount of their incomes being used to provide for the well-being of their children. It is during the latter part of this period that most families reach their maximum earning level. The later years of life bring a relatively fixed income for most couples. Decisions about housing, health care, and lifestyle may need reconsideration as children become independent, and retirement from the work force becomes a reality.

KEY CONCEPTS

Budget	Fixed income
Credit	Inflation
Open credit	Unemployment
Installment credit	Underemployment
Collateral	Social Security
Income taxes	

QUESTIONS

1. Children sometimes complain that although their parents provided them with many material things during their childhood years, they received very little love, especially from their fathers. Discuss how such resources as love and money may become confused and misused in family interaction.
2. On the basis of your personal experience and observations, discuss what you think are the primary reasons for poor financial management in the early years of marriage.
3. Using the information presented in this chapter, analyze the way you use your money by preparing a personal weekly and monthly budget. What changes, if any, would you like to make? How have your spending habits and general attitudes about money been influenced by earlier socialization experiences?
4. Investigate consumer-protection agencies and other services available in your community designed to help individuals and families manage their financial resources and achieve some control over the quality of purchased goods and services.
5. On the basis of the information presented in this chapter, list your financial planning recommendations for couples approaching retirement. Include the major decisions that will need consideration in the later years of life.
6. Discuss the advantages and disadvantages of using various types of credit. Indicate specific credit situations that should be avoided.
7. Imagine yourself a single parent with two children; you work at a low-paying job and are threatened with unemployment. If you should lose your job, what are some realistic ways that you might obtain the necessary resources to support yourself and your family? Categorize your alternatives according to short-term and long-term plans.

SUGGESTED READINGS

- Aldous, Joan, ed. *Journal of Family Issues* 2, no. 2 (June 1981). This entire journal issue is devoted to exploring the special circumstances of dual-earner families. Topics include women's jobs, the adjustment of families to working wives and mothers, the effects of marriage on occupational attainment, work roles and marital solidarity, and housework by husbands.
- Consumers Union of United States, Inc. *Consumer Reports*. Mount Vernon, N.Y. A popular consumers' magazine published monthly by Consumers Union, an organization whose aims are to provide information on consumer goods and services and to supply information on all aspects relating to the expenditure of family income. All products and services

are purchased on the open market and independently rated through laboratory tests or judgments by experts. This is a good resource for evaluating and comparing goods and services.

- Goldberg, Herb, and Lewis, Robert T. *Money Madness: The Psychology of Saving, Spending, Loving and Hating Money.* New York: New American Library, 1978. A book exploring the origins of attitudes and values related to money. The authors include discussions of the symbolic meaning of money and the effects that individual behavior in financial matters can have on intimate relationships. One objective of the book is to present an approach to achieving "money sanity."

- Mackevich, Gene. *The Woman's Money Book.* Washington, D.C.: Acropolis Books, 1979. A practical guide written especially for women on how to expand financial resources and make money work for you. Contents include discussions on understanding the marketplace, plus the advantages and disadvantages of various investment possibilities: stocks, bonds, gold, real estate, and insurance.

- Moen, Phyllis. "Developing Family Indicators: Financial Hardship, A Case in Point." *Journal of Family Issues*, no. 1 (March 1980): 5–30. A discussion of ways to view the family as a system, with a particular emphasis on families who are experiencing economic hardship. Significant relationships are found between the level of deprivation (for example, a decrease of income versus a more severe level of poverty) and the life-cycle stage of the family.

- Porter, Sylvia. *Sylvia Porter's New Money Book for the 80's.* Garden City, N.Y.: Doubleday, 1979. A comprehensive and practical guide to earning, spending, saving, and investing. Porter covers a wide range of common financial decisions for families, including planning for food, clothing, housing, transportation, and educational expenses. Information on budgeting, use of credit, and financial record-keeping is also discussed, along with long-term financial planning. A section on how and where to get help on consumer problems is included.

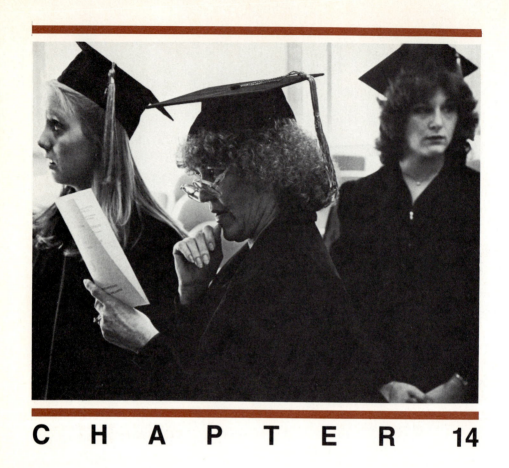

C H A P T E R 14

The Challenges of Adulthood

HE: I just want to try something new.

SHE: But you've got security there now, and a good pension later.

HE: I've got boredom and frustration, too.

SHE: You have to put up with some of that in any job.

HE: I've put up with 15 years of it.

SHE: But it's *my* turn. I've registered for the fall quarter. If you don't have a salary, how can we manage?

HE: We'll take a second mortgage on the house.

SHE: Do you know what kind of interest rates we'd have to pay?

HE: Look, we're talking about the rest of my life.

SHE: And mine.

HE: I don't want 25 more years of quiet desperation.

SHE: If you do take time off to write this novel, will we have any income?

HE: I figured I'd advertise as a handyman. You know I'm good at that.

SHE: Handyman!

HE: I like to work with my hands.

SHE: And I like to work with my head, but if you remember, I quit college so you could finish.

HE: Is there a martyr in our midst?

SHE: . . . and then the kids came.

HE: We'll nominate you for canonization on the next ballot.

SHE: You say you've felt desperate, but you had choices; I didn't.

HE: O.K. I'll go back to the job, but don't expect much in the way of an exciting mate.

SHE: Oh, I see, I'm supposed to sacrifice cheerfully for your education and your career, but when it's my turn, I get a bored, frustrated, bitter companion—that's great, just great!

INTRODUCTION

Growth and development do not stop at adolescence—they continue throughout a lifetime. The changes in adults are more subtle than those in children, and until the twentieth century, the developmental aspects of early and middle adulthood were virtually ignored. But due to increases in life expectancy and demographic shifts, people in early and middle adulthood now make up a larger proportion of our population. These shifts have given many researchers a new perspective—often referred to as the *life-cycle approach*—which we have used throughout this book. In this chapter we shall look at adulthood as a series of developmental challenges, concentrating on the tasks confronting mature and middle-aged men and women. We shall consider the effects of social norms on adults, the ways in which the expectations of society influence personal attitudes about the departure of children and other predictable events of middle age.

Theories concerning adult development have been based largely on men and the way males respond to the challenges of adulthood. We shall look at some of these findings, providing examples of how men feel when they face ages 30, 40, 50. But the life cycle offers different experiences for men and women, as has been pointed out in our discussions of male and female socialization, role patterns, and parenting. We shall suggest some ways in which adulthood and middle age differ for men and women, providing examples from the small body of research specifically on women. We shall also raise questions as to how these differences are likely to affect marriage and family life. Finally, we shall report results from a major study of satisfaction over the life cycle, looking at how such factors as marriage and the presence of children influence one's feelings of satisfaction.

The new research on adulthood suggests many possibilities for coping with life changes, whether one is married or single, a parent or childless. As we shall see at the end of the chapter, when we look at changes over the life cycle for single people, there are a variety of paths for satisfying the basic human need for intimacy in adult life.

MAPPING THE LIFE CYCLE

The exact timing of adulthood and middle age is difficult to establish, for there are numerous individual and class differences. For example, the age at which women finish school, marry, and have their first child or their first grandchild is significantly affected by their class status, as Figure 14.1 demonstrates. Roughly, the two stages on which we shall concentrate in this chapter—adulthood and middle age—cover a period that begins about age 22 and ends about age 60.

People are living longer, and that increased longevity has transformed the middle years from a period that used to encompass aging and death into a time of growth, change, and even new beginnings: "The average life expectancy in the eighteenth century was 35; by 1900 it was 50; and today it is 70" (Steinmetz 1978). According to census figures (reflected in Table 14.1), life expectancy has increased even more dramatically for women than for men. In terms of demography, the postwar baby boom and the decline in fertility in recent decades have created a larger proportion of adults in our current population, with the prospect of an even larger proportion of middle-aged and elderly people in future decades (Masnick and Bane 1980).

Persons no longer move abruptly from adulthood to old age, but instead go through a relatively long interval when physical vigor remains high, when family responsibilities are diminished, and when commitment to work continues. . . . Specific work roles may change, as when women reenter the labor market in their 40's and 50's and when men's work patterns become modified. (Neugarten and Hagestad 1976, p. 46)

The dramatic changes in the life span occurring in the twentieth century have been accompanied by major explorations into the phases of the human life cycle. Beginning with Freud's work on infancy and adulthood, students of behavior have mapped and divided each period of the life cycle, "as if the human psyche were a new continent gradually being explored and understood." Thus, "the number of recognizable life periods has been increasing, at least as described by historians and other observers" (Neugarten and Hagestad 1976). Until the seventeenth and eighteenth centuries, childhood was not recognized as a specific period of life (Aries 1962). The concept that infancy and early childhood experiences have a lifelong impact on the individual—Freud's unique contribution—was not accepted until the twentieth century. Working at about the same time as Freud, Emile Durkheim, one of the first sociologists, set the pattern for the study of social organizations. In his examination of suicide, Durk-

FIGURE 14.1 Median Ages at Which Women of Different Social Classes Reached Successive Events in the Family Cycle

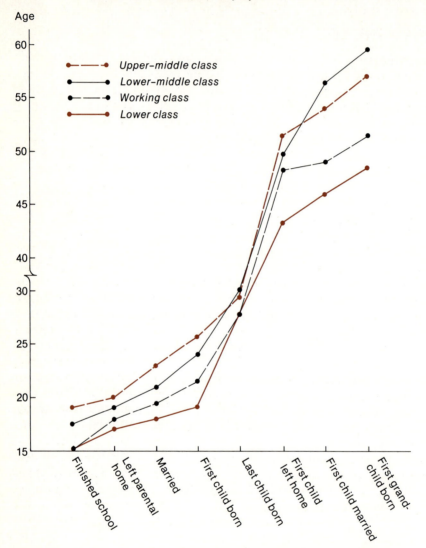

Source: Kenneth M. Olsen, "Social Class and Age-Group Differences in the Timing of Family Status Changes: A Study of Age-Norms in American Society," unpublished Ph.D. dissertation, University of Chicago, 1969.

TABLE 14.1 Life Expectancy at Birth, 1920–1975

Year	Total	Male	Female
1920	54.1	53.6	54.6
1930	59.7	58.1	61.6
1950	68.2	65.6	71.1
1955	69.6	66.7	72.8
1960	69.7	66.6	73.1
1965	70.2	66.8	73.7
1970	70.9	67.1	74.8
1971	71.1	67.4	75.0
1972	71.1	67.4	75.1
1973	71.3	67.6	75.3
1974	71.9	68.2	75.9
1975	72.5	68.7	76.5

Source: U.S. Bureau of the Census, *Current Population Reports*, Series P-20, No. 312, "Marriage, Divorce, Widowhood and Re-marriage and Family Characteristics: June 1975," U.S. Government Printing Office, Washington, D.C., 1977.

heim (1951) integrated biological, psychological, and sociological perspectives, considering the influences of religion, nationality, and socio-economic class. This use of several disciplines to understand changes in human behavior became a foundation stone of the life-cycle approach.

Carl Jung provided a bridge to current studies of adult development. It was Jung who proposed the idea that, in their thirties, men and women begin a process of individuation or self-realization. Jung was more sensitive than Freud to differences in this process for men and women. At the same time, Jung established what seems now a uniquely modern belief— the presence in every man and woman of both male and female components. The importance of active and passive traits within both sexes becomes more apparent as couples move away from the biological functions of parenthood and childbearing. When people have half a lifetime left after the childbearing years, they also have the possibility of discovering untapped resources in themselves. With increased longevity, the empty nest can offer a new beginning.

CHALLENGES OF ADULTHOOD

Erik Erikson's formulation of the life-cycle theory is the basis of most of the current work on development over the life span. We have already examined some of Erikson's contributions in terms of childhood and adolescence. Here we shall dwell on his conceptions concerning the next stages. In Erikson's scheme, the years between 22 and 60 embrace two stages—*young adulthood* and *adulthood*, or *middle age*. Each of these stages has its particular challenges. Between age 22 and roughly age 40, the primary challenge is that of *intimacy* versus *isolation*. Between ages 40 and 60, what we are calling "middle age" and what Erikson calls "adulthood," the major challenge is to move toward *generativity* and to avoid *stagnation*.

Intimacy is the capacity to make enduring commitments. As Erikson defines it, intimacy is the individual's capacity to commit himself or herself

to concrete affiliations and partnerships and to develop the ethical strength to abide by such commitments, even though they may call for significant sacrifices and compromises. . . . The counterpart of intimacy is distantiation: the readiness to isolate and, if necessary, destroy those forces and people whose essence seems dangerous to one's own and whose "territory" seems to encroach on the extent of one's intimate relations. (1968, pp. 263–264)

Erikson considered intimacy the challenge of young adulthood. But today, with marriage often postponed, divorce prevalent, and remarriage possible in later life, intimacy appears to be a challenge that is posed again and again throughout adult life. Traditionally, the challenge of intimacy has been met through the tasks of finding and cherishing a loved one, marrying, bearing and rearing children, finding productive work, and enjoying recreation.

Generativity is primarily "the concern in establishing and guiding the next generation." Failure to achieve generativity may result in stagnation or personal impoverishment, in indulging oneself as if one were alone in the world, the "one and only child" (Erikson 1968, p. 138). Generativity is a prominent challenge for middle age. This challenge may be met by guiding one's own children or by serving as a guide or mentor to the next generation.

Social Clocks

Erikson's view of adulthood accounts for the interaction between psychological developments and social influences, but it stresses the psychological aspects of adult development, particularly as experienced by men. Those who follow this formulation see a number of crises occurring during adulthood. For example, according to Daniel Levinson (1978, p. 57), during early adulthood comes the age-30 transition, when one must judge whether intimacy and other tasks of the period—settling in, marrying, finding an occupation—have actually been accomplished. Still another crisis comes between the ages of 40 and 45, when one moves from early adulthood to middle adulthood. (Levinson's approach is discussed in more detail on pages 455–461.)

Another approach is taken by Bernice Neugarten and others, who stress the sociological aspects of aging. In that framework, though one is re-

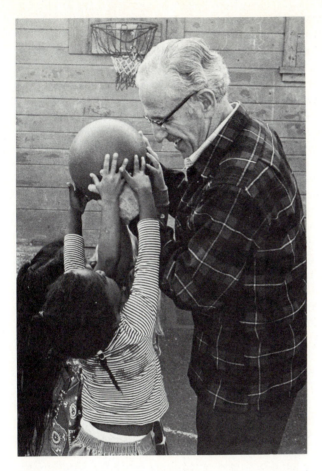

Generativity—guiding one's own children or other members of
the next generation—is a prominent challenge of middle age.
(Elizabeth Crews)

minded of psychological stages and individual expectations, the individual is seen in the group context. Crisis results only when the individual
is "out of sync" with his or her particular age group. The theory of *social
clocks* developed by Neugarten and her colleagues at the University of
Chicago is an outstanding example of the sociological approach to adult
development.

It is Neugarten's contention, and she has gathered substantial evidence
for it, that people are aware not only of the order in which life events
should go, but also of the schedule set by their society for such events.
Groups she has studied have known, for example, that they should first
marry, then raise children, reach a high point of productivity at home or
work, see their children leave home, deal with this time of postparenting,

and, finally, retire. They also have known whether they are early, late, or on time with these various family and occupational events.

As Neugarten sees it, the fact that a person has reached the age of 40, 50, or 60 is not so important as the question "How am I doing for my age?" She suggests that people have a "mental time clock telling them where they are and whether they are on time or off time." Who sets that clock? Who determines which "hour" is appropriate? Neugarten believes there are social factors that dictate, in general terms, when the normal time is for events to occur. She calls these social time schedules "social clocks" (Neugarten 1979, p. 888).

Neugarten, Moore, and Lowe (1968) sampled 400 men and women in three age groups: 20 to 29, 30 to 55, and over 65. As Table 14.2 demonstrates, the majority of the people in the 30-to-55 age group seemed to run their lives according to social clocks; the younger men and women felt that they were under more rigid age constraints than did the older ones. According to this theory, it is not the change from young adulthood to middle age that necessarily produces a crisis. Rather, it is the failure to conform to the social clock that causes anxiety and dissatisfaction.

Thus, it is "normal" to leave one's parents' home, to marry, to become a parent, to become a grandparent, and so on. It is true that these events "call forth changes in self-concept and identity, but whether or not they produce crises depends on their timing" (Neugarten 1979, p. 889). The so-called empty nest need not be a crisis for the mother and father, but may actually be a time of great happiness. It is not the predictable departure of the child, but the failure of the child to leave the house "on time" that could trigger a crisis. Neugarten finds that "even death is a normal and expectable event for the old. Death is tragic only when it occurs at too young an age. Even the death of one's spouse, if it occurs on time, does not create a psychiatric crisis for most men or women" (p. 889). The key for Neugarten is *preparation and timing:*

Most such events, when they finally occur on time, have been anticipated and rehearsed, the grief work completed, and the reconciliation accomplished without shattering the sense of continuity of the life cycle or the individual's coping strategies. (p. 889)

She divides the major psychological preoccupations of adulthood into two periods: young adulthood and middle age. In young adulthood,

the major tasks are to achieve a balance between settling down and moving forward; growing new roots while striving for achievement; meeting new obligations, especially toward spouse and children; and investing oneself in the lives of a few significant others to whom one will be bound for years to come, while at the same time achieving individuation, competency, and job mastery. (p. 890)

TABLE 14.2 Consensus in a Middle-Class, Middle-Aged Sample on Various Age-Related Characteristics

Characteristic	Appropriate or Expected Age Range	Percentage of Men Who Concur	Percentage of Women Who Concur
Best age for a man to marry	20–25	80	90
Best age for a woman to marry	19–24	85	90
When most people should become grandparents	45–50	84	79
Best age for most people to finish school and go to work	20–22	86	82
When most men should be settled in a career	24–26	74	64
When most men hold their top jobs	45–50	71	58
When most people should be ready to retire	60–65	83	86
Age of a young man	18–22	84	83
Age of a middle-aged man	40–50	86	75
Age of an old man	65–75	75	57
Age of a young woman	18–24	89	88
Age of a middle-aged woman	40–50	87	77
Age of an old woman	60–75	83	87
When a man has the most responsibilities	35–50	79	75
When a man accomplishes most	40–50	82	71
The prime of life for a man	35–50	86	80
When a woman has the most responsibilities	25–40	93	91
When a woman accomplishes most	30–45	94	92
Age of a good-looking woman	20–35	92	82

Source: Adapted from Bernice L. Neugarten, Joan W. Moore, and John C. Lowe, "Age Norms, Age Constraints, and Adult Socialization," in *Middle Age and Aging,* Bernice L. Neugarten (ed.), University of Chicago Press, 1968, p. 24. Copyright © 1968 by The University of Chicago. All rights reserved.

In middle age there are different tasks:

the reworking of relationships between husbands and wives, with new expectations of what it means to be male or female; the changing sense of self as children grow up and as one's victories and defeats are reckoned by how well the child is turning out; the need to quickly establish an intimate relationship with a stranger when a son-in-law or daughter-in-law appears; for increasing numbers of middle-aged people, the need to adjust quickly to a child's divorce; the appearance of a grandchild who brings a new awareness of aging but also a new source of gratification; and the awareness of the self as the bridge between the generations. (p. 890)

There are other issues for middle age as well: the possibility of marital difficulties as one faces a marriage now free of clear-cut parental pressures

Grandchildren bring a new awareness of aging but also a new source of gratification. (Florence Sharp)

or role distinctions and considers the possibility of divorce, remarriage, or the challenge of another type of intimate relationship. Caring for one's aging parents may be a new and consuming consideration. For women there may be new freedoms, and for both men and women middle age may be a period of reflection.

Resetting Social Clocks.   Social clocks can change. While individuals are undergoing personal changes because of different life events—marriage, children, departure of children—they are also responding to sociological factors. The age structure of the society, and certain historical changes, may alter social clocks. Norms regarding how people of different ages should behave and how different age groups should relate to one another may change over time (Neugarten, Moore, and Lowe 1968, p. 143). For example, the man reaching age 50 in 1930 may have been unemployed, burdened with family responsibility, committed to his role as exclusive breadwinner, yet facing poor prospects for his future and that of his children. The man turning 50 in 1960 had more security and a better hope of meeting the challenge of generativity. In fact, his earlier war experiences may have caused him to attach more importance to home and family. By

1970 the man turning 50 might have been thrown into doubt again concerning his children's future. Attacked by the younger generation for clinging to old institutions that fostered war, racism, and sexism, this man may have found that his sense of generativity was seriously shaken.

By 1980 the demographic pendulum had swung once more. Men and women turning 50 make up a larger cohort (or age-related segment) of the population than ever before. Their life span is longer; their options more numerous. They face turning points that other middle-aged people have faced before them: they are aware of being at a place in life clearly separate from the young and the old; they are likely to be taking stock and facing changes in health (Neugarten et al. 1968) or physical condition (see Box 14.1). They also may be making new beginnings that would not have been undertaken by middle-aged people of previous generations. This pattern of new beginnings in middle age is particularly applicable to women, who may choose to return to school or start a new career. Social institutions such as universities have changed to make midlife career changes or beginnings possible. Today it is common to see older students on college campuses; a mother might be returning to school at the same time her daughter is entering college. Given divorce and remarriage trends, a man might become both a father and a grandfather at 50. Thus the life cycle is becoming more fluid in our culture, as Hirschhorn (1977) has suggested, and social clocks are altered or reset. Yet the "perceptions, the expectations, and the actual occurrences of life events" continue to be "socially regulated" (Neugarten et al. 1968, p. 145).

Male and Female Differences in Life-Cycle Events

Most major theories of human behavior and life-cycle development have originated with male scientists. Their findings are based largely on data for males, and so the male pattern of behavior and development has been regarded as normal. Female development, while recognized as different, has often been regarded simply as deviating from this normative male pattern and, therefore, being of less interest and importance. Work is now being done, however, on defining and explaining female behavior and development over the life span, though much of the theoretical conceptualization and research remain to be done. In the next sections, we shall discuss some of the experiences and predictable crises unique to adult men and some of the experiences unique to women, keeping in mind the fact that as roles and socialization become somewhat less rigid, adulthood experiences of women and men may become more alike.

MEN IN ADULTHOOD

Daniel J. Levinson and his colleagues at Yale University conducted an in-depth study of adult development in men, published as *The Seasons of a*

BOX 14.1   Male and Female "Menopause"

Female menopause "is the dramatic change which signals the end of the reproductive phase of life" (Strauss and Mitzner 1977). Menopause starts, on the average, between the ages of 40 and 53, although there are great individual variations that extend the range of years even further. Menopause itself is not a sudden event but a gradual one, which takes on the average between two and five years. Estrogen secretion decreases; ovarian function diminishes and ceases; menstruation stops. Some women experience hot flashes and sweats in this process, or excessive or irregular bleeding may occur before menstruation stops. But for many women, the physical aspects of menopause are not severe (Strauss and Mitzner 1977). Episodes of anxiety and depression may occur before or during menopause, but the vast majority of women do not experience these severe emotional upsets.

The menopause can actually be seen as a remarkable and uniquely human grace period in which the woman is free from reproductive demands and yet still able-bodied and healthy. Life expectancy has increased faster than menopause expectancy: "While the age of onset of menopause has moved from the early forties to the late forties and early fifties, life expectancy has progressed from 54.6 years in 1920 to 74.5 years today" (Strauss and Mitzner 1977, p. 365). Menopause, then, in light of female longevity and current role changes, may be an added impetus for women to restructure their lives, examine new possibilities, and even begin a new career.

The biological changes in males during middle age are less universal. Generally, there are some hormonal changes—pituitary gonadotropic hormones are increasing while testosterone levels are decreasing. The age range of these events is even broader than that for menopausal changes in women. They occur most commonly between ages 48 and 60, with some changes not becoming evident until the period between 58 and 68. Endocrinologist Herbert S. Kupperman suggests that this kind of "change of life" or *climacterium*, in terms of specific laboratory findings, is experienced by only 35 percent of men during middle age (Strauss and Mitzner 1977, p. 306). Testosterone levels decline more gradually in most males, with physiological changes not becoming marked until about age 70. Even then, sexual activity can continue on into old age. Because males in their sexual socialization have been oriented to "performance," any reduction in their sexual capacity may be viewed with alarm. Despite undergoing fewer marked biological changes than women during middle age, men may experience greater anxiety.

Man's Life (1978). As Figure 14.2 indicates, Levinson concentrated much of his research in the areas of early and middle adulthood, from about ages 22 to 55. The major thrust of the investigation focused on the period of men's lives that begins at about age 40 and ends at about age 45. Levinson calls this the "mid-life transition"; the majority of the men he studied experienced a "moderate or severe crisis" during this transition (1978, p. 199).

Levinson's sample of 40 men included 10 each of hourly workers, business executives, academic biologists, and novelists. The 40 men had a wide

FIGURE 14.2   Developmental Periods for Men In Early and Middle Adulthood

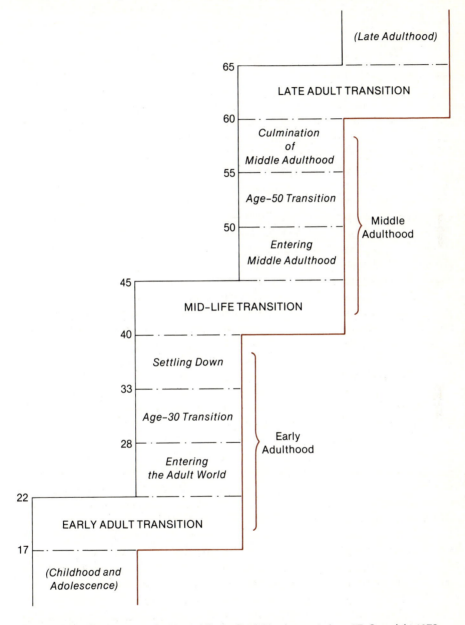

Source: From *The Seasons of a Man's Life*, by Daniel Levinson et al., p. 57. Copyright 1978 by Daniel Levinson. Reprinted by permission of Alfred A. Knopf, Inc.

variety of racial, ethnic, socioeconomic, religious, and educational back-grounds. The study was sensitive to social factors, but it relied heavily on the subjects' interpersonal behavior and, especially, their personal feelings about themselves.

Crisis Periods

Levinson found that most men experience at least two crisis periods in their lives. The first crisis period occurs around the ages of 28 to 33; the second crisis begins around age 40 and lasts about five years. The first crisis is generally less severe than the second. These crisis points are the major markers in Levinson's model for the developmental periods in early and middle adulthood.

At about age 30, nearly two-thirds (62 percent) of the men in Levinson's group experienced a moderate or severe crisis. At this stage of life, a man has taken the first firm steps in building a structured life; he has chosen a career, friends, often a spouse, but he wonders if these are indeed the choices he wishes to live with. If they are, then perhaps the years he will spend in his thirties will be fairly satisfying. But if the choices he has made do not mesh with his "dreams, talents, and external possibilities," then he must change directions—and quickly (p. 59). A man experiencing the age-30 crisis is like "a man alone, on a body of water trying to get from Island Past to Island Future" (p. 86). The man feels caught, trapped, and on the verge of drowning; all is in doubt; he asks himself: "Do I really want to be a (mechanic, business executive, scientist, writer)? If so, then I'd better work hard, very hard indeed. But if I want to do something different, I'd better make the change quickly. There's not a lot of time left. They still call me a young man, but I no longer consider myself young. And my marriage may not be all I hoped it would be. What can I do about that ... if anything?"

When a man nears the age of 40, he is likely to question all the choices he has made; just about everything in his life seems up for grabs. He may embark on a total reappraisal of his life choices and his life course. He may be seen by others as acting "irrational," "upset," or "sick," but in most cases, he is not. Rather, he is coming to grips with what Levinson calls his "Dream," his personal myth (p. 246)—a dream of himself-as-hero, which was created in his youth and has dominated his life choices until now. At about age 40, he realizes he has not fulfilled every aspect of his Dream, and this realization may cause him to view his entire life as a failure.

In the midst of this brutal self-appraisal, the man on the brink of middle age hears other internal voices, which may have been muted for years:

A man hears the voice of an identity prematurely rejected; of a love lost or not pursued; of a valued interest or relationship given up in acquiescence to parental or other authority;

of an internal figure who wants to be an athlete or nomad or artist, to marry for love or remain a bachelor, to get rich or enter the clergy or live a sensual carefree life—possibilities set aside earlier to become what he is now. (p. 200)

After a number of false or tentative starts, the man in his early forties is prepared to enter middle adulthood with a new or modified dream of what he can do with the rest of his life. As Box 14.2 indicates, midlife turmoil is often balanced by new satisfactions.

Early Adulthood

According to Levinson's model, the early adult period begins at about age 17 and ends at about age 40.

Early Adult Transition.   :vinson believes there are two tasks for the man between ages 17 and 22. (All age assignments Levinson makes have a flexibility of about two years in either direction.) The first task of this period is to "move out of the pre-adult world" and begin to change or end existing relationships (p. 56). One leaves adolescence, departing from an often tumultuous, uncertain world. The second task for this period is to "step into the adult world." Now the young man can begin to explore realistically the adult world and its possibilities. In adolescence, entry to this world of adult affairs was denied him. Now he can test his dreams of a future against actual experience.

Entering the Adult World.   At about age 22 to 28, the man now struggles to achieve a balance between "two primary yet antithetical tasks." The first task is to keep as many options open as possible, exploring, experimenting, rejecting, tasting a variety of experiences. The second task is to set down certain firm foundations upon which he may build a "stable life structure" (pp. 57–58).

Age-30 Transition.   t roughly age 28 to 33, a man begins to want to be taken seriously. He is no longer the fumbling adolescent, nor is he the experimenting young adult. He hears an inner voice say, "If I am to change my life—if there are things in it I want to modify or exclude, or things missing I want to add—I must now make a start for soon it will be too late" (p. 58). Often this is a stressful period; "the age-30 crisis" is a recognition that the present form of his life is intolerable, yet he appears unable to create a better life.

Settling Down.   This period begins at the end of the age-30 transition and continues to about age 40. The full force of the man's life is now directed at

BOX 14.2 Life After Harvard

In 1937, a project later known as the "Grant Study of Adult Development" was conceived. In all, 268 young men, specially selected from classes at Harvard University (1939 through 1944), were chosen for long-term study. These were young men judged most likely to make the most of their natural intellectual abilities, men who appeared to be the least troubled and the best adjusted. The obvious bias of the study is readily acknowledged. The young men were subject to early in-depth interviews, as were their families, and they were asked to fill out lengthy questionnaires each year about the state of their life. George E. Vaillant gathered all the material, conducted interviews with 94 of the Grant Study men, and published the results in *Adaptation to Life* (1977).

The men in Vaillant's study used many methods of coping with change. Some denied or distorted reality; others were at times immature or neurotic. By far the happiest men in the study used what Vaillant calls "mature" defenses, including altruism, humor, suppression, anticipation, and sublimation as means of dealing with the natural stresses of life. Interestingly, those men who were judged to have adjusted and dealt with reality the most satisfactorily did experience inner turmoil during the period of 35 to 45, yet these men also described that period as the happiest in their lives (p. 226). Vaillant found more support in his sample for the social-clocks view than for the midlife-crisis position.

Another group of studies is being conducted at the Center for the Study of Aging and Human Development at Duke University (Strauss and Mitzner 1977, p. 367). In these longitudinal studies of 500 persons from middle and upper socioeconomic levels, preliminary indications suggest that the work environment is the primary cause of problems for men, especially older men. Men appear to have difficulty dealing with their images—how they see themselves as contrasted with what they suspect others think of them. Some men suffer at this time from the feeling that their futures, especially their occupational futures, are out of their own hands. Planning for some work disengagement or investing in activities other than work may help men to maintain a sense of controlling their lives. In the Duke studies, those men who appear to be in control of their lives seem to be happiest.

achieving his major goals: "A man seeks to involve himself in the major components of the structure (work, family, friendships, leisure, community—whatever is most central to him) and to realize his youthful aspiration and goals" (p. 59). The man again has two tasks: (1) to establish himself, to develop, and to be recognized for developing competency, and (2) to build a better life for himself and be recognized for that.

Levinson uses the image of the "ladder"; it is important for the man to climb the ladder of prestige and add to his life those elements—social and personal—that acknowledge and affirm his climb to success. For a working-class man, success might mean becoming a foreman or obtaining an important position in a union, while a middle-class man might climb the ladder by rising to an executive or a managerial position.

Middle Adulthood

The Midlife Transition: Moving from Early to Middle Adulthood. This is the second crisis period, at roughly age 40 to 45. There are new developmental tasks, the first of which is to ask some of the most terrible and painful questions a person can ask: "What have I done with my life? What do I really get from and give to my wife, children, friends, work community—and self? What is it I truly want for myself and others?" (p. 60).

It is the period that has become known as the "mid-life crisis," a period of "emotional turmoil, despair, and sense of not knowing where to turn or of being stagnant and unable to move at all" (p. 199). By about age 45, the man has used the midlife transition to reappraise, explore, test choices, and create the basis for a new life.

Entering Middle Adulthood: Building a New Life Structure. After the midlife upheaval comes a new beginning: "Now he must make his choices and begin a new life structure." For some men, it will be an unhappy period, the past defeats so damaging that they have no more resources left. For others, it will mean a life that is just lived, one "lacking in inner excitement and meaning." But for others it will be a special time, "the fullest and most creative season in the life cycle" (pp. 61–62).

Age-50 Transition. The man from about age 50 to 55 can now continue to modify the life structure formulated in the mid-40s. If there has been no crisis in the midlife transition, Levinson believes, a man is likely to experience a crisis now.

Culmination of Middle Adulthood. This period, from about age 55 to 60, allows the man to complete middle adulthood; it is a time for rejuvenation and enrichment in life.

Late Adult Transition

The man now ends middle adulthood and begins late adulthood. At this major turning point in the life cycle, from about age 60 to 65, it is time to prepare for the final stages of life, a time to truly confront one's own mortality.

WOMEN IN ADULTHOOD

At the present time, information on women that is comparable in quantity and quality to the data on men is not available. The limited number of studies now available suggest some important differences between men and women in adulthood, especially in terms of satisfaction over the life cycle. In an address on the subject of women and midlife, Gunhild Hagestad (1975) remarked: "We've tended to judge women by a short-sighted male model which attempts to squeeze most of human becoming into the first two decades of adulthood." Hagestad contends that the tendency to dwell on the first two or three decades of adulthood emphasizes the conflicted aspect of women's lives. Women are raised with a greater investment in family and kin, although they may also receive the same education as males and be trained as if they will tackle the same achievement tasks. The result is "double-tracking"—family and work—while boys and young men are raised much more on the single track of work-achievement. During the period of mate selection, young women may feel some conflict between these two tracks. As was shown in Matina Horner's research (1972), women have often avoided success because they fear that it may threaten interpersonal relations; achievement may undermine their other goals—marriage and family. We discussed in Chapter 7 some changes occurring in role expectations, yet some of the ambivalence concerning achievement remains.

In young adulthood there is a "life-cycle squeeze" as women hasten to finish school, start a career, get married, and have children. We have noted that women may be subjected during their twenties and early thirties to a good deal of role strain, whether they are working outside the home or inside the home. As Hagestad (1975) puts it, "It is rough when two people in the same household need a good wife. The research shows that the man is more likely to get that spousely support than is the woman in a dual-career marriage."

But while women's double-track socialization creates some degree of strain and conflict in young adulthood, Hagestad asserts that it seems to have certain benefits in later adulthood or middle age: "With dual-track upbringing, women gain flexibility and a greater array of skills than most men possess." Her interviews with middle-aged, middle-class women indicate that the double investment in family and achievement makes them more hopeful and better able to deal with the transitions of the middle years.

Women in their late thirties and early forties face some of the multiple tasks and stresses that also confront men at those ages. They, too, must contend with more than one developmental event—for example, menopause and their children's adolescence or departure from home. Married women are also dealing with the anxieties that may be afflicting their husbands on the brink of middle age. But Hagestad's research indicates that the departure of children to college or to their own jobs and apartments is not necessarily traumatic for women. While the realignment of relationships with their adolescent children may produce great strains, the emptying of the nest apparently does not: "Women relish the release from some of the day-to-day demands in the mother role. When asked about the best part of being their current age, the most common answer given by middle-aged women that I studied was 'freedom.'"

The women Hagestad interviewed welcomed the freedom to use time, energy, and money at their own discretion rather than make the constant "contingency plans" of their twenties and thirties, when they would (or could) do certain things if their husband did this and their children did that. These contingencies, this series of "ifs," may have interfered with career planning and achievement patterns in earlier years. In the middle years, freedom from these contingencies can be exhilarating. Women in Hagestad's sample said:

"It's a great time of my life. The bargain basement struggle is over."
"I'm accepting myself as I am. I realize my tremendous growth since my twenties."
"I don't care what other people say or do any more. I'm my own person now."

Middle-aged women do have concerns related to the physical aging process. They told Hagestad that the most difficult part about being their age was their growing sense of the weakness of the body and the finitude of life, along with their awareness that they might not be able to accomplish many of the things they had wanted to do.

Yet the majority of the women were engaged in a remarkable exploration of "nonfamily spheres," including participation in the labor force, which reaches its peak in the middle years (see Figure 14.3). In Hagestad's middle-class sample, 60 percent of the women were taking two or more courses; two-thirds of them had embarked on a new activity, ranging from running for political office to belly dancing and scuba diving. The majority of these women had been influenced by their children, encouraged by them to change their appearance and take the leap into the world of work or school. Here again, the double-tracking becomes significant: Women continue to have regular contact with their children, while men do not.

Hagestad polled 760 college students and found that 80 percent of the college women and 60 percent of the college men reported that their mothers had discussed personal problems with them; very few reported that their fathers talked with them about personal concerns and worries. "Mothers were ushered into the next era by their children, by their continuing interaction with them" (Hagestad 1975). If, as Margaret Mead has noted, parents are "immigrants in time" (1970), continuing interaction with the next generation can help them make that passage and orient themselves to the new era.

FIGURE 14.3 Percentage of Women Working Year-Round Full-time, by Age, 1960–1977

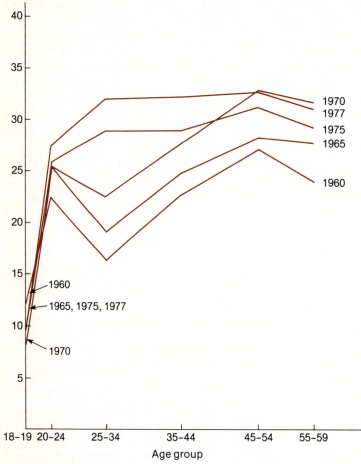

Percentage of women
working year-round full-time

Age group

Source: George Masnick and Mary Jo Bane, *The Nation's Families: 1960–1990*, Joint Center for Urban Studies of M.I.T. and Harvard University, Cambridge, Mass., p. 80.

Hagestad concludes, then, that "because of the dual track, women are better able to restructure a second life in the middle years than are men." It will be interesting to see whether the trend to a growing investment in parenting by men will bring them benefits in middle age.

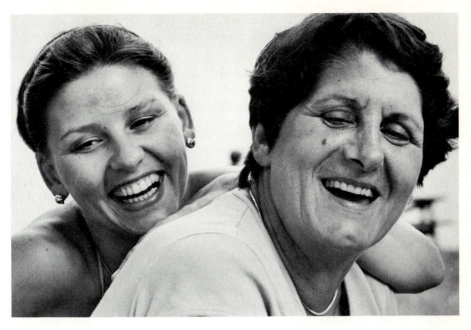

Mothers usually continue to have regular contact with their adult children. (Jean-Claude Lejeune)

So far, there has been no clear-cut formulation of the life cycle for women comparable to Erikson's and Levinson's for men. But a number of researchers, including Notman (1980) and Miller (1976), are attempting to point to areas where women's development over the life span differs from that of men.

Notman suggests, for example, that for women, autonomy and identity may not be followed by intimacy, as Erikson's scheme suggests. In female development, these events tend to be more nearly simultaneous. Women are more embedded in social interaction and personal relationships than men, and this training in intimacy begins in early childhood. Women seem to define their own life cycles more in terms of their children's ages or their family's stage of development than do men. Midlife may begin for a man when he is displaced at work by younger competitors and when he takes on the mentoring role; for women, middle age may be the time when children leave home and they can give attention to personal needs and development. Educational and career development may come later for women, especially those who are mothers, so that women in their forties face some of the tasks typically faced by men in their late twenties and early thirties. (Box 14.3 discusses some cross-cultural life-cycle patterns for men and women.)

For both sexes a more hopeful view of middle age seems to be emerging, a view of life (as Hagestad expresses it) as a series of "seizings and becomings, seizings and becomings" (1975).

SATISFACTIONS AND STRESSES OVER THE LIFE CYCLE

Investigations of what has come to be known as "quality of life" can provide further information concerning the stresses and satisfactions of young and middle adulthood, especially as related to intimate lifestyle patterns. Research aimed at finding out how individuals perceive their lives in terms of satisfaction or happiness began in the 1950s. Since then, numer-

---

BOX 14.3 Cross-Cultural Patterns

David Gutmann's cross-cultural work provides us with one version of the way husband and wife may serve complementary functions in each other's life cycles, "taking turns," as it were, in utilizing their passive (or traditionally feminine) and aggressive (or traditionally masculine) traits. Gutmann examined the psychology of aging in four groups: urban, middle-class, white Americans; Mayan Indians of Yucatan and Chiapas; traditional (Western) Navajo Indians; and Druze agriculturalists of the Galilee and Golan Heights in Israel (1972, p. 417).

Gutmann finds in all these cultures an "almost universal phasing out of aggressive motives in men during late middle life, and their replacement by more tender, affiliative sentiments" (p. 419). As the children grow up and are able to care for and take responsibility for themselves, the father and mother have "the luxury of living out the potentials and pleasures that they had to relinquish early on, in the service of their particular parental task." At middle life, both husband and wife experience a dramatic shift in emphasis in their personality characteristics: "Just as men reclaim title to their denied 'femininity,' women in late middle life repossess the 'masculinity' that they once had to send out of the house and live out vicariously through their husbands." Now both husband and wife, as they journey from middle life to old age, "move closer together, psychologically, each partner becoming what the other used to be, and there is ushered in the unisex of later life" (pp. 423–424).

It is important to note that Gutmann is not proposing that this is the way the normal life cycle *should be,* but rather reporting the way that he and others have observed that it *is* in many different cultures. There are already signs, in the late twentieth century, that certain aspects of this complementary male/female life-cycle pattern are changing. If this is so, we may find ourselves living in a country where different groups have different social clocks. We shall continue to go through stages of adulthood, but our expectations and our coping strategies may become extremely varied. Many adults will be like jazz musicians, improvising the tune as they grow through adult life.

ous studies have been made, using a variety of methods for measuring happiness and satisfaction with one's life circumstances.

The basic data for the following discussion are from a major work by Campbell, Converse, and Rodgers (1976) based on a probability sample of households within the United States and personal interviews with 2,164 persons, 18 years of age or older. The lengthy interview questionnaire covered the respondent's perception of his or her satisfaction with numerous aspects of life, including overall satisfaction with life in general. The findings of this study differ from those of the studies we have already discussed in this chapter, because they represent what individuals actually say about the satisfactions of their lives. It is not a theoretical analysis based on clinical work or a theory-building attempt based on empirical data (though the researchers attempt to explain the results on some issues). It presents the raw data regarding what respondents say about life, much like a detailed opinion poll. There are pros and cons for this approach, but it seems particularly instructive in exploring new areas where little previous work exists.

A variety of factors have been found to affect one's perception of satisfaction, including age, sex, level of education, health, socioeconomic status, and stage of family life cycle. Figure 14.4 illustrates how one's gender, age, and stage in the family life cycle correspond to one's general level of satisfaction. As we shall see, satisfaction with marriage and family life plays a paramount role in the lives of many Americans.

Patterns of Marital Satisfaction

Among those who were married, most of the respondents in the Campbell, Converse, and Rodgers study described their marriages in "very positive" terms. The authors qualify this finding, noting that the married people in their survey might have had time to get a divorce had they wanted one. Levels of satisfaction with marriage may be higher than would have been the case, say, 30 years ago, when even the unhappily married tended to remain together. The reports of marital satisfaction may also be somewhat inflated because of what the authors call "a good deal of denial." That is, people tend to deny dissatisfactions. Satisfaction levels for men and women differ in a number of ways, and women tend to view their marriages more critically than men, yet both rated "good health" and "a happy marriage" as the two most important values.

The authors discovered what might be called a U-shaped pattern to satisfaction in marital relationships. The relationship seems to begin with an intense high "just after commitment" of the couple to one another; it is followed by "a period of decay in marriage satisfaction out to nearly the twentieth year of marriage," which is then followed by an upswing in

FIGURE 14.4   Life Satisfaction of Women and Men at Stages of the Life Cycle

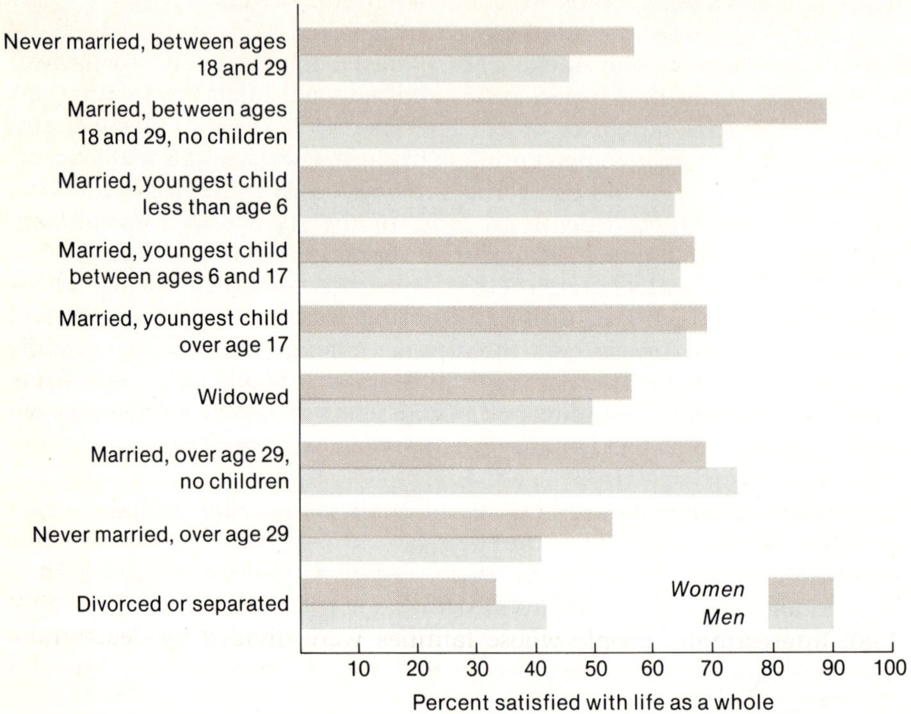

Source: From *The Quality of American Life: Perceptions, Evaluations, and Satisfactions*, by A. Campbell et al. Copyright © 1976 by Russell Sage Foundation. Reprinted by permission of the publisher.

marriage satisfaction into old age (p. 325). There was a modest correlation between the number of children in the family and marital satisfaction. It seemed that those couples who had no children in the home (that is, either very young couples or older couples whose children were grown and gone from home) showed the highest degree of marital satisfaction. The more children at home, the greater the dissatisfaction. The authors note that, while "the presence of numbers of small children in the home no doubt has its rewards," it can be financially as well as psychologically draining (p. 327). The U-shaped curve of marital satisfaction, especially the dip in satisfaction following the birth of the first child, is a phenomenon that has been identified in several studies.

Education.   The education of the couples also had a strong impact on their degree of satisfaction. The higher the education attained by the spouses, the *lower* their satisfaction with marriage. The authors believe there is a correlation between the amount of education and the tendency to be critical about one's marital role: "The higher educated people were most likely to express dissatisfaction with their performance as husbands or wives" (p. 328). The authors also note a finding by Gurin, Veroff, and Feld that "people with more education tend to be more introspective about themselves," act more judgmentally, and, according to Campbell, Converse, and Rodgers, "bring a richer awareness of alternatives to these judgments, so that they are more likely to see ways in which they fall short of their aspirations" (p. 328).

The authors are loath to point to any single attribute as a "predictor" of marital satisfaction or dissatisfaction. "The assessment of marital relationships," claim the authors, "is more correctly determined by the conditions of the marriage (particularly by the age of the children) and reflects the psychological cost which the married person is paying in disagreements, misunderstanding, and lack of companionship" (p. 336).

Family History. Campbell, Converse, and Rodgers found that those people who had grown up in an intact family with both parents present (until age 16) "were more likely to describe their own family life as satisfactory than people whose families were divided by divorce or separation" (pp. 337–338). Interestingly, people whose families were divided by death more closely resembled those people coming from intact families than they did those from divorced families.

Married versus Single

Of the population studied—married, widowed, divorced or separated, and never-married—"married people, both women and men, are the most content with their family life. Widowed women, however, are equally positive in their appraisals [of family life] in sharp contrast to widowed men, who are considerably more negative" (p. 339). Campbell, Converse, and Rodgers were not surprised to find divorced and separated people more dissatisfied than married people (even married people with children). Women and men who had not married were also more dissatisfied than married people; and, again, the single men expressed more negative feelings than did the single women. The authors state: "The presence of a spouse is apparently less essential to a woman's sense of satisfaction with family life than it is to a man's" (p. 339). Other studies of divorced men also reveal a deep sense of loss, men suffering higher rates of physical and mental illness and even of suicide than divorced women (Gilder 1973). The notion that marriage and children are somehow more essential to women than to men is dispelled by such findings.

Both unmarried women and unmarried men apparently failed to find much satisfaction in their singlehood. They were aware of enjoying good health (one of the factors in overall satisfaction), but that was about it. It appears that their work did not bring them a high degree of satisfaction, nor did their nonwork activities, nor the community, neighborhood, city, or country. "The free, unfettered life of the single girl and her male counterpart does not seem as attractive to those who are living it as one might have predicted" (Campbell, Converse, and Rodgers 1976, p. 402).

In sharp contrast to their married but childless counterparts, unmarried women over 29 describe their lives "in very negative terms" (p. 417). Nonetheless, these single women still do not see their lives as unfavorably as their single male counterparts do: "Men who do not marry appear to suffer more from the absence of a wife than unmarried women do from the absence of a husband" (p. 419).

There are a number of possible reasons for this greater negativism on the part of older unmarried men. In light of what we have discussed about male and female socialization, we can see that women tend to form intimate friendships from early childhood, while male friendships tend to be based on the solidarity that emerges from a shared activity. Marriage may be the only situation in which most grown men can experience the openness and emotional sharing of a truly intimate relationship, while single women may find it easier to share intensely with other women and men. Marriage is one of many places where women can experience intimacy.

The data in the final section suggest that satisfaction with singlehood, men's willingness to share emotionally with friends, and other aspects of remaining single may change as this cohort of the population increases. It should also be kept in mind that this study did not differentiate between those who were single by choice and those who wanted to marry but, for any of a number of reasons, did not. Nor did it distinguish between unmarried heterosexuals and unmarried homosexuals. People who have chosen to remain single might be expected to be happier than those whose desires for marriage have been thwarted.

The Divorced and Separated.   Divorced women regard their lives very unfavorably overall, as compared with other women's levels of satisfaction, and somewhat more negatively even than divorced men. Divorced women are particularly dissatisfied with their standard of living and their savings. This is not at all surprising, considering the facts that (1) their standard of living was higher when they were married and (2) women still suffer from economic discrimination in the job market as well as less adequate preparation for careers. In short (as discussed in Chapter 12), divorce brings more economic hardship for women and in this sense is often more stressful for women than for men. Women also are more likely to head single-parent households, an additional stress.

Life-Cycle Satisfaction for Women

Campbell, Converse, and Rodgers thoroughly studied the life cycles of women in terms of satisfaction. They looked at three stages: youth and singlehood, marriage and parenthood, and widowhood. They also looked at three categories that they considered to diverge from the norm: childless married women over 30, never-married women over 30, and divorced or separated women. In terms of overall satisfaction, divorced women and then unmarried women were the least satisfied; young married women without children were among the most satisfied.

If a young woman remains single, she is likely to continue her role as a student, particularly if she is from the middle class. If she marries, however, it is likely that she will either take a job or assume the role of housewife. She is thus effectively removed from advanced education and so is handicapped if she enters or re-enters the work force. (Marriage does not, however, prevent young men from continuing as students.) When the young women in the study were asked why they terminated their formal education following marriage, almost half gave marriage itself as the reason (p. 399).

It would appear that tradition also plays a significant part in women's decision not to return to school. It may be also that women who work while their husbands continue school consider their decision as part of a financial as well as an emotional investment in their marriages. That is, if the husband becomes a more effective breadwinner, they both will have more security. Some women who have made such a sacrifice and then are divorced feel their husbands owe them the education they put aside. In one of the first cases in which a divorce-court judge recognized the justice of such a claim, a woman who had put her husband through medical school and wanted to be a doctor herself was given tuition and support through school as part of her divorce agreement.

Married women who worked were asked to state which was more important—work for pay or housework. Thirty-seven percent said their housework was more important, 41 percent said a job was more important, and 22 percent said the two were of equal importance (p. 401). The younger the women, the more likely they were to consider their job more important than housework. Married women with small children gave their jobs the lowest priority.

Housewives generally described their lives as easier than working wives did, with the exception of homemakers who had graduated from college: "It is the highly educated housewife who does not have an outside job whose marriage seems most likely to be beset by disagreements, lack of understanding and companionship, doubts and dissatisfactions" (pp. 425, 427). College-educated housewives were more likely than other nonworking wives to think about divorce, although they did not generally actualize their divorce fantasies, a finding that surprised the authors. The authors also found that a wife's choice to work outside the home had no negative effect on the way her husband felt about their relationship (p. 432).

Campbell, Converse, and Rodgers assumed that the traditional woman's role would not find many adherents among young women, and they did find that young unmarried women were the most liberated from housework and the most work-oriented. On the other hand, they were surprised by the traditionalism of young women who were married, but did not yet have children. One reason for this finding might be that those young women who did opt for marriage would have a more traditional attitude than those women who had not chosen (or might never choose) to marry.

Stages of Marital Satisfaction

The Happiest Time. Young married women (ages 18–29) with no children reported a satisfaction rate of nearly 90 percent (higher than any other group), a remarkable contrast with the 57 percent rate for their unmarried counterparts in the same age range. Their satisfaction scores were even higher than those for young married men with no children, although these men appear more satisfied than any other group of men in the study. According to Campbell, Converse, and Rodgers, "The fact which is remarkable is that while young unmarried people are also rather negative about the general quality of their lives (as well as dissatisfied with jobs, government, and other institutions), the young married people (without children) are extraordinarily positive" (p. 403). This corresponds to the initial "high" in the U-shaped correlation between satisfaction and the stages of family life cycles.

Still, this preparent stage is not without its problems, especially for the young male. Men are considerably more worried than their wives about meeting their bills: "[Preparent men] are one of the few categories of men who more often report concern about a nervous breakdown than do women" (p. 405).

The Family with Young Children. Children, especially young children, present the greatest problems for their primary caretaker, the mother. The satisfaction scales in this period dip low in terms of "standards of living, savings, and housing." There is the burden of child rearing, as well as housework. Other studies throughout the 1970s have substantiated the negative impact of the birth of the first child on most marriages, especially for wives (Lerner and Spanier 1978; Russell 1974).

The presence of a child cuts down on the amount of time husband and wife have for each other. It may also be a crisis time for both, as we have suggested in Chapters 10 and 11. In answer to the question whether the person ever wished she or he had married someone else, "mothers of young children are the most ready to admit that this thought has crossed their minds." At other points in the life cycle, both married women and married men are about equally likely to answer "yes." About two out of five mothers of small children wished they could be free from the responsibility of motherhood. Almost one-fourth of the mothers worried about having a nervous breakdown (pp. 408–409). Indicators of psychological stress, shown in Table 14.3, suggest that this is also a stressful time for men, though not as intensely disturbing as it is for women. Generally, mothers report significantly greater difficulties than fathers in adjusting to their infants, and the discrepancy is slightly greater for black mothers and fathers (Hobbs and Wimbish 1977). Recall from Chapter 11 that new mothers are likely to feel some conflicts, whether they continue working or remain at home.

There are numerous personal and interpersonal psychological factors that the Campbell, Converse, and Rodgers study did not explore. For example, do couples who delay childbearing express any higher degree of satisfaction than couples who have children soon after they marry? Are couples who have an egalitarian marriage more satisfied or less satisfied when children come along? Does the birth of a child usually go along with a drop in frequency of sexual relations? Will the couples who go through a dissatisfied period during child rearing ultimately feel a greater sense of generativity and less sense of stagnation? Are childless couples ultimately more prone to despair? In the short run at least, this study does seem to suggest that children do not automatically bring completeness and satisfaction to a marriage.

The Family with School-Age Children.   Married women's evaluation of satisfaction at this stage in the life cycle is more favorable than that of their husbands, but neither husbands nor wives report as much satisfaction as during the preparent stage. Disagreements over money occur less often than in earlier years, women are now more likely to feel that their husbands understand them, and women do not fantasize as often about being married to someone else or about getting a divorce (pp. 409–410). Women who are well educated, or those who have trained for a job, may experience dissatisfaction with the role of housewife once their children have started school.

The Family with Young-Adult Children.   The findings of Campbell, Converse, and Rodgers seem to dispel the myth of the empty nest, the time when the last child leaves home and the two parents allegedly have nothing to do but stare at each other: "Whatever remorse or loneliness these people feel

TABLE 14.3 Indicators of Psychological Stress at Stages of the Life Cycle, by Sex (Percentages of Respondents)

Stage	Feel Life Is Hard		Feel Tied Down		Always Feel Rushed		Worry Some About Bills		Feel Frightened		Worry About Nervous Breakdown	
	M	F	M	F	M	F	M	F	M	F	M	F
18–29, never married	27	35	15	19	13	16	22	33	44	58	13	18
18–29, married, no children	34	18	14	4	24	13	38	20	36	47	12	7
Married, youngest child under 6	34	28	25	25	23	28	47	46	43	46	12	19
Married, youngest child aged 6–17	30	24	14	11	29	28	44	38	38	46	11	15
Married, youngest child over 17	25	15	7	12	21	17	24	24	36	43	8	10
Widowed	28	23	6	12	8	12	27	29	22	41	0	11
Over 29, married, no children	20	18	11	12	18	25	22	24	30	50	7	18
Over 29, never married	23	19	10	13	5	26	28	39	39	51	13	8
Divorced or separated	25	42	15	20	12	34	35	63	29	60	8	25
Total	28	24	15	15	21	23	35	36	38	47	10	15

Source: Adapted from *The Quality of American Life: Perceptions, Evaluations, and Satisfactions*, by Campbell, Converse, and Rodgers, p. 404, copyright © 1976 by Russell Sage Foundation. Reprinted by permission of the publisher.

at no longer having children in the house does not seem to affect their general outlook on life very seriously." These people are generally very positive about their economic situation, standard of living, savings, and housing. Only health is a major concern. It is a time of contentment (pp. 411, 413).

Childless, Over-30 Couples. These couples have an overall sense of well-being higher than the average, second only to the younger childless couples' satisfaction levels. "Husbands of these childless marriages are one of the most positive life cycle groups among men . . . similar to those of married men with grown children" (p. 415). In reviewing the interaction of married women and men who have no children, the authors conclude that "parenthood is clearly not essential to a sense of family and a satisfaction with that association" (p. 416). A couple can apparently feel like a family and experience a sense of completeness with or without children.

Conclusions

Campbell, Converse, and Rodgers were not able to sustain or confirm Jessie Bernard's findings that "the psychological costs of marriage seem to be considerably greater for wives than husbands and the benefits considerably fewer" (1972, p. 28). The authors found no differences between the way married women and married men assessed their general well-being. In fact, women were "generally more positive in their description of their marital relationships" than men were, although better-educated women tended to be more critical than other women (p. 434). The arrival of children puts a strain on both spouses, with a more severe strain on mothers than fathers. The authors reached four conclusions (pp. 435–436):

1. Married women and men without children are more positive about their life experience than never-married people of comparable age.
2. This discrepancy is greater among older men than older women.
3. Never-married women are more positive about their lives than [never-married] men of comparable age.
4. Never-married people do not become more positive about their lives as they grow older.

In short, the authors concluded that, "whatever the psychological costs of marriage, the costs of being single are greater" (p. 438).

The authors also found no support for Bernard's contention that "childless marriages that do survive tend to be happier than marriages with children" (1972, p. 60). While this survey did find that childless married people, especially the wives, described their lives in very positive terms, "the majority of these young people expect to become parents at a later point and will in fact become such" (p. 438). The Campbell, Converse, and Rodgers research did not have a sufficient number of middle-aged or elderly childless couples to compare with the middle-aged or elderly couples with children. The authors could certainly not conclude that parenthood was a dimension of human unhappiness. But they did determine that parenthood was becoming a unique dimension of life involving periods of dissatisfaction and satisfaction, rather than "an essential dimension of human experience" (p. 439).

Finally, it is important to note that satisfaction for married and single people during adulthood relates to the intimate aspects of their lives as opposed to the less personal domain. Four national satisfaction surveys conducted in 1972 and 1973 by Stephen B. Withey and Frank M. Andrews of the National Science Foundation report that adults are most pleased with areas of their lives that involve other people. Analyzing whether people's concerns were personal, local, or national, Withey and Andrews found a steplike progression from *personal* concerns, where satisfaction is very high; to *neighborhood* and *community* concerns; and finally to *national* concerns, where dissatisfaction predominates (Institute for Social Research 1974). Personal concerns and intimate relations are paramount to adult satisfaction.

SINGLEHOOD OVER THE LIFE CYCLE

Today many people are satisfying their intimacy needs without marriage. Whether satisfaction with singlehood will increase as the population of never-married men and women increases is still an unknown. But the growing number of never-marrieds is beginning to receive more recognition by sociologists. Duberman suggests that lack of research on the unmarried "reflects our adherence to the ideal that everyone marry and that, if a person really wants, anyone can" (1977, p. 118). This cultural bias, Duberman claims, has affected the field of sociology as well as such areas as social service delivery and the work place. Social services and career advancement may be limited for the person who remains single. Census data show that among all adults in the United States aged 18 and over, 21 percent of all men and 15 percent of all women have never been married (see Table 14.4). Projections made for 1990 indicate that the number of never-marrieds will increase, particularly those under 30 (Masnick and Bane 1980).

In his review of the recent research on singles, Peter J. Stein (1978) points out that 47 million men and women over 18 are currently unmarried. A substantial number of these single people are likely to remain single. They include men and women who choose not to marry, single parents who do not wish to remarry, and older widows and divorced people who have accepted singlehood as a way of life, even though they

TABLE 14.4 Marital Status of the U.S. Population (Age 18 and Over) by Sex and Age, 1979

Marital Status	Total Population (18 and Over)	Percentage of Total Population	18-19	20-24	25-29	30-34	35-39	40-44	45-54	55-64	65-74	75 and Over
Men:												
Single	16,970,000	23.3%	94.9%	67.4%	30.2%	14.9%	8.2%	8.4%	6.9%	5.2%	5.6%	4.9%
Separated	1,513,000	2.1	0.2	1.2	2.0	3.1	2.6	2.8	2.4	2.2	2.1	1.2
Divorced	3,471,000	4.8	0.1	1.7	5.5	7.3	6.9	7.1	5.7	4.7	3.9	2.2
Widowed	1,945,000	2.7	0.0	0.0	0.2	0.2	0.2	0.6	1.8	3.4	9.3	24.0
Married	48,816,000	67.1	4.8	29.7	62.1	74.6	82.2	81.2	83.2	84.4	79.2	67.7
Total	72,715,000	100.0%										
Women:												
Single	13,644,000	16.9%	83.1%	49.4%	19.6%	9.5%	6.6%	5.1%	4.4%	4.6%	6.0%	6.2%
Separated	2,409,000	3.0	1.2	3.1	4.3	4.3	4.1	4.6	3.3	2.0	1.4	0.4
Divorced	5,355,000	6.6	0.9	3.2	7.8	10.2	9.8	11.1	8.2	6.5	4.0	2.2
Widowed	10,449,000	13.0	0.0	0.1	0.5	0.8	1.6	2.8	7.6	18.8	41.2	69.7
Married	48,771,000	60.5	14.8	44.2	67.7	75.2	78.0	76.5	76.3	68.1	47.5	21.5
Total	80,628,000	100.0%										

Source: U.S. Bureau of the Census, *Current Population Reports*, Series P-20, No. 349, "Marital Status and Living Arrangements: March 1979," U.S. Government Printing Office, Washington, D.C., 1980.

may have wished to marry. Higher proportions of blacks than whites remain unmarried at any given age, though the trend toward singlehood is evident for both blacks and whites. Table 14.5 shows changes in the number of single men and women over a 16-year period.

Table 14.6 shows the pushes and pulls that may affect one's choice of marriage or singlehood. The pulls to marry may be weakening, while the pulls to remain single, particularly the premium placed on autonomy and career opportunities, are increasing. Stein also notes that recent surveys of college and noncollege youth show "more uncertainty about the desirability of marriage, whether or not people will marry, and whether the traditional family structure works" (1978, p. 5). With this in mind, he urges further research, the enhancement of support systems for singles, and an examination of practices that discriminate against advancing unmarried people to executive positions. Based on Stein's 1978 review, the life cycle of single adults seems to follow these outlines:

1. **Young Adulthood.**   This is a period when commitment is delayed through experiments made in the world of work, independent living, and friendship. Young unmarried adults often pursue higher education. Women who, in earlier times, married and delayed their education or their childbearing now postpone marriage instead. Nearly three times as many women were enrolled in college in 1972 as in 1962, an increase from 1.2 million to 3.5 million (Stein 1978, p. 5). Remembering that education seemed to decrease satisfaction in marriage, while increasing earning capacity outside of marriage, this tremendous upswing in education may serve to keep a certain number of the young singles permanently single. Demographer Paul Glick states: "It is too early to predict with confidence that the increase in singleness among the young will lead to an eventual decline in life-time marriages" (1975, p. 18). Yet certain "deficits" are not made up. "Just as cohorts of young women who have postponed childbearing for an unusually long time seldom make up for the child deficit as they grow

TABLE 14.5 Change in Men and Women Remaining Single, 1960–1976

	1960	1970	1976
Women remaining single:			
Ages 20–24	28.4%	35.8%	42.6%
Ages 25–29	10.5%	10.5%	14.8%
Men remaining single:			
Ages 20–24	53.1%	54.7%	62.1%
Ages 25–29	20.8%	19.1%	24.9%

Source: U.S. Bureau of the Census. "Marital Status and Living Arrangements: March 1976," *Current Population Reports*, Series P-20, No. 306. Washington, D.C.: U.S. Government Printing Office, 1977, Table C, page 3.

TABLE 14.6   Pushes and Pulls Toward Marriage and Singlehood

Marriage	
Pushes (negatives in present situations)	Pulls (attractions in potential situations)
Socialization	Approval of parents
Pressure from parents	Desire for children and own family
Desire to leave home	Example of peers
Fear of independence	Romanticization of marriage
Loneliness	Physical attraction
No knowledge or perception of alternatives	Love, emotional attachment
Job availability, wage structure, and promotions	Security, social status, social prestige
Social policies favoring the married and the responses of social institutions	Legitimation of sexual experiences

Singlehood	
Pushes (to leave permanent relationships)	Pulls (to remain single or return to singlehood)
Lack of friends, isolation, loneliness	Career opportunities and development
Restricted availability of new experiences	Availability of sexual experiences
Suffocating one-to-one relationship, feeling trapped	Exciting lifestyle, variety of experiences, freedom to change
Obstacles to self-development	Psychological and social autonomy, self-sufficiency
Boredom, unhappiness, and anger	Support structures: sustaining friendships, women's and men's groups, political groups, therapeutic groups, collegial groups
Role playing and conformity to expectations	
Poor communication with mate	
Sexual frustration	

Source: Reprinted from "The Lifestyles and Life Chances of the Never-Married," by Peter J. Stein, in *Marriage & Family Review* Vol. 1, No. 4 (1978): 4. Copyright © 1978 by The Haworth Press, Inc. All rights reserved. Used with permission.

older, so also young people who are delaying marriage may never make up for the marriage deficit later on. They may try alternatives to marriage and they may like them" (p. 18).

2. The Age-30 Transition.   This is a particularly difficult period, characterized by intense societal and parental pressure and, for many singles, a decline in self-esteem (Stein 1978, p. 6). In this period, more than half the unmarrieds find the pulls of marriage great enough to offset the pulls of singlehood. Those who remain single now may see singlehood as a way of life, whereas before, their single state had a transitory quality. They may return to school, attempt to establish greater economic independence and security, find a new living place, invest more heavily in work, strengthen friendships, and explore new activities. As Stein suggests, singles can find their own way of settling in: "There are different ways of 'building a nest,' including those that accommodate only one person or two persons living together outside of marriage" (p. 7). Never-marrieds seem to delay commitment until the age-30 transition. At this point, although they do not necessarily commit to another individual for life, they strengthen their affiliations and abandon some of the experimentation that has characterized their lives. In this sense, they deal with some of the tasks of intimacy.

3. Middle Years. At this stage of life, the never-marrieds are in a distinct minority. Within this minority, women and men exhibit very different characteristics. The women seem more likely to accomplish the generativity tasks of middle age; unmarried men seem more threatened by stagnation (Stein, p. 7). Women in their middle years who have never married are much more likely to be upwardly mobile in terms of education and occupation than men, notes Jessie Bernard (1972). They are also more likely to experience satisfaction (Campbell, Converse, and Rodgers 1976, p. 419). Men in middle years who are single have higher rates of mental illness. They are generally less successful than married men in terms of education, income, and occupation.

4. Old Age. There is very little research available on the never-married elderly. In the past these people were more likely to have been social isolates or "loners." But as singlehood becomes a viable alternative lifestyle, the cohort of single elderly people is more likely to be a diverse group that includes many sociable individuals (Stein, p. 8). The never-married elderly may suffer less from loneliness because they are accustomed to living alone. They may, according to one of the few studies of being single in old age, be more positive in certain ways than the widowed or the divorced because they have not suffered the desolation of loss or bereavement (Gubrium 1975). On the other hand, the never-married person may have failed to achieve the sense of generativity and ego integrity that may be achieved by people who have parented, grandparented, and enjoyed the intimate sharing that is possible in marriage.

The recent research on singles and the new information on women serve as reminders that there are many coping strategies that can be used to deal with the challenges of adulthood.

Research into the life cycle can shed light on the many patterns of adult development. It is not intended to be a grid that locks male and female, single, divorced, and married, into the same boxes. What adults seem to share, regardless of lifestyle, is a concern for the areas of their lives that involve other people, a tendency to find the greatest satisfaction with those parts of their lives that are most intimate and personal.

SUMMARY

1. The major objectives of this chapter are, first, to define the stages and tasks of adult life; second, to discuss the theories of Neugarten and Levinson on the social and psychological forces of adult development;

third, to review the satisfactions and stresses of adult life as related to marital and family status; and fourth, to explore developmental stages for single adults.

2. Scientific interest in adult life is a recent development compared with the study of childhood and adolescence. Erikson's contributions focus on the development of intimacy during young adulthood and of generativity during the midlife period, which are viewed as significant tasks for the years following adolescence.

3. Some disagreement exists among theorists about the impact and intensity of internal and external factors in adult development. For example, Neugarten emphasizes the role of social clocks in adult life. She indicates that all individuals are aware of socially defined time sequences for such major life events as marriage, parenthood, and even the death of one's parents or spouse. According to this view, we anticipate major life transitions and prepare for them so that the actual event does not create a serious crisis unless it occurs at an unexpected time. A somewhat different view is offered by Levinson and others, who stress the internal psychological conflicts that occur during the adult years and must be resolved for growth to take place.

4. Some studies of the overall quality of life in the United States, which rely on personal interviews or questionnaires, indicate how perceived satisfaction with several aspects of life is related to stages in the family life cycle. The research of Campbell, Converse, and Rodgers suggests that satisfaction with one's marriage, family, and life in general is highest during the initial period of marital commitment. Satisfaction levels decline sharply for couples with young children and then gradually increase as children get older and become young adults. Higher levels of satisfaction characterize the middle and later stages of life.

5. A number of factors influence one's perceived satisfaction with life circumstances. For example, younger people report less satisfaction than those in the middle and later years of life, with the exception of young married couples without children, who consistently report high levels of satisfaction. College-educated respondents tend to report lower levels of satisfaction with marital and family relations than do those with less education. Individuals without spouses, including those never-married, divorced and separated, and widowed, also report lower levels of satisfaction. This is especially true for men without marital partners.

6. The satisfactions, stresses, and transitions of those who choose alternative life patterns such as singlehood represent new areas for research and theory development. It is important to recognize that variations in adult development are influenced by several factors, such as culture, sex, and intimate life patterns. It is possible that future investigations of adult life will reveal several patterns that facilitate growth as well as multiple ways of satisfactorily coping with the stresses of these years.

KEY CONCEPTS

Life cycle	Crisis periods
Intimacy	Male-female life-cycle
Generativity	differences
Social clocks	Life-cycle satisfactions
	and stresses

QUESTIONS

1. Based on the information presented in this chapter, discuss the major problems or stresses of young and middle adulthood for women and men. How much do you think sex differences in adulthood are a result of earlier sex-role socialization? Illustrate your answer with some examples.

2. In considering Neugarten's concept of social clocks, what major events have occurred in your life that were anticipated and took place within the expected time sequence? Have any major events occurred in your life that were not in the expected time sequence? If so, do you think these events were more difficult to cope with or caused more stress? What major transitions do you expect to take place within the near future? How might anticipation of such events decrease problems associated with major changes?

3. Explain what is meant by the term "midlife crisis." On the basis of your reading, do you think that such a crisis is necessary in adulthood for continued growth and development? Why or why not?

4. What reasons do you think best explain why college-educated adults tend to report lower levels of satisfaction with marriage relationships than non-college-educated adults? Do you agree with the finding that marital and family systems are more important for men than for women? Whether you agree or not, what reasonable explanation can be given for this finding?

5. Why do you think adults in the middle and later years tend to express higher levels of satisfaction with life in general than do younger adults?

6. What do you view as the most significant problems or stresses over the life cycle for those who choose to remain single? What are the most significant benefits? What are some reasons that a person might choose to remain single?

SUGGESTED READINGS

- Gould, Roger L. *Transformations: Growth and Change in Adult Life.* New York: Simon & Schuster, 1978. A presentation of the author's theory about the changes and crises of adult life and how to cope with them creatively. It is based on Dr. Gould's own research plus observations by other social scientists. This is an easy-to-read and provocative book that may lead to personal insight, understanding, and growth.

- Kerckhoff, Richard K. "Marriage and Middle Age." *The Family Coordinator* 25, no. 1 (1976): 5–11. This brief article explores some of the typical problems that confront couples in the middle years of adulthood. Examples from literature and findings from research studies are included, along with suggestions for coping with stresses in a growth-producing way.

- Levinson, Daniel. *The Seasons of a Man's Life*. New York: Ballantine Books, 1978. The summary report of Levinson and his research team's efforts over several years to study adult development in males. It indicates that adult life has its own variations and crises just as the earlier years of childhood and adolescence do. In the brief time since publication, this book has become a basic reference for those interested in studying the transitions of adulthood.

- Miller, Jean Baker. *Toward a New Psychology of Women*. Boston: Beacon Press, 1976. A reasonably short, easy-to-read work that provides an important step toward building a framework for understanding the psychology of women. The author focuses especially on building self-esteem for women and indicates some possibilities for defining a broader theory of female development.

- Rubin, Lillian B. *Women of a Certain Age: The Midlife Search for Self*. New York: Harper Colophon Books, 1979. An interesting account of the author's interviews with 160 women between the ages of 35 and 54. The strengths and stresses of women in the middle years of life are vividly presented through numerous examples taken directly from the interview sessions. Feelings about marriage, sexual satisfaction, children leaving home, and work-related issues are emphasized.

- Sheehy, Gail. *Passages*. New York: E. P. Dutton, 1974. One of the first popular books to be published about young adulthood and the middle years. It includes numerous excerpts from 115 in-depth interviews carried out over a three-year period. Particular attention is given to the transitions and crises of the twenties, thirties, and forties.

- Troll, Lillian E. *Early and Middle Adulthood*. Monterey, Calif.: Brooks/Cole Publishing, 1975. A good, comprehensive source for reviewing major developments in young and middle adulthood. Topics covered include physical, intellectual, and personality development, plus adult development in the family and job world.

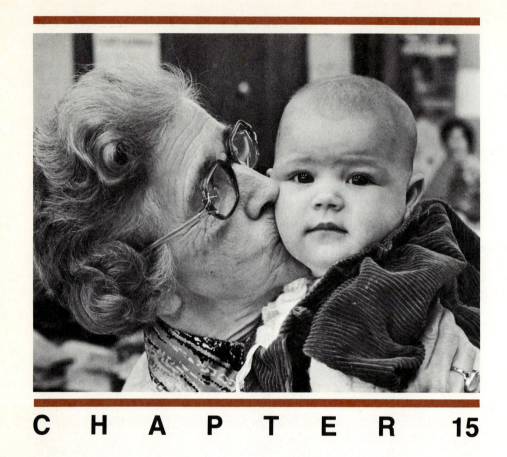

C H A P T E R 15

Family Interaction in
the Later Years

HE: One year from today, we'll be starting a new life: no more flak from the boss, no more tense weekends building myself up to ask for a raise, no more ulcer medicine.

SHE: I'm glad you're looking forward to that, dear.

HE: I thought we might take a trip to Florida this winter, look around at condominiums.

SHE: Oh, I wouldn't want to move yet, not until I get to know my new granddaughter.

HE: We could take her down with us and maybe teach her to swim.

SHE: I don't think we want to move just yet.

HE: Come on, take a chance. We'll make new friends, learn golf. I used to think golf was boring, but now it seems to be just about my speed.

SHE: Dear, it's Mother. She really can't live by herself any more. The doctor says she needs care. Her mind is still active, but after that last fall she really shouldn't be out shopping for herself and carrying bundles.

HE: Can't you hire someone to live with her?

SHE: That would be very expensive. I promised the kids we'd help with a down payment on a house next year. They'll need a yard for the baby.

HE: But you'll be completely tied down. We've waited so long for this freedom. We were going to travel, maybe even take a trip around the world.

SHE: Mother has been so wonderful to us. I don't want her to live out her days with some hired helper. She put aside her travels, and now she needs us. We'll be such a source of comfort to her, and we do have the extra room now that Bob's in college.

HE: Ever since I met you, I've been trying to get some time alone with you, some time for just the two of us.

SHE: Don't make me choose between you and Mother. I just couldn't live with myself if I knew I'd neglected her. We've got lots of time. . . . I don't think she does.

INTRODUCTION

In the later years, individuals and their families face new challenges. They must come to grips with their own reduced powers and, finally, their own mortality. They may also experience, from their vantage point, an appreciation of life in all its beauty and a gratitude for the special contribution made to their lives by their own parents. There is a satisfaction that may come at this time from recognizing the continuity existing from one generation to the next. In the book *American Dreams: Lost and Found* (1980), Studs Terkel has recorded some of these feelings of gratification experienced in later life by the fulfilled human being. Here are the reflections of a professor emeritus at the University of Chicago, Norman Maclean, at age 75:

One of my father's biggest dreams was the dream of great education in this country, and the necessity of every person to be educated. I was the first person in his family not to make his living with his hands. . . .

As I've grown older, I've tried to put together the dreams into my own life. . . . You have to be gifted with a long life to attain a dream and make it harmonious. I feel infinitely grateful in my old age that I've had in this country, within my family, the training needed to be the best that was in me. It's no great thing, but at 75, I'm fulfilled. There aren't any big pieces in me that never got a chance to come out. They may say at the end of my life I have no alibis. I have two children of my own, whom I admire and love and try not to annoy very much. I see my father going right on with my children. You've got to pass the ball along. (Terkel 1980)

The basic theme of this chapter is the family in the later years. We shall deal with questions such as: What is old? How do the young, the middle-aged, and the old themselves view the aging process? What kinds of satisfactions and dissatisfactions do the aging years bring to intimate relationships? Is there sex after 60? Are there any special developmental tasks that the elderly must perform? How are physical, social, and psychological needs met in later life?

There are approximately 22 million people over 65 in the United States today. More than 5,000 persons turn 65 every single day. About 3,600 persons aged 65 and older die every day. That means there is a yearly increase of about 460,000 persons 65 and older in this country (Crandall 1980, p. 11). Table 15.1 shows the change in the elderly population in this century.

Although more males are conceived than females, the mortality rate of males is higher at the fetal stage as well as in childhood and adolescence. In the 65-and-over age group, there are about 69 males for every 100 females. In the 75-and-over age group, there are about 58 males for every 100 females. Three-quarters of the aged reside in urban areas, and most of the elderly live in some kind of family setting (Crandall 1980). Although the experts disagree about the number of elderly who reside in institutions, the disagreement is slight; only about four to five percent of the aged live in homes for the aged, and for many of them, as we shall see, only an institution can provide the care they need.

Seventy-five percent of older men are married, as compared to 37 percent of older women (see Table 15.2). The majority of older women are widows, so a section of this chapter is devoted to the special problems of widows. Though a certain percentage of the elderly are poor, others enjoy relative affluence at this period and experience few financial demands. The majority of older people continue to see their children frequently and to offer them emotional support and, sometimes, financial assistance. Links to the next generation, through grandparenting or mentoring, provide a sense of continuity and meaning to the aging person.

DEVELOPMENTAL TASKS OF THE LATER YEARS

Erik Erikson (1963) thought of maturity as the task of later life, worked out between the poles of ego integrity and despair. But long before Erikson set

TABLE 15.1 Percentage Distribution of the Elderly in Age Groups (1900–1990)

Age group	1900	1930	1950	1960	1970	1975	1990*
65–69 years	42.3	41.7	40.7	36.6	33.9	36.2	34.2
70–74 years	28.7	29.3	27.8	28.6	28.0	25.8	26.8
75–79 years	{29	{29	17.4	18.5	18.6	17.9	19.5
80 years and over			14.1	15.3	19.6	20.2	19.5

* Projected

Source: U.S. Bureau of the Census, "Demographic Aspects of Aging and the Older Population in the United States," *Current Population Reports*, Seres P-23, No. 59, Washington, D.C.: U.S. Government Printing Office, May 1976.

TABLE 15.2 Distribution of Men and Women Aged 65 and Over by Marital Status, 1900 and 1978

Marital Status	1978		1900	
	Percentage of Men	Percentage of Women	Percentage of Men	Percentage of Women
Married	75	37	67.3	34.3
Widowed	14	52	26.5	59.5
Divorced	6	5	0.5	0.3
Never married	5	6	5.8	6.0
Total	100.0	100.0	100.0	100.0

Source: U.S. Department of Health, Education and Welfare, "Facts about Older Americans," Pub. No. (OHD) 75-20006, Washington, D.C.: U.S. Government Printing Office, 1975; and U.S. Department of Commerce, Bureau of the Census, "Social and Economic Characteristics of the Older Population," Washington, D.C.: U.S. Government Printing Office, 1978, p. 3.

down his developmental scheme, great thinkers and poets were aware of these same poles of the aging experience. In *King Lear* and *The Tempest*, Shakespeare illustrated, perhaps better than any research report, the two radically different outcomes that can confront the individual in old age (see Box 15.1).

UNDERSTANDING AGING

Research and interviewing can help students of human behavior to understand the practical and emotional issues of aging. Bernice Neugarten (1979), using a more refined scheme than Erikson provided, believes that the following guidelines will improve our understanding of the lives of old people:

1. Middle age and old age should not be viewed "primarily in terms of problems and losses [but rather in terms of] its freedoms and gains" (p. 891). Thus, instead of viewing retirement as the *loss* of status and self-esteem through work, retirement can be seen as gaining freedom from the narrow confines of stultifying work while gaining access to more satisfying pursuits. Literary and social critic Edmund Wilson was in his late fifties when he decided to study Hebrew and biblical manuscripts—a significant departure from his previous literary efforts. The result was *Scrolls from the Dead Sea* (1955), considered a major work of scholarship and reporting, published when Wilson was 60.

2. The longer one lives, the more choices and commitments one accumulates. While this can be viewed as a narrowing of the individual, it can just as easily be understood in terms of refining a person's uniqueness. While the "final biological decrements may sometimes reduce the diversity

among individuals" (Neugarten 1979, p. 891), aging in most people does not reduce individuality. Anna Mary Robertson Moses began painting in her seventies. The wife of a farmer, her so-called American primitive paintings attracted worldwide attention and gave rise to her colloquial name "Grandma Moses."

3. Most persons, upon reaching age 40, 50, or 60, do not wish to be young again, though it is natural to wish to *feel* young. Most people want "to grow old with equanimity and with the assurance that they will have had a full measure of life's experiences" (Neugarten 1979, p. 891). One can see older people as they continue to seek that "full measure of life's experiences." Cicero wrote *De Senecture* when he was 62; Simone de Beauvoir authored *Coming of Age* when she was 60; Emerson wrote *Old Age* at 57. Old age did not impair the faculties or drive of Sophocles or Michelangelo, Picasso or Georgia O'Keefe, Lillian Hellman or Artur Rubinstein. John L. Lewis, founder and leader of the 500,000-member United Mine Workers, was nearly 70 when he was interviewed by Saul Alinsky. His remarks reflect one older man's refusal to sip from the cup of regret:

As this is written, John L. Lewis stands on the threshhold of three score and ten years. . . . One gloomy late afternoon, during a meeting with Lewis, the writer referred to certain parts of Lewis's life with the remark that if Lewis had acted differently in a number of crises or if certain factors, both international and domestic, had not impinged as and when they did, the history of our nation would have been radically changed, that a third major political party would have emerged in a climate of revolution.

Lewis's answer came slowly as he almost seemed to weigh each word, "The doors of history swing on tiny hinges. Nothing is more barren and futile than speculation on what might have been." His head sank further, and for some moments there was silence as his eyes were fixed on the floor. Suddenly he tossed his head back; his face seemed to light up as he spoke. "I care not what might have been. I care only for today and the wonder of life itself, the sunrise of tomorrow and the new dawn. For this and in this I live." (Alinsky 1970, pp. 371–372)

Disengagement

Cumming and Henry (1961) suggest that older people go through a natural developmental "disengagement" from life. The older person has done his or her life's work, has contributed, and has been useful. Now it is time for others, those younger and more vigorous, to perform useful services. Many aging people cannot choose, as Prospero did, the time when they wish to set aside their staffs. Society allows older persons to withdraw from service and sometimes forces them to retire before they wish to do so. Increasingly, however, the elderly person determines the timing and the degree of his or her disengagement.

BOX 15.1 Prospero and Lear: Ego Integrity and Despair

Shakespeare created the powerful characters of King Lear, who shows the tragic outcome of despair in old age, and Prospero, who epitomizes ego integrity.

King Lear makes the decision to divide his kingdom, believing that at his advanced period of life he should "shake all cares and business from our age, conferring them on younger strengths, while we unburden'd crawl toward death." The decision to cut himself off in this way may be his first mistake. But the more tragic error comes when he believes the false words of devotion mouthed by his daughters Goneril and Regan, and then vents his rage on his honest but reticent daughter, Cordelia. He cuts her off from her inheritance because she admits that when she marries she will give half her love to her husband: "Sure, I shall never marry like my sisters, to love my father all."

Later, after Goneril receives half of King Lear's kingdom, she insists that her father reduce the number of his retainers (servants). Lear, cut to the quick by this ingratitude, curses her with barrenness, and worse:

If she must teem,
Create her child of spleen, that it may live
And be a thwart disnatur'd torment to her!
Let it stamp wrinkles in her brow of youth,
With cadent tears fret channels in her cheeks,
Turn all her mother's pains and benefits
To laughter and contempt, that she may feel
How sharper than a serpent's tooth it is
To have a thankless child!

(Act I, Scene IV, lines 303–311)

Lear's second daughter, Regan, also evicts him, and Lear spends the rest of the play on the heath, with a terrible realization of his error and the errors and evil of all humankind. His tendency to curse those who thwart him now is turned to all of creation:

Blow, winds, and crack your cheeks! Rage! Blow!
You cataracts and hurricanoes, spout
Till you have drench'd our steeples, drown'd the cocks!
You sulph'rous and thought-executing fires,
Vaunt-couriers to oak-cleaving thunderbolts,
Singe my white head! And thou, all-shaking thunder,
Strike flat the thick rotundity o' the world!
Crack nature's moulds, all germens spill at once,
That make ingrateful man!

(Act III, Scene II, lines 1–9)

Finally, Lear sees Cordelia again and begs her forgiveness, but it is too late. Events overtake them, and Cordelia is killed. Her death drives Lear to distraction and a final sense of life's unfairness: "Why should a dog, a horse, a rat, have life, And thou no

BOX 15.1 (Continued)

breath at all?" When Lear dies, Kent, his faithful retainer, sees death for him as a release:

O! let him pass; He hates him
That would upon the rack of this tough world
Stretch him out longer.

         (Act V, Scene III, lines 313–314)

Many people still see the death of an old person as a release from suffering. Elderly people still make terrible mistakes in favoring one child over the other, and still have thankless children.

At the other pole of the aging experience is the elderly Prospero, completely in control of his island domain when *The Tempest* begins. He is acting as the teacher and guide of his beloved daughter, still trying to humanize the primitive Caliban, and now preparing to pardon even his treacherous brother. Prospero has faced a terrible injustice in his lifetime—he was usurped and expelled from his dukedom and country by his own brother. But unlike Lear, Prospero has mastered his fate. He brings about the tempest in order to pardon the wrongdoing of his brother, while bringing Miranda, as well as himself, back to civilization, and mortality. Before Prospero relinquishes his magical powers, he makes sure that Miranda has found an eligible mate so that the next generation will thrive.

As we have seen, the elderly still can feel responsible and can be instrumental in setting the younger generation on a prosperous course. Prospero knows that returning to Milan will bring him closer to death. In the real world, the aged must come to grips with their mortality. As he says of his return: "Every third thought shall be my grave." Yet he must leave the island where he has magical powers to allow his daughter to marry and have children of her own. There is a sense that the aging Prospero has chosen the time to relinquish those powers, thus lending his diminished position a sense of dignity:

I have bedimm'd
The noontide sun, call'd forth the mutinous winds,
And 'twixt the green sea and the azur'd vault
Set roaring war; to the dread rattling thunder
Have I given fire, and rifted Jove's stout oak
With his own bolt; the strong-bas'd promontory
Have I made shake, and by the spurs pluck'd up
The pine and cedar; graves at my command
Have wak'd their sleepers, op'd, and let 'em forth
By my so potent art. But this rough magic
I here abjure; and, when I have requir'd
Some heavenly music, which even now I do,
To work mine end upon their senses that
This airy charm is for, I'll break my staff,

BOX 15.1 (Continued)
Bury it certain fathoms in the earth,
And deeper than did ever plummet sound,
I'll drown my book.

(Act V, Scene I, lines 41–57)

This is an exit suited to a king. Some say it was Shakespeare's way of facing his own death. Prospero's rich appreciation of all life's magic and beauty, as well as its treachery and evil, creates a final sense of affirmation. If we are, as Prospero says, "such stuff as dreams are made of," then this final vision of personal integrity—the fruits of a rich life as parent, teacher, friend—is a dream of the way our lives might end in the best of all possible worlds.

Stages of Aging

Robert Peck (1956) has suggested three stages of old age. Peck calls the first stage "ego differentiation versus work-role preoccupation." This is the stage in which the individual reappraises and redefines his or her self-worth. For example, a man approaching retirement may look back on his work career and wonder if his devotion to his trade or profession, the single-minded pursuit of success, has been worth it; a woman may have devoted forty years to being an accomplished wife and mother, submerging her own particular talents, and then wonder if she may have cheated herself. There are fewer years for these people to live, and so they may seek ways to live that are personally satisfying, rather than conforming to life-styles selected by family, friends, or society.

Peck's second stage, "body transcendence versus body preoccupation," is the stage in which natural biological deterioration takes place. Hearing may be somewhat impaired; there may be a decline in eyesight; eating habits may change because of a loss of teeth; overall stamina decreases as the body mechanisms work less vigorously and efficiently. Some people may fiercely reject these unmistakable signs of mortality, while others may accept the diminution of their physical capabilities as they continue their satisfying human relations.

A woman who has played tennis all her young adult life may find that she no longer has the stamina to play singles, but can play doubles. As the aging process continues, she may not have the strength to play tennis at all. And as she grows older, her brisk walk may even change to a slow, labored gait. As limitations to the body's activities become more evident, one person may scale down activities, while another, angry and resentful at any limitations, may reject the natural aging process.

Peck's final stage, "ego transcendence versus ego preoccupation" comes when the older person realizes that death may occur at any time. Peck calls this period "the night of the ego." The final door of life has opened and is now about to close. It is a time when one's end is certain. Yet it may also be a time to stress the continuity and meaningfulness of life, knowing full well there will be others who will live on after one's death. The chain of life has not really been broken.

Life Review

Robert N. Butler (1968) offers us still another aspect of aging—that of the "life review." Older persons, according to Butler, universally go through a mental process of increased reminiscences. Far from being a psychological dysfunction, Butler believes, reminiscences represent unresolved conflicts that can now be re-examined and successfully reintegrated before death. "In its mild form, the life review is reflected in increased reminiscences, mild nostalgia, mild regret; in severe form [life review results] in anxiety, guilt, despair, and depression. In the extreme, it may involve the obsessive preoccupation of the older person with his [or her] past and may proceed to a stage approximating terror and result in suicide" (pp. 488–489).

Adult children, as well as grandchildren, have an opportunity to play a significant role in the older person's life-review process. Listening to the reminiscences, commenting on them, and asking questions that support the act of reminiscing not only aid the older person, but provide a sound basis for the adult children and grandchildren to know more about their family "roots." While it is true that some of the "stories" may be repeated, they still represent significant milestones in the older person's life; the repetition of these stories makes them an integral part of the family heritage, passed on from generation to generation.

The Young-Old and the Old-Old

The aged population is not one monolithic group, but rather a large and varied segment of society, which should be divided by age, activity level, and other distinguishing features. One of the most creative divisions of the aging population was developed by Neugarten. She sees two basic aging populations: the *young-old* and the *old-old*. "The young-old, drawn mainly from those aged 55 to 75, is a group who are relatively healthy and vigorous, relatively comfortable in economic terms and relatively free from the traditional responsibilities of both work and parenthood. Better educated than earlier cohorts of the same age, politically active, and with large amounts of free time available, this age group seeks primarily for

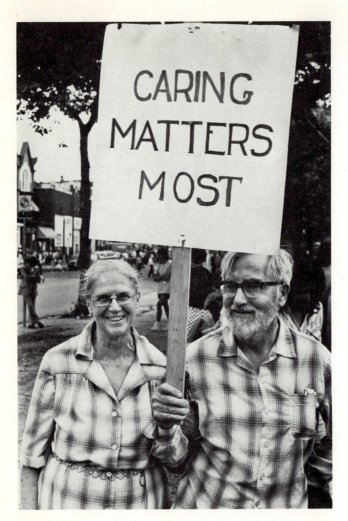

"Gray power" has become a viable political force. (George Cohen, Stock Boston)

meaningful ways of self-fulfillment and community service" (Neugarten and Hagestad 1976, p. 46). The old-old are likely to be over 75. However, they fall into this category not simply because of their having reached a certain age, but because of failing health or vigor, physical or psychological dependency.

Like other periods in the life cycle, the aging or maturity period cannot be easily broken down by chronological age assignments. Thus, while one may generalize that the young-old may be from 55 to 75, someone who is 60 may show all the mental and physical impairments of the so-called old-old, while a 78-year-old may be active, alert, and vigorous.

Ageism refers to the stereotyping of older people, the assumption that elderly persons are ill and tired, passive and selfish, cranky and conservative. Discriminating against people because of their age, denying them employment or housing, is also called ageism (Butler 1969). If we maintain our ability to respond to individual people rather than to age categories, we shall find that there are many people for whom age is irrelevant. Psychological attitudes and relative physical health provide the more significant boundaries between the young-old and old-old.

As life expectancy increases and the U.S. population shifts—there are now 22 million people in this country over 65—more and more Americans will find themselves confronted with an aging parent who requires care. The young-old person, especially the young-old woman, is often called upon to take care of her old-old mother, father, or aging in-laws. It is a task both physically taxing and emotionally disturbing, since the child must face the imminent death of the cherished parent.

Maggie Kuhn—founder of the Gray Panthers activist group, which promotes the interests of the elderly—is a perfect example of the individual who continues to be vital and assertive, involved in immediate family as well as world politics, social change, and education. One of Ms. Kuhn's tasks as a young-old person was to care for her aging mother. She remembers feeling rage mingled with compassion and pity when caring for her own mother, who died at the age of 92. Maggie Kuhn claims the thing that helped her most during those last trying years with her mother was the friendship she had established with her mother when she was in her late 20s and early 30s. It was easier to move from that base of friendship and equality gradually into her role of caretaker. Kuhn believes that people in their middle years need to be educated to prepare for the role reversal that inevitably comes when aging parents require care. Even with this preparation, and assuming children take on this responsibility out of love rather than greed or guilt, witnessing the aging of one's own parent is painful.

"My mother was a beautiful woman," Kuhn recalls (Koch and Koch 1980, p. 14). "She had beautiful blue eyes that never faded. And she would look up at me and say, 'I'm not a person anymore,' and I would put my arms around her and we would both cry. At a time like that, there's nothing else to do." Parent-child relationships can deteriorate as the burden of caring persists. A family that takes on this responsibility must share the tasks involved. Support systems for caretakers of aging parents are virtually nonexistent. Though only 1 person in 50 needs long-term care when they are between 65 and 72, 1 out of 15 persons at age 73 requires long-term care. Since there will soon be millions of people living to that age and beyond, we will need new networks, formal and informal, of self-help groups and services to help the middle-aged and young-old family accomplish this complicated role of becoming parents to their own aging parents. As Maggie Kuhn has put it: "When the parent becomes the child, the child must become the parent" (Koch and Koch 1980, p. 16).

THE STATUS OF THE ELDERLY IN THE UNITED STATES

In our nation's earliest times, the elderly constituted only two percent of the population, as compared with ten percent today. But the small number of people over 65 controlled the country. They owned the land and held political office, controlling both until death. "The idea of equality destroyed the hierarchy of age," claims historian David Hackett Fischer (1977, p. 225). When they had ironclad dominion over property and public office, they were venerated but not loved, as Fischer observes. The social status of old age declined during the nineteenth century, although old people began to be regarded with more affection.

Early in the twentieth century, the idea of the elderly as society's responsibility began to take hold. Private laws for pensions began to be proposed, and discussion of the proper role of government toward its elderly citizens was in the air. Social Security was enacted in 1935, and soon private pension plans increased in number. The elderly began to assume responsibility for their political and social rights. In fact, Pratt (1976) argues that the elderly, more than any other age group, have become aggressive in combating stereotyping of and discrimination against themselves and lobbying for programs that will meet their needs. This "gray power" is manifested in terms of visible governmental lobbying groups in Washington, D.C., as well as in the high percentage of elderly who vote. Now there are Medicare and Medicaid programs to meet the medical needs of the elderly, as well as various other supplemental-income programs for the aged who are in need of financial help. These programs prevent some of the more severe privations suffered by the elderly in the past.

There is no doubt that some people continue to enter old age without funds—especially women who are single heads of households—but the problem appears to be lessening. Many older people are able to maintain themselves and even contribute toward the support of their children and their grandchildren. Fewer people grow old without resources of their own. Poverty now afflicts less than five percent of the elderly. But the poverty line set by the U.S. Bureau of Labor Statistics was only $6,200 for a family of four in 1981. Those who live at or somewhat above this poverty line can be considered severely deprived (Chambers 1981). Lack of funds in old age can be a source of despair. This is especially true if the aging poor are forced to live in substandard institutions, as Box 15.2 makes clear.

Most older people whose health is not seriously impaired are able to live

---

BOX 15.2 The Nursing-Home Dilemma

Only a small portion of older persons (four percent) live in age-segregated housing such as institutions, primary nursing homes, and extended-care facilities (Neugarten and Hagestad 1976). Despite the fact that nursing homes are among the most closely regulated of all institutions, hardly a year goes by when newspapers fail to point out scandalous conditions in some nursing homes. "The most comprehensive survey of nursing home problems ever undertaken in this country, that of the Subcommittee on Long-Term Care of the Senate's Subcommittee on Aging [1974], bears the title 'Nursing Home Care in the United States: Failure in Public Policy.' It is impossible to be more succinct than that" (Vladeck 1980, p. 3). While it appears that the majority of nursing homes do not severely neglect their patients, "the best government estimate is that roughly half of the nation's nursing homes are 'substandard' " (p. 3). Of the nearly 18,000 nursing homes in the United States, thousands fail to provide even the minimal conditions for humane treatment, and some can be categorized only as subhuman. In such so-called homes,

infirm old people are left lying for hours in their own excrement; severely scalded or even drowned in presumably attended bathtubs; illegally restrained in "geriatric" chairs; or attacked, sometimes suffering broken limbs, by nursing home employees . . . in these [homes], residents live out the last of their days in an enclosed society without privacy, dignity, or pleasure, subsisting on minimally palatable diets, multiple sedatives, and large doses of television—even dying, one suspects, at least partially out of boredom. (Vladeck 1980, p. 4)

It also appears that those older persons who are forced to survive under such despicable conditions are often without family, friends, or relatives who might monitor the care of the aged.

Yet it would be a serious error to suggest that there are *no* occasions when the elderly should be institutionalized. When the elderly become seriously ill, when physical and mental conditions have substantially deteriorated, when the social support systems have broken down, when the family resources—emotional, physical, and financial—have been taxed beyond endurance, institutional care may be the only solution.

It is largely beyond the capacity of any one individual, no matter how caring or dedicated, to provide adequate care outside an institutional setting to someone who really is extremely senile, or who acts for some other reason as though he is. A high proportion of such people end up in nursing homes. . . . In fact, there is general consensus in the professional community that families are far more likely to wait too long for outside assistance, particularly institutional assistance, especially in cases of mental or emotional problems, than not wait too long. (Vladeck 1980, p. 16) physically separate from their children. Less than one-quarter of the aged live in the same household with their offspring. "Older people usually desire to live independently of their children for as long as they possibly can, not only to avoid impinging upon the freedom of the younger people but also to retain their own sense of competence and their privacy, independence and self-determination" (Kalish 1975, p. 77).

OLDER MARRIED COUPLES

Reviewing several longitudinal studies of older couples, Joan Aldous (1978) found that marital satisfaction in later years is high, perhaps even the highest of any period in the history of the marriage. In "Rabbi Ben Ezra," the poet Robert Browning expressed the anticipation of those companionable later years:

Grow old along with me!
The best is yet to be,
The last of life, for which the first was made:
Our times are in His hand
Who saith "A whole I planned,
Youth shows but half; trust God: see all nor be afraid!"

Yet older married couples face a number of new challenges. Researchers have found that as couples grow older, husbands and wives undergo profound changes in their roles (Troll, Miller, and Atchley 1979; Lowenthal 1975). Lowenthal explored attitudes of older couples and compared them to those of newlywed couples. Newlywed husbands described their wives as overly dependent, but it was the wife in later years who complained about her husband's dependency. "Where men tended to describe their dependent feelings as *tender*, women described them as *clinging*" (Lowenthal et al. 1975, p. 38). The older husband's lack of achievement goals, combined with the wife's highly critical attitudes and resistance to her mate's dependency, can create friction for the older couple.

One major reason for the change in the dynamics of the marital relationship is the change in work roles. This shift is especially apparent in one-worker families when the husband, once employed outside the home, retires from work. His presence at home for many hours during the day may create a problem for the wife if the home has been her exclusive domain. She may discover that her husband is tinkering, commenting, puttering around the house—"underfoot" as it were; the balance she maintained in the household has changed. The husband may feel under considerable pressure to redefine his social function and marital role. Without a job to go to, what does he do? When does he do it? With whom does he do it? These are the issues he must grapple with.

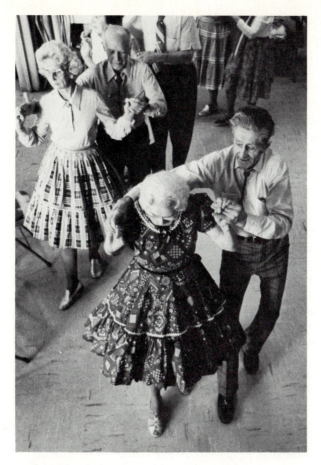

Marital satisfaction in the later years is reported as very high.
(Elizabeth Crews)

Role changes in later life are not without difficulties for women. With their husbands at home and actively partaking in household chores, wives who did not work outside the home may find that they have less work to do and fewer planned activities with which to take up the day. Wives who have worked all their lives may, like their husbands, experience a letdown after retirement.

The key to solving these role changes appears to be flexibility and responsiveness—each spouse somewhat modifying behavior patterns to accommodate the other. When such an empathic understanding occurs, elderly couples express a very high degree of marital satisfaction, according to current research. Lowenthal et al. (1975) found that married people facing retirement expressed renewed interest in the personalities of their spouses. Eighty-two percent of the men and women participating in the study gave positive descriptions of their mates, and the majority felt that their marriages had improved since their children had left home. Some couples even declare that this particular period of time is the most satisfactory of any period in the marriage (Rollins and Cannon 1974; Spanier, Lewis, and Cole 1975).

One can only speculate how older couples in the future will deal with role shifts in later life. Perhaps today's marriages will veer toward a more egalitarian style, with men and women sharing in the role of work in and out of the home. Couples will find that they have prepared well for the roles of equal partners that they are likely to assume in old age.

Sexuality in the Aging Couple

One aspect of a loving relationship between husband and wife is the very basic, elemental, and continual need for physical affection ranging from touch to coitus. It appears that aging has a greater impact on the sexuality of men than on that of women. A 70- or 80-year-old man is no longer able to experience the intense and numerous orgasms of his youth, nor may he be able to redevelop erections with as much rapidity. While the aging process may produce a diminution in the sheer number of orgasms an older man can achieve, this need not affect his overall sexuality. "Older men simply require more intense physical stimulation and time in order to enjoy sex fully" (Kaplan 1974, p. 108). Men over 50 may well need longer and more intense stimulation from their partner to achieve erection and ejaculation, but these men may also make highly satisfactory, erotic, and imaginative lovers as age frees them from some of the sexual inhibitions of earlier years (Kaplan 1974, p. 105–109).

Age does not take a similar toll, however, on the sexuality of women. It does, as we shall see, sometimes create a problem, especially for those women who do not have partners. The fact is that "age has no comparable effect on women, who remain capable of multiple orgastic response . . . throughout life" (Kaplan 1974, p. 105). Women tend to reach the height of their sexual responsiveness in their thirties and forties. Some women do experience fluctuations in sexual responsiveness during menopause. Kaplan suggests that a woman of 65 may be "less preoccupied" with sex than she was at 40, "but still may seek out and certainly can respond to sexual opportunities" (1974, p. 112). Kaplan reports that studies indicate 25 percent of 70-year-old women masturbate.

If we take into consideration the "normal" societal constraints attached to sexuality and tack on the societal constraints associated with aging, it should not be surprising that there are few positive images of sexuality in old age. These attitudes are especially burdensome for the older woman who is widowed or unmarried, even though she may have once had an active, healthy sex life. "For women past fifty, widowhood is usually a permanent status, though not necessarily a preferred one" (Troll, Miller, and Atchley 1979, p. 69). The widowed woman may not be able to find a sex partner. Lyn Kobosa-Munro (1977), reviewing the literature, points out that the most important factor in an older woman's sexuality—more important than "health factors, marital status, previous sexual experience, previous sexual interest, continuity of life style [—is] the availability of a socially sanctioned partner" (p. 77). Kaplan notes that when women lose their sexual partners, "they do not tend to actively seek replacements unless they are unusually active and secure and possess exceptional personal assets" (1974, p. 112).

In the over-65 population, the majority of male partners available to older women are younger men. Society has yet to accept with equanimity the idea of an older woman taking a younger man as a sexual partner, while it sanctions and perhaps even applauds the idea of an older man having a younger woman as his sexual partner. Hopefully, this double standard will change with time.

Gerontologists associated with institutions for the aging appear to have some difficulty accepting the possibility of sexual interest in the aged. "Have you ever seen a double bed in an institution? I never have," reports Irene Mortenson Burnside (1975, p. 47). The opportunity for an institutionalized man and woman to share a few private moments, giving and receiving physical affection, appears to be almost nonexistent.

WIDOWHOOD

One role that few older people are prepared for is that of the surviving spouse. Because males, on the average, die at a younger age than females do (see Figure 15.1), widowhood is likely to be the role of more than half of older married women sooner or later. Yet, as a group, widows are not well represented in the media or in the realm of politics. Although there are 10 million women who have experienced widowhood and reorganized their lives to meet their new "status," these women nevertheless remain, as Helen Z. Lopata has observed, "rather invisible" politically (1979, p. 378).

The situation of widows is of particular concern since there are about ten widows for every five widowers (Butler 1979; Troll, Miller, and Atchley 1979). Seventy-nine percent of older men are married while only 39 percent of older women are married (Harris 1978). According to one estimate (Hiltz 1978), less than five percent of women who are widowed after the age of 55 ever remarry. Hiltz makes a striking analogy about the length of time spent in widowhood, noting that if a woman is widowed at 55 and lives until 75, she "is likely to spend as much time as a widow as she does raising children." Yet, as Hiltz notes, the woman has been socialized from her earliest years for the role of wife and mother. "She typically has had no

FIGURE 15.1   Sex Ratios in the Older Ages, 1900 to 1990

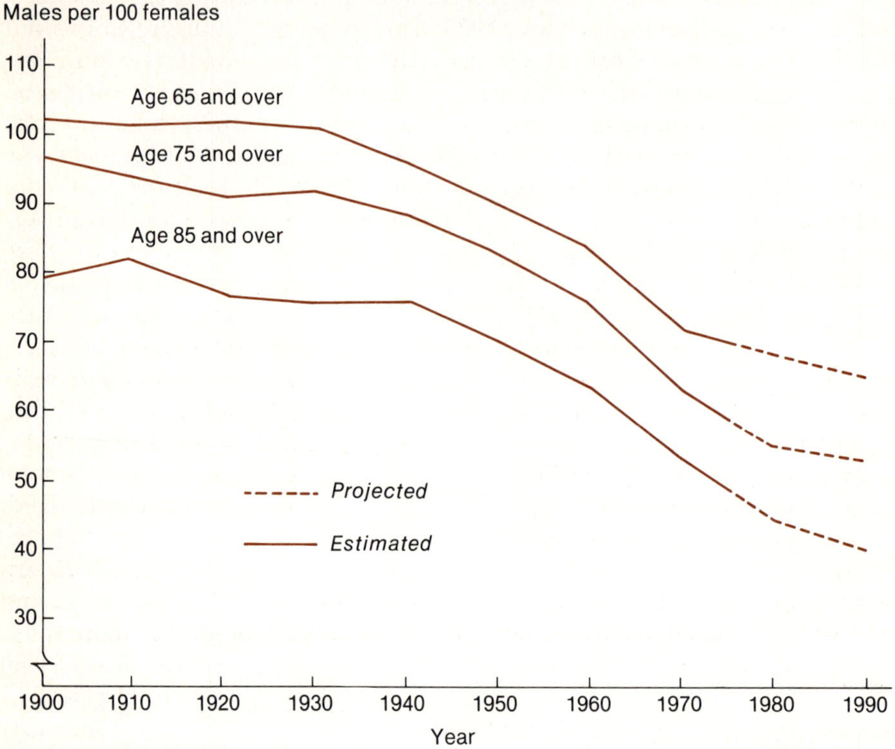

Males per 100 females

Source: U.S. Bureau of the Census, "Demographic Aspects of Aging and the Older Population in the United States," *Current Population Reports*, Series P-23, No. 59 (May 1976).

preparation for the widowhood role" (Hiltz 1978, p. 6). Hiltz flatly states that the whole subject of widowhood has been taboo, and thus few, if any, women have been adequately prepared ahead of time for a role most of them will have to assume.

The anticipation and rehearsal of widowhood, according to Neugarten, may diminish the impact of the loss. Thus, even the death of a spouse, if it occurs at the expected "time," as measured by "social clocks," and it has been anticipated through the general aging process or by long illness, should not create a psychiatric crisis for either men or women (1979, p. 889). Nonetheless, people who have spent a lifetime together naturally suffer when their cherished partner dies.

The Emotional Reaction to Widowhood

The person who survives the death of a loved one must "work" to separate himself or herself from the loved one. This is often a long and painful process because of the power of the bonds or ties that link the survivor with the one who has died. Those bonds are a mixture of the many positive and negative emotional elements that made up the relationship—love, hostility, warmth, irritability. The mourner, over a period of time that can be measured only in years, must come to grips with the many memories of the lost one. At last the memory no longer dominates the survivor's life, but occupies a realistic and healthy part of the survivor's emotional makeup. Mourning is a long and difficult process. In recent years researchers have finally begun to build on Freud's seminal work, *Mourning and Melancholia* (1917), recording and analyzing people's emotional and psychological reactions to death.

Troll, Miller, and Atchley (1979) suggest three elements to the period of mourning: physical, emotional, and intellectual. A person who has lost a loved one may experience shortness of breath, a tightness or constricted feeling in the chest, stomach upsets, as well as a general lack of strength. The emotional reaction, according to Parkes (1972), includes anger, guilt, sadness, anxiety—the common kinds of emotions that come into play during an involvement with a loved one. In terms of the intellectual process of mourning, most widows remember or talk about only the good side of the departed. Troll et al. (1979, p. 71) call this "sanctifying the memory of the dead spouse." With deliberate, conscious effort, the surviving spouse recalls only idealized, positive memories of the dead spouse. It is more than just not speaking ill of the dead; it involves a gross exaggeration of the positive virtues, while totally blocking out any aspect of the dead person's life that would sully the perfect memory picture. Ultimately, surviving spouses must deal with the real people they have lost, recalling their faults as well as their virtues. Finally, they must detach themselves and gradually rebuild their own lives.

Social Roles for Widows

It would seem futile to argue about who suffers a greater loss—the surviving husband or the surviving wife. Each loss has to be viewed individually, noting however that the problems of the widow may be different from those of the widower. Widows may face a greater identity crisis, especially if they have played a traditional role. What is the individual identity of the woman who has always thought of herself as Mrs. Brown, the wife of Mr. Brown, the mother of his children, the grandmother of his grandchildren? Women who have devoted their lives to such an affiliative identity may find themselves wondering who they are as individuals when their husbands die. Women who have identified so closely with their husbands, virtually merging with their husbands' identity, may experience severe feelings of loneliness.

Yet the picture of widowhood is not totally bleak. Widows who have job skills, typically those in the middle class, may find new lives for themselves once they have worked through some of the mourning process. These women may choose to work or become active in community affairs, while strengthening intergenerational ties (Troll et al. 1979). Whether or not such a new beginning can be undertaken depends to some extent on the age of the widow. Obviously the 50-year-old widow is in a more favorable position for new vistas than one in her seventies.

Women who are now in their seventies have had the "lowest fertility of any cohort of women in the United States" (NIH 1979). This means that about one-fourth of women now over 70 have no living children. If these women lose their husbands, they alone must provide for their own emotional, financial, and social support systems. Women now in their fifties have several advantages over this older widowed group. Not only do they have more education and more work experience, but they have had "the highest fertility rates ever recorded in this country" (NIH 1979, p. 17). Thus, when these women reach their seventies and many assume the role of widow, they will have education and work resources to call upon, as well as children from whom they might garner emotional support.

Social Roles for Widowers

The impact of widowhood on men has not yet been thoroughly researched (Troll et al. 1979). From the information we do have, it appears that the older men grow, the more they become dependent on their wives for direction of their daily activities. The social network they may have developed through work tends to dissipate or disappear once they retire. Women continue to be more closely involved with kin and friends. Lowenthal and Havens (1968) found that men were more likely to say that their wives were their confidantes than were wives to cite their husbands as confidants. In fact, women were twice as likely to say that a child or another relative or a friend was their confidant. Thus when a man loses his wife, he has lost his confidante as well. Women who lose their husbands may still continue to have a child, relative, or friend as their confidant (Lowenthal and Havens 1968, pp. 20–30).

Other research into widowers points to their lack of preparation for doing daily household chores. Widows have their housekeeping tasks, which lends some continuity to their lives following the loss of a spouse. In terms of the day-to-day chores, they are usually more self-sufficient than the elderly widower. As we suggested in Chapter 14, men are less likely to have intergenerational contact and seem to show less flexibility in midlife and after. Other data suggest that men are less invested in the role of husband than women are in the role of wife and that men have more work skills than women and thus are better off financially when widowhood occurs.

Most widowers under 70 remarry. They have ample opportunity to select from a large number of younger widowed, divorced, or single women, since custom in this country encourages the man to marry a woman younger than he. More research is needed to determine how generational differences may affect those remarriage relations.

ONGOING FAMILY RELATIONSHIPS

The Myth of Isolation

"An American myth, widely held, is that old people are isolated from their families. In the mass media—in newspapers, magazines, and television—when the aged are considered at all, the prototype old person is usually an older lady, physically decrepit, living in a single room surrounded by filth and squalor. Such old ladies are always reported as completely alone, without relatives, without anyone who cares" (Shanas 1977, p. 300). Isolation is particularly depressing in old age, and the plight of the lonely person should be a matter of concern. Fortunately, most elderly people in the United States are not isolated.

The majority of older people maintain contacts with family and friends. In a national survey, Shanas found that 52 percent of elderly persons not living with a child had seen their children sometime within the past 24 hours, and 78 percent of the elderly had seen their children within the past seven days (p. 304). Further, about 40 percent of the older persons had seen a living sibling sometime during the past week. Other surveys by Shanas indicate that those percentages can rise to as much as 84 percent of old persons with living children having had contact with their children within the past week and 90 percent having seen them within the last month.

Most older people want to live near their children, but not with them. When it does become impossible for an older person to live independently (and if the option of institutionalization has been rejected—at least temporarily), people over 65 are more likely to move in with an unmarried child than with a married one and are more likely to live with a daughter than a son. In cases where the children are married and have children, older people will move in when the grandchildren have moved out. Thus we see more two-generation families than three-generation families (Troll, Miller, and Atchley 1979, p. 85).

Varieties of Intergenerational Contact

Another myth that seems to permeate our society is that of a one-way street between old people and their adult children—with all the help moving from the children to the parents. But as Table 15.3 indicates, there is a two-way flow of help that goes from grandparents *to* parents *to* married

TABLE 15.3   Percentage of Help Received and Help Given by Generation for Chief Problem Areas

| | Type of Crisis | | | | | | | | | |
| | Economic | | Emotional Gratification | | Household Management | | Child Care | | Illness | |
	Gave	Received	Gave	Received	Gave	Received	Gave	Received	Gave	Received
Grandparents	26	34	23	42	21	52	16	0	32	61
Parents	41	17	47	37	47	23	50	23	21	21
Married children	34	49	31	21	33	25	34	78	47	18

Note: Percentages may not total 100 due to rounding.
Source: Adapted from Lillian E. Troll, Sheila J. Miller, and Robert C. Atchley, *Families in Later Life*, Wadsworth, 1979, p. 80. Reprinted with permission.

children, and from parents and married children *to* grandparents. One can surmise that when the grandparents are poor, help will flow to them; but middle-class grandparents who have maintained their resources are in a position to aid their children and grandchildren financially. In the areas of emotional gratification, household management, and illness, grandparents receive more help than they give, while in the area of child care, grandparents obviously give rather than receive. As Troll, Miller, and Atchley point out: "As a general rule it would seem that parents continue to give to their children one way or another for as long as they are able" (1979, p. 90).

In a thorough review of the literature on intergenerational relationships, University of Chicago psychologist Bertram J. Cohler (in press) found the following significant factors:

1. While there was frequent contact between adults and their own parents, greater contact was maintained between the wife and her parents than between the husband and his parents.
2. The single most important tie within the modified extended family is that between adult mother and her own mother, which provides the basis for family continuity.
3. This tie between adult mother and her own mother is particularly significant within working-class families—here, as we have indicated, families are more likely to live in the same neighborhood, and generally, working-class socialization has favored close ties from woman to woman.

Familial closeness between a mother and her adult female child may have its drawbacks, especially in terms of child rearing. Grandparents are not always anxious to help with child care (Cohler and Grunebaum 1980). Grandparents didn't choose to be grandparents in the same fashion they chose to be parents. Being a grandparent is a sign of aging. And tensions arise between grandmother and daughter over different child-rearing attitudes and practices, with the grandparents generally being more conservative and less flexible than their daughters in terms of discipline for the young child.

Still, there are subtle influences that may offset intergenerational conflicts. Hess and Waring (1978) believe that "the aged parent is often coping with situations which will one day be the lot of the adult child, and the latter is attempting to demonstrate ways of gracious aging for the older parent to emulate." Another kind of "modeling" is also taking place in such situations—that of the lesson the parent is teaching the young child about caring for older people. For example, a mother, by caring for her own aging mother, is, in effect, showing and telling her young child: "See,

Women maintain strong kinship ties and benefit from these relationships. (Charles Gatewood)

this is the way I am treating my mother when she is old. I hope this is the way you will treat me when I am old.''

Grandparenting is one way that older people can relate productively to the younger generations; mentoring is another way, as explained in Box 15.3.

Styles of Grandparenting

From the point of view of the older person, the role of grandparent may take many different forms. Neugarten and Weinstein (1964) found five major styles of grandparenting: (1) the *formal*, the grandparent who provides presents and treats for his or her grandchildren and serves as occasional babysitter; (2) the *fun seeker*, the grandparent who is interested in the grandchildren, who plays with them, but who leaves the parenting and discipline of the grandchildren to the parents; (3) the *surrogate*, the grandparent who takes an active role in the raising of the grandchildren, usually in the instance where there is a single parent who must work or where both parents are working full-time; (4) the *reservoir of family wisdom*, the grandparent who is an authoritarian model, possessor of real or imagined

BOX 15.3   Mentoring

Intergenerational relationships can be satisfying to old and young. One such unique and highly important relationship between adults of different age groups is the "mentor" relationship. As Levinson (1978) points out, the mentor acts as teacher, sponsor, host, guide, exemplar, and counselor to a younger person, as well as supporting the younger person in his or her attempt to achieve certain idealistic ambitions. Levinson notes that the mentoring relationship generally has been one of the older man and the young man, a relationship that often perpetuates what is known as "the old-boy network."

Women have recently begun to set up formal and informal networks of their own to redress the imbalance. It is now more common to find women mentoring women; however, because men have traditionally dominated the upper echelons of most professions, women often have mentors who are male. Levinson notes that "cross-gender mentoring can be of great value" (p. 98), but he cautions that in many instances, especially those involving older men and younger women, the mentoring relationship may bring with it sexual pressures between the mentor and the mentored. Levinson feels that the mentoring relationship is very important. Women can find a satisfying new role in later life as mentors to younger women and younger men. One can expect to see this type of mentoring relationship become more prevalent as women enter their fifties and sixties with high attainments in education and substantial work experience.

power within the family structure; and (5) the *distant figure,* the grandparent who is remote, distant, and rarely accessible to the grandchildren.

In studying the kinds of interaction between grandparent and grandchild, Smith (1965) found four styles of contact: (1) visits that were either extended, or brief; (2) visits on holidays, birthdays, and other occasions on which gifts were given and received; (3) less personal exchanges, such as phone calls and letters; and (4) personal contacts that resulted in the intimate exchange of experience with the grandchildren. It is this last type of contact that provides the continuity between generations. Here one finds grandparents following the progress, the growth, and the explorations of their young grandchildren in personal contacts; the children can experience and delight in the history and wisdom of their grandparents, and they can also find a source of support and love that supplements that of the parents. Grandparents can also serve as alternative confidants when the child cannot confide in the parents.

The elderly can add a special dimension to the lives of young children, especially if their contacts with them are frequent and intimate. They may have a greater capacity for stimulating creativity, because they are less intensely invested in their grandchildren than are the parents and are often less judgmental. They may be in the best position to recognize and savor the individual strengths of each child. This may also be true of older people who take on the care of children, such as nannies, foster parents,

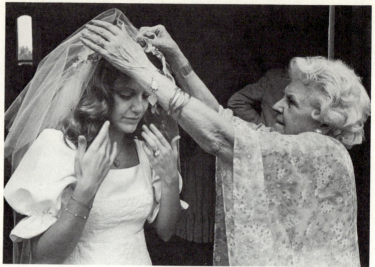

↑ Grandmother of the bride (Jean-Claude Lejeune)

← Grandfather and grandson fishing (Jean Shapiro)

↓ Grandchild visiting his sick grandmother (Jerry Howard, Positive Images)

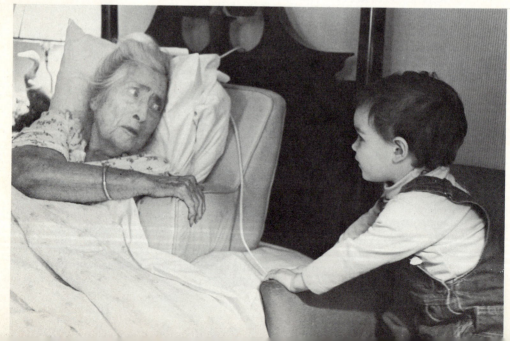

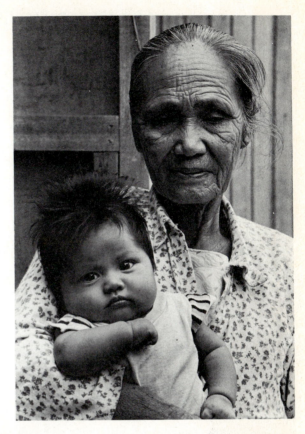

Grandmother and her infant grandchild
(Jerry Howard, Positive Images) →

Grandfather and granddaughter in conversation (Jerry Howard, Positive Images) ↓

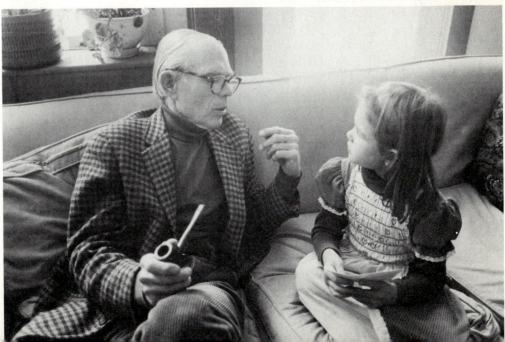

and committed babysitters. Psychoanalyst E. James Anthony (1980) calls this special type of loving care "othering." He points to many creative individuals, including England's great statesman Winston Churchill, the major Russian dramatist Maxim Gorky, and anthropologist Margaret Mead, who reaped the benefits of othering. Margaret Mead, for example, called her grandmother the most decisive influence in her life.

In a Turkish fairy tale told by Anthony (1980), the young hero, Iskender, is put into a casket and set adrift on the ocean. A green bird appears each time Iskender is in danger. After each rescue from a terrible threat, the green bird reassures the young ward with the words: "Know that you are never deserted." Anthony calls grandparents and other surrogate parents the "green birds" of our age, reminding children, when their parents are away or unavailable or unable to understand their feelings, that they are not deserted, and reassuring them that they have special and valuable qualities to offer to the world. These green birds also reassure the family as a whole, reminding them that despite the many social changes that take place from one generation to the next, there is continuity and the hope of understanding between the old and the young.

SUMMARY

1. The major purpose of this chapter is to present a developmental perspective on the aging years that focuses on potential strengths of later life, as well as on some of the special needs and problems of this stage of the life cycle. Particular attention is given to the lifestyles and satisfactions of older married couples, sexuality in the aging years, intergenerational relationships, and widowhood.

2. Various theories of aging emphasize a continuing necessity to confront and resolve certain developmental tasks in the later years. Such tasks typically involve a redefinition of one's identity in relation to the changes that come with retirement from the active work force, acceptance of some biological or physical limitations, and the recognition, as the end of life approaches, of the meaning of one's existence. This later task may be aided by the process of life review, which involves reminiscing about the significant events in one's life.

3. According to some historians, the position of the elderly in the United States has changed over time from one of significant power and control, but little affection, to a position of less power combined with more love. With the loss of power and the increasing numbers of aging individuals in the population, several government programs such as Social Security were enacted to help meet the needs of aging citizens.

4. The elderly population is composed of numerous individuals who represent various life patterns. Ageism is the refusal to recognize such differences by characterizing all or most elderly persons in negative terms. One useful way to divide the aging population is to distinguish

between the young-old, who are relatively healthy and vigorous and free of work or parental responsibilities, from the old-old, who are likely to be less able and more dependent. Most older people live with relative independence, but about four to five percent reside in institutions, half of which may present substandard conditions.

5. Older married couples frequently find the internal dynamics of their relationship changing as their social roles change. Recent research suggests that each spouse may begin to take on some of the traditional characteristics of the other spouse. For example, husbands may become more tender, wives more independent. For the majority of aging couples, satisfaction with the marital relationship is high.

6. While the older male may experience more decline in sexual ability than the older female, the barriers associated with the continuation of fulfilling sexual interaction in the later years are more likely to be a result of negative social attitudes than of an actual biological decline of sexual function.

7. Widowhood is a pervasive role in the later stages of the life cycle, especially for women. This role involves both the psychological task of working through the loss and grief associated with the death of the loved one and the re-establishment of a social identity separate from the spouse. Age and sex are two variables that are likely to influence individual adjustment to widowhood.

8. Contrary to popular opinion, a number of research studies have verified that most elderly people in this country have considerable contact with their adult children, grandchildren, and other relatives. These same studies reveal that intergenerational patterns represent a two-way flow of help that moves to the elderly from other family members and from the elderly to their children and grandchildren. For many elderly persons, grandparenting and mentoring provide meaningful roles that can actualize continuity from generation to generation, even in the wake of significant social change.

KEY CONCEPTS

Disengagement   Ageism
Life review   Intergenerational relationships
Young-old   Mentoring
Old-old   Widowhood

QUESTIONS

1. Considering the information presented in this chapter, describe two common myths about the aging years of the life cycle. Discuss the evidence that indicates such beliefs are false.

2. If you could interview various couples in the old-old stage of the life cycle, what questions would you ask them about their relationships?
3. Discuss three factors that you think influence the quality of relationships between adult children and their aging parents.
4. Though widowhood is a common role in later life, it does involve special problems. Discuss the kinds of information that educational programs could present in order to help individuals cope with this role.
5. The effects of ageism and age segregation often lead us to view the later years in a negative way. There are, however, a number of strengths the aging years can bring. Discuss some of the potential strengths of aging, and indicate how our society could utilize and enhance these strengths.

SUGGESTED READINGS

- Bengtson, Vern L. *The Social Psychology of Aging.* Indianapolis, Ind.: Bobbs-Merrill, 1973. A good overview for those interested in learning more about the later years of life. This brief monograph covers current theories of aging, dimensions of historical and developmental time, aging and the social system, and aging and the personal system.

- Downs, Hugh. *Thirty Dirty Lies About Aging.* Niles, Ill.: Argus Communications, 1979. A provocative, easy-to-read book that quickly breaks down the stereotypes of growing old that exist in such areas as learning, memory, health, retirement, and sex. Hugh Downs, the original television host of "Over Easy," a show on aging, discusses thirty myths about the later years.

- Foner, Anne, and Schwab, Karen. *Aging and Retirement.* Monterey, Calif.: Brooks/Cole Publishing, 1981. A short yet comprehensive review of the process and meaning of retirement. Topics covered include myths about older workers, profiles of the retired population, early retirement, retirement policy, and family, community, and societal aspects of retirement.

- Jacobs, Ruth H., and Vinick, Barbara H. *Re-engagement in Later Life: Re-employment and Remarriage.* Stanford, Conn.: Greylock, 1977. An informative look at elderly persons who confront losses due to employment and widowhood. The senior citizens who are the main focus of this book cope with these losses through finding other jobs and through remarriage.

- Kalish, Richard A. *Late Adulthood: Perspectives on Human Development.* Monterey, Calif.: Brooks/Cole, 1975. A comprehensive introduction to the later years that discusses research and theory related to the demographics of aging, basic processes and changes with age in sensory and cognitive functioning, mental health and illness, and primary relationships with family and friends in later life.

- National Council on Family Relations. *The Family Coordinator* 27, no. 4 (October 1978). The entire issue of this journal is devoted to the topic of "Aging in a Changing Family Context." Content includes articles on family relationships in the later years, remarriage in old age, support networks for the elderly, and alternative family forms for older persons.
- Troll, Lillian; Miller, Sheila; and Atchley, Robert. *Families in Later Life.* Belmont, Calif.: Wadsworth, 1979. A work that covers in some detail the satisfactions and stresses of older adults in their family-related roles. Particular attention is given to the older married couple, the older unmarried person, relationships between parents and adult children, and the role of grandparenthood.

Glossary

Agape. A kind of love characterized as primarily spiritual in nature.

Ageism. The stereotyping of older people in negative terms without regard for individual differences.

Agent of socialization. A transmitter of the manners, morals, tools, and techniques of a culture to its members. Usually parents are the first and primary transmitters of culture to infants and young children.

Alternative attractions. External factors that exert pressure toward terminating a marriage; for example, other intimate partners or enhanced status outside the relationship.

Androgyny. The merging of masculine and feminine characteristics in attitudes and behavior; resulting in decreased sex-role differentiation.

Attachment behavior. Biologically based behavior by infants that engages parents and thus insures satisfaction of physical and emotional needs.

Attractions to marriage. Internal factors, such as economic security and affection, that are influential in holding a marriage together.

Authoritarian parenting. A style of parenting in which obedience to parents is demanded, and few rights or choices are available to children. (See also *Authoritative parenting*; *Permissive parenting*.)

Authoritative parenting. A style of parenting that combines love and control appropriate to a child's age and stage of development. (See also *Authoritarian parenting*; *Permissive parenting*.)

Barriers to divorce. External factors, such as the disapproval of divorce by family or the presence of children, that are influential in preventing divorce.

Basic conflict. A struggle or disagreement over fundamental rules or expectations of a relationship. In marriage, basic conflicts often involve economic or expressive functions. (See also *Conflict*; *Nonbasic conflict*; *Personality conflict*; *Situational conflict*.)

Bonding. The beginning of affection between human beings as a result of mutual need satisfaction and the development of trust. In marital communication, bonding involves meeting a partner's needs through listening and reciprocity. (See also *Discrepant bonding*.)

Budget. A plan that records financial resources and indicates how such resources are being distributed or used.

Child abuse. The physical or emotional injury of a child by parents or guardians.

Children's rights. Rights that belong to a child by nature or law; for example, the right of a child to have food and shelter and not to be abused.

Climacterium. A period in men's lives, beginning in later middle age and extending into older adulthood, in which sexual drive and potency gradually decline, sometimes accompanied by other symptoms such as fatigue and irritability. Also refers to menopause in females. (See also *Menopause*.)

Clitoral stimulation. Manipulation of the clitoris in females for sexual arousal and orgasm.

Cohabitation. A more or less permanent relationship between two unmarried persons of the opposite sex who typically share living quarters, sexual and affectional access, and sometimes economic resources.

Cohort. A group of individuals who share a common condition such as age or social class.

Collateral. Material goods or investments of value against which money may be borrowed. If the money is not repaid, the lender keeps the goods or investments.

Commune. An intimate group usually including members of both sexes who share living arrangements and other resources. The details of commune living vary from group to group, but there is often a general commitment to certain ideals, such as shared intimacy with group members as a replacement for the nuclear family pattern.

Communication. The exchange of common meanings with another person through the use of both nonverbal signs and verbal symbols, or language. (See also *Complementary style of communication*; *Symmetrical style of communication*.)

Complementary style of communication. A style of communication in which interacting persons respond to each other with opposite but complementing behaviors: he explodes, she calms him down; she withdraws, he initiates responses. (See also *Communication*; *Symmetrical style of communication*.)

Conflict. A struggle or disagreement over two or more opposing or incompatible needs, goals, or values. (See also *Basic conflict*; *Nonbasic conflict*; *Personality conflict*; *Situational conflict*.)

Conflict, processes of. Observable stages through which disagreements between intimates pass regardless of the conflict issue being disputed.

Congruence. Correspondence between expected behaviors and actual behaviors.

Contraception. The intentional prevention of pregnancy through one of several possible methods of birth control.

Courtly love. A view of love that combines passion and respect, placing women on a pedestal as motivators of noble thoughts and deeds and as objects of devotion.

Credit. A temporary loan of money, usually involving a charge known as interest. (See also *Installment credit*; *Open credit*.)

Culture. The manners, morals, tools, and techniques that bind a particular group or society together.

Developmental framework. A perspective or view of individual or family life that defines specific stages in human growth and development. Certain tasks that need to be achieved within these periods in order for growth to proceed are also outlined.

Developmental stages. Specific periods within the individual and family life cycles characterized by particular kinds of growth and responsibilities. (See also *Individual developmental stages*; *Stages of family development*.)

Developmental tasks. Challenges that arise at certain periods of a person's life and that must be accomplished to some degree in order for growth to proceed. Erikson's theory poses such challenges as opposites or polarities, such as trust versus mistrust, to indicate the range of possible outcomes at any developmental stage.

Discipline. The establishment and enforcement of appropriate boundaries or limits on behavior.

Discrepant bonding. A communication pattern in which conflicting (and often negative) states are linked together: she expresses anger, he becomes silent; he becomes silent, she gets angry. (See also *Bonding*.)

Discretionary expenses. Purchases or expenditures over which the individual has some control or choice, such as food, clothing, and entertainment. (See also *Fixed expenses*.)

Disengagement. The process, in aging people, of gradually withdrawing from one's major roles and responsibilities of life. This is a shared process with society, which expects and supports such withdrawal.

Disqualification. Undermining another person's self-esteem through one's verbal and nonverbal messages; for example, ignoring someone's attempts to communicate.

Divorce. The termination of a marriage through legal means.

Dominant culture. A group within a society that imposes its culture upon other groups by virtue of its greater numbers or power or both.

Double bind. A situation in which conflicting messages or demands are communicated in the same message, without an acknowledgment that there is any contradiction; over time, this situation leads to distorted communication patterns. Schizophrenics have sometimes been victims in childhood of the double bind.

Double message. Two conflicting commands or responses communicated at the same time.

Double standard. A code or standard for sexual behavior that is more restrictive for women than for men.

Empathy. The ability to feel as another feels, to experience another's feelings indirectly or vicariously. (See also *Parental empathy*.)

Endogamy. Marriage between persons who are from the same social group and share such similarities as religion, ethnicity, and class.

Eros. A kind of love characterized as primarily carnal or sexual in nature.

Ethnicity. Identification of an individual or group on the basis of race, national origin, religion, or language. A sense of common identity with one's ethnic group is a typical component of ethnicity.

Exogamy. Marriage between persons who are from different social groups in situations in which such unions are required by law or custom; for example, a marriage between persons who are not blood relations.

Expressive characteristics. Qualities associated with the expression of feelings and emotional involvement with others. (See also *Instrumental characteristics*.)

Extended family. A social system that is larger and more complex than the nuclear family; often including three or more generations within the same household. (See also *Nuclear family*.)

Familism. A value system in which the importance of the family unit is emphasized over that of the individual.

Fixed expenses. Financial obligations that must be met to carry on daily life, such as rent, transportation, and mortgage payments. (See also *Discretionary expenses*.)

Fixed income. Earnings that vary little from pay period to pay period; situations in which income is not likely to increase regardless of other circumstances, such as when retired persons must live on social security or small pension payments.

Game transactions. Eric Berne's term for communication patterns designed to trap one's partner or defend one's ego.

Generativity. A sense of concern for the next generation, which may be expressed in parenting or by guiding others who are younger.

Homosexuality. Sexual preferences for or orientation toward members of one's own sex.

Homosocial. Having a preference for engaging in social interaction and activities with members of one's own sex.

Identification. A process by which individuals become like or take on certain characteristics of a loved or respected other.

Identity. A sense of self; of one's own uniqueness and consistency over the life course. Erik Erikson poses the consolidation of identity as the major challenge of adolescence.

Incest taboo. The social and legal prohibition banning sexual contact between certain closely related family members, such as siblings or parents and children.

Income tax. A graduated tax based on various kinds of earnings, such as wages, business profits, rents, royalties, interest on savings accounts, and investments.

Individual developmental stages. Periods within a person's life that represent particular levels of growth along several dimensions. Each stage is thought to be dependent upon the level of growth attained in the preceding stage. (See also *Developmental stages*; *Stages of family development*.)

Individuation. A process that defines the unique development of each individual in which certain potentials are encouraged and actualized, or the process of defining oneself as different from one's mate.

Installment credit. A type of credit that is based on an initial down payment and regular payments thereafter and that typically involves interest or a finance fee. (See also *Credit*; *Open credit*.)

Instrumental characteristics. Qualities associated with work and mastery, with getting the job done. (See also *Expressive characteristics*.)

Intergenerational relationships. Relationships between members of different generations; for example, parents and young children, adult children and their parents.

Intermarriage. Marriage between persons who are from different social groups and may not share the same background or values in such areas as religion, ethnicity, or social class.

Intimacy. A closeness between persons characterized by warmth, sharing, and mutual regard. Intimacy is a characteristic typical of most primary relationships.

Libido. A term used by Sigmund Freud to refer to the psychosexual energies that he believed to be the basic force fueling human behavior.

Life-course perspective. A framework for viewing life from birth until death as grounded in on-time, expected events appropriate for age and stage of development. (See also *Life-cycle perspective*.)

Life-cycle perspective. A framework for viewing life from birth until death as a series of developmental stages or periods that typically involve predictable tasks to be completed or crises to be resolved. (See also *Life-course perspective*.)

Life-cycle satisfactions. Satisfactions related to one's accomplishments during particular stages or periods of the life cycle.

Life review. The process of recall and reminiscence through which most aging individuals attempt to re-examine and integrate their life experiences.

Marital quality. The degree of satisfaction or happiness obtained by both partners from a marriage relationship.

Marital stability. The longevity of a marriage; the absence of divorce.

Marital structure. The type or form of a marriage as reflected by sex-role expectations and behaviors and by the relative power of the spouses; for example, head-complement, junior partner-senior partner.

Masturbation. Stimulation of the sexual organs to orgasm through means other than intercourse.

Menopause. The time in a woman's life when ovulation and menstruation cease, thus making conception no longer possible. This typically occurs between the ages of 45 and 55. (See also *Climacterium*.)

Metacommunication. The process of discussing and clarifying messages; communication about communication.

Neglect. Failure by parents or guardians to provide for the basic needs of their children; indifference to their children's physical and emotional needs.

Negotiation. The process of decreasing discrepancies between expectations and behavior through communication.

Nonbasic conflict. A struggle or disagreement over an issue that may seem important at the time, but will not threaten the existence of the relationship if left unresolved. (See also *Basic conflict*; *Conflict*; *Personality conflict*; *Situational conflict*.)

Nuclear family. A small social unit that includes husband, wife, and their children; also known as the *conjugal family*. (See also *Extended family*.)

Old-old. A term applied to those in the later years who are usually over age 75 and show signs of physical or mental impairment and withdrawal from active life.

Open credit. A type of credit on which no down payment is required and no interest charged if the account is paid within 30 days. (See also *Credit*; *Installment credit*.)

Open marriage. A marriage that allows both partners freedom of action and expression. (See also *Sexually open marriage*.)

Pair rapport. A process between two individuals that begins with self-disclosure and leads to a sense of comfort, affinity, and the discovery of common interests or backgrounds.

Parental empathy. The ability of parents or parenting figures to feel what their child is feeling; putting oneself in the place of one's offspring. (See also *Empathy*.)

Permissive parenting. A style of parenting tnat acknowledges the equality of children with parents with little or no enforcement of boundaries or limits on behavior. (See also *Authoritarian parenting*; *Authoritative parenting*.)

Personality conflict. A struggle or disagreement that arises or exists because of discrepancies between needs and capacities of partners; for example, one partner needs constant demonstrations of love while the other neither is demonstrative nor seeks frequent expressions of affection. (See also *Basic conflict*; *Conflict*; *Nonbasic conflict*; *Situational conflict*.)

Pronatalist attitudes. Opposition to or disapproval of abortion and sometimes to other contraceptive methods as well.

Propinquity. Physical or geographical proximity; physical nearness.

Quality of life. The degree of satisfaction or happiness that people obtain from various aspects of their lives, such as family relationships, employment situations, and community activities.

Relationship need. The need and desire of human beings for physical and emotional affection from others.

Religious homogamy. Marriage between persons of the same religion.

Role. A cluster of traits and tasks associated with a particular social position; a set of expectations for behavior considered appropriate in various situations.

Role induction. A method or means of trying to resolve conflict by employing techniques designed to change one's partner without altering oneself.

Role modification. A method or means of trying to resolve conflict by employing techniques designed to bring about change in both partners.

Role strain. Tensions arising from the gap or discrepancy between what one expects of a mate (role expectations) and what the mate actually does (role behavior); often the result of changes in marital structure.

Self-disclosure. Revealing personal information and feelings to another.

Sex roles. Traits and tasks expected of or assigned to individuals on the basis of their sex.

Sexual dysfunction. Abnormal or impaired functioning in sexual interaction, such as the inability to achieve orgasm.

Sexual identity. A part of individual identity that typically develops during adolescence as a sense of oneself as a sexual being.

Sexual response. As indicated by the research of Masters and Johnson, this term refers to four stages of sexual function: excitement, plateau, orgasm, and recovery.

Sexually open marriage. A marital union that, by mutual consent of the partners, does not include sexual exclusivity. (See also *Open Marriage*.)

Singlehood. The state of being unmarried that may occur either by choice or through life events such as the loss of one's spouse.

Situational conflict. A struggle or disagreement arising from unfair or unjust social conditions; for example, unequal distribution of power by sex or race. (See also *Basic conflict*; *Conflict*; *Nonbasic conflict*; *Personality conflict*.)

Social clocks. A term used by Bernice Neugarten to indicate the mental "clocks" that tell people how the expected sequence of events in their lives should proceed. Such a sequence is primarily determined by one's society and becomes problematic only when events in one's life are "out of sync" with social expectations; for example, marrying while still in high school.

Social cognition. Understanding the world of human interaction, sometimes referred to as *social understanding*, which involves role taking and perspective taking.

Socialization. The process by which the manners, morals, tools, and techniques of a culture are transmitted to its members, especially the young.

Social-learning theory. A theory of human behavior that emphasizes observation and modeling as important components for acquiring the significant elements of one's culture.

Social position. A particular location within a social group to which rights and duties are assigned.

Society. A group of people living and working together with some degree of permanence.

Stages of divorce. According to Paul Bohannan, divorce is a process that happens over time and includes several steps involving the emotional, legal, economic, coparental, community, and psychic aspects of terminating a marriage.

Stages of family development. Periods within the life cycle of families that are characterized by skills and activities needing major attention. Stages of family development are usually specified by age or stage of children, such as the preschool years or the school years. (See also *Developmental stages*; *Individual developmental stages*.)

Subculture. A group within a society that shares a common country of origin, race, language, or religion.

Symmetrical style of communication. A style of communication in which interacting persons mirror each other in approach and form of message that they share: he responds to her hostility with hostility; she responds to his hug with a hug. (See also *Communication*; *Complementary style of communication*.)

Traditional marriage. A legal union between one male and one female that is usually characterized by sexual exclusivity between the pair and a specified division of labor according to sex; also known as *traditional monogamy*.

Trimesters of pregnancy. The nine-month period from conception to birth divided into three periods of three months each.

Voluntary childlessness. The life pattern of couples who choose not to have children.

Young-old. A term applied to those in the later years who are usually between the ages of 55 and 75 and are still relatively active and involved participants in life.

Bibliography

Adams, Bert N. 1979. "Mate Selection in the United States: A Theoretical Summarization." In Wesley R. Burr, Reuben Hill, F. Ivan Nye, and Ira L. Reiss (eds.). *Contemporary Theories About the Family. Vol. 1: Research-Based Theories*. New York: The Free Press.

Adams, Bert N. 1980. *The Family: A Sociological Interpretation* (3rd ed.). Boston: Houghton Mifflin.

Aldous, Joan. 1978. *Family Careers: Developmental Change in Families*. New York: John Wiley and Sons.

Alinsky, Saul. 1970. *John L. Lewis: An Unauthorized Biography*. New York: Vintage Books.

Anderson, Ralph E., and Carter, Irl. 1978. *Human Behavior in the Social Environment* (2nd ed.). Chicago: Aldine.

Andrews, Frank M., and Withey, Stephen B. 1974. "Developing Measures of Perceived Life Quality: Results from Several National Surveys." *Journal of Social Indicators Research* 1.

Anthony, E. James. 1980. "The Creative Aspects of Parenthood." Paper Delivered at the Conference on Parenthood as an Adult Experience. Chicago: Michael Reese Hospital (March 7).

Aries, Philippe. 1962. *Centuries of Childhood: A Social History of Family Life*. Translated by Robert Baldick. New York: Knopf.

Arnold, Fred, et al. 1975. *The Value of Children: A Cross-National Study*. Honolulu, Hawaii: East-West Population Institute, East-West Center.

Aron, A. 1974. "Relationships with Opposite-Sex Parents and Mate Choice." *Human Relations* 27: 17–24.

Austen, Jane. 1965 (originally published in 1818). *Northanger Abbey*. New York: Signet, New American Library.

Babson, S. G., and Benson, R. C. 1971. *Management of High-Risk Pregnancy and Intensive Care of the Neonate*. St. Louis: Mosby.

Bach, George, and Wyden, Peter. 1968. *The Intimate Enemy*. New York: Avon.

Bahr, Stephen J. 1979. "The Effects of Welfare on Marital Stability and Remarriage." *Journal of Marriage and the Family* 41 (August): 553–560.

Banducci, R. 1967. "The Effect of Mother's Employment on the Achievement, Aspirations, and Expectations of the Child." *Personnel and Guidance Journal* 46: 263–267.

Bandura, Albert. 1977. *Social Learning Theory*. Englewood Cliffs, N.J.: Prentice-Hall.

Bandura, Albert; Ross, D.; and Ross, S. A. 1963. "Imitation of Film-Mediated Aggressive Models." *Journal of Abnormal and Social Psychology* 66: 3–11.

Bandura, Albert, and Walters, Richard H. 1963. *Social Learning and Personality Development*. New York: Holt, Rinehart and Winston.

Bane, Mary Jo. 1979. "Marital Disruption and the Lives of Children." In George Levinger and Oliver Moles (eds.). *Divorce and Separation*. New York: Basic Books.

Barbach, Lonnie G. 1975. *For Yourself: The Fulfillment of Female Sexuality*. New York: Doubleday.

Bateson, Gregory; Jackson, Don D.; Haley, Jay; and Weakland, John. 1956. "Toward a Theory of Schizophrenia." *Behavioral Science* 1: 251–264.

Baumrind, Diana. 1967. "Child Care Practices Anteceding Three Patterns of Preschool Behavior." *Genetic Psychology Monographs* 75: 43–88.

Baumrind, Diana. 1971. "Current Patterns of Parental Authority." *Developmental Psychology Monographs* 4, no. 1: 1–102.

Baumrind, Diana. 1973. "The Development of Instrumental Competence Through Socialization." In A. D. Pick (ed.). *Minnesota Symposium of Child Psychology*, Vol. 7. Minneapolis: University of Minnesota Press.

Baumrind, Diana. 1977. "Socialization Determinants of Personal Aging." Paper presented at the Biennial Meeting of the Society for Research in child Development. New Orleans (March).

Baumrind, Diana. 1979. "Sex Related Socialization Effects." Paper presented at the Biennial Meeting of the Society for Research in Child Development. San Francisco (March).

Beauvoir, Simone de. 1973. *Coming of Age*. New York: Warner Communications.

Beck, Dorothy Fahs, and Jones, Mary Ann. 1973. *Progress on Family Problems*. New York: Family Service Association of America.

Becker, Howard S. 1963. *Outsiders: Studies in the Sociology of Deviance*. New York: The Free Press.

Bell, Alan P., and Weinberg, Martin S. 1979. *Homosexualities: A Study of Diversity Among Men and Women*. New York: Simon and Schuster.

Bell, Alan P.; Weinberg, Martin S.; and Hammersmith, Sue K. 1981. *Sexual Preference*. Bloomington, Indiana: Indiana University Press.

Bell, R., and Peltz, O. 1974. "Extra-Marital Sex Among Women." *Medical Aspects of Human Sexuality* 8: 10–31.

Bem, Sandra L. 1975. "Sex-Role Adaptability: One Consequence of Psychological Androgyny." *Journal of Personality and Social Psychology* 31: 634–643.

Benedict, Ruth. 1934. *Patterns of Culture*. Boston: Houghton Mifflin.

Berger, Michael; Foster, Marsha; and Wallston, Barbara Strudler. 1978. "Finding Two Jobs." In Robert Rapoport and Rhona Rapoport (eds.). *Working Couples*. New York: Harper Colophon Books.

Bernard, Jessie. 1972. *The Future of Marriage*. New York: World.

Bernard, Jessie. 1974. *The Future of Motherhood*. New York: Dial Press.

Bernard, Jessie. 1977. "Infidelity: Some Moral and Social Issues." In Roger W. Libby and Robert N. Whitehurst (eds.). *Marriage and Alternatives: Exploring Intimate Relationships*. Glenview, Ill.: Scott, Foresman.

Berne, Eric. 1964. *Games People Play*. New York: Grove Press.

Bianchi, Suzanne, and Farley, Reynolds. 1979. "Racial Differences in Family Living Arrangements and Economic Well-Being: An Analysis of Recent Trends." *Journal of Marriage and the Family* 41 (August): 537–552.

Birdwhistell, Ray L. 1970. *Kinesics and Context: Essays on Body Motion Communication*. Philadelphia: University of Pennsylvania Press.

Blehar, Mary C. 1979. "Family Adjustment to Unemployment." In Eunice Corfman (ed.). *Families Today*. Vol. 1. National Institute of Mental Health. DHEW pub. no. (ADM) 79-815. Washington, D.C.: U.S. Government Printing Office.

Bohannan, Paul (ed.). 1970. *Divorce and After*. Garden City, N.Y.: Doubleday.

Bower, Donald W., and Christopherson, Victor A. 1977. "University Student Cohabitation: A Regional Comparison of Selected Attitudes and Behaviors." *Journal of Marriage and the Family* 39 (August): 447–453.

Bowlby, John. 1980. *Attachment and Loss*. Vol. 3. New York: Basic Books.

Brackbill, Y. 1979. "Obstetrical Medication and Infant Behavior." In J. D. Osofsky (ed.). *Handbook of Infant Development*. New York: Wiley Interscience.

Brunner, Jerome. 1968. *Toward a Theory of Instruction*. New York: Norton.

Bukstel, Lee; Roeder, Gregory; Killmann, Peter; Laughlin, James; and Sotile, Wayne. 1978. "Projected Extramarital Sexual Involvement in Unmarried College Students." *Journal of Marriage and the Family* 40 (May): 337–340.

Bullough, Vern, and Bullough, Bonnie. 1977. *Sin, Sickness and Sanity: A History of Sexual Attitudes*. New York: Meridian Books, New American Library.

Bumpass, Larry L., and Presser, Harriet B. 1973. "The Increasing Acceptance of Sterilization and Abortion." In Charles F. Westoff (ed.). *Toward the End of Growth: Population in America*. Englewood Cliffs, N.J.: Prentice-Hall.

Burnside, Irene M. (ed.). 1975. *Sexuality and Aging*. University of Southern California Press.

Burr, Wesley R. 1973. *Theory Construction and the Sociology of the Family*. New York: Wiley.

Burr, Wesley R. 1976. *Successful Marriage: A Principles Approach*. Homewood, Ill.: The Dorsey Press.

Burrows, P. 1980. "Mexican Parental Roles: Differences Between Mother's and Father's Behavior to Children." Paper presented at the Annual Meeting of the Society for Cross-Cultural Research, Philadelphia (February).

Butler, Robert N. 1968. "The Life Review: An Interpretation of Reminiscence in the Aged." In Bernice L. Neugarten (ed.). *Middle Age and Aging*. Chicago: University of Chicago Press.

Butler, Robert N. 1969. "Agism: Another Form of Bigotry." *The Gerontologist* 9, no. 4, Part I: 243–246.

Butler, Robert N. 1979. "Sexual Intimacy for Older Folks." *Geriatrics* 34, no. 1: 9, 27.

Byrne, Doran. 1971. "What Makes People Sexually Appealing?" *Sexual Behavior* (June): 75–77.

Byrne, D., and Clove, G. L. 1967. "Effectance Arousal and Attraction." *Journal of Personality and Social Psychology* 6, no. 4.

Campbell, Angus; Converse, Philip; and Rodgers, Willard. 1976. *The Quality of American Life: Perceptions, Evaluations, and Satisfactions*. New York: Russell Sage Foundation.

Campbell, Sally R. 1976. "How to Create Your Own Financial Master Plan." *New Marriage*. Nashville, Tenn.: Approach Corporation 13–30.

Card, Josefina, and Wife, Lauress. 1978. "Teenage Mothers and Teenage Fathers: The Impact of Early Childbearing on the Parents' Personal and Professional Lives." *Family Planning Perspectives* 10, no. 4 (July/August).

Catton, William R. 1964. "A Comparison of Mathematical Models for the Effect of Residential Propinquity on Mate Selection." *American Sociological Review* 29: 529.

Cavan, Ruth S. 1969. *The American Family*. New York: Crowell.

Cavan, Ruth S., and Cavan, Jordan T. 1975. "Cultural Patterns, Functions, and Dysfunctions of Endogamy and Intermarriage." In Ruth E. Albrecht and E. Wilbur Bock (eds.). *Encounter: Love, Marriage, and Family*. Boston: Holbrook Press.

Chafetz, Janet Saltzman. 1974. *Masculine/Feminine or Human*. Itasca, Ill.: Peacock Publishers.

Chambers, Donald E. 1981. "Another Look at Poverty Lives in England and the United States." *Social Service Review* 55 (September): 472–483.

Chestang, Leon W. 1980. "Character Development in a Hostile Environment." In Martin Bloom (ed.). *Life Span Development*. New York: Macmillan.

Chilman, Catherine S. 1976. "Public Social Policy and Families in the 1970's." In Evelyn Eldridge and Nancy Meridith (eds.). *Environmental Issues: Family Impact*. Minneapolis: Burgess.

Cicero, Marcus Tullius. 1969. *De Senectute* ("On Old Age"). E. S. Shuckburgh (ed.). New York: St. Martin's Press.

Clarke-Stewart, Alison. 1978. "Popular Primers for Parents." *American Psychologist* 33: 359–369.

Clarke-Stewart, Alison, and Koch, Joanne. 1983. *Children: Development Through Adolescence*. New York: Wiley (in press).

Clayton, Richard R., and Voss, Harwin L. 1977. "Shacking Up: Cohabitation in the 1970's." *Journal of Marriage and the Family* 39 (May): 273–283.

Cohler, Bertram J. 1983. "Autonomy and Interdependence in the Family of Adulthood: A Psychological Perspective." *The Gerontologist* (in press).

Cohler, Bertram J., and Grunebaum, Henry V. 1980. *Mothers, Grandmothers and Daughters*. New York: John Wiley.

Coleman, James. 1974. *Youth: Transition to Adulthood*. Chicago: University of Chicago Press.

Conover, P. W. 1975. "An Analysis of Communes and Intentional Communities With Particular Attention to Sexual and Gender Relations." *The Family Coordinator* 24 (October): 453–464.

Cooper, Pamela; Cumber, Barbara; and Hartner, Robin. 1978. "Decision-Making Patterns and Postdecision Adjustment of Childfree Husbands and Wives." *Alternative Lifestyles* 1 (February): 71–94.

Cory, Donald Webster. 1951. *The Homosexual in America*. New York: Greenberg.

Coser, Lewis A. 1968. "Conflict: Social Aspects." *International Encyclopedia of the Social Sciences* 3: 232.

Crandall, Richard C. 1980. *Gerontology: A Behavioral Science Approach*. Reading, Mass.: Addison-Wesley.

Cuber, John F., and Harroff, Peggy B. 1965. *Sex and the Significant Americans*. Baltimore: Penguin.

Cummings, E., and Henry, W. E. 1961. *Growing Old*. New York: Basic Books.

Cutright, P. 1971. "Income and Family Events: Marital Stability." *Journal of Marriage and the Family* 33 (May): 291–306.

Datan, Nancy. 1977. "The Narcissism of the Life Cycle: The Dialectics of Fairy Tales." *Human Development* 20, no. 4.

Datan, Nancy. 1980. "Midas and Other Mid-Life Crises." In W. A. Norman and T. S. Scaramella (eds.). *Mid-Life Crisis: Clinical Issues and Implications*. New York: Brunner/Mazel.

Davis, Flora. 1974. "How to Read Body Language." In Jean M. Civikly (ed.). *Messages: A Reader in Human Communication*. New York: Random House.

DeLora, Joann S.; Warren, Carol A. B.; and Ellison, Carol Rinkleib. 1981. *Understanding Sexual Interaction* (2nd ed.). Boston: Houghton Mifflin Company.

Demos, John. 1970. *A Little Commonwealth: Family Life in Plymouth Colony*. New York: Oxford University Press.

Demos, John. 1976. "Myth and Realities in the History of American Family Life." In Henry Grunebaum and Jacob Christ (eds.). *Contemporary Marriage: Structure, Dynamics and Theory*. Boston: Little, Brown.

Demos, John. 1977. "The American Family and Social Change." In Arlene S. Skolnick and Jerome H. Skolnick (eds.). *Family in Transition* (2nd ed.). Boston: Little, Brown.

Denfield, Duane. 1974. "Dropouts from Swinging." *The Family Coordinator* 23 (January): 45–49.

Derlega, Valerian J., and Chaikin, Alan L. 1975. *Sharing Intimacy: What We Reveal to Others and Why*. Englewood Cliffs, N.J.: Prentice-Hall.

DeRougemont, Denis. 1956. *Love in the Western World*. New York: Pantheon.

Dibble, Ursula, and Straus, Murray A. 1980. "Some Social Structure Determinants of Inconsistency Between Attitudes and Behavior: The Case of Family Violence." *Journal of Marriage and the Family* 42, no. 1 (February): 71–80.

Douvan, Elizabeth. 1963. "Employment and the Adolescent." In F. Ivan Nye and Lois W. Hoffman (eds.). *The Employed Mother in America*. Chicago: Rand McNally.

Douvan, Elizabeth, and Adelson, Joseph. 1966. *The Adolescent Experience*. New York: Wiley and Sons.

Douvan, Elizabeth, and Pleck, Joseph. 1978. "Separation as Support." In Robert N. Rapoport and Rhona Rapoport (eds.). *Working Couples*. New York: Harper Colophon Books.

Draper, Thomas. 1981. "On the Relationship Between Welfare and Marital Stability: A Research Note." *Journal of Marriage and the Family* 43 (May): 293–299.

Dressell, Paula L., and Avant, W. Ray. 1978. "Neogamy and Older Persons: An Examination of Alternatives for Intimacy in Later Years." *Alternative Lifestyles* 1 (February): 13–36.

Drinan, Robert F. 1975. "American Laws Regulating the Formation of the Marriage Contract." In Ruth E. Albrecht and E. Wilbur Bock (eds). *Encounter: Love, Marriage and Family*. Boston: Holbrook Press.

Duberman, Lucile. 1975. *The Reconstituted Family: A Study of Remarried Couples and Their Children*. Chicago: Nelson-Hall.

Duberman, Lucile. 1977. *Marriage and Other Alternatives* (2nd ed.). New York: Praeger.

Dunphy, Dexter C. 1963. "The Social Structure of Adolescent Peer Groups." *Sociometry* 26: 230–246.

Durkheim, Emile. 1951. *Suicide: A Study of Sociology*. New York: The Free Press of Glencoe.

Duvall, Evelyn Millis. 1962. *Family Development* (2nd ed.). New York: J. B. Lippincott Company.

Duvall, Evelyn M., and Hill, Reuben. 1975. "How Can You Cope With Conflict Constructively?" In Ruth E. Albrecht and E. Wilbur Bock (eds.). *Encounter: Love, Marriage and Family*. Boston: Holbrook Press.

Edwards, Carolyn S. 1981. "USDA Estimates of the Cost of Raising a Child: A Guide to Their Use and Interpretation." Hyattsville, Md.: U.S. Department of Agriculture, Miscellaneous Publication 1411.

Elder, Glen H. 1974. *Children of the Great Depression–Social Change in Life Experience*. Chicago: University of Chicago Press.

Ellison, Ralph. 1953. *Invisible Man*. New York: Signet Books.

Emerson, Ralph Waldo. 1922. "Old Age." In E. Rhys (ed.). *Modern English Essays*. Vol. 1. New York: Dutton.

Epstein, Joseph. 1974. *Divorced in America*. New York: E. P. Dutton.

Erikson, Erik. 1963. *Childhood and Society* (2nd ed.). New York: Norton.

Erikson, Erik. 1968. *Identity, Youth and Crisis*. New York: Norton.

Etaugh, Claire. 1974. "Effect of Maternal Employment on Children: A Review of Recent Research." *Merrill-Palmer Quarterly* 20, no. 2 (April).

Etzkowitz, Henry, and Stein, Peter. 1978. "The Life Spiral: Human Needs and Adult Roles." *Alternative Lifestyles* 1 (November): 434–446.

Fasteau, Marc. 1972. "Men: Why Aren't We Talking?" *Ms.* (July): 16.

Ferguson, Lucy Rau. 1970. *Personality Development*. Belmont, Calif.: Wadsworth.

Feshbach, N., and Feshbach, 1972. "Children's Aggression." In W. W. Hartup (ed.). *The Young Child: A Review of Research*. Vol. 2. Washington: NEAYC.

Feshbach, N., and Roe, K. 1968. "Empathy in Six and Seven Year Olds." *Child Development* 39: 133–145.

Fischer, David Hackett. 1977. *Growing Old in America*. New York: Oxford University Press.

Flanagan, Geraldine. 1962. *The First Nine Months of Life*. New York: Simon and Schuster.

Fleming, Ann Taylor. 1980. "New Frontiers of Conception." *New York Times Sunday Magazine* (July 20).

Ford, Clellan S., and Beach, Frank A. 1951. *Patterns of Sexual Behavior*. New York: Harper & Row.

Ford, Kathleen. 1980. "Widespread Contraceptive Use Found in Britain: Condom Popular." *Family Planning Perspectives* 12, no. 2.

Francoeur, Anna K., and Francoeur, Robert T. 1974. *Hot and Cool Sex: Cultures in Conflict*. New York: Harcourt, Brace, Jovanovich.

Franke, Linda B. 1978. *The Ambivalence of Abortion*. New York: Random House.

Franke, Linda B.; Sherman, Diane; Simons, Pamela E.; Abrahamson, Pamela; Zaborsky, Marsha; Huck, Janet; and Whitman, Lisa. 1980. "Children of Divorce." *Newsweek* (February 11).

Frazier, E. Franklin. 1962. *Black Bourgeoisie*. New York: Collier Books.

Freud, Sigmund. 1900. "The Interpretation of Dreams." In A. A. Brill (editor/translator). *The Basic Writings of Sigmund Freud*. 1938. New York: Random House.

Freud, Sigmund. 1905. "Three Contributions to the Theory of Sex." In A. A. Brill (editor/translator). *The Basic Writings of Sigmund Freud*. 1938. New York: Random House.

Freud, Sigmund. 1917. "Mourning and Melancholia." In A. A. Brill (editor/translator). *The Basic Writings of Sigmund Freud*. 1938. New York: Random House.

Freud, Sigmund. 1920. *Group Psychology and the Analysis of the Ego*. Edited and translated by James Stachey. 1959. New York: Norton.

Friedan, Betty. 1963. *The Feminine Mystique*. New York: Dell.

Frommer, E. A., and O'Shea, G. 1973. "Antenatal Identification of Women Liable to Have Problems in Managing Their Infants." *British Journal of Psychiatry* 123: 149–156.

Fullerton, Gail P. 1977. *Survival in Marriage* (2nd ed.). Hinsdale, Ill. Dryden Press.

Furman, Erna. 1974. *A Child's Parent Dies: Studies in Childhood Bereavement*. New Haven: Yale University Press.

Gagnon, John. 1972. "The Creation of the Sexual." In Jerome Kagan and Robert Coles (eds.). *Twelve to Sixteen: Early Adolescence*. New York: Norton.

Galenson, Eleanor. 1979. "Development from One to Two Years: Object Relation and Psychosexual Development." In Joseph Noshiptz (ed.). *Basic Handbook of Child Psychiatry*. Vol. 1. New York: Basic Books.

Gerbner, G. 1972. "Violence in Television Drama: Trends and Symbolic Functions." In G. A. Comstock and E. A. Rubinstein (eds.). *Television and Social Behavior: Media Contents and Control*. Vol. 1. Washington, D.C.: U.S. Government Printing Office.

Gershman, Carl. 1980. "A Matter of Class." *New York Times Sunday Magazine* (October 5).

Gibson, Guadalupe. 1980. "Chicanos and Their Support Systems in Interaction with Social Institutions." In Martin Bloom (ed.). *Life Span Development*. New York: Macmillan.

Gilder, George F. 1973. *Sexual Suicide*. New York: Quadrangle/The New York Times Book Co.

Gilmartin, Brian G. 1977. "Swinging: Who Gets Involved and How?" In Roger W. Libby and Robert Whitehurst (eds.). *Marriage and Alternatives: Exploring Intimate Relationships*. Glenview, Ill. Scott, Foresman and Company.

Gitman, Lawrence J. 1978. *Personal Finance*. Hinsdale, Ill.: Dryden Press.

Glasser, Ira. 1978. "Prisoners of Benevolence: Power Versus Liberty in the Welfare State." In Willard Gaylin; Ira Glasser; Steven Marcus; and David Rothman (eds.). *Doing Good: The Limits of Benevolence*. New York: Pantheon.

Glick, Paul C. 1975. "A Demographic Look at American Families." *Journal of Marriage and the Family* 37 (February): 15–27.

Glick, Paul C. 1975. "Some Recent Changes in American Families." *Current Population Reports*, Series P-23, No. 52. U.S. Bureau of the Census. Washington, D.C.: U.S. Government Printing Office.

Glick, Paul C. 1976. *American Families*. New York: Russell.

Glick, Paul C. 1977. "Updating the Life Cycle of the Family." *Journal of Marriage and the Family* 39, no. 1 (February): 5–13.

Glick, Paul C., and Norton, Arthur J. 1977. "Marrying, Divorcing, and Living Together in the U.S. Today." *Population Bulletin* 32, no. 5 (October): 5

Glick, Paul C., and Spanier, Graham B. 1980. "Married and Unmarried Cohabitation in the United States." *Journal of Marriage and the Family* 42, no. 1 (February).

Gluck, Louis (ed.). 1977. *Intrauterine Asphyxia and the Developing Fetal Brain*. Chicago: Year Book Medical Publishers.

Golanty, Eric, and Harris, Barbara B. 1982. *Marriage and Family Life*. Boston: Houghton Mifflin.

Goldstein, Joseph; Freud, Anna; and Solnit, Albert. 1973. *Beyond the Best Interests of the Child*. New York: The Free Press.

Goodfield, June. 1977. *Playing God*. New York: Random House.

Goodman, M. E., and Beman, A. 1971. "Child's-Eye-Views of Life in an Urban Barrio." In N. Wagner and M. Haug (eds.). *Chicanos: Social and Psychological Perspectives*. St. Louis: C. V. Mosby.

Gordon, Leland J., and Lee, Stewart M. 1977. *Economics for Consumers*. New York: D. Van Nostrand.

Gottman, John M. 1979. *Marital Interaction*. New York: Academic Press.

Gough, Kathleen. 1977. "The Origin of the Family." *Journal of Marriage and the Family* 33 (November): 760–770.

Gowler, Dan, and Legge, Karen. 1978. "Hidden and Open Contracts in Marriage." In Robert N. Rapoport and Rhona Rapoport (eds.). *Working Couples*. New York: Harper Colophon Books.

Greeley, Andrew. 1971. *Why Can't They Be More Like Us?* New York: E. P. Dutton.

Gubrium, J. F. 1975. "Being Single in Old Age." *International Journal of Aging and Human Development* 6: 29–41.

Gurin, G.; Veroff, J.; and Feld, S. 1960. *Americans View Their Mental Health*. New York: Basic Books.

Gutman, Herbert. 1976. *The Black Family in Slavery and Freedom: 1750–1925*. New York: Pantheon Books.

Gutmann, David. 1972. "The Premature Gerontocracy: Themes of Aging and Death in the Youth Culture." *Social Research* 39: 416.

Gutmann, David. 1975. "Parenthood: A Key to the Comparative Study of the Life Cycle." In Nancy Datan and Leon H. Ginsberg (eds.). *Life-Span Developmental Psychology: Normative Life Crisis*. New York: Academic Press.

Guttmacher Institute. 1976. *Eleven Million Teenagers*. The Alan Guttmacher Institute, 360 Park Ave. South, New York.

Guttmacher Institute. 1981. *Teenage Pregnancy: The Problem That Hasn't Gone Away*. The Alan Guttmacher Institute, 360 Park Ave. South, New York.

Hacker, Andrew. 1979. "Divorce a la Mode." *New York Review of Books* (May 3).

Hagestad, Gunhild O. 1975. "Role Change and the Life Course: Toward a Conceptual Framework." Unpublished paper on file. Committee on Human Development. Chicago: University of Chicago.

Harlow, Harry F. 1974. *Learning to Love*. New York: Jason Aronson.

Harlow, H. F., and Mears, C. 1979. *The Human Model: Primate Perspectives*. New York: Halsted Press.

Harris, Charles S. 1978. *Fact Book on Aging: A Profile of America's Older Population*. Washington D.C.: The National Council on the Aging, Inc.

Hart, Gavin. 1977. *Sexual Maladjustment and Disease: An Introduction to Modern Venereology.* Chicago: Nelson-Hall.

Hartley, Ruth E. 1960. "Children's Concepts of Male and Female Roles." *Merrill-Palmer Quarterly* 6: 83–91.

Harvard Encyclopedia of American Ethnic Groups. 1980. Cambridge: Harvard University Press.

Hawthorne, Nathaniel. 1958. *The Blithedale Romance.* New York: Norton.

Heer, David M. 1974. "The Prevalence of Black-White Marriage in the United States, 1960 and 1970." *Journal of Marriage and the Family* 36: 246–258.

Hemingway, Ernest. 1940. *For Whom the Bell Tolls.* New York: Charles Scribner's Sons.

Henschel, Anne-Marie. 1973. "Swinging: A Study of Decision-Making in Marriage." *American Journal of Sociology* 78 (January): 885–891.

Herzog, Elizabeth, and Sudia, Cecilia. 1973. "Children in Fatherless Families." In B. M. Caldwell and H. N. Ricciuti (eds.). *Review of Child Development Research.* Vol. 3. Chicago: University of Chicago Press.

Hess, Beth, and Waring, Joan. 1978. "Parent and Child in Later Life: Rethinking the Relationship." In Richard Lerner and Graham Spanier (eds.). *Child Influences on Marital and Family Interaction: A Life-Span Perspective.* New York: Academic Press.

Hess, Robert D., and Camera, Kathleen A. 1979. "Post-Divorce Family Relationships as Mediating Factors in the Consequences of Divorce for Children." *Journal of Social Issues* 35, no. 4 (March): 79–96.

Hess, Robert D., and Handel, Gerald. 1974. *Family Worlds.* Chicago: University of Chicago Press.

Hetherington, E. Mavis. 1972. "Effects of Paternal Absence on Personality Development in Adolescent Girls." *Developmental Psychology* 7: 313–326.

Hetherington, E. Mavis; Cox, Martha; and Cox, Roger. 1976. "Divorced Fathers." *Family Coordinator* 25: 417–428.

Hetherington, E. Mavis; Cox, Martha; and Cox, Roger. 1978. "The Aftermath of Divorce." In J. H. Stevens and Marilyn Mathews (eds.). *Mother-Child, Father-Child Relations.* Washington, D.C.: National Association for the Education of Young Children.

Hetherington, E. Mavis, and Parke, Ross. 1975. *Child Psychology: A Contemporary Viewpoint.* New York: McGraw-Hill.

Hill, Charles T.; Rubin, Zick; and Peplau, Letitia A. 1979. "Breakups Before Marriage: The End of 103 Affairs." In George Levinger and Oliver Moles (eds.). *Divorce and Separation.* New York: Basic Books.

Hill, Robert. 1972. *The Strengths of Black Families.* New York: National Urban League.

Hill, Robert. 1977. *Informal Adoption Among Black Families.* Washington, D.C.: National Urban League Research Department.

Hiltz, Roxanne S. 1978. "Widowhood: A Roleless Role." *Marriage and Family Review* 1, no. 6 (November/December).

Hirsch, Barbara. 1976. *Living Together: A Guide to the Law for Unmarried Couples.* Boston: Houghton Mifflin.

Hirschhorn, Larry. 1977. "Social Policy and the Life Cycle: A Developmental Perspective." *Social Service Review* 51 (September): 434–450.

Hite, Shere. 1976. *The Hite Report.* New York: Macmillan.

Hittelman, Joan, and Simons, Richard. 1977. "Pregnancy and the Expectant Couple." In Richard C. Simons and Herbert Pardes (eds.). *Understanding Human Behavior in Health and Illness.* Baltimore: Williams and Wilkins.

Hobbs, D. F., and Wimbish, J. M. 1977. "Transition to Parenthood by Black Couples." *Journal of Marriage and Family* 39 (November): 677–687.

Hofferth, Sandra L. 1979. "Day Care in the Next Decade: 1980-1990." *Journal of Marriage and the Family* 41 (August): 649–657.

Hoffman, Lois W. 1974. "Effects of Maternal Employment on the Child: A Review of the Research." *Developmental Psychology* 10, no. 2: 204–208.

Hoffman, Lois W., and Mavis, Jean D. 1977. "Influences of Children on Marital Interaction and Parental Satisfactions and Dissatisfactions." Paper presented at Conference on Human and Family Development, Pennsylvania State University (April).

Holmes, T. H., and Rahe, R. H. 1967. "The Social Readjustment Rating Scale." *Journal of Psychosomatic Research* 11: 213–218.

Holtzer, Marion. 1980. "Swinging Doesn't Work." An Interview with Jack Mabley. *Chicago Tribune* (August 25).

Hooker, Evelyn. 1957. "The Adjustment of the Male Overt Homosexual." *Journal of Projective Techniques* 21: 18-31.

Horner, Matina. 1972. "Towards an Understanding of Achievement Related Conflict in Women." *Journal of Social Science* 28, no. 2: 157-174.

Horowitz, Irving L. 1967. "Consensus, Conflict, and Cooperation." In N. J. Demerath and R. A. Peterson (eds.). *System, Change, and Conflict*. New York: The Free Press.

Huange, Lucy J. 1972. "Mate Selection and Marital Happiness in the Mainland Chinese Family." *International Journal of Sociology of the Family* 2: 121-138.

Hughey, Michael J.; McElin, Thomas W.; and Young, Tod. 1978. "Maternal and Fetal Outcome of Lamaze Prepared Patients." *Obstetrics and Gynecology* 51, no. 6 (June): 643-647.

Hunt, Morton. 1959. *The Natural History of Love*. New York: Knopf.

Hunt, Morton 1966. *The World of the Formerly Married*. New York: McGraw-Hill.

Hunt, Morton. 1972. "The Future of Marriage." In J. S. DeLora and J. R. DeLora (eds.). *Intimate Life Styles*. Pacific Palisades, Calif.: Goodyear.

Hunt, Morton. 1974. *Sexual Behavior in the Seventies*. Chicago: Playboy Press.

Hunt, Morton, and Hunt, Bernice. 1977. *The Divorce Experience*. New York: McGraw-Hill.

Jackson, Brooks, and Witt, Evan. 1976. "Regulations—Quietly Pervading the Daily Life of a U.S. Family." In Evelyn Eldridge and Nancy Meredith (eds.). *Environmental Issues: Family Impact*. Minneapolis: Burgess Publishing.

Jaffe, Sondra, and Viertel, Jack. 1979. *Becoming Parents*. New York: Atheneum.

James, Henry. 1956 (First Published 1881). *Portrait of a Lady*. Edited and with an introduction by Leon Edel. Boston: Houghton Mifflin.

Jerrick, Stephen J. 1978. "Federal Efforts to Control Sexually Transmitted Diseases." *Journal of School Health* 48, no. 7 (September): 428-432.

Jessor, Shirley L., and Jessor, Richard. 1975. "Transition from Virginity to Nonvirginity Among Youth: A Social-Psychological Study Over Time." *Developmental Psychology* 11: 483-484.

Johnson, Kenneth R. 1974. "Black Kinesics—Some Non-Verbal Communication Patterns in the Black Culture." In Jean M. Civikly (ed.). *Messages: A Reader in Human Communication*. New York: Random House.

Jones, Ann. 1980. *Women Who Kill*. New York: Fawcett Columbine.

Jong, Erica. 1973. *Fear of Flying*. New York: Holt, Rinehart and Winston.

Jung, Carl. 1966. "Two Essays on Analytical Psychology." In *The Collected Works of C. G. Jung*. Vol. 7 (2nd ed.). Princeton, N.J.: Princeton University Press.

Kafka, Franz. 1952. *The Metamorphosis*. New York: Random House.

Kagan, J., and Moss, H. 1962. *Birth to Maturity: A Study in Psychological Development*. New York: John Wiley and Sons.

Kagan, S., and Madsen, M. D. 1971. "Cooperation and Competition of Mexican-American and Anglo-American Children." *Developmental Psychology* 5: 32-39.

Kalish, Richard A. 1975. *Late Adulthood: Perspectives on Human Development*. Monterey, Calif.: Brooks/Cole.

Kanter, Rosabeth Moss. 1977. "Getting It All Together: Some Group Issues in Communes." In Arlene S. Skolnick and Jerome H. Skolnick (eds.). *Family in Transition* (2nd ed.). Boston: Little, Brown.

Kantner, John F., and Zelnick, Melvin. 1973. "Contraception and Pregnancy: Experience of Young Unmarried Women in the United States." *Family Planning Perspectives* 5, no. 1 (Winter): 21-35.

Kaplan, Helen S. 1974. *The New Sex Therapy*. New York: Brunner/Mazel.

Kappel, B. E., and Lambert, R. D. 1972. *Self Worth Among Children of Working Mothers*. Unpublished manuscript. Waterloo, Ontario: University of Waterloo.

Katchadourian, Herant A., and Lunde, Donald T. 1972. *Fundamentals of Human Sexuality*. New York: Holt, Rinehart and Winston.

Katz, P. 1973. "Perception of Racial Cues in Preschool Children: A New Look." *Developmental Psychology* 8: 295-299.

Katz, Stanford M. 1971. *When Parents Fail*. Boston: Beacon Press.

Kazan, Elia. 1967. *The Arrangement*. New York: Stein and Day.

Kellam, Sheppard; Adams, Rebecca; Brown, C. H.; and Ensminger, Margaret. 1980. "The Long-Term Evolution of the Family Structure of Teenage and Older Mothers." Unpublished report from the Social Psychiatry Center, 5811 S. Kenwood, University of Chicago, Chicago, Ill.

Kelly, Joan, and Wallerstein, Judith. 1976. "The Effects of Parental Divorce: Experiences of the Child in Early Latency." *American Journal of Orthopsychiatry* 46: 20.

Kempe, C. Henry, and Helfer, Ray E. (eds.). 1972. *Helping the Battered Child and His Family.* Philadelphia: J. B. Lippincott Co.

Kerckhoff, Richard K. 1976. "Marriage and Middle Age." *The Family Coordinator* 25: 9.

Kessler, I. I. 1979. "On the Etiology and Prevention of Cervical Cancer: A Status Report." *Obstetrics and Gynecological Survey* 34: 790–794.

Kikumura, Akemi, and Kitano, Harry H. 1973. "Interracial Marriage: A Picture of the Japanese-Americans." *Journal of Social Issues* 29: 67–81.

Kinsey, Alfred C.; Pomeroy, Wardell B.; and Martin, Clyde E. 1948. *Sexual Behavior in the Human Male.* Philadelphia: Saunders.

Kinsey, Alfred C.; Pomeroy, Wardell B.; Martin, Clyde E.; and Gebhard, Paul H. 1953. *Sexual Behavior in the Human Female.* Philadelphia: Saunders.

Klaus, M. H., and Kennell, J. H. 1976. *Maternal-Infant Bonding: The Impact of Early Separation or Loss on Family Development.* St. Louis: C. V. Mosby.

Klemer, Richard H. 1971. "Self-Esteem and College Dating Experiences as Factors in Mate Selection and Marital Happiness: A Longitudinal Study." *Journal of Marriage and the Family* 33 (February): 183–187.

Kobosa-Munro, Lyn. 1977. "Sexuality in the Aging Woman." *Health and Social Work* 2, no. 4 (November).

Koch, H. 1955. "Some Personality Correlates of Sex, Sibling Position, and Spacing Among Five-and-Six-Year-Old Children." *Genetic Psychology Monographs* 52.

Koch, H. 1956. "Some Emotional Attitudes of the Young Child in Relation to Characteristics of His Siblings." *Child Development* 27: 393–426.

Koch, Joanne. 1971. "It All Comes Out On The Ravich Flyer." *Chicago Tribune Sunday Magazine* (March 28): 48–53.

Koch, Joanne. 1977. "When Children Meet Death." *Psychology Today* (August).

Koch, Joanne, and Koch, Lewis. 1974. "Family Lib." New York: Newspaper Enterprise Association (August 30).

Koch, Joanne, and Koch, Lewis. 1976. *The Marriage Savers.* New York: Coward, McCann & Geoghegan, Inc.

Koch, Joanne, and Koch, Lewis. 1980. "Parent Abuse—A New Plague." *Parade Magazine* (January 27).

Koch, Lewis. 1975. "Divorce, Chicago Style." *Chicago* magazine.

Koch, Lewis, and Koch, Joanne. 1980. "To Your Happiness." *Washingtonian* (August): 55–56.

Koff, Richard. 1979. *Home Computers.* New York: Harcourt, Brace, Jovanovich.

Kohn, Melvin L. 1963. "Social Class and Parent-Child Relationships: An Interpretation." *American Journal of Sociology* 68: 471–480.

Kohn, Melvin L. 1977. *Class and Conformity: A Study of Values* (2nd ed.) Chicago: University of Chicago Press.

Kohn, Melvin, and Carroll, Eleanor E. 1960. "Social Class and the Allocation of Parental Responsibilities." *Sociometry* 23: 372–392.

Kohut, Heinz. 1977. *The Restoration of the Self.* New York: International Universities Press.

Komarovsky, Mirra. 1946. "Cultural Contradictions and Sex Roles." *American Journal of Sociology* 52 (November): 182–189.

Komarovsky, Mirra. 1967. *Blue Collar Marriage.* New York: Random House.

Komarovsky, Mirra. 1973. "Cultural Contradictions and Sex Roles: The Masculine Case." *American Journal of Sociology* 78: 873–884.

Konopka, Gisela. 1976. *Young Girls: A Portrait of Adolescence.* Englewood Cliffs, N.J.: Prentice-Hall.

Koos, Earl L. 1946. *Families in Trouble.* New York: Columbia University Press.

Laing, R. D. 1972. *Knots.* New York: Random House (Vintage).

Landis, Judson T. 1949. "Marriages of Mixed or Non-mixed Religious Faith." *American Sociological Review* 14: 401–407.

Lardner, J. 1972. *Tomorrow's Tomorrow:*

The Black Woman. Garden City, N.Y.: Doubleday.

Lawick-Goodall, Jane. 1971. *In the Shadow of Man*. Boston: Houghton Mifflin.

Lederer, William J., and Jackson, Don D. 1968. *The Mirages of Marriage*. New York: W. W. Norton.

Lefkowitz, Monroe M.; Eron, Leonard D.; Walder, Leopold O.; and Huesman, L. Rowell. 1977. *Growing Up to Be Violent: A Longitudinal Study of the Development of Aggression*. New York: Pergamon Press.

Lein, Laura. 1979. "Male Participation in Home Life: Impact of Social Supports and Breadwinner Responsibility on the Allocation of Tasks." *The Family Coordinator* 28 (October): 489–495.

LeMasters, E. E. 1977. *Parents in Modern America* (3rd ed.). Homewood, Ill.: The Dorsey Press.

Lerner, Richard M., and Spanier, Graham B. (eds.). 1978. *Child Influences on Marital and Family Interaction*. New York: Academic Press.

Levande, Diane I. 1976. "Family Theory as a Necessary Component of Family Therapy." *Social Casework* 57, no. 5 (May): 291–295.

Levande, Diane I. 1980. "Sex-Role Expectations and Filial Responsibility." In Nick Stinnett, Barbara Chesser, John DeFrain, and Patricia Knaub (eds.). *Family Strengths: Positive Models for Family Life*. Lincoln, Neb.: University of Nebraska Press.

Levande, Diane I. 1982. "Content and Structure in Moral Development: A Crucial Distinction." In Albert Cafagna, Richard Peterson, and Craig Staudenbaur (eds.). *Child Nurturance: Philosophy, Children, and the Family*, Vol. I. New York: Plenum Press.

Levande, Diane I., and Levande, James S. 1979. "The Encouragement of Pro-Social Behavior." *Middle School Journal* X, no. 4 (November): 12–13, 31.

Levinger, George. 1979. "A Social Psychological Perspective on Marital Dissolution." In George Levinger and Oliver Moles (eds.). *Divorce and Separation*. New York: Basic Books.

Levinson, Daniel J. 1978. *The Seasons of a Man's Life*. New York: Knopf.

Levi-Strauss, Claude. 1957. "The Principle of Reciprocity." In Lewis Coser and Bernard Rosenberg (eds.). *Sociological Theory*. New York: Macmillan.

Levitan, Max, and Montagu, Ashley. 1971. *Textbook of Human Genetics*. Cambridge, England: Oxford University Press.

Lewin, Kurt. 1935. *Dynamic Theory of Personality*. New York: McGraw-Hill.

Lewin, Kurt. 1948. *Resolving Social Conflicts: Selected Papers on Group Dynamics*. New York: Harper and Brothers.

Lewis, Robert. 1973. "A Longitudinal Test of a Developmental Framework for Premarital Dyadic Formation." *Journal of Marriage and the Family* 35 (February): 16–25.

Lewis, Robert, and Spanier, Graham B. 1979. "Theorizing About the Quality and Stability of Marriage." In Burr, Wesley; Hill, Reuben; Nye, F. Ivan; and Reiss, Ira (eds.). *Contemporary Theories About the Family*. Vol. 1. New York: The Free Press.

Lewis, Sasha G. 1979. *Sunday's Women: A Report on Lesbian Life Today*. Boston: Beacon Press.

Liebert, Robert M., and Poulos, Rita W. 1975. "Television and Personality Development: The Socializing Effects of an Entertainment Medium." In A. Davids (ed.). *Child Personality and Psychopathology: Current Topics*. Vol. 2. New York: Wiley.

Loevinger, Jane. 1976. *Ego Development*. San Francisco: Jossey-Bass.

Longfellow, Cynthia. 1979. "Divorce in Context: Its Impact on Children." In George Levinger and Oliver Moles (eds.). *Divorce and Separation*. New York: Basic Books.

Lopata, Helen Z. 1979. *Women as Widows*. New York: Elsevier.

Lorenz, Konrad. 1966. *On Aggression*. New York: Harcourt Brace Jovanovich.

Lowenthal, Marjorie F., and Haven, Clayton. 1968. "Interaction and Adaptation: Intimacy as a Critical Variable." *American Sociological Review* 33: 20–31.

Lowenthal, Marjorie F.: Thurnher, Majada; and Chiriboga, David. 1975. *Four Stages of Life*. San Francisco: Jossey-Bass.

Maccoby, Eleanor E., and Jacklin, Carol N. 1974. *The Psychology of Sex Differences*. Stanford, Calif.: Stanford University Press.

Mack, Delores. 1978. "The Power Relationship in Black Families and White Families." In Robert Staples (ed.). *The Black Family: Essays and Studies*. Belmont, Calif.: Wadsworth.

Macklin, Eleanor D. 1972. "Heterosexual Cohabitation Among Unmarried College Students." *The Family Coordinator* 21 (October): 463–472.

Macklin, Eleanor D. 1980. "Nontraditional Family Forms: A Decade of Research." *Journal of Marriage and the Family* 42, no. 4: 905–922.

Malone, Margaret. 1977. "Child Care: The Federal Role." Issue Brief Number IB 77034. Washington, D.C.: The Library of Congress, Congressional Research Service.

Marshall, Donald S., and Suggs, R. C. 1971. *Human Sexual Behavior*. Englewood Cliffs, N.J.: Prentice Hall.

Maslow, Abraham H. 1962. *Toward a Psychology of Being*. Princeton, N.J.: Van Nostrand.

Masnick, George, and Bane, Mary Jo. 1980. *The Nation's Families: 1960–1990*. Boston: Auburn House.

Masters, William H., and Johnson, Virginia E. 1966. *Human Sexual Response*. Boston: Little, Brown.

Masters, William H., and Johnson, Virginia E. 1970. *Human Sexual Inadequacy*. Boston: Little, Brown.

Masters, William H., and Johnson, Virginia E. 1980. *Homosexuality in Perspective*. Boston: Little, Brown.

Masters, William H.; Johnson, Virginia E.; and Kolodny, Robert C. 1982. *Human Sexuality*. Boston: Little, Brown.

Matras, J. 1973. "On Changing Matchmaking, Marriage and Fertility in Israel: Some Findings, Problems and Hypotheses." *American Journal of Sociology* 79: 364–368.

Mayer, Jean. 1970. "On the Life Sciences." *Vital Speeches of the Day* 36 (April): 402–407.

McBroom, Patricia. 1980. "Is Modern Television Showing—Or Shaping—Our Thoughts?" *Chicago Tribune* (August 13).

McCord, J.; McCord, W.; and Thurber, E. 1963. "Effects of Maternal Employment on Lower-Class Boys." *Journal of Abnormal and Social Psychology* 67: 177–182.

McCracken, Samuel. 1980. "Are Homosexuals Gay?" *Commentary* (January).

McCraven, Marilyn. 1980. "Women Are Turning Away from IUD's as the 'Horror Stories' Mount." *Chicago Tribune* (September 7), section 12, p. 3.

McCray, Carrie A. 1980. "The Black Woman and Family Roles." In La Frances Rodgers-Rose (ed.). *The Black Woman*. Beverly Hills, Calif.: Sage.

Mead, Margaret. 1966. "Marriage in Two Steps." *Redbook* 127 (July): 48–49.

Mead, Margaret. 1970. *Culture and Commitment: A Study of The Generation Gap*. New York: Doubleday.

Mead, Margaret. 1973. *Male and Female: A Study of Sexes in the Changing World*. New York: Dell.

Mehrabian, Albert. 1974. "Communication Without Words." In Jean M. Civikly (ed.). *Messages: A Reader in Human Communication*. New York: Random House.

Merton, Robert K. 1938. "Social Structure and Anomie." *American Sociological Review* 3 (October).

Merton, Robert K., and Barber, Elinor. 1963. "Sociological Ambivalence." In E. A. Teryakian (ed.). *Sociological Theory, Values and Socio-Cultural Change*. Glencoe, Ill.: The Free Press.

Middleton, Russell, and Putney, Snell. 1960. "Dominance in Decisions in the Family: Race and Class Differences." In C. V. Willie (ed.). *The Family Life of Black People*. Columbus, Ohio: Merrill.

Mill, John Stuart. 1970 (first published in 1869). "The Subjection of Women." In Alice S. Rossi (ed.). *Essays on Sex Equality*. Chicago: University of Chicago Press.

Miller, D. 1980. "The Native American Family: The Urban Way." In E. Corfman (ed.). *Families Today*. Washington, D.C.: U.S. Government Printing Office.

Miller, Jean B. 1976. *Towards a New Psychology of Women*. Boston: Beacon Press.

Miller, Roger Leroy. 1975. *Economic Issues for Consumers*. St. Paul, Minn.: West Publishing.

Mindel, Charles H., and Habenstein, Robert W. 1981. *Ethnic Families in America* (2nd ed.). New York: Elsevier.

Monahan, Thomas P. 1976. "An Overview of Statistics on Interracial Marriage in the United States with Data on Its Extent from 1963–1970." *Journal of Marriage and the Family* 38: 223–231.

Montagu, A. 1962. *Prenatal Influences*. Springfield, Ill. Thomas.

Morton, R. S. 1977. "Venereal Disease." In

John Money and Herman Musaph (eds.). *Handbook of Sexology*. New York: Elsevier North—Holland.

"Mothers' Contribution to the Family Money Economy in Europe and America." 1979. *Joint Center Policy Note*, 12. Cambridge, Mass.: M.I.T.–Harvard Joint Center for Urban Studies.

Moynihan, Daniel Patrick. 1965. *The Negro Family: The Case for National Action*. Washington, D.C.: U.S. Government Printing Office.

Murphy, Patrick. 1974. *Our Kindly Parent, The State*. New York: Viking.

Murstein, Bernard I. 1976. *Who Will Marry Whom? Theories and Research in Marital Choice*. New York: Springer.

Murstein, Bernard I. 1978. "Swinging, or Comarital Sex." In Bernard I. Murstein (ed.). *Exploring Intimate Lifestyles*. New York: Springer.

Murstein, Bernard I. 1980. "Mate Selection in the 1970's." *Journal of Marriage and the Family* 42, no. 4 (November): 777–792.

Mussen, Paul H., and Eisenberg-Berg, Nancy. 1977. *Roots of Caring, Sharing and Helping*. San Francisco: W. H. Freeman.

Napier, Augustus Y. 1971. "The Marriage of Families: Cross-Generational Complementarity." *Family Process* 9: 373–395.

National Commission on Families and Public Policies. 1978. *Families and Public Policies in the United States*. National Conference on Social Welfare, 22 W. Gay Street, Columbus, Ohio.

National Institute of Health. 1979. National Institute on Aging. Special Report on Aging. Bethesda, Md.: Department of Health, Education, and Welfare, Public Health Service. Washington, D.C.: U.S. Government Printing Office.

Neisser, Edith. 1960. "Emotional and Social Values Attached to Money." *Marriage and Family Living* 22 (May): 132–138.

Neugarten, Bernice L. 1974. "Age Groups in American Society and the Rise of the Young-Old." *Annals of the American Academy of Political and Social Science* (September): 187–198.

Neugarten, Bernice L. 1979. "Time, Age, and the Life Cycle." *American Journal of Psychiatry* 163: 887–894.

Neugarten, Bernice L., and Datan, Nancy N. 1973. "Sociological Perspectives on the Life Cycle." In Paul B. Baltes and K. Warner Schaie (eds.). *Life-Span Developmental Psychology: Personality and Socialization*. New York: Academic Press.

Neugarten, Bernice L., and Hagestad, Gunhild. 1976. "Age and the Life Course." In R. H. Binstock and Ethel Shanas (eds). *Handbook of Aging and the Social Sciences*. New York: Van Nostrand Reinhold.

Neugarten, Bernice L.; Moore, Joan W.; and Lowe, John C. 1968. "Age Norms, Age Constraints and Adult Socialization." In Bernice Neugarten (ed.). *Middle Age and Aging*. Chicago: University of Chicago Press.

Neugarten, Bernice L., and Weinstein, Karol K. 1964. "The Changing American Grandparent." *Journal of Marriage and Family* 26: 199–204.

Nielsen, J. M. 1978. *Sex in Society: Perspectives on Stratification*. Belmont, Calif.: Wadsworth.

Norton, Arthur J., and Glick, Paul C. 1979. "Marital Instability in America: Past, Present, and Future." In George Levinger and Oliver Moles (eds.). *Divorce and Separation*. New York: Basic Books.

Notman, Malkah T. 1980. "Changing Roles for Women in Mid-Life." In W. H. Norman and T. J. Scaramella (eds.) *Mid-Life: Developmental and Clinical Issues*. New York: Brunner/Mazel.

Novak, Michael. 1972. *The Rise of the Unmeltable Ethnics*. New York: Macmillan.

Nye, F. Ivan. 1957. "Child Adjustment in Broken and in Unhappy Unbroken Homes." *Marriage and Family Living* 19: 356–360.

Olsen, Kenneth M. 1960. "Social Class and Age-Group Differences in the Timing of Family Status Changes: A Study of Age-Norms in American Society." Unpublished Ph.D. dissertation. University of Chicago.

O'Neill, Eugene. 1956. *Long Day's Journey Into Night*. New Haven: Yale University Press.

O'Neill, Nina, and O'Neill, George. 1972. *Open Marriage: A New Life Style for Couples*. New York: Evans.

Oshman, H. F., and Manosevitz, M. 1976. "Father Absence: Effects of Stepfathers upon Psychosocial Development in Males." *Developmental Psychology* 12, no. 5: 479–480.

Paolucci, Beatrice; Hall, Olive A.; and Axinn,

Nancy. 1977. *Family Decision Making: An Ecosystem Approach*. New York: John Wiley and Sons.

Parke, Ross D. 1977. "Punishment in Children: Effects, Side Effects, and Alternative Strategies." In H. Horn and P. Robinson (eds.). *Psychological Processes in Early Education*. New York: Academic Press.

Parke, Ross D. 1978. "Children's Home Environments: Social and Cognitive Effects." In Irwin Altman and Joachim F. Wohlwill (eds.). *Children and the Environment*. New York: Plenum.

Parkes, C. Murray. 1972. *Bereavement*. New York: International Universities Press.

Parsons, Talcott. 1955. "The American Family: Its Relation to Personality and Social Structure." In Talcott Parsons and Robert Bales (eds.). *Family, Socialization and Interaction Process*. New York: The Free Press.

Patterson, G. R., and Cobb, J. A. 1971. "A Dyadic Analysis of Aggressive Behaviors." In J. P. Hill (ed.). *Minnesota Symposium on Child Psychology* 5. Minneapolis: University of Minnesota Press.

Paul, E. W.; Pipel, H.; and Weschler, N. F. 1976. "Pregnancy, Teenagers and the Law." *Family Planning Perspectives* 8: 16.

Paul, Norman L. 1970. "Parental Empathy." In E. James Anthony and Therese Benedek (eds.). *Parenthood: Its Psychology and Psychopathogy*. Boston: Little, Brown.

Peck, Ellen. 1971. *The Baby Trap*. New York: Bernard Geis.

Peck, Robert. 1956. "Psychological Developments in the Second Half of Life." In John E. Anderson (ed.). *Psychological Aspects of Aging*. Washington, D.C.: American Psychological Association.

Peters, Marie, and de Ford, Cecile. 1978. "The Solo Mother." In Robert Staples (ed.). *The Black Family: Essays and Studies* (2nd ed.). Belmont, Calif.: Wadsworth.

Pleck, Joseph H. 1979. "Men's Family Work: Three Perspectives and Some New Data." *The Family Coordinator* 28 (October): 481–488.

Pogrebin, Letty. 1975. *Getting Yours*. New York: McKay.

Pomeroy, Wardell. 1972. *Dr. Kinsey and the Institute for Sex Research*. New York: Harper and Row.

Pratt, Henry J. 1976. *The Grey Lobby*. Chicago: University of Chicago Press.

Prescott, Peter S. 1981. *The Child Savers: Juvenile Justice Observed*. New York: Knopf.

Prevey, Esther E. 1945. "A Quantitative Study of Family Practices in Training Children in the Use of Money." *Journal of Educational Psychology* 36: 411–428.

Propper, A. M. 1972. "The Relationship of Maternal Employment to Adolescent Roles, Activities, and Parental Relationships." *Journal of Marriage and the Family* 34: 417–421.

Rallings, E. M., and Nye, F. Ivan. 1979. "Wife-Mother Employment, Family, and Society." In Burr, et al. *Contemporary Theories About the Family. Vol. 1: Research Based Theories*. New York: The Free Press.

Rapoport, Rhona, and Rapoport, Robert N. 1971. *Dual-Career Families*. Baltimore: Penguin.

Reiss, Ira L.; Banwart, Albert; and Foreman, Harry. 1974. "Premarital Contraceptive Usage: A Study and Some Theoretical Explorations." *Journal of Marriage and the Family* 37 (August): 619–630.

Reyner, F. C. 1975. "The Venereal Factor in Cervical Cancer." *Medical Aspects of Human Sexuality* (August): 77.

Rodgers-Rose, LaFrances. 1980. *The Black Woman*. Beverly Hills: Sage Publications.

Rollins, Boyd C., and Cannon, Kenneth L. 1974. "Marital Satisfaction Over The Family Life Cycle." *Journal of Marriage and the Family* 36 (May): 271–282.

Roman, Mel, and Haddad, William. 1978. "The Case for Joint Custody." *Psychology Today* 12, no. 4 (September).

Rome, Esther R.; Ansley, Fran; and Schwarz, Abby. 1976. "Venereal Disease." In *Our Bodies, Ourselves*. Edited by Boston Women's Health Book Cooperative. New York: Simon and Schuster.

Rosenberg, Morris. 1965. *Society and the Adolescent Self-Image*. Princeton, N.J.: Princeton University Press.

Rossi, Alice S. 1968. "Transition to Parenthood." *Journal of Marriage and the Family* 30 (February): 26–39.

Rowse, A. L. 1977. *Homosexuals in History*. New York: Macmillan.

Roy, P. 1963. "Adolescent Roles: Rural-Urban Differentials." In F. Ivan Nye and Lois

W. Hoffman (eds.). *The Employed Mother in America*. Chicago: Rand McNally.

Rubin, Zick. 1973. *Liking and Loving*. New York: Holt, Rinehart, and Winston.

Rugh, R., and Shettles, L. B. 1971. *From Conception to Birth: The Drama of Life's Beginnings*. New York: Harper and Row.

Russell, Candyce S. 1974. "Transition to Parenthood: Problems and Gratifications." *Journal of Marriage and the Family* 36 (May): 294.

Rutter, M. 1971. "Parent-Child Separation: Psychological Effects on the Children." *Journal of Child Psychology and Psychiatry* 12: 233–260.

Salaff, Janet W. 1973. "The Emerging Conjugal Relationship in the People's Republic of China." *Journal of Marriage and the Family* 35 (November): 705–717.

Samovar, Larry A., and Rintye, Edward D. 1974. "Interpersonal Communication: Some Working Principles." In Jean M. Civikly (ed.). *Messages: A Reader in Human Communication*. New York: Random House.

Satir, Virginia. 1972. *Peoplemaking*. Palo Alto, Calif.: Science and Behavior.

Satir, Virginia. 1974. "Communication: A Verbal and Nonverbal Process of Making Requests of the Receiver." In Jean M. Civikly (ed.). *Messages: A Reader in Human Communication*. New York: Random House.

Saxton, Lloyd. 1980. *The Individual, Marriage, and the Family* (4th ed.) Belmont, Calif.: Wadsworth.

Scanzoni, John. 1972. *Sexual Bargaining*. Englewood Cliffs, N.J.: Prentice-Hall.

Scanzoni, John. 1978. *Sex Roles, Women's Work, and Marital Conflict: A Study of Family Change*. Lexington, Mass.: Lexington Books.

Scanzoni, John, and Fox, Greer Litton. 1980. "Sex Roles, Family and Society: The Seventies and Beyond." *Journal of Marriage and the Family* 42 (November): 743–756.

Scanzoni, Letha, and Scanzoni, John. 1976. *Men, Women, and Change*. New York: McGraw-Hill.

Schelling, Thomas C. 1960. *The Strategy of Conflict*. New York: Oxford University Press.

Schopenhauer, Arthur. 1928. *The Philosophy of Schopenhauer*. Irwin Edman (ed.). New York: The Modern Library, Inc.

Schramm, Wilbur. 1974. "How Communication Works." In Jean M. Civikly (ed.).

Messages: A Reader in Human Communication. New York: Random House.

Schulz, David A., and Rodgers, Stanley F. 1975. *Marriage, the Family, and Personal Fullfillment*. Englewood Cliffs, N.J.: Prentice-Hall.

Scoresby, A. Lynn. 1977. *The Marriage Dialogue*. Reading, Mass.: Addison-Wesley.

Seaman, Barbara. 1972. *Free and Female*. New York: Coward, McCann & Geoghegan.

Seaman, Barbara. 1975. "How Late Can You Wait to Have a Baby?" *Ms.* (January).

Seaman, Barbara, and Seaman, Gideon. 1977. *Women and the Crisis in Sex Hormones*. New York: Rawson.

Sears, R. R.; Rau, L.; and Alpert, R. 1965. *Identification and Child Rearing*. Stanford, Calif.: Stanford University Press.

Seifer, Nancy. 1973. *Absent from the Majority: Working Class Women in America*. New York: National Project on Ethnic America.

Selman, Robert L. 1981. "The Child as a Friendship Philosopher." In Steven Asher and John Gottman (eds.). *The Development of Children's Friendships*. New York: Cambridge University Press.

Selman, Robert L., and Byrne, Diane F. 1974. "A Structural-Developmental Analysis of Levels of Role Taking in Middle Childhood." *Child Development* 45: 803–806.

Shakespeare, William. 1942, 1970. "King Lear." In William Allan Neilson and Charles Jarvis Hill (eds.). *The Complete Plays and Poems of William Shakespeare*. Boston: Houghton Mifflin.

Shakespeare, William. 1942, 1970. "The Tempest." In William Allan Neilson and Charles Jarvis Hill (eds.). *The Complete Plays and Poems of William Shakespeare*. Boston: Houghton Mifflin.

Shanas, Ethel. 1977. "Family-Kin Networks and Aging in Cross-Cultural Perspective." In P. J. Stein, J. Richman, and N. Hannon (eds.). *The Family*. Reading, Mass.: Addison-Wesley.

Shantz, C. U. 1975. "The Development of Social Cognition." In E. M. Hetherington (ed.). *Review of Child Development Research*. Vol. 5. Chicago: University of Chicago Press.

Shereshefsky, Pauline, and Yarrow, Leon. 1973. *Psychological Aspects of a First Pregnancy and Early Postnatal Adaptation*. New York: Raven Press.

Sherfey, Mary J. 1966. "The Evolution and Nature of Female Sexuality in Relation to Psychoanalytic Theory." *Journal of the American Psychoanalytic Association* 14: 50.

Shostak, Arthur B. 1980. "Middle-Aged Blue-Collarites at Home: Changing Expectations of the Roles of Men and Women." In Martin Bloom (ed.). *Life Span Development*. New York: Macmillan.

Silverstein, B., and Krate, R. 1975. *Children of the Dark Ghetto*. New York: Praeger.

Siman, Michael L. 1977. "Application of a New Model of Peer Group Influence to Naturally Existing Adolescent Friendship Groups." *Child Development* 48: 270–274.

Simmel, Georg. 1959. "The Sociology of Sociability." Translated by Everett C. Hughes. *American Journal of Sociology* 55 (November): 254–261.

Simon, William, and Gagnon, John H. 1977. "Psychosexual Development." In Peter J. Stein, Judith Richman, and Natalie Hannon (eds.). *The Family*. Reading, Mass.: Addison-Wesley.

Singer, June. 1973. *Boundaries of the Soul*. New York: Anchor Books.

Skolnick, Arlene. 1978. *The Intimate Environment* (2nd ed.). Boston: Little, Brown.

Smith, Harold E. 1965. "Family Interaction Patterns of the Aged: A Review." In Arnold Rose and Warren Peterson (eds.). *Older People and Their Social World*. Philadelphia: F. A. Davis.

Sorensen, Robert C. 1973. *Adolescent Sexuality in Contemporary America*. New York: World Publishing.

Sowell, Thomas. 1981. *In Ethnic America*. New York: Basic Books.

Spanier, Graham B., and Anderson, Elaine A. 1979. "The Impact of the Legal System on Adjustment to Marital Separation." *Journal of Marriage and the Family* (August): 605–613.

Spanier, Graham B.; Lewis, Robert A.; and Cole, Charles L. 1975. "Marital Adjustment Over the Family Life Cycle: The Issue of Curvilinearity." *Journal of Marriage and the Family* 37 (May): 363–375.

Sprey, Jetze. 1969. "The Family as a System in Conflict." *Journal of Marriage and the Family* 31, 699–706.

Stein, A. H., and Friedrich, L. K. 1975. "Impact of Television on Children and Youth." In E. M. Hetherington (ed.). *Child Development Research*. Vol. 5. Chicago: University of Chicago Press.

Stein, Peter J. 1976. *Single*. Englewood Cliffs, N.J.: Prentice-Hall.

Stein, Peter, J. 1978. "The Lifestyles and Life Chances of the Never-Married." *Marriage and Family Review* 1 (July/August): 1–11.

Steiner, Claude. 1974. *Scripts People Live*. New York: Grove Press.

Steinmetz, Suzanne K. 1978. "Battered Parents." *Society* (July/August).

Steinmetz, Suzanne K. Testimony of February 15, 1978. "Research Into Violent Behavior: Domestic Violence." Hearings before the Subcommittee of the Commission on Science and Technology. U.S. House of Representatives 95th Congress, No. 60. Washington, D.C.: U.S. Government Printing Office.

Sternglanz, S. H., and Serbin, L. A. 1974. "Sex-Role Stereotyping in Children's Television Programs." *Developmental Psychology* 10: 710–715.

Stolte-Heiskanen, Veronica. 1975. "Family Needs and Societal Institutions: Potential Empirical Linkage Mechanisms." *Journal of Marriage and the Family* 37, no. 4 (November): 903–916.

Strange, H. 1976. "Continuity and Change: Patterns of Mate Selection and Marriage Ritual in a Malay Village." *Journal of Marriage and the Family* 38: 561–571.

Straus, Murray A. 1974. "Leveling, Civility, and Violence in the Family." *Journal of Marriage and the Family* 36, no. 1 (February).

Straus, Murray A. Testimony of February 14, 1978. "Research into Violent Behavior: Domestic Violence." Hearings before the Subcommittee on Domestic and International Scientific Planning, Analysis and Cooperation of the Commission on Science and Technology. U.S. House of Representatives 95th Congress, No. 60. Washington, D.C.: U.S. Government Printing Office.

Straus, Murray A. 1979. "Measuring Intrafamily Conflict and Violence: The Conflict Tactics (CT) Scales." *Journal of Marriage and the Family* 41 (February): 75–88.

Strauss, Dorothy, and Mitzner, George L. 1977. "Middle Age and the Climacterium." In Richard Simons and Herbert Pardes (eds.). *Understanding Human Behavior in*

Health and Illness. Baltimore: Williams and Wilkins.

Sullivan, Harry S. 1953. *The Interpersonal Theory of Psychiatry*. New York: Norton.

Sutton-Smith, Brian, and Rosenberg, B. G. 1970. *The Sibling*. New York: Holt, Rinehart and Winston.

Talese, Gay. 1980. *Thy Neighbor's Wife*. New York: Doubleday.

Tanner, Donna M. 1978. *The Lesbian Couple*. Lexington, Mass.: Lexington Books.

Tanzer, Deborah, and Block, J. L. 1976. *Why Natural Childbirth? A Psychologist's Report to Mothers, Fathers, and Babies*. New York: Doubleday.

Tawney, R. H. 1926. *Religion and the Rise of Capitalism*. New York: Harcourt, Brace.

TenHouten, Warren D. 1970. "The Black Family: Myth and Reality." *Psychiatry* 23 (May): 145–173.

Terkel, Studs. 1974. *Working*. New York: Pantheon Books.

Terkel, Studs. 1980. *American Dreams: Lost and Found*. New York: Pantheon Books.

The American Heritage Dictionary. 1969. Boston: American Heritage Publishing Company and Houghton Mifflin.

The Family Banker. 1979. Continental Illinois National Bank and Trust Company 13, no. 6 (July/August).

Thomas, Alexander, and Chess, Stella. 1977. *Temperament and Development*. New York: Brunner/Mazel.

Thomas, Edwin J. 1977. *Marital Communication and Decision Making*. New York: The Free Press.

Tietze, Christopher. 1979. "Unintended Pregnancies in the United States, 1970–1972." *Family Planning Perspectives* 11, no. 3 (May/June): 186–188.

Time. 1979. "How Gay Is Gay? Homosexuality in America" (April 23): 72–78.

Time. 1980. "Reassessing the Pill's Risks" (June 30): 40.

Tinker, John N. 1973. "Intermarriage and Ethnic Boundaries: The Japanese-American Case." *Journal of Social Issues* 29: 49–66.

Toffler, Alvin. 1980. *The Third Wave*. New York: William Morrow.

Tolstoy, Leo. 1964 (first published in 1877). *Anna Karenina*. Translated by David Magarshack. New York: New American Library.

Tolstoy, Leo. 1961 (first published in 1869). *War and Peace*. Translated by Rosemary Edmonds. Baltimore: Penguin Books.

Troll, Lillian E.; Miller, Sheila J.; Atchley, Robert C. 1979. *Families in Later Life*. Belmont, Calif.: Wadsworth.

Trost, Jan. 1975. "Married and Unmarried Cohabitation: The Case of Sweden, with Some Comparisons." *Journal of Marriage and the Family* 37 (August): 677–682.

Turner, Ralph H. 1970. *Family Interaction*. New York: John Wiley and Sons.

Udry, J. Richard. 1974. *The Social Context of Marriage* (3rd ed.). Philadelphia: J. B. Lippincott.

U.S. Bureau of the Census. 1967. "A Survey of Economic Opportunity." Washington, D.C.: U.S. Government Printing Office.

U.S. Bureau of the Census. 1976. "Demographic Aspects of Aging and the Older Population in the United States." *Current Population Reports*, Series P-23, No. 59. Washington, D.C.: U.S. Government Printing Office (May).

U.S. Bureau of the Census. 1977. "Marital Status and Living Arrangements: March 1976." *Current Population Reports*, Series P-20, No. 306, Table C. Washington, D.C.: U.S. Government Printing Office.

U.S. Bureau of the Census. 1977. "Marriage, Divorce, Widowhood and Remarriage and Family Characteristics: June 1975." *Current Population Reports*, Series P-20, No. 312. Washington, D.C.: U.S. Government Printing Office.

U.S. Bureau of the Census. 1978. *Statistical Abstracts of the United States*. Washington, D.C.: U.S. Government Printing Office.

U.S. Bureau of the Census. 1979. "Household and Family Characteristics: March 1979." *Current Population Reports*, Series P-20, No. 340, Table A. Washington, D.C.: U.S. Government Printing Office.

U.S. Bureau of the Census. 1979C. "Population Profile of the United States: 1978." *Current Population Reports*, Series P-20, No. 336. Washington, D.C.: U.S. Government Printing Office.

U.S. Bureau of the Census. 1980. "Marital Status and Living Arrangements: March 1979." *Current Population Reports*, Series P-20, No. 349. Washington, D.C.: U.S. Government Printing Office.

U.S. Department of Commerce, Bureau of the Census. 1978. *Consumer Income Series*, P-20, No. 74. Washington, D.C.: U.S. Government Printing Office (September).

U.S. Department of Commerce, Bureau of the Census. 1978. "Social and Economic Characteristics of the Older Population." Washington, D.C.: U.S. Government Printing Office.

U.S. Department of Health, Education, and Welfare. 1975. "Facts About Older Americans." Pub. No. (OHD) 75-20006. Washington, D.C.: U.S. Government Printing Office.

Vaillant, George E. 1977. *Adaptation to Life*. Boston: Little, Brown.

Veevers, Jean E. 1979. "Voluntary Childlessness: A Review of Issues and Evidence." *Marriage and Family Review* 2 (Summer): 1–26.

Victor, Jeffrey S. 1980. *Human Sexuality: A Social Psychological Approach*. Englewood Cliffs, N.J.: Prentice-Hall.

Vladeck, Bruce C. 1980. *Unloving Care: The Nursing Home Tragedy*. New York: Basic Books.

Vogel, S. R.; Broverman, I. K.; Broverman, D. M.; Clarkson, F. E.; and Rosekrantz, P. S. 1970. "Maternal Employment and Perception of Sex Roles Among College Students." *Developmental Psychology* 3: 384–391.

Wachowiak, Dale, and Bragg, Hannelore. 1980. "Open Marriage and Marital Adjustment." *Journal of Marriage and the Family* 42 (February): 57–62.

Walker, Lenore E. 1977–78. "Battered Women and Helplessness." *Victimology* 2, nos. 3 and 4: 525–534.

Walker, Lenore E. 1978. "Response to Presentation by Murray Straus, 'Wife Beating: Causes, Treatment and Research Needs.'" In *Battered Women: Issues of Public Policy*. U.S. Commission on Civil Rights, Washington, D.C. 20425.

Waller, W. 1938. *The Family: A Dynamic Interpretation*. New York: Dryden.

Wallerstein, Judith S., and Kelly, Joan B. 1974. "The Effects of Parental Divorce: The Adolescent Experience." In E. J. Anthony and C. Koupernik (eds.). *The Child and His Family: Children at Psychiatric Risk*. Vol. 3. New York: Wiley.

Wallerstein, Judith S., and Kelly, Joan B. 1975. "The Effects of Parental Divorce: Experiences of the Preschool Child." *Journal of the American Academy of Child Psychiatry* 14: 600–616.

Wallerstein, Judith S., and Kelly, Joan B. 1976. "The Effects of Parental Divorce: Experience of the Child in Later Latency." *American Journal of Orthopsychiatry* 46: 256–269.

Wallin, Paul. 1950. "Cultural Contradictions and Sex Roles: A Repeat Study." *American Sociological Review* 15 (April): 288–293.

Walster, Elaine. 1966. "Importance of Physical Attractiveness in Dating Behavior." *Journal of Personality and Social Psychology* 4: 508–516.

Warshak, Richard, and Santrock, John W. 1979. "The Effects of Father and Mother Custody on Children's Social Development." Paper presented at the Society for Research and Child Development. San Francisco (March).

Watt, Ian. 1957. *The Rise of the Novel*. Berkeley: University of California Press.

Westoff, Charles F. 1973. *Toward the End of Growth: Population in America*. Englewood Cliffs, N.J.: Prentice-Hall.

Whelan, Elizabeth. 1975. *A Baby . . . Maybe*. New York: Bobbs-Merrill.

White, Edmund. 1980. *States of Desire: Travels in Gay America*. New York: Dutton.

Will, George. 1982. *The Pursuit of Virtue and Other Tory Notions*. New York: Simon & Schuster.

Willie, Charles V. 1976. *A New Look at Black Families*. Bayside, N.Y.: General Hall.

Willie, Charles V., and Greenblatt, Susan. 1978. "Four Classic Studies of Power Relationships in Black Families: A Review and Look to the Future." *Journal of Marriage and the Family* 40 (November): 691–694.

Wilson, Edward O. 1978. *On Human Nature*. New York: Harvard University Press.

Wilson, William J. 1980. *The Declining Significance of Race* (2nd ed.). Chicago: University of Chicago Press.

Winch, Robert F. 1958. *Mate-Selection: A Study of Complementary Needs*. New York: Harper and Brothers.

Winett, R., and Neale, M. 1980. "Results of Experimental Study on Flexitime and Family Life." *Monthly Labor Review* 103 (November): 29–32.

Wolff, K. H. (ed.). 1950. *The Sociology of Georg Simmel*. Glencoe, Ill.: The Free Press.

Wolkind, S.; Hall, F.; and Pawlby, S. 1977. "Individual Differences in Mothering Behavior: A Combined Epidemiological and Observational Approach." In P. J. Graham (ed.). *Epidemiological Approaches in Child Psychiatry*. New York: Academic Press.

Woods, M. B. 1972. "The Unsupervised Child of the Working Mother." *Developmental Psychology* 6: 14–25.

Yankelovich, Daniel. 1974. *The New Moral Majority: A Profile of American Youth in the 70's*. New York: McGraw-Hill.

Yenckel, James T. 1981. "Money: IRA on My Mind." *The Washington Post* (December 23).

Yllo, Kersti A. 1978. "Non-Marital Cohabitation: Beyond the College Campus." *Alternative Lifestyles* 1 (February): 37–54.

Zelnick, Melvin, and Kantner, John F. 1977. "Sexual and Contraceptive Experience of Young Unmarried Women in the United States, 1976 and 1971." *Family Planning Perspectives* 9: 55.

Zilbergeld, Bernie, and Evans, Michael. 1980. "The Inadequacy of Masters and Johnson." *Psychology Today* (August).

Zill, N. 1978. "Divorce, Marital Happiness and the Mental Health of Children: Findings from the Foundation of Child Development National Survey of Children." Paper prepared for National Institute of Mental Health Workshop on Divorce and Children. Bethesda, Maryland.

Zunin, Leonard, and Zunin, Natalie. 1972. *Contact: The First Four Minutes*. New York: Ballantine.

Credits

INDEX